BN43984

OF THE STATE OF DELAWARE

Company

D1569751

SEE REVERSE FOR CERTAIN DEFINITIONS

is the owner of

BY

COUNTERSIGNED:

BANK OF AMERICA

NATIONAL TRUST AND SAVINGS ASSOCIATION

(SAN FRANCISCO)

TRANSFER AGENT

AUTHORIZED OFFICER

CUSIP 345370 10 0

DRED

E PAR VALUE OF TWO DOLLARS AND FIFTY CENTS ($2⁵⁰) EACH OF

*corporation by the holder hereof in person or by duly authorized
certificate and the shares represented hereby are issued and shall
n and all amendments thereto (copies of which are on file at
acceptance hereof expressly assents. This certificate is not
Transfer Clerk and registered by the Registrar.
facsimile signatures of its duly authorized officers.*

SPECIMEN

Henry ___

CHAIRMAN OF THE BOARD

NOTE COMPANY

A Practical Introduction to Business

A Practical Introduction to Business

Harold Koontz
University of California
at Los Angeles

and

Robert M. Fulmer
Trinity University

1975

RICHARD D. IRWIN, INC.   Homewood, Illinois   60430
Irwin-Dorsey International, Arundel, Sussex   BN18 9AB
Irwin-Dorsey Limited, Georgetown, Ontario   L7G 4B3

First Printing, January 1975
Second Printing, July 1975
Third Printing, November 1975
Fourth Printing, January 1976
Fifth Printing, February 1976
Sixth Printing, July 1976

ISBN 0-256-01616-X
Library of Congress Catalog Card No. 74–79468

Printed in the United States of America

To Karen, Jeanne, Jeff, and Burt

Rationale of
A Practical
Introduction to
Business

The approach of this book is prompted by three concerns. One is the belief that far too many college students do not appreciate the role and significance of business, whether privately or publicly owned, in making available the goods and services our society must have if it is to exist and thrive. They sometimes do not understand that making our standard of living possible depends upon what people working together in business can produce and earn.

A second concern arises from our review of many leading "Introduction to Business" books. These often seem to present the basics of business in a scattered and encyclopedic way with too much emphasis on too many facts and too little on the practical operating nature and problems of business. While these books present material pertinent to understanding business, their approach can hardly be expected to give a student a feeling of the unity, importance, and excitement of business operations.

The third concern arises out of the second. Widespread reports indicate that students find the typical "Introduction to Business" courses to be dull and not relevant to their lives. Too many college students today are not challenged by, and interested in business, and some have found "business is for the birds." This situation should present a challenge to every teacher of business subjects. No one can deny the importance of business. It is up to these teachers to convey, particularly in the "Introduction to Business" courses, not only the importance of business but the opportunities for an exciting career offered those who enter a business enterprise.

We hope to deal with these concerns by presenting a *practical* introduction to business. Both of the authors have had years of experience in and with business as employees, supervisors, executives, consultants, corporate directors, or business manager seminar leaders. We have attempted to draw on this experience to present an introduction that tells how business operates in practice.

We have tried to treat this subject in an orderly way. Part One— "Business and Its Environment" deals with the role of business, its environment and social responsibilities, and the part government plays in the United States as policeman and partner of business. This part is aimed toward describing the task of business in the American society, its competitive nature, the monopoly elements in business, the role of capital and profits, and how business relates to its entire environment and to the government in particular.

In Part Two—"Establishing a Business" our focus is on the major facilities and tools that must exist before a business, at least as we know it in the United States, can exist. In this part, we look at the legal forms a business can use, giving special emphasis to the corporation. We also introduce the basic elements of accounting and treat this subject as the principal way we keep and know the score in business. Because business is so dependent on financial resources for its initial and continuing existence, special attention is given to raising money through the banking system and the public money markets. This part concludes with a practical chapter on how businesses are started and financed and the financing pitfalls a businessman often faces.

In Part Three—"Operating a Business" we deal with the various areas of business operations. It is logical to start out with how customers are created and, through a study of marketing, how customers and products are brought together. At this point we introduce international business operations since they are growing fast and involve reaching into the global market by an increasing number of American businessmen.

Succeeding chapters in Part Three have to do with practical operations in creating goods and services, in making them available, and in securing the human resources to make a business work. Because business involves risks of a wide variety, the practice of reducing the impact of risks through insurance is discussed here. Also, it has become dramatically clear in recent years that business needs information, as well as human and material resources. The problems of managing information and utilizing the computer effectively for obtaining information are seen as key elements in operating a business.

Experience has shown that businesses, almost without exception, succeed or fail to the extent that they are well managed. Management is as essential a part of any business as money, operations, and people. For this reason and because the authors see managers as the catalysts for business success, Part Four—"Managing a Business" is devoted to this area of business effectiveness. Our interest is not to make this a management book or to cover the entire area of a basic management course. It is, rather, to identify the role of managers in business and to highlight some of their major problem areas in planning, organizing for teamwork, energizing the business through leadership, and assuring success through effective controls. We have also chosen to present the subject of unions here, since organized labor affects business management in so many ways.

As a concluding section of this book we present a thought-provoking chapter on future developments in business. We also place at the end of the book a chapter on what these developments mean in terms of opportunities for a challenging career in business.

Material is included in Appendix "A" to describe the financial flows in the United States economy. This is intended to be useful to those teachers who find it desirable to expand on the role of business in our total economic system. In Appendix "B" may be found a quite complete, but selective, bibliography of information available on careers in business. Some of this has been carefully annotated and the material is organized to be helpful to students with special career interests in business.

There is also included an extensive "Glossary of Key Terms and Concepts." While this is a more complete glossary than is usually found in books of this kind, it has been constructed with a view to being of maximum help to the student. All key terms and concepts noted at the end of each chapter are included in the Glossary and, to the extent possible, they are expressed in the practical language found in the book.

We have attempted to add to the sense of reality and excitement of business by using the story of Walt Disney and the highly successful business he founded to introduce each major part of the book. We have also included in each chapter a biographical summary of an outstanding leader in the world of business. We have further tried to contribute to the reality of the book by references to many real life incidents and examples which are spread throughout the text.

As will be quickly noted, we have used the second color in this book not just to improve its attractiveness, but more especially to assist students. The second color is planned to help the reader see more clearly the outline of the book and as a device for emphasizing key concepts, terms, and thoughts. In so doing, we use color as a means of stressing materials which we would underline if we were studying the book.

ACKNOWLEDGMENTS

In undertaking this book we have sought and received valued assistance from many persons. Realizing that the best advisers on a textbook are those who are actually teaching the course, we have gone directly to a number of prominent teachers of the "Introduction to Business" course in our community colleges and our four-year colleges and universities.

The original rationale and detailed plan for the book were carefully reviewed and many valuable suggestions were received from David H. Bowen of the University of Colorado; J. Jackson Davis of Western State College (Colorado); John Flood of Regis College; Earl Goddard of Oregon State University; Ethel Jorgenson of Los Angeles Valley College; Gene Logan of Diablo Valley College; Mark Mathews of California Lutheran University; Jon Pierce of St. Cloud State College; Donald Sedik of William Rainey Harper College; James F. Snyder of Arizona State University; and Norman Woodin of Kalamazoo Valley Community College.

The manuscript itself was carefully reviewed and many valuable suggestions received from Sonya Brett of McComb County Community College; Ben Compaine of Philadelphia Community College; Max Douglas of Indiana State University; John Flood of Regis College; Harold L. Goldman of Los Angeles Pierce College; George Katz of San Antonio Junior College; Gene Logan of Diablo Valley College; Paul N. Loveday of the University of Nevada; Jack C. Routson of the University of Wyoming; and James F. Snyder of Arizona State University.

It goes without saying that we are deeply indebted to all of these persons who have had so much experience with the course this book is intended to serve. Without their help, this book could not have been written. Yet, we recognize that none of them can share any responsibility for any shortcomings the book may have.

Among the many others who have helped with the book, we would like to acknowledge the great assistance of the top executives of Walt Disney Productions, including Cardon Walker, James Stewart, and Thomas Craven. John W. Enell of the American Management Associations was of considerable help in putting together the career bibliography in Appendix "B." James Haine of Catto and Catto, San Antonio insurance brokers, provided special assistance on the chapter on insurance. Judy Robinson, Picture Librarian for the *San Antonio Express-News*, was an invaluable resource in locating photographs for the chapter openings. Research assistance for the backgrounds of various business leaders was given by George Jacobs of Georgia State University and Thomas Bates of Trinity University, and Betty Ullman of Trinity University deserves a special vote of thanks for her assistance in handling permissions and correspondence with business leaders whose biographies are featured in the text.

A special debt is owed to Frank Pierce of Glencoe, Illinois, and formerly with *Encyclopaedia Britannica* for his thorough, intelligent, and rigorous editing of the manuscript. Although his editing often wounded the pride of the authors, we are now certain that he contributed much to the book's clarity and to assuring a reading level students should find acceptable.

An exceptional expression of gratitude is due Helen Schwartz of the University of California, Los Angeles. She conscientiously managed the preparation of the manuscript with rare intelligence and care.

We also appreciate the cooperation of the executives featured throughout the book in providing us with photographs and information about their careers.

As the reader can see, if this book fails in any way to meet the goals we have set, it will not be due to the lack of intelligent assistance we have been fortunate enough to receive.

HAROLD KOONTZ
ROBERT M. FULMER

December 1974

Notes to Students

All too frequently, textbooks are written for professors rather than students. This book is different in that it was written with you in mind.

Certainly, we are interested in what other professors think of the book. Yet, we did not write to impress them with our sophistication or linguistic abilities. We hope that this book will be all that its name implies. We hope you find it practical, easy to understand, and even enjoyable to read.

Some of you will enter this course to find out more about the world of business and to help you decide if business offers an opportunity for a career that would be meaningful and rewarding to you. Others may have already decided upon business as a college major. We hope that the book will help you to learn what to expect in the real world of business, and to prepare you for success in your chosen profession.

Too often, people think that business offers little challenge and only material rewards. This book should help dispel that prejudice.

As you begin your study of business as a profession or vocation, you might like to test your own knowledge of some of the subjects covered within this book. Already you have considerable experience as a customer of business. Maybe your mother or father, an aunt or uncle or some other close relative is or has been in some branch of business. Perhaps you yourself have worked for a business firm to help pay some of your college expenses. But, how much do you really understand about the foundations of our business system? To help answer this question, we are including a simple test you should take before you begin reading the book. Your professor may wish to spend some time discussing the answers—although they will be discussed in much greater detail throughout the book.

This book and the course which uses it as a text may be a turning point in your career plans. We hope it will open up new avenues of thought and new vistas of understanding about business—its opportunities and its challenges. In future editions of this book, we may be able to include your biography as an example of how business success can still be achieved.

Regardless of your eventual career or degree of success, we hope that you will enjoy this exposure to the wonderful worlds of business.

Erroneous Perceptions of Business

1. The average rate of profit on sales (after taxes) for U.S. corporations is between 15 and 25 percent.
2. The proprietorship and partnership form of organization is for small business activities.
3. Most workers in the United States are members of labor unions.
4. Personal savings of owners are the means that businessmen ordinarily use to finance their operations.
5. U.S. productivity is growing faster than that of any other major nation.
6. Railroad cars are the major means of transportation used by businessmen to transport their finished goods.
7. Insurance in the United States is written to protect the lives of individuals.
8. The key to successful marketing is to produce the very best product.
9. Men make better managers than women.
10. The key to motivation of workers is to provide good working conditions.
11. The United States sells far more of its production to other nations than it buys from other nations.
12. The majority of American business firms are involved in the manufacturing of products.
13. The majority of management jobs in American business can be found in large corporations.
14. The American business system is based on democracy.

15. Originally, the federal government was intended to protect the consumer from exploitation by business.

16. Computers are smarter than most managers.

17. Most businesses fail because of lack of information.

18. The primary challenges of a businessman is to prevent personnel turnover (employees leaving his firm).

19. The corporate form of business organization is for big firms.

20. Most business corporations are listed on the New York Stock Exchange.

21. All money used in business is created by the federal government.

22. Farming is not a business.

23. Par value of common stocks represents the minimum value of shares and indicates the amount that a corporation owes stockholders for their investment.

24. Large businesses far outnumber small businesses in the United States.

25. The advantage of bonds is that they are completely safe since they are fixed promises to pay.

Contents

part one

Business and Its Environment

© Walt Disney Productions.

Walt Disney's Wonderful World of Business

Walter Elias Disney was the American dream come true. Biographers will always revel in his life. He came to Hollywood from the Middle West with only $40 and a headful of new ideas, and proceeded to parlay those assets into a multimillion-dollar empire. To the student of business management, Disney's success is more astonishing than his screen fantasies. He was able to practice in business the same perfectionism that made his movies the peak experiences of many a childhood.

No success story can ever be reduced to a simple formula. Being in the right place at the right time with the right idea can't be explained as just a matter of luck, hard work, or courage. Walt Disney brought many other assets to the West Coast, as we can see from the following list of his possessions. They were certainly appropriate attributes for anybody contemplating the construction of a multimillion-dollar empire.

Walt had an idea . . . called pleasure. He knew what gave him pleasure and he set out to give it to others. From his early days with the slapstick cartoon until his last days of planning model urban environment, Walt always had a new idea for turning people on. His medium for bringing pleasure matured with him, and grew along with his financial resources. He moved from laugh-making to dream-making to future-making . . . but his starting point remained the same: think of a way to give people pleasure . . . and do it.

Walt had dedication to his idea . . . called quality. Probably the greatest thing that can be said of him is that success never spoiled his dedication to quality. Many people have started out with a good idea and then gradually succumbed to the need to make production quotas and meet profit margins until they lost the idea. Disney not only stuck to his idea, he created a company in his own image. The operations and philosophy of Walt Disney Productions show that the Disney dedication lives on. "Walt left us with the habit of crossing division lines, and freely getting involved in each other's department," says one vice president.

The *idea* remains king at Disney. Whatever it takes to make the idea a reality, is the thing to be done. At Disneyland the trash cans are gorgeous—they cost $70 each to paint. But the *idea* is cleanliness, and if $70 trash cans will serve the idea, then the cans get painted.

Walt had a brother . . . called Roy. Roy Disney was the financial genius who balanced the books and kept Walt free to play with his ideas. Roy once commented on the relationship: "Together we're a success. Separately, Walt would have been a cartoonist for the Kansas City Star and I would have been a bank teller." Executives within the firm feel that Roy was far too modest in his assessment of their talents. Yet they agree that the brothers were a unique example of balanced management teamwork.

There were times when Walt's plans were a little outside Roy's budget. One time, Walt decided that Disneyland really needed its own Matterhorn. The artificial Swiss ALP would cost $7 million, and Roy explained that they couldn't afford to spend $7 million to build a mountain. While Roy was away in Europe, Walt called an executive meeting. "We're going to build a Matterhorn," he informed them. "And when Roy gets back from Europe, let *him* figure out how to pay for it."

A little thing like a $7 million mountain has been known to come between brothers. But Roy and Walt had the relationship between ideas and dollars all worked out. And they seem to have succeeded in passing this critical relationship on to the surviving corporation.

Walt had a genius . . . called timing. His Mickey Mouse cartoons arrived at just the right time to please audiences. During World War II he turned to training and propaganda films. Disneyland came along just when the sprawling and unstructured market of southern California could use a tourist attracting focal point.

The Disney timing, too, has been inherited by the Disney enterprises. At a moment when people are conscious of the need for better cities and a cleaner environment, the Florida community and amusement center of Disney World introduces the cleanest place around, with clean water, clean air, and no smog-generating automobiles. The corporation has other big plans for future projects but is wary of rushing into them—it's not the Disney way.

Walt had the magic wand . . . called money. Finance was never exactly carefree, but Roy Disney and the corporation he created knew how to use a dollar. While other companies demand that all of their divisions be profit makers, Disney looks for the *experience* to be right, regardless of the cost. In money matters, such idealism is a luxury that only a few can afford. When Walt decided to build Disneyland, he borrowed $100,000 against his own insurance to finish the project. The gamble paid off, and the Walt Disney concept ("get the idea right regardless of the cost") was incorporated into the entire Disney World approach.

One hundred million dollars has been spent by the developers of the new town of Columbia, Maryland. Eighty-five million has been put into Reston, Virginia. But Disney Productions has sunk over $600 million into Walt Disney World, and is ready to add several hundred million more. Walt and Roy had the rare opportunity to live and work by a financial principle that is opposed by every school of business: "The folks who win financially are the ones who don't worry about money."

Most important of all, *Walt had control* . . . and held onto it. He and the Disney enterprises occasionally subcontracted parts of a business to others to raise construction capital, but in the end they bought back each contract to assure that things would be done the Disney way. The food service at Disneyland, for example, was originally contracted out to a subsidiary of the American Broadcasting Company; but some years later, Disney bought out ABC's interest for $7.5 million and took over the food service as soon as the leases could be terminated. Disney reasoned that concessionaires tend to view the business from the standpoint of their own units and therefore cut corners to maintain their profits. The Disney philosophy dictates that there is nothing wrong in losing money on a hot dog if it enhances the visitor's total experience.

It takes a special kind of man to build an organization with a unique management style, in which channels are always open. Walt Disney—that special kind of man—is still very much alive in the management of Disney Productions. When top management speaks, it is as if Walt or Roy were standing behind them, nodding approval. "My greatest accomplishment," said Walt Disney, "was that I built an organization of people that enabled me to do the things I wanted to do all my life." And anybody who knew Walt will tell you that the thing he wanted to do . . . was to give people pleasure.

AP Wirephoto.

1

The Role of Business

Any person, group, company, or government department or agency whose purpose is to produce or sell products or services is a business. We often think of mammoth companies, like General Motors or the Bank of America, as representing the business element in our society. But the small grocery store, the beauty parlor down the street, and the shine stand on the corner are also businesses. There is also a tendency to let references made to "business" bring to mind only those enterprises owned by individuals, partners, or stockholders. If this were true, Soviet Russia would have few businesses and we could not regard the U.S. Postal Service, the Tennessee Valley Authority, or the Los Angeles Airport as businesses.

Neither size nor kind of ownership determines what is a business. The real distinguishing feature is the production and sale of goods and services. A moment's reflection will show how much this definition includes. Doesn't a city fire department "produce" fire protection services which are "bought" by taxpayers? Doesn't a school "produce" educational services and "sell" them to students and taxpayers? As will be seen later, there is not much difference between what is commonly thought of as "business" and any other kind of operation that produces and markets products or services.

THE BUSINESS OF BUSINESS IS BUSINESS

In order to keep the subject manageable, we must draw some boundaries. Let us say that the business of business is business. In other words, let us limit ourselves to *economic* enterprises, those operations that produce a service or a product and sell these to people who want and can buy them. They may be large or small. They may be owned privately or by a government.

In this book, major attention will be given to privately owned businesses. While a fairly large portion of business operations are government owned, even in the United States, it is still true that by far most of the goods and services we buy—what we eat, wear, live in, ride in, treat our illnesses with, and are entertained by—are furnished by privately owned businesses. Virtually all of the total of $1,081 billion spent in 1973 for personal consumption and government purchases, in the United States, as well as the $209 billion of private investments, was used to purchase goods from some kind of business, and over 80 percent of these goods came from privately owned businesses. It is worth noting that government agencies consume a large part of the output of business. In 1973 federal, state, and local governments bought $276 billion of goods and services, an amount equal to 34 percent of all purchases by all other consumers.

THE FUNCTIONS OF ALL ECONOMIC SYSTEMS

People on our planet Earth differ greatly in national origin, race, geographical location, education, customs, and attitudes. But we all have a common characteristic in our need for food, clothing, and shelter, as well as our desires for a variety of other goods and services which can better our standard of living. Indeed, we have an even more common bond—we depend upon our planet Earth for the natural resources needed to provide these goods and services.

The Task of All Economic Systems Is the Same

Every country has to have some way of producing the goods and services its people need. If a society is rural and without the advancements brought by civilization, people work on the land they occupy to meet their own basic needs. However, as civilization grows and advances, more can be produced if workers specialize in making certain things for each other. Organizations are formed to employ them in their specialized work. Each individual then depends increasingly on others for most of his needs and wants.

Some method of marketing must be established to bring goods and services to the customer. Distribution and transportation systems must be developed, and these require other types of specialized organizations. To complete the picture, money is necessary to facilitate the transfer of the goods and services; this requires banks and other financial organizations.

The organizations set up to produce, market, distribute, and exchange the goods and services of a nation have a common goal—to meet the needs and wants of the people. They must be managed so that the goal is accomplished as efficiently as possible, no matter what economic or political system is used. All systems utilize some kind of business organization. All systems employ the available land and capital. All systems depend upon the work of people. In this way, we are all alike in our economic activities.

How Economic Systems Differ: Capitalism and Socialism

So, where do the systems differ, if it is not in "what" is being done? It is the "how to go about it" that the dfifference has become greater over the past 200 years. It has only been within this period that our civilization has grown to the point of urbanization and specialization. Consequently, it has been within this period that two quite opposite philosophies have developed in regard to the accomplishment of the economic function.

In some countries a system of capitalism or "free enterprise" has developed. This is based upon individual initiative rather than upon government action. It is often referred to as "laissez faire" (French for "let be," or "allow to act"). This system promotes and encourages private ownership of property as the means by which individuals produce or distribute goods and services. It carries with it a "government stay out" attitude. It rewards with "profits" the individual who can successfully establish and operate an organization meeting economic needs. Such a person may hope to increase his wealth, and even to become rich, by meeting other people's needs and wants.

Many people do not accept capitalism as the best economic system. They feel it has defects which outweigh its advantages. These critics of capitalism oppose the principle of private enterprise. Rather, they look to the government to control the economy and to make the major decisions. We shall refer to this as "controlled enterprise," or socialism. In many countries this is the predominant system.

BUSINESS UNDER PRIVATE OWNERSHIP: THE CAPITALISTIC SYSTEM

The distinguishing feature of American business throughout history has been private ownership. This concept of privately owned business, the heart of our capitalistic system, means not only that business is owned directly or indirectly by individuals. Traditionally it has also involved certain freedoms: (1) the right of the owners to receive the profits a business makes (while assuming the risks of loss); (2) the right to start up any lawful business and to liquidate it; (3) the right to invest or to refrain from investing; (4) the right to make contracts; (5) the right to buy from and sell to whomever one pleases; and (6) the right to set whatever prices one wishes and can get. Some freedoms of business have been limited by laws passed over the years.

Historically, the rights attached to ownership have also been accompanied by a number of political freedoms. These include (1) the right to free speech and press, (2) the right to a fair trial and due process of law, (3) the right to religious freedom, (4) the right to vote for political candidates of one's choice, and (5) the right to equal and fair protection of the law. Some would argue that we can have freedom in political matters without a high degree of freedom in business matters. However, in countries in which the rights of private ownership have been largely abandoned, political freedoms have also tended to disappear.

One characteristic common to almost all human beings is the desire to own things—and the willingness to work to get them. Once people have the minimum requirements of life, such as personal security, food to stave off hunger, and clothing and shelter to provide protection from the elements, they begin to want to buy and consume freely. This has happened to a great degree even in the Soviet Union, where private enterprise has been discouraged. The recent Soviet government policy making available more consumer goods, and the growing use of profits to guide the production of state enterprises, show that the Soviet leaders recognize the importance of personal incentives. Wherever private enterprise is not forbidden, it is safe to say that when there is a demand for a product somebody will go into business to supply it.

FIGURE 1-1

Economic Systems

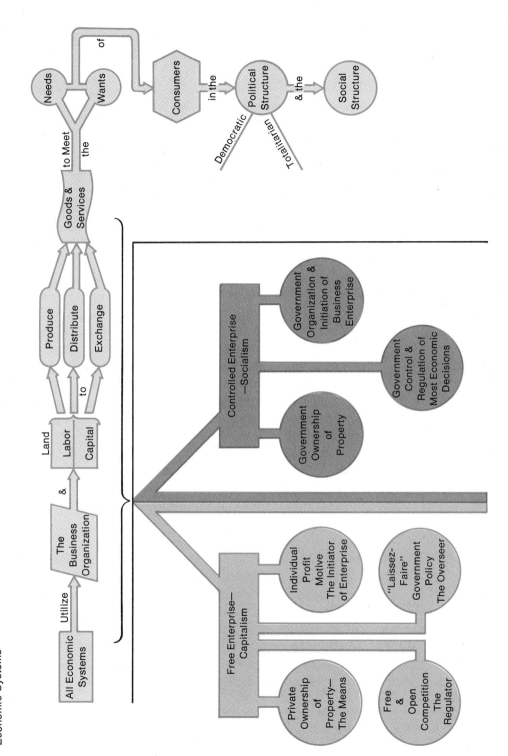

History and Capitalism

This is exactly what happened in England in the 18th century. A series of mechanical inventions sparked the development of the factory system. Among these were Kay's invention in 1733 of the flying shuttle for weaving, Hargreaves's invention of the spinning jenny in 1770, and Watts's invention of the steam engine in 1781. These inventions required large investments to put them to use. England's foreign trade had been growing rapidly. The stage was set for a move toward freedom from restrictive government regulations. Along with these great changes came increased trading to market the products of factories, and migration of farmers and tradesmen to factories, enticed by the higher wages they could make there.

These developments were given strong social and political support by various thinkers and economists. The most influential of them was Adam Smith, who published his *Wealth of Nations* in 1776—the very year of American independence. Smith argued that interference by government in economic matters only hindered the natural tendency of men, pursuing their individual interests, to obtain the maximum satisfaction of their wants from the limited available resources. Government intereference, he argued, thus prevented resources from being used in the most efficient way for improving the well-being of individuals and society.

These ideas were in the air when the United States of America was born. In America, as well as in most of Europe, people believed that free men competing with each other to produce what the public wanted, goaded by the desire to make a profit, and controlled by the lash of competition to keep prices low, would create the most vigorous and successful economic system possible.

To be sure, it was recognized that many things people wanted could not be produced and marketed by private businessmen.* The provision for national defense, the safeguarding of persons and property, and even the construction of certain large business projects such as canals and waterways, were seen as falling outside the sphere of private enterprise. But the dominant idea on which private capitalism thrived in the United States was that government intervention should be minimized. Instead, the economy was based on private ownership and

---

* Although the authors use the terms "businessmen" and "businessman" throughout this book they do not mean to imply that all people in business are men. Indeed, an increasing number of women have careers and have become influential in business. Thus, these terms must be interpreted to mean *both* men and women in business.

production for the market. Business activity was controlled by what Adam Smith had called the "invisible hand" of competition.

Success of Private Capitalism in America

Anyone can see that this system has been successful in the United States. From an undeveloped nation two centuries ago, the U.S. has become undisputably the leading industrial nation of the world. With less than 6 percent of the world's population, it has over 40 percent of the world's wealth and production. The Soviet Union, on the other hand, has one-fifth more population than the United States but produces less than one-third the output of the United States.

The U.S. achievement of a high material standard of living cannot be accounted for by natural resources alone. Other countries, such as Brazil, have vast natural resources. Other countries also have large educated populations. Many competent observers have claimed that our prosperity is the result of a long tradition of private ownership *plus* the regulation and drive supplied by legally enforced competition.

Defects of Private Capitalism in America

In stressing the good points of private capitalism, we should not overlook its defects. In the 19th century the factory system was accompanied by intolerable working conditions, long hours, low pay, and the exploitation of women and children. Most of these abuses have since been eliminated by the efforts of government, labor unions, and enlightened management. In the 19th century, some capitalists exploited their positions of power to develop monopolistic positions. They jacked up prices, fought against the efforts of workers to organize unions, rode rough-shod over weaker competitors, sold worthless stocks, and even forced legislators to give them favorable treatment. But laws passed half a century ago have now made such abuses of power very difficult. While cases of price-fixing, stock manipulation, misleading advertising, and other illegal or unethical behavior still occur, they are relatively few. There is no evidence that the private capitalists, or businessmen, include in their ranks any more breakers of laws and moral codes than other groups in society.

It is true that economic growth has brought with it many social problems. Poverty still exists in the midst of unprecedented wealth. Pollution of water, land, and air has become a major problem. People who want jobs cannot always find them. Motor vehicles kill hundreds of thousands. The growth of large cities has led to a host of other problems. But most of these problems also exist in countries where there is little private ownership. Moreover, so long as a country has the material resources, political freedoms, and a responsive elected government, there is promise that most major social problems can be solved. Without these strengths and without a high degree of economic productivity, such problems cannot be solved in any society.

BUSINESS UNDER PUBLIC OWNERSHIP: SOCIALISM AND COMMUNISM

As pointed out above, some societies believe that business operates best when it is publicly owned. This view is held in the Soviet Union, the People's Republic of China, Egypt, Yugoslavia, and other countries. But even in these countries some small-scale private ownership is allowed. In Russia, small farmers peddle produce in city markets. In Egypt the large farms have been broken up and given to small farmers. Private ownership is also allowed in many other small Egyptian businesses, such as truckers having less than five trucks, or shopkeepers with fewer than five employees, and many small manufacturing companies.

A national system of public ownership is almost invariably accompanied by central government planning of what will be produced and sold. Central planning has at times been fairly effective in marshalling national efforts in well-defined directions. In the Soviet Union, for example, when national needs were clearly for defense, food, and minimal shelter and clothing, these were provided through public planning and ownership. Even in capitalist countries, public ownership has been useful in accomplishing certain programs. In the United States one might mention, among other things, the Panama Canal, the Alaska Railroad, irrigation and power dams, highways and waterways, Army ordnance plants, and national parks.

Public planning and ownership are most effective when needs are clear. The Russians have found that when needs become more a matter of individual taste, such as styles of clothing, and when people have the money to pay for what they want, the market place becomes the only workable mechanism for expressing their demands. That is why in recent years they have been experimenting with reforms of their planning system. It is impossible for any central planner to know the tastes and desires of a nation of consumers and to provide the right things in the right amounts in the right places. Many Russians have come to believe that even under socialism it is necessary to allow businesses to make profits by furnishing what is wanted.

It is often forgotten that the Soviet system is a *political* system involving *government* ownership of business. In theory this political system aims at community sharing of all wealth—"from each according to his ability, to each according to his need." As actually practiced, it is a system of public ownership in which the government is controlled by the few (in the Soviet Union by the few leaders of some 30 million members of the Communist Party, which represents only 12 percent of the population). Those in control have imposed many restrictions on individual freedoms: on freedom of expression, on the freedom to move from one job to another or from one housing unit to another, and on economic freedom. Many things people want, and have the money to buy, are either unavailable or strictly rationed. Thus few Soviet citizens can buy an automobile, even if they have the money to do so.

MIXED SYSTEMS

Many countries have systems of mixed public and private ownership of business. In the United States, as in all so-called private capitalistic countries, many businesses and other facilities are publicly owned. The so-called Communist countries have, for their part, found it necessary to allow varying degrees of private ownership.

Private capitalism may be modified in other ways. The U.S. government has increasingly controlled private business by a multitude of regulations, as well as by various aids and subsidies. When government agencies hand out gifts, certain controls usually follow since government givers characteristically attach strings to their generosity. For example, needy people given food stamps cannot buy whatever they want with them, and publicly supported schools must usually purchase "approved" textbooks. In addition, government agencies, as the nation's largest single buyers of goods and services, exercise great power over companies that sell to them. A defense contractor, for example, is told how to keep his accounts, what reports he has to make, and often how much profit he can earn.

PRIVATE OWNERSHIP VERSUS PUBLIC OWNERSHIP

As we have already seen, neither private ownership nor public ownership of business is "perfect" for all circumstances. Every country's system is to some extent "mixed." Both capitalism and socialism have their defects. A privately owned capitalist system cannot guarantee full employment; it cannot guarantee the elimination of poverty; it must be regulated to prevent "sharp" practices (such as the former practice by loan companies of implying that their interest rates are lower than they are); it may produce air and water pollution; and it cannot assure that people will buy what they need rather than what they believe they want. On the other hand, a government-owned business system may stifle initiative and innovation. It may not be quickly responsive to public desires for products and services. And it may severely limit the freedom of people to work where they wish, buy what they want, and live as they wish.

As in all things in life, political-economic systems are not "perfect" or wholly "good" or "bad". Life is a matter of "trade-offs"—the giving up of some things to get others. In the United States most people believe our mixed system of private and government ownership is better for us than any other alternative. We like the opportunities for greater freedom in buying and living. We prefer a system that gives us the opportunity to own property, to go into our own business, to make profits, and to enjoy with minimum control the fruits of our labor. We do not believe it is perfect, but we prefer its combination of virtues and defects to those of other systems.

THE ROLE OF COMPETITION

A successful private enterprise system depends on the maintenance of effective and responsible competition. Without competition, consumers would be at the mercy of greedy sellers, and workmen would be at the mercy of unscrupulous employers. For that matter, without competition between customers, businessmen would be at the mercy of those to whom they sell; and without competition between workers for jobs, employers would be at the mercy of their employees. Competition is a basic element of our economic system. To meet the goals of society, however, competition must be effective and responsible.

Effective Competition

For competition to be effective, suppliers of goods and services must be in open rivalry for customers. One seller's loss must be another seller's gain. Sometimes competition takes the form of rivalry over price. Sometimes, however, competition is based on real or imagined differences in products or services, as in the airlines, cosmetics, and packaged foods industries. The basic price of a ticket on one airline is the same as on another, but the lines compete in other ways—in the services they offer, or in their scheduling, or perhaps just in the smiles of their stewardesses.

In some cases competition will not work, as with telephone companies, electric utilities, and most local buslines. In these cases, competition would only result in higher costs and poorer service to the public. In industries such as these it has been the practice to allow single-company operation—that is, a monopoly. Government agencies then step in to regulate prices, quality of service, and freedom to enter into or abandon a business.

Responsible Competition

Competition cannot be allowed to become reckless or to follow the law of the jungle. Government agencies have increasingly been given power to regulate competition by enforcing reasonableness and responsibility. Companies that use competition with a view to destroying others or to discriminating unfairly against rivals have been carefully controlled. For example, chain grocery stores such as the A. & P. have been brought under certain rules to keep them from gaining unfair advantage over independent stores. Unfair methods of competition, such as dishonest advertising, discrediting of competitors, failure to be truthful in product claims, and many others, are investigated by various government commissions. Many other steps have been taken to enforce a degree of fairness and social responsibility in competition.

Competition May Be Varied

Competition may be between sellers of the same product, who seek to win customers from each other. Newspapers, magazines, radio broadcasts, and television shows are full of advertisements designed to convince buyers of the superiority of one company's products or services. All of us have seen and heard the commercials attesting to the superiority of "Crest" toothpaste, the superior whiteness of "Clorox" bleach, the greater freshness of "Salem" cigarettes, or the special "Finger-Lickin'" goodness of Kentucky Fried Chicken.

Competition can also take the form of rivalry among different products. The dairy industry tries to get people to consume their proteins in cheese or milk rather than meat. Savings banks and mutual

J. Willard Marriott

Courtesy of Capitol and
Glogau Photographers.

J. Willard Marriott, son of a poor Utah sheep rancher, founded Marriott Corporation, one of the largest and fastest growing companies in the food and lodging business in America. Mr. Marriott's leadership of the company spans more than 45 years. In 1974 he was still active in policy matters and planning as Chairman of the Board.

Marriott was born in 1900 near Ogden, Utah, the second of eight children. He tended sheep for his father, and at 14 made the first of many trips by rail to market the sheep. A Mormon, he went to New England at age 18 where he served two years as a missionary. When he returned, his father's bankruptcy required him to work while attending school at Weber State College and the University of Utah. He received his B. A. degree in 1926 and began teaching at Weber soon after.

At college he had noticed the success of a drink stand in Salt Lake City which sold a type of root beer. Not finding the challenge and opportunity he sought in teaching, he purchased the Washington, D.C., area franchise for the root beer product and set up business in a rented half of a bakeshop in downtown Washington. In 1927 he married. He and his wife had great success in selling root beer while the weather was hot and muggy, but sales started to taper off as winter approached. He switched to a barbecue, chili, and tamales format based on recipes he acquired from the chef at the nearby Mexican Embassy.

His success was immediate, and by

funds compete for the saver's money. There can even be competition within a business, such as the urge of the purchasing department to be given the same important position accorded the sales department.

The essence of competition is rivalry, whether between businesses, baseball teams, or individuals striving for recognition. Many psychologists believe that competitiveness is a basic part of human nature. This does not mean that it is always good. Competitiveness may take the form of cheating, striving for undue advantage, and even immoral behavior. But it also results in accomplishment and superiority. Competition underlies the development of new products and new methods, the founding of new businesses, the lowering of costs, and the whole

1932 he had built a chain of seven Hot Shoppes restaurants in the Washington area. The outlets were family-oriented, offering good food and service at moderate prices. He introduced the first drive-in eating accommodations east of the Rocky Mountains, and his company grew steadily during the depression years. The company was the first to cater meals for airlines, beginning in 1937. World War II was a difficult period, but the business thrived again in the postwar years.

In 1957 Marriott entered the hotel business, opening the Twin Bridges Marriott Motor Hotel in the metropolitan Washington, D.C., area. By 1973 there were 20 Marriott hotels in operation, including the Essex House in New York City, Camelback Inn in Arizona, and the Paraiso Marriott in Acapulco, Mexico. Seventeen more company-owned or -managed hotels were under construction or planned, including three in Europe. In addition, expansion was planned for the existing chain of a dozen franchised Marriott Inns. Marriott's Hotel Group also operated cruise ships, a world travel division, and resort hotel condominiums.

The food service end of the business was not forgotten. The airline catering arm of Marriott Corporation, In-Flite Services, grew to become the world's largest independent airline food supplier with kitchens located in most major United States airports as well as in South America, Europe, Africa, and the Far East.

By mid-1972, the company's Restaurant Operations Group included about 1,200 units, of which it owned 400 directly, the remainder being franchises. The company was active in institutional and industrial feeding, and had its own food production and distribution facilitly. Marriott also planned to develop three regional family entertainment centers in the San Francisco, Chicago, and Washington, D.C., areas as an important part of its program for growth and diversification in the leisure time and family markets.

Marriott management is considered exemplary by the industry. Labor relations are benevolent and paternalistic; the company enjoys remarkable loyalty among its 39,000 employees, who consistently reject union organizing efforts because of the benefits the company provides and its progressive employee relations.

In the 1960s and 1970s, Marriott Corporation doubled its sales and profits on an average of every five years. The management was confident of its ability to continue this growth. Sales rose from $84.7 million in 1964 to $538 million in 1973, and were expected to top $700 million by 1975.

Marriott has been director of American Motors and has served on the boards of the Riggs National Bank and the Chesapeake & Potomac Telephone Company. He has held high office in the Mormon church and has received several awards and honors in professional and public life, including honorary doctorates from Brigham Young University, the University of Utah, and Weber State College.

movement toward a better way of life. Although some persons would strive for the new and better without the pressures of competition, most probably would not. Most of our material improvements—homes, automobiles, transportation services, entertainment, television sets, new life-saving drugs, and even better colleges—have come about largely because of the desire to beat rivals.

SOME BUSINESSES ARE MONOPOLIES

When there is only one seller in an industry, he is said to have a monopoly. The monopolist may be a business, a labor union, or a government agency. The definition of a monopoly is that it is the only source of supply of its product. The monopoly may be privately or publicly owned. It may be an association, such as a labor union, which controls the supply of a particular kind of labor. A monopolist can—if it is not controlled—charge buyers whatever it wishes. The amount it sells will depend on the extent to which buyers want or must have its products or services and are willing to pay for them—no monopolist of beef can force us to buy beef rather than chicken.

Only a rare monopolist would have control over something for which there was no substitute. An example of such a monopolist would be the sole possessor of water on a desert island, or a seller of food where no other food is available. Monopolists seldom if ever have so much power. Even water can usually be obtained from sources other than a city water system. It is possible to live without electricity or telephone service. Moreover, any monopolist interested in making the greatest possible profit must take into account the price a buyer will be willing to pay rather than accept a substitute service or product, or even go without.

Sometimes a buyer may have a monopoly too. Where there is only one buyer for the product of a business, this situation is referred to by economists as a "monopsony." Obviously, the power of this buyer can be great, as many companies wholly dependent on the Defense Department to buy their products have found out. But the power of the monopsonist is not absolute either, since the seller may well decide that he would rather go without an order than sell at a loss. This is what many defense suppliers did when they refused to accept government orders a few years ago; they had been given no choice but to take orders at a fixed price, and they considered the risk of losses in the project to be too high to assume.

The best-known instances of monopolistic businesses in this country are public utilities—companies producing and selling electricity, water, gas, telephone service, street railway and bus services, and sometimes other items. The public gains by allowing these to be monopolies. Competitive telephone companies in the same city, for example, would mean a proliferation of wires and phones if people wished to communicate freely with each other. This actually happened in the early days of telephones when it was common to have more than one telephone company in a community. Unless a person had more than one telephone, he could not call all those he wished to reach.

The importance of public utility services has often led local governments to take over ownership of them. Government ownership is common in water services, and frequent in electric service and local transit lines. Private ownership predominates in telephone and fuel gas services.

Because of their importance and the fact that they are monopolies, public utilities are more extensively regulated than other businesses. Government commissions have been set up to regulate the prices utilities charge, the quality and quantity of service they give, and the extension or abandonment of their services. All privately owned utilities, and many government-owned utilities, are subject to detailed regulation, particularly by federal and state governments. But government-owned utilities may also be controlled by a city council, or by a state or federal legislature. There has, moreover, been a growing tendency to place publicly owned utilities under the same controls as those applicable to privately owned.

MONOPOLY ELEMENTS IN COMPETITIVE BUSINESSES

Even among businesses that are predominantly competitive, there are often elements of monopoly. The most important of these are oligopoly, product differentiation, and trademark, copyright, and patent monopolies.

Oligopolies and Presumption of Monopolistic Behavior

When there are so few sellers in a market that what any one of them does to influence buyers will be immediately and definitely felt by the others, this is called an oligopoly (from Greek, meaning "few sellers"). Oligopolies exist among the automobile manufacturers, the steel and aluminum companies, the larger tobacco companies, the major soap and detergent companies, the airlines, and in many other industries.

Because of the fact that one seller's competitive actions will be noted and felt by others, it is easy to assume that members of an oligopoly do not really compete. Since they know that price cutting, for example, will soon bring retaliation from the others, or that a new product or service will soon be copied, it is assumed that each seller has an incentive to leave well enough alone and not rock the boat. The result may be price stability, and perhaps a live-and-let-live policy that resembles monopoly pricing. This will naturally depend on the ease or difficulty with which new suppliers can come into a market. If an oligopolistic industry requires heavy capital investment or a large and expensive marketing organization, it is not easy for new suppliers to come into the field. For example, no new automobile manufacturing company has been able successfully to start up in the United States for more than half a century.

But the fact that price competition is limited among oligopolists does not rule out strong competition for customers through advertising, special customer services, product changes, and other forms of nonprice competition. We only have to look at the active competition among the soap companies and the automobile manufacturers to understand this. A more realistic view of the competitive situation is given by what may be called the "theory of the aggressor." In its fundamentals, this states that when a situation becomes too comfortable and profitable there always seems to be one seller who sees an opportunity to gain by introducing a new product or sales gimmick, a special advertising program, a product or service improvement, or even a price concession. The aggressor is not always the same seller; this role tends to shift.

For example, in the airline business, which is certainly oligopolistic and even regulated by the government, companies are continually offering new special fares and services to attract more passengers. Thus American Airlines introduces a new family fare, Continental starts the "coach lounge" fad, Western offers its champagne breakfasts, and Braniff brings out its colorful airplanes and stewardess costumes.

Similar examples can be found in almost every oligopolistic industry. Purex pioneered plastic bottles for detergents and bleaches. RCA pioneered color television. Procter & Gamble moved ahead by putting fluorides in toothpaste. Reynolds Aluminum became the first company in its industry to go after the ordinary consumer by marketing aluminum foil wrap and aluminum house siding. Countless other examples might be given. The notion that few sellers mean there is little competition is simply not borne out by the facts.

Monopolistic Competition: Product Differentiation

One of the most common variations of competition is the practice by otherwise competitive companies of making buyers believe that their individual products are different, whether they are or not. If a soap manufacturer puts more lanolin into his soap and persuades people that his product is therefore superior and unique, he gains an advantage. He has introduced an element of monopoly. The same is the case if he leads people to think his product is substantially unique by means of effective advertising and the establishment of a known brand name.

The various brands of beer, aspirin, tires, detergents, shaving lotions, bread, household paints, and transistor radios are good examples of this monopolistic competition.

Sometimes there are real differences among these products, and in certain cases there may be substantial differences. But the authors have seen examples of product differentiation in which the differences existed only in the buyer's mind. Once they heard two housewives debating the advantages of their favorite brands of detergents, when in fact the only differences between them were the colors and the brand names. The purpose of product differentiation is to make a buyer *believe* that a given product is superior to others he might buy. To the extent that a seller is successful in this he has gained a monopoly-type position.

Trademark, Copyright, and Patent Monopolies

Governments generally permit sellers to register trademarks and copyrights and to patent new products, processes, and services so that these become their property and cannot be used by others without their permission. This is done to protect an individual's investment and to prevent others from making money out of his work. As can be seen, these devices represent monopolistic elements in an otherwise competitive situation.

Thus no one but General Motors can manufacture and sell "Chevrolet" or "Cadillac," at least in those countries where the trademarks are registered. No one but General Electric has "Hotpoint" ranges or refrigerators. And no one but Bulova can make an "Accutron" watch. This "monopoly" exists if the trademark is properly registered and if the owner will take upon himself to defend it from infringement. In the United States, exclusive right of use of a trademark is given for 20 years and may be renewed for an additional 20 years.

A copyright is a special privilege given to an author or a publisher granting him the exclusive right to own, sell, or otherwise use a written work—a book, poem, song, play, or even a photograph. In the United States, copyrights are good for 28 years and may usually be renewed. But, as with trademarks, it is up to the author or publisher to prosecute those who copy.

A patent, likewise, is a right given to an inventor, or to someone to whom he may assign this right, for the exclusive ownership and use of a novel idea. The idea may be a product, a chemical or physical composition, a process, or a design. The right is given for a period of 17 years. While it legally confers a "monopoly" position on the patent holder, many holders have found that the right does not mean anything until it has been successfully defended in court against an infringer. These lawsuits often fail because a court may decide that an idea was not really novel and that the patent was therefore not legally valid.

Having a trademark, copyright, or patent in the United States does not necessarily give the holder protection outside this country. It is true that most countries have signed international agreements honoring copyrights issued by each other. A fair number of countries have likewise signed an agreement with respect to trademarks, and a number of countries have done so with patents. But with respect to both trademarks and patents, holders concerned with foreign competition find it wise to register them also in other key countries where competition may arise.

THE MANY INTERFERENCES WITH COMPETITION

Competition tends to be limited by many factors other than the monopolistic elements mentioned above. Examining only a few of them, it is remarkable that competition works as well as it does.

Lack of Information

Competitors often suffer from lack of information as to what their costs or markets are and what their rivals plan to do. This makes it difficult to compete effectively.

Capital Requirements

The capital requirements for entering many businesses are so great that few people are able to embark in them. Newcomers have found it difficult to break into the automobile, steel, aluminum, industrial chemicals, or oil businesses. There are always exceptions, however. A number of oil and steel companies set up expensive industrial chemical plants in the 1960s, resulting in temporary overcapacity in that industry. The Occidental Petroleum Corporation became a three-billion-dollar fuel and chemical company in 12 short years after being founded in 1957.

Strong Engineering, Marketing, and Service Organization

The difficulty of breaking into an industry is not always that of capital requirements for plant and equipment. Sometimes the existing companies have developed such a strong engineering, marketing, or service organization that newcomers find it difficult to compete with them. This has been a major factor in the commanding position of International Business Machines Corporation in electronic data processing, of the Hughes Tool Company in oil drilling bits, and of the Electro-Motive Division of General Motors in diesel locomotives. The recent dominant position of Winnebago in the motor home business has been due primarily to the fact that it was the first in its field to set up a strong national dealer organization. This power exists in many industries of which the automobile industry is noteworthy.

The Power of Advertising and Sales Promotion

Another factor that tends to limit competition is the power of some companies to make volume sales and to expend large sums on advertising. This is nowhere better illustrated than by the practices of the Procter and Gamble Company in the soap and detergent business. By far the largest U.S. company in the field, Procter and Gamble is reputed to spend one fifth of every sales dollar on advertising and sales promotion. Even large companies like Colgate and Lever Brothers, whose sales are much smaller, find it difficult to compete at this game. And when Procter and Gamble does heavy "investment" advertising on a new product, its competitive edge approaches monopoly strength. When Procter and Gamble introduced its "Comet" household cleanser, it reportedly spent more in launching the product than the entire annual sales of the cleanser industry. The new product was immediately thrust into the leading position, and many smaller competitors lost part of their share of the market. Unquestionably Procter and Gamble recovered its costs in a few years through its sales volume and its dominance of the cleanser market.

Government Actions

Many government actions tend to interfere with competition. Tariffs and subsidies put some sellers in an advantageous position. Governmental power to grant or withhold licenses can strongly affect competition. For example, the Yellow Cab Company was given a monopoly in downtown Los Angeles for many years. The Federal Communications Commission can practically dictate the competitive behavior of broadcasting companies through its power to grant or withdraw broadcasting privileges.

By requiring companies to publish certain financial information, such as the profitability of product divisions within a company, the Securities and Exchange Commission may force companies to give information beneficial to competitors. Such data may tell competitors where profitable opportunities for expansion lie, or what other companies' costs are.

The Pure Food and Drug Administration may spend so much time testing a new drug product that undue advantage is given to those already in the market with a similar product. One major pharmaceutical company was delayed in putting its new birth control pills on the American market for seven years, though it was able to market them in other western countries several years before. Although it was strictly interpreting the law, the action of the U.S. government in outlawing cyclamates in soft drinks in 1970 caused a heavy blow to many firms in the business, and gave at least temporary advantage to competitors. This action was taken because a dosage of cyclamates apparently caused bladder cancers in 6 out of 12 laboratory rats. However, to consume an equivalent amount of cyclamates, a human being would have to drink several cases of cyclamate-sweetened soft drinks every day for most of his life span.[1]

WHY CAPITAL?

It is easy to see that human labor and natural resources are needed in order to produce economic goods. But not everyone fully appreciates the need for capital—machinery, buildings, inventories of goods, office equipment, and tools of all kinds. Few products or services could be made without these. It is estimated that nearly $50,000 of capital is required to create a single job for a production worker in U.S. manufacturing. In 1973, capital invested per company employee, including those in factories and elsewhere, was around $35,000.

But where does capital come from? Basically, from the labor of many people over the years who produced more than they consumed. People used their time and effort and natural resources to make something that in turn could be used to make something else. This kind of roundabout production, in which people work to produce something that cannot be directly consumed but can only be used to make something else, is essential in the modern economy. Even a musician, who

[1] George A. Steiner, *Business and Society* (New York: Random House, Inc., 1971), p. 464.

provides a service that is directly consumed, needs instruments, sheet music, a concert hall, seats for listeners, and many other items of capital equipment. Clearly, without capital, life as we know it would not be possible.

Every society, and every advanced one in particular, has amassed a huge amount of capital from the efforts of those in the past. But this capital must continually be replaced as it wears out or grows obsolete. Additional capital becomes necessary as new methods are developed and additional goods and services have to be produced. It is possible, of course, for a society to consume more than it produces by using up some of its capital accumulated from the past. Some companies have been known to do this by deferring the repair of machinery and equipment for a time. Individuals can do it through the miracle of the credit card, which enables them to buy now and pay later. If this continues for long, of course, the factory will cease to function and the individual will go bankrupt.

What is true of a company or an individual is also true of a society or a nation. No society can consume what has not been produced. And even if it tries to buy on credit or use up some of its capital resources, it cannot continue to do so indefinitely. There is no such thing as a free lunch. What we consume today must have already been produced by someone. This simple truth should have meaning for those who hold to the mistaken notion that "the government" can solve any problem simply by appropriating money for it. Except for things such as electricity, national park facilities, and water systems, government agencies do not produce goods that can be consumed or the capital with which to make them. Instead, they draw savings from businesses and individuals through taxes, and redistribute these funds to the beneficiaries of various programs. Or a government may raise funds by printing money, resulting usually in higher prices which take purchasing power away from those whose incomes do not increase as fast as prices.

The extent of annual capital formation is considerable. In 1973, for example, $115 billion was put into new plant and equipment and new inventories in the United States. In the same year consumers invested $189 billion in capital items, such as automobiles, housing, and household appliances. Obviously, these huge sums had to come from somewhere. Some people and companies in the United States had to produce more than they consumed that year. (The financial flows of the American economic system are further explained in Appendix A.)

WHY PROFITS?

One of the most misunderstood features of the capitalistic system is the fact that businesses strive to make profits. Some people look upon profits as unfair, and profit-making as an antisocial action carried on by unscrupulous businessmen. But the part profits play in our life takes on a different meaning when one realizes what the role of profits is, that they are not as great as most people think, and that they tend to serve social ends.

Profits as "Surplus"

The nature of business profits is often misunderstood. They are really only a measure of the surplus of business income over expenses. Surplus is logically the goal of every manager, whether in business or in other fields. It seems both logical and in the social interest for every manager, in any kind of enterprise and at any level in an enterprise, to manage his operation so that his group will accomplish its purpose at the least cost—whether in money, time, effort, discomfort, or materials—or will accomplish as much of the purpose as possible with the resources available.

In a business we call this surplus "profit" because we measure outputs as well as inputs by use of dollars. But does it not seem reasonable that a police chief should deliver to a city the best possible police protection he can with the resources made available to him? And should it not be the goal of the fire chief and his subordinate managers to do the same with fire protection service? Should not the dean of a university, college, or division do his best to operate as a manager so that professors will deliver the best possible teaching and research services? Most nonbusiness operations, of course, do not have any means of measuring their outputs so they do not know how much "surplus," if any, is being produced.

Profits as a Regulator of Efficiency and Effectiveness

The concept of profits as a surplus suggests the way they act as a regulator of efficiency in operations. People who accomplish objectives with the least cost, and therefore make profits, will tend to surpass and often replace people who do not. Thus there is a strong presumption, particularly under competitive conditions, that profitable companies are using their human and material resources better than others. If a business is to continue profitable over a period of years, it must be responsive to the various economic, technological, and social forces that influence all businesses.

The quest for profits does more than help to keep costs down. To succeed, a business must meet the demands of its customers. It is not enough to produce something at low cost if people do not want it or find it too expensive. Profits are a guide to effectiveness as well as efficiency.

The way profits function as a regulator in business suggests that a "surplus" approach might benefit many nonbusiness enterprises as well. If governments, schools, universities, nonprofit foundations, and religious organizations could somehow be judged by the amount of surplus they create over costs, what differences in their operations we might see!

Competition and Profits Allocate Resources

In a competitive system, the quest for profits tends to send labor, materials, and other resources into the production of things that the buying public wants most. The very fact that companies compete with each other for customers' dollars indicates that those who serve customers best will make the most sales. And only those companies that can make sales at a profit will stay in business. Thus profits act as a strong inducement to put resources into those economic operations that serve the public best. By buying what he wants at the lowest price, the customer, who is all of us, "votes" in favor of allocating resources in certain ways.

Profits as Pay for Use of Capital

One of the major purposes of profits is to compensate the millions of owners—proprietors, partners, or stockholders—for the use of the capital they have invested in a business. Profits also must compensate them for taking the risk that their capital may be lost should the business fail. If it were not for this hope of compensation, few people would want to invest in a business.

Profits as Source of Capital

One of the major sources of a company's capital is its profits. To be sure, not all of its profits are plowed back into the business. Some are paid out to investors who furnish a large portion of the capital used by the typical company. Moreover, since businesses also borrow money so that they can have the necessary funds to carry on their operations, they must make enough before profits to pay interest and to "save" enough from profits to pay debts as they are due.

It should not be forgotten that payments to stockholders and other owners for the use of their capital are not all spent by them on living expenses. A large percentage of such payments are saved and go back into business either directly through purchases of stock or by being deposited in banks or invested in life insurance.

Profits Yield Mutual Benefits to Investors and Society

We see, then, that "profits" is not a dirty word. Profits yield a socially desirable benefit to those who have capital to invest. It is true that some businessmen and investors make profits only because they are lucky. Many of the small machine and electrical shops located on the West Coast before World War II made sizeable profits during the war because they were in the right business in the right place at the right time. So were the movie studios that suddenly found their old films had increased in value because they could be used in television. Everyone has heard of greedy people who take advantage of temporary shortages to make a lot of money. Many automobile dealers did this at the close of World War II when new cars were scarce and the demand for them was high.

While the profit system has its shortcomings, the fact remains that without profits there would be no reason for the existence of private enterprise. Even under government ownership of business, as the Russians have found, there is no better single measure of how well a business is serving society than the measure of profit.

Profits as noted above, often go back into business and are thus an important source of capital. Without capital we could not have our system of industrial production with its increasing standard of living. Also, about half of profits in this country go to federal, state, and local governments in the form of taxes; the revenue from profits is then used to finance many government-run programs of social improvement.

Whatever our social goals are, it makes sense that they need to be accomplished efficiently. What is needed is to extend the profit, or "surplus," measurement to nonbusiness as well as to business enterprises.

How High Are Business Profits?

People greatly exaggerate the size of business profits. McGraw-Hill's Opinion Research Corporation conducted a survey in 1970 and found that people on the average thought profits to be 28¢ out of each dollar of sales. The average woman guessed 34¢, teenagers guessed 33¢, stock owners estimated 23¢, and farmers 21¢. An interesting twist of this survey was that most people thought that even these exaggerated business profits were reasonable. The fact is that in 1970 American manufacturing companies averaged only 4¢ profit after taxes on every sales dollar. The average for all manufacturing companies throughout the 1960s was less than 5¢. For corporations generally the average was closer to 3¢.

According to The Conference Board, corporations as a whole made approximately $65 billion after taxes in 1973, $50 billion in 1972, $43 billion in 1971, and averaged approximately $39 billion in the previous 10 years. We may compare these figures with the level of government expenditures. In 1973, the federal government spent over $264 billion. Had *all* corporate profits been confiscated through taxes, they would have financed the national government for a little more than two months. Even the country's top profit-making company, General Motors, which made $2.4 billion after taxes in very profitable 1973, would have been able to finance the federal government for roughly three days if all (instead of half) of its profits had been taken in taxes. And this would have left the company's 1,285,000 stockholders with no return on their $12 billion of investment.

It is worth noting that U.S. business corporations in 1973 invested an amount far more than their total profits in new machinery and equipment, new buildings, and additional inventory needed for production. Not all of this came from profits, to be sure, but profits account for as much as 25 percent of such expenditures in good years and 5 percent in a poor year. Without reasonable profits, a business would find it difficult to borrow from banks or to get investors to put up new money—which it must do if it is going to expand.

BUSINESS MUST RESPOND TO ITS ENVIRONMENT

Like individuals, businesses must be responsive to the total environment in which they operate. It would be stupid for a businessman to produce something people did not want to buy. Likewise, it would be foolish for him to try to sell something at a price that people would not pay. Thus, a first rule of business is to be aware of and respond to the economic environment.

In the same way, a successful businessman must respond to his technological environment. He must keep up with the technical changes affecting his operation or output. The introduction of the radial tire has greatly changed the tire business. The invention of synthetic fibers has revolutionized the textile and clothing business. And computerized machine tools have greatly changed the economics of making machined parts.

But economic and technological factors are only a part of the business environment. The successful business must also be aware of and responsive to the social and cultural forces, to the political setting, and to legal pressures and requirements. Otherwise it may lose money and even fail. Responsiveness to the total environment is in a businessman's own interest.

SUMMARY

Before we go on to see how businesses are established, how they operate, and how they are managed, it is important to know something of the role of businesses in the United States. A business is any person, group, company, or government department or agency whose purpose is to produce or sell products. In this book, we limit ourselves to economic enterprises, those operations that produce services or products and sell them to people who can buy them. About 85 percent of the products and services produced and sold in the United States are furnished by privately owned businesses, and the remainder by government agencies. In Communist countries such as Russia and China the situation is reversed: Most important products and services are provided by the publicly owned businesses, although some private enterprise still exists.

The American private business system is based on competition—rivalry between businesses for customers, between customers for products and services, between workers for jobs, and between investors for opportunities to make money from their savings. In some industries, where competition would not benefit the public, we allow monopolies such as public utilities. We also allow monopoly elements in the form of trademarks, copyrights, and patents. Other monopoly elements arise in industries where there are few sellers (called "oligopolies"), from the practice of making products appear to be different through "product differentiation," from lack of information among competitors, from the difficulty of entering certain businesses, and from government actions.

Any business requires capital. The average manufacturing business in the United States needs an investment of $35,000 for each worker's job. The tremendous accumulation of capital in modern society comes from the fact that over the years people have produced more than they have consumed. Companies have reinvested their profits, and individuals have saved and invested.

Profits are important to any economic system and in particular to a capitalistic system. They are really only a surplus of income over expenses. In the sense of "surplus," even nonbusiness operations should strive for accomplishing the most possible at the least cost. In this sense, profits help to bring about efficiency and effectiveness in business operations. They also provide a return on capital invested, create more capital, and contribute to government tax revenues. Profits are much lower than most people believe, although most people do not believe profits to be too high.

If businesses, like individuals, are to succeed, they must be responsive to life around them. This means being aware of, and taking into account in their everyday operations the economic, technical, social, and ethical factors of the society in which they live.

KEY TERMS AND CONCEPTS FOR REVIEW

What a business is	Role of competition
The business of business	Monopoly
An economic system	Monopsony
The task of economic systems	Oligopoly
Capitalism	Monopolistic competition—product
Private capitalism	differentiation
Socialism	Trademark, copyright, and patent
Communism	monopolies.
Public ownership of business	Capital
Effective competition	Profits
Responsible competition	Business responsiveness

QUESTIONS FOR ANALYSIS AND DISCUSSION

1. If the distinguishing feature of business is the production and sale of goods and services, can we think of a university as a "business"? Or a city police department? A state highway department? What is the distinction made in this book?

2. If all kinds of economic systems require business organizations, in what ways are business organizations in the United States and in the Soviet Union different?

3. If the concept of privately owned business is the heart of the capitalist system, can we say we have such a system in this country?

4. How, if at all, are rights attached to ownership of property related to our other rights?

5. Government (or public) planning and ownership are likely to be most effective when needs of people are clear and specific; they are likely to be least effective when individual tastes and desires predominate. Analyze and comment.

6. It is said that a private enterprise system depends largely on the existence of effective and responsible competition. Why is this so? How can we be assured that competition is effective and responsible? What do we do in private businesses when competition cannot work?

7. "Competition between businesses need not be price competition in order to be active and strong." Comment.

8. Even in the American business system, monopolies of various kinds exist. Identify the kinds. Why are they allowed to exist?

9. "Oligopolies in business are equivalent to monopolies, since companies in an oligopolistic industry do not compete." Comment.

10. Why do we need capital?

11. "There is no such thing as a free lunch." What does this mean, and what significance does it have for you?

12. Why should businesses be allowed to make profits? How do profits benefit our society? Are business profits too high? How high should they be? What would happen if the government took all private business profits?

SUGGESTED READINGS

Berg, I. *The Business of America.* New York: Harcourt, Brace & World, Inc., 1969.

Bjork, G. C. *Private Enterprise and Public Interest: The Development of American Capitalism.* Englewood Cliffs, N.J.: Prentice-Hall, 1969.

Bock, B. *Concentration, Oligopoly and Profit: Concepts and Data.* New York: The Conference Board, 1972.

Cohen, J. C. *America, Inc.: Who Owns and Operates the United States.* New York: Dial Press, 1971.

Eels, R. *The Meaning of Modern Business.* New York: Columbia University Press, 1960.

Galbraith, J. K. *The New Industrial State.* Boston: Houghton Mifflin, 1967.

2

Business Environment and Social Responsibility

We noted at the close of the previous chapter that every business, and indeed every person, must be responsive to the forces around him, whether social, technological, economic, political, or ethical. Business is often criticized for lacking social responsibility. This is not new. Businesses have been similarly criticized since the days of the 18th-century Industrial Revolution. Most people seem to feel that business has done fairly well over the years in handling purely economic problems, but has been less than sensitive in dealing with social problems. In the last few years, this public feeling has been reflected in many of the reports issued by corporations to their stockholders.

In a message to his shareholders late in 1971, the Chairman of Exxon Corporation (formerly Standard Oil Company of New Jersey) said:

Our company's basic role in society is economic. But we know that we must also respond to public needs and shifts in public attitudes, remain sensitive to human values, and alert to the effects of every company action on society and the environment. We must listen to the marketplace—and we must look beyond it.

Similar sentiments have been expressed by many other top executives.

This appears to represent a sincere, although for many businessmen a belated, recognition that they cannot ignore any part of their environment. The primary task of business, of course, must be to produce and sell products and services that people want and can buy. Businesses are not charitable enterprises. But it would be short-sighted of them to operate in a vacuum. To begin with, they must take into account markets and the demands of buyers. They must also consider changes in technology that affect them. It appears that they must also be aware of and responsive to social, political, and ethical influences.

This is not to say that the task of business is to solve the world's social problems. Its task is still to produce and sell economic goods and services. But it must do so in the total environment in which it operates.

THE SOCIAL AND CULTURAL ENVIRONMENT: POPULATION

In every kind of nation every business, whether privately or publicly owned, must operate within a social and cultural environment. Basically what is meant by this is that every society is comprised of people. The number of people, their age and educational composition have great significance for business. But also important is the fact that people have attitudes, desires, degrees of intelligence and education, beliefs, problems, and customs, most of which they have learned from their families, their schools, their friends, community, and work place. This, of course, represents a highly complex matter. For example, take any of your own attitudes, say, toward race, political party, money, or school. Why do you feel about these the way you do? The chances are that this will be found to be a very difficult question to answer.

Population: Growth

Let us first look at population growth and composition.

Concern with growing population in the world, and even in the United States, has given rise to much discussion of what is sometimes called the "population explosion" or even "population pollution."

Early in the 19th century an English clergyman and economist, T. R. Malthus, became famous for his argument that population was expanding at a faster rate than food production, and that unless people stopped multiplying there would eventually be widespread poverty and starvation. Malthus was overly pessimistic. European and American living standards continued to rise, not because of any remarkable slowdown in population growth, but primarily because of rising efficiency in food production. In the early 19th century in the United States, the average farmer could only grow enough food and fiber to supply 4 persons, but today he can supply 45 persons. In 1850, approximately two thirds of all employed persons in the U.S. worked on farms; by 1960 the proportion had fallen to about 8 percent, and it is expected to be only 2.6 percent by 1980.

This is not to say that population growth is not a social problem. In parts of Asia and Africa, the predictions of Malthus have been borne out in famine and warfare. In China with its 800 million population and India with its 550 million, producing the needs for life and efficiently utilizing the hands and minds of a growing population are prime social problems. Yet in the United States the standard of living has continued to rise despite an increase of population from 31,000,000 in 1860 to over 210,000,000 today.

For the businessman, population growth presents both opportunities and problems. Opportunities arise from the fact that there are continually more consumers to buy business output and more workers to produce and sell it. Problems are caused by the fact that, as more people want and need jobs, business must make them available. That this problem can be difficult, even in a prosperous country, may be seen from the numbers of people available for employment in the United States. There were 64 million people employed or looking for jobs in 1950, 86 million in 1970, and in 1985 forecasts indicate a work force of 107 million.

Population: Composition

The businessman studying the market for his product will want to know how the population is composed. Young people are likely to be interested in sport clothes and equipment, in the sportier automobiles, in furniture, and in musical instruments. Older people are likely to be interested in retirement homes, health foods, medical care, comfortable automobiles, and travel. Higher-income people can afford to satisfy tastes that people of lower incomes cannot. Thus, the composition of a population affects the demand for the output of most businesses.

While there are many ways of looking at the composition of a population, let us examine it in terms of age groups, level of educational attainment, allocation among various occupations, and income per household.

In the United States the proportion of the population over 65 years of age is increasing, primarily because of better health care. It rose

FIGURE 2–1

Educational Attainment and the Work Force

A. The Rising Educational Level of the Civilian Labor Force, Persons 18–64 (percent distribution)

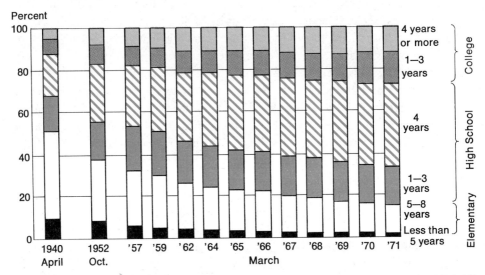

B. Occupations of Employed Persons and Years of School Completed, March 1971 (18 years of age and over)

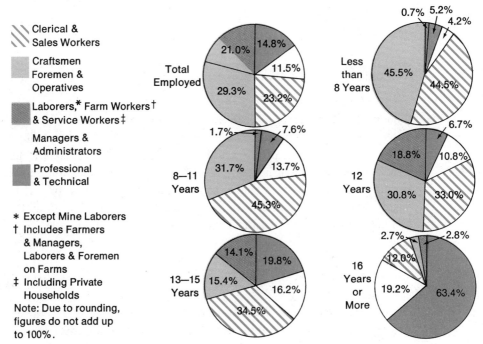

FIGURE 2–1—*Continued*

Education is one of several activities—sometimes termed investments in human capital—that raise potential future income by increasing resources in people. In most cases, education at the high school and college levels provides *general* training (mathematics, for example), which is applicable in a wide variety of job situations and thus benefits both the firm (potentially higher productivity) and the worker (potentially higher earnings). General training also benefits the individual because it acts as a hedge against the technological displacement of specific skills. *Specific* training (such as vocational courses), while less widely applicable, also raises potential productivity and earnings.

For at least a half century, there has been a continual rise in the educational attainment of American workers. For example, median years of school completed by the U.S. labor force rose from 9.1 years in 1940 to 12.4 years in 1971, and education began much earlier. During this period, the proportion of labor force participants with 12 years or more of formal education grew from 32 percent to 68 percent. The educational upgrading of the work force—necessitated by the increasingly complex nature of the economy and the concomitant growing demands for skilled workers—has played an integral role in boosting productivity.

Source: U.S. Department of Labor; The Conference Board, *Road Maps of Industry*, No. 1690, May 15, 1972.

from 5 percent in 1925 to nearly 10 percent in 1970. On the other hand, the proportion of those of working age, 18 to 65, stayed about the same, dropping slightly from 58 percent in 1925 to 56 percent in 1970.

The level of educational attainment is significant in the study of employee qualifications and markets. In the United States this has changed rather fast. In 1940 only 24.4 percent of the population over 25 years of age were high school graduates, and only 10.1 percent had some college or were college graduates. By 1970 over 55 percent were high school graduates and 21.4 percent had gone to college. It is forecast that by 1985 15.4 percent of the population 25 years of age or older will have graduated from college and another 12 percent will have been to college without graduating, for a total college group of 27.4 percent. It is hardly any wonder that businessmen today accept and support the demands of their employees for more interesting and worthwhile job opportunities.

Changes have also occurred in the relative numbers of people working at various occupations. Professional and technical jobs have been increasing and are expected to increase still more, as shown in Table 2–1 and Figure 2–2. The same is true of clerical jobs. The numbers of managers, officials, and proprietors are also expanding rapidly, but the numbers of farm workers have declined. The opportunities for operatives and non-farm laborers are increasing relatively slowly.

If we look at occupational groupings in other ways, we find some pronounced shifts. These have been caused by changes in the demand

TABLE 2–1

Civilian Employment by Occupation (millions of persons)

	1960	1970	1980
Accounting, stenographic and other clerical workers..........................	9.8	13.7	17.3
Professional, technical.....................	7.5	11.1	15.5
Operatives, nonfarm laborers..............	15.7	17.6	18.9
Service workers............................	8.3	9.7	13.1
Craftsmen, foremen.......................	8.6	10.2	12.2
Managers, officials, proprietors...........	7.1	8.3	9.5
Sales workers.............................	4.4	4.9	6.0
Farm workers.............................	5.4	3.1	2.6
Total Employed.....................	66.7	78.6	95.1

Source: The Conference Board, Inc., *A Guide to Consumer Markets, 1971–1972* (1971).

for goods and services combined with rises in the level of technology and productivity in certain industries. Thus we have seen and will see a lessening in the need for farm workers and for most types of blue-collar workers, such as machine operators, craftsmen, and laborers. There has been fast growth in the service industries—transportation,

FIGURE 2–2

Civilian Employment by Occupation

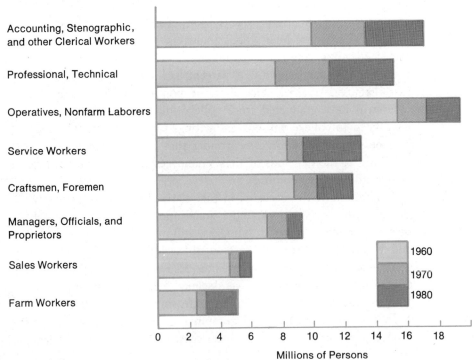

communication, utilities, trade, finance, education, health, government, and other business and personal services—where white collar workers predominate. The occupational shifts have been and will continue to be, toward jobs with higher formal educational requirements.

Another fact of great interest to the businessman is the growth of family incomes. The median family income in the United States increased from $3,031 in 1947 to nearly $10,000 in 1970. (This means that half of the families in 1970 had less than $10,000 while half had more.) Even if these figures are adjusted for price increases, the median income in terms of purchasing power doubled in those 23 years. This means that the businessman's market for products and services also doubled.

Many other population factors bear on the environment of a business. Among these we may mention the pronounced shift of population to the Pacific Southwestern, and Mountain states, the declining size of families, and the continuing increase of women in the work force—with more and more women being placed in responsible positions.

THE SOCIAL AND CULTURAL ENVIRONMENT: SOCIAL ATTITUDES AND BELIEFS

Many businesses have been justly criticized for not being as alert as they should have in the area of social attitudes and beliefs. Just as individuals have their various attitudes and beliefs, so do groups, societies, and even nations. Workers are likely to have different attitudes than employers, college students than alumni, capitalists than those who must stretch cash between paydays, Californians than Vermonters, engineers than accountants, and so on.

People are not born with their attitudes, and beliefs. They learn them from their families, friends, teachers, coworkers; political leaders, and others who touch their lives. It is not surprising that many college students, influenced by their new freedom of life and coming into contact with new friends and new ideas, tend to be highly critical of what they call the "establishment." Yet years afterward, out of college, they usually become a part of the establishment themselves.

It is impossible to deal in this book with all the social attitudes that affect business. In Japan, it has long been the rule for people to spend their lives working for the same company, even though this attitude appears to be changing somewhat in recent years. In Great Britain, until recently, business owners were regarded highly but professional managers not so highly. In the Soviet Union, autocratic control by the leaders of the Communist Party is generally believed to be for the good of all the people, and party members are regarded with high respect. Anyone moving from one society or group to another must take into account their different patterns of belief if he expects to operate a business, take a job, or even live congenially within a group.

The Major Traditional American Beliefs

In the centuries of American business development, there have been four dominant social beliefs of significance to the business climate:

1. The belief, derived from the experience of the frontier, that opportunities of all kinds exist for those willing to work to take advantage of them;
2. Faith in business and a high esteem for businessmen;
3. Belief in competition and competitiveness in all aspects of life, but particularly in business;
4. Belief in the importance of change and in experimenting to find better ways of doing things.

These beliefs have been worn away somewhat as the country has become more populous and as social problems have forced more government intervention in everyone's life. But they are still strong. They are supported by the real opportunities that have existed in this country, and by the conviction brought over originally by the early settlers and later by the hordes of immigrants, that honest work is good and enjoyment of the fruits of labor every man's right. They are supported by the Constitution which spells out limitations on the power of government and guarantees the rights of individuals. Although much of the original intent of the framers of the Constitution has been modified by court decisions and legislative actions, its guarantees of individual freedom still stand.

Tied in with these historical beliefs are a number of attitudes widely held by Americans. Among them are respect for individuals regardless of their race, religion, or creed; respect for authority arising from ownership of private property and elected or appointed political position; a strong regard for education; and a faith in logical processes, in science, and in technology. These beliefs and attitudes have had a considerable impact on business.

The Recent Upsurge of Social Beliefs

In recent years, Americans have supplemented and somewhat modified their traditional beliefs. They have come to feel that every individual has a right to a job, or to material support if he cannot get or hold a job because of age, illness, or other sufficient reasons. More and more Americans have come to believe that everyone is entitled to adequate medical care. Other strong beliefs favor the abolition of discrimination with respect to race, religion, political party, age, or sex; an environment cleansed of air and water pollution; and livable communities with decent housing, safe streets, efficient transportation, and educational and cultural opportunities.

To a very great extent these recent demands for a better life stem from the very success of the economic system that so many criticize. More and more citizens are able to live their lives without the hardships of urgent economic need. Most Americans have been able to afford food, clothing, shelter, health, transportation, and educational opportunities on a scale never achieved by the citizens of any other nation. Even with a threefold increase in population since 1890 and greatly increased taxes, the amount of money people have to spend has more than tripled while the time required for gainful work has diminished by half.

But the demands for a better life are real. People believe they are achievable and will not cease pressing for them. To the businessman, this is a fact of life that he cannot afford to ignore.

THE ECONOMIC ENVIRONMENT

Social pressures have not been a favorite subject of board meetings, at least in the past, and to a large degree it was long possible to ignore them. Few businesses, however, can afford to ignore their economic environment.

Desires, Customers, and Markets

As Peter Drucker said years ago, "the purpose of business is to create a customer." However, Drucker could not have meant that a business should create customers at any cost. One cannot imagine the chief executive of a business saying at the end of a financially disastrous year: "We had a great year. We created a million new customers. But, by the way, we lost ten million dollars and went bankrupt doing it."

Without customers, of course, a business cannot exist. Customers are people who want the product or service a business offers and have the money to buy it. This naturally puts pressure on a business to produce what people want and to sell it at as low a price as possible. As a rule, the forces of competition tend to keep prices, costs, and profits low. The main exceptions to this are those few goods produced by monopolies whose prices are invariably regulated.

It is not easy to predict what people will buy. For one thing tastes change, as the automobile manufacturers found out when the once despised German "beetle," the Volkswagen, burst into the American market. For another thing, substitutes appear for old products, as the magazine publishers found out when advertisers shifted from them to television. And people buy for different reasons: some want a sailboat, others want a power boat, and still others would not have the cost and responsibility of a boat at all. In the case of industrial buyers, who buy materials or machinery to use in production, demand changes as their final products change, as new processes are found, and as different equipment comes on the market.

Timing is important. The businessman must anticipate demand early enough to be ready for the market. Except for very simple products, it takes time to develop an item, get it into production, and put it on the market. It is a rare product that does not take three or more years to get to market from the time it is thought of. A new airplane is likely to take five or more years. A certain detergent manufacturer required five years to get his new dishwashing detergent designed and on the market.

Availability and Price of Capital

Business requires capital. While some capital can be generated within a business, much of it must come from outside investors or bankers. Moreover, capital must not cost too much since its cost must be covered by the price at which a product or service is sold.

One of the problems of every developing country is to obtain capital for its expanding industry. The early railroads in the U.S. were largely built with capital lent by European investors. Much of the recent development of transportation and productive resources in Canada has been financed by British and American investors.

Availability and Price of Labor

Labor is an important business resource. In Japan the availability of a well educated and hardworking population has contributed much to that country's business development. The early beginnings of the automobile industry in Detroit, the tire industry in Akron, and the aircraft industry in Southern California gave rise to a skilled labor supply in these areas, and this contributed to the further growth of the same industries there.

The price of labor is also an important factor. While the rise of wages in the United States has been gratifying, it has led to cost problems for the American producer who wants to sell abroad. Until recently labor costs in Europe were half those in the United States, in Mexico one quarter and in Taiwan one tenth. It is not difficult to see that products having a high amount of labor in them have often been made at less cost outside the United States.

Even within the United States there used to be great differences in wages from one region to another. The movement of the textile industry from New England to the South was primarily the result of lower labor costs there. Many companies have moved from large cities to suburban or agricultural areas for the same reason. But the adoption of minimum wage laws and the growth of unionism have tended to reduce wage differentials within the United States.

Level of Productivity

How much are capital and labor worth to the businessman? This depends on their productivity, that is, on what a dollar's worth of capital or labor will produce. We measure productivity by the total amount produced per employee—for example, tons of steel per worker or the number of cases of soap per man-hour. We can even add up the value of all the goods and services produced in the United States (gross national product) and divide it by the total hours worked to get national output per man-hour (Figure 2–3).

It is hard to say what causes an increase in output per man-hour. The equipment may have been improved, the workers may have become more skillful, management may be using better methods, or something else may have changed. When a company installs a new machine that lowers the cost of making a product, we can assume that the higher productivity is the result of capital improvements. But might it not also be the result of making labor more efficient? Therefore when we say that there has been an increase in output per labor-hour (or man-hour), we do not necessarily mean that the increase was caused by labor.

America's success in competing on the world market has been the result of high productivity in this country. But productivity has been increasing rapidly in other such countries as Germany and Japan, and is even rising in developing nations such as the U.S.S.R. and Iran. Thus

FIGURE 2–3

Trends in Productivity (Indexes: 1967 = 100)

A. Output per Man-Hour in the private Economy   B.   Sector Trends in Productivity

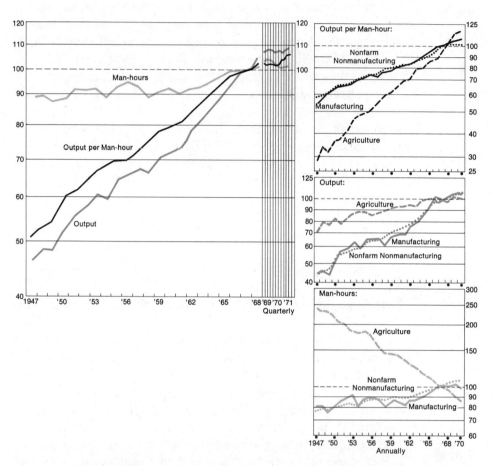

Advances in productivity are responsible for a large share of economic growth in the United States. Productivity is affected by such factors as the amount and quality of equipment used, technical improvements, managerial efficiency, and the skill and efforts of workers. But because some of these input classes are so varied, their effects so hard to separate, and their outputs so diverse, the level of, and the change in, productivity are extremely difficult to measure.

The relationship between output and man-hours is frequently used to attempt to measure changes in productivity, partly because of the relative ease in obtaining data on man-hours—though it is admitted that it is probably an inaccurate simplification to pool the hours worked by persons with a wide range of skills. It should be noted that output per man-hour expresses not only the efforts and skill levels of workers, but also the general efficiency in the use of labor; hence it reflects the effects on productivity of other factors as well.

Source: Bureau of Labor Statistics; The Conference Board, *Road Maps of Industry*, No. 1675, October 1, 1971.

FIGURE 2–4

International Labor Costs and Productivity in Manufacturing (selected countries)

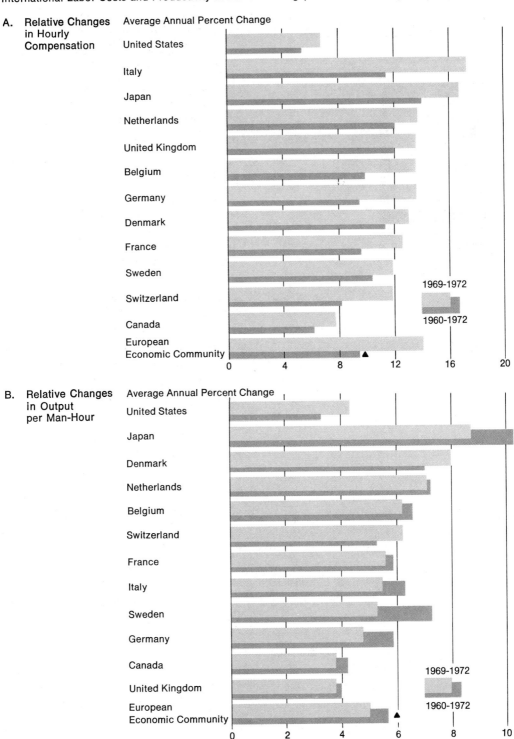

Source: Department of Labor; The Conference Board, *Road Maps of Industry*, No. 1733, March 1, 1974.

J. Paul Austin

J. Paul Austin was elected the tenth president of the Coca-Cola Company in 1962 at the age of 47. In 1970 he became chairman of the board and chief executive officer of the world's leading soft drink producer.

Austin was born in 1915 at Lagrange, Georgia. He attended Culver Military Academy and Harvard University, from which he was graduated in 1937 with a liberal arts degree. He received his law degree from Harvard Law School in 1940, after which he entered private practice in New York City.

During World War II he served with a motor torpedo squadron in the Pacific. He attained the rank of Lieutenant Commander and was decorated with the Legion of Merit. After the war he returned to his law practice in New York.

In 1949 Austin joined the Coca-Cola Company's legal department and pursued assignments in New York and Chicago. A year later he was transferred to the Coca-Cola Export Corporation, and in 1951 appointed assistant to its president. In 1952 he was elected a vice president of the Export Corporation.

He went abroad in 1954 to direct operations in Africa from the company's office in Johannesburg, South Africa. He was promoted to executive vice president and director in 1958, advancing to the export

---

the advantage of the United States in the world market is diminishing. In many products, such as transistor radios, steel, automobiles, and many textiles, the advantage has tended to appear.

To be sure, the record of American productivity has been good. It increased at an average rate of 2.2 percent a year over the period 1958–1973, and is expected to continue at 2.5 percent a year in the period 1974–1988. But this is a low rate of increase compared to Japan's average, at least until recently, of approximately 10 percent.

The need for higher productivity exists in every field. Most service businesses—movie making, home and building construction, health care, and others—are slow in increasing productivity. Yet the service industries are the fastest growing portion of American business which explains why we pay so much for their products nowadays. Productivity

company's presidency in 1959. In 1961 he was elected to the additional post of executive vice president of the parent organization, headquartered in Atlanta, Georgia. After stepping up to the presidency in 1962, he also assumed the role of chief executive officer in 1966.

Austin's job has been described as "managing success." Coke, with 41 percent of the soft drink market, has had uninterrupted earnings gains. Sales have exceeded $1 billion annually since 1966, and Coca-Cola products are marketed in 130 countries.

But the dynamic society in which Austin has had to manage this success has not failed to generate enough crises for the company to keep the executive team's adrenalin flowing. Austin has had to face the cyclamate scare, a promotional bingo game scandal, widespread publicity about the deplorable living conditions of migratory citrus laborers employed by its subsidiary Minute Maid, the Federal Trade Commission's charge that Hi-C advertising was making false claims, and the cries of millions of environmentalists in outrage against Coke's one-way bottles and cans. Complaints have also been filed by the Federal Trade Commission against the company and other firms in the industry, attacking the validity of territorial provisions in bottlers' contracts. The company has affirmed its intention to defend vigorously the integrity of its contracts with bottlers, although it is likely that litigation could continue over a period of years.

Ecology is the big problem, however. Coke finds itself in the middle of the growing conflict between the traditional American demands for ease and convenience on the one hand, and the newer dedication to a cleaner environment on the other. Alienation of an important segment of the consumer market is the result, whatever the fate of the nonreturnable bottle. The company is trying to demonstrate its sensitivity to the expectations of our dynamic society. It has described the constant need to find ways to respond affirmatively as "a never-ending, dynamic process."

Austin phrased this philosophy, in a 1972 speech to an international food distributors' association in Vienna, as follows: "If we are to ameliorate the environmental crises that confront us . . . if we are to help restore ecological peace to an earth with which we have so long been engaged in violent war . . . if our concerns are now to turn from quantity to *quality* of life . . . then we must redefine our priorities and reorder our lives, even to the point of accepting *psychic* rewards in place of some types of physical progress."

does not seem to increase very much at all in education or government, despite the fact that almost a third of our dollars go for these.

Productivity is a mixture of many things: labor-saving machinery; the willingness to work efficiently; the availability of good managers; and people's ingenuity in developing new equipment and processes. Perhaps the most important of all is a widespread understanding that we cannot increase our standard of living and improve our quality of living without producing more efficiently.

The Quality of Imaginative Entrepreneurship

An entrepreneur is a person who sees an opportunity, gets together the capital he needs, and starts a business—taking, of course, the risks of failure while hoping to reap the gains of success. America has been especially blessed by many creative entrepreneurs over the years. Much of this has been the result of the great opportunities present in an expanding country in which private ownership has been supported and profit-making regarded as respectable.

Are the opportunities for entrepreneurship declining now that the United States is a developed country and the frontier is gone? We should not forget that more than four fifths of the 5 million businesses in America are still owned by individuals, and that the number of business firms is growing at the rate of 50 thousand per year. It is true that 10 to 15 thousand businesses fail every year, and that in addition many businesses stop operating when the owners get tired and quit. Most of these businesses, as one would expect, are retail stores, small repair shops, builders, and other service activities.

Almost every large business in the United States, let us note, was started by one or two entrepreneurs or is made up of a merger of several businesses started by entrepreneurs. Henry Ford, George Eastman, H. J. Heinz, Andrew Carnegie, Henry Kaiser, and R. H. Macy are only a few of the names that come easily to mind. To show that large businesses are still being started by individuals, we need only recall Edwin H. Land with his Polaroid camera, Charles Thornton and Roy Ash of Litton Industries, Howard Hughes and the Hughes Aircraft Company, Armand Hammer and the Occidental Petroleum Corporation, and Mr. and Mrs. Eliot Handler and their Mattel Toy Company. All of these were founded in the past two or three decades.

The importance of imaginative entrepreneurship is not limited to the founding of a new business. It is also a highly desirable quality in existing businesses. The ability to see an opportunity, talent for putting together a successful operation, and the willingness to take personal risks are qualities prized even by large companies. A top executive of the General Electric Company has said that what his company wants most from the young people they hire is the ability to act like entrepreneurs.

Intelligent and Able Managers

One of the advantages of American business has been the existence, particularly in the past three decades, of increasing numbers of intelligent and able managers. The United States has been generally regarded as leading the world in quality of management. The importance of managerial skills can hardly be overestimated. As we shall see in later chapters, it is the task of managers to design and maintain an environment in which individuals can work effectively together in

groups. It is not enough for a society to have capital and skilled workers; leadership is needed so that they can work together efficiently. The countries that benefited most from the huge American aid program after World War II were those in which managerial skills were best applied.

Market Size

Some businesses produce goods for relatively small markets (for example, luxury goods), while others sell to millions of customers. The larger a market is, in terms of customers and purchasing power, the more of a given product can be sold and the more cheaply it can be made by means of large-scale production.

The United States has had an advantage over many countries because of its large internal market, particularly as compared to the more advanced countries of Europe. However, now that European countries have joined together in the European Economic Community, often called the Common Market, they have achieved a market approximately the size of the U. S. market. This need for a large market helps to explain why Japan is so keenly interested in the maintenance of a high degree of freedom in international trade.

Price Levels and Inflation

It is difficult to do business when prices keep changing. A businessman has to know what his costs will be six months or a year from now so that he can set his prices to cover them, hopefully with a profit. Most businesses need to borrow money, and if prices are rising rapidly a lender will want to charge very high interest rates because the money he gets back will have less purchasing power. Even then he will probably want to limit his lending to short periods of time. A business finds it difficult to operate on short-term credit.

Business can tolerate moderate rises in price levels, and business in Brazil has learned to live with price rises of 15 or 20 percent a year or more. But the uncertainty does tend to increase costs, to make capital less available, and to increase the difficulty of paying adequate and fair wages. One need only think what would happen if last week's wages were barely enough to buy a pair of shoes this week, as happened at the height of the German inflation of a half century ago.

It is no accident that the best business development has come in countries with a fair degree of price stability. The fact that the

Mexican peso has remained fairly stable in value for several decades, while currencies of most South American countries have suffered from considerable inflation, is a major reason why Mexican business has developed so well in this period.

Government Fiscal and Monetary Policy

Fiscal policy comprises the taxing and spending actions of government. Monetary policy involves government actions that affect the supply of money and credit (to be discussed in a later chapter on banking). If the government spends a lot more than it takes in through taxes, it will have to borrow from the banking system. If the banking system makes too much credit available, the result will be more dollars seeking things to buy than are available on the market. This will tend to push prices up. On the other hand, if the government spends much less than it takes in, or makes too little credit available, the result can also be disruptive. There will be fewer dollars chasing more goods and services. People will not be able to buy the goods and services available, production will fall and unemployment will rise.

It can be seen that what a government does in its spending and in its influence on the availability of money is important to the businessman. To be sure, inflation is not altogether bad; business tends to expand during inflation because demand increases. But when prices go up, suppliers want more money for materials while labor understandably wants higher wages. Consequently, a vicious spiral may result in which nobody ever quite catches up, like the proverbial dog chasing his tail.

Government Tax Policy

The level of taxation is just as important as the level of government spending. The more a government spends, the more it must get in taxes if it is to avoid inflation. The *way* a government levies its taxes is as important to businesses and to people generally as the *amount* of taxes collected. If taxes are too heavy on profits, the incentive to go into or stay in a business tends to drop and investors will look elsewhere to invest their capital. If taxes are too heavy on income, people will not only be able to buy less but will feel less inclined to work hard because so much of their earnings are taken away from them. If taxes are levied on sales, prices rise and buyers get less for their money. If taxes become too high on real estate, people will find, as many have in recent years, that it is too expensive to own a house and they will look for cheaper and less comfortable living quarters. Also, as taxes get high, people will reasonably ask for higher wages and salaries, thereby raising business, government, and other costs.

What is especially important to business is whether the existing taxes and the attitude of taxing authorities make it difficult to carry on a business. Corporate income taxes, if too high, tend to do this. Special taxes levied on products, called excise taxes, may if they are too high put one product at a disadvantage as against another. Very high taxes on a product can even drive it out of the market, as happened in this country for many years when taxes on oleomargarine colored to look like butter were so high in some states that only white margarine could be sold.

As we shall see later, there is much more to be said about the impact of taxes on business. There have been periods (and it is even true to a great extent now) when one of the major things to consider in making a business decision was the taxes which might result.

THE TECHNOLOGICAL ENVIRONMENT

Technology is an all-encompassing term used to mean the knowledge we have of ways to do things. Technology includes inventions, such as Edison's electric light or the office copying machine. It includes science, that vast store of organized knowledge about everything from aerodynamics to zoology. We are concerned here with technology as it affects the production and selling of products or services.

There has always been a strong link between business and technology. Any business that wishes to survive in a changing world must use technology to develop and modernize its products or services, and also to meet cost competition and to improve its marketing. A study made of important new inventions since 1800 has shown that most of them occurred because someone was looking for ways of making a profit.

The alert businessman must not only be aware of technological changes affecting his operations and his customers; he needs to forecast the state of the art so that he will have time to use it successfully before he finds his products or processes obsolete. It is not safe to wait until a competitor puts new technology on the market and offers something new to customers. By then it may be too late to catch up with him. The steam locomotive manufacturers found this out with the advent of the diesel locomotive, and had to close their factories.

Categories of Technological Change

Looking back, we often speak of the adoption of machinery and electric power or the advent of the computer as "revolutions." But technological growth is really much broader in scope. Taken all together, the various kinds of technological change can be grouped as follows (for each of which examples are given):

1. Increased ability to master time and distance for the movement of materials and people: railroads, automobiles and trucks, airplanes, and, to some extent, space vehicles.
2. Increased ability to generate, store, transport, and distribute energy: electricity, nuclear power, and perhaps the laser.
3. Increased ability to design new materials and change the properties of others so that they better serve needs: steel alloys, plastics, synthetic fibers, new drugs.
4. Mechanization or automation of physical processes: the host of labor-saving or labor-substituting devices from Hargreave's spinning jenny of 1770 to the largely automatic San Francisco subway system of 1974.
5. The mechanization or automation of mental processes: the computer, which greatly expands man's ability to store, manipulate, and select or supply data.
6. Extension of human ability to sense things: radar, the electron microscope.
7. Increased understanding of individual and group behavior: psychology of motivation and of group behavior, better managerial techniques.
8. Increased understanding of individual disease and its treatment: inoculations for polio, kidney transplants, antibiotic treatment of infections.

Should Technology Be Curbed?

At every stage of technological growth, fears have been expressed that technology is advancing too fast. The early railroad train was charged with upsetting the quiet pace of life. The first automobiles were regarded as rich men's dangerous playthings. The mechanical developments of the early 20th century were blamed for the unemployment of the Great Depression of the 1930s. Today there are people who want to stop the space program, whose efforts have halted the development of the supersonic airplane in this country, who oppose the use of nuclear energy for power generation, and who would even slow down all technological development because they fear it will bring more unemployment, pollution, and spoilage of the environment. Some of them blame business for pushing technological growth just to make a profit, regardless of the consequences.

Although unemployment remains a serious problem in this country, the United States has been able to double the number of jobs in the last 40 years. Certainly much of this expansion would not have been possible without new products, techniques, and processes. The advances of technology have undeniably brought social problems such as pollution and other damage to the environment, but they have also brought an expanded standard of living.

Dr. Wernher von Braun, renowned space scientist and pioneer, has said of the drive to slow down technology:

> It is irrational because those most vocal in their hostility toward science and technology are the very ones professing the greatest concern about poverty, poor housing, hunger, and quality of the environment. All of these problems depend in varying degree upon our technological capabilities, and certainly upon increased productivity for their solutions.

THE POLITICAL ENVIRONMENT

It is difficult to separate the political environment of business from that which we choose to call the legal environment. Laws and their administration by various commissions and bureaucrats are naturally a reflection of the political environment, particularly that of the past, since laws and regulations, once on the books, are not easily changed. For example, the railroads were subjected to close regulation three quarters of a century ago because they had a strong monopoly power in transportation. Subsequently there arose vigorous competition from trucks, automobiles, pipelines, and airlines, but most of the old regulations still exist.

A political environment unlike laws, tends to change with the ebb and flow of events and social pressures. The patriotic fervor of World War II and its effect on political and government action can be contrasted to the disillusionment with respect to the Vietnam conflict. Some of the United States Senators who strongly backed our going into Vietnam completely changed their minds as people became disenchanted with the conflict. The same shifts occur in attributes toward business. Franklin D. Roosevelt's vow to "throw the money changers

out of the temple" during the Great Depression changed to a pro-
business attitude when more output was needed for World War II.
John F. Kennedy's crackdown on the steel industry because of price
increases in 1962 was followed by efforts to reassure and to woo business
when he saw that businessmen's lack of confidence in him might lead
to a business slowdown and unemployment. Strong moves to combat
pollution have changed to softer attitudes in some communities when
it turned out that a plant unable to meet pollution-control standards
would have to shut down. The shortage of petroleum in the 1970s has
caused many people to change their minds about not using high-sulfur
oil and coal, or adopting pollution control devices on automobiles that
reduce the miles driven per gallon of gas, or banning off-shore oil
drilling, or opposing the construction of atomic energy generating
plants.

Even within cities and states, political attitudes vary. Delaware has
long been regarded as a state favorable to business corporations and
one where business regulations and political attitudes are not likely to
change. Consequently a large number of businesses have been incorporated under the laws of that state. The fact that political leaders—
those in government office and those who help elect office holders—in
many medium-sized cities of the Midwest are known to be favorable to
business has led many companies to locate their plants in those places.

When top management sets out to establish a new business or a
new plant or office, one of its first considerations will be the political
climate of the area. Is the state or city likely to levy taxes disadvantageous to business, such as a local income tax or a discriminatory
property tax? Does the political system tolerate or encourage various
forms of bribery among party leaders and government officials? Do
present regulations, as well as those that might be passed, impose excessive costs?

While political pressures and government actions tend to change
greatly over time, in many countries the basic political system remains
highly stable. American businessmen can have a high degree of confidence that we will continue as a predominantly democratic society
with ultimate power in the hands of voters and with a dictatorship
being unlikely. On the other hand, businesses in most South American
and African nations cannot be sure that the policy toward private
business will remain from one decade to the next. For example, in Chile
the landowners, mining companies, and large manufacturers faced a
completely new situation when President Allende came into power in
1971. And this changed again when Allende was later deposed.

If a business is to thrive, it needs some assurance of basic political stability. Investments in plant and equipment must be made. Systems of selling must be established, employees hired and trained. A businessman can learn to live in almost any stable political environment that allows him to exist at all. But to try to live in a radically changing one is like playing roulette.

Political environments are basically a matter of the customs of a society. As we know, the long tradition in America has been one of individual freedom, the right to vote and select government leaders, belief in private ownership and competitive business. This has also been largely true of the western European nations. But such traditions are by no means universal. Both the Russians and the Chinese have had a long history of political and economic rule by the few. Egypt, before the socialization of major economic activities in 1962, was predominantly controlled by large landowners and large companies. It is no exaggeration to say that politics is "the art of the possible," meaning possible in terms of what people have been taught to think, believe, and want.

THE LEGAL ENVIRONMENT

Every business is encircled by a complex web of laws, regulations, and court decisions. Some of them are designed to restrict what a business can or cannot do. Some are intended to protect workers, consumers, and communities. Some, like patents and laws to make contracts enforceable, exist to protect business and its operations. In almost every decision a businessman makes he is subject to a law or a regulation. He is in continual need of legal counsel, either from an outside law firm or from a lawyer employed by the company. The nature of these legal supports and controls will be discussed in the following chapter.

Regulations are necessary, even though they may often be burdensome. Without laws power-hungry and greedy individuals might gain the upper hand in an industry; then workable and responsible competition would probably disappear. Healthy working conditions would certainly not be as universal if it were not for laws and governments, nor would the rights of workers be so well protected. Investors could be freely bilked by unscrupulous confidence men selling fraudulent stocks.

Strict regulation in many areas is necessary just to make our system of competition work. The honest businessman would find it difficult to compete with sharpers who were able to pay substandard wages, misrepresent the quality or weight of their products, mislead investors through false earnings reports, or get out of paying taxes.

Regulation does more than protect the honest against the dishonest. It forces everyone to play by the same rules. Some of the side effects of modern industry, such as pollution, cannot be eliminated without laws and regulations that apply to everyone. Many businesses have contributed to the pollution of Lake Erie. If only one of them had tried to do something about it, by not dumping harmful wastes into the lake, it would have incurred costs greater than those of its competitors who still allowed their wastes to go into the lake. If one automobile manufacturer had put out a smog-free car several years ago, raising the price by several hundred dollars, he would have been at a competitive disadvantage. How many car buyers who spent hundreds of dollars for optional automatic transmissions and air conditioning would have bought the smog-eliminating "extra"?

WHAT IS THE SOCIAL RESPONSIBILITY OF BUSINESS?

There is probably no question that has received more attention by businesses, governments, politicians, and people in general in the past few years than what the social responsibility of business is. Some people say that social problems are no business of business. Others believe that almost all of our social problems are caused by business and that business should do something about them. Even a young teacher of business in a community college has strongly expressed the belief that business *causes* recessions, unemployment, inflation, and pollution. In a nutshell, there appears to be a feeling that business has been effective in dealing with economic problems, but is narrow, selfish, and insensitive in dealing with social problems.

Businessmen face a dilemma in this area. If they respond to the demands of many interest groups that they do something about social problems, they may undertake actions that run counter to a program of some government agency to which handling of the problems has been given. If a business spends too much on the effort to solve social problems, its costs may go so high that it cannot sell its products and earnings might suffer so that it would be unable to attract the capital investments needed to continue and expand operations.

Social Responsibility Is Social Responsiveness

The purpose of business, of course is to produce goods and services that the public wants and can buy. It is not the job of business to furnish public school education, religious services, or police protection. But, as we have seen throughout this chapter, business must live within its environment—social, economic, technological, political, and legal.

To live within an environment is to take into account those elements of our surroundings that are important to us. We certainly do this when we drive on the right side of the street, wear clothes, work for a living, use a power mower on our yard, vote, go to church at certain hours, or pay taxes. Some of these things we do in order to live more compatibly with our neighbors. Some we do because we get satisfaction from them. And some we do because society, through its laws, requires us to do them.

In other words, we respond to our environment. Business must do the same. While its major purpose is economic, its very survival depends on doing those things that are compatible with its environment.

As pointed out in previous sections of this chapter, to respond requires first of all that we know what our total environment is. Since a business, like a university or government agency, cannot expect to respond very quickly to new problems, it must develop ways of anticipating them. An alert company does not wait until its product is obsolete and sales have fallen off before coming out with a new or improved product. And it should not wait for other problems to develop before preparing to face them.

The point can be illustrated by what happened in the case of the automobile industry and the smog problem. We can hardly blame the auto makers for not doing anything about smog 10 or 20 years ago when buyers would almost surely not have paid more money for a smog-free car. But we can criticize them for not seeing the problem earlier and for not getting ready, through research and development, to make the technical changes quickly when laws were passed.

What Can Business Do and Still Be Business?

Beyond obeying the laws, there are a number of things a business can do in society's interest and in its own. These go beyond the normal social expectation that a business be efficient and productive, serve its customers well, act responsibly and competitively, help the economy grow, furnish meaningful jobs to people, and pay good wages.

Since an educationally qualified work force is essential to business, firms can and do support education through direct financial aid to schools in their communities, and by giving their employees opportunities for training and development. A company may find it advantageous to recruit and train persons suffering from physical and mental deficiencies, so that they become useful members of the work force. Companies can justifiably take leadership and even give financial aid to improve the general quality of life in their communities, because better living conditions mean better employees. For the same reasons, it can be in a company's best interest to help design and operate health care and recreational facilities. And since virtually all businesses use natural resources, they have an interest in taking steps to conserve them.

But Control by the Government Is Often Necessary

Some firms have found special advantages for themselves in these programs. The Union Carbide Company, for example, discovered that in filtering the smoke that went out of its smokestacks it obtained minerals and gases that made the cleaning of air profitable. Many oil companies have found that removing sulfur from their products yielded a profitable by-product. Companies that took the lead in hiring and training minority races and disadvantaged persons often found that they developed a loyal and competent employee group.

It is easy to see that all businesses in a community may benefit from the efforts and expenditures of a few. Better public education, improved housing and transportation, less air and water pollution, and improved health care become the property of everyone. Businesses that do not spend their funds to accomplish these things may get a "free ride" from those that do.

To assure that no company gets even a temporary cost advantage by not responding to social forces, government regulation may be necessary. It is unlikely that a smog-free automobile would have been produced without such controls. We would never be able to reduce the pollution of our rivers, lakes, and oceans without legal action, particularly since many cities that dump raw sewage into them have been found to be far greater polluters than businesses. Nor is it likely that discrimination in the employment of minority groups, women, and older persons would have been reduced without legal action. Social prejudices and short-term selfish interests must often be curbed by the power of government.

Social Action Often Presents Opportunities for Business

We have already mentioned the profits one company found in filtering smokestack pollutants. Many others can be cited. Compulsory insurance schemes have led to more profitable hospitals, higher incomes for physicians, and a boom for those who supply medicines and medical equipment. Two New York City corporations made a profit in setting up a joint venture to build low-cost apartments in ghetto areas. The largest bank in Georgia has, for some years, found a profit in being reasonably liberal in extending housing and business loans to poorer blacks and whites in that state. Manufacturers of safety devices for automobiles and other machines have done a thriving business. A West Coast air filtering company discovered that costly, high-efficiency air filtering systems in office buildings more than paid for themselves in lower cleaning and painting costs, so that clean air for office workers became a profitable free dividend.

In other words, contributing to the solution of social problems does not always involve net expenses. But we may need the bludgeoning force of government action to get them under way.

Use of Business Talents in Solving Social Problems

While we can't expect business to solve major social problems, there is much to be said for borrowing business talent to help deal with these problems. The quality of management in business generally exceeds that in other fields. Long subject to the spur of competition, business-men have had to be innovative, careful with costs, concerned with the consumer, and generally competent and responsible. If more of these qualities were brought to bear on government agencies and universities, we might get more and better service from them at lower costs.

To some extent this has been done. The government has granted various forms of aid to businesses to encourage them to train disad-vantaged persons, rebuild ghettos, help blacks and others establish businesses, make more liberal loans for home and apartment building, establish better pension plans, and so on.

Sometimes government agencies contract out some of their func-tions to private businesses. This has been done in the fields of defense and space exploration, the majority of the contracts providing in-centives for efficient performance and penalties for inadequate results. The Social Security Administration contracts out some of its handling of claims under the Medicare program to private insurance companies. The government has also cooperated with private corporations in joint ventures. Comsat (Communications Satellite Corporation), which furnishes satellite communications services, is financed and operated by both government and business. Amtrak (National Railroad Passenger Corporation) is a joint government-business enterprise set up to handle most of the nation's rail passenger service. In 1970, Gary, Indiana became the first city in the United States to contract out an elementary school to a private business concern; the contract provided that the company would refund the fee for any student whose grade level did not rise to at least one third above what the average had been.

SUMMARY

Any business firm must live within its total environment if it expects to survive. While the basic purpose of business is economic, it must be responsive not only to market and economic factors but also to other elements in its environment—social, economic technological, political, and ethical.

The social and cultural influences affecting business include people's attitudes, desires, degrees of intelligence and education, beliefs, problems, and customs. Other important factors are the size and location of the population, people's occupations, and their incomes. These affect business operations because they influence customers, workers, managers, and investors. The major traditional American beliefs in private property, competition, and finding better ways of doing things have provided a climate for business growth and success for many years. In more recent times, increased emphasis has been put on human rights, especially the right of all people to a better life without discrimination because of sex, race, religion, or age.

Businesses are by their very nature economic organizations, and must consider the desires of customers who expect to purchase goods at the lowest possible prices. Other economic factors of great importance to businessmen are the availability and cost of capital, the level of productivity, the quality of imaginative entrepreneurship, the availability of intelligent and able managers, the size of the market in which goods and services are to be sold, the stability of price levels, and the nature of government fiscal and monetary policies.

Every businessman must be concerned with technical developments in his field. The alert businessman must forecast changes that may affect his operations and his customers, so that he will have time to adapt to them before he finds his products or processes obsolete.

The political and legal situation is extremely important to business: whether political leaders are sympathetic to business needs, whether laws support sound and ethical business practices or make them difficult, and whether the political and legal system is reasonably stable. To operate a business effectively requires knowing the rules of the game and also what they are likely to be in the future.

Businesses must also fit in with their social environment. Sometimes government controls help businessmen to assure their social responsibilities by ensuring that no company will be put at a disadvantage. Being responsive to social needs can even open opportunities for profits. Perhaps in time everyone will come to recognize that being a helpful member of society is also good business.

KEY TERMS AND CONCEPTS FOR REVIEW

Social responsibility	Entrepreneurship
Social responsiveness	Price levels and inflation
Environment of business	Government fiscal policy
Social and cultural environment	Government tax policy
Social attitudes and beliefs	Technology
Major traditional American beliefs	Technological environment
Recent explosion of social concern	Political environment
Economic environment	Legal environment
Productivity	Social action

QUESTIONS FOR ANALYSIS AND DISCUSSION

1. If the task of business is to produce and sell goods and services that people need and want, how can we expect business to be socially responsible?

2. Why must any business continually be responsive to its entire external environment? What are the major areas in this environment to which a business should be responsive? Can you distinguish between social responsibility and social responsiveness?

3. Why are population growth and composition important to a businessman?

4. Why are attitudes and beliefs of both individuals and social groups important to the businessman? How should he take them into account? How has the recent explosion of social beliefs affected business?

5. Peter Drucker has said that "the purpose of business is to create a customer." Do you agree with this statement? Assuming there is truth in it, how do businesses reflect this purpose?

6. Business cannot exist without capital and labor. Every business wants to use these resources productively. How can a businessman know he is doing so?

7. Imaginative entrepreneurship is essential to business success. Explain how this is so.

8. Price levels, inflation, and government fiscal and monetary policies are of great importance to business. Explain how and why this is so.

9. How can a business respond best to technological change? Would it be a good thing for business if technological change were curbed?

10. Elements in the social, political, and legal environment of business tend to be intertwined. Does this close relationship have important meaning to business? How?

11. Laws and regulations applicable to business are usually thought of as pro-

tecting people from dishonest or unethical business practices. However, sometimes laws and regulations are necessary to assure accomplishment of social goals even where business firms are honest and ethical. Explain.

12. To what extent are social problems the concern of business? What can and should business do about them?

13. Do the ideas of profit, capitalism, and social responsibility seem to you to be in conflict? How? How not?

SUGGESTED READINGS

Committee for Economic Development *Social Responsibilities of Business Corporations.* New York: Committee for Economic Development, 1971.

Jacoby, N. H. *Corporate Power and Social Responsibility.* New York: Macmillan Publishing Co., Inc., 1973.

Kuhn, J. W., and I. Berg *Values in a Business Society: Issues and Analyses.* New York: Harcourt, Brace & World, Inc., 1968.

Monsen, R. J. *Business and the Changing Environment.* New York: McGraw-Hill Book Company, 1973.

Sethi, S. P. (ed.) *The Unstable Ground: Corporate Social Policy in a Dynamic Society.* Los Angeles: Melnille Publishing Company, 1974.

Steiner, G. A. *Business and Society.* New York: Random House, 1971.

Photo courtesy Washington Convention and Visitors Bureau.

3

The Government: Policeman and Partner of Business

A prominent business executive once said that the government is a partner of every business in the country, and that for many businesses it has become a controlling partner. American society was grounded on belief in individual freedom, private ownership, and free competition, and Americans have traditionally distrusted government power. In recent years, however, they have relied increasingly on government to solve economic and social problems. Even businessmen have often welcomed government intervention, especially when it is designed to help them and protect them from actions of other businessmen.

PATTERNS OF GOVERNMENT INVOLVEMENT IN BUSINESS

Protection of Businesses, Competitors, and Customers

Some government involvement in business has taken the form of protection. As early as 1789, taxes on goods imported from a foreign country, called tariffs, were introduced, partly for revenue and partly to protect American businesses from foreign competition. In 1836 Rhode Island created a commission to inquire into railroad "transactions and proceedings" so that the people of that state might "secure . . . the full and equal privileges of the transportation of persons and property." Disgruntled farmers provided the real stimulus to the regulation of railroads in the 1860s and 1870s. Concerned over high transportation rates and the fact that they paid higher charges for railroad service than certain industrialists did, and aroused also by the arrogant attitude of railroad executives, farmers pressed for regulation of railroad rates and services.

State laws were soon followed by a federal law, the Interstate Commerce Act of 1887 and its many later amendments, which brought the federal government into detailed regulation of all forms of transportation services sold to the public. Today, of course, both state and national government agencies regulate various aspects of railroads, water carriers, pipelines, highway carriers, and air carriers offering their services for sale to the public.

It was only a step from regulation of the rates and services of railroads to government control of the various public utilities—companies selling electric, gas, water, telephone, telegraph, broadcasting, and local transit services.

Public utility regulation differs from that of railroads in one interesting way: while government regulation tended to force competition among the rail carriers, it has encouraged monopoly among the public utilities. The reason for this is that public utility services are provided more efficiently by monopolies than by competing companies. Competition in the utility field usually leads to poor service and high costs. But the consuming public realized that if they were to have monopoly they must be protected by strict regulation of prices and service.

The desire for protection against the abuses of business power resulted at the close of the 19th century in laws breaking up monopolistic combinations of businesses and enforcing competition. The Sherman Anti-Trust Act of 1890 and the many additional pieces of similar legislation over the years have done much to strengthen the competitive nature of American industry.

The laws against monopolistic combinations of business have been supplemented since the early 20th century by a host of state and national laws to outlaw unfair competition. What is "unfair" is often difficult to determine, but the laws, however, extend to a large variety of practices, including unfair methods of pricing, advertising, and packaging. The effort to regulate competition in "big" business has served to bring about the regulation of competition among small businesses as well.

Protection through Enforcement of Contracts

The pattern of protection of people in business dealing has taken many other forms. Perhaps the most important to business have been the various laws that are designed to clarify various forms of contracts and make them enforceable. A moment's reflection will make us see that most of business—buying, selling, borrowing money, hiring people, or getting materials—depends upon a system of agreements and understandings. Contracts serve to make these arrangements clear and to spell out the obligations of each party. If contracts were not enforceable, business as we know it would not be possible. Modern business is therefore dependent upon laws designed to clarify the various forms of contracts and make them enforceable.

Matters of contract terms have traditionally been left to the states. Since state laws have tended to differ, one of the most important developments of recent years has been the enactment of uniform state laws following the Uniform Commercial Code devised by the American Bar Association in 1952 and approved by all states except Louisiana. This complex piece of legislation spells out in detail the nature and handling of contracts in business sales and purchases.

Safeguarding Workers

We also have laws that seek to protect workers by setting a floor under wages, limiting hours of work, and regulating conditions of work. One of the most far-reaching of these laws has been the federal law protecting the right of workers to join labor unions. This law has had the effect of encouraging and strengthening unions.

Protecting Consumers

Other laws and regulations are designed to protect buyers. Laws enforcing fair competition serve to some extent to protect the unwary buyer from being duped by the slick-talking seller. In recent years, the authority of the Pure Food and Drug Administration to protect consumers of foods and drugs has been greatly expanded. Other laws in the broad category of consumer protection include the many state and national laws regulating security transactions, which are designed to protect investors against unscrupulous sellers of securities and which will assure that all sellers give adequate and accurate information to buyers.

Aids to Business

Still other patterns of government involvement have arisen from the various kinds of aid that government has extended to business. Long before 1900, these included tariff protection against foreign competition; the provision of patents, trademarks, and copyrights; the getting of standards of correct weight and measures; land grants to railroads to encourage their construction; services for farmers; and assistance in foreign trade.

The maintenance of a sound monetary system has been important to business, as have the laws governing the setting up of corporations and those protecting investors in case a business becomes bankrupt.

Perhaps the most direct and important of all government supports to business are the many programs of financial aid and support. These include: the guaranteeing of bank loans for the purchase of homes and the financing of defense facilities; subsidies to American ocean shipping companies; the construction of highways and airports; direct subsidies to farmers; the establishment of the National Railroad Passenger Corporation, or Amtrak, to take the burden of intercity passenger service off the railroads; and the giving of grants to communities for improving public transportation.

These programs, it should be pointed out, also result in government controls on business. Governments, whether national, state, or local, do not extend aid without attaching strings limiting the way it may be spent and who is entitled to it.

Government Ownership

Another pattern of government influence may be seen in the many instances of government ownership. To be sure, in most cases government enters into business when private businesses either will not or cannot respond to a public need. Whether it be the United States Postal Service, the Alaska Railroad, the Panama Canal, the Tennessee Valley Authority that provides for flood control and electric power generation, government-owned airports or highways, national parks and forests, or government-owned public housing, the effect is the same. These government enterprises all set rules for those who use their services, buy from them, or sell to them.

Social Programs

The large social programs that have been developed in the past four decades have also brought government into the field of business. The provision of pensions, medical, and other benefits through Social Security has given rise to a government insurance program that dwarfs even the largest private insurance companies.

The Government as a Buyer

Nor should anyone studying the impact of government on business overlook the tremendous power the government has as a buyer of goods and services. The national, state, and local governments buy nearly one-fourth of everything produced in the United States. Businessmen who sell to the government must abide by its terms and requirements.

An exhaustive study of the many government controls and supports affecting business would require a large book in itself. In the following sections we will, however, look at a few of them in more detail so that we can appreciate why and how government has become a policeman or a partner of every business, large or small.

TRANSPORTATION AND PUBLIC UTILITIES

Transportation companies, except for those in local transit operations, are highly competitive. Almost all companies usually referred to as public utilities tend to be highly monopolistic. Both types of companies are subject to basically the same kind of regulation. Local utilities, such as electricity, gas, water, and telephone companies, are predominantly regulated by state governments. But the clearly interstate nature of most transportation companies has brought them under the control of the national government. The two areas are not mutually exclusive, since state and federal government agencies exercise some control over both kinds of companies.

The reader may wonder why railroad, truck, and airline companies are regulated as though they were monopolies, despite the vigorous competition that exists among them for freight and passenger business. The laws regulating them were set up nearly a century ago to control the railroad monopolies, and were later extended to other carriers. The basic approach has been kept in the face of many special studies recommending changes in the law to reflect the fact that these carriers strongly compete. This is a good example of how government regulation, once undertaken, tends to persist even when the original situation no longer exists.

The Level of Rates

Regulation of the rates charged by transportation and public utility businesses falls into two major types. One type has to do with the level of rates and the other with the fair charging of rates to different kinds of customers. In setting the level of rates, the attempt is made to arrive at rates approximating those which would exist under competition. These are thought of as covering reasonable operating expenses plus a reasonable return on investment. The return on investment should be enough to lead investors to put money into the business for its expansion, when necessary.

Regulatory commissions in recent years have generally allowed rates of return ranging from 6 or 7 to 10 percent. For local utilities, such as electricity and gas, these rates have seemed to be adequate. With railroads, all but a very few carriers find that they are unable to earn as much as the allowable return because of high costs and heavy competition. On the average—recognizing that a few railroads like Southern Pacific and the Norfolk and Western do much better—the railroads have earned from 2 to 4 percent on their investment. Even airlines have usually earned far less than the 9 or 10 percent permitted by the Civil Aeronautics Board.

One of the problems in rate level regulation is that competition may not allow prices to rise to the level permitted by the regulators. Moreover, there is no way to discriminate among carriers when they are competing with each other. If a Norfolk and Western Railroad or a Delta Airlines is already making the highest allowable rate of return on its investment, and a direct competitor is not, to allow the competitor to raise its fares while holding Norfolk and Western or Delta's fares down would, of course, be self-defeating because the lower fare carriers would attract the business.

Rates to Different Customers

Perhaps the most difficult part of price regulation in the transport and utility fields is the determination of fairness of rates to different customers. This is called rate discrimination, and it is made necessary by differences in quantities purchased by customers, differences in costs of serving customers, and variations in customers' ability or willingness to pay.

Transportation and utility companies usually have relatively high constant, or fixed, costs. This is because of their equipment requirements. Railroad track and terminal facilities must be developed and maintained almost without regard to the volume of traffic handled. An electric company must have almost the same transmission and distribution lines regardless of the amount of electricity consumed. And an unsold airline seat must still be provided. This means that the special, or out-of-pocket, costs for serving a customer tend to be relatively small compared to the *total* cost of serving him. For example, a passenger who occupies a seat on an airplane that would otherwise remain empty does not add much to the cost of a flight. Special rates for some customers are good for business when they yield sales dollars above out-of-pocket costs especially if these revenues could not be otherwise obtained.

It is very difficult for a businessman or a government regulator to know what is fair. A person shipping a ton of freight can hardly expect as low a rate as a person shipping a carload. And a residential electricity customer can hardly expect to pay as little for a kilowatt-hour used in the peak evening hours as an industrial user who consumes larger quantities in off-peak hours.

The question is how great a difference in prices may be considered fair and reasonable. As a general rule, regulators will not allow sellers to go below out-of-pocket costs, as these costs are calculated by the government. Regulators also watch for discrimination between customers that seems clearly unreasonable. In the setting of transport rates particularly, government commissions are careful to see that individual rates are not set at levels that would put carrier competitors at so great a disadvantage as to destroy their ability to compete.

Service Controls

If a transport or utility company could start or abandon a service at will, or if the quality of service offered were not controlled, much of the purpose of regulation would be defeated. If companies were allowed to enter freely, or expand their services without control, destructive competition could result. Unqualified suppliers might enter, offering the public an inadequate service. If companies could abandon their operations without government approval, there would be a natural tendency to serve only the more profitable markets and some of the public might be left without an essential service.

Likewise, if the quality of service were left uncontrolled, the regulation of price might have little meaning. Prices are presumably set to provide the public with the service it needs. In utilities, especially when there is no practical way of buying service elsewhere, regulation is necessary to assure that consumers get what they pay for.

Entry into, and abandonment of service are handled by government commissions through their authority to issue what are called certificates of convenience and necessity. Generally, government agencies have authority to order a company serving an area to expand its service if this is determined to be in the public interest. Many electric companies have been forced to serve outlying areas even when they would prefer not to do so. It is not always sufficient for a company to show that it is losing money on a service to secure permission to abandon it. For example, railroads have often been required to operate a branch line to a few grain elevators even though losses were demonstrable. Even airline companies are often forced to serve points they would rather drop. The President of Eastern Airlines said in 1972 that 20 percent of its routes were profitable, 40 percent barely covered costs, and 40 percent lost money. But the Civil Aeronautics Board apparently feels that the Eastern Airlines system is profitable enough overall to afford its losses on some routes.

Regulators have found it difficult to police the quality of service, although the laws generally provide that they must. State commissions keep records on breakdowns of electric service and on overloaded telephone trunk lines. Federal commissions monitor the availability of railroad cars for autumn grain shipments, the adequacy of airline schedules between certain points, the degree of on-time performance, and the instances when airlines oversell their seats and are unable to confirm reservations.

Perhaps the best-known application of service regulation is that imposed on the television broadcasting companies. By government edict in 1972, stations were required to set aside a certain amount of prime evening time for non-network shows. Stations are also required to program educational shows, to provide equal free time for major political candidates, to refuse cigarette advertising, and to offer shows that are not obscene or in clearly bad taste.

Service regulation of transport and utility companies is heaviest in the area of safety. Since they deal with the public generally, and utilize public rights of way for transporting and distributing their service, carriers must honor safety regulations that are more extensive and detailed than those applied to other businesses.

Accounting and Finance

To show how regulation tends to expand, beyond the area of prices and services, we should add that regulatory bodies are always given authority to oversee how a company keeps its accounts and how it raises its money. To regulate prices, a commission needs to be certain that expenses and investments are accurately and clearly recorded. Likewise, it needs to be sure that a company does not weaken itself or unduly increase its costs through the improper issuance of stocks or bonds.

LAWS TO ENFORCE COMPETITION

As noted above, among the oldest and most thorough sets of government controls over business are the state and national laws to assure competition. Some of them date back to the latter part of the 19th century. Basically, they are of two kinds: (1) those designed to prevent the destruction of competition through combinations that tend toward monopoly; and (2) those designed to enforce a degree of fair and responsible competition. No other nation in the world has been so devoted to enforcing competition as the United States, although in the European Common Market and in a few other countries similar controls are now developing.

These laws reflect the traditional American belief in competition. Indeed, as mentioned in the first chapter, there is good reason to believe that the vigor and growth of the American economy have been due in past to these laws.

The Antitrust Laws

Toward the end of the 19th century a number of states, inflamed by the growth of large monopolistic combinations such as John D. Rockefeller's Standard Oil Company and the large railroad combinations, passed legislation outlawing them. But because their businesses spread across state lines, the cornerstone of national antimonopoly law was laid by the Sherman Act of 1890 and the Clayton Act of 1914, together with their many revisions in succeeding years. At the time the early laws were passed, many of these business combinations used a legal form called the "trust," which placed the control of companies in the hands of a legal owner or "trustee," and hence they have been called antitrust laws.

The antitrust laws essentially forbid attempts to develop monopolies or to "restrain trade" (that is, to eliminate competition through mergers and other kinds of combinations). They have not been applied to public utilities and to combinations approved by such regulatory commissions as the Interstate Commerce Commission (for railroads and truck lines) or the Civil Aeronautics Board (for airlines), or to labor unions and farmers' cooperatives.

The meanings of "tending" toward monopoly and "restraining trade" were not clearly defined in the laws. Consequently the laws have had a long history of interpretation by the courts, particularly the United States Supreme Court, with the result that their full meaning cannot be simply stated.

When Does a Business "Monopolize"?

There are still questions as to what constitutes an unlawful combination, or whether or not the laws apply to a particular case. The more important guidelines can be summarized as follows:

1. Not all combinations of two or more businesses are forbidden, but only those that have an "unreasonable" effect in reducing competition. What is "unreasonable" is determined by the courts in individual cases. In 1916, the courts approved the merger of companies which became American Can Company having 90 percent of the market. This was found to be "reasonable" in 1916. But in 1945, when the American Aluminum Company had a similar share of the market, it was "unreasonable." American Aluminum had become dominant not through mergers but by internal growth and the development of patents.
2. An important point in determining unlawfulness has always been the way a company acts. If it does not use its power of size to throttle competition, a combination has on occasion been held to be lawful. The Supreme Court decided in favor of the United States Steel Corporation on this count in 1920.
3. Any joint fixing of prices among businesses has been consistently found to be unlawful.
4. Any combination of companies designed primarily to squeeze out competitors or put them at a disadvantage has also been consistently held to be unlawful.
5. If a combination of two companies leads to unusual power that might substantially reduce competition, the law has not permitted it. For example, when the Procter and Gamble Company (makers

of "Ivory Soap," "Tide," and "Crest") acquired "Clorox" bleach, the Supreme Court found that the great power of Procter and Gamble as the nation's largest advertiser might enable it to reduce considerably the competition in the sale of household bleach. Procter and Gamble was consequently forced to sell the Clorox Company.

While the above guidelines do not fully summarize the meaning of the antitrust or antimonopoly laws, they are adequate to indicate that U.S. law means what it says when it outlaws any combination of companies that might materially reduce competition, or any action of executives of competing companies that might do the same. There are many gray areas in the definition of unlawful behavior, but there can be little doubt in any intelligent businessman's mind that certain behavior is unlawful. A few years ago, executives of some of our most prominent companies, including General Electric, Westinghouse, and Allis Chalmers, were caught conspiring together to fix the prices of certain electrical equipment; they were fined and seven of them were imprisoned. Their behavior was clearly illegal, since the test of clear illegality is whether two or more companies are working together to fix prices, and no excuse can be made for this behavior.

Controls Enforcing Fair Competition

To supplement the antitrust laws, enforced by the United States Department of Justice, the Federal Trade Commission Act of 1914 established a commission of five appointed members. The Commission was charged with maintaining competition through controlling various kinds of unfair competition. While this law and its many amendments over the years specify a number of instances of unfair competition, the Commission has added its own interpretations of the law, which, often supported by the courts, have given it an enormous amount of power over business.

Price Discrimination

One of the major kinds of trade regulation, greatly strengthened by the Robinson Patman Act of 1936, is directed against unreasonable price discrimination. It is unlawful for a seller to engage in price cutting designed to destroy a competitor. It is also held to be unlawful for a seller to discriminate between buyers by selling at a lower price to one buyer than to another, unless these differences relate to different goods

Donald M. Kendall

© Karsch, Ottawa.

Donald M. Kendall was one of the organizers of PepsiCo, Inc., a worldwide consumer products and services company with sales in 1974 of over $1.4 billion. Its market extends to over a billion people in the United States and 129 other countries.

PepsiCo's major divisions include Pepsi-Cola Company, Frito-Lay, Inc., PepsiCo International, Wilson Sporting Goods, Co., PepsiCo Transportation, Rheingold Corporation, PepsiCo Leasing, and Monsieur Henri Wines, Ltd.

Born in Sequim, Washington, he attended Western Kentucky State College, where he played tackle on the football team. During World War II he was a naval aviator. Afterward he joined Pepsi-Cola as a fountain syrup sales representative. Within five years he was named president of Pepsi-Cola's overseas operations. Under his leadership, Pepsi-Cola's international growth showed dramatic expansion. The number of countries in which Pepsi-Cola was sold more than doubled. Sales of this division tripled and income rose sharply to the point where it provided a major portion of company earnings.

As a result of these successes, Kendall

or are for quantities clearly justified by cost differences. Likewise, price reductions not available to all customers buying the same good or quantity are held to be unlawful. Thus if a manufacturer of soaps and detergents sells to a supermarket chain at lower prices than to an independent grocer who can buy in the same quantity, and if quantity discounts are not based on a clear demonstration of cost differences, this is unlawful. It is no wonder that most businesses have become extremely careful in setting and changing prices, and usually have a competent lawyer available to advise them when price changes are made.

Unfair or Deceptive Practices

Another major area of regulation by the Federal Trade Commission is that of unfair or deceptive practices. These are exceedingly varied. They include, among other things, false and misleading advertising, misbranding of commodities, simulation of trade names, procuring of business or trade secrets by spying or bribery, making of false or disparaging statements concerning a competitor's products, and cutting

was named president of Pepsi-Cola Company in 1963. He quickly launched a series of marketing and management innovations that accelerated the sales of Pepsi-Cola, and added new products, such as Diet Pepsi-Cola and Mountain Dew.

Kendall engineered the merger that in 1965 brought Pepsi-Cola Company together with Frito-Lay, the nation's leading snack food marketer, and assumed the presidency of the company that resulted—PepsiCo, Inc. He was president and chief executive officer until May 5, 1971, when he became chairman and chief executive officer.

In 1969 Kendall was appointed to a one-year term as chairman of the National Alliance of Businessmen by President Nixon. The NAB is a voluntary, non-profit organization manned by business executives, labor officials, and government officers, whose goal is locating jobs in the private sector of the economy for the hard-core unemployed. In November, 1970, he was elected to the chairmanship of the National Center for Resource Recovery, Inc. an organization founded by a large group of industrialists to work on the country's solid waste and litter problems. He also served as chairman of the Emergency Committee for American Trade, an organization of heads of 54 corporations organized to fight restrictions on international trade and investment. In 1972 Kendall was national chairman of the Business and Industry Committee for the Re-Election of the President. In this position he took the unusual step of asking his stockholders to back a political candidate.

Kendall's outside directorships include memberships on the boards of Pan American World Airways, Inc., Atlantic Richfield Company, the Investors Diversified Services mutual fund, Boys Clubs of America, Boy Scouts of America, and the Metropolitan Opera Association, Inc.

He is also a trustee of the Nixon Foundation, the Council of the International Chamber of Commerce, the Committee for Economic Development, and Whittier College in Whittier, California.

To keep in trim, Kendall plays tennis and runs four miles every morning. He is married to the former Baroness Ruedt von Collenberg.

off of a competitor's source of supply. One manufacturer was forced to stop calling his textiles "woolen" when they contained some cotton. The automobile companies were stopped from advertising a "6 percent plan" for financing automobiles when the actual annual interest rate was 11½ percent.

Taken together, the antitrust laws and the laws outlawing unfair and deceptive practices in competition represent a strong policy of enforcing *responsible* competition. Other countries have not gone this far. Even in some of the advanced capitalist countries overseas it is still legal for one competitor to agree with another to set prices, or for a company to cut off supplies to one of its customers who has become an important competitor.

Moreover, even in the United States, some companies break the law knowingly or unknowingly. Like traffic policemen who cannot catch all the speeders, the government cannot stop all who break the law on fair competition. One very large TV advertiser has the reputation of frequently misusing consumer "tests" and testimonials to demonstrate the superiority of its product, by showing on television commercials only those persons who liked the company's products. By the time the Federal Trade Commission can stop the practice, the company is willing to discard the commercial because it has already got the advertising it wanted.

In fairness to many businessmen, the laws prohibiting business combinations or competitive practices are so complex, and their interpretations by the law enforcement agencies so uncertain, that it is hard to know what is truly unlawful. As a federal judge once said, "I doubt that any judge in the land would assert that he knows what does or does not involve a violation of the law in any and all instances."

LAWS TO PROTECT CONSUMERS

The Federal Trade Commission has taken many actions designed to protect consumers by enforcing a level of responsible competition. A number of other laws have been passed to protect consumers from dishonest, misleading, and even dangerous practices. These include the various pure food and drug laws administered by the Department of Agriculture and the Food and Drug Administration, laws on product packaging and labeling, various health and sanitation laws, legislation limiting interest charges borrowers must pay and requiring that they be told the actual interest charges when they borrow, and the laws in every local community establishing zoning for the use of real estate. All of these understandably have considerable impact on business and the way a business may operate.

Pure Food and Drug Laws

In many areas, the government closely controls the quality of a product a business may make and sell. Although the first federal act was passed in 1906, the more comprehensive Food, Drug, and Cosmetic Act of 1938, along with various amendments since that time, has authorized the Food and Drug Administration to establish minimum quality standards for many food products. Regulation of the quality of foods is also undertaken by the Department of Agriculture, which inspects or grades meat, poultry, eggs, fruits, vegetables, and dairy products.

Especially important to many businesses are the laws administered by the Food and Drug Administration prohibiting sale of any food, drug, therapeutic device, or cosmetic that may endanger public health. The Administration may withhold its approval from any new drug until it has reason to believe that it is safe, and may order removal from the market of any food, drug, health device, or cosmetic if it finds the product may endanger public health.

The powers over business of the Department of Agriculture and the Food and Drug Administration are enormous. Pharmaceutical companies often are forced to withhold drugs from the American market for years even after they are found to be safe for sale in other advanced western countries. The outlawing of cyclamates in soft drinks, the removal of cranberries from the market, and the scare over mercury in tuna fish, are only a few recent instances demonstrating the power of the law. They suggest that overly strict laws or their too cautious administration may destroy a whole product line, and perhaps a business, even though the danger to public health has not been clearly shown. However there is a clear need for strict and sensible government regulation in these areas, as was shown when the baby-deforming drug thalidomide was kept off the market in the United States.

Laws on Product Packaging and Labeling

Another group of state and federal laws require businesses to package and label goods so that the consumer can see what he is getting. The national Fair Packaging and Labeling Act (1967) is the most important of these. The requirements of such laws include the disclosure of product identity, the name and location of the packer or distributor, the net quantity of contents (measure, weight, numerical count, or quantity of servings), and a warning if the product is dangerous or habit-forming (for example, "The Surgeon General has determined that cigarette smoking is dangerous to your health."). Other regulations require that textile products be labeled to show the kind of fibers and percentage of each, as well as the country of origin if the fiber is imported. Of special importance to drug makers is the requirement that they not make unsupported claims, such as stating that a drug is a "cure" when it is not. States have many regulations. For example, Florida requires orange juice packers who add sugar to certain oranges in making juice, to label the juice as "substandard."

Health and Sanitation Laws

Various state and federal laws require certain standards of cleanliness in the manufacturing, packing, and handling of foods, drugs, and other items for internal human consumption. State and local laws have similar requirements for restaurants, grocery stores, and like establishments. Regular inspections, backed by fines and penalties, are used to enforce these laws.

It would obviously be impossible to enforce all the laws governing drugs, foods, and cosmetics. The Food and Drug Administration estimates that in the area of food alone it is responsible for inspecting 32,000 manufacturers and processors and 28,000 warehouses, grain elevators, and repacking and relabeling plants. With only 210 inspectors working full time on food, and making perhaps 9,000 inspections a year, it would take 6.7 years to get around to all the plants. But actions taken in a few cases have a strong deterrent effect on other companies.

Regulations on Behalf of Borrowers

For centuries, governments have set limits on the rates of interest that moneylenders may charge borrowers. These are sometimes known as usury laws. They are not nowadays very restrictive; many state laws permit interest rates as high as 24 to 30 percent per year. The national Truth in Lending Act of 1971 has added a new requirement that may be more effective in protecting borrowers. It requires lenders, including merchants who sell goods on time payments, to spell out clearly for the borrower exactly what interest he is paying. A nominal interest rate of 6 percent a year may actually be 12 percent if the loan is paid off in installments. By making this clear, it is hoped that people will not be taken in by lenders who make time payments seem so easy.

Local Zoning Laws

Every businessman is aware of real estate zoning laws, since they often add to his costs. Local governments commonly limit the use that may be made of land in particular areas by dividing it into residential zones, commercial zones (stores and service operations), light industrial zones (such as an electronics factory), and heavy industrial zones (such as a steel mill or a chemical plant). These laws are designed to protect owners of residential property against the incursion of businesses and factories.

The impact of zoning restrictions on business may be considerable. In the Los Angeles area, for example, a residential acre may cost $40,000; an acre zoned for apartment building near a residential area may cost $80,000; and an acre in an industrial tract may cost $160,000, largely because of the limited space available. Zoning may also limit the specific use that may be made of land and buildings. In one city, a factory manufacturing paint found that it could not make adhesives in the same building.

Environmental Control Regulations

The most ambitious of all programs to protect consumers is the effort to improve the environment that began in the 1960s. A wave of public concern resulted in a number of antipollution and environmental control laws on the national, state, and local levels. The National Environmental Policy Act of 1970 created the United States Environmental Protection Agency, charged with mounting a strong and integrated attack on all kinds of pollution. Its aims include air pollution control, assurance of clean water, the disposal of solid wastes such as garbage and trash, protection from radiation, safeguards against excessive use of chemical pesticides, and elimination of the health hazards of excessive noise. Although there have been laws dealing with some aspect of environment control for many years (including one passed in 1899, but not really enforced until 1972, giving the Army Corps of Engineers the power to control dumping of industrial wastes in navigable waters or their tributaries), most of the environmental control laws were passed in the 1960s. With the new Environmental Protection Agency, a nationwide coordinated effort to protect the quality of life has been undertaken.

The magnitude of this task is readily apparent. About 200 million tons of man-made waste products are released into the air each year. Reducing the emissions from automotive vehicles, which contribute less than half these pollutants, has been an extraordinarily difficult task. When it is considered that, in 1972, some 1,300 communities dumped raw sewage into waterways and 240,000 water-using industrial plants generated pollutants, the problem of cleaning waterways and water supplies needs no emphasis. Americans constitute only 7 percent of the world's population, but they consume nearly half the earth's raw materials; in doing so, they create 4.3 billion tons of waste each year.

If the problems of the environment are to be solved, we can expect continuing and greater control of both business and individuals now and in the coming years. The problem will ever be one of tradeoffs. How many plants should be closed and jobs lost and how fast? How much more should we pay for automobiles and other necessities and comforts of life? How much by way of taxes should we pay in order to solve community waste and sewage problems? How much should we restrict air transportation to reduce noise? These and many other questions present hard decisions. But no one would deny that the harm to the earth's environment cannot be allowed to continue unchecked.

There is hardly a business that is unaffected by environmental controls. Many companies have been forced to make large expenditures to meet the various pollution standards established by law. This aspect of governmental control over business may be the most important one in the years to come.

LAWS TO PROTECT INVESTORS

Another important area in which government controls materially affect business operations are the laws designed to protect depositors in banks, holders of insurance policies, and investors in corporation stocks and bonds. The public interest in banks and life insurance companies is not difficult to see. These institutions receive funds from individuals and businesses to safeguard. They invest them and lend them out in various ways to make a profit. People who entrust their money to banks and life insurance companies want to be sure that it doesn't fall into dishonest or incompetent hands. Those who borrow want a flow of funds that is adequate for business and personal needs. Everyone concerned wants the system to operate efficiently so that interest rates paid by borrowers will be no higher than necessary and the returns to investors will be as high as feasible.

But the public interest in this area extends beyond the reasonable desires of investors and borrowers. Our whole society is interested in the flow of private capital, since that underlies the American system of private business enterprise. It has long been a policy of the government to try to assure that investors and borrowers are not deceived or cheated in their financial dealings.

Banking

As we shall see in Chapter 7, both state and federal governments exercise considerable control over banks. Every bank must have a permit from a state or federal government agency. Banks are also regulated in various aspects of their operations. These include, among other things, the quality of their loans and investments, the interest rates they pay depositors and charge borrowers, and the amount of cash reserves they must hold.

Insurance Companies

More than 80 percent of American adults carry some form of life insurance. In 1973, privately owned life insurance companies in the U.S. held $252 billion of assets. Other large amounts were held by companies that insure against casualties such as automobile accidents and fires.

As one might expect, the regulations applied to insurance companies are similar to those covering banks. Entry into the business is controlled, and the companies are regulated as to premium charges, the quality of investments held on behalf of the public, and the responsibility and honesty of their employees.

Investment in Securities

Government controls on the issuance of stocks and bonds will be discussed more fully in Chapter 8. Most states try to assure that the security to be issued is not fraudulent or deceptive. The federal government actively entered the field through the Securities Act of 1933, aimed primarily at protecting investors, and the Securities Exchange Act of 1934, designed mainly to regulate trading of securities. The Securities Act does not apply to all securities; certain securities, such as those of government agencies and those closely regulated by other government commissions, are exempt from the law, which also applies only to issues above $300,000 sold to the public.

The national securities laws, have their main impact on business in requiring companies to provide investors with a complete, accurate, and fair disclosure of information. A company issuing stock must file a registration statement with the government which is available for public inspection, and issue a prospectus to interested investors, thus providing a vast amount of information. The accuracy and completeness of this information are assured by making a number of parties liable for losses if it should prove misleading or if material facts are omitted.

Every company selling a security on a public exchange must continue to file information of importance to investors. Trading practices are also closely controlled so that brokers and dealers cannot take advantage of investors by manipulating the market.

LAWS TO PROTECT WORKERS

Legislation to protect workers was one of the earliest forms of government intereference with business. Massachusetts and Connecticut enacted laws in 1842 limiting the labor of children under twelve years of age to ten hours a day in manufacturing establishments. Pennsylvania prohibited labor by children under twelve in manufacturing plants in 1848. A ten-hour day for women was prescribed in New Hampshire in 1847. But the real development of labor legislation belongs to the 20th century.

Expansion of Labor Laws

Labor laws enacted since the early 1930s require every businessman to reckon with the government in dealing with his workers. He must keep one eye on the law in setting hours and wages, determining the physical conditions under which people work, and in avoiding discrimination in hiring with respect to age, race, religion, or sex.

He must also provide for the insurance of his workers against accidental injury, occupational disease, old age, and unemployment, either through paying taxes or by purchasing insurance policies. When he hires, pays, promotes, or discharges workers, he may have to take into account the rights guaranteed them to organize into unions and bargain collectively. And if his plant or office has a contract with a union, he is obligated to abide by its conditions.

The state and federal laws aimed at protecting workers are too numerous and complex to discuss here. Let us only note that there is little a business can do regarding workers and their unions that is not subject to some law or ruling of a government commission.

Growing Power of the Federal Government

State agencies still have a major part in regulating hours that women can work, in assuring safe and healthful working conditions, and in providing compensation for workers injured on the job or suffering from a disease caused by their occupation.

But in recent years the federal government has become increasingly powerful. It is predominant in the area of child labor, in requiring a 40-hour week (beyond which an overtime rate of 1½ times the hourly rate must be paid), in requiring employers in most businesses to pay a minimum hourly rate, and in seeing that employers recognize and bargain with a duly elected labor union.

Payment of unemployment benefits is handled by the states, with benefits varying somewhat among the states. However, it is the national government that has required them to set up their systems of unemployment compensation. It has established certain standards of payment by levying taxes on payrolls and then returning most of the money collected to the states, provided they meet the federal standards.

Likewise, the national government has required protection of workers from the economic hazards of old age and disability. Social Security is provided for all workers except government employees, those in certain nonprofit institutions, and a few other groups (generally those having their own pension plans). In 1974, approximately 90 percent of all workers in the United States were covered by some kind of pension plan.

In general, Social Security provides for full retirement benefits at the age of 65 and somewhat reduced benefits if a person retires at 62. In addition, persons covered by Social Security receive retirement benefits at any age if they are disabled, and if they die their dependents receive benefits. In recent years, medical benefits have been added for those, retired or not, who have reached 65. The Social Security program is, of course, expensive, costing approximately $90 billion in 1973 (including old age, disability, medical, and unemployment benefits) and is expected to require much more in future years.

GOVERNMENT AIDS

Both state and federal governments have given aid to business of various kinds. Some aids are direct, in the form of loans or subsidies. Some work indirectly by helping customers buy the products of business, as with the guarantee of housing loans for veterans. Some aids help business operate effectively, as do those government provisions making contracts legally enforceable and allowing corporations to be formed. Some aids consist in giving valuable rights to individuals and companies through patents, copyrights, and registration of trademarks. A few examples follow.

Aid through Tariffs and Quotas

As noted earlier in this book, throughout its history the United States has given protection to many businesses through tariffs, which are special taxes levied on goods imported into the country. Sometimes these taxes have been so high as to keep certain imports out, but more often they are intended to equalize the costs of foreign and domestic goods. Thus, manufactured cotton goods, allowed to come in free in 1789, were subjected to a 25 percent duty in 1816 in order to encourage domestic industry. That tariffs are not always effective in protecting domestic industry is indicated by the fact that American jeweled watch movement manufacturers have been driven out by Swiss and Japanese competition, despite tariffs on imported watch movements.

Some businesses have been aided by government quotas limiting the quantity of a product that can be imported. Such quotas were for a long time applied to crude oil with a view to holding up prices and thereby encouraging domestic oil exploration and production.

Transportation Aids

Over a century ago, the federal government gave certain railroads, particularly in the western part of the country, large gifts of land to encourage construction of new lines. These subsidies helped to open the country up for trade and agriculture. They were more than repaid through the reduced rates required to be given for government shipments until 1946; the total value of the rate reductions has been estimated at more than $600 million, an amount several times the value of the land grants at the time they were made.

Substantial government aid has also been given to the development of the air transportation system. Airlines have been subsidized in carrying mail, a practice now all but discontinued. Much larger sums were given for building airports and setting up flight facilities, though in recent years costs have been recovered from taxes on air traffic and fuel.

The extensive network of interstate highways built since 1960 has been financed by the federal government from taxes on motor fuel raised specifically for that purpose. The federal government has also begun subsidizing rail passenger service, and has undertaken a significant program of subsidies for improving urban transportation. For example, the subsidy to the new San Francisco Bay Area Transportation system (BART) has amounted to more than $600 million. Such subsidies are not really aids to business so much as to urban communities as a whole and to their working people who benefit from improved service.

Agriculture

For more than 40 years the American farmer has received direct government aid. Through various support programs, the federal government has subsidized such crops as wheat, corn, cotton, oats, and peanuts. Despite the great increase in farm productivity over these years, and the fact that many farming operations have become big business, these supports, introduced during the depressed 1930s, cost American taxpayers more than $4 billion dollars as late as 1973.

Special Lending and Loan Guarantee Programs

Of great importance to many businesses are the lending and loan guarantee programs that the federal government has instituted. Agencies in the fields of housing and agriculture have established special banks and provisions for guaranteeing loans. The agencies borrow their funds from investors and have not generally required tax support. They had nearly $40 billion in loans outstanding during 1972.

In a few cases, loans have been made directly to business. The U.S. Small Business Administration made more than 16,000 loans to small businesses in 1971, totalling more than $1 billion dollars. However, 83 percent of the funds provided came from private banks with the government only guaranteeing or helping to arrange the loans.

Business loans are generally not made by the government but rather by private lenders, often with a government guarantee. Even the much-publicized loan guarantee for $250 million to the Lockheed Corporation in 1972 was not a loan of taxpayers' funds but a loan from private banks, guaranteed by the federal government. Since the loan guaranteed by the government took priority over those of other lenders, there could not be any cost to taxpayers until the company had lost all its ownership and some $500 million of bank loans then outstanding would have been written off as a loss. Only then would the taxpayers be called upon to put in funds. In other words, the company would have to lose over $1 billion before the taxpayers would be called upon to contribute a cent! This underscores what most businessmen well know—that the government seldom makes or guarantees loans without a lot of protection. In this area, the government is no "patsy."

By far the largest government loan programs are those to support housing by guarantees of mortgages to homeowners under the Federal Housing Administration (FHA) or the Veterans Administration (VA). These insured and guaranteed loans totalled approximately $140 billion in 1973. Because the government charges a fee for this insurance, and defaults have been negligible, it has made a profit of from $100 to $200 million annually on this program. These loans are designed to aid homeowners rather than businesses, although they have unquestionably helped the housing industry.

Information

There is hardly a government agency, federal or state, that does not gather information and make it available to business. This information ranges from the population data of the Census Bureau to the crop reports of the Department of Agriculture, and includes transportation data from the Department of Transportation, industry sales and other data from the Department of Commerce, and economic forecasts from the President's Council of Economic Advisers. Neither its cost, nor its value can be estimated, but certainly business would be at a disadvantage without such information.

SUMMARY

Government is both policeman and partner of business. As policeman, it regulates business. As partner, it gives business considerable assistance. Both regulation and aid "help" to make business more effective in serving the needs of society. In some cases, such as the continued regulation of railroads as though they were still monopolies, the government has interfered with effective management.

The businesses most subject to regulation have been transportation companies, public utilities, banks, and insurance companies. Because of special public interest in their services, government has been given extensive control over the prices they charge, the services they provide, and their continuance in business.

Some of the laws regulating business are designed to maintain a level of effective and responsible competition. Except for public utilities, where monopoly is regarded as being in the public interest, and for labor unions and farmers' cooperatives, virtually all businesses are subject to antitrust laws and laws to enforce competition. These laws not only forbid monopolies and monopolistic practices, but also attempt to require a level of competitive behavior regarded as "fair."

Controls of great importance to businesses have also arisen from the desire to protect consumers, investors, and workers. These include laws relating to foods, drugs, and cosmetics, and laws protecting borrowers. Zoning laws and environmental controls aim to protect the consumer as a member of the community.

Protection of the consumer extends to close regulation of banks, insurance companies, and securities transactions. As a worker, the consumer is safeguarded by an array of programs dealing with wages and hours, conditions of work, discrimination in employment, union organization and activity, and personal security.

Government agencies also give assistance of various kinds to business. Laws making contracts clearly enforceable and providing for business organizations such as corporations are obviously important in almost all fields of business. Most businessmen also gain from the great volume of information made available by government. Other forms of assistance include tariffs and import quotas.

A few businesses, including farmers and ocean shipping companies, have received direct subsidies. In earlier days railroads, highways, and airlines received direct subsidies. Many businesses have been assisted by government loan and loan guarantee programs, although most of these have been designed to encourage ownership of farms and homes rather than to aid businesses as such.

KEY TERMS AND CONCEPTS FOR REVIEW

Import tariffs and quotas
Interstate Commerce Act
Antitrust laws
Federal Trade Commission Act
Level of public utility and transportation rates
Public utility and transportation rate discrimination
Entry into and abandonment of service
Quality of public utility and transportation service
Monopolistic combinations
When a business "monopolizes"

Robinson-Patman Act and price discrimination
Unfair competition
Pure food and drug laws
Product packaging and labeling laws
Health and sanitation laws
Usury laws
Truth in Lending Act
Zoning laws
Environmental control laws
Securities Act of 1933
Securities and Exchange Act of 1934
Social Security
Agricultural support programs

QUESTIONS FOR ANALYSIS AND DISCUSSION

1. In what ways is the government a policeman of business and in what ways a partner? Why should the government act as a policeman? When the government acts as a partner, to what extent does it exert control over business, and how?

2. How does the regulation of transportation and public utilities differ from the regulation of other businesses? Why?

3. In what ways is government regulation beneficial to business?

4. Why should the government control entry into and abandonment of service by public utility and transportation companies?

5. It has been said that antitrust and fair competition laws, which are an American invention, have contributed much to the economic growth of the United States. Why could this be true?

6. The Robinson-Patman Act regulating price discrimination has been regarded as a major means of keeping large businesses from putting smaller businesses at a serious disadvantage. How does it do this?

7. If the antitrust and fair completition laws have the clear purpose of enforcing responsible and effective competition, why are there so many uncertainties about their application?

8. Many laws have been passed to protect consumers. What are these various laws, what consumer groups are they designed to protect, and how do they do so?

9. Laws intended to protect the environment may require certain compromises, or trade-offs. Why is this likely to be true? Should we accept these?

10. The laws designed to protect investors affect businesses in many ways. How?

11. Laws to protect workers affect business in almost every aspect of hiring and dealing with labor. If you were a businessman, what are some of the areas in which you would be affected?

12. Businesses benefit from government aid in many ways. Name three ways and analyze whether, in your opinion, we should extend such help.

SUGGESTED READINGS

Corley, R.N., and R.L. Black   *The Legal Environment of Business.* New York: McGraw-Hill Book Company, 1968.

Phillips, C. F., Jr.   *The Economics of Regulation.* Homewood, Ill.: Richard D. Irwin, Inc., 1969.

Steiner, G. A.   *Business and Society.* New York: Random House, 1971.

Stocking, G. W.   *Workable Competition and Anti-Trust Policy.* Nashville: Vanderbilt University Press, 1961.

Wilcox, C.   *Public Policies Toward Business* (4th ed.).   Homewood, Ill.: Richard D. Irwin, Inc., 1971.

part two

Establishing a Business

Disney's System of Money Management and Control

The folks around Orlando, Florida, were very pleased in the early 60s when several development and holding companies began purchasing alligator-infested land. Companies with names like "Tomahawk" and "Compass East" purchased 27,443 acres for an average cost of about $200 an acre. When in October, 1965, the announcement was made that the entire tract was now owned by subsidiaries of Walt Disney Productions and would become the site of a Florida Disneyland; land values skyrocketed. Soon propeprty near the Disney site was selling for as much as $125,000 an acre.

Walt Disney World and the other enterprises of Walt Disney Productions have the crafty financial expertise of Roy Disney stamped all over them. Seemingly offhand decisions turn out later to have been well-planned expansions of the corporate empire.

The real heart of the Disney empire is its movie business. As the corporation diversifies, the percentage of gross revenues from movies decreases. But the screen has been the place where the public first met Mickey Mouse, Donald Duck, and a host of other personages later to be encountered at Disneyland and Disney World. The films remain ever fresh, as each succeeding generation of parents introduces a new set of children to Bambi and Captain Hook. Thirty years after it was made, the film classic "Snow White" was re-released for the fifth time and grossed $5,200,000 in the United States alone. That was a million more than it made when it first came out in 1937.

The Disney philosophy not only dictated that productions be top quality. It demanded that ownership be retained completely. As a result of this decision, it is said that Disney could stop now . . . never produce another film . . . and re-release parts of its library every year and make forty or fifty million dollars annually.

The corporation follows a continuing policy of internal diversification within the family entertainment and recreation fields. The divisions of the Disney empire include "The Wonderful World of Disney," now in its second decade on NBC-TV; Walt Disney Educational Films; Disney on Parade, a traveling live show for indoor arenas and coliseums; Disneyland, 230 acres of dreams-come-true at Anaheim, California; Walt Disney World, in Orlando, Florida, which will carry the Disney creativity into urban planning and ecological study as well as family entertainment; and many other smaller concerns set up to merchandise publications, records, comic strips, home films, educational materials, and sheet music. These major interests are supported by a number of lesser activities such as companies to buy land, build things, and manage people.

Disney World provides its own internal postal service and fire department. It has its own power supply and garbage removal system. The corporation also owns nearly 300 water craft, the "ninth largest navy in the world."

Every operation is supportive of the other operations, as can be seen in the diagram, drawn before the creation of Walt Disney World. According to a top Disney executive, the chart has not been redrawn because today's operations would make the diagram hopelessly complicated.

The Disney managers are wise enough to place significant financial valuation on two factors many firms overlook. Chairman Donn B. Tatum has said of one of these factors, "Perhaps our greatest asset is the high platform of public acceptance which attaches to the Disney name and to all the activities and products to which it is attached around the world. To continue to merit this confidence is to us a great trust— and to try to do so is potently good business."

The company places equal stress on the second factor, its people. The employees who create, produce, construct, operate, and administer for the company are possessed with a special attitude toward themselves and their mission. Gray-haired managers take turns wearing the Mickey Mouse suits at Disneyland and Disney World. This esprit de corps makes a dollars-and-cents difference in all the Disney operations.

As it entered the mid-70s, the company seemed to be in a period of

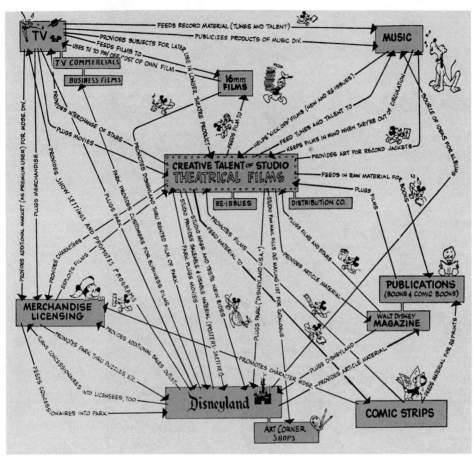

© 1974 Walt Disney Productions.

unparalleled growth and opportunity. All its divisions were operating profitably, with short-range prospects very good and long-range prospects excellent.

Prophets of doom rise up occasionally to predict that one of these mammoth gambles will end in bankruptcy. But as Disney touches another orange grove or swamp and turns it to gold, the skeptics are stilled. The Disney philosophy may be to "wish upon a star," but the financial plans of the company are very definitely on paper.

4

Legal Forms of Business Ownership: Proprietorships, Partnerships, and Trusts

A business enterprise may encompass billions of dollars' worth of resources, or it may consist only of a corner drugstore, an antique shop, or a used car lot. It may engage in repairing faulty plumbing, selling furniture, rendering telephone service, or growing wheat. In short, a business enterprise may engage in any kind of productive activity.

As we have seen in previous chapters, a business may even be owned by a government, as are the post office and the city airports of the U.S. A business may also be partly owned by government and partly owned by private investors. In the United States, however, nearly all business enterprises are privately owned and operated. That is to say, the decision to enter a business is made by individuals; the ownership of the resources used is largely private; and the control over operations is mainly in private hands.

While one-man businesses are by no means uncommon, such as those of farmers or television repairmen, most of the business volume of the country is carried on by enterprises employing groups of people. They range from the small retailer with one or two clerks to the huge General Motors Corporation with 800,000 employees. Some businesses, usually small, are owned by one man. Others are owned by a number of people, ranging from two or three persons in a partnership to the 3,000,000 owners of the American Telephone and Telegraph Company. Some are financed entirely by their owners' money, but most operate in part with money borrowed from banks and other sources.

ESTABLISHING A BUSINESS

Businesses do not just happen. At some time someone starts them. Sometimes these have been individuals who founded a blacksmith shop, a store, or a printing establishment. As a matter of fact, in 1830 most businesses were run by one or a few owners and had, on the average, only seven wage earners (though there were cotton mills in New England with hundreds of workers). Sometimes, though, groups of investors started businesses such as insurance companies and banks.

The first colonizing expeditions to America were business ventures organized by groups of investors with an eye to making money from settling the new world. A group of 715 investors subscribed $218,000 and received a charter from the British government in 1606 to form the Virginia Company and send colonists to Jamestown. A few years later other investors sent colonists to Plymouth, Massachusetts. Since these early beginnings in the United States, millions of other businesses have been established.

No matter who starts a business, certain initial decisions have to be made. One concerns the form of ownership that is to be used. The oldest and most common form is the proprietorship, a business owned by one person. Another is the partnership, in which two or more persons share in direct ownership. A third form is the corporation, used when the investors wish to divorce themselves from the liabilities of direct ownership; this is now the most important in terms of total business sales. The advantages and disadvantages of the corporation are discussed in Chapter 5. Proprietorships, partnerships, and corporations are the three basic forms of business ownership, although other forms are sometimes used.

Those who run a business must have some way of keeping score. This is done through a system known as accounting. Accounting enables a businessman to know how much he is taking in and paying out, whether he is making a profit and how much, the value of his property, the amount of his debts, and how much the company is worth. Accounting also gives him guidance in making decisions, shows him whether the business is meeting its profit goals, and furnishes him information he can use to control his operations. Methods of accounting are described in Chapter 6.

To establish a business also requires money. It may be a fairly small amount in the case of a shoe repair shop, or a very large amount in the case of a steel mill or an automobile factory. The owners of a very small business may furnish all or most of the money necessary to get started. But most businesses have to borrow. Corporations can raise money by selling shares of stock. All businesses borrow from time to time from banks and other institutions whose function is to lend money. As will be pointed out in Chapters 7 and 8, the banking system and the stock and bond markets are the major sources of funds for all but the smallest businesses. But, as we shall see in Chapter 9, there are not only opportunities but many problems involved in financing a business.

BUSINESS OWNERSHIP

People sometimes think that ownership means the holding of something valuable—cash, buildings, machinery and equipment, materials, and other items of marketable value. But ownership is only the right to these things and even this right is always limited by the amount that is owed on them. Thus it cannot be said that a person "owns" a house worth $50,000 if he owes his mortgage company $30,000 on a loan against it. What he really owns and therefore what is referred to as his "equity," is $50,000 minus $30,000, or $20,000.

It is the same in business. A man may own a restaurant that he could sell for $100,000 but if he owes other people $80,000—his banker, his food suppliers, his employees—it can be seen that his true ownership, or equity, is only $20,000. If we remember this difference between property and equity, we will not make the mistake of assuming that a millionaire has a million dollars in cash. As J. Paul Getty has said, people often forget that his many millions—some say over a billion— are tied up in factories, oil wells, pipelines, refineries, real estate, and other investments, so that very little of his estimated fortune is in cash.

When we speak of the equity of a proprietorship, a partnership, or a corporation, we are therefore not speaking of cash or other property. Rather, as will be seen more clearly in Chapter 6, we are speaking of the claims owners have against property, after debts and other obligations are deducted. This simple distinction is essential to understanding the forms used in setting up a business and financing it.

A number of legal forms and arrangements have been developed for establishing and operating a business. The principal ones are described in this and the following chapter: (1) the individual proprietorship; (2) the partnership; (3) the business trust; (4) the corporation; and (5) special variations of the corporation such as co-operatives and mutual companies.

FACTORS WHICH INFLUENCE SELECTION OF A LEGAL FORM OF BUSINESS OWNERSHIP

Each legal form of business ownership has its own characteristics and its own advantages and disadvantages. A businessman will adopt the form that seems most appropriate to his purpose. In deciding which form to use, he will take certain factors into account.

First, he must decide *how much capital* the enterprise is likely to need.

Second, he must make up his mind *how much of his own property he is willing to risk* in the business.

Third, he will have to decide *how much control* over the enterprise he wishes to retain.

Fourth, he must decide whether he wants the internal affairs of the business kept relatively *secret,* or whether he is willing to open much of his financial affairs to *public inspection.*

Fifth, he must inquire into and consider the *ease and cost of organizing* the business.

Sixth, he must take into account the need for *stability and continuity in operation* of the business and the ease or difficulty of transferring his ownership.

Seventh, he must consider his *liability for taxes* in each of the different forms.

To appreciate the considerations that a businessman must take into account, we shall examine each form in relation to these seven important factors.

THE INDIVIDUAL PROPRIETORSHIP

The individual proprietorship is a business owned and controlled by one person. For that reason, proprietors are often referred to as "self-employed." The proprietorship was the earliest form of business organization and is still by far the largest in terms of numbers. There are approximately nine and a half million proprietorships in the United States, including three and a half million farmers who own and operate their farms. Proprietorships are also commonly found in retail trade and in many service businesses, such as repair shops, insurance and real estate firms, bars, and small restaurants.

But while the 9.5 million proprietorships include approximately 83 percent of all businesses, they account for only about 12 percent of all business sales. The major part of American business is carried on by 1.7 million corporations, with over 83 percent of total sales. There are also approximately 900,000 partnerships in the country, which have 5 percent of the sales.

Individual proprietorships are usually quite small businesses, many of which are small firms and part-time businesses, with average annual receipts of about $35,000 and profits of $5,000 although there are a few large ones. The latter are rare because the corporation form has important advantages for a large enterprise. Even the Hughes Tool Company, a portion of which was sold in 1972 for $148,000,000 and which had been solely owned by Howard Hughes for nearly 50 years, is a corporation.

Advantages of the Proprietorship

The proprietorship vests in the owner complete control over his business, subject only to the many government regulations applicable to all businesses. No other form has such concentration of control. The owner does not have to share his plans, policies, and manner of operation with anyone else. This form also furnishes an incentive for efficiency and devoted management that cannot be easily equalled in other forms, involving as it does the sole right to profits—and losses—of the business.

A proprietorship enjoys the maximum amount of secrecy and freedom from making public reports. To be sure, the proprietor, like any other person, must file information on income and other taxes, hours worked by his employees, and the many other things required by business regulations. But this information is not normally made available to the public.

Another advantage of the proprietorship is the ease and low cost of organizing the business (as well as of dissolving it). No contract need be entered into, as in the case of the partnership, and no incorporation papers taken out, as with a corporation. The proprietor may organize the business when he wishes by simply starting it up, and he may retire from it with a little ceremony. Even if he wishes to use a fictitous name for his business, such as the "Superior Pharmacy," all he needs to do in most states is to register the name and place a few notices in a newspaper that he is "Hilton Smith, doing business as the Superior Pharmacy."

A major advantage of the proprietorship as compared to a corporation, lies in the fact that it pays no income taxes. The proprietor pays the taxes as an individual, on his own income. A corporation pays income taxes on its profits as a corporation, and its shareholders pay taxes on their dividends as well, the proprietorship, *as a business form,* pays no taxes.

Disadvantages

On the other hand, the proprietorship has several disadvantages. The proprietor is usually at a disadvantage in raising a large amount of capital. The ownership investment is limited to his own resources, since there can be no stockholders. This likewise limits the amount he can borrow, unless he has a large personal estate, in which case creditors would be willing to lend on that. Since few investors possess great fortunes, businesses requiring large capital outlays are seldom organized as a proprietorship. It has been said that a steel plant of efficient size requires an investment of more than a billion dollars, and an oil refinery $100–200 million. Individuals are few indeed who can raise this kind of capital. Even the proprietor of a small drugstore, clothing store, or repair shop often finds capital limitations a serious disadvantage. Bankruptcies supply thousands of examples each year of proprietorships failing from lack of capital.

Another major disadvantage of a proprietorship lies in the relatively high personal risk involved. The proprietor, being an individual, is legally liable for all debts of the business, even to the extent of his own personal property. While state and national bankruptcy laws allow a few minor exceptions, this unlimited liability means that a proprietor may not separate his business from his personal property in settling claims with creditors. It is easy to see that, if a proprietor is well-to-do, creditors will be willing to lend him funds, but this is precisely the reason why wealthy owners prefer not to use the proprietorship form.

The concentration of control in a proprietorship, which is an advantage, can also have drawbacks. Many persons with high-grade managerial ability prefer to work for a business in which they can acquire a financial interest. They may also dislike the idea that their security depends on the character and health of a single man. Furthermore, most proprietorships are small and often cannot afford high-salaried executives. Thus the proprietor may find it difficult to hire and keep highly trained and motivated managers for those parts of the business that he has neither the time nor the ability to administer himself.

The very ease and cheapness of entering business as a proprietor may be disadvantageous. Many people go into business with too little capital or too little training, or find their dream of being "boss" dashed by the fierce competition of existing firms.

Finally, the proprietorship is not as stable a business form as might be desired. It ends with the retirement, death, or bankruptcy of the owner. While the business may be sold to others, the point is that the individual proprietorship ends. This may not be a serious matter for some small businesses in which continuity is not important. But even for a retail store or a building contracting firm, continuity may be highly desirable. For a bank, insurance company, or large manufacturing business, continuity is an absolute necessity.

THE PARTNERSHIP

A partnership is a form of business organization in which two or more owners are associated. It is thus similar to a proprietorship in most respects except the number of owners. A partnership may be based on a written contract or simply on an oral arrangement which, by law, is nonetheless a binding contract. The law regards individuals as partners when they act in such a way as to make reasonable people believe that they are associated in business, even though no definite arrangement exists. It is unwise, of course, for anyone to enter a partnership without a careful and clearly written contract.

As pointed out above, partnerships in the United States are far fewer than proprietorships, and even fewer than corporations. They are common in retail and wholesale trade, in the service businesses, and in insurance and real estate. Professional men, such as lawyers, doctors, and accountants, form partnerships. Until recent years before the stock exchanges permitted their members to be corporations, it was the form commonly taken by stock brokerage and underwriting firms, and it is still that of most smaller firms in the field.

General Partners

There are a number of kinds of partners. Unless otherwise specified, a partner is assumed to be a *general* partner. A general partner, regardless of the percentage of ownership he might have contributed, has authority to act as an agent for the partnership, normally participates in its management, and is liable, just as a sole proprietor is, for all of the debts of the business. Also, unless provision is made to the con-

George R. Brown

*Courtesy of
Brown & Root, Inc.*

In 1921, George R. Brown, a recent graduate of the Colorado School of Mines, was recuperating from injuries received in a mine cave-in in Montana. His older brother Herman, who ran a struggling road-building and earth-moving company named Brown and Root (named for Herman and Dan Root, Herman's brother-in-law), persuaded George to go to work for him. A flood in Central Texas had washed out several bridges and the firm of Brown and Root won contracts to rebuild four of them. Setting piers for one of these bridges required dynamiting the rock bottom of the San Gabriel River. Herman Brown was unfamiliar with underwater blasting, so he put his brother in charge of the San Gabriel River job.

In 1926 George Brown moved to Houston with his bride and set up a branch office for Brown and Root. In those days the assets of the partnership were so limited that the partners feared one good flood could wipe them out. For every bridge-building job George got in wet South Texas, Herman tried to negotiate another contract in dry West Texas as a hedge against disaster.

After Dan Root's death in 1928, George Brown acquired his interest and in 1929 the brothers decided to incorporate as Brown & Root, Inc., with Herman as President and George as Executive Vice President. In 1941, after continued growth, the brothers took over a Navy contract to build a shipyard on the Houston ship

trary, he may share in partnership profits equally with all other partners, regardless of his ownership contribution.

In his authority to act as an agent, a general partner can bind the partnership in any business deal he makes. To be sure, partners usually have a special agreement with each other in the handling of matters committing the partnership. Partner A may be put in charge of buying, partner B may be responsible for sales, and partner C may be given authority over financial matters. But unless outsiders clearly understand that such an agreement has been made, the partnership is fully responsible for the acts of any general partner.

In the matter of debts, the liability of general partners is unlimited and may extend to their personal property. However, should the

channel, which also required them to build ships. No one in the company had ever seen a ship built, but the Browns invested two million dollars in the Brown Shipbuilding Company which by 1945 delivered 359 destroyer escorts and landing craft to the Navy.

This phase of their business ended with the war, leaving the company with a surplus of engineering talent. George Brown brought in a contract to design and engineer a chemical plant, putting the technical personnel back to work. At the same time, he began to hire engineers to design gasoline plants which he believed held promise.

On the international scene, Brown & Root played a part in the reconstruction of Guam after World War II. Later they managed the reconstruction of NATO air bases in France, built bases for the Air Force and Navy in Spain, and worked on ground installations for American forces in South Vietnam.

In recent years, Brown & Root has completed hundreds of projects in foreign lands—dams in Haiti, Thailand, Mexico, and Australia; gas compressor stations in Venezuela and Canada; power plants in Puerto Rico and Italy; drilling platforms in the North Sea and off the coast of Peru; and gas and oil transport projects in the Soviet Union.

Brown & Root designed and built the compressor stations that converted the "Big Inch" and "Little Big Inch" feed pipelines of World War II into the first major cross-country natural gas transmission system, now known as the Texas-Houston Transmission System.

George Brown's career with Brown & Root has seen its transition from a family-related partnership to a closely-held corporation. The firm grew from an initial capitalization of 18 mules, 4 road-scrapers, and a pair of plows to one of the largest construction companies in the world with revenues in excess of a billion dollars a year. His interests remain diversified and widespread, ranging from oil, engineering, and construction to ranching, real estate, and education.

In 1960, Herman Brown, then 68, underwent heart surgery. The following year the brothers decided to give the stock of Brown & Root to the Brown Foundation, which in 1962 sold 95 percent of it to the Halliburton Company for almost $37 million.

George Brown continues to serve as Chairman of the Board of Brown & Root, Inc. and as a director or director emeritus of nine corporations, including ITT, Trans-World Airlines, Armco Steel, and Rice University. He has also served on various government councils for Presidents Eisenhower, Kennedy, and Johnson.

Since 1951, the Brown Foundation has given over $60 million to various educational and philanthropic activities.

partnership go bankrupt and all the partners have enough personal resources, debts of the firm will usually be allocated in a prearranged ratio. If there is no agreement covering this, the law provides that partners share losses in accordance with their share of profits.

A partnership agreement stipulates how the profits of the partnership will be divided. Among general partners, it is customary that profits be divided according to the amounts invested. However, there is no reason why an agreement may not provide for any other basis of division desired by the partners. For example, the partner who puts in most of the investment may wish to take a fairly inactive role and be satisfied with far less than a proportionate share of the profits. There can be other considerations. In a certain small electronics company, profits and ownership interest were shared equally by three partners despite the fact that only one partner put up the cash and credit needed. Another partner had the idea for the company and managed it, and the third partner was an engineer who brought product ideas to the firm.

Limited Partners

While all partnerships must have at least one general partner, it is possible for some partners to be *limited* or *special* partners. A limited partner, sometimes called a "silent" or "dormant" partner, usually contributes capital and shares in profits in accordance with some agreed-upon ratio, but his liability for loss is limited to his capital contribution. A limited partner may take an active part in the management of a partnership but, if he does so, his limited status must be known to creditors.

While a "silent" or "dormant" partner may be a general partner, he is normally a limited one. A "silent" partner is usually known to the public while a "dormant" partner may not be known.

Advantages of the Partnership

The partnership has many of the advantages and disadvantages of the proprietorship. This is understandable since it is essentially only an association of individual owners. Except as otherwise provided in a partnership agreement, each partner exercises control over the business and shares in profits and losses, with the result that the motivation to succeed is great.

Because the partnership may have any number of members—though most partnerships are not larger than two or three members—it is possible for individuals with talents in different operations of a business to team together. Moreover, employees with ability and ambition may be induced to stay on with a hope of being eventually admitted to membership in the firm. This is a common practice in accounting, law, and management consulting firms.

Because a partnership is formed as a private contract between the members, and no government permission is necessary, there is little more government regulation than in a proprietorship. Business matters normally need not be shared with any person other than the partners. Thus where secrecy is advantageous, as in many professional and financial businesses, one is likely to find the partnership form used.

Another advantage growing out of the private contractual nature of the partnership is that it is relatively easy and inexpensive to organize. An oral agreement can be made in minutes, and even a written agreement (much to be preferred) can be drawn up within a short time and at modest legal expense.

An important advantage of the partnership as compared with the individual proprietorship is that it often enables the firm to secure a greater capital investment. By pooling resources several individuals may be able to go into business when one person alone could not. Since the personal assets of more individuals are subject to liability for the debts of the firm (to the extent that the members are general partners), creditors may be more willing to make loans to the partnership.

There may also be tax advantages with a partnership, at least as compared to a corporation. A corporation pays income taxes and its shareholders also pay income taxes on the dividends they receive. In a partnership, as with a proprietorship, the members pay taxes on their earnings as these accrue, but the partnership as such does not pay income taxes. To be sure, until recent years, because taxes on corporation income were at a lower rate (approximately 50 percent) than those paid by individuals in high tax brackets (70 to 90 percent), it was advantageous for some persons to operate as a corporation. With the federal income tax ceiling for earned income reduced to 50 percent in 1971, the partnership may now have a decided tax advantage.

Disadvantages of the Partnership

The major disadvantage of the partnership is the unlimited personal liability of general partners. Even limited partners must take care that those who deal with their company know of their limited status if they are not to be held liable for more than their investment. While the law does not limit the number of partners a firm may have, the dangers of legal liability certainly do.

When it is also considered that any general partner has the legal right to act as an agent and bind the firm to contracts and other obligations, the problem of liability becomes even greater. Imagine a partnership of 1,000 members, each member having unlimited liability, the right to participate in management, and the right to bind the firm! It is no wonder that partnerships tend to be small in size and to have few partners. One could not expect hundreds of small investors to place their capital in a partnership. Nor would it generally be wise for persons of large means to risk everything on the success of a venture organized as a partnership.

A further disadvantage of the partnership is its instability. Some partnerships apparently endure for long periods of time. But whenever a partner dies, retires, or withdraws from the partnership, a new partnership must legally be established. If a partner withdraws, even a limited one, his share must be liquidated. Usually it is sold to a person whom the other partners will accept, for those in the firm must be responsible for the ability and integrity of the new member. If his interest is liquidated, he must be paid an acceptable price unless a price is already stipulated in the partnership agreement.

Thus one of the major disadvantages of a partnership is the lack of free transferability of ownership. This alone should give one pause before investing much in a partnership. A sole proprietor, or a shareholder in a small corporation, may have difficulty in finding a buyer for his interest, but a partner may face even greater difficulty because he is not a free agent in the transaction.

The Importance of a Clear Partnership Agreement

A clear partnership agreement is essential to avoid difficulties such as those mentioned above. One must bear in mind that a partnership represents a legal contract between the partners. Although it is legally binding only on the partners and on those outsiders who are clearly informed of it, the agreement should be treated with the same care as any other contract. A first step is to put it in writing. An agreement should include the following items:

1. The name of each partner, and whether he is a general or a limited partner.
2. The name of the firm, the kind of business to be conducted, and its location.
3. The duration of the agreement, especially if the partnership is being formed to accomplish a specific objective.
4. The amount of money to be invested by each partner.
5. How profits and losses are to be divided among the partners.
6. The authority of each partner to bind the firm to particular kinds of contract commitments and arrangements, or to spend the firm's money.
7. The amount of time and effort each partner is to give the business (some partners may not give it their full time).
8. The responsibilities of each partner in the firm (for example, one partner may be put in charge of selling, another of buying, another of accounting and financial arrangements).

9. An agreement by each partner to protect the partnership from claims made by his personal creditors (since a partnership interest is personal property like a house or automobile, creditors may go after a person's partnership interest if a personal debt is not satisfied).
10. The amounts of partners' salaries if, as is usually the case, partners are to be paid for their time and effort beyond what they would receive from partnership profits.
11. The amounts of money a partner may withdraw, either from his original investment (his "capital") or from the profits, and under what conditions.
12. Provisions for the payment of interest on money in the partnership, especially if one partner leaves more in the partnership or withdraws less than the others.
13. How the accounts of the partnership are to be kept and how they are to be audited for accuracy and completeness.
14. Procedures for handling the withdrawal of a partner from the firm and admitting new partners.
15. Procedures for dissolving the partnership.
16. Procedures for resolving disagreements among partners.

Evidently there is much more to starting a partnership than a handshake. Even between the best of friends there can be misunderstandings and difficulties as time goes on. The best way to avoid these is to anticipate them and to provide ways for handling them if they should occur.

JOINT VENTURES OR SYNDICATES

There are many variations of the partnership, usually designed for special purposes and to avoid certain problems. Among the most common are joint ventures or syndicates. These are usually set up for specific purposes, are normally of short duration ending when the purpose is accomplished, provide for one or a few general partners who may manage the venture, and include provisions that death or withdrawal of a partner does not affect the life of the partnership.

A common form of joint venture is one set up to sell a specific stock or bond issue. It is usually known as a syndicate. Figure 4-1, shows a group of underwriting firms that have joined together in a temporary partnership to sell 1,900,000 shares of Canteen Corporation stock. The four managing partners shown at the top of the list bear responsibility for the entire issue while the other partners have under-

FIGURE 4–1

NOT A NEW ISSUE

1,900,000 Shares

Canteen Corporation

Common Stock
(Par Value $1 Per Share)

Price $22 Per Share

Copies of the Prospectus may be obtained in any state in which this an-
nouncement is circulated only from such of the underwriters as may legally
offer these securities in compliance with the securities laws of such State.

Lazard Frères & Co.

Kuhn, Loeb & Co.

Merrill Lynch, Pierce, Fenner & Smith
Incorporated

Paine, Webber, Jackson & Curtis
Incorporated

Blyth Eastman Dillon & Co. Incorporated	The First Boston Corporation	Dillon, Read & Co. Inc.	Drexel Firestone Incorporated
duPont Glore Forgan Incorporated	Goldman, Sachs & Co.	Halsey, Stuart & Co. Inc.	Hornblower & Weeks-Hemphill, Noyes Incorporated
Kidder, Peabody & Co. Incorporated	Loeb, Rhoades & Co.	Salomon Brothers	Stone & Webster Securities Corporation
Wertheim & Co., Inc.	White, Weld & Co. Incorporated	Dean Witter & Co. Incorporated	Bache & Co. Incorporated
E. F. Hutton & Company Inc.	Reynolds Securities Inc.		Shearson, Hammill & Co. Incorporated
ABD Securities Corporation	Allen & Company Incorporated	Basle Securities Corporation	Bear, Stearns & Co.
A. G. Becker & Co. Incorporated	Burnham & Company Inc.	Clark, Dodge & Co. Incorporated	F. Eberstadt & Co., Inc.
EuroPartners Securities Corporation		Robert Fleming Incorporated	Hallgarten & Co.
Harris, Upham & Co. Incorporated	Hayden Stone Inc.	Hill Samuel Securities Corporation	W. E. Hutton & Co.
Kleinwort, Benson Incorporated	Ladenburg, Thalmann & Co. Inc.		Model, Roland & Co., Inc.
New Court Securities Corporation	Paribas Corporation		L. F. Rothschild & Co.
Shields Securities Corporation	Spencer Trask & Co. Incorporated		Swiss American Corporation
UBS-DB Corporation	G. H. Walker & Co. Incorporated	Walston & Co., Inc.	Wood, Struthers & Winthrop Inc.

Amsterdam-Rotterdam Bank N.V.	Banca Commerciale Italiana	Banque Nationale de Paris
Kuhn, Loeb & Co. International	Lazard Brothers & Co. Ltd.	Lazard Frères et Cie
Merrill Lynch, Pierce, Fenner & Smith Securities Underwriters Limited	National Westminster Bank Group London	Skandinaviska Enskilda Banken
Société Générale de Banque S. A.	M. M. Warburg-Brinckmann, Wirtz und Co.	S. G. Warburg & Co. Ltd.

Westdeutsche Landesbank
GIROZENTRALE

January 26, 1973

taken to sell specific amounts. Once the issue is sold, the syndicate will be dissolved.

A similar use of the syndicate, or joint venture, is common in the purchase of real estate. For example, in one purchase of land, ten persons each contributed $15,000, for a total of $150,000, to use as a half payment on some land. One person was designated the general partner with unlimited liability and the right to sell or otherwise dispose of the land when he saw fit. For acting in this capacity he was given a one-eleventh share of the profits.

The main advantages of such syndicates are that they allow most members limited liability, are easy to form, can be dissolved easily, and give their members the tax advantages of being owners.

MINING PARTNERSHIPS

Some western states of the U.S. have legalized another form of special partnership known as the mining partnership. This is similar to the syndicate in that usually only one member is a general partner and manages the business. But unlike other partnerships, the mining partnership allows its limited members to own shares and dispose of their shares to anyone without affecting the life of the business. Since mining often involves high risks and long periods of time, such a means of enabling investors to get together has real advantages.

BUSINESS TRUSTS

The trust is used for many business purposes, most commonly to hold securities for investors. Originally it was known as the "Massachusetts trust" because it was a form used in that state when laws forbade corporations to buy and sell real estate. Many investment trusts, called mutual funds, hold billions of dollars of securities on behalf of many thousands of investors.

Under this form of doing business, a trustee or group of trustees is created by a legal agreement. The trustees are the actual holders of property and can accept funds from investors to whom they issue certificates of beneficial interest, referred to as trust shares. These shares are merely evidences that the holder has transferred funds to a trustee and has a right to benefit from the proceeds of the trust. But the shareholder has no right to vote for trustees or otherwise control them so long as they act in accordance with the trust agreement. Since the trustees really own the property and run the business, the shareholders have no liability beyond the possible loss of their investment.

While it would appear that the business trust has all the advantages of the corporation without the need to go through the formalities of incorporating, this is not necessarily so. Lawyers must draw trust agreements carefully to gain all the advantages, particularly that of limited liability of shareholders. In most cases the trust cannot be given perpetual life. And businessmen and investors do not always understand the trust form, which lack of understanding, along with the fact that the trust has been used by some fly-by-night business operations, tends to make it far less popular than the corporation.

SUMMARY

Business ownership may take any of various forms provided by law. By far the most common are proprietorships, partnerships, trusts, and corporations. Each form has certain advantages and disadvantages. (The corporation form, so widely used in business, is discussed at length in the following chapter.)

Factors that influence businessmen in selecting one form rather than another are (1) the amount of capital the business enterprise will need, (2) how much of his property a person is willing to risk in a business, (3) how much control an owner wishes to retain, (4) the extent to which he wants secrecy in his operations, (5) the ease and cost of organizing a business, (6) the extent to which stability and continuity are needed, and (7) the liability for income taxes of the different forms.

A business owned and controlled by a single person is referred to as a proprietorship. This form has advantages from the point of view of control, secrecy, ease and low cost of organizing, and not having to pay income taxes. The disadvantages of the proprietorship are the limited funds an individual can normally raise, the unlimited liability of the owner, the difficulty a single owner may have in hiring and keeping highly qualified persons, the fact that the ease of setting up a proprietorship may lead people to go into business too casually, and the fact that its life and stability depend on those of an individual person.

A partnership is a business in which two or more owners are associated. There may be a number of different partners. A general partner has the authority to act for the partnership and bind it, participates equally in management with other partners, and has liability for the debts of the business in the same way an individual proprietor does. A limited, or special, partner is limited in his liability for debts, cannot bind the partnership, and may or may not participate in the management of the business.

The partnership has many of the advantages of the proprietorship. Because of his ownership interest and control, each partner tends to have the same desire to succeed as an individual owner. A partnership can be easy and inexpensive to form, permits a high degree of secrecy, and usually allows a business to raise more capital than a proprietorship can because of the number of owners. There are also advantages with respect to income taxes, at least as compared to a corporation, because the business as such is not taxed; only the earnings of the partners are taxed.

The major disadvantage of a partnership is the unlimited liability of the general partners. When it is considered that each general partner can act for the partnership, this risk may be great. Another disadvantage is the lack of stability of the partnership form since the death or withdrawal of a partner legally requires a new partnership to be formed. Also, an important disadvantage is that an individual partner cannot easily sell or otherwise transfer his ownership interest. Because of these and other problems, it is of the greatest importance that a clear and complete partnership agreement be drawn up before people go into a partnership.

There are many variations of the partnership, usually designed to avoid some of its disadvantages. Among the two most prominent are the joint venture, or syndicate, and the mining partnership. In these, members can be clearly and easily given limited liability; they are also easy to form, and the transfer or change of ownership is fairly easy.

A special form of business organization is the business trust, *often used to handle financing arrangements. In this form, trustees are created by legal agreement. The trustees hold the property of the business for the interest and benefit of others, usually persons who have invested money. This gives investors the advantage of limited liability and many of the advantages of the corporate form. But trusts do not have perpetual life. Because the trust agreement is so important, it must be drawn carefully by competent lawyers.*

KEY TERMS AND CONCEPTS FOR REVIEW

Proprietorship	Silent, or dormant, partner
Partnership	Partnership agreement
Ownership	Transferability of ownership
Equity	Joint ventures
Unlimited liability	Syndicates
General partner	Mining partnership
Limited, or special, partner	Business trust
	Investment trust

QUESTIONS FOR ANALYSIS AND DISCUSSION

1. Why are there so many proprietorships in the United States, yet they do such a small part of the nation's business?

2. Why is an understanding of the concept of ownership or equity so important to an understanding of the legal form a business may use?

3. Since so many businesses are founded and operated as proprietorships, there must be many advantages to the proprietorship form. What are they? Would these appeal to you if you were to start a small business?

4. Since most proprietorships are small businesses, there must be certain disadvantages to using the proprietorship form. What disadvantages would concern you most if you were to go into business?

5. Partnerships have many of the advantages and disadvantages of proprietorships. What are these? How are partnerships different from proprietorships?

6. If you were a partner, would you rather be a general partner or a limited partner? Why?

7. Why is it important that a partnership agreement be drawn up in writing and with great care?

8. Why do you suppose that underwriting firms often set up partnerships, referred to as syndicates, when they join together to sell stocks or bonds? Why are joint ventures, or syndicates, often used in real estate purchases?

9. How do mining partnerships differ from ordinary business partnerships? Why have these been legalized in so many western states?

10. How does a business trust differ from an ordinary business partnership? Why do we have so many investment trusts?

SUGGESTED READINGS

Anderson, R. A. *Business Law* (9th ed.). Cincinnati: South-Western Publishing Company, 1972, Chapters 44–53.

Lusk, H. F. et al. *Business Law: Principles and Cases* (3d U.C.C. ed.). Homewood; Ill.: Richard D. Irwin, Inc., 1974, Part V.

Van Horne, J. C. *Fundamentals of Financial Management* (2d ed.). Englewood Cliffs, N.J.: Prentice-Hall, Inc., 1974.

Votaw, D. *Legal Aspects of Business Administration* (3d ed.). Englewood Cliffs, N.J.: Prentice-Hall, Inc., 1969, Part 3.

Williamson, J. P., and R. W. Austin *Law in Business Administration.* Boston: Allyn and Bacon, Inc., 1962, Chapter 3.

5

Legal Forms of Business Ownership: The Corporation

We have already noted the importance of the corporate form of business enterprise, and that corporations account for over 83 percent of the nation's business sales. There are over 1.7 million profit-seeking corporations in the U.S., in every field of economic activity. There are also many corporations that are not conducted for private profit and do not have private stockholders. These so-called nonprofit corporations are numerous in governmental activities and among religious bodies, charitable institutions, educational organizations, and scientific societies.

If proprietorships and partnerships were the only forms of business ownership, the industrial giants of today with their hundreds of millions of dollars in assets would be inconceivable. The *Fortune* "Directory of the 500 Largest U.S. Industrial Corporations" shows that all but a few have more than $100 million in assets; in 1973, some 138 had assets of more than a billion dollars. These 500 largest companies handled two thirds of the sales of all industrial corporations in the United States.

The corporate form is also used by small-scale businesses. In fact, more than 95 percent of all U.S. corporations have assets and annual sales of less than one million dollars.

Because of its importance in business life, the corporate form of enterprise

117

merits extended discussion. We shall pay particular attention to (1) the nature of the corporation; (2) how a corporation is formed; (3) the types of corporations; (4) how corporations are financed; (5) how corporations are governed; (6) the advantages of the corporate form; and (7) the disadvantages of the corporate form.

THE NATURE OF THE CORPORATION

The most widely quoted definition of a corporation was that made by Chief Justice Marshall of the United States in 1819. He referred to a corporation as "an artificial being, invisible, intangible, and existing only in contemplation of the law." In other words, a corporation is an artificial being endowed by law with the rights, powers, and duties of a natural person. The fiction exists in the fact that a corporation is not a natural person but is treated by the law very much as if it were.

Like natural persons, a corporation may own property, incur debts, and be sued for damages. Legally it is the corporation, and not its stockholders or officers, that buys buildings and machinery, sells goods, borrows money, and engages in lawsuits. Unlike natural persons, a corporation may not vote and cannot be sent to jail. However, natural persons may own a corporation and do determine and carry out its policies. At the same time these natural persons own none of the property of the corporation. These relationships are illustrated in the accompanying diagram and explained in more detail in the following paragraphs.

HOW A CORPORATION IS FORMED

The corporation is not exactly a modern invention. In the Middle Ages, the corporate form was used by the Catholic Church and by the towns as a device for holding property separate from the property of individuals. The corporate device was also used centuries ago in the fields of banking, insurance, and transportation. But the practice of placing general business ownership and control in the corporation is relatively recent. At first, the corporation was regarded with considerable suspicion in the United States, and was used only in cases specifically approved by national and state legislatures. In 1830, however, New York State extended the use of the corporation to businesses generally and by 1860 most of the other states had followed suit. Today, the organization of corporations is an everyday occurrence and it is not

FIGURE 5-1

The Corporation and Its Relationships

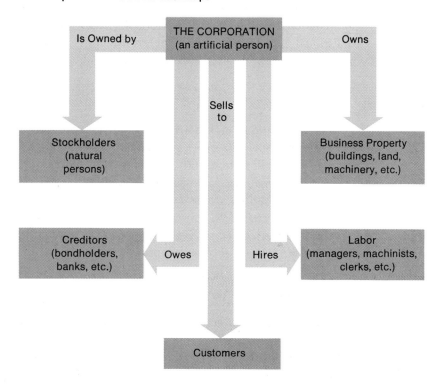

unusual for an individual state to charter several thousand corporations in a single month.

To establish a corporation is usually an easy matter. States have general incorporation laws that standardize the procedure for doing so. Most states require that at least three persons join to establish a corporation. These persons fill out application forms which are then sent to some designated state official. If the information supplied is adequate, if the individuals have complied with the incorporation law and have paid a small fee, they receive a corporate charter. This charter is essentially a contract between the state and the incorporating natural persons allowing the latter to set up a corporation. In fact, this is so simple a matter that many lawyers will handle all the paper work and the incorporation fees for a few hundred dollars.

In the U.S., most corporations are formed under the laws of one of the 50 states. In special cases, the federal government issues corporate charters; it does so for national banks, federal credit unions, and federal savings and loan associations. Some government-owned corporations are federally incorporated; others are incorporated by states. Other corporations chartered by the federal government include certain scientific and educational organizations. But Congress has not yet passed any general incorporation law applying to businesses and other organizations.

TYPES OF CORPORATIONS

Most corporations in the United States are privately owned and operated for profit. But many government corporations also exist, organized by federal, state, county, city, and other political entities. Still other corporations own and operate charitable, religious, educational, or social organizations; these are normally not operated to make a profit and are referred to as nonprofit corporations. Universities and colleges are incorporated, as are churches, social fraternities, the Red Cross, and all manner of other nonprofit enterprises.

HOW CORPORATIONS ARE FINANCED

Corporations, like other forms of business, secure their productive resources either by the use of money, by trading securities directly for them, or by leasing facilities and paying rent. Money is obtained through selling goods or services at more than cost—profits, by selling shares of ownership—stock, or by borrowing from banks or from investors through the sale of bonds or notes.

Common Stock

When a corporation sells stock, it gives each purchaser a share in the ownership. Stock is divided into two classes, *common* and *preferred*. Stock ownership is evidenced by a certificate, as shown in Figure 5–2. The front of the certificate attests that the named person is the owner of a specified number of shares. It is signed by officers of the issuing company, and also by a trust company certifying that the shares are properly issued. On the back of the certificate is a form to be filled out when the owner wishes to transfer the shares.

Common stock ordinarily carries with it the right to vote for directors who represent the owners in the management of the corporation. It also carries the right to share in the earnings of the corporation whenever dividends are declared. Common stockholders also have the

FIGURE 6-2

Typical Common Stock Certificate (front)

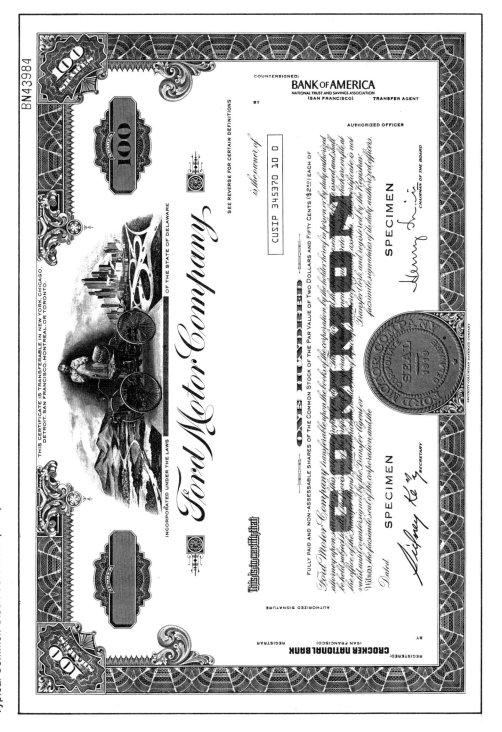

FIGURE 5–2 (*Continued*)

Typical Common Stock Certificate (back)

FORD MOTOR COMPANY

The Corporation will furnish without charge to each stockholder who so requests, the designations, preferences and relative, participating, optional or other special rights of each class of stock or series thereof and the qualifications, limitations or restrictions of such preferences and/or rights. Any such request should be addressed to the Secretary of Ford Motor Company, The American Road, Dearborn, Michigan, or to the Transfer Agent named on the face of this certificate.

The following abbreviations, when used in the inscription on the face of this certificate, shall be construed as though they were written out in full according to applicable laws or regulations:

TEN COM—as tenants in common	UNIF GIFT MIN ACT—............... Custodian ....
TEN ENT —as tenants by the entireties	(Cust) (Minor)
JT TEN —as joint tenants with right of	under Uniform Gifts to Minors
survivorship and not as tenants	Act..............
in common	(State)

Additional abbreviations may also be used though not in the above list.

For Value Received _____ *hereby sell, assign and transfer unto*

PLEASE INSERT SOCIAL SECURITY OR OTHER
IDENTIFYING NUMBER OF ASSIGNEE

_____

PLEASE PRINT OR TYPEWRITE NAME AND ADDRESS OF ASSIGNEE

_____

Shares of the stock represented by the within Certificate, and do hereby irrevocably constitute and appoint

_____ *Attorney,*

to transfer the said stock on the books of the within named Corporation with full power of substitution in the premises.

Dated, _____

X_____

NOTICE: THE SIGNATURE TO THIS ASSIGNMENT MUST CORRESPOND WITH THE NAME AS WRITTEN UPON THE FACE OF THE CERTIFICATE, IN EVERY PARTICULAR, WITHOUT ALTERATION OR ENLARGEMENT, OR ANY CHANGE WHATEVER.

THIS SPACE MUST NOT BE COVERED IN ANY WAY

right to share in the assets of the corporation should it be liquidated, after the claims of creditors and preferred stockholders have been paid.

Stocks often have a *par value*. To say that a stock has a par value of $100 per share is only to say that $100 was supposed to have been contributed in money or property by the original stockholders when they received the stock. Par value is a stated value which has little significance once a corporation is operating. A share of stock is simply evidence of part ownership in the corporation, and it matters little whether the share has a par value of $1 or $100. A share of stock, like anything else, is worth what people will pay for it. This depends upon such things as the company's earnings, its growth outlook, and the cash dividends it has paid. For example the common stock of General Motors has a par value of $1.67 even when selling for $80.

Par value has been misleading to investors who often think incorrectly that a $100 or $10 par value gives them a right to collect that much from a corporation. Since the law does require that something of value at least equal to par be paid in when stock is originally issued, it is difficult to sell new stock when the market price is below par. As a result stock of no par value has come into common use. This simply means that no stated value is given to such a stock and a share is what it actually is, a portion of the company's ownership. If 10,000 shares of a corporation's stock have been issued, a holder of 100 shares has ownership claims to 1/100 of the corporation's assets, after all prior claims are deducted, whether the share of stock has a par value of $100, $50, $1, or no par value.

Preferred Stock

Preferred stock, while still representing ownership, has other rights of its own. It is commonly *preferred as to dividends,* that is, the holders receive their dividends before anything can be paid to common stockholders. Preferred stockholders are usually limited to dividends in the amount of their preference, say $6 per share, and can get no more. Occasionally preferred shareholders may *participate* with the common in dividends. For example, there may be a provision that if preferred shares receive a $6 dividend, they can participate in dividends after common shares receive $6. Or the participation may be based on percentages of par value or on some other formula.

A preferred stock may also be *cumulative* or *noncumulative*. If it is cumulative its dividends, when not paid in any particular year, accumulate from year to year. No dividends can be paid in any year to common stockholders until the preferred dividends, including accumulated amounts from prior years, are paid in full. Thus if a cumulative preferred stock with a preference of $6 per year received no dividends in 1972 and 1973, no dividends could be declared on common stock in 1974 until preferred dividends for 1972 and 1973 as well as 1974— or $18 per share—had been paid on the preferred. Note that these dividends in arrears are not debts of the corporation in the sense that the company *owes* these dividends to preferred stockholders. They are merely obligations to pay such dividends before any dividends are paid to the common stockholders *if dividends are paid at all.*

If preferred stock is noncumulative, a corporation that does not declare a dividend in one year has no obligation to pay preferred stockholders back dividends in a later year when dividends are paid. The preferred only have the right to be paid ahead of common stockholders in that year. In the example given above, with noncumulative preferred, dividends could have been paid to common stockholders in 1974 after the regular $6 per share preferred dividends for that year were paid, and the preferred stockholders would have had no right for the dividends passed in 1972 and 1973.

Borrowing by Use of Bonds

A corporation may raise some of its funds by borrowing. Lenders receive bonds, notes, or are carried on the books of the corporation as accounts to be paid. This last form of indebtedness arises as the result of normal business operations when items such as raw materials are bought and delivered to be paid for at a later date. Such "accounts payable" credit is very important in business finance, and will be discussed in the following chapters.

Bonds are evidences of debt that the corporation owes to a special group of creditors. A bond is backed by a special agreement between the corporation and a trustee acting for the bondholders. The specific credit position of these lenders is spelled out in the agreement, as are the things the corporation will or will not do to protect the bondholders. Thus a corporation may promise not to pay dividends to stockholders if earnings drop below a particular level, or not to endanger the bondholders' position by additional borrowing without their consent.

A bondholder may lend his money permanently or for a very long period of time, such as 99 years or even longer, but usually he expects to have his money repaid at a certain future date. There are many bonds, like certain Pacific Gas and Electric Corporation bonds, not due until 2003. In the meantime, the bondholder receives *interest*.

Corporate bonds are usually issued in $500 and $1,000 denominations, bearing interest annually at a certain percentage of their face value, and running for a period of more than 10 years. A 6 percent bond of $1,000 denomination, issued in 1965 for a term of 30 years, would bind the corporation to pay $60 interest each year until 1995 and to repay the $1,000 at that time.

Bonds are of several kinds. Because lenders may desire a definite guarantee of repayment, bonds may be secured by some kind of valuable property. If the underlying security is certain business property on which a mortgage—similar to the ordinary house mortgage—has been placed, the bond is called a *mortgage bond*. Many railroad bonds have been secured in this way. If the security back of a bond consists of stocks and bonds of other companies held by the borrowing corporation, and if these are specifically pledged, it is called a *collateral trust bond*.

Most bonds issued in recent years are secured not by specific property but by the general assets, not otherwise pledged against loans, and earnings of the corporation. These bonds, called *debenture bonds,* are simply promises to pay. Normally the promise is supported by the usual contractual provisions that the corporation will not pay dividends when earnings or cash fall below certain levels, will limit its uses of leases in obtaining property, and will not pledge company assets for other loans. Sometimes, as in the case of the Ford Motor Company 8⅛ percent debentures, the company also promises to reduce the bonds outstanding by repurchasing them on a schedule over the years, or depositing funds with the trustee to repurchase them. This is called a "sinking fund," and the bonds are referred to as *sinking fund bonds.*

The relatively unsecured nature of the debenture bond does not mean that it is riskier than other bonds. In many corporations with good earnings and a record of success, a general promise to pay means more than does a secured promise of a business whose security is a piece of property with no earning value and which can only be sold for junk. It is obvious that a holder of General Electric debentures has a better chance of receiving interest and repayment than does a holder of a railroad mortgage bond when the railroad is in bankruptcy. General Electric debentures were selling in 1973 at approximately their original issue price, while Erie Railroad mortgage bonds were selling at between 3 and 4 percent of their issue price.

Bonds sometimes carry the provision that they may be traded for

FIGURE 5-3

$5,000 Sinking Fund Debenture of Ford Motor Company

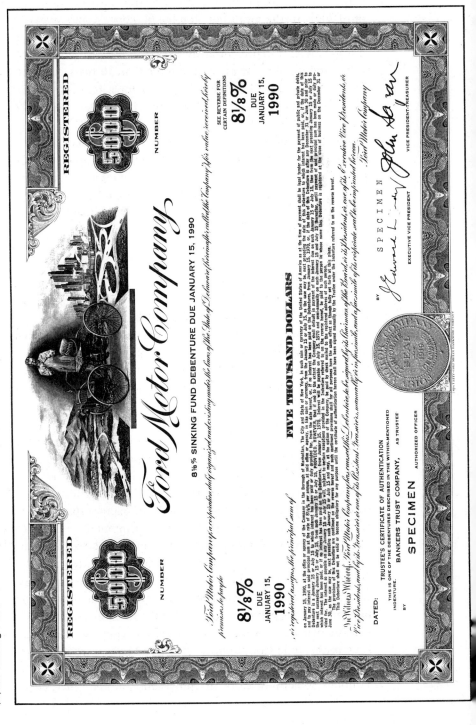

common stock in the issuing company. These are called *convertible bonds*. For example, Occidental Oil Corporation 7½ percent bonds, issued in 1971 and due in 1996, carry the provision that each $1,000 bond may be converted into 50 shares of common stock at the option of the holder. If Occidental common stock should rise above $20 per share, the holder would have a value in the bond above its face value. Such bonds offer investors the security of a bond and the growth potential of common stock. The latter is sometimes considerable. For example, Xerox convertible bonds in 1973 were valued on the market at almost double their issue price of a few years earlier, because they were convertible into Xerox stock which had approximately that value.

Corporations Obtain Funds in Other Ways

Corporations, like other business enterprises, may obtain funds through the issuance of notes, which are simple promises to pay. They may also get possession of physical assets by leasing them—buildings, machinery, and various kinds of equipment ranging from typewriters and automobiles to computers. These ways of obtaining funds are discussed in Chapters 8 and 9.

HOW THE CORPORATION IS GOVERNED

A corporation is managed by a board of directors elected by the common stockholders. Usually each share of common stock entitles the holder to one vote. The preferred stockholders may also have voting rights, on the same basis as common stockholders.

How a Stockholder Votes

Voting in a corporation election is different from voting in a city or state election. In a political election, all voters are equal; they have the same number of votes. In a corporation election, the number of votes a person has depends on the number of shares he owns. Consequently, one or a few large stockholders can prevail over many others.

In some states, such as California, cumulative voting is required. This provides that a stockholder be given the right to have as many votes for directors as his number of shares multiplied by the number of directors to be elected, and that he can give as many of his votes to one director as he wishes. In this way he can accumulate his votes for one or more directors, so that a minority group of holders may be able to place one or more directors on the board.

Hugh Marston Hefner

Courtesy: Playboy.

Hugh Marston Hefner was born on April 9, 1926, in a quiet middleclass section of Chicago where his parents still live. Glenn and Grace (Swanson) Hefner were of German-Swedish extraction and had moved in 1920 from the farm country of Nebraska to Chicago, where the elder Hefner had been offered a job with an accounting firm.

Hugh Hefner's childhood and adolescence were fairly typical of middle-class American family life in the 1930s.

After unsuccessful efforts as an independent cartoonist, he went to work for a cardboard carton manufacturing company as assistant personnel manager. He quit the box company as soon as he found another job as advertising copywriter for a Chicago department store.

Next he landed a job as a subscription promotion copywriter for *Esquire* magazine, whose editorial offices were then located in Chicago. He had long been an avid reader of the magazine, and since high school days he had dreamed of publishing his own men's magazine.

By 1952 Hefner was convinced that there was now room on the nation's newsstands for a younger version of *Esquire*— and that he was the man to publish it.

Hefner learned that launching a national magazine with little money and less experience was a nearly impossible task. "The only reason I tried it was because I had no conception of the almost insurmountable difficulties and the odds against my success," Hefner said recently. "If I had known then what I know now, I doubt if I would have even tried. But once I had made up my mind, I worked on the idea with everything I had, and for the first time in my life I felt truly free. It was like a mission—to publish a magazine that would thumb its nose at all the phony puritan values of the world in which I had grown up."

To support himself while working on his idea, Hefner took a job as circulation managers to hired professionals. Shapiro was raise money for the initial production costs, he mortgaged his furniture, borrowed a few hundred dollars from various friends and relatives, and sold $10,000 worth of stock in his newly incorporated enterprise to random social acquaint-

Once a board of directors is elected, it has the authority to appoint officers and make most company decisions (except for a few matters, such as deciding to issue additional stock). The board, as the representative of all the stockholders and their interests, has the power to manage the corporation. Technically, the stockholders have the right to change the membership of the board if they do not like its performance.

ances. Hefner's personal investment in the project amounted to only $600.

In the summer of 1953, Hefner put together a mock-up of his proposed magazine with the help of Art Paul, who is still *Playboy*'s art director. It featured a full-color reproduction of the already famous nude calendar photograph of Marilyn Monroe, and an assortment of cartoons, party jokes, feature articles, and fiction that was remarkably prophetic of the editorial content of *Playboy* magazine years later. With the mock-up as a sales tool, Hefner found a distributing company that agreed to put the magazine on newsstands all over the country, if he could manage to get it printed. He then found a printing company that agreed to produce the magazine, if Hefner would assign it first rights to the proceeds from newsstands sales.

Fifty-one thousand copies were sold of the first issue, enough to pay the paper and printing bills and to provide enough profit for a second issue which carried the date "January 1954." After that, Hefner never doubted the inevitability of *Playboy*'s success.

The first three issues of *Playboy* were planned, edited, and laid out on the kitchen table of Hefner's modest apartment at 61st and Harper on Chicago's South Side. He then rented office space in a converted Victorian residence at 11 East Superior Street near Chicago's night club district, and began to assemble a staff. By mid-1955 he had a dozen employees, his magazine was making a modest profit, and circulation had passed 300,000.

The results of continued hard work are now apparent to all. By 1971 the Playboy Clubs, which Hefner had launched 11 years earlier, had grown to a chain of clubs in 15 U.S. cities, plus Montreal and London, plus posh resort hotels in Miami Beach and Jamaica and Wisconsin, with another resort hotel under construction in New Jersey. Hefner also found time to launch such subsidiaries as the Playboy Model Agency, Playboy Press (a book publishing firm), the Playboy Theater, Playboy Products, (a line of playboy-oriented gifts), Playboy Limousine, Inc., and Playboy Productions, created to produce feature-length motion pictures and TV specials.

By 1971 *Playboy* magazine's circulation had reached the 6 million mark and its advertising sales had grown to more than $32 million annually. In the meantime, Hefner's company had grown from 10 employees in 1954 to 4,000 in the late 1960s. He leased the 37-story Palmolive Building, one of Chicago's landmarks, remodeled the interior, renamed it, and moved his staff into the Playboy Building in June 1967.

To facilitate his new involvement in show business, Hefner established a West coast base of operations by acquiring Playboy Mansion West, a baronial estate in the Holmby Hills section of Los Angeles. He commutes between his two headquarters in The Big Bunny, a stretch DC-9 jet that is specially designed to provide Hefner with comfortable working and living accommodations as he travels about the world overseeing his far-flung business operations.

Only recently the respected *Sunday Times* of London selected Hefner as one of the 1,000 most influential people of this century. Hefner, explained the *Times,* had "struck an answering chord in the young urban American male. His fantasies became their fantasies."

The Power of Insiders

In large corporations, the stockholders do not in fact exercise much control. Often a certain group, usually allied with or consisting of the top management of the corporation, is able to maintain control for a long period of time without owning anywhere near the majority of the voting stock. If a stockholder is one of thousands who own a few shares of stock, he may have little choice but to vote for directors nominated by the controlling stockholders or the inside management group, if he votes at all. When stock in a corporation is owned in small lots and by thousands of individuals scattered across the country, the directors or top managers may effectively keep control away from the real owners of the corporation.

This inside control is made possible by the use of "proxies" in corporation elections. A proxy is a certificate signed by the shareholder giving someone else the right to exercise his vote (see Figure 5–4). The officers of a corporation have the list of shareholders and can use

FIGURE 5–4

Front and Back of Typical Proxy

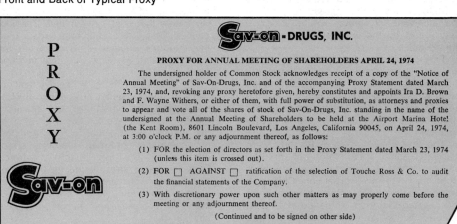

Sav-on-DRUGS, INC.

PROXY FOR ANNUAL MEETING OF SHAREHOLDERS APRIL 24, 1974

The undersigned holder of Common Stock acknowledges receipt of a copy of the "Notice of Annual Meeting" of Sav-On-Drugs, Inc. and of the accompanying Proxy Statement dated March 23, 1974, and, revoking any proxy heretofore given, hereby constitutes and appoints Ira D. Brown and F. Wayne Withers, or either of them, with full power of substitution, as attorneys and proxies to appear and vote all of the shares of stock of Sav-On-Drugs, Inc. standing in the name of the undersigned at the Annual Meeting of Shareholders to be held at the Airport Marina Hotel (the Kent Room), 8601 Lincoln Boulevard, Los Angeles, California 90045, on April 24, 1974, at 3:00 o'clock P.M. or any adjournment thereof, as follows:

(1) FOR the election of directors as set forth in the Proxy Statement dated March 23, 1974 (unless this item is crossed out).

(2) FOR ☐ AGAINST ☐ ratification of the selection of Touche Ross & Co. to audit the financial statements of the Company.

(3) With discretionary power upon such other matters as may properly come before the meeting or any adjournment thereof.

(Continued and to be signed on other side)

THIS PROXY IS SOLICITED BY, AND ON BEHALF OF, MANAGEMENT AND MAY BE REVOKED PRIOR TO ITS EXERCISE. This proxy will be voted as directed but if no direction is indicated, it will be voted for the nominees for directors listed in the Proxy Statement and for ratification of the selection of Touche Ross & Co. as auditors.

Date 1974

....

220-84453   67054   400

MR HAROLD D KOONTZ   C
4838 GLORIA AVE
ENCINO CA 91316

....
(Please sign EXACTLY as your name appears hereon)

When signing as attorney, executor, administrator, trustee or guardian please give full title. If more than one trustee, all should sign. All joint owners must sign.

**PLEASE SIGN, DATE AND RETURN YOUR PROXY
PROMPTLY IN THE POST-PAID ENVELOPE PROVIDED**

company funds to solicit such proxies, thus maintaining control over the voting. This is easy in the case of a large company like American Telephone and Telegraph with its 3,000,000 shareholders, very few of whom ever attend an annual meeting in person.

But the same holds for many smaller companies. In one small and poorly run company, the top managers were able to maintain themselves in control by spending company money in actively soliciting proxies all over the country from some 1,200 small shareholders, despite the fact that their opponents owned more than one third of the stock while the management group owned less than one percent of it.

ADVANTAGES OF THE CORPORATE FORM

The widespread use of the corporate form for both large and small businesses suggests that it has certain advantages over other forms of ownership. These advantages arise mainly from its wider appeal to investors.

Limited Liability

Stockholders have no liability for the debts of the corporation. The corporation, as a legal person, is really the proprietor or owner of the business. As such it is the corporation that is legally responsible for its debts, while those who own the corporation, the stockholders, are not. Obviously, it is easier to raise capital if investors know that their risk of loss is limited to the amount they have put in, and that creditors cannot lay claim to their property.

Delegation of Management

The owners of the corporation, the stockholders, may delegate their power of management to the board of directors and, through the board, to a group of hired managers. It is the board and the managers who can bind the corporation to contracts and other relationships, not the stockholders. This, along with limited liability, makes it less needful for corporation owners to be concerned with who their fellow owners are than if they were members of a partnership.

Through delegation of management, it is possible to place the corporation's affairs in the hands of competent specialists. This is especially important for larger corporations, where size allows the selection of outstanding managerial talent and the payment of high compensation. The directors have the power to replace those who do not perform well. Smaller corporations may not have this advantage since the managers are usually large stockholders. Even in large corporations, managerial groups may be able to perpetuate themselves regardless of their competence because of their control over shareholder lists and proxy voting.

Ability to Attract Competent Talent

The very separation of ownership and management in the corporation, through allowing non-owners to hold positions of status and power, tends to permit the attraction of competent talent. Moreover, through allowing key managers to obtain shares of stock, often on advantageous terms, a part in ownership can be enjoyed by many managers.

Transferability of Ownership

Another advantage of the corporation form is the easy transferability of ownership. A stockholder may sell his shares to whomever he pleases, at any price he can obtain, and whenever he wishes. Sale of stock in unknown corporations may not be easy. But the stocks of almost all important corporations are readily saleable in the stock markets; all a person need do is notify his broker. Investors who would not want to tie up their capital in a business from which they might not be able to take it out will readily invest in corporate stocks.

In fact it is primarily through his freedom to buy and sell stock that an investor "votes." If he likes the company and the way it is going, he buys. If he does not, he sells.

Long Life and Stability

Ordinarily a corporation is chartered for perpetual life, until its dissolution. The death, retirement, or withdrawal of any stockholder need not affect the life of the corporation. Its policies may change after the withdrawal of a controlling stockholder, but the corporation goes on. As one airline worker remarked after a controlling stockholder died, "Even on the day of Mr. Quigley's funeral, the planes still ran on time."

Larger Size

The corporation form permits larger businesses than are possible under a proprietorship or partnership. By combining the ownership shares of thousands or hundreds of thousands of stockholders, the giant enterprises of today are made possible.

The use of the corporate form is virtually a "must" for a large or growing business, unless it can finance itself from profits and grow as opportunities present themselves—something few businesses can do, especially in this era of high income taxes. Individual proprietors or even partnerships seldom have the resources for large size and growth. Even the stock exchanges, which for many years did not permit their brokerage firm members to be incorporated, finally permitted incorporation as the needs for capital grew with the rise in stock sales in recent years.

DISADVANTAGES OF THE CORPORATE FORM

For all its great advantages, the corporate device does have certain drawbacks. That is why there are still so many proprietorships and partnerships, particularly in smaller business operations.

Taxation

A corporation has to pay income taxes on its profits. Its stockholders must also pay income taxes on the dividends they receive. The disadvantages of this double taxation are shown in Table 5–1. As the table also shows, under present tax laws a small corporation with no more than 10 stockholders can elect to report income and be taxed as though it were a partnership. But most corporations and their stockholders suffer the disadvantage of having to pay taxes twice. (Federal tax laws allow a small deduction for dividends received, but this is hardly important.)

Inadequate Control by Owners

As mentioned above, individual stockholders are not likely to have any control over the corporation. In large corporations they have no real choice but to vote for the slate of directors proposed by the corporation's management group. This is also likely to be the case in smaller businesses where an individual stockholder does not have a majority of

TABLE 5–1

Double Taxation in Corporations for a Typical Year

Financial Statement	Corporations with More Than Ten Stockholders		Corporations** with Ten or Fewer Stockholders*	Partnership or Proprietorship*
	Assuming All Earnings Paid Out as Dividends	*Assuming No Earnings Paid Out as Dividends*		
Business sales..................	$5,000,000	$5,000,000	$5,000,000	$5,000,000
Business expenses.............	4,000,000	4,000,000	4,000,000	4,000,000
Profits before income taxes......	$1,000,000	$1,000,000	$1,000,000	$1,000,000
Income taxes on business (approximately)...............	500,000	500,000		
Business profits after taxes......	$ 500,000	$ 500,000	$1,000,000	$1,000,000
Taxes paid by stockholders, partners, or proprietor†........	200,000	††	400,000	400,000
Net income to stockholders, partners, or proprietor.........	$ 300,000	††	$ 600,000*	$ 600,000*

* Whether profits are kept in the business or paid out to owners in cash.
** Electing to be taxed as a partnership.
† Assuming that owners are paying personal income taxes at a 40 percent rate. Note that in the case of corporation stockholders, the personal income tax may be slightly less since each stockholder is allowed to deduct a small amount of his *total* dividends from all sources for personal income tax purposes.
†† If earnings are kept in the corporation and no dividends are paid out, the stockholders have realized no cash income and no personal income taxes are owed by them.

the shares outstanding. The only real vote the shareholder usually has is the one he exercises by selling or buying stock.

Expense and Difficulty of Organization

Although the expense and difficulty of organizing a corporation are small (the costs ranging from a few hundred to a few thousand dollars), it is not as easy as setting up a proprietorship or partnership. For a very small business, going through the legal formalities and paying the costs of incorporation may be an important consideration.

Danger of Lack of Personal Interest

Because management and ownership are separated in all but the smallest corporations, management may not have a direct interest in the profitable growth of the company. Officers and managers are, of course, employees of the corporation. They draw their salaries from the corporation, and as long as they remain on the payroll they receive their salaries regardless of the performance of the company.

Most well-managed companies encourage key officers and managers to own stock in the company so that they will have a positive incentive to feel and act like owners. But this is not always true. One small shareholder in a fairly large corporation (with sales of more than $100 million) was shocked and dismayed to find that no director or officer of the company owned as many shares as he did, despite the fact that the president drew a salary in excess of $150,000 per year. (On noting this, he sold his stock in the company).

Lack of Secrecy and Greater Government Supervision

Since a corporation is set up by law, it is subject to certain governmental requirements that do not apply to proprietors and partners. For one thing, reports must be made to stockholders, when there are many stockholders there can be little secrecy with respect to assets, profits, costs, and sales. And a corporation chartered in one state may be restricted in doing business in another state unless reports are filed and taxes paid in that state.

Governmental control is felt most in the issuance of stock. State and federal laws call for very thorough supervision of stock issues, except for very small offerings to a few stockholders. The company may have to disclose detailed information about its assets and operations.

Credit and the Small Company

Those who lend money to corporations have to think about getting it back. If a corporation should go bankrupt, its creditors could look only to its assets for satisfaction of their claims. In a partnership, as we have seen, creditors can also look to the personal assets of the general partners. Consequently, in the case of a small corporation, banks or other creditors may seek more security on their loans by requiring the major shareholders to sign notes in their capacity as individuals.

COOPERATIVES

A form of business ownership that has become increasingly important in the last half century is the *cooperative association,* or co-op, as it is usually called. While many cooperatives are incorporated, and hence differ little from corporations or partnerships, almost all states now make special legal provision for them.

Certain principles are common to cooperatives that are not usual in other forms of business:

1. Each cooperative is owned by its user-members.
2. The capital of the cooperative is subscribed by the members and there is usually a limit to the amount any member may subscribe.
3. Members are paid interest on their investment.
4. Each member has only one vote regardless of the size of his investment or the number of shares he owns.
5. Members share in profits—after payment of interest on their investment—in accordance with their patronage, that is, the amount of business each does with the cooperative.

Cooperatives are of various types. There are producers' cooperatives, marketing cooperatives, and consumer cooperatives. Most of the well-known cooperatives in agriculture are really marketing cooperatives, associations engaged in the marketing of agricultural products grown by their many members, such as "Sunkist" oranges and "Sun Maid Raisins." They are common among producers of citrus fruits, dairy products, grains, livestock, eggs, and certain vegetables.

Consumer or buying cooperatives are not as numerous or as large. They engage in the buying of seeds, groceries, gasoline, and farm machinery. Notable exceptions to the small size of these cooperatives are the rural electricity distributing enterprises set up under the encouragement of the Rural Electrification Administration. As a matter of fact, there are over 1,000 such cooperatives in the United States providing electricity to more than 6 million members.

Another prominent type of cooperative is the credit union. These are common among the employees of businesses, government agencies, and universities. They are really savings and loan cooperatives whose members purchase shares entitling them to participate in the earnings from loans made to members. A member can purchase as many shares as he wants, just as a depositor in a savings bank can make as many deposits of funds as he wishes. But only a member of the credit union can borrow from it.

MUTUAL COMPANIES

Mutual companies are similar to cooperatives in that their owners are users of the service they provide. Many large life insurance companies are mutual companies, as are all federally chartered savings and loan associations, many state-chartered savings and loan associations, and many state savings and loan banks. The savings and loan associations are primarily devoted to lending money to home owners, while the savings and loan banks make a variety of investments and may lend money for purposes other than home ownership, although home mortgages are by far their most important investments.

In 1973, two thirds of the $252 billion of assets held by all life insurance companies were in mutual companies, as were most of the $232 billion of assets of savings and loan associations. Mutual savings banks had $100 billion of assets. As can be seen, mutual companies dominate the field of personal savings institutions.

Mutual companies are much like other kinds of corporations, but they do not issue stock. The members own the company and can vote for the directors, but do not receive dividends in the same way that other business stockholders do. The "dividends" of mutual life insurance companies, based on their earnings from investments, are not regarded as taxable income to policyholders but rather as a return of excess premiums charged. As one observer of these companies noted: "This is the only business that charges its customers more than the services cost, returns to them what the management cannot spend, and makes them happy to receive a dividend."

In savings banks and in savings and loan associations, on the other hand, members receive interest on their deposits, which may vary from year to year depending on earnings. This interest is regarded as taxable income to the saver, just as if he had bought an industrial bond or lent money to an individual. Since the amount savings institutions can pay their members is limited by law, the highly successful companies may accumulate large surpluses of earnings. If such companies were not mutuals, they could pay these surplus earnings to their stockholders.

SUMMARY

Most of the business in this country is carried on by corporations. A corporation is an artificial being, or "person," endowed by law with most of the rights, powers, and obligations of natural persons. It may own property, incur debts, and be sued for damages. The attractiveness of the corporation form of ownership lies in the fact that the corporation is liable for its debts, and not the stockholders.

A corporation can be easily and inexpensively formed. Usually all that is required is that three or more persons file certain papers with a government agency and pay certain fees. All 50 states have laws for setting up corporations. While there is no federal law permitting incorporation of all kinds of businesses, some corporations are chartered by the national government, including all national banks, federal credit unions, federal savings and loan associations, and most national government-owned corporations.

Corporations obtain funds from investors and lenders by issuing common and preferred stocks, bonds, and notes. Common and preferred stocks represent ownership in a corporation, while bonds and notes are ways of borrowing money. A corporation may also borrow property, by leasing it.

Stockholders are the owners of a corporation. They elect a board of directors to represent them. The board of directors, in turn, is responsible for managing the corporation and for selecting its officers. Even though stockholders have legal control of the corporation in this manner, in most companies their real power is not very great. Directors and officers, many of whom are directors themselves, have ready access to the list of stockholders and can use company funds to solicit the votes of stockholders by means of proxies. In the larger companies stockholders are very numerous, own only a few shares each, and can seldom attend meetings to vote on directors. They have little choice but to vote for the management slate of directors.

There are many advantages to the corporate form. These include the limited liability of stockholders, easy delegation of management by owners, the ability of the corporation to attract competent talent since managers need not be owners, the ease of transferring stock ownership, and the long life and stability of the organization. The corporation form of ownership permits business firms to be much larger than is possible with a proprietorship or a partnership.

There are disadvantages, however, in the use of the corporate form. A major drawback is the double taxation of earnings, first as profits and then as dividends. Other disadvantages include inadequate control by owners, the expense and difficulty of organizing a corporation (for small businesses), the danger that corporation managers may not have enough personal interest in the prosperity of the corporation, the greater government supervision, and the lack of secrecy.

Important variations of the corporate form are cooperatives and mutual companies. They differ from the usual business corporation in that their owners are the members and users. Thus in a marketing cooperative such as "Sunkist" oranges, orchardmen who market their fruit through the cooperative are the owners. In a mutual life insurance company, the policy holders are the owners. This arrangement makes a material difference in the operation of these companies, primarily in the voting power of owners and the way earnings are distributed.

KEY TERMS AND CONCEPTS FOR REVIEW

Corporation
Nonprofit corporation
Incorporation laws
Corporation charter
Common stock
Preferred stock
Dividends
Par value
No par value
Participating preferred stock
Cumulative or noncumulative preferred stock
Bonds
Bondholder trustee

Interest
Mortgage bond
Collateral trust bond
Debenture bond
Sinking fund bond
Convertible bond
Board of directors
Cumulative voting
Proxy
Limited liability
Double taxation
Cooperative associations
Mutual companies

QUESTIONS FOR ANALYSIS AND DISCUSSION

1. Explain what a corporation is and how this makes logical the limited liability of stockholders.

2. "Not all corporations are business corporations." Explain.

3. Neither common nor preferred stockholders own the buildings, machinery, materials, or other assets of a corporation. Explain why this is so, and what it is that stockholders own.

4. Why may stock with a par value of $1.00 per share sometimes be more valuable than stock with a par value of $10.00 per share? Would a no-par-value stock be worth more or less than a par-value stock?

5. A preferred stock has certain features differentiating it from common stock. What are the usual features? Does the fact that a stock is preferred mean that it must be paid dividends?

6. Why would a business issue a preferred stock?

7. Why would a lender want to invest in bonds that do not fall due for a long period of time, such as 99 years?

8. Is a mortgage or collateral trust bond safer than a debenture bond? Why, or why not?

9. What is the attraction to investors of convertible bonds, and why would a company want to sell them?

10. Voting by stockholders of a corporation is different from voting for candidates in a government election. How is this so? Why should it be?

11. Especially in large corporations, it is possible for certain persons to control a corporation even though they may own very few shares of stock. How is this accomplished?

12. Considering the advantages and disadvantages of the corporate form, when would you expect a business to use the corporation? Under what conditions would you expect a business might not want to be a corporation?

13. How does a cooperative differ from a business corporation? A partnership? Why are cooperative associations so often used in certain areas?

14. Can you suggest reasons why so many life insurance companies and savings and loan associations have been organized as mutual companies?

SUGGESTED READINGS

Krainin, H. L. *What You Should Know About Operating Your Business as a Corporation.* Dobbs Ferry, New York: Oceana Publications, 1967.

Lusk, H. F. et al. *Business Law: Principles and Cases* (3d U.C.C. ed.). Homewood, Ill.: Richard D. Irwin, Inc., 1974, Part VI.

Van Horne, J. C. *Fundamentals of Financial Management* (2d ed.) Englewood Cliffs, N.J.: Prentice-Hall, Inc., 1974, Chapters 2, 20–22.

Williamson, J. P., and R. W. Austin *Law in Business Administration.* Boston: Allyn and Bacon, Inc., 1962, Chapter 4.

6

Knowing
the Score
in Business

In every game we keep score so that we will know how well we are doing and who wins the game. It could hardly be imagined how baffling it would be to play a game and have no way to keep score. Even though the penalty for losing is greater, it is the same way in business. Because our principal measurements of how we are doing are profits and the soundness of our financial condition, this is the way score is kept in business.

Profits may seem to be a cold and mercenary way of judging human activity. But business, after all, is the economic instrument of society, and profits are merely the way we ascertain whether we are getting more for what we produce—sales—than we are paying to produce it—expenses. The only way yet found to measure the results of the many activities carried on by a business is to convert them to sums of money.

In nonbusiness enterprises we can't always do this. We can calculate our costs in monetary terms but not our output, since it is not sold for dollars. For example, except for fines collected, the output of a police department is measured by such things as the number of arrests, the reduction in crime rates, or the miles of street patrolled. The military keep score by counting the number of trained men available, missions flown, enemy planes knocked down, or enemy installations destroyed.

In business, monetary measurements prevail. But money is not all there is to business, anymore than touchdowns and field goals are all there is to football. Financial transactions and statements are really the windows through which we see what is happening in a business.

What kinds of things do we particularly want to know about a business? They include the following major questions:

What are we selling and what does it cost us to produce what we sell?

What profit (or loss) are we making? Have we a surplus of sales dollars over expense dollars?

What cash are we taking in and what cash are we spending?

What things of value—assets—are we using in the business?

How much do people owe us, and how much do we owe other people?

How much of the business assets are owned by the owners of the business?

How does our ownership interest change as our business enters into various transactions?

What is happening inside the business with respect to costs and revenues?

What do people who lend us money or invest in our company look for in measuring our success and financial soundness?

In summary, every businessman wants to know how well his business is doing, how financially sound it is, and why. To the extent that the knowledge of these things can be reduced to monetary terms, this is the task of accounting. The accountant records, summarizes, and interprets financial transactions. Those who want to understand business must know how score is kept and comprehend at least the basics of the science and art of accounting.

THE BASIC THEORY OF ACCOUNTING

Accounting can become extremely complex, so that almost every business hires specialists to do it. But the basic nature of accounting is not hard to grasp. It rests on the fact that every business uses property, that property is subject to certain rights, that business operations produce changes in property and property rights, and that such changes can be expressed in terms of dollars and cents.

Property Is Necessary to Operate a Business

Everyone in business uses property to conduct his operations. The manufacturer uses buildings, machinery, office equipment, raw materials, and purchased parts. The storeowner uses buildings, shelves, cash registers, and a stock of merchandise. Even a law firm must have offices, desks, chairs, typewriters, books, and supplies. And every business must have cash with which to pay its bills.

These are called the *assets* of a business. Whether a business is small or large, whether it is a proprietorship, a partnership, or a corporation, it must have property to operate. Sometimes it must have a very large amount, as in the case of the American Telephone and Telegraph Company with its more than $70 billion of assets, and Exxon with its $25 billion of assets. Some businesses need very little, like the Miller Electrical Repair Shop with its thousand dollars of assets.

All Property Is Subject to Property Rights

All property is subject to some right or claim against it. Some of the rights are those of owners as in the case of an individual or a partnership owning a business outright. This ownership is referred to on the accounts of the firm as *proprietorship* or *capital* or *net worth*. Some of the claims against property are those of creditors who have lent funds to a business. The claims of all kinds of creditors are called *liabilities* in accounting terms.

Those to whom a business owes money, or who have some claim against the assets, are not limited to people from whom it has borrowed money in the usual sense. They include employees, who are paid weekly, semimonthly, or monthly. When a worker is paid on a Friday evening his check may only cover his work through the preceding Wednesday, so that the company may have time to make out paychecks. Consequently, there will almost always be a period of time for which a company owes its employees money. These amounts are part of its liabilities.

In the same way, a business may owe taxes that do not have to be paid until April of the following year. This also represents a liability— a claim by a creditor—even though the company has not borrowed money in the usual sense. Many other liabilities arise in the course of doing business.

The relationship of property and rights against it is somewhat complicated by the existence of the corporation. As will be recalled, the corporation is an artificial person. It owns the assets of the business. Rights or claims against these assets are against the corporation. Stockholders own the corporation through their ownership of stock, but they do not owe the corporation's creditors. The value of their ownership in a corporation is called *stockholders' equity,* an amount which includes their original investment plus accumulated profits that have not been paid out in dividends.

Accounting Is Built around Property and Rights

All modern accounting is built around the recording of property and the rights or claims against it. Accounting can be reduced to the simple formula.

$$\text{Assets} = \text{Liabilities} + \text{Proprietorship (or Equity or Capital)}$$

This means that all assets held by a business are subject to two types of claims: those arising from the rights of creditors and those arising from the rights of owners (or proprietors or stockholders). The amount of ownership can at all times be determined by ascertaining the total of assets and subtracting from it the claims of creditors. In this case, the simple equation becomes

$$\text{Assets} - \text{Liabilities} = \text{Proprietorship (or Equity or Capital)}$$

Every transaction made by a business involves some change in one or more of the elements of this formula. If a businessman buys a new machine, his assets in terms of machinery are increased; if he pays cash for it, his cash assets are reduced. On the other hand, if he buys the machine on credit, both his assets and his liabilities will increase.

If a businessman borrows from a bank, his cash assets increase and his liabilities also increase by the amount of the loan. When he hires labor, his assets increase by the amount the labor produces, and his liabilities rise by the amount of wages he owes his workers. If the work performed can be sold for more than it costs, a profit results and proprietorship is increased.

If a business sells goods to a buyer today to be paid for 30 days later, assets in the form of finished goods on hand are decreased. The amount owed by the buyer, called an *account receivable*, represents an asset increase to the business. If the businessman sells the goods to a buyer at a price higher than they cost him, the difference is profit. The account receivable from this sale, being higher than the cost of the goods sold, causes an increase in proprietorship or equity. Likewise, if a business buys raw materials to use in production and will pay for them 30 days later, the result is to increase an asset—the stock of materials, called *inventory*—and also to increase the firm's liabilities, expressed in *accounts payable*.

As Figure 6–1 shows, we can go through every transaction of a

FIGURE 6–1

Some Ways Assets, Liabilities, and Equity Change in a Business

A. Borrowing from a bank

	Before Borrowing	*After Borrowing $2,000*
	ASSETS	
Cash	$ 500	$ 2,500
Owed by customers	1,000	1,000
Inventory	2,000	2,000
Machinery	4,000	4,000
Building	15,000	15,000
Total	$22,500	$24,500
	LIABILITIES AND EQUITY	
Liabilities:		
Owed to bank	—	$2,000
Owed to suppliers ......$	4,000	4,000
Owed to workers	500	500
Equity	18,000	18,000
Total	$22,500	$24,500

B. After using bank loan to pay some suppliers

	Before Paying	*After Paying $2,000*
	ASSETS	
Cash	$ 2,500	$ 500
Owed by customers	1,000	1,000
Inventory	2,000	2,000
Machinery	4,000	4,000
Building	15,000	15,000
Total	$24,500	$22,500
	LIABILITIES AND EQUITY	
Liabilities:		
Owed to bank ....$	2,000	$ 2,000
Owed to suppliers	4,000	2,000
Owed to workers	500	500
Equity	18,000	18,000
Total	$24,500	$22,500

C. Business sells goods which it carries in inventory at a cost of $1,500 to customers at a price of $2,000, thus making a profit of $500 over cost

	Before Selling	*After Selling*
	ASSETS	
Cash	$ 500	$ 500
Owed by customers	1,000	3,000
Inventory	2,000	500
Machinery	4,000	4,000
Building	15,000	15,000
Total	$22,500	$23,000
	LIABILITIES AND EQUITY	
Liabilities:		
Owed to bank ....$	2,000	$ 2,000
Owed to suppliers	2,000	2,000
Owed to workers	500	500
Equity	18,000	18,500
Total	$22,500	$23,000

company and see that it does one or more of the following things: (1) increases assets; (2) reduces assets; (3) changes the kind of assets (as happens when we buy an asset for cash); (4) increases liabilities; (5) reduces liabilities; (6) changes the kind of liabilities (as happens when we borrow money from a bank and use it to pay off suppliers for amounts owed them); (7) increases proprietorship; or (8) reduces proprietorship.

In accounting language, anything that increases assets or reduces liabilities or proprietorship is called a *debit*. Any transaction that decreases assets or increases liabilities or proprietorship is called a *credit*.

The Essence of Accounting Procedure Is Balance

As can be seen, every property carries a right, or has a claim against it. The total cost value of the property owned by a business must, of course, be equal to all financial claims against the business by creditors and owners. This is what is meant by *double entry* bookkeeping.

It is possible for a business to have more claims against its property than it has property. This unfortunate state of affairs usually happens as the result of operating losses, when a company sells its goods and services for less than they cost. As long as the losses do not exceed the company's proprietorship, or net worth, the result is only to reduce the claims of the owners. But sometimes the losses are greater than a company's net worth, so that creditors' claims, or liabilities, exceed the value of property or assets. This means that the company is technically *insolvent*, that is, the assets will not cover the claims against them. Occasionally it can sell these assets for more than their cost entered on the books, and get enough cash to satisfy the creditors' claims. Until it does, however, accountants label the difference as a *deficit* and show it as a negative asset or a negative net worth.

Accounting Is Based on Costs and Sales

Almost invariably, assets are entered in the books at cost. A company may have bought a building for $500,000 which now, because of rising real estate values, is worth twice as much. But it is carried on the books at cost, less a reduction each year for *depreciation*—the term accountants use to indicate loss of value due to the wearing out of an asset or its becoming out-of-date. One company on the West Coast near the Los Angeles Airport bought ten acres of land some years ago for $60,000. Today the market value of this land is more than $600,000. But it is carried on the company's books at cost.

Sales are likewise entered at what a product actually brings. The list price may be $10 per unit, but if 1,000 units are sold at $6 each the amount entered on the books will be $6,000.

ACCOUNTING IS NOT PERFECTLY ACCURATE

Although accounting has the appearance of being perfectly logical and numbers give it a look of being accurate to the last penny, it is not an accurate science. Of course, assets must balance with a total of liabilities and proprietorship. But there are often places where there is no alternative but to use judgment in arriving at figures that go into the books and financial statements.

The Question of Costs and Assets

In many cases costs do not reflect values. Sometimes the assets are worth more than they originally cost, and sometimes they are worth less. A piece of machinery may have cost $30,000, but if the company can no longer use it and no one wants to buy it, it is only worth what it will bring as scrap. Some valuable assets are not even carried on the books. For example, Bristol-Myers, makers of many drugs and cosmetic products from Bufferin to Vitalis, spent over $260 million in a period of ten years on product development; yet none of this clearly valuable asset is carried on its balance sheet.

Depreciation

Over the years, businesses write off what they have invested in machinery and equipment, in the form of *depreciation* charges (an expense). Often, this reduction in asset costs carried on the books is much greater than the real loss of value from wear or obsolescence; sometimes it is less. Depreciation can almost never be exact because it is, at best, an estimate.

Inventory

Businesses customarily accumulate raw materials, parts, and finished goods as *inventory*. It is not unusual for much more inventory to be acquired than can be sold, or for some of it to become worthless because a new product appears on the market or customers prefer other things. The inventory may be carried on the books at cost, but is it really worth what the books say? In a time of rising prices, the inventory may be worth more. If some inventory items turn out to be valueless, the inventory may be greatly overstated. In one small company that had an inventory of more than $4 million dollars, it was discovered that nearly half was worthless. The resulting adjustment to the books, or writedown, made the company show a large loss and was followed by a sharp drop in the value of the company's stock.

Accounts may not be strictly accurate in other respects. Estimates must often be made, as when today's market value is different from yesterday's costs, or in cases in which we cannot know how to allocate costs among different products (how much of the president's salary should be allocated to a ton of steel in the U.S. Steel Company?).

Even though accounting is not an exact science, it is still the best way we have of keeping score in a business. It usually gives the general picture of how a company is faring financially. But the wise businessman or investor will realize that there are areas of potential inaccuracy. These inaccuracies are not ordinarily matters of deception, but of judgment. There can be no exact answers to such questions as: What are our accounts receivable really worth—how many customers will actually pay what they owe and how many will not? What is an accurate measure of depreciation? How much have our assets appreciated above costs? To what extent is our inventory saleable and useful? What is the value of the research and development that have gone into our products and have not been entered in our books as assets? Have our costs been accurately computed?

While we recognize that accounting is not an exact science, that we use judgment in determining many items, and costs entered on a balance sheet may not correctly represent present values (as in the case of the company's land values discussed above), we should not get the idea that accounting is useless guesswork. Accountants have had to make a trade-off between stating things in terms of cost or trying to use present market values. Accountants have so far chosen to use costs since they do usually represent historically valid figures, while market values are subject to a wide variety of interpretations of people, at least until an item is actually sold on the market.

Moreover, what is important about accounting data is that it gives us an ability to compare results over time, to see changes from year to year. So long as accounts are kept consistently, the kind and size of *changes* in assets, liabilities, and equity are the really important considerations for businessmen, creditors, and investors.

THE BALANCE SHEET: SNAPSHOT PICTURE
OF FINANCIAL POSITION

The balance sheet is the most basic of all accounting statements. It is the statement that summarizes the assets, on the one hand, and the claims against them on the other. Balance sheets may be simple, as in most small companies, or they may be complex. They may be presented in considerable detail or only in summary form.

A balance sheet is a kind of snapshot picture of a company. It tells, as well as accountants can, what the status of the property and property rights of a company was at the close of business on a certain date. The actual balance sheet may be different a day or two later or different several days before. Every business transaction changes the amount of assets and the claims against them. No company could issue a new balance sheet every time a change was made in its assets, liabilities, or net worth. Instead it prepares a balance sheet (takes a snapshot picture) on a periodic basis—perhaps monthly, or more usually quarterly or annually.

Current and Long-Term Assets and Liabilities

Every balance sheet distinguishes between current assets and fixed, or long-term, assets; it makes the same distinction between current and long-term liabilities. An *asset* is classified as current if it is to be turned into cash within a year. This is naturally true of cash, but it is likewise true of customers' accounts receivable, and inventories.

A *liability is* classified as current if it is expected the company will be required to pay it within a year. Some bank loans, usually those made for a short period of 90 days, are classified as current; other bank loans due over a period of years are regarded as long-term. However, that portion of a long-term loan which is due in the coming year will be classified as current.

This distinction between current and long-term is made in balance sheets to indicate to readers the extent to which a company has assets that it can expect to convert into cash in a short time, and liabilities that will have to be paid in a short time. As we shall see, bankers and financial analysts make a considerable point of this distinction.

Balance Sheet: Small Company

Some balance sheets are very simple. One for a small dry cleaning business looked as shown in Figure 6–2 as of June 30, 1974. This bal-

A Practical Introduction to Business

FIGURE 6–2

Balance Sheet of a Small Company

FRANK'S DRY CLEANERS
Balance Sheet, June 30, 1974

ASSETS (what we have)		LIABILITIES (what we owe)	
Current Assets		Current Liabilities:	
Cash	$ 567.46	Loan from bank	$ 1,200.00
Accounts due from customers	862.80	Due to suppliers	126.75
Supplies on hand	585.55	Due to employees	137.50
Total Current Assets	$2,015.81	Total Current Liabilities	$ 1,464.25
Property, Plant, and Equipment:		Long-Term Liabilities:	
Land	$ 6,000.00	Mortgage on land and	
Building	22,800.00	building	$16,250.00
Equipment	5,780.86	Total Liabilities	$17,714.25
Total	$34,580.86		
Less: Accumulated		PROPRIETORSHIP	
depreciation	3,859.00	Original investment	$10,000.00
Total	$30,721.86	Accumulated profits	5,023.42
		Total	$15,023.42
		Total Liabilities and	
Total	$32,737.67	Proprietorship	$32,737.67

ance sheet shows several significant things. The company has made modest profits since it started. The owner put in $10,000 to start the business. If we can assume, as is probable, that the building is being depreciated over 30 years and the equipment over 10 years (land, of course, does not depreciate), the business has probably been going for around three years. It shows that the business does not have much cash and that, for a dry cleaning business where most customers would be expected to pay in cash, accounts receivable appear to be rather high. We would, however, need more information to be sure of this since the company may be extending more credit to its customers than is usual with dry cleaning establishments.

Balance Sheet: Large Company

Large companies have much more complex balance sheets. That of the Union Carbide Corporation may be used as an example. This is a *consolidated balance sheet* since it represents the accounts both of the Union Carbide Corporation and of other companies in which it has a substantial interest. In 1972, this corporation had $3,261 million of sales in chemicals, plastics, gases, metals and carbons, machinery for handling materials, and various consumer items such as Eveready batteries.

A somewhat simplified balance sheet of this company for the years 1972 and 1971 may be found in Figure 6–3. Some of the items on this balance sheet may need some special explanation.

The item *Time deposits and short-term marketable securities* represents money carried on deposit and earning interest in banks for a period of time, say six months, plus investments the company has made in government bonds, stocks, or other securities that can readily be sold. The combination of these items plus the amount shown as cash represents assets that are the equivalent of cash.

As can be seen, the company's cash items grew from $114.7 million in 1971 to $261.6 million in 1972. This may seem like a very large amount of cash. However, the company's large sales volume and the necessity of carrying huge amounts of accounts receivable and inventories—which could easily rise considerably if sales increase—may require this much cash. The reader will note that the company has accrued income and other taxes of $142.4 million, plus payments due on its long-term debt of $57.1 million, both of which would probably require cash in the months after the end of the year.

The item *Prepaid expenses* includes such things as rent and insurance premiums paid in advance, and office supplies that have been paid for but will be used over a period in the future.

Construction in progress, as the term indicates, includes buildings, machinery, mines, and similar items for which funds have been spent but which are not yet ready for use.

Investments and advances is a customary item found on larger company balance sheets. It indicates that the company has purchased stock in various companies and has made advances (loans) of funds to some of these companies.

Accrued income and other taxes amounts to a considerable portion of the current liabilities. These represent mostly taxes owed on income, both to the United States and its state governments and to foreign countries. As indicated in the discussion of cash above, there is a strong likelihood that these taxes will have to be paid early in the following year.

Minority stockholders equity in consolidated subsidiaries arises from the fact that Union Carbide has consolidated in this balance sheet the assets, liabilities, and profits of some companies in which it owns considerable blocks of stock. But Union Carbide does not own all the equity in these companies, so that it has to deduct an amount equal to the stock it does not own.

FIGURE 6–3

Balance Sheet of a Large Company

UNION CARBIDE CORPORATION AND SUBSIDIARIES
Consolidated Balance Sheet as of December 31, 1972 and 1971
(millions of dollars)

	1972	1971
ASSETS		
Current Assets		
Cash	$ 99.7	$ 71.8
Time deposits and marketable securities	161.9	42.9
Total Cash Items	261.6	114.7
Notes and accounts receivable	576.9	513.2
Inventories	743.2	756.1
Prepaid expenses	46.5	45.8
Total Current Assets	1,628.2	1,429.8
Fixed Assets		
Land and improvements	268.4	245.9
Buildings	608.2	606.9
Machinery and equipment	3,683.6	3,403.7
Construction in progress and other	169.4	473.8
	4,729.6	4,730.3
Less: Accumulated depreciation	2,775.7	2,743.3
Total Fixed Assets	1,953.9	1,987.0
Investments and Advances		
Ownership in subsidiary companies	76.0	65.8
Other	8.2	6.2
Total Investments and Advances	84.2	72.0
Other Assets	52.0	65.9
Total Assets	$3,718.3	$3,554.7
LIABILITIES AND STOCKHOLDERS' EQUITY		
Current Liabilities		
Accounts payable	$ 158.6	$ 137.7
Short-term borrowings	68.8	105.8
Payments due within one year on long-term debt	57.1	32.3
Accrued income and other taxes	142.4	118.9
Other accrued liabilities	203.9	164.4
Total Current Liabilities	630.8	559.1
Deferred liabilities (income taxes that have been deferred to later years by special tax provisions)	117.5	108.2
Long-term debt	901.1	915.9
Minority stockholders' equity in consolidated subsidiaries	135.3	127.2
Union Carbide Stockholders' Equity—Common Stock		
Original investment of stockholders	322.9	317.8
Retained earnings	1,610.7	1,526.5
Total Common Stock Equity	1,933.6	1,844.3
Total Liabilities and Stockholders' Equity	$3,718.3	$3,554.7

INTERPRETING A BALANCE SHEET

We shall use the Union Carbide Corporation balance sheet to show what can be learned from such a financial statement even without looking at the company's record of sales, expenses, and profits. Keeping in mind that a balance sheet is a snapshot of the relationship between property and claims against property at a given time, we can make the following observations.

1. *Cash.* We can see that "Cash" and "Cash items" in 1972 appear to be quite large, especially as compared to 1971. Yet, even though these have increased by $146.9 million, we can also see that "Accounts payable" (amounts the company owes to others on a short-term basis) have risen, as have "Payments due within one year on long-term debt," and "Accrued income and other taxes."

2. *Accounts and Notes Receivable.* The increase in "Notes and accounts receivable" may indicate that sales were up in 1972 over 1971, since higher sales usually require more receivables. It might, on the other hand, indicate that customers were slower in paying their bills in 1972.

3. *Construction in Progress.* The decrease in "Construction in progress" in 1972, from 1971, as well as the large increase in investment in "Machinery and equipment," indicates that the company was finishing its huge capital expansion program under way in 1971.

4. *Short-Term Borrowings.* These borrowings have declined in 1972 by $37 million. This is an indication that the company may have had excess cash during the year, suggesting higher profits. However, one should note also that "Accumulated depreciation" increased by $32.4 million in 1972. Although depreciation is an expense of doing business, it is not an expense which requires cash payments, and this undoubtedly helped the company's cash position.

The item "Short-term borrowings" is very low for a company of this size. As we shall see in the following chapter, banks ordinarily are quite willing to lend money on accounts receivable. Loans against these of 50 percent of their value are not unusual. This indicates that Union Carbide could probably have borrowed nearly $290 million from the banks if it wished, instead of the $68.8 million it apparently did. This makes one even more sure that the company has or can get considerable amounts of cash if necessary.

5. *Long-Term Debt.* "Long-term debt" is high, being over $900 million. While it is well secured by assets, and while current assets more than equal current liabilities plus long-term debt, such a large

Irving S. Shapiro

*Courtesy of E. I. du Pont
de Nemours & Co.*

Irving S. Shapiro's ascent to the chairmanship of Du Pont in December 1973, was like a dramatization of the American dream of success and social advancement through education and hard work. It also symbolized the well-established shift in American business from owner-managers to hired professionals. Shapiro was born in 1916 to Jewish immigrants from Lithuania who had settled in Minneapolis. His father was a pants presser by trade. In 1924, with a loan of $500, he opened his own dry cleaning shop. Despite hard work and long hours, the Shapiros went through times when there was barely enough to eat.

Although Shapiro was interested in an accounting career, his father persuaded him to study law. Through part time employment, a $200 loan, and an uncanny ability at poker, he was able to graduate from the University of Minneapolis Law School in 1941. After a poor start in school—he "flunked" kindergarten—Shapiro graduated fourth in his law school class.

Rejected by the armed services because of asthma, he went to work for the wartime Office of Price Administration. Able attorneys were needed to develop

debt means heavy interest charges. If earnings before interest payments should decline in a serious recession, this high interest cost might give the company some difficulty.

6. *Stockholders Equity.* These figures tell the analyst two interesting things. In the first place, the company has probably done most of its ownership financing, in recent years at least, from earnings retained in the business and not paid out to the stockholders in dividends. In the second place, the increase in "Retained earnings" of $84.2 million in 1972 shows that the company made a profit that year, since this is the amount retained *after* paying dividends. (In fact, the company paid dividends in 1972 of $121.3 million to nearly 200,000 stockholders.)

THE INCOME STATEMENT

As can be seen by our analysis of the balance sheet, this statement, as important as it is, does not give us an adequate score on a company's activities. It does not tell us precisely what happened during the year.

price control regulations. With an annual salary of $2,000, he felt economically secure enough to get married. When he confided to his fiancée that some day he wanted to make as much as $5,000 a year, she responded, "You're selling yourself short. You're worth at least $7,000 a year."

After a successful career at OPA, Shapiro got a job with the Criminal Division of the Justice Department where he became known as an articulate debater, a skillful writer of briefs, and a brilliant analyst of critical points of law. He argued his first case before the Supreme Court when he was 30.

After one case that was attended with a good deal of publicity, Shapiro was asked to join the legal department at Du Pont. The challenge, and the $12,000 annual salary, were irresistible. He was assigned to the antitrust section at Du Pont, where, because of the company's active program of antitrust litigation during the 50s, he became well known to top management. His professional achievements, and his ability to put complex and emotional issues into simple and practical terms, made him Assistant General Counsel in 1965. Within the company he was known as the "can do" attorney: while other lawyers emphasized what could not be done, Shapiro stressed the possible.

Another major impetus in Shapiro's meteoric rise at Du Pont was Brel McCoy, Chairman of the Board. McCoy was the first top executive at Du Pont who had not been associated with the family. He is credited with transforming Du Pont from a private fiefdom to a professionally managed institution. McCoy was impressed with Shapiro's ability and dedication, and in 1970 had him leapfrogged to Senior Vice President, director, and member of the all-powerful Executive Committee. In July, 1973, he became Vice Chairman.

At 57, Shapiro was elected head of the 23rd largest industrial enterprise in the world, with 113,000 employees and 224 plants in 27 countries. Du Pont's worldwide sales were more than $5 billion in 1973, and its assets more than $4 billion. Shapiro is the first person with a nontechnical background to head Du Pont, and is its first Jewish chief executive. With an annual salary of about $300,000, he has proved that his wife was right, he was worth more than $5,000 a year.

It does not tell us what the company's sales or expenses were, and only gives us a clue as to its profits. For this information we must look to the income statement, often called a profit and loss statement, or a statement of income.

What the Income Statement Is

The income statement summarizes sales for a period of time—a month, three months, or a year—and subtracts the expenses incurred in the same period, showing either a profit or loss. This is why it is often called a profit and loss statement.

The income statement is generally regarded as the most important score card of a business. Any business, if it is to exist for long, must show a profit. Decisions to stay in business or to expand or contract will usually be based on profits. Creditors, and banks especially, are interested in this statement because they know that a company's ability to repay loans will depend mainly on whether it makes profits.

They look at a business in exactly the same way that a savings and loan company looks at a person applying for a home mortgage. The house may be worth what he is paying, and the mortgage may be amply secured. But the loan company wants to be sure that the borrower will be able to keep up his payments so it will not have to take over the house to get its money back.

Major Parts of the Income Statement

The normal income statement develops by identifying, adding or subtracting the following items:

Sales. This is the total amount of goods or services a business sells in a given period. A "sale" is made when the product or service is delivered to the buyer, whether it is paid for in cash or through an account receivable (that is, "charged").

Net Sales. This item is actual sales less any returned merchandise, any discounts allowed for prompt payment, or any other allowance, such as a reduction in price for defective goods.

Cost of Goods Sold or Cost of Production. This is the record of what goods cost to produce, including (1) the cost of materials used; (2) the cost of labor directly utilized in the production of a good or service ("direct labor"), and (3) the overhead or "burden" costs involved in production, such as supervision, electricity, production machine maintenance, and direct labor "fringes" such as vacation and sick pay, medical insurance, and Social Security.

Gross Profit. This is net sales minus cost of goods sold.

Operating Expenses. These include various expenses not directly related to the cost of actually producing a good or service, such as rent, most utilities, engineering, sales expenses, insurance, depreciation of buildings, accounting expenses, and the expenses of the general managers and officers of the company.

Income from Operations. This is gross profit minus operating expenses. It is the profit of the company before deducting or adding interest payments, income or expense not directly related to the business (such as royalty income from patents, income from investments of company funds, and losses suffered when a customer does not pay his account), and income taxes.

Income before Income Taxes. This is the profit of the company after deducting from, or adding to, income from operations the net of various miscellaneous expenses and income; because interest expenses are deducted at this point, income before income taxes is usually less than income from operations.

Income Taxes. This is the amount of taxes the company owes to various government agencies for the income earned during the period.

Net Income (or Profit). This is the true profit of a company after all expenses and taxes. It is the amount the company has available to pay dividends to stockholders or to reinvest in the business. Of course, a negative amount represents a loss.

Income Statement: Small Company

To show how an income statement might look in a small company, we shall use the statement of Frank's Dry Cleaners, whose balance sheet we showed earlier. It is for the year ending June 30, 1974, and is shown in Figure 6–4.

Review of this income statement tells us several things. Assuming that it is a corporation, completely owned by Frank Cole, we can see

FIGURE 6–4

Income Statement of a Small Company

FRANK'S DRY CLEANERS
Income Statement for Year Ended June 30, 1974

Sales		$35,666.90
Less: refunds		102.50
Net sales		$35,564.40
Cost of dry cleaning services:		
Direct labor	6,350.00	
Materials used	895.62	
Plant overhead	1,681.33	
Total cost of dry cleaning services		$ 8,926.95
Gross profit		$26,637.45
Operating expenses:		
Electricity, gas, and water	487.25	
Telephone	221.67	
Delivery expenses	2,577.80	
Office expenses	265.75	
Office salaries (office girl and bookkeeper)	5,675.00	
General manager's salary (Frank Cole)	12,600.00	
Insurance	496.00	
Miscellaneous	537.80	
Total operating expenses		$22,861.27
Income from operations		3,776.18
Interest expense		1,137.50
Income before income taxes		$ 2,638.68
Income taxes		782.47
Net income		1,856.21

that the owner is making in profits after taxes a good yearly return on his original investment (see the balance sheet) of $10,000, or 18.5 percent, after taking a fair salary for himself. It indicates that there is only one full-time worker handling the cleaning and pressing duties, although the owner probably spends some of his time working on these.

The statement also indicates that profits could be materially increased if the company did not deliver. However, the delivery service may be one of Frank's main sales advantages. The relatively small amount of income taxes reflects the lower tax rates applicable to small businesses. The bank and the mortgage holder should feel rather comfortable about Frank's ability to repay the loans, because of his solid earnings.

Income Statement: A Large Company

The income statement of a large company is naturally more complex, though presented here in a condensed and summarized form. The statement is that of the Union Carbide Corporation (Figure 6–5), whose balance sheet was shown earlier. Even in its condensed form, some interesting observations can be made.

1. *Profits.* The company had a considerable improvement in profits in 1972. Profits after taxes increased by over 30 percent on a sales increase of only 8 percent. In looking to see how this could happen, we find that gross profit increased somewhat more than sales (10 percent), indicating either slightly higher prices or increased efficiency in plant and distribution costs, or both. We find also that research and development expenses were down, and that selling, general, and administrative costs held firm even with higher sales. Interest costs were down slightly as the result of reducing loans. Income taxes, while up considerably, did not increase as fast as income before taxes. (See the explanation of income taxes below.)

2. *Depreciation and Depletion.* Although we have discussed depreciation, some explanation of depletion may be necessary. This is a special term used with oil wells, mines, and other natural resources to indicate a loss of value when oil or minerals are taken from the ground. It is similar to depreciation in that it represents a loss of value through use. In the case of Union Carbide, these depreciation and depletion expense deductions are quite high, mainly because of its large investment in buildings, machinery, equipment, and mining operations. It should be noted that, while these are truly expenses of doing busi-

FIGURE 6–5

Income Statement of a Large Company

UNION CARBIDE CORPORATION AND SUBSIDIARIES
Consolidated Statement of Income for Years Ended December 31, 1972 and 1971
(millions of dollars)

	Year Ended December 31, 1972	Year Ended December 31, 1971
Net sales	$ 3,261.3	$ 3,037.5
Cost of sales: Plant cost and distribution expense	$ 2,169.8	2,044.2
Gross profit	$ 1,091.5	$ 993.3
Operating expenses:		
Research and development expenses	69.6	78.3
Selling, general, and administrative expenses	348.4	343.2
Depreciation and depletion	245.2	229.3
Total operating expenses	$ 663.2	$ 650.8
Income from operations	428.3	342.5
Other income and (expense)—mostly interest expense	(50.5)	(53.6)
Income before provision for income taxes	$ 377.8	288.9
Income taxes	156.2	124.6
Less: Minority stockholders' share and special items	16.4	6.5
Net income	$ 205.2	$ 157.8
Earnings per share (in dollars):		
Number of common shares outstanding	60,569,016	60,538,572
Net income per share	$ 3.38	$ 2.53
Disposition of net income (millions of dollars)		
Payment of dividends to stockholders	$ 121.3	$ 121.1
Retained in the business	$ 73.8	36.7

---

ness, they do not require cash for their payment. They are, instead, a using up of assets.

3. *Income Taxes.* Most corporations in the United States pay income taxes of approximately half their net income before taxes. Union Carbide, however, paid taxes averaging 43 percent of its income in 1971 and 41 percent in 1972. This is probably because of the company's very large program of investment in fixed assets, which the government has encouraged by granting companies a slight reduction of taxes. It may also be in part a consequence of its exploration and mining operations, which carry some tax benefits.

4. *Minority Stockholders' Share and Special Items.* These deductions from income may arouse some curiosity. In regard to the minority stockholders' share, it will be recalled that in our discussion of the company's balance sheet we pointed out that the company had consolidated the accounts of certain companies which it did not own completely. Stockholders other than those of Union Carbide owned stock in these companies. Their ownership interest was eliminated from the

corporation's equity in the balance sheet, and for the same reason the income on their ownership must be deducted in the income statement.

The term "special items" refers to various expenses and profits that do not arise in the usual course of business. They are usually small; they comprise such things as Union Carbide's gains from the sale of a subsidiary company, and its losses and gains from changes in the value of the dollar in foreign countries.

KEEPING SCORE ON CASH

While profits are extremely important to a company, perhaps the availability of cash is even more important. A company can take losses and still stay in business if it has cash. A company can show profits and have difficulty in staying in business if it does not have cash.

Even the cursory review of balance sheets and income statements undertaken here should make it clear that profits are not necessarily cash. Proprietorship, equity, or profits are simply claims on the assets of a company. If the assets are tied up in inventory, accounts receivable, buildings, or machinery and equipment, and the company has no cash, it is obviously in trouble. Workers cannot be paid with inventory or machinery, and taxes can only be paid in cash.

We can tell how much cash a company has by looking at its balance sheet. We can also get an idea of how much a bank would be willing to lend by looking at such assets as accounts receivable, which are believed to be convertible in a short time into cash. A bank will also be impressed by a record of profitable performance, on the assumption that profits will eventually give rise to cash.

Factors That Affect the Generation of Cash

To determine how much cash a company's operations are generating or can be made to generate, we look at several things. These are important not only to bankers and investors, but, above all, to the top business manager himself. They are as important to small businesses as to large businesses.

1. *The Amount of Expenses Payable in Cash.* Most business expenses are payable in cash, usually in a short time. But some, especially depreciation, are not. As pointed out above, being an expense to give effect to the wasting away of assets, depreciation does not require cash payments. Again, under certain circumstances, the government may allow income taxes to be deferred to a later year. Both of these items can

be considerable. Union Carbide had $245.2 million in depreciation and depletion in 1972, and was able to defer $15.4 million of taxes. Both of these items were expenses but required no cash payments, at least in the immediate future.

2. *Profits.* Profits can give rise to cash if the company does not invest them in assets other than cash.

3. *Loans and Ownership Investments.* New cash can be brought into a business, either through borrowing money or by additional investment from owners.

4. *Increase in Accounts Payable.* If a company increases its accounts payable to suppliers and others, this has the same effect as borrowing money. The company receives assets for use in the business, but by not paying for them immediately it "borrows" from its suppliers.

5. *Reduction of Assets through Obtaining Cash.* The sale of any asset may give rise either to cash or to accounts receivable. If a company reduces its accounts receivable or inventories, cash will be increased unless, of course, this is offset by the increase of other assets.

6. *Increase of Accounts Receivable and Inventories.* On the other hand, an increase in accounts receivable and inventories, assuming no other change, will increase the need for cash.

7. *Capital Expenditures.* Expenditures for new buildings, machinery, and equipment, referred to as *capital expenditures* because they represent long-term investment in assets, will require cash.

8. *Reduction of Loans.* When loans of a company are reduced, the presumption is that this has been done with cash and cash will be spent in the process.

9. *Payment of Cash Dividends.* The payment of cash dividends to stockholders will reduce cash.

10. *Reduction of Accounts Payable.* Accounts payable, being amounts due to suppliers and others, may be reduced and this will cause a reduction of cash.

11. *Reduction of Inventories.* Just as an increase in inventories causes demands on cash, a reduction will tend to generate cash.

Determining Cash Available

As can be seen from the foregoing, the cash available in a company is influenced by so many actions that it takes careful consideration to determine how much cash will be available when, and why. Many people have started businesses with enough cash to buy machinery and equipment, pay rent, and meet payrolls only to find that they did not have enough to meet the requirements for accounts receivable and inventories. It is a rare business that can grow quickly enough and make profits fast enough to pay its taxes and still have enough cash to finance these assets.

Every business, small or large, must therefore anticipate its cash requirements and develop ways of meeting them. More businesses get into trouble for lack of cash than for lack of profits.

RATIOS USED IN BALANCE SHEET ANALYSIS

Many people have reason to analyze a company's financial condition: lenders, investors interested in putting money into the business, creditors who may allow the company to increase its accounts payable, and the company managers themselves. One common method of analyzing a balance sheet is known as ratio analysis. A ratio measures the relationship between two different things, such as assets and liabilities. By using ratios it is possible to compare how a company stands in relation to other companies in the same industry.

In general, these ratios may be classified into two groups. One group of ratios have to do with the balance sheet. The other group of ratios are concerned with the income statement.

Some of the most commonly used ratios are described below.

Current Ratio. This ratio measures the relationship of current assets to current liabilities. It is important to all kinds of creditors, especially bankers who lend money and sellers who allow businesses to charge their purchases. As a general rule, lenders like to see current assets twice as large as current liabilities, a ratio of 2 to 1. With such a ratio, it is assumed that the business will always be able to meet its current liabilities. The reasoning is that a company's current assets may shrink because it can't collect accounts receivable or because it has losses on its inventories, but that its current liabilities will remain constant.

Frank's Dry Cleaners had a current ratio of roughly 1.4 to 1. This was well below the standard 2, but since the company had few receivables and only a small inventory of supplies, it was probably not dangerous. In fact, the typical airline or electric utility may have a current ratio of only 1 to 1. In those industries, accounts receivable and inventories are low, and customers pay their bills regularly.

The balance sheet of Union Carbide shows a current ratio of 2.6 to 1, probably a comfortable ratio. Of course, if the current assets were in unsalable inventory or uncollectible accounts receivable, the high ratio would not mean much. Most large and well financed companies have such higher ratios, probably to give them an unquestioned credit standing.

Acid Test or Quick Assets Ratio. This is the ratio of cash plus accounts receivable to current liabilities. It excludes inventories and only includes assets that can be converted to cash on short notice to meet current liabilities. The generally accepted standard for this ratio is 1 to 1. Both Frank's Dry Cleaners and Union Carbide amply meet this standard.

Debt to Net Worth Ratio. This is the ratio of the total debt to stockholders' equity, or proprietorship. It measures the amount of money put into the company by owners, as compared to the amount put in by all creditors. Banks like to see debts equal to no more than 50 percent of ownership, although they may not be uncomfortable if debt is as much as net worth, particularly if the company is profitable.

In the case of Frank's Dry Cleaners, this ratio is somewhat more than 1 to 1. However, Mr. Cole could sell his building and rent it back, thereby obtaining a very low debt to net worth ratio. Consequently the bank is probably not concerned about it. With Union Carbide, the debt to net worth ratio is well below 1 to 1, despite a large long-term debt. Since maintaining a large long-term debt is not generally regarded as good policy for manufacturing companies that are likely to have severe ups and downs in earnings, we are likely to find much lower ratios among them. For example, General Motors' ratio of debt to net worth is roughly 1 to 2.

Inventory Turnover Ratio. This is the ratio of sales to inventory and measures, in relation to sales, the average number of times an inventory "turns over" in a year. As pointed out earlier, inventory is usually a considerable investment for a company; there is always the danger, especially if inventories get too high, of losses from unsalable materials. Moreover, high inventories are costly to carry. Counting the interest on funds tied up in inventory, the costs of handling and storing, insurance, taxes, and the possibility of obsolescence or declines in prices, a reasonable estimate would be that stocks of materials, parts, and finished goods cost a company 25 to 30 percent of their value each year. If a company can operate with a million dollars less of inventory, it will probably improve its profits before taxes by a quarter of a million dollars or more each year.

There is no standard ratio for inventory turnover. One rule of thumb for manufacturing companies is that the ratio should not be lower than six; in other words, inventory should not exceed the equivalent of two months of sales, and preferably it should be less. But in some businesses the ratio is much higher than six. In dairies it ranges between 25 and 50, because milk must be processed quickly and buttter, ice cream, or bottled milk cannot be kept long in stock. In supermarkets the ratio is also quite high, averaging around 20.

The businessman who wants to compare his inventory turnover ratio with that of other companies may find figures for a wide variety of industries in Dun and Bradstreet's *Dun's Review,* a monthly journal.

Collection Period of Accounts Receivable. This is a way of looking at a business balance sheet to determine whether the level of accounts receivable is a cause for concern. It consists of calculating the number of days of sales these accounts represent. We divide the figure for sales by the value of accounts receivable to get the number of times the accounts turn over in a year, and convert this to days of sales. In the case of Union Carbide, for example, when we divide annual sales of $3,261.3 million by accounts and notes receivable of $576.9 million, we get a turnover ratio of 5.65. Translating this into days of sales (365 days divided by 5.65), we find that receivables represent nearly 65 days of sales. This means that customers pay Union Carbide, on the average, 65 calendar days after a sale is made.

Most businesses have a collection period of less than 65 days, although 50 to 60 days is common for manufacturing companies. If the collection period is much longer, an analyst is likely to be concerned that too many of the customers' debts to the company will turn out to be uncollectible. If the collection period is much shorter, the firm can be encouraged that collection losses should be low and savings will occur through reducing the assets it needs in the business. Collection periods, like inventories, vary with the kind of business. A supermarket that sells only for cash will not have a collection period.

But whatever the collection period, the person who goes into a business, like manufacturing, where customers seldom pay, on the average, faster than in 45 days and more often in 50 or 60 days, he will have to provide for this by money he has available for operating the business. As indicated above in our discussion of cash, one of the major errors people make in starting a business is overlooking the amount of cash they need to carry customers' accounts as well as inventories.

RATIOS USED IN INCOME STATEMENT ANALYSIS

Like ratios used for the analysis of balance sheets, there are many used to evaluate the earnings of a company. Among the most generally used in analyzing income statements are the following:

Gross Profit Margin. This ratio is the percentage that gross profit (after deducting the cost of services or products, and before deducting operating expenses, taxes, and other items) bears to total sales. It represents the amount a business has available to cover those expenses not directly related to the production of a service or product. Gross profit margins range from 25 percent to 35 percent in most successful manufacturing companies. The margin is 35 percent in Union Carbide, but approximately 25 percent in Ford and General Motors where a considerable amount of expenses are purchased parts and accessories and operating expenses are relatively low. It was 38 percent in profitable Du Pont in 1973. As might be expected for Safeway Stores in 1973, the gross profit margin was only 19 percent because it mainly buys finished goods and sells them in its stores with a high inventory turnover of some 12 times in 1973.

The gross profit margin is considered the most useful basis for comparing companies in the same kind of business. It shows what various companies are making above their costs of production, and what they have available to cover their operating expenses plus a profit. It is generally believed that if a business cannot make a gross profit at least equal to the average in its line of business, it will probably not be a success.

Pretax Profit Margin. This is the percentage of a company's profits before taxes to its sales. Because tax calculations can vary due to special tax provisions, this ratio is usually looked upon as the true measure of a company's profitability. It measures the percentage of the sales dollar that is carried down into profits before taxes.

Manufacturing companies usually average pretax profit margins of 8 to 10 percent of the sales dollar. There are wide variations among industries, ranging from nearly 20 percent in drugs and medicines, and 16 percent in office equipment and computers, to slightly more than 3 percent in meatpacking. Food chain stores generally have pretax profit margins of slightly less than 2 percent, because of the large volume of sales in relation to the amount invested in the business. However, Safeway Stores had pretax profits in 1973 of 2.3 percent.

Ratio of Profit after Taxes to Sales. Another measure of profitability is the amount a company earns after income taxes. Although individual companies differ, depending on certain legal provisions for paying taxes, income taxes generally amount to 50 percent of net income before taxes. As a consequence, the percentage of net income to sales after taxes is usually about half that of pretax income to sales. While ratios for individual companies may be higher or lower, the percentage of profit after taxes to sales has been averaging about 4 or 5 percent.

Ratio of Profit after Taxes to Net Worth. This ratio measures what the owners of a company are making on their investment. It consists of profits after taxes divided by the total net worth, or proprietorship, of the company. For Union Carbide in 1972, the return was 10.6 percent, approximately the average for all manufacturing companies. Many nonmanufacturing companies, such as department stores and food chains have a similar rate of return. It is considerably higher than the 3 percent earned by railroads and the 6 percent earned by airlines in 1972, and considerably below the handsome return of nearly 20 percent earned by the trucking companies in recent years.

Although 1972 was a good year, and 1973 was better for many companies, most companies do not appear to be making excessive returns. Some of those that fell below the average would have been better off if they could have liquidated their entire businesses at costs carried on the balance sheet and invested their funds in high interest-bearing savings accounts or even in government bonds.

INTERPRETING FINANCIAL REPORTS

With the information given above, anyone can make a fairly intelligent approach to interpreting the principal financial reports of a business. He will not be an expert analyst, but he can understand how the score is kept if he (1) knows how to read balance sheets, (2) understands income statements and how they are constructed, and (3) is able to work out a few ratios and apply them. By understanding the fundamentals of these three areas, he can interpret the essentials of financial statements and reports. Accounting and statement analysis are really nothing more than a logical system for handling business financial information and making it meaningful.

WHAT RATIOS MEAN TO THE BUSINESSMAN

The purpose of financial statements and reports is to show anyone concerned with a business how well it has done in terms of sales and profits and how financially sound it is. The use of ratios makes it easier for owners, lenders, and others to see the condition of a company and where its weak spots are. Also, by comparing ratios for a given company with those of other companies in the same line of business, the businessmen can get an idea of how he is doing competitively. He must also know what is happening to his accounts receivable, his inventories, his investments in machinery and equipment, and the cash withdrawals of owners. These, along with profitability, are of continuous concern to him.

Other than the understandable desire to stay in business and not go bankrupt, and to make as large profits as possible, there are no absolute standards of what is best in business. It is much like any game or competitive sport. Every businessman wants to be a winner. He certainly does not want to be a dismal loser.

SUMMARY

In the game of business, the main way we keep score of our progress is through measurements of our profitability and the soundness of our financial condition. It must be remembered that profits are merely a measure of the surplus of what is produced and sold—sales—over the cost of producing it—expenses. The financial soundness of a business is closely tied to the various items of property a business has, and to the changing claims of owners and creditors against them.

What every businessman, owner, creditor, tax collector, and others concerned with business want to know is how well the business is doing, how financially sound it is, and why these things are occurring. To the extent that these can be reduced to monetary terms, this is the task of accounting: to record, summarize, and interpret financial transactions. To understand business, one must know how score is kept and comprehend at least the basics of the science and art of accounting.

To do this, he must understand that a balance sheet is a way of showing what a business owns and the claims of creditors and owners against the things owned. We call those things of value owned by a business "assets," and the claims against assets made by creditors "liabilities." When liabilities are subtracted from assets, the remaining claims represent "proprietorship," "net worth," or "equity." A balance sheet shows these relationships only at an instant of time like a snapshot. We must look to the income (or profit and loss) statement to find out what happened over a period of time.

Accounting and financial statements are windows through which we see what is happening in a business. To aid us in seeing, certain ratios have been developed. These ratios are especially useful in showing how one business is doing in comparison with others. Ratios are also used by lenders and investors to measure how well a business is doing and how soundly it is financed.

Certain ratios deal primarily with the balance sheet. Among the most widely used of these ratios are current assets to current liabilities, quick assets to current liabilities, total debt to net worth or equity, inventory turnover, and collection period of accounts receivable.

Other widely used ratios are designed to help analyze the income, or profit and loss, statement. They include such ratios as gross profit margin, pretax margin, profit after taxes to sales, and profit after taxes to net worth.

There is more to understanding and interpreting financial reports of businesses than we have covered in this chapter. But the fundamentals of keeping and knowing the score in business presented here can give the reader considerable understanding of what financial statements and reports show about a business. It is amazing how many people, working in business and constantly rubbing elbows with businessmen, watch the game without knowing how the score is kept. With a little practice in using the essentials outlined in this chapter, the reader will be surprised how much he can learn about a business—what it does, how well it does it, and how effective its management is.

KEY TERMS AND CONCEPTS

Property
Property rights
Assets
Proprietorship, capital, or net worth
Liabilities
Stockholders' equity
Account receivable
Note receivable
Inventory
Account payable
Debit
Credit
Double entry bookkeeping
Insolvent
Deficit
Depreciation
Depletion
Balance sheet
Current liabilities

Current assets
Long-term liabilities
Short-term liabilities
Time deposits
Prepaid expenses
Accrued taxes
Income statement
Net sales
Cost of goods sold or cost of production
Gross profit
Operating expenses
Income from operations
Income before income taxes
Net income (or profit)
Capital expenditures
Current ratio
Acid test or quick assets ratio
Debt to net worth ratio
Inventory turnover

QUESTIONS FOR ANALYSIS AND DISCUSSION

1. Why is it important for a businessman to keep and know the score in business through the use of accounting? How else could he know the score?

2. Distinguish between property and property rights in business. Why is this distinction important in determining a company's net worth or equity? Could you apply the same thinking to determine your personal net worth (or deficit)?

3. In the final analysis, all accounting can be reduced to the simple formula ASSETS = LIABILITIES + PROPRIETORSHIP (or Equity, Capital, or Net Worth). Taking the transactions in Figure 6–1, show how this is true. Could you do the same thing in calculating your own property and net worth?

4. Despite its use of numbers, balance sheets, and income statements, accounting is not perfectly accurate. Why? Can you suggest how it might be made more accurate? Do the elements of inaccuracy mean that accounting has limited use for business?

5. Why do the authors of this book refer to the balance sheet as a "snapshot picture"? Could you say the same for an income statement? How does an income statement fit into a balance sheet?

6. Why are banks and other creditors likely to be more interested in the results shown on an income statement than those in a company's balance sheet?

7. What are the major differences between the balance sheets and income statements of Frank's Dry Cleaners and the Union Carbide Corporation? Given the sizes of the two companies, do these differences seem reasonable to you?

8. Why is it said that knowing the score on cash is probably more important than knowing the score on profits in a business? How can we determine the cash a business will generate? How does the procedure in determining cash illustrate the basic accounting equation of Assets = Liabilities + Net Worth?

9. Explain why you would expect bankers lending money to a business to be interested in balance sheet ratios. Which ones are likely to be of greatest concern to them? In which income statement ratios would you expect them to have the greatest interest? Why?

10. If you were in business and wanted to watch the score carefully to assure that the business made a profit and did not get into financial difficulties, what items on the balance sheet and income statement would you watch most closely? Why? Would you be as concerned as bankers or other lenders with the various financial ratios? Why?

SUGGESTED READING

Carson, A. B., A. E. Carlson, and C. Bolina *College Accounting* (9th ed.). Cincinnati: South-Western Publishing Company, 1972.

Homgren, C. T. *Accounting for Managerial Control.* Englewood Cliffs, N.J.: Prentice-Hall, Inc., 1970.

Meigs, W. B., A. N. Mosick, and C. E. Johnson *Accounting: The Basis for Business Decisions* (3d ed.). New York: McGraw-Hill Book Company, 1972.

Myer, J. N. *Accounting for Non-Accountants.* New York: Hawthorn Books, 1970.

Still, J. W. *A Guide to Managerial Accounting in Small Companies.* Englewood Cliffs, N.J.: Prentice-Hall, Inc., 1969.

Van Horne, J. C. *Fundamentals of Financial Management* (2d ed.). Englewood Cliffs, N.J. Prentice-Hall, Inc., 1974, Chapters 3–4.

Weston, J. F., and E. F. Brigham *Essentials of Managerial Finance* (3d ed.). Hinsdale, Ill.: The Dryden Press, 1974, Chapter 3.

7

Raising Money: The Banking System

To start a business takes money. Money is needed to finance such assets as machinery and equipment, accounts receivable, and inventories, and to pay for labor, materials and supplies, and taxes. These needs often rise faster than profits. That is why most companies cannot make enough from profits after taxes to finance considerable growth unless, of course, a very large investment has been made by the original owners.

To raise the funds necessary to operate, a business has three major sources: (1) investments by the owners, (2) borrowing, or (3) funds generated by the business through depreciation charges and profits. In Chapter 8 we shall deal with one way of raising funds, by selling stock or bonds to the public. In this chapter we shall discuss another source of funds, the banking system.

HOW BANKS SERVE BUSINESSES

Banks, like other businesses, operate to make a profit. They do this by selling their services—to individuals, businesses, government agencies, churches, schools and colleges, and anyone else who uses money. In the United States, all banks are privately owned, although they have many close ties to government agencies.

Banks serve business in many ways other than as lenders of money. While their most important function is to provide funds, they offer other services essential to business operations. Among the most important are the following:

1. Providing a place where cash may be deposited for safekeeping.
2. Making it possible for depositors to draw funds from their accounts and pay them to any designated party by merely signing a piece of paper, referred to as a check or draft.
3. Making short-term loans for periods ranging from 30 to 180 days.
4. Making long-term loans for periods ranging from a year to five years, and, in some instances, for much longer periods of time.
5. Making loans to business customers so that they may purchase products or services.
6. Providing a place where a business may deposit surplus cash for a period of time and earn interest on it.
7. Providing cash or checks in a foreign currency so that a business may buy from a foreign seller, as well as converting foreign money into American dollars when a customer in another country wants to use his money to buy from an American business.
8. Handling the registration and transfer of company securities, such as stocks and bonds.
9. Providing a department called a trust department which is licensed by the government to safeguard various assets and contracts entrusted to the bank by its customers, and to buy or sell property and securities for them.
10. Often helping businessmen find individuals willing to invest in ownership in businesses or in their securities; this is a primary function of investment banks, which will be discussed later, but other banks often give business customers some assistance in their search.
11. Giving businessmen information and advice concerning the credit reputation and the standing of all people with whom they do business.

THE DIFFERENT KINDS OF BANKS AND LENDING INSTITUTIONS

There are a number of different kinds of banks and lending institutions where companies can put funds for safekeeping and where they may borrow money. One major type, known as investment banks, are mainly concerned with selling corporation securities to the public. But all the rest are in the business of safeguarding and investing funds, supplying credit, and performing in various degrees the services outlined above.

Commercial Banks

Of special importance to businesses, but also to nonbusiness organizations and individuals are commercial banks. Commercial banks specialize in (1) accepting deposits of money and making funds readily available on demand to depositors, and (2) lending money. Most so-called commercial banks also have a savings department where time deposits can be made, and offer other services. But the principal role of commercial banks in the United States is to handle demand deposits and make loans, usually on a short-term basis, such as 30, 60, 90, or 120 days.

Unlike some foreign countries, all commercial banks in the United States are owned by individuals through their purchase of common stock in them. Banks which are chartered (incorporated) by the federal government are called *national banks,* and those chartered by the states are called *state banks.* Anyone can start a bank if he meets certain strict requirements. A minimum of cash must be invested by the stockholders (customarily from $50,000 to $200,000), the organizers must stand thorough scrutiny by the authorities, and, a government agency must find that there is reasonable evidence of need for the bank's services. A bank must also meet regulatory requirements, and must open its books and accounts to government auditors.

Savings Banks

While not nearly as common as commercial banks, these banks have been designed to serve smaller savers as a means whereby their savings can be pooled, investments made by the bank, and interest arising from these investment earnings be paid to depositors. Savings banks started in New York and New England early in the 19th century. They were organized as *mutual* banks, owned by depositors rather than stockholders.

Most of the present 500 mutual savings banks are in New York and the New England states, with New York alone having nearly three-fifths of all mutual savings bank assets in the country. Total assets were $101 billion in 1973.

Mutual savings banks have been largely superseded elsewhere by other savings institutions. In the southern and western states, there are some stockholder-owned savings banks. However, most of these stock savings banks have become commercial banks as well, and almost all commercial banks have their own savings departments. Even the world's largest privately owned commercial bank, the Bank of America, has as its complete corporate title "The Bank of America National Trust and Savings Association."

Because savings banks invest most of their funds in government securities and loans secured by real estate (mortgages), they are not of prime importance to business. However, they sometimes finance buildings and land belonging to business firms.

Savings and Loan Associations

Savings and loan associations are similar to savings banks, except that their lending is limited to mortgages on homes and other real estate. They began 150 years ago as temporary associations of people who pooled their savings and lent them to one of their number to build a home. The idea was that if each of 20 individuals wanted to build a $10,000 house but could only save $500 each year, it would be in their interest to pool their savings so that one house could be built every year. Obviously, those waiting the longest would gain from interest paid by the people who got the earlier houses.

From these commonsense associations of individuals have grown today's savings and loan companies. Some are mutual companies, owned by the savers. Others are stock companies owned by a group of stockholders who pay interest to the savers but also accumulate profit for themselves. There are approximately 4,000 state-chartered companies and 2,000 nationally chartered companies.

The savings and loan companies have had an exceptional growth, particularly since World War II. Their assets rose from less than those of the savings banks in 1950 to more than double those of the savings banks in 1973, or approximately $232 billion. The distinction between the two institutions has tended to become blurred. Savings banks were established to pool savings in any safe investment (generally other than common stocks) but now lend money primarily on real estate, as do the savings and loan associations. Both institutions are chiefly of interest to businessmen in financing the purchase of real estate.

Credit Unions

As indicated in Chapter 5, credit unions are really cooperative savings associations of people who have some common tie, such as an employer or a union. They help small savers to make deposits easily and regularly, usually by deductions from their pay checks. Being operated by the savers themselves, their expenses tend to be low and, in order to encourage thrift, many employers provide credit unions with office facilities and other assistance. Their loans are normally small personal loans made to their members. They are especially active in helping people with installment purchases of appliances, furniture, and automobiles.

There are 24,000 credit unions in the United States, with more than 22 million members and total assets of over $25 billion. These associations are fairly important to business. They give employees an easy means of saving, and they provide a bank where people can get installment loans for many of their purchases at fairly low interest rates.

Life Insurance Companies

While life insurance companies are not banks in any sense, they have become large holders of people's savings. With their $252 billion of assets in 1973, life insurance companies held more savings than any other kind of company.

These companies accumulate assets as the result of selling life insurance policies for prices much higher than the probable cost of death benefits at the time they are sold. In the earlier years of a person's life, the sums collected on a whole life policy are more than the amount required to meet the likelihood of his dying. As he gets older and his chances of death increase, his premium remains the same, but enough has been accumulated from previous payments and accrued interest to cover possible death benefits. In fact, the total premiums paid each year by all policyholders in the United States are roughly three times the death benefits paid out by the companies.

Insurance companies invest their assets in corporation bonds and stocks and in home mortgages. They also lend directly to businesses. Much of their lending takes the form of real estate mortgages to finance buildings and plants. But some of it is for other capital equipment. For example, ever since the Equitable Life Assurance Company lent money to Trans World Airlines in 1946 to help it acquire new airplanes, life insurance companies have been prominent lenders of funds to airlines. They also lend long-term money to business firms by buying notes or bonds from them.

Investment Banks

Although they are not commercial banks, investment banks are very important to business. Since their main function is to aid businesses in selling securities to the general public, their activities will be discussed in Chapter 8, which describes how funds are raised on the public market.

Commercial Finance Companies

These are companies which help businesses turn their accounts receivable into cash. They purchase receivables at a discount, in effect lending the money on the assumption that the customers will pay. If an account remains unpaid, the borrowing business firm must make good the loss.

The companies also make loans on business inventory, and sometimes on machinery and equipment. The interest rates of these companies are likely to be high, often double bank lending rates, because of the higher risks involved and the expense of administering the loans. When company assets are taken as security, the commercial finance companies must not only keep close watch over the assets but also place many restrictions on the way company management may operate. Finance companies have often rescued hard-pressed companies from possible bankruptcy.

Factoring Companies

These operate in much the same way as commercial finance companies, with one important exception. A factoring company purchases accounts receivable from a business at a discount but, if a customer does not pay his account, the factor takes the loss. Since the factoring company's risk is correspondingly greater it charges a higher discount, although it will be understandably careful in selecting the accounts receivable it purchases. When a business sells its accounts receivable to a factor, the customers pay their bills directly to the factoring company. Occasionally, like commercial finance companies, factoring companies lend money to businesses on the security of inventory as well as on accounts receivable.

In general, factoring companies are used by smaller firms since the larger ones can ordinarily finance their credit needs through commercial banks. In certain industries, such as clothing manufacture, the use of factoring companies is the common practice. Some clothing manufacturers even find it advantageous to use a factoring organization because of its care in granting credit to their customers. In other fields, however, companies tend to avoid using factors since this is usually more expensive than commercial bank financing, and may give a company a poor reputation of not having a good enough credit rating to deal with commercial banks.

Sales Finance Companies

An important source of credit for customers buying from businesses is the sales finance company. These companies finance installment credit on individual purchases of automobiles, refrigerators, freezers, television sets, home furnishings, and other durable goods. Without them, most merchants would have neither the resources nor the inclination to sell to many customers on credit.

When a customer buys an item on the installment plan, the item bought becomes the security for the loan. If he fails to keep up his payments, the finance company can repossess it. Sometimes the finance company can also look to the original merchant to cover a loss due to a bad loan. But competition among finance companies has made this practice less general than it was a few years ago. Because of the cost of making and collecting installment loans, and the risks involved, they tend to bear a fairly high interest rate, varying from 18 to 30 percent per year.

Many sales finance companies handle installment sales to businesses as well. If a businessman wants to buy a new machine, install air conditioning equipment, or purchase store fixtures, he may buy on the installment plan like anyone else. But most companies do better to pay for such equipment by regular bank financing, the sale of ownership equity, or cash generated from business profits.

There are a number of large sales finance companies. Certain corporations such as General Electric and General Motors have their own companies which are usually quite large: the General Motors Acceptance Corporation had over $14 billion of assets in 1974. Most commercial banks, attracted by the volume of installment business and the high interest rates, have set up special departments for consumer financing.

Consumer Finance Companies

These are the "small loan" companies that specialize in making personal loans for any purpose. Such loans usually carry interest rates of 2 percent per month or more. The security for the loan, which is seldom more than $2,500, is minimal: the borrower's credit standing, his salary, and his ability to repay. These companies sometimes lend on the additional security of automobiles or furniture.

Consumer finance companies are of no particular interest to the general businessman. They may, however, make it possible for customers to buy merchandise they would not otherwise be able to purchase.

COMMERCIAL BANKING

The most important source of funds for businesses are the commercial banks. As we have already seen, their basic functions are to accept demand deposits against which checks can be drawn and to make short-term loans. In addition, commercial banks normally provide all the services outlined at the beginning of this chapter.

There are approximately 14,000 commercial banks in the United States, holding more than $500 billion in deposits. They are found in all but the smallest towns and villages. Nearly 5,000 commercial banks are chartered by the federal government through the Comptroller of the Currency. The remaining 9,000 have state charters.

Some banks have only a few hundred thousand dollars of assets. The nation's largest bank, the Bank of America, had more than $49 billion of assets in 1973. New York City is headquarters for seven banks with more than $10 billion in assets each, ranging from the First National City with $44 billion in 1973 to the Marine Midland with $13 billion. Of the 25 largest corporations in the country in 1973, as measured by asets, 13 were commercial banks, each of which had more assets than Sears Roebuck, the country's largest retailer.

Demand Deposits

Individuals can open a checking account (place a demand deposit) in a bank with a minimum of difficulty. Generally all a bank is concerned with is having a deposit in cash or valid checks on another bank and having the depositor's signature on file so that the checks he writes may be verified and honored. An account for a partnership is essentially as simple to open. But the opening of a corporation account usually requires a resolution by the bank's board of directors authorizing the account and permitting certain officers of the corporation to draw checks against it.

These demand deposits draw no interest. If the depositor keeps a certain minimum balance in the account, usually no charge is made for handling his checks.

Time Deposits

Commercial banks also accept deposits that are to be kept for a period of time and to draw interest. There are two kinds of these: *savings deposits* and *certificates of deposit*. Savings deposits are for smaller savers and ordinarily may not exceed a certain amount, usually $5,000 to $25,000. While the bank can require 30 days or more notice by a depositor before withdrawal, this restriction is seldom imposed. Only individuals and nonprofit organizations, such as churches, are allowed to have savings deposits in commercial banks, principally because the rate of interest paid on them has been designed for individual savers who will keep their money there, rather than for business firms with temporary excess cash.

However, banks also offer certificates of deposit for business firms as well as individuals. They require that the deposit be made for a certain period of time and that it not be withdrawn for 30 or more days. Certificates were long issued only in large denominations of $100,000 or more, but in recent years they have been available to savers in denominations of $1,000 and occasionally less. They are also often made negotiable, so that a bank can sell them to other banks or investors.

Short-Term Loans

As mentioned earlier, the principal business of a commercial bank and its main source of income is making short-term loans to business firms and individuals. Interest is charged on these loans at varying rates. Larger customers with an unquestioned credit rating, like Ford Motor Company or International Business Machines Corporation, are charged the lowest rate, called the "prime rate." Other customers are charged rates above prime, ranging from as little as ¼ percent higher to 2 or even 3 percent higher, depending on the borrower's credit standing. Prime rates in recent years have tended to vary considerably as the demand for and supply of loanable funds changed. In 1971, prime rates fell as low as 4.5 percent and in 1974 they rose to 12 percent.

Loans may be *secured* or *unsecured*. On loans to many individuals and to companies whose credit has not been well established, a bank may require the borrower to deposit *collateral* as security for the loan. This may be stocks, bonds, life insurance policies, accounts receivable, equipment, inventories, and other things of value that the bank could sell if the borrower did not pay. But loans for some individuals and most companies are unsecured in the sense that nothing is required except the borrower's promise to pay. Such loans are made to borrowers

David Rockefeller

*Courtesy of the Chase
Manhattan Bank.*

David Rockefeller has gained a world-wide reputation as a spokesman for the American business community. He has spearheaded the Chase Manhattan Bank's expansion both internationally and throughout the metropolitan New York area and has helped the bank play a significant role as a corporate citizen.

Rockefeller was born June 12, 1915, in New York City, the youngest of the five sons of John D. Rockefeller, Jr. He graduated from Harvard in 1936 with a bachelor of science degree, went on to graduate study at Harvard and the London School of Economics, and received a Ph.D. degree in economics from the University of Chicago in 1940.

After Pearl Harbor Rockefeller enlisted as a private in the U.S. Army, and was discharged as a captain in 1945. He was awarded the U.S. Legion of Merit, the U.S. Army Commendation Ribbon, and the French Legion of Honor.

In 1946 he joined the Chase National Bank, of which his uncle Winthrop Aldrich was board chairman. By 1949 he had advanced from assistant manager in the foreign department to a vice presidency. From 1950 to 1952 he ran Chase's business in Latin America. He was named a senior vice president in 1952 with responsibility for the economic research department and customer relations in the metropolitan New York area, including all the New York City branches.

When Chase National merged with the

who have established credit and whose business operations or personal income and estate provide assurance that the loan will be repaid.

Intermediate-Term and Long-Term Loans

Commercial banks increasingly make loans to businesses for periods of one, three, or even five or more years. Some commercial banks have even made business loans for as long as 10 years or more. In general, however, they view their function as the financing of accounts receivable, inventories, and similar short-term needs. Their position has been that businesses needing funds for a longer period should raise

Bank of the Manhattan Company in 1955, David Rockefeller was appointed an executive vice president in charge of the development department. On January 1, 1957, he became vice chairman of the board of directors, with responsibility for the administrative and planning functions of the bank as a whole. He was named president of the bank and chairman of the executive committee of the board of directors on January 1, 1961. On March 1, 1969, Rockefeller became chairman of the board of directors and chief executive officer.

Speaking of his career, Rockefeller has said, "Having the name Rockefeller can be an advantage, but it also means people . . . assume anything you achieve is the result of the name rather than doing something yourself. So it makes it doubly important that you do twice as well as the other person to justify things."

His career as board chairman has not been without its worries. In October 1972 he made front-page headlines by firing the bank's president, who hadn't been able to pull Chase Manhattan along fast enough in the race with its chief competitor, First National City Bank. The performance of National City has been better in recent years by all the standards bankers use in keeping score. In 1968 Chase had assets of $19.4 billion, compared to First National City Bank's $19.6 billion. By October 1973, Chase Manhattan had $35 billion but National City had $41 billion.

David Rockefeller frequently meets and negotiates with foreign heads of state, ranging from Sadat of Egypt to Kosygin of the Soviet Union and Chou En-lai of China. In May 1973 Chase Manhattan announced the opening of a representative office in Moscow—the first presence of an American bank on Russian soil in over half a century. Chase has also been named correspondent for the Bank of China.

Rockefeller is not exactly a man of leisure. For many years he has played a leading role in the affairs of the Rockefeller Institute for Medical Research, founded by his famous grandfather in 1901. In 1947 he helped organize Morningside Heights, Inc., a group of educational, religious, medical, and welfare institutions concerned with the development of upper Manhattan. He followed this by becoming chairman of the Downtown-Lower Manhattan Association which produced a $1.2 billion program for the redevelopment of lower Manhattan. It hopes to draw back middle-class residents who have fled the urban jungle for the suburbs.

Busy as he is with intellectual, cultural, and civic projects, Rockefeller estimates that he spends at least two thirds of his time on bank-related business. He has said that "the conduct of modern enterprise is so complex that a person who knows and understands something about philosophy, literature, the arts, and history is the type of person who is most likely to succeed in business."

them through sales of stocks or bonds, by mortgaging real estate, or going to financial institutions specializing in this kind of credit.

How Banks "Create" Money

One of the most interesting features of commercial banking, and the most difficult to understand, is the ability of banks to increase the supply of money. They don't print currency or issue coins: that is done by the government. But they do permit checks to be drawn against their deposits, and checks can be used as money.

When a bank makes a loan, it enters this on its balance sheet as an asset (a note receivable) and a liability (a deposit). It has, in effect, created funds. To be sure, if it made a hundred loans and the borrowers all immediately drew out their funds in cash, or paid bills by checks to merchants who then deposited these checks in another bank, the lending bank could lose cash. But, borrowers seldom draw out their loans in cash; even if they did, and used the cash to pay bills, some or all of this cash would be returned to the bank as a deposit. When borrowers write checks to pay their bills, at least some of these checks will be deposited by recipients in the borrowers' bank. Furthermore, people receiving checks drawn on other banks may deposit these checks in the lending bank. The result is that in a system of thousands of banks, checks drawn on Bank A will be deposited in that bank or in another bank, and some checks drawn on other banks will be deposited in Bank A.

We can see how banks "create money" by thinking of a town having a single bank. The bank lends an individual $1,000 and deposits that amount in his checking account. This borrower pays his electric company $25, his department store $500 for a new television set, his furniture store $300 for some chairs, and his Ford dealer $75 for work on his car. He has drawn $900 of his deposit. The electric company, department store, furniture store, and Ford dealer, however, do not draw out cash from the bank but deposit the $900 in checks in the bank. The result is the bank has lost no cash, the total new deposits remain at $1,000, and purchasing power in the town has been increased by that amount.

To be sure, in real life it is not as simple as this. The borrower may draw out some cash. The persons receiving his checks may deposit them in other banks, or if they don't they may draw checks against this deposit payable to someone in a city miles away. For example, the department store may use the $500 to buy television sets from a manufacturer in another city.

To safeguard against the possibility that a bank making loans will not receive enough return deposits from local customers or from banks in another city, commercial banks are required to maintain a certain level of reserves. In other words, a bank must have available enough funds either in cash or in items that can be converted into cash quickly —government bonds or deposits in other banks—to cover possible needs.

State and federal regulations require banks to maintain certain levels of cash or cash-equivalent items. These required reserves are expressed as a percentage of deposits, and may vary over time and as between smaller and larger banks from as little as 7 percent of demand deposits to as much as 22 percent. Most banks like to keep their reserves above legal requirements so that they will not be caught short. It can be seen, however, that the requirement for reserves limits the amount of deposits, and thus limits the amount a bank can lend. While an individual bank standing alone cannot "create" much money, a system of banks can, as shown in Figure 7–1.

Deposit Insurance

Since banks cannot hold enough cash reserves to cover all deposits without limiting their ability to lend money to the actual amount of cash on hand, the danger exists that if all of a bank's depositors showed up on the same day at the tellers' windows and asked for cash, the bank would be in trouble. This is exactly what happened to many banks in 1932 and early 1933. The "runs" on banks forced many banks to be unable to pay their depositors and to close their doors. Many went bankrupt because they could not collect on their outstanding loans soon enough, and many depositors lost money.

To guard against this happening again, the federal government established the Federal Deposit Insurance Corporation in 1935 to insure depositors against losing their money. Since that time, similar government deposit insurance has been provided for a variety of other financial institutions, including savings banks and savings and loan companies. Deposits are now insured up to $20,000 on any single account.

All nationally chartered banks are required to carry deposit insurance, and most state banks have elected to do so. Fewer than two percent of the nation's commercial banks, holding less than ½ of 1 percent of total deposits, are not so insured. Insured banks pay a small fee (in 1973, 1/30 of 1 percent of deposits) for this insurance, which, after expenses, goes into a fund to support banks that get into trouble. Since most depositors in banks have accounts below the maximum of $20,000 insured, and it is the small depositor who is most likely to start a "run" on a bank, the fact of insurance has all but eliminated "runs" on banks.

Banks Are Closely Regulated

The Federal Deposit Insurance Corporation keeps close watch over insured banks so that they are unlikely to get into trouble. Banks are also regulated by other governmental agencies including the Federal

FIGURE 7–1

How Banks "Create" Money

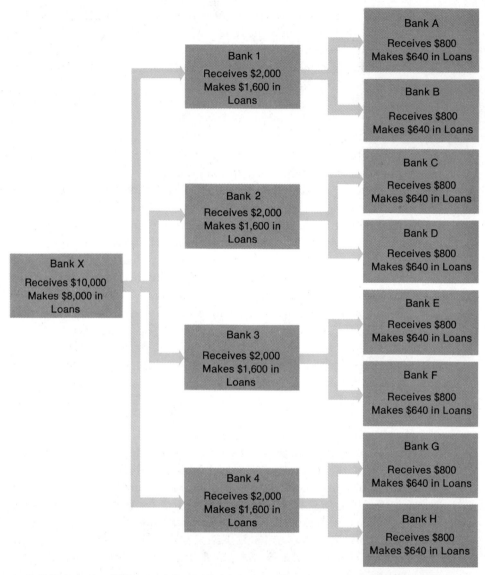

In this very simplified example, Bank X received $10,000 in new deposits. If the bank keeps a reserve of 20 percent against deposits, it can make new loans of 80 percent of $10,000, or $8,000. Let us suppose that the loans are used by customers to pay bills, and that the persons to whom the payments are made deposit their receipts in Banks 1, 2, 3, and 4. These banks now have new deposits of $2,000 each. If Banks 1, 2, 3, and 4 keep reserves of 20 percent against deposits, each can make new loans of $1,600. If these loans in turn are used by customers to pay bills, and the persons to whom the payments are made deposit their receipts in Banks A, B, C, D, E, F, G, and H, these banks can make loans of $640 if they keep reserves of 20 percent. If we add up all of these loans, we see that the original cash inflow of $10,000 to Bank X has resulted in new loans totaling $19,520. Obviously, if reserves are lower than 20 percent, the total of possible new loans and deposits would be larger.

Reserve System, the Comptroller of the Currency for national banks, and the various state banking agencies. Banking is probably the most closely regulated of all businesses.

The regulation of banking is only natural, since banks hold the deposits of millions of people. They also control the supply of money, as we have seen. Through their lending operations they are an integral part of the nation's business system. It would be harmful to almost everyone in the country if we permitted a dishonest, irresponsible, or weak banking system.

Bank regulation takes many forms. The legal requirements of minimum reserves have been mentioned. Banks are also restricted as to the kinds of securities in which they may invest, and their loans are subject to careful review. Government agencies establish the maximum interest rates banks may pay on deposits.

Much of the regulation is carried on through periodic and unannounced audits by government agents. The audits are concerned not only with honesty and accounting accuracy, but also with the quality of loans and investments. All members of the Federal Deposit Insurance Corporation—that is, most banks—are audited by that agency. All nationally chartered banks are further audited by representatives of the Comptroller of the Currency. All state banks are audited by state banking departments. There is little opportunity for a bank to stray far from legal requirements and reasonably sound banking practices.

THE FEDERAL RESERVE SYSTEM

American commercial banking cannot be understood without some familiarity with the Federal Reserve System. This was established in 1913 for the purpose of providing a central banking authority that would correspond to the central banks of other countries. Before 1913, the thousands of separate privately owned banks borrowed from each other when they needed funds. This worked all right when some banks were in a position to lend. But when most or all of the banks in the country needed funds at the same time, there was no place to borrow and many banks would fail.

In other countries this problem had been met by having a central bank—a "banker's bank"—with the power to make loans to banks and "create" necessary money in the same way that individual commercial banks do. Most of the central banks of foreign countries, such as the Bank of England and Bank of France, have been owned by the government. With the vast resources and powers of governments behind them, these banks could lend any necessary funds to the commercial banks.

The Federal Reserve System is such a central bank. Although the 12 District Federal Reserve Banks in this system are privately rather than governmentally owned, their operations are federally controlled. Their main task is to lend money to individual commercial banks; since they are held to no reserve requirements, their ability to lend is virtually unlimited. By choosing to lend or not to lend to banks, this central banking system can and does exert considerable control over the expansion of bank credit.

Organization of the Federal Reserve System

The United States, as noted, instead of having a single central bank has a system of 12 District Federal Reserve Banks, one for each geographic region. They are located in Boston, New York, Philadelphia, Cleveland, Richmond, Atlanta, Chicago, St. Louis, Minneapolis, Kansas City, Dallas, and San Francisco.

Although each of the Federal Reserve Banks is owned through stock purchased by member banks in each district, the stockholders cannot vote according to their shares as most stockholders do. To avoid the dominance of the larger banks, since they are required to purchase shares in accordance with their size, the governing board of directors of each Federal Reserve Bank is chosen in the following way. Of the total of nine directors, only three may be bankers; three must represent borrowers such as businessmen or farmers; and three are selected as representatives of the general public by the Board of Governors of the Federal Reserve System, and cannot be connected with the operation of any bank. The first two categories of directors are elected by member banks, but the large banks can only elect one in each category; the middle-sized banks also elect one in each category, and the small banks do the same.

Member Banks. All national banks are required to be members of the Federal Reserve System. State banks are not compelled to join, but may do so if they can comply with certain requirements as to capital and reserves and quality of management. Of the 14,000 commercial banks in the country, less than half are member banks. However, the members include all the larger and more important banks, and their total deposits are more than four times those of nonmember banks.

The Board of Governors. The activities of the 12 District Federal Reserve Banks, are directed and coordinated by a Board of Governors of seven members. These are appointed by the President of the United States, serve 14-year terms to give them a degree of political independence, and may not be reappointed. Not more than one can come from a single Federal Reserve Bank District.

The Board of Governors of the Federal Reserve System has the power to raise, lower, or suspend member bank reserve requirements. It also has the authority to approve the interest rates that each of the 12 Federal Reserve Banks charges its commercial bank borrowers. And through its Open Market Committee it can require the Reserve Banks to buy or sell government securities. This gives the Board of Governors tremendous power to influence the amount of commercial bank lending and thus the total money supply. (The various ways in which the Federal Reserve can increase or decrease the amount of money available are summarized in Figure 7–2.) It can also set the maximum interest rates commercial banks can pay on time deposits.

FIGURE 7–2

Ways the Federal Reserve System Can Increase or Decrease the Money Supply

Words in boldface represent actions that increase the money supply. Words in parentheses represent actions that decrease the money supply.

Action	Result	Further Result
Buy (sell) U.S. government bonds	**Increases** (decreases) money in banks and increases (decreases) bank reserves	**Increases** (decreases) banks' ability to lend
Lower (raise) ratio of reserves banks must hold against deposits	Requires banks to hold **less** (more) cash or cash equivalents such as government bonds	**Increases** (decreases) banks' ability to lend
Encourage (discourage) member bank borrowing from Federal Reserve	**Increases** (decreases) member bank reserves, since deposits in the Federal Reserve Banks are counted as reserves	**Increases** (decreases) banks' ability to lend
Lower (raise) rate of interest banks must pay Federal Reserve Banks for loans or discounts	Makes borrowing from the Federal Reserve **less** (more) costly	**Increases** (decreases) banks' willingness to lend
Lower (raise) the percentage or "margin" that security purchasers must pay down to buy securities	Makes it possible for purchasers to buy **more** (fewer) securities on credit.	
Raise (lower) the maximum interest rates banks can pay on savings accounts	Makes it **easier** (more difficult) to get and hold savings	**Increases** (decreases) cash available for banks to use in making loans

The Board of Governors has the right to audit the books and operations of each of the 12 district banks. It also conducts research and publishes statistics on banking and money.

The Federal Open Market Committee.   Closely allied to the Board of Governors is the Federal Open Market Committee. It is composed of the Board of Governors plus five representatives from the 12 Federal Reserve Banks. This Committee has the power to *require* the Federal Reserve Banks to buy or sell government securities. When the Federal Reserve Banks buy securities, they create deposits of member commercial banks in the Reserve Banks; when they sell, they reduce these deposits. Since, for the most part, deposits in the Federal Reserve Banks are also reserves of the member banks, these actions tend to increase or reduce member bank reserves.

In this way, the Open Market Committee can influence the volume of business loans outstanding and, in doing so, the amount of money available to the public. What the Federal Reserve System really does by buying government securities is to add to the total money supply (cash and deposits). When it sells them it subtracts from the total money supply.

Borrowing from Federal Reserve Banks

As mentioned above, any member commercial bank may borrow from its District Federal Reserve Bank. The deposits in the Federal Reserve Banks resulting from such loans can become legal reserves against which the member bank may expand its volume of loans. The member bank borrows in two ways. It may sell certain of its notes receivable to the Federal Reserve Bank which will buy them at their value, less a discount to cover interest. This is called *rediscounting.* Or the member bank may borrow from the Reserve Bank like any individual borrowing from a bank, putting up notes, securities, or other valuable business paper as security. These loans are called *advances.*

Increasing or Decreasing the Money Supply

We can sum up what has been said above about the Federal Reserve System's powers to increase or decrease the money supply. If the Federal Reserve thinks we are heading into price inflation—when too many dollars are competing for the goods and services available—it can reduce the dollars in the hands of the public. It can do just the opposite when more dollars are needed. For example, if a business recession appears to be coming, the Federal Reserve can take several steps to increase the money supply: It can lower the reserve requirements of the commercial banks; it can buy government securities; and it can lower the rates at which it will purchase (rediscount) business loans sold to it by the commercial banks.

Check Clearing Services

An important service the Federal Reserve System does for its members is to handle the clearing of checks. When a merchant in Houston pays a bill to a manufacturer in Chicago and uses a check drawn on his Houston bank, there must be some way in which a Chicago bank—where the manufacturer deposits the check—can get its money. The Chicago bank may send it to the Chicago Federal Reserve Bank, which sends it to the Dallas Federal Reserve Bank, which charges it to the account of the Houston bank.

Since 90 percent of all business transactions are handled by checks, it can readily be seen that the process of clearing checks through different banks involves a large amount of paperwork. Much, but not all, clearing of checks is handled through the Federal Reserve Banks. Commercial banks in the same city will usually have their own clearing system. Some checks are sent from smaller banks to larger banks in which the smaller banks keep accounts, and the larger banks handle the collection. A simplified example of how a clearing house works is shown in Figure 7–3.

During the clearing process, with a very large volume of checks moving to and from the various banks, the amounts credited to a bank and charged to it tend to balance out. As a result, the actual net transfer of funds between banks tends to be a small percentage of the total value of all checks. And these transfers are to a great extent made by book transactions on the accounts of the banks involved.

Truth-in-Lending Regulation

Congress passed the Consumer Protection Act in 1968. This law requires all banks, loan companies, retailers, or other businesses selling on an installment basis to disclose to buyers the actual interest rate they are charging per year. For example, automobile finance companies formerly advertised that new cars would be financed on a 6 percent basis. Actually, they charged 6 percent per year on the total amount borrowed. But since the customer was paying off part of the loan each

FIGURE 7–3

How a Clearing House Works: A Typical Day's Clearances among Three Banks

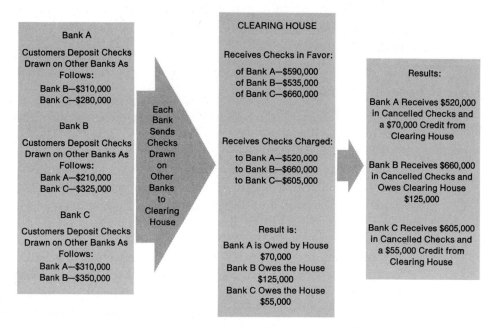

month, the average amount borrowed over a period of time was roughly half the original amount.[1] This meant that the interest rate was much higher than stated, usually amounting to around 11.33 percent per year. A store that formerly listed a charge account rate of 1.5 percent per month must now state it at 18 percent per year. Administration of this law, which took effect July 1, 1969, was placed under the Board of Governors of the Federal Reserve System.

The law, popularly known as the "truth-in-lending" bill, applies only to home mortgages, consumer loans, and time purchases up to $25,000, with a few minor exceptions such as credit purchases under $25. It does not apply to commercial or business transactions. What effect has this law had on the public's buying habits? Disclosure of the interest rates people are really paying does not seem to have had much effect on borrowers, especially on consumers who use charge accounts or buy on the installment plan. They think mostly of how large the monthly payments will be, and not of the interest percentage being charged.

---

[1] Note that, if an individual borrows $1,000 and pays $100 per month on the loan, plus interest, he really has for his use over ten months only a little more, on the average, than $500.

LEASING COMPANIES AND ARRANGEMENTS AS MEANS FOR FINANCING

Businesses and individuals often acquire fixed assets by leasing, or renting, them. People rent houses and apartments, and even furniture. Business firms rent stores, offices, factory buildings, and warehouses. For many years, railroads have leased cars and locomotives. In recent years it has become possible for a business to lease almost any important asset—machinery, typewriters, photocopiers, computers, and automobiles.

Specialized companies have grown up that lease assets to businesses. Insurance companies often purchase buildings and lease them back to the user, as do many individual investors. Airlines lease their planes with funds lent by banks and other financial companies. Special real estate development associations have been established to construct buildings and lease them to the users. Safeway Stores has financed most of its stores for four decades by such special lease arrangements; in 1973, it had long-term leases on 2,796 properties, requiring annual payments of more than $100 million.

Leasing Is Equivalent to Borrowing

While the business of leasing is not the same as banking, leasing does take the place of borrowing from banks. Moreover, much of the money used to buy and lease property comes from financial institutions.

The costs of a typical lease are, as would be expected, higher than the interest on loans. The lessor (the person or company making the lease) must charge the lessee (person or company renting the property under lease) more than interest. He must also receive profit for his risk and for arranging the lease, as well as payment for the depreciation of the item leased—the amount of depreciation depending on the period of the lease and the value of the property at the end of the lease. A truck, for example, leased for four years would carry a lower lease rate than one rented for two years.

Why Does a Company Lease?

A company leases buildings or equipment to avoid using its cash resources for buying them. By doing so, it will not have to resort to borrowing or selling shares of stock. Many companies, like Safeway Stores, take the position that their business is to produce and sell products or services, and that their funds should be used to expand these operations rather than for assets that can be leased. Also, lease costs are tax-deductible expenses, so that leasing may be cheaper than using stockholders' funds and figuring depreciation.

Another important consideration in leasing is that it often gives a company an opportunity to avoid long-term asset commitments. Many companies lease special machines for a few years and then turn them back to the lessor to lease to someone else. The leasing of computers has been popular, in part for financial reasons, but also because a company's computer needs may change, or new and more attractive models may appear.

Leasing is not without its drawbacks. Leasing normally costs more than borrowing money, and a company with adequate funds may find it preferable to purchase the assets, especially if it can charge off part of the costs against its income taxes as depreciation allowance. Leases also commit the company to fixed payments that can become a burden in time of difficulty. Moreover, as often happens with land and buildings, the value of the leased property may increase with the benefit going to the property owner rather than the lessee.

TYPICAL CREDIT INSTRUMENTS

When a company borrows funds, it may pledge some of its assets as security. The assets may be securities, accounts receivable, various rights to ownership (such as warehouse receipts showing that the borrower has certain goods in a warehouse, or bills of lading which show that the borrower has ownership of some goods being transported by a transportation company), inventory, and sometimes machinery and equipment. In fact, anything that is saleable may be pledged. For a farmer, the security may be livestock, grain, or farm implements.

Promissory Notes

A *promissory note*, usually called simply a "note," is a promise by the borrower (the "maker") to pay the lender (the "payee") a certain amount of money plus a specified amount of interest after a certain period of time, or on a specified date. Notes are commonly used credit instruments. A business borrowing from a bank customarily gives the bank such a note. Sellers of goods or services may accept such a note instead of cash. Individuals who borrow for personal needs usually give promissory notes to lenders.

A promissory note may be *negotiable*—that is, the payee can sell it to someone else who will then have the same claim against the borrower

FIGURE 7–4

Promissory Note

NOTE: INTEREST IN INSTALMENTS OR AT MATURITY

CHECK APPROPRIATE BLOCK
☐ INDIVIDUAL ☒ CORPORATION
☐ PARTNERSHIP ☐ ASSOCIATION

ACCOUNT (5)	CLASS (3)	LOAN (5)

$ 10,000.00   Los Angeles   , California, May 1   , 19 74

On April 30, 1975

for value received, the undersigned promises to pay in lawful money of the United States of America to the

BANK OF AMERICA
order of the NATIONAL TRUST AND SAVINGS ASSOCIATION at its Westwood   Branch the

principal sum of Ten Thousand and no/100 ------------------------------DOLLARS,

with interest in like lawful money from May 1, 1974 at the rate of 8 per cent per annum,

computed on the basis of a three hundred sixty (360) day year and actual days elapsed,

interest payable on November 1, 1974 and April 30, 1975.

If default be made in the payment when due of any part or instalment of interest, then the whole sum of principal and interest shall become immediately due and payable at the option of the holder of this note, without notice.

In the event of commencement of suit to enforce payment of this note, the undersigned agrees to pay such additional sum as attorney fees as the court may adjudge reasonable. This note binds each of the undersigned, if more than one, jointly and severally.

IN WITNESS WHEREOF, the undersigned has caused this note to be executed by its officers thereunto duly authorized and directed by a resolution of its Board of Directors duly passed and adopted by a majority of said Board at a meeting thereof duly called, noticed, and held.

(BORROWER SIGN HERE)

(BORROWER SIGN HERE)

(BORROWER SIGN HERE)

Jones Lumber Company   A Corporation
(BORROWER)
By _____ President
By _____ Secretary

Telephone No. 213-774-9126
Mail Address: 7562 Main Street
Los Angeles, California 90024

that the original payee had. Suppose a feed company takes a note from a farmer in payment for $5,000 of feed, to be paid in 120 days plus interest at 9 percent per year. The feed company, not wishing to have its money tied up so long, sells the note to its local bank, perhaps at a price less than $5,000 if the bank is not satisfied with the interest rate on the note. The farmer then pays the bank the $5,000 plus the 9 percent interest when the note is due. If the farmer fails to pay, the bank can ask the feed company to make good on the note. This is called selling the note *with recourse*.

The note described above carries interest that will be paid as an addition to the amount due. Thus 120 days later the farmer will pay $5,000 plus $150 in interest ($\frac{120}{360} \times .09 \times \$5,000$). Sometimes interest is paid on a *discount* basis. The borrower signs a note for $5,000 at 9 percent, but the interest is deducted from the loan and he receives $4,850. Since he will actually have the use of an amount smaller than the loan, his real interest rate is slightly higher than 9 percent, or approximately 9.3 percent. It can be seen why banks prefer a discount basis of making loans.

Drafts

Another common form of credit instrument is the *draft*. This is an order made in writing by one party (the "drawer") addressed to a second party (the "drawee") ordering the drawee to pay to a third party (the "payee") a certain sum of money. A draft may be distinguished from a promissory note in that it is an order to pay, while a note is a promise to pay. As can be seen, an ordinary bank check is a draft. If Richard Smith wants to pay his electric bill by check, he (the drawer) writes a check ordering his bank (the drawee) to pay the electric company (the payee) a sum of money.

In business dealings, drafts may be used when a selling company does not wish to extend credit and wants payment for goods before the buyer takes possession. This arrangement is customary in dealings with foreign customers. A manufacturer in the United States selling some machinery to a purchaser in Brazil may draw a draft requiring payment to his bank in Miami before the machinery can be loaded on a boat to Brazil.

A draft may be a *demand*, or *sight*, draft, meaning that it is payable whenever the payee presents it to the drawee. Or it may be a *time* draft, payable at a certain future date. A draft need not name a specific payee, but can be made out to the *bearer*. Then, anyone in possession of the draft is the legal payee. In the case of bank checks, we accomplish the same thing by making the check payable to "cash."

Acceptances

A special form of time draft is known as a *trade*, or *bank, acceptance*. It is drawn by a seller, sent to the drawee, and when he accepts it by signing his name on it as being binding on him, it becomes negotiable paper, that is, it can be bought and sold. **When accepted by a business firm, it is a** trade acceptance; **when accepted by a bank it is a** bank acceptance. **Acceptances are normally employed only in the sale and purchase of goods. When accepted by banks or companies with unquestioned credit rating, they are easily negotiable and even the Federal Reserve Banks will buy them on a discounted basis.**

Special Types of Checks

The kind of check most of us are familiar with is the one we draw on our own bank to pay bills. But sometimes the payee wants assurance

FIGURE 7–5
Sight Draft

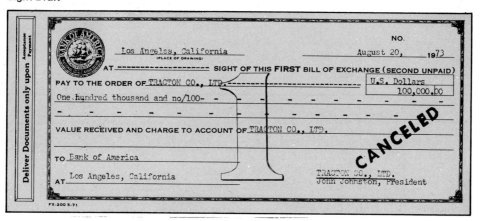

FIGURE 7–6
Time Draft

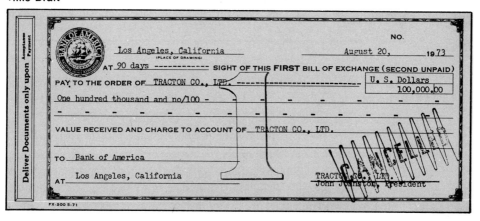

FIGURE 7–7

Bank Acceptance

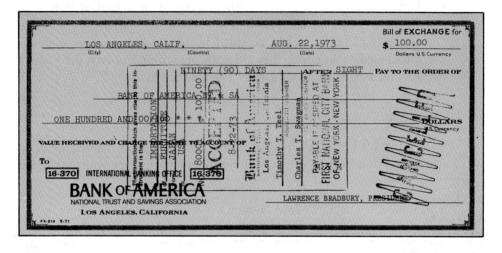

FIGURE 7–8

Certified Check

that the check is good before accepting it in payment. Sellers who do not know a purchaser, or who may not have confidence in his credit standing, may not be willing to accept an ordinary check.

To fill this need, bankers issue at a modest fee a *certified check* or a *cashier's check*. In the case of a certified check, the bank merely stamps an individual's or a company's check as "certified" and immediately deducts that amount from the issuer's account. This assures that the funds to cover the check are available. In the case of a cashier's check,

FIGURE 7–9

Cashier's Check

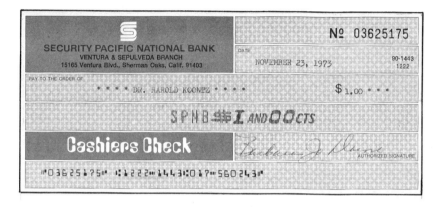

the bank itself writes the check payable to a specified payee and receives the money for it, or charges the person's account. Since the bank is a safe credit risk, the payee readily accepts the check, particularly if the bank is well known.

TYPICAL BANK LOAN AND INTEREST PROVISIONS

Most lending by commercial banks is done on a short-term basis to help finance accounts receivable, inventories, and other short-term operating needs.

Obtaining a Line of Credit

A company intending to borrow short-term funds goes to its bank and obtains a line of credit, that is, the right to borrow from time to time as needed up to a certain amount, whether $50 thousand or $50 million. If the company's financial standing is satisfactory—that is, if its earnings, quality of management, record of loan repayment, and other factors lead the bank to feel that the company is a good credit risk and can repay the loan—the credit will be granted, normally on an unsecured basis.

One of the evidences bankers want to see from any company is a forecast of the company's earnings, expected needs for cash, and the amount of cash it will have available from business operations in the future. From the point of view of a banker the best assurance that a loan can be repaid is that the company will have the necessary cash to repay it.

Revolving Credit

A bank may guarantee a company a line of credit over a period of months or years, usually at an interest rate equal to or above the current prime rate. It may charge a fee, such as ¼ percent of the amount of unused credit, to compensate for holding the funds available for the company.

Compensating Balances

In recent years banks have increasingly insisted that a borrower maintain in his deposit account a minimum balance, usually an amount equal to 15 percent of his loan. The banks' argument is that a borrower should also be a depositor. This thinly veiled argument is actually a means of charging a higher rate of interest. If a company borrows $100,000 from a bank at 10 percent interest, but is required by the bank to hold a deposit of $15,000, it has really only borrowed $85,000 and is therefore paying an interest rate of 11.8 percent.

Sometimes a businessman can induce his bank to waive the requirement of a compensating balance if it is eager to have his account. In effect, it will be offering him a lower rate of interest than it charges on its other accounts.

Some Loan Arrangements Carry Restrictions

When a company is small, or when a line of credit is regarded as large for a certain company, its promissory note and other lending arrangements may carry restrictions on the company's financial operations. The bank may, for example, require the company to maintain a current ratio (current assets to current liabilities) of not less than 1.75. It may limit the amount of dividends paid to stockholders. Or it may provide that the company cannot invest in capital expenditures, such as equipment or buildings, more than an amount equal to depreciation charges plus one half its annual earnings. It is also common for the agreement to prohibit additional borrowing from other sources without prior approval of the bank.

SUMMARY

Business operations would not be possible without the facilities and services of the banking system. Unlike most other countries in the world, the banking system in the United States is privately owned, although the government regulates and assists banks in various ways.

Banks are essential to business operations because they provide a place for safekeeping of cash, furnish facilities for handling checks or drafts, make loans to businesses and their customers, handle transactions in foreign currencies, take care of the registration and transfer of stocks and bonds, provide various trust services, and help in such matters as raising outside capital and determining the credit standing of customers.

The banks most important to business are the commercial banks. Other lending organizations are of significance to businesses, their customers, and others with whom they deal. These include savings banks, savings and loan associations, credit unions, life insurance companies, investment banks, commercial finance companies, factoring companies, sales finance companies, and consumer finance companies.

Commercial banks offer many services essential to business in addition to their primary function of accepting deposits and making loans. Acting together they also have the important ability to "create" money by lending far more than they have available as cash in their vaults or on deposit in other banks.

To assure that our banking system works well, the government regulates banks thoroughly in the interest of financial soundness, and assists them in various ways. A major kind of government assistance, especially for commercial banks and other saving and lending institutions, is deposit insurance. Under the present provisions, depositors with accounts up to $20,000 are guaranteed against loss in case a bank should fail.

Special assistance is also given by the Federal Reserve System. Through 12 District Federal Reserve Banks, privately owned but closely controlled by the government, funds are made available to commercial banks so that they can meet the legitimate needs of businesses for loans. The Board of Governors of the Federal Reserve System has the power to expand or contract the supply of money (including deposits) by buying or selling government bonds and business notes, setting reserve requirements for member commercial banks, and regulating interest rates. The Federal Reserve System also provides facilities for the clearing of checks, which are used in 90 percent of all business transactions.

Businesses can also borrow by leasing assets. Specialized companies lease assets of various kinds, from machinery and automobiles to airplanes. Leasing has certain advantages, particularly with assets such as buildings and expensive equipment like computers; it also frees company funds for other business operations. However, leasing normally costs more than direct borrowing, and often has other disadvantages.

Credit instruments used in business include promissory notes, drafts, acceptances, and special types of checks. Banks often require business borrowers to retain a percentage of their loans as deposits. These so-called "compensatory balances" have the effect of increasing the interest charged. A bank may also place restrictions on the borrower's business operations, such as requiring a minimum current ratio, limiting the dividends given to stockholders, or limiting the amount of money that can be invested in such capital expenditures in buildings and equipment.

KEY TERMS AND CONCEPTS

Commercial banks	Deposit Insurance
Demand deposits	Federal Reserve System
Time deposits	Board of Governors
Savings deposits	Open Market Committee
Certificates of deposit	Rediscounting
National banks	Advances
State banks	Clearing house
Savings banks	Leasing companies
Mutual banks	Promissory notes
Savings and loan associations	Negotiable notes
Credit unions	With recourse
Investment banks	Discount
Commercial finance companies	Demand drafts
Sales finance companies	Time or sight drafts
Factoring companies	Trade, or bank, acceptances
Consumer finance companies	Certified check
Prime rate	Cashier's check
Secured loans	Line of credit
Unsecured loans	Revolving credit
Collateral	Compensating balances

QUESTIONS FOR ANALYSIS AND DISCUSSION

1. Banks serve businesses in many more ways than giving them a place to deposit cash or lending them money. What are these ways and why and how might each of them be important to business?

2. Why are commercial banks of special importance to business?

3. In what ways are savings banks and savings and loan associations important to business? Could you say the same things about credit unions, commercial finance companies, factoring companies, or sales finance companies?

4. Life insurance companies are clearly beneficial to individuals. But they have become of increasing importance to businesses. Why?

5. Why would individuals and business firms be interested in making demand deposits with a commercial bank, since interest is not normally paid on these deposits?

6. If a company gets a short-term loan and must pay 2 percent over "prime," what does this mean? If a company is required to hold 15 percent of its loan as a "compensating balance," of what significance is this to the company?

7. Since a secured loan always has the pledge of valuable assets back of it as security, why wouldn't a bank insist on making only secured loans?

8. Commercial banks have a way of "creating" money. How do they do this? Does this seem to you to be somewhat tricky? Can you see how this ability to "create" money makes it possible for the Federal Reserve Board and the Open Market Committee to control the amount of money businesses and the public have?

9. Describe how the Federal Reserve System operates to help businesses when they need money for expansion. Also, in what ways does the Federal Reserve System regulate both companies and individuals? What do you believe would happen if we did not have a Federal Reserve System?

10. Why would a business firm want to use a leasing company to acquire buildings, stores, warehouses, machinery, or equipment. Why not merely borrow the money from bondholders or from a bank?

11. How would a company use the various credit instruments described in this book? Would every company use them all? Would you use any of them?

SUGGESTED READINGS

Campbell, C. D., and R. G. Campbell *An Introduction to Money and Banking.* New York: Holt, Rinehart & Winston, 1972.

Johnson, R. W. *Financial Management* (4th ed.). Boston: Allyn and Bacon, Inc., 1971, Chapters 12–14.

Kaufman, G. C. *Money, the Financial System, and the Economy.* Chicago: Rand McNally & Company, 1973, Chapters 4–7, 10–11.

Klise, E. S. *Money and Banking* (5th ed.). Cincinnati: South-Western Publishing Company, 1972.

Smith, H. M. *The Essentials of Money and Banking.* New York: Random House, 1968.

8

Raising Money: The Public Market

We have already mentioned several ways in which business firms raise money. A firm can raise some ownership money from its founders and their friends. It can obtain money from banks and lending organizations. It will generate its own funds out of profits and allowances for depreciation. But if a company is to grow, sooner or late it must obtain funds from the investing public. It may obtain them by selling ownership in the firm—that is, shares of stock. Or it may borrow from the public through the sale of bonds.

To obtain funds from public investors, it is almost essential that a business be a corporation. As we saw in Chapter 5, corporation stockholders have the advantage of limited liability. Many investors do not wish to take the risks of being an owner in a partnership; a corporation frees them from the risk of losing more than they invest. Also, it is difficult for companies that are not corporations to raise money through sale of bonds.

There are exceptions to every rule, of course—some fairly large companies have been able to grow and finance themselves without going to the public for funds. The U.S. Time Corporation, makers of "Timex" watches, has grown to sales of more than $200 million per year without public financing. Howard Hughes developed his billion-dollar empire without selling either stock or bonds to the public. He owned his Hughes Tool Company outright, and this company alone had sales of oil drilling bits and equipment well above $100 million per year. After he bought his controlling interest of more than 70 percent of the stock in Trans World Airlines, he did not permit that company to make sales of stock to the public as long as he controlled it although it did borrow large amounts from banks and insurance companies. He sold his controlling interest in the airline in 1965 for $541 million.

But such exceptions are few. Most companies must go to the public for funds, and most, as we shall see, wish to do so.

WHAT THE PUBLIC MARKET IS

When we speak of the public market for money, we are referring to the thousands of individual and other investors who buy and sell business corporation stocks and bonds and the channels through which the transactions are made. It is estimated that more than 31 million persons in the United States own one or more shares of corporation stock. The public market also includes the many institutional owners of securities: company, union, and other pension funds; insurance companies; investment trusts or "mutual funds," which invest money for millions of individuals; commercial and savings banks and loan companies; business firms that buy securities in other companies; government agencies that buy and sell various kinds of government bonds; investment banks that have inventories of securities for resale; brokerage firms that buy and sell securities for customers and often keep an inventory of securities on hand; universities and colleges, charitable organizations, churches, hospitals, and philanthropic establishments, with their billions of dollars of endowment; and nonprofit foundations like the Ford Foundation; and many other institutions which have reason to invest funds.

When it is considered that most citizens have some of their savings invested in one or more of these ways, we can see why the American business system is sometimes called "people's capitalism." But many people, such as those with pensions or life insurance, do not realize that they have funds invested in American business. Nearly 80 percent of all the business securities bought and sold from day to day in the United States are for the account of institutional investors.

THE IMPORTANCE OF PUBLIC MARKETS FOR BUSINESSES

The existence of a public market enabling individuals and financial organizations to invest their money has obvious importance to business firms that need money to finance their operations and growth. It would be impossible to have a privately owned American Telephone and Telegraph Company with its $70 billion in assets, most of which have been furnished by investors in bonds and stocks, without a large public market. Or the much smaller Cessna Aircraft Company with its stockholders' equity of $100 million. Even much smaller companies, making and selling a few million dollars of product, use the public market as a means of raising funds through the sale of stock.

The public market also serves other functions. It allows investors to sell their holdings as well as buy, and to do so without hunting for a buyer or seller. This very fact—the easy purchase and sale of securities—makes investors of all kinds willing to put their money in the public markets.

By offering ready purchasers and sellers, the public market enables investors and company managers to find out what their securities are worth. The small grocery store or machine shop owner without publicly held stock has no way of accurately knowing the value of his business. He may know approximately what his inventory and equipment are worth. But what is his business worth as a going operation? It is obviously worth what someone will pay for it, but who is that? Without a market on which stocks and bonds are regularly traded, no businessman has much of a basis on which to make such an appraisal. Individual holders of securities also need to know what their investments are worth. If a person wants to borrow from a bank, the bank may want to know the value of his property. If he dies, his executor will need to know its value in order to pay the taxes on his estate.

Moreover, the public market furnishes a means of appraising the quality of a company's operations. If its profit or growth performance is poor, its stock will not be in much demand, and the price of it will fall. When profit or growth performance is good or promises to be good, investors buy the company's stock and its price on the market goes up. When Litton Industries was growing fast and making increased profits each year, its common stock reached a price of $120 per share in the late 1960s, but when the company suffered losses its common stock fell to less than $7 per share in 1972 and to $4 in 1974.

INVESTMENT BANKERS: SELLERS OF NEW SECURITIES

Although they are called bankers, investment bankers do not perform any of the functions of commercial banks. They specialize in the marketing of new issues of stocks and bonds. They sell them to the general public or to pension funds, insurance companies, or other large investing institutions.

What these houses usually do is to "underwrite" a corporation's new security issue. Investment bankers agree with a corporation to market its securities by buying them and then selling them to the investing public. In other words, security houses guarantee the sale of a company's securities and deliver a check to it for these new securities. They make their profit by charging a commission, which may vary from 3 to 10 percent or more, of the proceeds of the sale.

Normally, investment banks know quite well that they can soon sell the stocks or bonds they purchase. The final agreement to underwrite is usually not signed until a day or two before the securities are put on the market. Occasionally an issue sells slowly and the investment bank may have to keep the securities in inventory for a period of time. In the slow bond market of 1973, the underwriters who guaranteed a sale of $200 million of Bell Telephone System bonds held over half the issue in inventory for a number of days before it was sold.

Sometimes, smaller underwriting houses take on the task of selling a corporation's securities on a "best efforts" basis. This means that the investment banker does not guarantee the sale of the issue of securities but only agrees to use its best efforts to sell them. From a company's point of view this is undesirable, both because it wants to be assured of getting the money and because its reputation among investors suffer if underwriters are unwilling to guarantee the sale of its securities. Larger investment bankers do not operate on this basis, and only the smaller and less known corporations are forced to resort to "best efforts" sales.

The contributions of investment bankers to business are obviously great. A business might be able to sell a few shares of stock to people known to it. But the distribution of any important volume of stock or bonds requires the services of specialists who have the offices and sales personnel to handle it. Their function is similar to that of a department store which buys goods from manufacturers and sells them to customers.

As a general rule, investment bankers cannot help very small companies because of the costs of marketing an issue of stock, and also because it is difficult to interest investors in such issues. Small investment bankers may market a stock issue as small as $200,000 to $300,000 for a promising company. But large investment banking houses, such as Merrill Lynch, Pierce, Fenner, and Smith, or Kuhn, Loeb and Company, find it difficult to be interested in issues of less than $2 or $3 million and prefer them larger. For one thing, a house with a large number of branch offices must have enough shares to distribute among them. For another thing the costs of arranging a small underwriting, other than salesmen's commissions, may be nearly as much as for a large one. Investment bankers are also concerned to get enough of a company's shares into the hands of enough people so that they can be readily bought and sold and a market price established.

BROKERAGE HOUSES: DEALERS IN EXISTING SECURITIES

Brokerage houses are firms that buy and sell securities on behalf of investors. They are essential to the working of the market. It would be impractical for a person who wanted to buy 100 shares of Chrysler Corporation common stock to go out and find someone who wanted to sell them to him; and it would be equally difficult for a person who wanted to sell 100 shares of Chrysler to find a buyer who would pay him the best possible price. It would be even more difficult than for a farmer having wheat to sell to find the flour mill wanting it, or for a person coming into a strange city to buy a house to find individual owners wanting to sell. In all these kinds of transactions we usually go through middlemen, called brokers.

Very large investors, such as pension funds, may deal directly with a large holder of securities, perhaps a mutual fund or another pension fund. But even in these cases, the services of a broker are customarily used to arrange the purchase or sale.

Almost all investment bankers also operate as brokers; they have special departments handling the buying and selling of issued securities. But not all brokerage firms engage in investment banking. Some brokerage houses, especially those with only one or a few offices, feel that they cannot do well with new issues; they are content to limit their business to buying and selling existing securities for their customers.

Brokerage firms make their money from commissions charged on purchases and sales. Since most of their buying and selling is handled through securities exchanges, as we shall see below, their commission rates are set by the exchanges and approved, informally at least, by the Securities and Exchange Commission of the federal government. Commissions on buying and selling securities are fairly modest, although they can become a major item of expense to investors who buy and sell large volumes of securities. For example, the commission on the purchase of 100 shares of Ford Motor Company stock, worth nearly $7,000, cost a buyer a commission of $65 in 1973, and the purchase of $5,000 of

Occidental Petroleum Corporation bonds carried a commission to the broker of only $25. However, as might be expected, smaller purchases or sales can cost, as a percent of the value of the transaction, much more. A purchase of $500 of stock can cost $25 or more.

SECURITY EXCHANGES AND MARKETS

Usually a broker buys and sells through a securities exchange or over-the-counter markets. As mentioned earlier, brokers, as well as investment bankers, may sometimes buy or sell directly from or to large investors. But most purchases and sales of issued securities are made through one of the established markets.

Security Exchanges

Security exchanges are merely places where exchange members buy and sell securities among themselves. Members are referred to as owning "seats" on the exchange. Brokerage firms have one or more partners or employees who are members of various organized exchanges. There are 16 organized exchanges in the United States, and many abroad. The general public is not permitted to handle security purchases and sales on the floors of these exchanges, only members of the exchange.

The best-known and largest exchange in this country is the New York Stock Exchange, which has 1,366 members. On a normal day, 10 to 20 million shares of stock worth from $600 million to $1.7 billion may be traded on the floor of this exchange, as well as $15 to $20 million of company bonds. The next largest stock exchange in the United States is the American Stock Exchange, also located in New York City. Its normal daily sales are 2 to 5 million shares with a value of from $50 to $150 million each day. Other exchanges are located in such cities as Chicago, Boston, Detroit, Los Angeles, and San Francisco.

Over-the-Counter Markets

Many stocks and bonds are not handled on any organized exchange, but by brokers and other dealers who trade in them like small retailers. These brokers buy stocks for inventory and sell them to other brokers who may need them for their customers. Individual brokers tend to specialize in certain stocks and carry an inventory of these stocks. In market language this is called "taking a position" in a stock or "making a market" for it.

Through an electronic information system, the thousands of brokers and dealers in the United States are able to know who has a supply of a particular stock, and what he will sell it for. In the same way, they can find a broker who will buy the stock. They charge a commission for their services, based on the difference between the buying and selling prices. Thus a dealer may offer to buy ("bid") Pabst Brewing Company stock at $47.25 and to sell it at $47.75 per share ("asked" price).

Many bank and insurance company stocks are handled exclusively on the over-the-counter market, as are state and municipal bonds. Stocks of many businesses are handled on both the over-the-counter market and the organized exchanges.

Listed and Unlisted Stocks

A "listed" stock is one that an organized exchange has put on the list of stocks that may be traded through its facilities. If a stock is only traded over-the-counter, it is called "unlisted."

The significance of this distinction is not as great as it once was. At one time many investors preferred listed stocks because a ready market for them existed and they could easily be bought or sold. It was simple to ascertain from the financial pages each market day how many shares had been sold and at what price. Some years ago, this was not true for many unlisted stocks and the investor had to call his broker who asked around to other brokers to find who was buying and selling the stock, and at what price. However, today, with a national system of electronically transmitted information, a broker anywhere in the country can find out what the bid and asked prices of most unlisted stocks are and who will buy or sell them by pushing a button. Also, the bid and asked prices for some 2,000 unlisted stocks are published each weekday in *The Wall Street Journal* and in many large city newspapers, along with the last price at which a security was bid on the preceding day.

Listing Requirements

Not every stock can be listed on an organized exchange, and many that can be listed on one exchange do not meet the requirements of another. The New York Stock Exchange requirements for listing are the strictest. A company had to meet the following qualifications in 1973:

1. Annual profits before federal income taxes must be at least $2.5 million for the previous year and at least $2 million in the two years preceding that.
2. A minimum of one million shares must be outstanding, of which at least 800,000 shares must be in the hands of a minimum of 2,000 public shareholders (that is, excluding shares owned by company insiders) of which number 1,700 must each own a minimum of 100 shares.
3. Shares in the hands of the public must have an aggregate market value of at least $16 million.
4. Net tangible assets must exceed liabilities by at least $16 million ("tangible assets" mean such assets as cash, receivables, inventory, and machinery, rather than such "intangible" assets as the value of a company's patents).

Obviously a company must be a fairly good-sized one before its stocks can be traded on the New York Stock Exchange. The members of this exchange have built a reputation of trading only in such stocks and believe this to be good business. Even so, the New York Stock Exchange has nearly 2,000 listed stocks.

Listing requirements on the American Stock Exchange are roughly one third to one fourth as high as on the New York Stock Exchange. The requirements are even lower on most other exchanges. But no organized exchange will list securities for which there are so few buyers and sellers as to make it uneconomical to provide facilities for their transactions.

For the small business, especially one that does not have many shares in the hands of the public, there are national and local over-the-counter markets where its stock can be traded if there is enough of it in the hands of the public to warrant a dealer's handling it.

Types of Exchange Members

Brokers do not all work in the same way. On the New York Stock Exchange, for example, the 1,366 members fall into one of the following four classes.

Commission Brokers. The largest group of members are the commission brokers, who maintain offices to take care of customers wanting to sell or buy. Some of these do not actually handle transactions on the floor but have their membership so that they can get a special commission rate from other members for handling purchases and sales. Some of these members have a single office, with nonmember broker partners in other cities, but many have branch offices throughout the country.

Registered Traders. These members, formerly called "floor traders" before special registration was required of them, buy and sell securities for their own accounts. They profit by their membership in that they do not have to pay commissions. Also, by being on the trading floor, they can often more readily see opportunities to make a profit.

Specialists. Some members are assigned to special locations in an exchange and specialize in a few stocks, buying and selling for their own account and executing orders for other brokers. By keeping a "book" on offers to sell and buy at various prices, as well as maintaining an inventory of stocks assigned to them, they are useful to other floor traders and brokers from whom they receive a commission.

Odd-Lot Dealers. It is customary on exchanges to have all trades made in 100-share lots, or "round lots" (although a very few high-priced or preferred shares are sold in lots of 10). Doing so reduces the paperwork and confusion involved in the handling of millions of shares of stock daily. In order to serve a customer who may not wish to buy or sell in 100-share lots—who may wish to buy 1, 10, or 50 shares— some members of the exchange specialize in handling smaller orders or "odd lots." These dealers buy and sell on the exchange in 100-share lots, and then "retail" smaller lots to brokers who need them for their customers. For this service an odd-lot dealer receives a special commission, normally varying from 12½¢ to 25¢ per share, depending on the price of the stock.

HOW EXCHANGES OPERATE

A security exchange, usually called a stock exchange, provides the facilities where stocks and bonds are bought and sold. The exchange itself does not buy or sell. Only the members of the exchange do the actual trading in securities. As noted above, each exchange allows its members, when trading on the floor, to buy and sell only the securities listed on the exchange.

Exchanges are organized as either corporations or voluntary associations, much like a partnership. A member owns a "seat" and may sell it, with a buyer subject to the approval of the exchange. An exchange is run by a board of governors elected by the members. The board elects the president and other operating officers of the exchange. The expenses of running an exchange are covered by dues or assessments from the members, much like any private club.

How Stocks and Bonds Are Quoted

Before discussing the actual operation of an exchange, it will be useful to know how stock and bond prices are quoted. Stocks are quoted in "points" which are the equivalent of dollars, except that parts of dollars are given in fractions rather than in decimals. The fractions are eighths, quarters, and halves. Thus quotations of 12⅝ and 46¼ mean $12.625 and $46.25 per share.

Bonds are quoted in points, in intervals of eighths, except for government bonds which are quoted in intervals of thirty-seconds of a point. Bonds are quoted on the basis of 100, regardless of whether the denomination of a bond is $500, $1,000, or $5,000. A quotation of 96½ for a $1,000 bond means that its cost to a buyer (before commission) is $965. A $500 bond at the same quotation sells for $482.50 and a $5,000 bond for $4,825. Government bonds are quoted differently: if a quotation reads 98.23, it means 98²³⁄₃₂ or $987.1875 in the case of a $1,000 bond.

How Trades Are Handled

Let us suppose that Richard Farr of Los Angeles decides to buy 100 shares of American Air Lines common stock. He calls his local broker in Los Angeles and asks what American is quoted at. The broker presses a button and the electronic display on his desk tells him it is 12 bid, 12¼ asked. Mr. Farr tells his broker to go ahead and buy at the market, in other words at the best price possible. The broker immediately teletypes the order to the firm's member partner on the floor of the New York Stock Exchange. The partner goes to the post in the exchange where American is traded, since all of the stocks traded on the exchange are assigned to various locations or "posts." He asks the specialist handling this stock, "How is American?" The specialist responds "12 at 12¼". This means that the specialist has bids to buy at 12 and offers to sell at 12¼. The broker representing Mr. Farr could readily buy at 12¼, but because he is required by exchange rules to try to buy for his customer at the lowest possible price, and knowing that bids are already in at 12, the broker will first bid 12⅛. The specialist, or another broker at the post trying to sell for someone, may not be willing to sell at this price. If the broker representing Mr. Farr does not get an offer to sell, he then bids 12¼. At this point the specialist or another broker with a sell order in his hand shouts "take it at 12¼." With this, the buying and selling traders each make a notation on a piece of paper, the broker representing Mr. Farr teletypes his Los Angeles Office, and the Los Angeles broker notifies Mr. Farr of his purchase.

The same process takes place in the selling of a security. In that instance the broker representing the seller will naturally try to get the highest price possible.

Sales and purchases of stocks and bonds worth many millions of dollars are handled each day on the floor of the exchange as informally as this; without written contracts, based on an oral agreement of the deal on the floor and merely by the jotting down of the sale on a small piece of paper by each trader. This is one reason why only members under strict control of the exchange are allowed to trade on the floor.

It should be noted in the example given above that Mr. Farr was willing to buy at the market. This is called a "market" order. Had he felt that American Airlines might go down, or if trading was brisk and he believed that the price might go up by the time his order was executed on the floor and he did not want to pay more than $12 per share, he might have told his broker in Los Angeles to buy at 12 or lower. This is called a "limited" order and will be handled by the trader on the floor that way.

Suppose, however, that Mr. Farr is going on vacation and wants to be sure of selling his 100 shares of American Airlines, which has now risen to 14. Fearing that the market price may fall while he is away, he puts in an order to sell at 13. This is called a "stop" order and is executed as soon as the market price reaches 13. A "stop" is used most often when a person has a stock which he expects to go up, but does not want to lose too much if it should go down. His stop order becomes a market order whenever the stock falls to that price.

The Ticker Tape

Immediately after a transaction is made on the floor of the exchange, a piece of paper is put on a conveyor and operators record it on a tape which is electronically transmitted to a large screen on the floor of the exchange and to brokerage offices all over the country in a running series of trades. Each stock is given a symbol. American Airlines is AMR, United States Steel is X, American Telephone and Telegraph Corporation is T, Bendix Corporation is BX, General Motors is GM, and so on.

Since sales of stock are in 100-share lots, smaller numbers of shares being sold only through odd-lot dealers, the number of shares shown on the tape is in hundreds. For 200 shares, a "2" and an "s" are shown before the price. If a transaction is for a thousand or more shares, the actual figure is shown. If sales are common stock, no designation is indicated, if preferred stock a "pf" precedes the number.

A typical segment of tape showing five transactions is displayed in Figure 8–1.

FIGURE 8–1

Segment of Ticker Tape

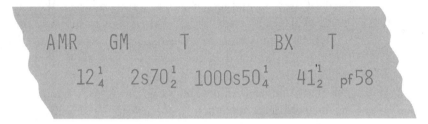

This, of course means that in the few seconds this part of the tape passes by:

100 shares of American Airlines common traded at 12¼.
200 shares of General Motors common traded at 70½.
1,000 shares of American Telephone and Telegraph common traded at 50¼.
100 shares of Bendix Corporation common traded at 41½.
100 shares of American Telephone and Telegraph preferred traded at 58.

Tapes are projected on wall displays in most brokerage offices for view by anyone who wishes to come in and watch. Most firms also have electronic desk displays linked to a computer memory system. This provides instant access to the prices of latest trades on all listed stocks, as well as current bid and asked prices on both listed and over-the-counter stocks. Instead of waiting for the tape to provide information on a particular stock, one merely punches in the symbol on the keyboard and the latest information flashes on the screen.

Margin Trading

Many purchasers of securities buy "on margin," that is, by borrowing from the broker a portion of the purchase price of a stock. If Mr. Farr has a margin account with his broker, he can buy the 100 shares of American Airlines at 12¼ by putting in, say, $650 in cash and borrowing the rest. This enables him to buy more shares of stock with the same amount of money than he could otherwise.

If the stock goes up in price, he makes money because he owns more shares. If it goes down, of course, he loses more. Because the broker in turn borrows from a bank on the security of the stock purchased by his customer, when the market price drops near to this amount borrowed he must ask his customer for more cash or sell out the shares to cover his loan.

At one time there was considerable abuse of margin trading. When customers were allowed in the 1920s to buy on margins of 10 or 20 percent of the value of the stock, profits piled up fast so long as prices rose. But when prices went down and the value of the stock got close to the loan made on it, the purchasers without adequate funds were sold out by their brokers. A large number of buyers were on thin margins in 1929. The tremendous volume of forced selling brought on when prices fell was a powerful factor in the stock market crash of that year.

Because of the danger of distress selling, and the fact that excessive borrowing tends to inflate stock prices, the Board of Governors of the Federal Reserve System has been given power to set minimum margins. Usually these are 50 percent, but in years of strong credit controls they have gone as high as 100 percent, meaning that people could not buy on margin at all.

Short Selling

Traders in stocks do not have to wait for prices to rise in order to make profits. They can also make money when prices are falling, by "selling short." A person who has an established account and credit rating with a broker can sell a stock he does not own. If he feels that General Electric stock, for example, will go down he may sell 200 shares at, say, 67. If the stock goes down to 57, he then buys 200 shares ("covers") and makes a profit of $2,000 less commissions. But if the stock goes up to 77 and stays there, he takes a loss of $2,000 plus commissions.

A person sells a stock he does not have by asking his broker to borrow the shares and sell them for him. Since many stock purchasers do not take delivery of their certificates when they buy but keep them deposited with a broker, and since many brokers also have an inventory of stock of their own for sale to customers, it is easy to borrow stock.

Short selling sounds like gambling, and sometimes it is. But buyers sometimes bid up a company's stock beyond reasonable levels, and

James J. Ling

James J. Ling, an innovative financial wizard and industrial empire builder, was born in 1922 in Hugo, Oklahoma, son of a railroad fireman. His mother died when he was 11, and he was sent to a Catholic boarding school. He dropped out of school after a few years and roamed around the country working at odd jobs. He married at 17, and when he was 19 he settled in Dallas as an assistant to an electrical contractor. He also worked evenings at an aircraft plant.

He took a correspondence course to qualify as a journeyman electrician. In 1944 he enlisted in the Navy, went to a naval electrical school, and worked at stringing power lines and recovering electrical equipment from destroyed ships. He returned to Dallas after his discharge in 1946 and set up a small electrical con-

tracting firm with $2,000 in capital he had raised by selling his home. In the beginning, the Ling Electric Company fixed doorbells, installed wall sockets, and wired new houses. But he soon turned to bidding on larger industrial jobs. His annual volume of business grew from $70,000 his first year to more than $1.5 million in 1955.

In 1955 Ling incorporated the company and obtained authorization to issue 800,000 shares of capital stock. Keeping half the shares for himself, he and three friends went out to sell the rest. In three months they had sold 400,000 shares, bringing in $738,000 in new capital. By 1960, according to Ling, the initial investment in the corporation had increased to six times its original value.

Ling then began to expand through acquisitions and mergers. He picked up a California vibration equipment manufacturer in financial difficulties. By 1958 gross revenues had reached $6.9 million, 60 percent of which was from the company's manufacturing activities. He then purchased a hi-fi sound equipment company, and in 1960 merged with Temco Electronic and Missiles Company, a defense contractor. His next goal was to get control of Chance-Vought, Inc., an aerospace firm, which he accomplished in 1961 after a bitter fight with that company's board. He chopped Chance-Vought's management roster from 700 to 166 over the next two years, and dumped its unprofitable side activities. He became chairman and chief executive officer of Ling-Temco-Vought in 1963.

In 1964 Ling instituted what he called Project Redeployment and separated the company's divisions into three subsidiaries, with 10 to 25 percent of each firm's stock being offered to the public. The next year he acquired the Okonite Company from

short selling can have a stabilizing effect on the market by bringing in more sellers.

BUYING SECURITIES FOR INVESTMENT

Anyone entering the stock market should first decide whether he wants to be an investor or a speculator. An investor is one who buys a

Kennecott Copper. In 1966 Okonite, operating as a fourth subsidiary, earned more than it had in all of the previous six years. *Fortune* magazine cited Ling-Temco-Vought as the fastest growing company in the nation for the decade 1955–65.

Ling scored again in a deal that he called Project Touchdown, in which he acquired Wilson & Company, meat packers, sporting goods, and chemical manufacturers. He estimated that $80 million would be necessary to buy control of Wilson. Because funds were tight in this country, he borrowed $50 million from European sources and the rest from non-bank lenders in this country. He then divided up Wilson into three smaller companies organized by product line—immediately nicknamed by Wall Street "Meatball" (meat processing), "Golfball" (sporting goods), and "Goofball" (pharmaceuticals). The Wilson debt was reduced through the sale of stock in the new subsidiaries. This practice of turning divisions into subsidiaries and selling their stock to the public was to bring difficulties for the parent corporation later.

In 1968 the Great American Corporation, a banking, insurance, and car rental holding company which also owned a majority interest in Braniff Airways, was brought into the LTV system. Later that year Ling made a bid for Allis-Chalmers, but failed because of opposition from that firm's management. He then acquired control of Jones & Laughlin Steel Company, the nation's sixth largest steel producer.

These acquisitions rocketed the company from 204th place among the country's top 500 industrial corporations in 1965 to 14th in 1968. Sales increased from $336 million to $2.8 billion in this three-year span.

In 1969 the Justice Department's antitrust division filed suit to force LTV to divest itself of control of Jones and Laughlin. In 1970 the Department offered an alternative—to sell Okonite and Braniff—which was accepted. But LTV's profits and stocks fell badly, and the firm's creditors got control of the board of directors and forced Ling to step down from chairman to president. After a new chief executive officer was appointed in July 1970, Ling left the company, although he was still the largest single shareholder.

In 1972 he formed an investment firm, the Omega-Alpha Corporation to try to build up another large company through buying control of sick companies, trying to make them profitable, selling some of their shares to the public to raise cash not only to pay for them but also to buy other companies. As a matter of fact, Ling's Omega-Alpha Corporation reached sales of $375 million by 1973. However, Ling's once highly regarded financial wizardry failed him when the companies acquired suffered huge losses and Omega-Alpha shares dropped from $6.50 to 35 cents.

Having also financed much of its growth through borrowing, Omega-Alpha found itself unable to repay its loans in 1974, and was forced to seek refuge under Chapter 11 of the federal Bankruptcy Act. Under this chapter a company is protected, for a time, against creditors' claims while it tries to work out a plan to pay its debts.

Ling's experience in LTV and Omega-Alpha demonstrates that an imaginative entrepreneur can reach the public market and that loans, once easy to get, can become a real source of weakness. It shows that a company built on debt and selling securities to the public market can only succeed if it makes good earnings. But, unless a company performs, it can be in real trouble.

stock or bond for long-term purposes rather than to take advantage of day-to-day or hour-to-hour changes. It is with the investor that we shall be concerned in what follows. An investor may have several objectives. His first concern may be with the safety of his investment, that is, with his "principal." Or he may be seeking income from his investment, either in interest or in dividends. Or he may hope to see the value of his investment increase. While it might be said that all three objectives are desirable, it is not practicable to achieve them all to the maximum extent at the same time.

Safety of Principal

The safest kind of investment, in terms of insuring against the loss of actual dollars of principal, is an account in a savings bank. These usually pay a lower interest rate than can be obtained on many bonds and industrial stocks. A high degree of safety of principal also exists in federal government bonds, at least if an investor is willing to keep them until the date they are due to be repaid. These investments assure the safety of the dollars put into them but not, of course, of the purchasing power of the dollars.

It is important to realize that even high grade bonds do not assure that the investor can get his original investment out at any time. If bonds carry a low interest rate, and the market rate of interest rises, the bonds will sell below their stated value. The market value of a bond is determined by a combination of the interest rate it carries, the market rate of interest, and the date it will be redeemed. In other words, investors pay for what a bond will "yield" them in interest plus payments made when the bonds are expected to be redeemed.

For example, in mid-1973 one issue of federal government bonds with an interest rate of 4 percent sold at just slightly under 100, while another government bond issue with a 4½ percent rate sold at 70. The difference was that the bond selling at just under its original price was to be paid off at face value in a few months, and the 4½ percent bond would not be redeemed until 1988. The actual yields (what the investor would be earning, taking into account interest and the difference between the present price and the redemption price) of these two bond issues were almost the same, with the 4 percent bond yielding 6.7 percent over the few months to maturity and the 4½ percent bond yielding 7 percent. It is important to note that the actual yields of the bonds were well above the interest rates at which they had been issued, because the market rate of interest had risen. The prices at which the bonds were selling reflected this fact.

To see why a bond may sell at a considerable discount, let us take the case of a United States Steel Corporation bond issued at an interest rate of 4⅝ percent. In the middle of 1974 this bond, which had a face value of $1,000, was selling for $635. It was due to be paid in 1996. At the same time similar high-grade bonds selling at face value paid 7½ to 8½ percent interest. The $635 price for the United States

Steel reflected two factors: (1) the fact that the going interest rate for similar bonds was much higher than 4⅝ percent, and (2) that an investment of $635 paying $46.25 per year would represent an annual return of 7.3 percent. Since the person who buys the bond in 1974 and holds it can look forward to receiving $1,000 in repayment in 1996 for his $635 investment, this gain has to be added to the interest rate of the bond. Allowing for the fact that he has to wait for 22 years for the extra $265, the actual amount this bond will yield an investor who holds it to maturity in 1996 is 8.25 percent per year.

If this bond had been due to be paid off in 1976, its price in 1974 would have been much higher because the investor could look forward to getting $1,000 for the bond in two years. In that case, if the bond were to yield 8.25 percent, it would have to sell at approximately $930.

The effect of dates of redemption ("maturity" dates), shown by the prices of two Union Pacific Railroad Company bonds in 1974. Both paid around 2¾ percent interest on their face value. But the one due to be paid in 1976 sold at $910 for a $1,000 bond and the other, due in 1991, sold at $490.

A bond can, of course, sell for a premium above its face value, if the interest rate on the bond is above the going market rate. Thus in 1973 an RCA bond paying 9¼ percent of its face value was selling at 109½, or $1,090 for a $1,000 bond.

With lower grade bonds the difference between current price and face value can be considerable. And when a company goes into bankruptcy, the price may plummet. Many Pennsylvania-Central Railroad bonds sold in 1973 at 12, meaning that an investor who bought these bonds for $1,000 several years earlier could only get $120 in 1973.

Annual Return

Some investors buy with a view to getting the highest annual return that they can with a reasonable degree of safety. In 1974 there were many good bonds and stocks on which an investor could earn 9 percent and more. Several issues of American Telephone and Telegraph Company bonds yielded this amount, and even AT&T's stock was yielding 7 percent.

As a general rule, bond yields tend to be higher than dividend yields on good stocks. This is because investors in stocks usually expect to gain by an increase in the price of stock as a company's profits increase, or the market improves, and will take a lower dividend yield.

Growth of Investment

A major objective of many investors is to put their money in something that will increase in value. They look for a "growth" stock or for a bond that is convertible, at the owner's option, into common stock. This kind of investor is not as interested in the size of the dividends a stock pays as in what the company earns and whether its earnings are likely to increase. In fact, the stocks of some companies have commanded a high price even though no cash dividends had been paid. As noted earlier, Litton Industries, for example, has never paid a cash dividend, but its stock reached a price at one time of $120. Even though the price dropped precipitously thereafter, the drop was caused not so much by the lack of dividends but by company losses and investor concern over future earnings.

Some companies have had a remarkable increase in profits over the years, with the result that their stock prices have risen considerably. If an investor had put $1,000 in International Business Machines Company stock in 1945 and held on to it, it would have been worth over $100,000 in 1972. This is an exceptional case, but there are many industrial stocks in which an investment of $1,000 in 1945 have appreciated to more than $10,000 in 1972.

Sound and fast-growing stocks tend to have a high "P/E" or price/earnings ratio, meaning that the market price per share divided by annual earnings per share tends to be high. Even in the depressed stock market of 1973, International Business Machines sold at $313 per share when its annual earnings were around $9.50—a price/earnings ratio of 33. Walt Disney Productions stock sold at $90 per share with earnings of less than $2, or a P/E ratio of 54. The stocks of drug manufacturing companies, with their high earnings and growth, were still selling at high prices in 1973. Eli Lilly, for example, sold at $88 per share in August, 1973, when earnings were a little over $2.10 per share, or at 40 times earnings. Needless to say, in more optimistic markets like that existing between 1967 and 1971, P/E ratios for such stocks were much higher.

In some years P/E ratios of some prosperous and well managed companies tend to be low. Ford Motor Company, for example, in its very prosperous year of 1973, was selling at a P/E ratio of 5, and even General Motors stock dropped to a P/E below 7. These unusually low ratios apparently reflected, in addition to general investor pessimism in 1973, concern with such matters as the gasoline shortage and the polution problem, and the effect these would have on future profits.

Company Performance, the Investor, and the Market

The price/earnings ratio reflects the existence of a common interest between a company and its investors. Investors in stocks, particularly common stocks, incur a risk when they put their money in a company. If the company goes bankrupt, they may lose their entire investment. If the company succeeds, they stand to gain both through cash dividends and through appreciation in the value of their shares. A stockholder thus has a right to expect payment both for the use of his money and for the risk he takes.

The managers of a company will want to secure the best possible return on the money invested by the owners. The rate of return on equity (percentage of earnings after taxes to stockholders' equity) is their measure of a company's profitability. The stock market P/E ratio is an assessment by investors of what they believe a company's earnings are worth at a certain time. If the P/E ratio is high relative to other stocks, it is a sign that investors believe in the solidity of the company and in the likelihood that its earnings will increase in the future. If the P/E ratio is low, the opposite beliefs prevail.

Thus the rate of return on equity and the price to earnings ratio are two sides of the same coin. What is good for a company is also good for a company's stock values. Stock values do not stay high for long without company profit performance, since investors normally do not put their money in a company that does not use it well. Such a company will decline or fail, not only from lack of profits but also from lack of capital with which to expand.

The Problem of Balancing Objectives

Every company interested in raising money by the sale of its stock must be concerned with investors and their objectives. Every investor must balance one objective against another. For younger people, the primary objective is growth, with a fair degree of security of principal. No investor can overlook the problem of inflation. As a matter of fact one of the authors put money into government bonds between 1938 and 1944 with plans to buy a house, but this was not enough to make an adequate down payment on a home in 1950, because of price rises during and after the war. For older people who have to be concerned with living on earnings from their investments, growth is of little importance; their current yield on stocks or bonds is what is important to them. No investor, of course, can overlook the danger of inflation; the purchasing power of his money may melt away if he puts it into a savings account or into long-term bonds.

Many people try to get all they can of everything—safety, earnings, and growth. Sometimes investment in a high-grade industrial stock of a good company in a growing industry accomplishes much of this. Sometimes a convertible bond will serve. But there is always a risk in going for all three objectives at once, and no investor can expect to maximize all three.

Perhaps the best course is to invest in companies that are well managed, particularly if they are in an industry that is likely to expand. Past earnings are an important criterion, but the best indicator is the quality of management. The better a company's management is, the more assurance an investor has that it will make the right decisions for the future. Part Four of this book attempts to give the reader some understanding of how businesses are managed, and what is necessary for good management.

SPECULATING IN SECURITIES

Some people like to speculate in stocks and bonds. Their primary concern is whether they can make money on the short-term price movements of securities. Often they try to enlarge their possibility of gain by buying on margin, as described above. This increases the amount of their loss if they guess wrong.

Since prices on the various public markets are always moving up and down as demand and supply varies, a speculator can make handsome profits in these changes *if* he picks the right security at the right price at the right time. To be a successful speculator, however, requires exceptional knowledge and skill. The speculator must be able to analyze and anticipate changes in investor attitudes. He must be able to pick the security that shows clear evidence of being undervalued or overvalued, ordinarily be satisfied with small profits, and be willing to take his losses when he guesses wrong. This is not a game for anyone with little cash who cannot risk losing, or who does not have the time and skill to study markets and individual securities carefully. Even persons exercising care and skill can get caught in "bear" markets—when prices of most stocks drop—while the most ordinary speculators may reap large profits in a "bull" market—when prices of almost all stocks go up.

REGULATION OF SECURITIES TRANSACTIONS

The issuance of new securities and their trading on the public market are carefully regulated. The history of stock swindles, market manipulations, deception, and the use by company insiders of information to make a profit for themselves or to mislead public investors, led to this regulation. It was first undertaken by the states, but really effective regulation did not come until the federal government stepped into the field in 1933 and 1934.

State Regulations

State laws, starting with legislation in Kansas in 1911 but now existing in every state except Nevada, are generally referred to as "blue sky" laws. They are called this because they deal almost exclusively with the issuance of new securities, and are aimed at preventing the sale of stocks or bonds that have nothing but "blue sky" back of them.

In general, state laws are designed to ensure that when a stock or bond is issued the issuing company sells something of value and gets something of value in return, whether money or other property. In other words, their purpose is to assure that the sale is not fraudulent. The laws cannot and do not attempt to guarantee that the stock is a "good buy." State laws also usually provide for registration of brokers and dealers with a view to assuring that only persons of integrity, competence, and good reputation are allowed to enter the business.

Federal Regulation of Securities

Because state laws varied and states could not reach interstate sales of securities, the federal government stepped into the field with the Securities Act of 1933 and with certain provisions of the Securities Exchange Act of 1934. These laws, so far as the issuance of new securities is concerned, have as their purpose to assure that full and adequate information is made available to the public concerning an issuing company and its securities. A similar requirement exists for securities traded on the stock exchanges and on the over-the-counter markets.

Certain securities are exempted from the federal law, such as government bonds, securities of such highly regulated companies as banks and railroads, and securities offered to a few private investors rather than to the public generally. However, the laws are vigorous in their application to most securities. A company's officers and directors, its auditors and underwriters, and any experts on whose information the company relies are made liable for misleading or inadequate information. They can be punished by fines or imprisonment, and are liable for any loss an investor can claim as a result of inadequate information.

Under the Securities Exchange Act of 1934 and its various amendments, essentially the same kind of information requirement is made for securities traded on exchanges and the over-the-counter market. It requires periodic filing of information with the Securities and Exchange Commission so that the public may be informed on a company's stocks and bonds and on company operations.

These regulations are designed only to be sure that the truth is told about a company and its securities. They cannot and do not keep an investor from making a poor investment. In instances of fraud, however, the federal as well as the state governments can act.

Regulation of Securities Trading

A number of trading practices are also regulated. The Securities Exchange Act of 1934 gives the Board of Governors of the Federal Reserve System authority to regulate margin trading by setting a minimum percentage that a security purchaser must put up in cash. Company officers, directors, and anyone else owning more than 10 percent of a company's stock are regarded as "insiders" and must file a report monthly with the Securities and Exchange Commission if they have bought or sold any of the company's stock. Any profit such an insider makes by buying and selling, or selling and buying, his company's stock within six months can be recovered if a stockholder or the company sues, and must be paid over to the company, on the assumption that the person traded on the basis of inside information. Insiders are not permitted to sell their company's stock "short." Manipulation of a stock through buying and selling at the same time to create an appearance of market interest is also forbidden.

In addition, the government has power over the operations of all stock exchanges and the over-the-counter market. Traders on them must be registered. While the authority of the government is extensive over all kinds of exchange practices, the Securities and Exchange Commission has largely allowed the exchanges to regulate themselves, but, given the broad power of the Commission, over exchange practices, the regulations tend to be in accordance with its wishes.

READING THE FINANCIAL NEWS

Just as a businessman needs to know some basic accounting in order to keep score within his business, so must he, as well as the thousands of investors, need to know the score with respect to trading in stocks and bonds. We have discussed the nature of stocks and bonds in Chapter 5, and the way their prices are quoted earlier in this chapter. With this background, we should find it easy to read the market pages of a newspaper.

Stocks

A portion of a daily report on stock transactions is shown in Figure 8–2. Reading the columns from left to right, we obtain the following information.

—1973— High Low	The highest and the lowest prices paid for this stock in 1973 through August 1.
Stock Div.	The name of the company stock in abbreviated form with the annual rate of dividend paid, based on the latest quarterly dividend. An "a" after this figure indicates that an extra dividend has been paid. A "b" indicates that a regular cash dividend has been paid plus an extra dividend in stock. Other letters have special meanings that can be ascertained by looking at the notes at the bottom of the financial page.
P-E Ratio	The price/earnings ratio of the stock. No numbers are given for preferred stock because their dividends come before those of common stock and a number would be meaningless. Also, no number is given where earnings do not exist.
Sales 100s	The volume of sales in the stock that day, expressed in hundreds of shares.
High	The highest price at which the stock sold that day.
Low	The lowest price at which the stock sold that day.
Close	The price at which the stock sold on its last sale of the day.
Net Chg.	The net change in price at close from that of the preceding trading day.

FIGURE 8–2

Portion of Financial Page Showing a Typical Day's Stock Sales and Quotations

New York Stock Exchange Transactions

Wednesday, August 1, 1973

A-B-C

—1973— High	—1973— Low	Stock Div.	P-E Ratio	Sales 100s	High	Low	Close	Net Chg.
80⅞	61	AbbtLb 1.20	22	26	71⅜	70¾	70¾	– ⅞
49¾	40½	ACF Ind2.40	11	12	48⅛	48	48	– ⅛
17⅛	12¼	AcmeClv .88	10	6	14½	14⅜	14⅜	....
26	16½	AcmeMkt 1	10	12	21	20½	20½	– ½
14¾	12	AdmE 1.15e	..	1	12⅞	12⅞	12⅞	....
8½	5½	Ad Millis .20	9	6	7	6⅞	6⅞	.....
34	11½	Addrsso .60	7	123	14¾	14¼	14½	..
18	7¼	Admiral	5	91	12¼	11⅜	11⅜	– ⅝
13¾	12¾	Advan Inv	.	51	12⅞	12⅝	12⅝	– ¼
76¾	57½	AetnLf 1.76a	10	276	72	71	71	– 2
31⅛	11½	Ahman .10e	6	60	13⅞	13⅝	13⅝	– ⅜
9	3⅞	Aileen Inc	17	16	5⅜	5¼	5⅜	+ ⅛
45¾	37	AirProd .20	26	335	44	43½	43½	– ¾
18¼	10¾	Airco .80	9	46	12⅜	12	12⅛	– ¼
3⅝	2	AJ Industris	7	23	2⅜	2¼	2¼	..
31¼	22⅜	Akzona 1.10	10	3	25¾	25¾	25¾	– ¼
17½	15	Ala Gas 1.18	6	43	15⅞	15	15⅜	– ½
109	100	AlaP pf8.28	...	z60	100	100	100	..
37⅞	24⅜	Alaska Intrs	22	73	30¾	30	30⅜	+ ⅛
29¼	9¼	AlbertoC .35	7	132	9¾	9⅛	9¾	..
17⅜	10½	Albtsn .36a	10	22	13¼	13	13¼	+ ⅛
33⅛	22⅞	AlcanAlu 1	16	x541	32½	31¾	32¼	– ⅜
10⅞	7⅛	AlcoStd .36	6	5	8¼	8¼	8¼	– ¼
42¾	29¼	AlconLb .16	48	29	35⅞	34¾	35¼	– ⅞
9½	3½	Alexdrs .10e	41	38	6½	6¼	6¼	– ¼
31⅞	23¼	AlisnM 2.94e	9	30	28	27¼	27¼	– ¾
15⅛	6¾	AllALfe .24	10	78	13⅝	13	13½	– ¼
14½	8⅜	AllegCp .28e	10	21	10¼	10⅛	10¼	– ⅛
29⅞	19¾	AllgLud 1.20	6	9	24⅝	24¼	24⅝	– ⅛
24½	19¼	AllgPw 1.44	8	198	19½	19⅛	19⅛	– ⅜
19⅜	9¼	AllenGp .65t	10	9	12¼	12	12¼	– ⅛
36⅞	28⅛	AlldCh 1.32	12	277	36½	36⅛	36¼	– ⅜
44⅞	27½	All Mnt .45b	22	22	33⅝	32¼	32¼	– 1⅞
22	14⅝	AlldPd .68	6	8	17⅜	16⅞	16⅞	– ½
39⅜	22½	AlldStr .140	7	31	27⅜	26⅝	26⅝	– ⅞
5½	3	Alld Supmkt	13	12	4½	4⅜	4⅜	– ¼
12⅝	8	AllisChl .21e	9	54	9⅞	9½	9⅝	– ⅛
15½	8	AllrtAut .50	8	7	9¼	8⅞	8⅞	– ⅜
17½	11⅛	AlphaPl .60	6	4	13½	13¼	13¼	– ¼
69	47⅞	Alcoa 1.94	12	453	66	64	65¼	– ¾
28⅜	22¼	AmalSg 1.60	8	7	24⅛	24⅛	24⅛	...
14¾	8⅝	AMBAC .50	7	11	10½	10⅜	10⅜	– ⅛
6½	4	Amcord .10e	6	4	4½	4⅜	4⅜	– ⅛
26¼	18½	Amerce 1.20	6	1	19	19	19	....
46	36⅛	Amrc pf2.60	...	1	38	38	38	– ¾
50½	31¼	A Hess .30b	18	68	33½	33	33	– ½
112½	70½	AmH pf3.50	..	22	74⅞	73¾	73¾	– ⅝
40	15½	AAirFilt .42	20	26	22	21½	21½	– ½
25⅜	9⅞	Am Airlin	...	869	11¼	11	11⅛	– ⅛
11¼	6⅛	A Baker .20	...	10	7⅛	7	7⅛	+ ⅜
45⅝	38	ABrnds 2.38	8	42	38⅞	38⅜	38½	– ½
31½	21	AmBdcst .64	12	124	26¾	26⅛	26½	...
47½	9⅝	AmBldM .28	10	11	15	14½	14½	– ⅝
34¾	29⅞	Am Can 2.20	9	57	30⅞	30½	30½	– ¼
26	22⅞	A Can pf1.75	..	3	23¼	23⅛	23¼	+ ⅛
26⅛	15⅞	ACentM 2.32	7	16	17⅝	17¼	17⅝	+ ⅛
26⅜	19¼	A Chain 1.20	7	5	24⅝	24⅜	24⅝	+ ¼
32⅛	22½	ACyan 1.25	9	460	24	23⅜	23⅜	– ¾
27½	17⅞	Am Distill 1	16	2	21½	21½	21½	..
61⅞	35⅜	AmDisTl .43	23	25	42⅝	42	42	– ½
11⅜	5½	AmDualVt	...	12	6⅞	6⅞	6⅞	...
13⅝	12⅛	ADul pf.84a	...	19	12¼	12	12	– ¼
30¾	25¼	A ElPw 1.90	9	440	26⅜	26	26¼	– ¼
3¼	11-16	AmExp Ind	...	22	13-16	11-16	¾	– 1-16
10¾	3⅛	AmExp pf	...	z20	3⅜	3⅜	3⅜	...
23⅝	15⅝	AmFin 1.10	10	123	20	19½	19½	– ½
28⅞	24½	AGeBd 1.92e	...	79	26	26	26	......
22⅞	17	AGnCv 1.39e	...	14	17¾	17½	17½	– ⅛
21⅛	13¼	A GnIns .60	7	26	16⅜	16⅛	16⅜	+ ⅛
29¾	22¾	CabCF 2.26e	10	25	24⅝	24	24⅜	– ¼
40¼	23⅜	Cabot Cp .92	6	34	26⅞	26½	26⅝	– ⅜
8⅜	3¼	Cadence Ind	3	5	4¼	4⅛	4¼	– ⅛
5½	3	Caesars Wrl	5	66	3⅞	3⅝	3⅝	– ⅛
7½	3⅝	Cal Finanl	4	30	4⅛	4	4	– ¼
13	8½	CallahM .34t	30	81	11½	11	11½	+ ⅛
32	24½	CamB 2.77e	9	x16	27⅞	27¼	27¼	– ⅜
71⅜	35⅛	CampR .50a	35	54	60¾	59⅝	60	+ 1
35	27¼	CampS 1.18	13	74	31⅛	30½	30¾	– ½
6⅜	4	Cdn Brew	60	6	4¼	4⅛	4¼	– ⅛
19⅜	15⅞	CdnPac .74e	12	32	17⅞	17⅝	17⅝	– ⅜
16⅜	12½	CanalR 1.10	11	1	13½	13½	13½	....
62½	35	CapCit Com	21	243	50¾	49⅞	50	– ½
31⅜	23⅜	CapHold .26	20	632	29⅜	27¾	28	– 1⅝
73¼	41	Carbrn 1.60	10	16	50¾	50	50¼	– ½
82	62½	CaroC&Oh 5	.	z170	64½	64	64	– ½
14⅜	8	CaroFrg .40	7	5	9¼	9⅛	9⅛	– ¼
30⅜	22¾	CaroPw 1.52	8	89	23¼	22⅞	23	+ ⅛
25¾	20	CarpTech 1	7	59	22⅛	21⅞	21⅞	– ⅜
30¼	18¼	CarrCp .52	15	236	22⅞	22¼	22¼	– ⅞
18⅜	12¾	CarGnl 1.27e		1	14¾	14¾	14¾	– ¼
27¼	9⅛	CartWa .40a	7	44	10½	10¼	10⅜	– ⅛
12¾	11⅝	CascNGs .92	7	2	12¼	12	12¼	......
17¾	12⅛	CastleC .60b	10	15	14⅝	14½	14½	– ¼
70⅝	53⅝	CaterTr 1.50	14	1041	62	59⅝	59¾	– 2⅜
6⅝	2½	Cavngh Cm	4	37	3⅝	3⅜	3½	....
4¾	2⅛	CCI Corp	..	25	2⅜	2¼	2¼	– ⅛
42¼	28¼	Celanese 2	7	76	33⅝	33	33¼	– ½
58⅞	55½	Celn pfA4.50	..	2	57	56½	56½	– ½
23⅝	9¾	CencoInc .20	10	79	15⅝	14¾	14¾	– ¾
28¾	10	Centex .09e	17	15	16⅞	16⅝	16⅝	– ⅛
24⅝	22	CenHud 1.60	7	9	22	21⅞	21⅞	– ⅜
25⅛	20⅛	CenIllLt 1.60	9	40	20⅝	20⅛	20⅝	+ ⅜
65½	58½	CnILt pf4.50	.	z20	58	58	58	– ½
19⅛	15	CenIIPS 1.20	10	56	15⅜	15	15⅛	...
25	20¾	CenLaE 1.16	11	5	21	21	21	– ⅛
18⅞	16¾	CeMPw 1.26	9	20	17½	16¾	17	+ ¼
23¾	20	CenSoW 1.08	12	128	20⅛	19⅞	20⅛	– ⅜
31	24⅛	Cent Soya 1	9	57	30⅞	30⅛	30⅝	– ⅛
25	20⅜	CenTlUt .96	13	92	24⅞	24⅜	24⅜	– ⅜
16⅞	12⅝	CerroCp .80	5	97	14⅞	14⅛	14¾	....
22⅜	14	Cert-teed .50	6	11	15½	15⅛	15⅛	– ½
43¼	29	Crt-ted pf.90	...	14	30½	30	30	– 1
34¾	16½	Cessna .80	7	39	22¼	21⅝	21¾	– ½
2¾	1¼	Chadbrn Inc	...	2	1½	1⅜	1⅜	......
3⅜	2⅛	Chadbrn pf	...	3	2⅛	2	2	– ⅛
23	14⅞	ChmpInt .84	7	136	16⅞	16½	16¾	...
24	18	Chml pf1.20	.	11	20¼	20	20¼	+ ⅛
17⅝	12¼	ChamSp .44	14	499	17⅜	16⅞	16⅞	– ⅛
30	13⅞	ChartrCo .30	10	9	25¼	24½	24½	– 1
35⅜	28⅜	Chartr NY 2	8	26	29¾	29⅜	29⅜	– ⅛
12	9⅛	ChaseFd .72	..	9	9¾	9¾	9¾	.....
60¼	41½	ChasManh 2	9	392	47⅝	46¼	47	– 1
70	48⅜	ChasT 5.09e	10	10	52	51¾	51¾	– ½
23	15	Checker Mt	15	1	20⅜	20⅜	20⅜	– ⅛
13⅜	6¾	Chelsea .30	4	9	7⅝	7½	7½	– ⅛
22	13¾	Chemetn .80	6	13	16¼	15¾	15¾	– ½
54⅛	40¾	ChmNY 2.88	9	255	46⅞	45⅜	45¾	– 1
38	29⅞	ChesVa 1.60	9	1	35	35	35	+ ¼
92	69⅝	Chsbgh 1.12	31	222	73¼	72	72¾	+ ⅜
54¼	40	ChessS 3.35e	6	25	43½	43⅛	43¼	– ¾
9⅜	5½	ChiMilw Cp	2	106	8¼	8	8	– ⅝
17¼	12	Chi Milw pf	...	4	14½	14	14	– ⅞
46⅜	30	ChiPneuT 2	10	13	34¼	33¼	33¼	– 1
26¾	10¾	ChRI ct UP	...	4	10¾	10¾	10¾	...
26½	10½	ChRI ct NW	...	3	11⅛	11⅛	11⅛	+ ⅛
7	4½	ChkFull .20r	16	37	5½	5⅜	5⅜	– ⅛
6⅝	3⅝	Chris Craft	45	37	4⅛	4	4⅛	+ ⅛
20⅞	11⅝	Chromal .70	6	48	13	12⅝	13	......
85	65½	Chroma pf 5	...	1	65½	65½	65½	– ½
44¼	22¾	Chryslr 1.40	4	373	25¾	25⅜	25⅝	– ⅜
18½	6¾	Chrysler wt	.	138	8⅝	8⅜	8⅜	– ⅜
25	16⅞	CI Mtg 2.57e	7	64	17	16⅛	16¼	– ⅝
22⅞	18¼	CinBell 1.30	9	12	19⅜	19⅛	19⅛	– ¼

STOCK INDEXES AND GENERAL MARKET INFORMATION

Figure 8–3 gives a summary of New York Stock Exchange transactions on August 1, 1973. It shows the 15 stocks[1] that traded in the heaviest volume that day, and various data on the volume of transactions and the number of stock advances and declines. It also shows the performance of the various stock indexes that are designed to reflect total market performance.

The most famous of these indexes is the Dow Jones Stock Average. These have been published since 1884. This index is an average of 65 leading stocks, including 30 industrial stocks, 20 transportation company stocks, and 15 public utility company stocks. The way it is calculated is too complex to discuss here, but it does show that the selected industrial stocks have over the years far outdistanced the utilities and transportation companies whose profits have been strictly regulated by the government.

Another widely used index is Standard & Poor's Averages. This is compiled from the prices of 500 stocks. Unlike the Dow Jones index, which reflects averages of current stock prices, the Standard & Poor's index uses percentage changes of stock prices; it takes as its base the average prices of the selected stocks for the period 1941–43, giving them a value of 10. This number was picked, rather than the customary index base of 100, since it more closely approximated the prices of stocks at that time. By August 1973 the index of 500 stocks had risen from 10 to over 100.

Perhaps the most accurate index of stock market movement is the New York Stock Exchange Index. It is an average of all stocks traded on the exchange, using 50 as the base number for prices of each group of stocks and of the composite of all stocks. The base of 50, in turn, is an arbitrary number selected to reflect average stock prices on December 31, 1965. Thus, with industrials at 63, we can say that, on the average, industrial company stocks were 26 percent above December 31, 1965 (that is, 63 divided by the base of 50). Banking and other financial institution stocks at 70 were up 40 percent, while transportation companies were down 30 percent and public utilities down 28 percent from 1965.

---

[1] It will be noted that one of the heavily traded "stocks" was "Amer. Tel. & Tel. Wt." This is not American Telephone and Telegraph Company common stock, but rather "warrants" entitling the holders to buy the common stock at a price of $52 per share until 1975.

FIGURE 8–3

Summary of New York Stock Exchange Transactions on a Typical Day

The New York Stock Exchange

Transactions for Wednesday, Aug. 1, 1973

THE LEADERS

	SALES	CLOSE	CHANGE
Westinghouse Elec.	151,500	36	−2⅛
Rio Grande Ind. .	142,200	10¼	− ⅜
Fairchild Camera .	140,000	49⅝	−1⅞
Int'l. Tel & Tel . . .	128,400	34¼	− ¾
Amer. Tel & Tel wt	126,700	5¼	− ¼
Tandy Corp.	123,400	21	−1½
Texasgulf Inc. . . .	118,300	25¾	+ ½
Boise Cascade . . .	114,900	12½	None
20th Century-Fox .	109,300	8	− ⅜
Levitz Furn.	106,200	7½	− ¼
Caterpillar Tractors	104,100	59¾	−2⅜
General Elec.	102,800	61¾	−1
Delta Air Lines . . .	101,800	50½	− ⅝
Amer. Tel & Tel . .	98,700	50	− ¼
Warner Commun. .	96,400	12⅝	+ ⅛

NEW YORK STOCK EXCHANGE INDEX

1973 HIGH	1973 LOW		HIGH	LOW	CLOSE	NET CHANGE POINTS	NET CHANGE PERCENT	HOURLY FLUCTUATIONS 11 A.M.	NOON	1 P.M.	2 P.M.	3 P.M.
65.48	53.36	Composite	57.15	56.90	56.90	— 0.75	— 1.30%	57.12	57.15	57.15	57.11	56.96
71.66	58.23	Industrials . . .	63.09	62.76	62.76	— 0.86	— 1.35%	63.05	63.09	63.08	63.02	62.84
47.96	32.22	Transportation .	35.00	34.86	34.87	— 0.41	— 1.16%	34.86	34.96	34.95	35.00	34.90
42.59	36.98	Utilities	36.66	36.62	▼36.62	— 0.36	— 0.97%	36.66	36.65	36.65	36.66	36.62
84.53	61.75	Finance	70.41	70.25	70.25	— 0.83	— 1.17%	70.27	70.28	70.41	70.40	70.25

DOW JONES STOCK AVERAGES

1973 HIGH	1973 LOW		HIGH*	LOW*	CLOSE	NET CHANGE POINTS	NET CHANGE PERCENT	HOURLY FLUCTUATIONS OPEN	11 A.M.	NOON	1 P.M.	2 P.M.	3 P.M.
1051.70	869.73	30 Indus.	924.37	907.28	912.18	—14.22	— 1.53%	921.06	915.86	916.54	916.32	914.58	913.00
228.10	154.36	20 Trans.	165.82	162.80	164.15	— 1.05	— 0.63%	164.85	163.84	164.27	164.23	164.50	164.35
120.72	99.31	15 Utils.	99.47	97.97	▼98.29	— 1.02	— 1.02%	99.21	98.83	98.73	98.61	98.51	98.61
334.08	266.27	65 Stocks	279.67	274.67	276.23	— 3.52	— 1.25%	278.58	277.05	277.30	277.18	276.91	276.60

SALES: 30 Industrials, 1,116,800 shares; 20 Transp., 340,200; 15 Utilities, 268,400; 65 Stocks, 1,725,400.

▲ New 1973 high ▼ New 1973 low

*Averages of the highs and lows reached at any time during the day by the individual stocks.

HOURLY VOLUME

11 A.M.	NOON	1 P.M.	2 P.M.	3 P.M.	3:30 P.M.
4,340,000	2,710,000	2,160,000	1,350,000	1,690,000	1,280,000

WHAT THE MARKET DID

	WED.	TUES.	MON.	FRI.	THURS.	WEEK AGO
Volume*	13,530	13,534	11,171	12,908	18,411	22,217
Issues Traded .	1,757	1,777	1,812	1,757	1,794	1,815
Advances	308	484	626	526	729	1,024
Declines	1,186	937	817	888	728	467
Unchanged . . .	263	356	369	343	337	324
New Highs . . .	2	27	16	17	41	61
New Lows	104	74	69	66	51	48

*Thousands of Shares

ANNUAL TRANSACTIONS

Jan. 1 to date 1973	1972	1971
2,259,681*	2,500,399*	2,424,455*

*Thousands of shares

ODD LOT TRANSACTIONS

	TUES.	MON.	FRI.	THURS.	WED.	TUES.
Purchases	227,495	240,332	222,356	298,234	306,722	268,146
Sales	355,658	362,050	333,578	398,989	423,531	370,571
Short Sales	2,963	5,041	3,336	4,809	5,649	4,049

STANDARD & POOR'S AVERAGES

1973 High	1973 Low		High	Low	Close	NET CHANGE Points	NET CHANGE Percent
120.24	101.28	500 Index	108.12	106.24	106.83	— 1.39	— 1.28%
134.54	113.21	425 Indus.	121.64	119.53	120.12	— 1.57	— 1.29%
44.91	33.53	15 Rails	35.38	34.94	35.12	— 0.26	— 0.73%
61.57	52.40	60 Utils.	52.38	51.36	▼51.69	— 0.71	— 1.35%

ADVANCE-DECLINE VOLUME

	WED.	TUES.	MON.	FRI.	THURS.	WEEK AGO
Advances*	2,000	3,981	4,256	4,265	8,706	15,377
Declines*	10,448	8,367	5,702	6,730	7,372	5,109
Unchanged*	1,082	1,182	1,212	1,915	2,332	1,734

*Thousands of Shares

Bonds

A portion of a financial page showing a day's bond transactions has been reproduced in Figure 8–4. These quotations are similar to those of stocks with certain differences. It will be noted that the name of the company is followed by several numbers and letters. These identify the bonds. For example, "ATT 8¾ 2000" means an American Telephone and Telegraph bond, carrying an interest rate of 8¾ percent, due for redemption in the year 2000.

The column entitled Cur Yld (Current Yield) gives the bond's current yield taking into account its interest rate and its present price. In many places in the Current Yield column the letters CV occur, indicating that the bonds are convertible into common stock and that, since their value depends on what happens to the company's common stock, an accurate yield figure cannot be given.

The Vol (Volume) column gives the number of $1,000 bonds exchanged that day. In the price and net change columns, the bonds are quoted on a basis of 100; a price of 100 means that a $1,000 face value bond will sell for $1,000, and a quotation of 72 means that it will sell for $720.

Bond Indexes

There are a number of indexes of bond performance. The Dow Jones Bond Averages are commonly used, as shown in Figure 8–4. This index is made up of an average of the prices of 40 selected bonds, equally divided between high-quality railroad bonds, second-quality railroad bonds, public utility bonds, and industrial bonds.

It may appear surprising that the average of all 40 bonds in the Dow Jones Bond Average was only slightly above 72, well below their face value of 100.

This is because the index was set up some years ago when the bonds selected were selling at full price on the basis of an interest rate around 4½ percent. The high interest rates prevalent in 1973 caused these bonds to sell at a substantial discount. Also, it is interesting that high-quality rail bonds appear to be selling at a lower average price than second-quality. This unusual situation is caused by the sad fortunes of the bonds of such leading railroads as the bankrupt Pennsylvania Central Railroad, which were formerly considered of high quality.

232 *A Practical Introduction to Business*

FIGURE 8–4

Portion of Page Showing a Typical Day's Bond Sales and Quotations

CORPORATION BONDS
Volume, $16,570,000

Bonds	Cur Yld	Vol	High	Low	Close	Net Chg
Abex 8¾77	8.7	7	100½	100½	100½	−1
AddM 9⅜95	9.1	12	103	102⅞	102⅞	−1
AlaP 9s2000	8.6	14	104¼	104	104	+ ⅛
Alaska 6s96	cv	15	125	125	125	.....
Alexn 5½96	cv	10	52	52	52	.....
AldCh 6.6s93	7.5	30	87½	87½	87½	..
AldCh 5.2s91	6.9	40	75¼	75¼	75¼	−1¼
AlldPd 7s84	8.9	11	78½	78¼	78½	.
AlldSt 4½92	cv	100	69¾	69¾	69¾	+ ¼
AldSu 5¾87	cv	36	57	57	57	....
Alcoa 9s95	8.6	21	104½	104	104½	− ½
Alcoa 5¼s91	cv	65	90	89⅜	90	−2
Alcoa 3s79	3.8	10	77⅝	77⅝	77⅝	+ ⅛
AAirFil 6s90	cv	10	95	95	95	....
AAirln 11s88	10.	61	105½	105	105	− ⅛
AAirl 10⅞88	10.	37	105½	105¼	105¼	− ⅝
AAirln 10s89	9.8	37	101¾	101½	101½	− ¼
AAirl 4¼s92	cv	46	56½	55	55	−1½
ABrnd 8⅞75	8.7	17	101½	101	101	−1
ACeM 6¾91	cv	10	70	70	70	− ½
ADist 4⅜s86	6.5	1	66½	66½	66½	
AExp 5¼93f	cv	51	11¾	11¼	11½	+ ¼
AForP 5s30	10.	110	49¾	49⅝	49⅝	− ⅛
AFoP 4.8s87	8.4	20	56¾	56½	56¾	+ ¾
AHoist 5½93	cv	19	75¾	75	75	− ¾
AHoist 4¾92	cv	18	85¼	84½	84½	−2½
AInvt 9½s76	9.3	12	102	101⅛	102	⅞
AMF 4¼s81	cv	9	80½	80½	80½	−1
AmMot 6s88	cv	51	81½	81	81	....
AS 5.3s93r		6	68⅛	68⅛	68⅛	..
ATT 8¾2000	8.4	935	104⅜	103⅛	103¾	− ¾
ATT 8.7s02	8.4	231	103¼	102½	103	
ATT 7.75s77	7.8	170	99	98½	98½	− ¾
ATT 7⅛s03	8.0	117	88⅜	87½	88⅛	−1
ATT 7s01	8.0	185	88	87	87¼	− ¾
ATT 6½s79	7.0	3	92½	92½	92½	
ATT 4⅜s85	5.9	14	73	72½	73	−1
ATT 4⅜s85r		10	72	72	72	..
ATT 3⅞s90	6.0	5	64	64	64	−1¼
ATT 3⅜s73	3.4	48	98	97 13-16	98	+3-16
ATT 3¼s84	4.9	24	65⅜	65¼	65¼	−1¼
ATT 2⅞s87	4.9	20	58¼	58	58	
ATT 2¾s75	3.0	4	90½	90½	90½	+ ½
ATT 2¾s80	3.8	17	73⅜	71⅝	71⅝	−1⅜
ATT 2¾s82	4.0	76	67¼	66¾	67¼	+ ¼
ATT 2⅝s86	4.5	21	57⅞	57	57½	− ⅜
Amfac 5¼94	cv	28	63	62½	62½	−1
Ampx 5½94	cv	29	45½	43½	43¾	−1¾
Anhser 6s92	7.5	4	79½	79½	79½	− ¾
AnnArb 4s95	12.	15	31½	31	31	− ½
ApcoO 5s88	cv	36	64½	64⅛	64½	− ⅜
APL 5¾s88	cv	4	68	68	68	− ½
AppalP 9s75	8.9	22	101	101	101	− ¾
AppP 8⅝s76	8.5	9	100½	100½	100½	+ ½
ARA 4⅝s96	cv	12	101½	101½	101½	−1½
Aristr 9½89	9.5	8	100	100	100	....
ArizP 8.5s75	8.5	11	101	100	100	
ArmSt 8¼75	8.2	4	99⅝	99⅝	99⅝	+ ⅜
Armr 5s84	7.4	5	67½	67½	67½	+ ¼
Ash 6.15s92	7.8	2	78½	78½	78½	−4
AshlO 4¾93	cv	5	75	75	75	−1½
AsCp 9¼90	8.9	10	103½	103	103	−1
AsCp 8½77	8.5	68	100	99	99	− ¼
AsInv 7⅜88	8.4	13	87	87	87	−5
AsInv 5¼77	5.7	8	91	91	91	...
AsInv 5⅛79	6.2	1	82½	82½	82½	− ⅝
AsInv 4½76	5.1	5	87	87	87	
Atchsn 4s95	6.4	1	62	62	62	+1
Atchn 4s95st	6.3	11	63⅛	63	63	
Atico 6¾82	9.1	9	74	74	74	−1
AtlRich 7s76	7.2	33	96½	96½	96½	
ARich 5⅝97	7.3	1	76	76	76	−2
AvcoF 11s90	10.	12	107½	106¼	106¼	−1¼
AvcoF 9¼89	9.0	11	102	102	102	− ½
Avco 7½93	10.	17	73	72	72	− ⅜
Avco 5½93	cv	3	59¾	59¾	59¾	..
AvcoF 9¼90	9.0	15	102	102	102	− ½
AvcoF 8⅞77	8.7	15	101	100⅞	100⅞	− ⅛
BalGE 8½74	8.5	10	100	100	100	+ ¼
B& O11s77	10.	4	110	110	110	−2
B&O 6¼s97	cv	5	78½	78½	78½	− ½
BO 4½s10A	cv	10	45	44½	44½	− ½
B&O 4s80	5.4	15	73½	73½	73½	....
BangP 6¼94	cv	5	87	86¾	87	....
BkNY 6¼94	cv	31	96	95¼	95¼	− ¾
BaxL 4⅜s91	cv	14	138	138	138	....
Beau 4¼s90	cv	17	61	60	60½	+ ¼
BectD 5s89	cv	13	80	80	80	−1½
BecD 4⅛s88	cv	10	95	95	95	+ ¾
BeecA 4¾93	cv	9	61	61	61	− ½
Belco [illegible]	[illegible]	1	57	57	57	

New York Exchange Bonds

Wednesday, August 1, 1973

Total Volume, $16,600,000

SALES SINCE JANUARY 1

1973	1972	1971
$2,641,315,300	$3,503,931,300	$3,990,605,900

	Domestic Wed	Domestic Tues	All Issues Wed	All Issues Tues
Issues traded	663	653	666	658
Advances	130	170	130	170
Declines	364	294	364	295
Unchanged	169	189	172	193
New highs, 1973	2	6	2	6
New lows, 1973	162	139	162	139

Dow Jones Bond Averages

—1971— High	—1971— Low	—1972— High	—1972— Low	—1973— High	—1973— Low		WEDNESDAY —1973—		WEDNESDAY —1972—		WEDNESDAY —1971	
73.39	68.62	75.07	73.41	75.34	72.38	40 Bonds	72.38	+ .05	73.94	+ .07	70.19	− .05
52.63	48.95	54.60	52.67	55.27	53.58	10 Hi Rails	53.78	+ .20	52.98	− .01	50.20	− .12
66.23	59.20	69.01	66.16	69.73	66.50	10 2nd Rails	66.50	..	67.26	+ .04	63.35	− .06
89.80	85.50	91.97	89.55	92.00	89.62	10 Utilities	89.62	− .03	90.75	....	86.40	− .02
84.96	80.22	86.09	84.05	85.90	79.63	10 Industrial	79.63	− .35	84.75	+ .23	80.82	...

Bonds	Cur Yld	Vol	High	Low	Close	Net Chg
EaAir 4¾93	cv	33	53⅝	53	53¼	− ½
Echlin 5¼91	cv	5	125	125	125	−1
EGG 3½s87	cv	6	58½	58½	58½	+ ¼
ElPas 8½95	cv	38	102⅛	102	102⅛	− ⅜
ElPaso 6s93	cv	8	80	79	80	+1
Englh 5¼97	cv	20	86	85	85	....
vjEri 3⅛90f		85	13½	13⅛	13⅛	−1⅜
Essex 9¼75	9.2	12	100½	100¼	100¼	− ¼
Evan 6¼94	cv	10	89⅝	89⅝	89⅝	+ ⅝
Exxon 6½98	7.5	52	86	86	86	−1
Exxon 6s97	7.4	21	81⅛	81	81⅛	− ⅜
Fairch 4⅜92	cv	20	48	48	48	− ½
Farah 5s94	cv	1	56	56	56	+2⅞
Feddrs 5s96	cv	16	66	65	65	−1¼
FedN 4⅜96	cv	408	99	95¾	97¼	+ ¾
FPac 5½87	cv	43	99	98	99	+1⅛
Fiber 4¾93	cv	16	68¾	68	68	− ¾
FstMge 9s78	9.0	3	99⅞	99⅞	99⅞	.....
FtNBo 6⅝79	7.1	5	93	93	93	.....
FishF 6½94	cv	7	82	82	82	+1½
FlexiV 4¾97	cv	1	83	83	83	+1
FlaPw 8⅛75	8.1	25	100	99½	99½	− ½
FlyT 6.6s80	7.2	1	90½	90½	90½	−3⅜
FMC 4¼92	cv	17	65	65	65	− ½
FoodF 4s79	5.5	1	72	72	72	....
Ford 8¼74	8.2	41	100	96½	99¾	+ ¾
Ford 8⅛90	8.0	81	101½	100¾	101½	− ½
Ford 7¼77	7.4	14	97¼	97¼	97¼	
Ford 6½79	7.0	7	93	92⅛	92⅜	−1⅜
FrdC 8¾75	8.6	34	101	100¾	100¾	+ ½
FrdC 8½91	8.4	5	101	101	101	...
FrdC 8⅜76	8.4	113	100⅛	99⅜	99⅜	− ⅞
FordCr 7s80	7.5	10	93⅛	93⅛	93⅛	− ¼
FrdC 4⅞98	cv	40	83¼	82	82	−1½
FrdC 4½96	cv	83	75½	74½	74½	−1½
FoMcK 6s94	cv	18	75⅞	75	75⅞	− ⅛
Fruehf 6s87	7.3	4	81½	81½	81½	− ¾
Frueh 5½94	cv	7	72⅜	72⅜	72⅜	+ ¼
FruF 8.7s75	8.7	20	100⅜	100	100	− ⅜
Fuqua 7s88	9.5	30	74⅛	73	73	−1½
GAC 5⅞s94	cv	56	34¾	33	33⅛	−1⅝
GAC C 12s75	17.	201	72½	70⅛	70⅛	−3⅞
GAC C 11s77	17.	236	62½	61	62	−2⅛
GAC 10¼s90	11.	132	93	90	93	− ½
GAC 8½74	8.8	135	94½	88	92¾	+4¾
GnEl 6¼79	6.8	5	91⅛	91	91	+ ⅝
GnEl 3½76	3.9	41	91	88	88	−1⅛
GElCr 8½76	8.4	55	101	100½	100½	−1⅜
GElCr 7s80	7.4	30	94¼	94¼	94¼	−2⅛
GFood 8⅞90	8.3	8	106	105⅞	106	− ½
GFood 8¾75	8.6	34	101⅝	101	101⅝	+ ⅝
GHost 6s90f		2	58	58	58	+1
GnInst 4¼85	cv	10	80⅛	80	80	+14¾
GMA 8¾77	8.5	45	103	102½	102½	− ½
GMAcc 8s93	8.2	30	98½	97½	97½	−1
GMA 7¾94	8.0	21	96⅜	96¼	96¼	....
GMA 7⅛90	7.9	20	90	90	90	−2
GMA 7⅛92	7.9	35	89¾	88¾	89¾	− ¼
GMA 6¼88	7.4	18	84	82½	84	+ ⅝
GMAcc 5s77	5.7	26	87¾	87½	87½	
GMAcc 5s80	6.2	48	82¾	80	80	−2⅝

Bonds	Cur Yld	Vol	High	Low	Close	Net Chg
MichB 7¾11	8.1	2	95	95	95	−1½
MichB 3⅛88	5.5	15	56½	56¼	56¼	−1¾
vjMchC 4½f		2	42¼	42¼	42¼	.....
Mile L 5¼94	cv	45	90	89	89	....
MKTex 4s90	11.	1	35	35	35	− ½
MoPac 5s45f	..	14	49	49	49	.....
M Pac 4¼90	7.2	5	59	59	59	.....
M Pac 4¼05	8.4	3	50⅛	50⅛	50⅛	....
Mob O 7⅜01	7.8	24	94⅜	94	94	− ¼
Moh D 5½94	cv	18	39	38	39	....
Mong 10½75	10.	6	101	101	101	+ ½
Mnt W 9¼90	8.8	5	105	105	105	.....
Mont W 9s89	8.8	6	102	102	102	+1
Mnt W 4⅞80	6.1	1	79⅜	79⅜	79⅜	....
MonyM 7s90	cv	10	102	102	102	.....
vjMrE 3½00		3	12¼	11¾	11¾	− ¼
MtS TT 9s10	8.4	13	107	107	107	....
MtS Tl 7¾13		79	94¼	93½	93¾	− ¾
MtS Tl 7⅜11	8.2	13	89½	89½	89½	
MtS Tl 6½77	6.9	1	94¼	94¼	94¼	− ¾
N Bisc 4¾87	6.8	10	70	69¾	69¾	−5
N Cash 6s95	cv	78	86½	85½	86	− ¾
N City 6½91	cv	42	70	68⅛	68⅛	−2⅞
N Dist 4½92	cv	20	67½	67½	67½	+ ⅜
N Ind 5¾88	cv	2	53½	53½	53½	− ½
Nat Stl 8s95	8.0	28	100	100	100	− ½
N EnT 8⅝09	8.4	10	102	101	102	+1
NEnT 8.2s04	8.2	14	99½	99	99	− ½
N EnT 6½79	7.1	10	90⅝	90⅝	90⅝	− ⅞
NEnTT 3s74	3.0	5	97	97	97	....
Newh L 6s95	cv	30	70½	70½	70½	−1¾
NJBl 9.35s10	8.5	21	110	109	109	−1
NJBTl 7⅜12	7.8	5	93⅞	93⅞	93⅞	....
NJBTl 7¼11	8.0	53	90½	90	90⅛	+ ⅛
vjNYC 6s80f	..	3	10	9½	9½	− ⅝
vjNYC 4½13	..	2	6¾	6¾	6¾	.....
vjNYC 4s98f	..	72	5½	5½	5½	.....
vjNYMC 98r	..	10	12¼	12¼	12¼	....
vjNYL 4s73f	..	15	13⅞	12⅝	13⅞	+ ½
vjNYH 4½sf	..	50	2⅜	2⅜	2⅜	....
NYPw 2¾75	3.0	2	90½	90½	90½	−1½
NY Tl 9¼10	8.5	24	109	108	108	− ½
NY Tel 8s08	8.2	38	97¾	97¼	97¼	..
NY Tl 7¾06	8.1	3	95⅜	95⅜	95⅜	− ⅛
NY Tl 7⅜11	8.1	61	90½	89⅜	90½	
NY Tl 4⅛93	6.6	5	61¾	61¾	61¾	−1⅜
NY Tl 3⅛78	3.9	10	79⅝	79⅝	79⅝	− ⅞
Ni MP 4⅞87	6.9	2	70¼	70¼	70¼	− ¼
Ni MP 3½83	5.0	5	69	69	69	−1
NorfWe 4s96	6.6	4	60½	60½	60½	+1
NoA Ph 4s92	cv	40	61⅜	61¼	61¼	− ⅝
No Pac 3s47	8.1	23	37	36¾	36¾	+ ¼
NoPac 3s47r		3	36½	36½	36½	
NoSP 8⅞s74	8.8	5	100⅜	100⅜	100⅜	−5-16
No St P 5s90	7.0	9	71	71	71	.....
NoSP 4⅞s91	6.6	4	72¾	72¾	72¾	...
NoSP 3⅛s84	4.8	12	67⅞	64	64	−3⅞
Nwst I 7½94	9.1	2	82	82	82	− ⅜
NwnBl 7⅞11	7.9	4	99	99	99	.....
Occidt 7½96	cv	22	82	81⅛	81⅛	− ⅜
Ogden 5s93	cv	13	61¼	61	61	...
OkGE [illegible]	[illegible]	3	69½	69½	69½	[illegible]

Other Financial News

Most large newspapers have, in addition to their stock and bond pages, several pages of general business news. These contain news of what companies are doing, earnings reports, items on new contracts, news on changes in management, reports of legal cases involving businesses, and many other things. The discussion of business in this book will provide a basis for the understanding of most such news.

There are a number of newspapers devoted exclusively to business matters. *The Wall Street Journal*, published since 1889 and available in special editions throughout the country, is the most widely read. Its daily index covers the following business areas:

Annual stockholders' meetings	Foreign exchange
Bond markets	Foreign markets
Commodities markets	Money markets
Dividend news	Securities markets
Earnings digests	Tax-exempt securities
Editorials	Who's news
Financing business	

Weekly and monthly periodicals for businessmen and investors include *Fortune, Business Week,* and *Dun's Review.* Of special interest to investors are *Forbes* and *Barrons.* Beyond these, every industry—from banking to supermarkets, and from aviation to zinc mining—has journals for people interested in a particular field.

There is plenty of business and financial news available. Such news can hardly be looked upon as of interest to the few. Business in all of its aspects is not only important to businessmen and investors, but to everyone who depends on business. And that means all of us.

SUMMARY

As businesses grow and need money, they usually have to go to the public market for funds. What we call the public market is the many thousands of individuals and other investors who buy and sell stocks and bonds. It also includes the many institutional buyers of securities— pension funds, insurance companies, investment trusts, commercial and savings banks, government agencies, foundations, and businesses with funds to invest. Without these sources of money, most businesses as we know them could hardly exist.

Two major types of business firms exist to bring owners and users of money together: investment bankers, whose principal task is to sell new securities to investors, and brokerage houses, that represent investors wishing to buy or sell issued securities. Often a financial company will have both an investment banking department and a brokerage department.

Issued securities are bought and sold on security exchanges, such as the New York Stock Exchange and the American Stock Exchange, which furnish trading floors and other facilities for brokers to use. There are 16 security exchanges in the United States and many abroad. It should be remembered that none of these exchanges buys or sells securities. They only furnish facilities where their broker members can easily buy and sell among themselves.

Many stocks and bonds that are not listed on organized exchanges are traded on over-the-counter markets. Transactions are made among the thousands of brokerage offices in the United States through an electronic information system.

On the organized exchanges, securities are entered for listing if they meet the exchange's requirements. These are called listed securities. Other securities are referred to as unlisted. Exchanges are organized either as corporations or as voluntary associations like partnerships. A broker member owns a membership or "seat," and only members can use an exchange's facilities. Usually, members fall into four classes in accordance with the way they operate on the exchange: commission brokers, registered traders, specialists, and odd-lot dealers.

Members of an organized exchange handle transactions, or "trades," by a simple bidding process on the floor of the exchange. The commission broker members buy and sell in accordance with instructions given them by investor customers. Other members buy and sell for their own account, and by doing so help to make an orderly and active market for the public. Investors sometimes buy on "margin" by having their brokers borrow money to help pay for the securities purchased. At other times, investors sell securities they do not own, called "selling short," by getting their brokers to borrow the securities. A person buying on margin hopes to gain by a price increase on his securities, and a person selling short hopes to profit by a price decline.

People buying securities may do so either for investment or for speculation. When they buy for investment they intend to hold the securities for a period of time, and hence they may be interested in any one or a combination of the following objectives: safety of principal, annual return on their money invested, or growth of their investment through long-term rises in price. Those who buy for speculation hold securities for a short period of time, hoping to make money on small increases or decreases in security prices.

Brokers and exchanges, as well as anyone offering securities for sale, are extensively regulated by both state and federal governments. Regulation of the issuance of new securities is designed to prevent sales of fraudulent securities and to provide investors with accurate and clear information. Stiff penalties are provided for issuers who hand out incomplete or misleading information. In the trading of securities by brokers, penalties are provided for those who use their middleman position to take advantage of the investing public.

Just as a businessman needs to know some basic accounting in order to keep score within his business, he also needs to know how score is kept in the stock and bond markets. This requires knowing how stocks and bonds are quoted, how to read the daily reports in the newspapers, what stock and bond indexes mean, and where to get and how to understand other financial news. This may seem complex. But with a little practice it is not difficult.

KEY TERMS AND CONCEPTS

Public market	"Limited" order
Investment banking	"Stop" order
Underwriting	Margin trading
Brokerage houses	Short selling
Security exchanges	Bond discount
Over-the-counter markets	Bond yield
Listed and unlisted stocks	Price/earnings (P/E) ratio
"Taking a position"	Security speculation
"Making a market"	"Bear" market
Commission brokers	"Bull" market
Registered traders	"Blue Sky" laws
Specialists	Company "insiders"
Odd-lot dealers	Dow-Jones Stock Averages
Stock exchange "seat"	Standard & Poor's Averages
Stock exchange "post"	New York Stock Exchange Index
"Market" order	Dow-Jones Bond Averages

QUESTIONS FOR ANALYSIS AND DISCUSSION

1. What is the "public market" for money? Why is it so important to business? Why is it sometimes said that the public market gives rise to a "people's capitalism?" Can every business firm take advantage of the public market?

2. Investment bankers are not really bankers, but they can be very important to a business in getting the funds it needs for expansion. Explain.

3. Distinguish between investment banking and brokerage operations. Why are both necessary to make the public market work?

4. What is the function of the security exchanges in business financing? How do the New York Stock Exchange and the over-the-counter market differ? Why would you suspect that many investors prefer to own a listed stock than an unlisted stock?

5. Describe the four different kinds of members of the New York Stock Exchange. Can you see why we may need all four kinds to make an exchange work?

6. Suppose that you were going to buy some stock in a company, say, the Ford Motor Company. How would you go about it? What would you do if you decided to sell these shares?

7. If you had some money to invest, would you be inclined to buy "on margin"? Why or why not? Why might you wish to do some "short selling"? Why do you suppose far more investors buy on margin than sell short?

8. Some people say that the safest kind of investment is to buy bonds. Is this always true? Why? Is it possible to lose money even by investing in government bonds?

9. Why do bondholders and stockholders pay so much attention to "yield"? What is it, and how would you calculate current yield? Why do stockholders pay even more attention to the Price/Earnings ratio? How would you calculate this for a particular stock?

10. Why do common stocks of the same company often yield less than bonds of that company, especially when bonds have a higher security than common stocks?

11. The regulation of securities and securities trading does not protect investors against loss. What does it attempt to do?

12. Of the various stock indexes, which would you prefer as an indicator of the trend of the stock market? Why?

13. Pick up the financial section of your daily newspaper. Can you understand it through your knowledge of the material given in this chapter?

SUGGESTED READINGS

Dauten, C. A., and M. T. Welshaus *Principles of Finance: Introduction to Capital Markets* (3d ed.). Cincinnati: South-Western Publishing Company, 1970, Chapters 8–15.

Johnson, R. W. *Financial Management* (4th ed.). Boston: Allyn and Bacon, Inc., 1971, Chapters 15–16,

Van Horne, J. C. *Fundamentals of Financial Management* (2d ed.). Englewood Cliffs, N.J.: Prentice-Hall, Inc., 1974, Chapters 18–19.

Weston, J. F., and E. F. Brigham *Essentials of Managerial Finance* (3d ed.). Hinsdale, Ill.: The Dryden Press, 1974, Chapter 13.

9

Financing Business

In establishing and maintaining a business, one encounters many problems. But it is problems that make business exciting, or for that matter any game or occupation. Problems are really opportunities for meaningful work and a feeling of accomplishment. In business, solving problems leads to financial rewards, not to mention the satisfaction we get from creating goods and services that our society wants.

These are some of the problem areas in business: How can we develop new products or services that will sell? How can we market them effectively? How can we produce and distribute them efficiently? How are we to manage the team of people who must work together to make all this happen? How shall we finance our operations so that we can start a business, stay in business, and do so profitably? We shall discuss many of these areas later in this book. Let us now look at some of the problems of financing a business.

We might begin with Henry Ford and the way he started the Ford Motor Company, or Thomas Watson and what he did with the International Business Machines Corporation, or Walt Disney and his company. But perhaps a better beginning is to look at two real examples of ordinary, successful business starts. Afterward we can go on to examine some of the pitfalls of financing a business, the question of how to use the banks, of when and how to go to the public markets, and other problems that arise in the financing of a business.

STARTING A RETAIL BUSINESS: THE LIPTONS[1]

Charles and Audrey Lipton started a specialty footwear business in Aspen, Colorado, in December 1969. It has turned out to be a successful and profitable small business in this Rocky Mountain town so noted for its ski slopes and year around vacation attractions. Although neither of the Liptons had even been in the retailing business, Charles Lipton had been a partner with his father in a family-owned oil fuel business in Bayonne, New Jersey, for 18 years. His principal job was to handle oil-burner repairs for the firm's customers. Mrs. Lipton had been interested in fashions and had worked for a year as a home-furnishing consultant with the Lord & Taylor women's wear company in New York City.

Why the Business Was Started

Tired of being an oil-burner repairman with his 80-hour, any time of the day or night, weeks, Charles Lipton took his first vacation in 10 years in 1966. A trip with his family to Aspen for skiing made the fuel oil business seem all the duller and more meaningless. As Charles told his father, "I am up to here in oil burners." His father was ready to retire anyway. He and Charles and another partner sold their business in New Jersey, and the Liptons moved to Aspen. Their assets included a house in New Jersey, some stocks and bonds, and $38,000 from their interest in the oil business.

This, then, is the picture. A couple, 39 and 37, with two small children, considerable savings from frugal living and hard work, and, above all, a desire to live in Aspen. They also wanted to be their own bosses, live their own life, and raise their children in a small community. While they had a desire to make money, they saw this only as a means of living the kind of life they wanted to live.

The Liptons did not know what sort of business they wanted to start. They thought of buying a lodge or a restaurant, but the cost of either was so high that they would have had to invest most of their savings and even borrow money. At the same time, they realized that small shops starting in Aspen had a high mortality rate and that almost

---

[1] Adapted from "The Liptons of Aspen," *Money*, August 1973, pp. 49–54.

one third of the new shops in this thriving community closed their doors within a year. They also knew that throughout the country small "mom-and-pop" retail businesses had a high rate of failure.

Audrey Lipton, long interested in fashion and clothes, thought of going into a specialty shoe business. She studied the various shops in Aspen and found no specialty shoe stores. She also took note that the people visiting Aspen were fairly well-to-do and sport-style conscious. She went to the La Piuma Shoe Company in New York, makers of her favorite shoes, and talked to the company's chief designer and part-time salesman. He told her to come back when she had made definite plans. After the Liptons decided to open such a store, specializing in that company's shoes in Aspen, the La Piuma chief designer helped them set up and stock their store.

Financing the Store

Drawing carefully from their savings, the Liptons rented a small 600-square-foot store, put $15,000 into the initial shoe inventory, and spent $8,000 for shelves, decoration, and fixtures. They also invested $15,000 in a condominium home. This still left them over $40,000 in other investments and savings accounts which, along with the rental income from their New Jersey home, gave them a comfortable cushion for unforeseen expenses.

Profitability of the Store

The store fortunately did well from the start. The Liptons had apparently discovered an untapped market. An unusual line of shoes, Mrs. Lipton's flair for style, the attractiveness and informality of the little store, and Mr. Lipton's care in handling the books and watching expenses all served to make the store a success. To this was added the willingness of both Liptons to work long hours, six days a week. Even their two small children pitched in with such after-school chores as cleaning and dusting.

The first year, from sales of $44,000, they netted profits before taxes of $10,000. In three years, sales had grown to $115,000 and profits before taxes to $35,000. They expected that in succeeding years, helped by a wider variety of items including specialty hats and women's clothing, sales would go to $200,000 per year with at least the same margin of profit.

Ingredients of Success

What were the ingredients of success in this small retail business? Perhaps the most important was the willingness of the Liptons to work hard. Another was the fact that they had gone into a business they liked with adequate cash for that kind of business. Had they chosen a more expensive lodge or restaurant, they might not have made it. Also important was Mrs. Lipton's flair for fashion and her idea of a specialty shoe store, plus the happenstance that they discovered an opportunity in a resort town that had gone unfilled.

STARTING AN ELECTRONICS COMPONENT BUSINESS: GENISTRON, INC.[2]

An electronic engineer, Fred J. Nichols, was West Coast manager of an electronic noise filter[3] division of a large eastern company. Nichols had long had the desire to be his own boss and to try to make some money that he could never make from a salary. Through his technical papers read at national electronic engineering meetings, he was well known in his field. One of his close friends was Millard Porter, also a specialist in electronic noise filters who worked as a top engineer for the same company. Another friend was Paul M. Kuefler who held a position similar to Nichols in the West Coast division of another large eastern company. Both Porter and Kuefler shared Nichols' feeling about wanting to have their own business. Moreover, because of certain headquarters decisions affecting West Coast operations, all three engineers were not completely satisfied with their large eastern companies' managements.

How the Business Was Started

The three engineers realized that they knew little about running a business and nothing about starting one. Nichols had a friend who was a management and financial consultant to small businesses. Nichols went over with him his ideas of starting a business. He suggested that the business should specialize in designing high-precision electronic noise filters, primarily for the defense industry, because there was too much competition from large companies in other types of filters. It

---

[2] From one of the authors' personal files.
[3] These are special electronic devices for filtering out various electric waves constantly on electric wires and in the air, which can interfere with the operation of electronically controlled devices ranging from radios to space vehicles.

would require a small staff of highly trained specialists, considerable expensive electrical measuring equipment, and a special room shielded in such a way as to exclude outside electrical noise from interfering with design experiments.

The consultant had had considerable experience with ambitious engineers who wanted to start their own businesses, and he knew the problems of developing a successful company from scratch. He did some research on the engineering talent in this field and discussed the market potential for filters with his many contacts in the defense electronics business. He found several interesting things. One was that the three engineers were among the eight most highly regarded engineers in the high-precision electronic filter field. Another was that a large market for high-precision filters was developing at that time (1958) in such defense programs as that for the "Minuteman" missile. The West Coast market for these high-precision devices was estimated by defense electronics engineers and buyers at $4 million annually, and was expected to double in three years and quadruple in six years. He found also that the three engineers had had experience in developing a similar operation, that they knew where the markets were and how to reach them, and were familiar with costs and prices.

The consultant also knew of several companies and investor groups interested in putting money into new electronic businesses. Although he had looked at dozens of small business proposals and found that nine out of ten were not worth doing anything about, he felt that this proposal was a good one. He was even willing to help finance it himself.

Making Objectives Practical

The three engineers had clear objectives. They wanted (1) to run their own company; (2) to build up a company in which they could feel a personal incentive for success; and (3) to make money out of their ownership. At first they also wanted to maintain a controlling interest in the company's stock, but together they could only raise $25,000 in cash. The consultant knew that an investment of $25,000 would never finance a successful small electronics component business.

Estimating cash needs in the first two years at something like $150,000 to $200,000, the consultant pointed out that banks would not lend them money until they were established and showed promise of profits and cash flow. He also informed them that an investor who might lend them the kind of money they needed would not be satisfied with interest payments but would want in addition a share of ownership. An investor who could provide "important" money would want control of the company, he told them, so that they would probably have to be satisfied with being minority shareholders. However, any investor who put money in their venture would only do so on the strength of their abilities and would want them to be tied into the company with an important stock interest. The right investor would not be out to "steal" the company from them, but would want to let them make money while he also made money.

The consultant had known of investors who financed engineers without requiring them to put their own money into the company. But too often those concerned, not having their own money in a company, tended to be careless in spending the investors' capital. Therefore, he had the conviction, and so informed the engineers, that they should put enough money of their own in the company that their invested dollars would be important to them. This, despite the fact their investment would be a small part of the total.

The three engineers agreed to modify their original objectives and to meet the conditions outlined by the consultant. The consultant took on the task of getting financing, organizing the company, and watching over it at no fee, asking only a small stock participation in the company if and when it was organized.

Forecasting Sales, Profits, and Cash Needs

Before the proposal for the new company could be taken to an investor, it was necessary to develop a forecast of sales, expenses, profits, and cash needs. Sales were forecast by months for the first 18 months, and by quarters for another 18 months. The forecast indicated no sales for the first two months and only $2,000 sales in the third month, but $30,000 in the twelfth month and $43,000 in the eighteenth month. By the third year, sales were expected to reach $750,000.

It was further forecast that the company would lose money each month until the eighth month of operations, and that the operating loss for the first year would be more than $10,000. In the second year a profit of $42,000 before taxes was forecast, and in the third year a profit of $150,000 before taxes. It was fairly easy to forecast operating expenses since the engineers knew what costs to expect for material, labor, and overhead. In the first eight months of operation it was important to add in the unusual costs of starting the operation, such as legal expenses, having people on the payroll before they could produce efficiently (the cost of learning), and special sales expenses. These start-up costs were estimated at $38,000.

In determining cash needs, it was necessary to estimate the cost of laboratory, production, and office equipment carefully. This came to $63,500. Losses in starting operations were expected to add another $38,000. On the assumption that defense industry customers would pay their bills on the average about 60 days after delivery of products, the volume of accounts receivable that would have to be financed in the first year was estimated at $55,000. Inventories were estimated to require $31,600 in the first year. Cash for unforeseen contingencies, and the need to have cash balances on hand to pay bills, added another $16,500. Thus, total cash needs for the first year were calculated to be a maximum of $204,600. It was further estimated that, even if bills were paid fairly promptly, accounts payable would still run $8,000. They hoped that by the tenth month the company's credit would be good enough that a commercial bank loan of $25,000 could be obtained. This would leave *net* cash needs by the end of the first year at $171,600 ($204,600–$33,000).

Similar estimates were made for the second and third years. These showed that, even with additional bank borrowings and assuming that all profits after taxes were reinvested in the business, the company might need an additional $55,000. Altogether, it would be necessary to see a total of $226,600 in cash available before the company could be started.

The Investment Arrangement

Several investors expressed interest in the new company. The three engineers, however, elected to be financed by a larger company that was interested in adding to its product line. In order to maintain investment incentive by the three founders, this company agreed to finance the engineers by establishing a company in which the engineers and the consultant would own $24,500 of stock, to be paid for in cash, and the investing company would have $25,500 in stock, giving it a controlling interest of 51 percent of the common stock. In addition, the investing company agreed to finance additional funds as needed by extending loans at an interest rate 1 percent above the cost of borrowing from its bank. In this way adequate cash would be available.

If the company failed, the founders might lose all their original investment while the investing company would probably be able to regain its loans from the sale of assets, leaving it with a loss of no more than the $25,500 of stock it had purchased. The agreement provided that, if the company succeeded, the investor company would buy the minority shares—those of the consultant and the three engineers—at the end of three years. It further provided that these shares would be purchased by exchange of parent company stock at a price calculated at 7½ times Genistron's third-year earnings.

What Happened?

The company turned out to be an unusual success. Sales and profits exceeded those forecast, and cash requirements were lower than projected. The result was that the founders benefited handsomely when the larger company purchased their minority shares three years later. The three engineers and the consultant received a total of more than $500,000 in stock of the parent company for their original investment of $24,500, and the investor company came into sole ownership of a highly profitable division.

Ingredients of Success

There were several ingredients in the success of this small company. One was the fact that the three engineers knew their field. Another was that they stepped into an expanding market. Still another factor was that they were adequately financed to meet the obligations of a fast growing company. Since they had money important to them in the company and stood to gain from running an aggressive, high-quality, low-cost operation, they worked long hours and watched every cent of expense. Also, they were intelligent enough to realize that, while they knew the market, knew engineering, and knew production, they did not know management or business finance. They kept the consultant involved in the company's management on a part-time basis and were willing to allow the more experienced financial management of the investor company to exercise control in this area.

PITFALLS IN FINANCING A BUSINESS

The cases of the two small companies outlined above illustrate many of the essentials in financing a business. For the sake of perspective, and to include some problems that any business encounters, let us look at major problem areas in which businesses often make mistakes.

Underestimating Cash Needs

As we have stressed already, one major mistake people starting small businesses make as well as those who have an operating business, is to underestimate cash needs. Any business, and especially a growing one, even if it leases its buildings, requires cash for equipment and machinery, for inventories, to finance accounts receivable, for start-up costs, and for a host of other things. In no part of a business is planning more important than in planning for cash.

The fact that a company's balance sheet shows it has millions of dollars of cash does not mean that it has all it needs. As we saw in the case of the Union Carbide Corporation in Chapter 6, a large amount of cash may be necessary to meet the company's particular needs. A small business may have urgent need for $50 thousand, a medium sized business for $500 thousand, a medium large business for $5 million, and a very large business for $100 million. The figures are different, but so are their needs for cash.

The best way to meet cash needs in a business is to provide for them before they become urgent. Banks are most willing to arrange for loans when a business is not urgently in need of money. Investors are most willing to invest when a company is financially healthy.

Underestimating Start-Up Costs

Another pitfall in financing a business is the underestimation of what it costs to start up a business, to embark on a new product development program, or to go into a new plant. There are always costs involved in doing something new, until we get to the point where we can operate efficiently. In the case of Genistron above, the three engineers were fortunate in having been forced to sit down and calculate how much they would need to spend before they could make any profits.

Underestimating the Need for Working Capital

The term working capital is used to indicate the amount by which current assets exceed current liabilities. As will be recalled, current assets are short-term assets such as accounts receivable and inventory, which a business must have to operate. Current liabilities are items such as accounts payable that represent amounts owed for a short time to those from whom we buy on a charge basis; they also include short-term borrowing from banks, and others to whom money is owed. Assuming

Baron Guy de Rothschild

Courtesy Drucker-Hilbert
Co., Inc.

Baron Guy de Rothschild is the senior member of the French branch of the House of Rothschild, the financial family that has figured so importantly in the history of Europe. He heads the Banque Rothschild which is not large as banks go, but is one of the most influential privately owned banks in the world, as well as the Compagnie du Nord, a holding company with far-flung mining, industrial, and financial interests.

Guy Edouard Alphonse de Rothschild was born in Paris on May 21, 1909. He is the great-great-grandson of the founder of the House of Rothschild, Mayer Anselm Rothschild. The family's financial history intertwines with that of almost every European nation. Napoleon Bonaparte, the Duke of Wellington, and Benjamin Disraeli are only a few of the illustrious men whose careers were influenced by the Rothschilds. In 1875, this outstanding family had England acquire title to the Suez Canal. In the early 1800s the family was investing in railroads even when a majority of experts believed that the human respiratory system could not stand a speed exceeding 15 miles per hour. Some experts predicted that the speed of the

a business pays its bills on time, its working capital represents an amount that must be available on a long-term basis because a company should always have more current assets than current liabilities. As mentioned in Chapter 6, banks and others like to see current assets at least double current liabilities.

As emphasized earlier, it is easy to underestimate the amount of money required for accounts receivable and inventories, especially if a business is expanding.

Failing to Watch Accounts Receivables and Inventories

Many companies, both small and large, get into trouble by allowing accounts receivable and inventories to get too large. In the desire to sell all it can, a company may permit its customers to be slow in paying their bills and may even acquire customers who cannot pay at all. Likewise, one of the most difficult things to do is to keep the company's

railroads would drive men to suicide and cause women to lapse into sexual orgies. Yet, the Rothschilds had the foresight to see the tremendous commercial potential which this invention possessed.

In 1936, Baron Guy entered the family firm of Monsieurs Rothschild Frères, the largest private bank in France. His business career was interrupted by the outbreak of World War II. Out of an original 26 officers in his battalion, Baron Guy de Rothschild was one of 3 to survive the heavy fighting that followed the German invasion of France in 1940. He was evacuated to England in May, but returned to France almost immediately and, for a short time, was a German prisoner of war. In 1941 he came to the United States with other members of his family. After reassembling that part of the Rothschild assets over which he could exercise control from the United States, he recrossed the Atlantic in 1943. His ship was torpedoed by a German submarine and he spent several hours in the water before being picked up by a British destroyer. Soon after his arrival in England he became a captain in the Free French Army and carried out several important missions.

Upon his return to civilian life, Baron Guy devoted himself to reconstructing and developing the family's inheritance. The Banque Rothschild is a deposit and branch bank, with assets of $400 million in 1972. He and his two cousins Alain and Elie control the holding company Compagnie du Nord, which owns 68 percent of Banque Rothschild. The rest of the bank is owned directly by the Rothschild family. Through the holding company they have gone into leasing, real estate, and other financial arrangements designed to secure growth. They have interests in nickel and other minerals, real estate companies, shipping, tourist enterprises, construction, food manufacturing, and cold storage.

The Baron is lean, athletic, silver-haired, and blue-eyed. He now limits his active sports to golfing and racing horses. He speaks impeccable English with a clipped British accent and insists on writing his own speeches. He and his wife maintain two magnificent residences—an 18th century mansion in Paris, and a 19th century chateau about 20 miles northeast of Paris.

administrators from buying more raw material, parts, and other supplies than necessary, or stocking more finished goods than are really required. Inventories cost money to carry, and if they are too large they may become obsolete and not salable except at distress prices.

In view of the amounts of money that can be tied up in accounts receivable and inventory, the costs of carrying them, and the danger of losses, the intelligent businessman will keep close watch over these.

Failing to Understand the Importance of Financial Forecasts

Another pitfall in financing any kind of business is failing to understand the importance of financial forecasts. By forecasting what sales and expenses will be, we are better able to see problems in making profits in time to do something about them. By forecasting our cash needs, we are less likely to run out of cash; we can provide for our cash needs well in advance, or else take steps to reduce our cash requirements if necessary.

Failing to Develop a Strong Credit Rating

Every business needs to have a strong credit rating. It needs a record of paying bills on time and of meeting loan and interest payments to banks when they are due. "Credit," let us note, comes from the Latin word meaning "trust." But to develop this trust, particularly in matters involving money, one must work at it. It calls for honesty in business dealing, meeting financial obligations as promised, and having the money to do so.

Failing to Use Bank Financing Properly

As shown in Chapter 7, commercial banks exist to lend funds to businesses as well as to individuals. But they are primarily concerned with making short-term loans for short-term needs. While in recent years they have been making long-term loans increasingly for their better customers, they are reluctant to have their loans used where the business should have more permanent investment either in the form of common stock, reinvested earnings, or long-term bonds and other loans.

Picking the Right Time to Go to the Public Market

Public investors are more willing to invest in company stocks or bonds at some times than at others. For a number of years prior to 1971, public investors were willing to put money into almost any security, common stock especially, of a company that looked promising. But by 1973 it was almost impossible to interest public investors in any new stock issue, and even the large electric and telephone companies had difficulty selling their highly secured bonds.

The "right" time to go to the public market for funds is when people will buy. But some times are more "right" than others, and 1973 was definitely "wrong." Picking the right time is mostly a matter of forecasting cash needs for years in advance so that the company hits the market with a new stock or bond issue when it is "right."

Failing to Budget Sales, Expenses, and Profits

As we shall see in Chapter 20, budgeting is simply giving numerical meaning to a company's plans. It involves, among other things, forecasting how much the company can expect to sell, what its costs will be, and the profits that will result. Some smaller businessmen (and even, on occasion, a few larger companies) go along selling what they can, paying bills, and waiting until the end of the year to see if they have made any money. This is called the "barrel" system of accounting— putting all your receipts in a barrel, withdrawing the cash needed for expenses, and what is left in the barrel at the end of the year is profits.

The trouble with the barrel approach is that the barrel may become empty before we get to the end of the year. The only way to be certain of making profits is to plan for them. This means planning sales and expenses so that profits result. It is the only way to know how much money a company will require for its operations and how much money it can expect to take in.

Failing to Budget Capital Expenditures

Sums spent for long-lived assets, such as buildings, machinery, office equipment, and computers, are classed as capital expenditures. Their importance can be seen from the fact that manufacturing requires an average of $35,000 of capital expenditures for every worker employed. Moreover, as wages and other labor costs increase, there is an incentive to use more labor-saving machinery.

It is not difficult to spend money for capital items. Anyone who has ever asked a production manager what he needs in the way of new machinery and equipment will be deluged by requests. Engineers always seem to need more test and measuring equipment. And office people can always use additional files, desks, computers, and typewriters. It is easy for any company, small or large, to find reasons for buying more capital equipment than it can afford.

Capital expenditures are locked up for a fairly long period of time, since these costs can only be recovered over a period of years through depreciation. Hence funds spent on capital must be invested in the company on a long-term basis. There are three main sources of such funds: the investment of stockholders, including earnings ploughed back into the company; long-term loans; and from such noncash expenses as depreciation charges.

Since long-term funds are almost invariably limited, and the demand for them within a company tends to be high, the only way capital expenditures can be controlled is to plan them carefully. And this means budgeting them.

Assuming Large Risks

There is almost no such thing as a safe thing in business. Almost every business operation involves some risk. Perhaps costs will be higher than anticipated. Perhaps that new product will not sell. Perhaps a competitor will develop a product or an advertising program that cuts into your sales. And so on. A company must assess its risks and avoid those it cannot afford.

One danger that haunts the small company is that it may take on a large contract—to build a special machine or to furnish a large customer with a large order—involving risks it cannot afford. In the urge to expand business, it is easy to overlook the risks. One small electronic equipment company that had built many special testing machines at prices from $2,000 to $5,000 each, took a contract for a new and exciting machine for a large aerospace company at a fixed price of $385,000. This almost led to the company's bankruptcy when difficulties were encountered in designing it and costs skyrocketed. The company finally delivered the machine more than a year late to an unhappy customer at an actual cost of more than $1,300,000. This kind of thing is, unfortunately, not unusual.

Large companies also make such mistakes. The Convair Division of General Dynamics Company undertook the development of jet airplanes in 1957, sold only 59 of them against a forecast of 260, ran into engineering and production problems, and lost $480 million. This was certainly an example of taking on a large risk without adequate assessment of it and with ineffective planning and control, after other companies had most of the large jet airplane market sewed up.

DEVELOPING A STRONG BANKING RELATIONSHIP

To show how a company develops a strong relationship with its bankers over a period of years, we may glance at the history of a middle-sized manufacturing company. This is a real company which has grown from a modest start to sales of $40 million in 1974. In the interest of confidence we will call it the XYZ Company.

The company was organized to manufacture and sell a simple product used in commercial buildings. The owners were a man and his two sons, who began it with $10,000. After an initial period when they worked in a garage, their business grew. The owners then received a fairly large order for which they could not finance necessary inventory and accounts receivable. Their banker gave them a 120-day loan for $20,000, on the security of their personal assets and reputation. At the end of the loan period, the large order had been produced and sold and the loan repaid. This was repeated from time to time as other large orders came in. The next loan from the bank was for $50,000 for an even larger order. This was repaid, and the next loan was for $80,000 which was also repaid on time.

As time went on and more and larger loans were made and repaid, the XYZ Company built a good credit reputation with the bank. The company operated profitably but the three owners took out no dividends, reinvesting their earnings in the business. This has gone on for 30 years. To be sure, the company brought in outside stockholders by selling stock to the public in 1960, and sold more stock to the public in 1967 and 1972. By 1973 the total equity of the stockholders was more than $7 million dollars and the short-term loans from the bank had reached more than $2 million. In that year, as business expanded and the company did not wish to sell more stock on a depressed stock market, the bank offered to meet the company's needs for expansion by agreeing to lend an additional $4 million on a five-year basis.

This history has been repeated over and over in American business. It shows that banking relationships and the borrowing of increased amounts of money depend on the ability of a company to build a reputation as a good credit risk. This, in turn, arises from a record of borrowing and repaying on time, of operating a business profitably, of raising stockholders' equity money to keep a reasonable debt-to-equity ratio, and of watching that cash requirements do not exceed cash available.

SUPPLEMENTING FINANCING BY USING LEASES

In the discussion of banking organizations in Chapter 7, we pointed out that there are companies which lease all sorts of equipment to businesses. Some of them lease office and plant buildings. Many individual investors and groups of investors will also lease plant and office buildings. The leasing of major assets is often an important source of company financing.

Some companies, as we have seen, consider that their chief function is producing and selling goods or services and not being in the real estate business. Safeway Stores was mentioned as an example of having leased most of its stores. Many companies rent such items of equipment as computers, automobiles, and typewriters. On the other hand, major items of machinery and equipment are usually purchased. Some large companies such as General Motors, Ford, Du Pont, and United States Steel, do little leasing, apparently feeling that they can finance their own major assets at costs lower than leasing.

When a company considers leasing in its program of financing it must also consider the costs. The company or investor from whom it leases assets must plan on making a satisfactory interest return on its investment, plus an allowance for depreciation, plus the costs of arranging and administering the lease, plus a profit. Moreover, at the end of the lease the property belongs to the lessor and not to the company. But leasing, as indicated in Chapter 7, cannot be overlooked as a way of raising money for needed company assets.

GOING TO THE PUBLIC MARKET

The nature of the public market for long-term funds was discussed in the previous chapter. Let us now take a look at how a company approaches that market.

Selecting an Underwriter

The first thing to do is to select an underwriter. The problem of selecting an underwriter to handle the company's distribution of securities is an important one for any company wishing to go to the public market for funds. Usually and certainly for a company's first trip to the public market, a single investment banker is selected. This security house then normally gets other investment bankers to participate with it in distributing an issue, particularly if the issue of securities is fairly large.

The investment banker does this by forming a temporary partnership, called a syndicate. A syndicate may be only two underwriters joining together. In other cases, a large group of investment bankers may participate. When Howard Hughes sold his Hughes Tool Company to the public in December 1972, the lead underwriter—Merrill Lynch, Pierce, Fenner & Smith—enlisted a total of 209 other underwriters to help sell the 5 million shares of common stock at a total price of approximately $145 million. Even underwriters for much smaller issues will gather a number of investment bankers in a syndicate. When the Farr Company, a West Coast air filter manufacturer with sales of $23 million in 1972, sold 250,000 common shares to the public near the end of that year at $14.50 per share, the two lead underwriters had 28 other investment bankers assisting in the distribution of this fairly small issue.

There are several reasons why the selection of an underwriter is important to a company. The reputation of the underwriter in the investment community is important in making an offering of stock and bonds acceptable to investors. A company will also want its securities to be sold at the best possible price and to as many buyers as possible. This is of special importance to a smaller company wishing to establish its stock in the market so that traders can readily buy and sell it. Nothing is worse from the standpoint of investors than a security that cannot be easily bought or sold.

Another important consideration in selecting an underwriter is that such relationships tend to last a fairly long time. To be sure, a company is not contractually bound to an underwriter for more than a single issue. But investment bankers, accustomed to working together in the marketing of securities, tend to become something of a club in which members do not "steal" customers from one another. As a practical matter, therefore, it is not easy to change underwriters.

Registering a Security

As mentioned in the previous chapter, all new securities sold to the public, with a few exceptions, must be registered by filing information with the Securities and Exchange Commission and making available to any interested investor a summary of this information, called a *prospectus.* Companies with existing security issues must regularly file similar information.

Because the penalties for omitting any "material" facts (facts that could influence an investor in his decision to buy or sell) or for giving misleading information are severe, registration of new securities is a difficult and expensive task. Among the information required are financial statements for five years; a detailed description of the company, its products, and its competition; the purpose for which the proceeds of the security sale are to be used; a description of the company's management and such internal matters as its employee relations; the number of shares of stock owned by directors, officers, and anyone else with 10 percent or more of the company's stock; the salaries of all directors and of the three top officers making over $30,000 per year; the bonus arrangements for executives; the underwriting arrangements, including the fee charged by the underwriters; the opinions of legal counsel for both the company and its underwriters; the opinion of any other expert relied on by the company for information; and the certified opinion of the company's accountants. All of these experts, as well as all directors and officers who sign the registration statement, are held personally liable to security buyers for inaccurate information.

To prepare, file, and print a registration is expensive. It is also expensive to get the opinions of legal counsel, experts, and accounting firms. For a small company wishing to register a few million dollars of securities, these expenses can easily run from $75,000 to $100,000. For larger and more complex companies, costs are, of course, much higher. Naturally, the larger and better known companies selling a large stock or bond issue will incur higher total costs than a small company, but the costs as a percentage of the money raised may be quite small.

IMPACT OF TAXATION ON FINANCING A BUSINESS

Taxes and the way they are levied have a great deal of influence on what is done in business. We have seen that income taxes take away approximately half of the profits of most corporations. Almost anyone who has ever held a job knows how social security and other payroll taxes bite into his pay, but few people are aware of the load these taxes impose on the employer. Businesses must also pay property taxes of various kinds on their assets.

The cost of raising money through loans, leases, or bonds—that is, interest or rent—is an expense deductible from profits *before* income taxes. But dividends on common or preferred stock are paid *after* taxes. This tends to make financing by borrowing or leasing somewhat more attractive to a company than financing by the issuance of stock. If state and federal income taxes average about 50 percent of total profits, we can see that it is cheaper for a company to pay interest at an annual rate of 10 percent on bonds than promise stockholders a dividend of 6 percent.

However, as we saw in Chapter 6, a company must be concerned with the amount of debt in relation to its stock otustanding. Owners and lenders understandably get uneasy when debt or long-term leases are high, because debt must at some time be repaid; moreover, interest and rental charges must be paid whether business is good or not. Dividends, on the other hand, do not have to be paid, and when business is bad many corporations skip a year or even several years.

Taxes can influence the financing and operating of a business in many other ways. Their impact is often very complex and difficult to understand. A businessman, whether in a small or large company, will do well to consult tax specialists on any matter in which money is involved.

PAYING DIVIDENDS

Any company that has sold preferred or common stock to public investors has to consider the problem of paying dividends. A dividend is a return to stockholders for the use of their money. Dividends may be paid in cash or in stock; they have, at times, even been paid in property. Years ago, several distillers paid dividends in bottles of whiskey, before taxes on whiskey became so high as to make this prohibitive.

Cash Dividends

Cash dividends are usually paid quarterly, although a company may pay them at any time. The power to determine whether to pay a dividend and how large it will be rests with the board of directors. However, most large companies that want to attract long-term investors follow the practice of paying dividends regularly.

Many companies take pride in their long history of regular dividend payments. It is not unusual to see a notice in the financial pages saying that a certain company has declared its hundredth or two-hundredth regular dividend. American Telephone and Telegraph Company has paid dividends each year since 1882, Procter & Gamble since 1898, General Electric since 1899, Eastman Kodak since 1902, and Du Pont since 1905. Such a record cannot help but stamp a company's stock as being of "investment quality."

Investors get in the habit of relying on regular dividends. For that reason a company that has had an especially profitable year and wishes to declare a higher dividend than usual may announce an "extra" dividend, so as not to encourage expectations that it will become a regular thing. This practice was formerly known as "cutting a melon."

Stock Dividends

Occasionally companies pay dividends in stock rather than in cash. A company may, for example, pay a 5 percent stock dividend by sending each holder of 100 shares another 5 shares. This does not change the value of the total stockholders' equity. Suppose that a corporation's balance sheet shows total stockholders' equity of $10,000,000 and that there are 1,000,000 shares of stock. The equity value of each share is $10. If a dividend of 5 percent is declared by the company, there will then be 1,050,000 shares outstanding but the stockholders' equity will still be $10,000,000. Each share will have an equity value of $9.524.

But why does a company give out a dividend that merely increases the number of shares without changing the equity value of each stockholder's ownership? There are several reasons. When stock dividends are declared there are usually grounds for believing that a company will maintain the same cash dividend per share. If the dividend had been $1.00 per share, the holder of 100 shares who receives 5 more can expect to receive $105 in cash dividends. Another reason is that a company may wish to get more shares into the hands of the public to create a more active market. Still another reason is that a company may have high enough earnings to justify higher than regular dividends, but prefers to retain more of its cash for financing expansion.

A company may split its stock, giving each shareholder an additional share for each one he holds. This doubles the number of shares outstanding but with no change in the total equity value. This is usually done when a company's earnings have been good and the price of its stock has risen considerably. It is generally believed that more people will buy stocks at lower prices than at higher. Had International Business Machines, for example, never split its stock over the years, each share would now be worth $6,000 and few people would be able to buy shares at this price.

Cash Dividends or No Cash Dividends

Most companies feel that investors in common stock want and should get regular cash dividends as payment for the use of their money. However, some companies have taken the attitude that cash dividends should not be paid at all, on the ground that their stockholders will be better off if their companies reinvest their earnings in expansion. Such companies confine themselves to issuing occasional stock dividends. As mentioned earlier, Litton Industries has never paid a dividend in its corporate life. Braniff International Airways has paid only stock dividends for many years, and the same is true of many smaller fast-growing companies.

There have even been times when paying cash dividends was regarded by some investors and corporation officials as a sign of weakness. Those who put growth above other considerations said that if a company was any good it could make more money for its stockholders by reinvesting profits than by handing out its cash to stockholders. Luckily for those owners of stock who like to have cash returns from their investments, this has by no means been a customary practice.

How Much to Pay Out in Cash Dividends

How much of a company's annual earnings should it pay out to stockholders in cash dividends? The answer will depend upon a number of factors. A company owned by a few stockholders, all of whom are officers of the company and obtain adequate salaries from it, will normally prefer not to pay any dividends. They get income from the company through salaries and, so long as these are reasonable, the amounts so paid can be deducted from profits before taxes, while dividends would have to be paid from profits after taxes. It is easy to see why closely owned companies often prefer not to pay dividends, but to reinvest their profits after taxes.

In one medium-sized company owned by three men, each of whom had 150,000 shares of stock and drew a salary of $60,000 per year, payment of dividends did not make much sense to them. Had they each taken a salary of $45,000 and paid themselves dividends of $15,000 each, the company would have had to pay taxes on its larger profits amounting to an extra $22,500 for the three.

Companies that need cash to grow may choose to pay small dividends or none at all. Still another factor influencing the amount of earnings a company pays out in dividends is the extent to which a company's earnings are stable. If a company has high earnings one year and low earnings the next, it may prefer to pay lower dividends in the high-profit years so that it will not have to reduce dividends in low-profit years.

Although there are wide variations in dividend policies, most established companies that have stock held largely by the public tend to pay around 60 percent of their earnings in dividends. In good years the percentage may be somewhat lower, and in poor years it may be higher. This policy has apparently met with wide acceptance among investors. It represents a compromise between the demands of stockholders for cash and the need of companies to plough earnings back into expansion.

SUMMARY

In establishing and maintaining a business there are many problem areas. One of the major problems is how to finance a business so that we can start it, stay in it, and do so profitably. This was the subject of this chapter. It would be more dramatic to talk of the history of some of the great pioneers like Henry Ford or Thomas Watson. But in this chapter we chose to discuss the starting of a small retail business and a small manufacturing business. Then, we looked at some of the pitfalls in financing a business, the importance of developing a strong banking relationship, supplementing financing through leasing, and how to go to the public market for funds. In addition, other financial problems were discussed.

Perhaps the best way to approach some of the financial problems in starting a business is to look at two real-life cases. One is the case of the Liptons who developed a specialty retail store in Aspen, Colorado. The other is the case of Genistron, an electronic components business started by three engineers in Los Angeles. In both cases, the businesses succeeded because those who started them saw an opportunity, were willing to work hard, and were careful to plan ahead so that they had enough funds to see them through the initial stages.

But not all businesses are successful. Many fail; and most of these fail because of poor management, as we will see in Part Four of this book. As an evidence of this cause of failure, many problems arise from financing. Pitfalls in financing a business are (1) underestimating cash needs, (2) underestimating the costs of starting up a business, (3) underestimating the need for working capital, (4) failing to watch accounts receivable and inventories, (5) failing to understand the importance of financial forecasts, (6) failing to develop a strong credit rating, (7) failing to use bank financing properly, (8) failing to pick the right time to go to the public market, (9) failing to budget sales, expenses, and profits, (10) failing to budget capital expenditures, and (11) assuming risks too large for the company to take.

It is important for a company is to develop a strong relationship with its bankers. Because businesses are almost invariably dependent to some extent on bank funds, they must try to develop banker confidence through careful borrowing and prompt repayment of loans.

A company can obtain assets such as buildings and equipment by leasing them rather than buying them outright. Even large companies such as Safeway Stores do this. But the company must consider the costs and whether it may not be better off if it raises money from other sources and buys the buildings and equipment.

As a company grows and finds it must go to the public market for funds, new problems arise. It must select an underwriter who will do a good job of distributing the company's securities to the public. Since it is not easy to change underwriters, this step is exceedingly important. It must also register the new securities so as to meet the stringent requirements of the government on full and adequate disclosure of information.

In financing a business, the impact of income taxes cannot be overlooked. When a company finances by borrowing or leasing, it can treat interest or rental costs as expenses which are deductible for tax purposes before profits are determined. The net cost after taxes is consequently around half of the actual amounts paid in interest on rent.

On the other hand, if financing is done by the sale of stock, the dividends will not be deductible and must be paid from company earnings after income taxes.

Companies that raise money from the sale of preferred or common stock must consider whether to pay dividends, and how. Preferred stock dividends are almost invariably paid in cash, and most common stock dividends are so paid. But some companies give their common stockholders dividends in the form of stock of the corporation. This does not require paying out cash, and really does nothing more than increase the number of shares of a company's stock an investor holds. Even so, there are often good reasons why stock dividends should be paid and are acceptable to investors.

A company always has to face the problem of how much in cash dividends to pay out and, indeed, whether to pay any dividends at all. Those companies which do pay cash dividends seldom pay out all their earnings, preferring to keep some cash in the company to finance growth. There are often good reasons for not paying cash dividends at all. If a company is owned by a few people, all of whom receive salaries and bonuses from the company, they may prefer not to receive dividends on which they would have to pay personal income taxes. Also, in some fast-growing companies, investors prefer to see earnings put back into the company for expansion, rather than receive cash dividends. They hope to profit by an eventual increase of stock values.

KEY TERMS AND CONCEPTS

Start-up costs	Registering a security
Working capital	Prospectus
Financial forecasts	Cash dividends
Credit rating	Stock dividends
Budgeting sales, expenses, and profits	Stock splits
Budgeting capital expenditures	

QUESTIONS FOR ANALYSIS AND DISCUSSION

1. Why do you think the Liptons succeeded in Aspen? Why do you think the Genistron business succeeded? Did different factors account for the success of these two businesses? Why did the Genistron engineers have to do more detailed planning than the Liptons?

2. Among the major pitfalls in financing a business, the danger of underestimating cash needs heads the list. Why is this so important? What other of the pitfalls we have noted have a bearing on cash needs and planning?

3. Do the pitfalls in financing apply to a large company as well as to a small one? Would Ford, General Motors, or Union Carbide have to be concerned with any of these pitfalls? Do you believe that any of them would be more or less important for Illinois Bell Telephone Company or Pacific Telephone Company?

4. If you wished to develop a strong banking relationship so that you would be assured of the best possible credit from a bank, what would you do?

5. How does a company go about selecting an underwriter, or an investment banker? Why is this likely to be a very important decision for a business?

6. Do you see why the registering of a security with the Securities and Exchange Commission can be costly and very important? Why should a company have to go through this?

7. How would taxes influence a business in its financing program? Is the impact of taxes important to both small and large businesses?

8. Should a company pay cash dividends? Why? How much?

9. What does a stockholder gain when a company pays him stock dividends? Why would a company want to do this?

10. Assuming you owned stock in a profitable fast-growing company, would you prefer: (1) cash dividends; (2) stock dividends; or (3) no dividends? Why?

SUGGESTED READINGS

Johnson, R. W. *Financial Management* (4th ed.). Boston: Allyn and Bacon, 1971, Chapters 4–11, 22.

Pfeffer, I. (ed.) *The Financing of Small Business*. New York: The Macmillan Company, 1967.

Summers, G. W. *Financing and Initial Operations of New Firms*. Englewood Cliffs, N.J.: Prentice-Hall, Inc., 1962.

Van Horne, J. C. *Fundamentals of Financial Management* (2d ed.). Englewood Cliffs, N.J.: Prentice-Hall, Inc., 1974, Chapters 5–8.

Weston, J. F., and E. F. Brigham *Essentials of Managerial Finance* (3d ed.). Hinsdale, Ill.: The Dryden Press, 1974, Chapters 5–9, 25.

part three

Operating a Business

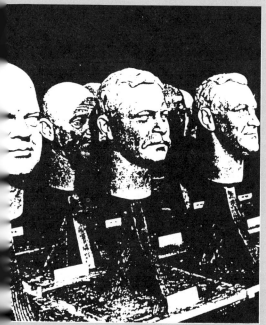

Disney's "Imagineering"

While most of the world's managers go plodding along in the footsteps of others, the managers of WED Enterprises, Inc., have the opportunity to forge out ahead of everybody and to do things that have never been done before. They call it "imagineering" WED Enterprises is the architectural, engineering, research, and development arm of Walt Disney Productions. It is a kind of paradise for a person with ideas, for it gives its employees the chance to dream dreams and try experiments that other companies would dismiss automatically. Under the Disney approach, fueled with the Disney bankroll, the *idea* is the thing to be accomplished.

When you're designing the world's magic kingdom of vacations for Walt Disney Productions, you can't just order things from a catalogue. The magic kingdom has to be created out of thin air. This makes it different from other businesses. At the same time, it contains a valuable lesson for every manager—that to manage is to imagine. The Disney empire was built up by doing things first . . . doing things that nobody else had done before. But the fact remains that *Disney does its work consistently better than others in the same business do theirs.*

Whether the business is amusement parks or steel mills, management has to take chances if it wants to lead. The activity of management requires risk-taking, and it is up to the individual manager to decide whether his risks will be big ones or so small as not to be risks at all. If a company wants to be a leader, it needs creative people in its policy-making offices. The creative people should not be confined to the art department or the advertising division.

When the creative doors are thrown open, a company tries things. It builds a new kind of recreation experience like Disneyland when amusement parks are closing down right and left. It spends millions on projects that could have been half-done for thousands. It goes all the way in an effort to achieve reality, authenticity, and perfection. In Disney's case, this dedication to quality paid off. It is true that the same approach might not work for other companies without the Disney name or the Disney resources, but there is always a reward for creativity in even the most mundane activity.

It is worthwhile to consider the way in which the Disney managers approach their tasks. Their product, of course, is entertainment. And every year it takes a little more to amuse that fickle tyrant the public. But the Disney approach is not simply to create something a little better than last year's model. Each project is attacked in the light of its potential, to see how far it can be developed. The landscaping of Disney World, for example, could have been quite acceptably accomplished with the traditional central Florida greenery. For a couple of million dollars, a local nursery would certainly have made the place neat and green enough for most purposes. However, the Disney philosophy calls for something more. "We are constantly aware," says a Disney landscape architect, "that we are designing for some of the world's largest and busiest 'stages' where guests are also a part of the scene. Our plantings must help create the environment of the past, or the future, or of fantasy, and in themselves add extra visual pleasure for our visitors." Work on the landscaping began three years before the park was even built. Fifty-five thousand trees and shrubs were brought in from all over the world—not for planting but for testing. The Jungle Cruise had to have real African flora. And Liberty Square could hardly be right without moving in a 32-ton Liberty Oak. The visitors to Disney World may never know the money and trouble that went into creating the landscape, but they will know that their day at Disney World was superb.

The same principle was followed in stocking the shops at Disney World. An acceptable line of souvenirs might have been obtained from a wholesale house. The customers would never have missed the curious and one-of-a-kind items that the Disney people came up with. Just as the shops must be unique, so must the boats be authentically reproduced and clean-running, and the people-moving systems convenient and safe. The logistics of all this require the coordinated efforts of 500 WED architects, engineers, research, and design experts, 6,000 construction workers, and an army of employees who are "cast" —not hired—to perform in the magic kingdom.

The businessman may scoff at the notion of creative management. "People don't pay for quality," he may object. To some extent, he is right. But the fact remains that people are willing to pay for the quality given them by the Disney enterprises.

10

Creating Customers

Ralph Waldo Emerson once said, "If a man will build a better mousetrap, the world will beat a path to his door." Everyone repeats this, and it goes well in pep talks to people involved in product development. But is it true? We like to think that if we make something better the world will reward us by buying it. The fact is, though, people being what they are, that quite a few other characteristics of a product are more important than having something new when you decide to sell it.

Chester M. Woolworth, president of the Animal Trap Company of America, took Emerson's advice seriously. His company since 1928 had produced millions of the classic wooden mousetraps. After listening to innumerable cocktail party references to the "better mousetrap," Mr. Woolworth decided that the time had come to improve his product.

The Animal Trap Company of America did careful and thorough research on product design. It studied the eating, crawling, and nesting habits of mice, the different sizes of mice, and the preferred sizes of holes. Woolworth field-tested his new product before putting it into full production, and decided that he had what the world was waiting for.

The new trap was modern, streamlined, and made of molded black plastic. It worked like a charm: the mouse, attracted by the easily-inserted bait, tripped a spring on top of the trap and was neatly strangled. When the spring was pushed down from the top, the dead mouse fell out. The trap was noiselsss, sanitary, and relatively cheap. The consumers who tested it declared it to be superior. Mr. Woolworth looked forward now to hearing the old saw about the "better mousetrap," for he would be able to reply that he had made money out of one.

After the new mousetrap hit the market, Mr. Woolworth was greatly surprised to find that the world did *not* beat a path to his door—that the sales of his better mousetrap were very poor. The company tried various first-aid measures to save the new product, but the conventional mousetrap outsold it by the million. Why was the better mousetrap such a tremendous commercial failure?

Mr. Woolworth began looking into consumer attitudes. He found that in making its product research, the company had not judged the market adequately. The majority of mousetrap buyers were urban dwellers who had to cope with only one or two mice at most. They set traps at night because of the roaming habits of the mice and the fear that their children might be injured in the daytime. Women disliked having anything to do with either the mouse or the trap, and expected their husbands to take care of setting the trap and disposing of the mouse. But in the morning, the average husband had to rush for his train or bus, leaving the disposal job to his wife. Since the trap was so inexpensive and the mouse was probably the only one in the house, the wife would throw away both trap and mouse, solving her problem quickly and easily.

The new mousetrap, however, with its sleek black exterior, looked too expensive to throw away, even though it cost only a little more than the wooden trap. It had to be emptied, cleaned, and put on a shelf where it remained a gruesome reminder of the possible presence of frightening and perhaps diseased creatures. When husbands bought the new mousetrap, wives would not let them use it or would not purchase it again.

The better mousetrap failed because the marketing study had been incomplete. As far as the mouse was concerned, the trap was almost perfect. As far as the consumer was concerned, it was completely unsatisfactory. It did not meet the standards, problems, needs, and habits of the 20th-century urban family.

Are You a "Logical" Buyer?

Consider your own most recent selection and purchase of a piece of clothing. What product characteristics did you seek out first? Were you looking primarily for durability and warmth? How much did the price affect your decision? Were you influenced by the number of other people who would be likely to wear a similar style or brand? To what extent were your perceptions of the garment shaped by advertising? Did you, in light of all these influences, purchase according to product quality or according to a constellation of other ideas. And just how definable is "quality" anyhow?

The more cynical might say, "If a man will build a better mousetrap . . . some mouse is going to make a million in the survival training business." Competition is not yet that keen between man and mouse, but it has reached an all-time high between man and man. The seemingly simple act of bringing customer and product together calls upon the coordinated efforts of several fields of endeavor.

Of course a product must have a certain amount of quality if the business is to be honest and long-term. Quality is the start, but definitely not the end. Selling a product requires the supportive effort of many skills and activities. Together these skills and activities comprise what we call marketing. Marketing is more than simple advertising or merchandising. It involves all the activities required to make a product the customer will buy and get it to the right place at the right price at the right time.

Marketing teachers often like to summarize what marketing is about in the words: Product, Price, Place, and Promotion. In the last analysis, however, regardless of the effort and expertise that go into the marketing plan, it is a failure unless the customer buys. The end result is what counts. If the product sells . . . the marketing approach must have been right.

CREATING CUSTOMERS OR CREATING *FOR* CUSTOMERS

In recent years, the marketing function has become more and more important in American industry. At first, the marketing department's primary responsibility was for sales activities. Soon it became obvious that the functions of advertising, public relations, and promotion were also an integral part of the marketing thrust. Further experience showed that other parts of a company's activities were also important to the marketing effort. Soon product development, marketing research, product servicing, and forecasting also began to come under the jurisdiction of the marketing director. The purpose was to help make the entire company more responsive to the consumer. In the 1950s firms such as Pillsbury and General Electric began to say that their entire business function should begin and end with the customer. They felt that they must discover his needs or wishes and try to fulfill them. This idea has been called the "total marketing concept," or "consumer-oriented management." A company which accepts this approach will alter its organizational chart and its philosophy until the marketing people have the facilities and power to bring about a unified customer-oriented operation.

This emphasis on customer service should not be brushed off as a lot of theorizing. Of course, the first concern of marketing is to make a profit for the company's investors. But management is coming increasingly to see customer satisfaction as the only basis for profitable operations in the long run.

The Essence of Consumer Satisfaction

The marketing task involves two phases. In the first phase the company or its marketing specialist tries to find out exactly what goods and services consumers are ready to buy. In the second phase the company undertakes to provide those items at the right time, place, and price.

Some people argue that the recent upsurge of criticism by consumer groups led by spokesmen such as Ralph Nader proves that the new marketing approach has made no difference, and that business really doesn't care about the consumer except on paper. But it is too soon to jump to this conclusion. It may be true, as the consumerists often say, that management is still thinking more of the dollar than of the customer. But any social change takes time.

Progress is being made. Management has usually been ready to adopt a consumer-oriented policy, and now the practical effects are beginning to appear. For example, when the public began to express concern about phosphates in detergents as a source of water pollution, Procter & Gamble, Colgate-Palmolive, and other firms began to produce soaps without phosphate. In Chicago, concerned citizens were able to prohibit the sale of regular phosphate detergents within the city limits. Many housewives, however, began to do their shopping in the suburbs in order to get the detergents they were accustomed to. Eventually, the loss of sales taxes prompted the city to lift the phosphate ban and shopping habits returned to normal. In this case a majority of the consumers got what they wanted despite the efforts of business, government, and environmentalists.

Make no mistake—business still operates to make a profit. The broadening of the marketing concept and the establishment of the customer-as-king philosophy were never adopted for the purpose of going out of business. The new approach was meant to keep business in continued contact with customers and their desires. It was a move away from the certain destruction of business by the profits-only philosophy.

WHO ARE THE CUSTOMERS?

When someone speaks of the American consumer most people think of a private citizen purchasing items in a retail store. But though he is always the *ultimate* consumer, John Doe is not the number one buyer of American products. Two other kinds of customer—the industrial customer and the commercial customer—precede the man on the street in the total volume of their purchases. This is because one purchase by John Doe may have been preceded by many prior purchases by businessmen. When a customer buys a television set or a week's stay in a hospital room, he is only making the final purchase in each case. The television set and the hospital room were brought into readiness for him through a multitude of previous purchases.

Industrial customers purchase goods for resale either as they are or in an altered form. Consider the number of raw material purchases required to bring together the printed book you are now reading. Timber was sold and processed by a paper mill, chemicals and dyes were combined to make the ink, and iron ore was mined, refined, and made into steel for printing presses. This does not include the camera and film used for pictures, or the skill of artists, editors, and reviewers. An amazing proliferation of industrial sales preceded your single purchase. Whenever we attempt to trace the string of buyer-seller situations which preceded our purchase of any article, we are amazed that the final product is still within our price range.

Commercial customers include hotels, offices, banks, schools, hospitals, and theaters. They do not generally alter the goods before resale. Many of the materials they buy are intended to be used up in the production of a service or resold without significant change. Typing paper, soap, chalk, pencils, and other supplies are examples of their purchases.

"Getting to Know You"

As we saw earlier, in the examples of Mr. Woolworth and his mousetrap, it is important for a businessman to know what his customers want. But to find out what customers want is sometimes exceedingly difficult. The customers themselves may not be able to tell you.

Provided with two or more alternatives, the customer can usually make a clear-cut decision. But he does not, as a rule, think in terms of new products or of refinements that might be made in an existing service. The public's inability to imagine in advance what it wants is complicated by a tendency to be rather fickle. Some manufacturers have learned bitter lessons from trying to give the public what the public said it wanted. For example, in the 1950s the Ford Motor Company conducted considerable market research into the feasibility of a new model line, and concluded that there were millions of potential buyers for it. But by the time the Edsel became a reality the public had changed its mind, and Ford lost $225 million.

Finding Out What Buyers Want

Researchers have used three different ways of establishing what the public really wants without asking it. The first way has been to study the consumer, sometimes through very elaborate questionnaires and interviews, to find out how buyers are likely to respond to a new product. The automobile industry has often been criticized for designing cars that appeal to the desire to be powerful or to look important. Detroit has merely discovered what people are most likely to buy, and is responding to the pressures of the market.

Because public needs are so difficult to determine, some firms use a second approach. They simply ignore what the public says it wants and make the product they think the public *ought* to want. Then they use advertising to make the public want it. Such an approach seems on the surface to reflect a total disregard for the customer. Yet in many cases business is actually better qualified to recognize a public need than is the public itself. An electronics engineer is obviously more competent to design an improvement on a television set, and to explain its advantages, than is the man in the street.

The third approach to the difficult task of establishing the public's true wants and needs is the use of a test market. It has become the growing practice for businesses to field-test a new product in a single city or in a representative sample of small areas. General Mills is reported to have spent almost $6,000,000 in 1973 to introduce its "Nature Valley" natural cereal to northwestern and western markets. Some other examples of test marketing are listed in Figure 10–1, taken from

FIGURE 10–1

News Briefs from One Issue of *Advertising Age,* August 13, 1973

● **Clorox Co.,** Oakland, on Aug. 13 will begin testing Cooking Ease, natural vegetable cooking spray in 6-oz. aerosol cans, via tv in Fort Wayne and in Fresno. Agency is Botsford Ketchum, San Francisco.

● **American Brands'** American Tobacco division is expanding into the western states and the Southeast with Twist, a new lemon menthol 100mm cigaret which entered Atlanta and San Diego test markets in late spring (AA, May 21). Twist is getting print support with introductory theme, "Our new menthol is a lemon." F. William Free & Co., New York, is the agency.

● **Alcon Laboratories,** Fort Worth, has introduced Lens-Mate all-purpose contact lens solution nationally, backed by a $500,000 campaign on NBC-TV's "Today" and "Tonight." Witherspoon & Associates is the agency.

● **Andrew Jergens Co.,** Cincinnati, is introducing Direct Aid hand lotion nationally after successful testing for about a year. A multi-media campaign, created by Cunningham & Walsh, is planned.

● **Warner-Lambert Co.,** Morris Plains, N.J., is introducing Effergrip denture adhesive in powder and cream forms, backed by a multi-million-dollar print, tv and couponing campaign. Meanwhile, Block Drug, Jersey City, is expanding its Poli-Grip line to include Super Poli-Grip for hard to hold dentures, supported by a $2,000,000 tv and print effort. Grey handles Super Poli-Grip; Bates has Effergrip.

● **Voir,** Chicago, first scheduled as a male-oriented magazine to bow in August, and later as a female-oriented magazine to bow in the '73 fourth quarter (AA, July 16), "has been postponed indefinitely due to the state of the market because of the recent Supreme Court obscenity ruling," according to Don Myrus, editor-in-chief of *Gallery, Voir's* parent. Mr. Myrus had been president of the subsidiary, Voir Publications Co.

● **Evinrude Motors,** division of Outboard Marine Corp., Milwaukee, has entered the electric outboard motor market with Scout, a model set to go on the market in October or November. Advertising for Scout, the company's first such entry, is through Cramer-Krasselt Co. Evinrude's sister company, Johnson Motors, Waukegan, Ill., also will have the unit available under its own name. Johnson's agency is Hoffman, York, Baker & Johnson, Milwaukee.

● **The two-month-old toiletries division** of Hoffmann-La Roche is testing Seven Reasons instant hair conditioner in Philadelphia and Louisville, using free trial offer ads in Sunday supplements. DKG Inc., New York, is the agency.

Advertising Age. While the field test is probably the most accurate gauge of public interest in a product, it is also the most complex. It involves all the costs of product development that would be incurred for full-scale production. This method is used in order to avoid the far greater costs that would be involved in marketing a product for which there was insufficient demand.

Background Knowledge for Marketing

In addition to the subjective desires of the consuming public, there are certain objective factors to be considered in setting up any marketing program. The planner must remember that buying patterns differ from one region to another. So do the characteristics of the population. He must find out where his customers are by studying reports on trends in the population, such as the migration of people from one region to another, or the kinds of jobs at which they work. He must know the age structure of the population—is he serving the teenage crowd or senior citizens? He must also try to determine whether these things will change by the time his product reaches the market. What income levels is his product intended to appeal to? Will the customer regard it as a luxury or as a necessity? Will it appeal to a particular racial or ethnic group? Should adjustments be made in the light of educational trends in the nation?

All of this information is available if the planner knows where to look. He can get varied and useful breakdowns of national census information from the Bureau of the Census, and other statistical data from specialized periodicals, from business sources such as the Conference Board, from university survey centers, from the Federal Reserve System, and even from some advertising agencies.

Understanding and serving the customer, whether an industrial or a commercial buyer or a private individual, requires a great deal of creativity. Effective customer-oriented marketing is not merely a matter of following formulas. It is a puzzle, a quest, a maze, and it can only be mastered by skilled and dedicated planners.

BUYER BEHAVIOR

Whatever the thinking that led to a certain product or service, the marketing specialist usually must devise the program for selling it. Even when products are carefully sculptured to meet customer requests, there are still the tasks of advertising, promotion, sales, and follow-through. Because marketing personnel are so closely involved with the customer and his responses, they are always interested in the various theories of human motivation.

Getting Inside the Mind of the Buyer

The main task of the marketer interested in selling a specific product or service is to get inside the mind of the prospective buyer. He must try to see the product as the buyer sees it. He must feel the pressures for and against buying just as the buyer feels them. Is the buyer one of the group called *final* purchasers, who will use the product himself? Or is he one of the *intermediate* purchasers, who will remake or resell what he has bought?

If the purchaser is a final customer, he will behave differently than if he is a purchasing agent for a company that is an intermediate purchaser. Typically, the ultimate consumer is swayed more by his emotions than is the professional buyer. His impulse to buy will spring from one or more of the following motives.

1. Satisfaction of the senses—he likes the way the product feels, tastes, smells, looks, or sounds.
2. Preservation of the species—he thinks it will help him or his family to live longer or better.
3. Fear—he is afraid of what may happen if he does not have the particular product.
4. Rest and recreation—it looks as if it is easy or fun.
5. Pride—he thinks this product may change the way others see him or the way he sees himself.
6. Striving—ownership of this product represents the accomplishment of a worthwhile goal.
7. Curiosity or mystery—the product looks new, different, excitingly unique.

Quantitative and Qualitative Data

It is difficult to tell how people will respond to a product. The motives of each individual are locked up inside of him. While it is important for the marketing planner to know how many male senior citizens live in a given marketing area, he must try to supplement such *quantitative* data with *qualitative* insights into the likely behavior of purchasers.

Qualitative information can be gathered in part through methods known as motivational research. But the planner must sift the information carefully in terms of what he can guess about the potential purchaser. This requires care: he must sift the information through his own feeling for the buyer, yet he must never assume that his own motivations are those of the consumer. He must balance the input from all sources, field-test as thoroughly as possible, and, in the end, recommend and take the entrepreneurial leap. The business of marketing is the heart of business.

Mary Wells Lawrence

Mary Wells Lawrence is living proof that some women have a place in the executive suite. She is founder, chairman, and guiding inspiration of the advertising firm of Wells, Rich, Greene, Inc., and holds the highest-paid job of any woman in America.

Born Mary Georgene Berg in 1928, she was a shy child whose mother sent her to an elocution class at the age of five to make her more outgoing. In succeeding years she took dancing, drama, and music lessons. At 17 she left Youngstown, Ohio, to go to a theatrical school in New York. A year later she moved to Pittsburgh, where she studied at Carnegie Tech and married Burt Wells. In 1950 they moved to New York.

She broke into advertising with Macy's department store, where at 23 she became fashion advertising manager. A year later she went to work for McCann-Erickson, Inc., as a copy group head. In 1957 she switched to Doyle Dane Bernbach, Inc., and at 35 was making $40,000 a year as associate copy chief and vice president. She established her reputation by her successful handling of major campaigns for several important accounts.

In 1964 she moved to Jack Tinker &

INTERMEDIATE PURCHASERS

Intermediate buyers are more logical and systematic in making their purchases than are final customers. They are likely to follow certain prescribed methods. There may be standard bidding procedures or other negotiations. Sometimes the approach is so ironclad that the sale is to a system rather than to a human representative of the system. But in the majority of cases, a purchasing agent or other official will be the focal point of the marketing strategy. The marketing planner's task is once again to get inside the mind and situation of that potential buyer. He must single out the concerns which motivate the purchasing agent. Some of the factors often cited by purchasing agents are:

1. Supply sources must be dependable.
2. Bulk buying is important (quantity purchases are less expensive).
3. Price is important, but is not the deciding factor.
4. Long-term use may change the price of a product (long-term customers get better prices or services).

Partners, an agency that functioned largely
as a service agency, supplying affiliated
agencies with ideas. There she worked
with two young men, Richard Rich and
Stewart Greene, creating the award-win-
ning series of Alka-Seltzer commercials
for television. Another project that made
them famous was a new image for Braniff
Airlines. The three devised a campaign
built around the theme, "The end of the
plain plane," which involved painting the
Braniff airplanes in bright new colors and
getting the Italian designer Emilio Pucci
to redress the stewardesses. Braniff became known as "the Easter-egg airline."

This colorful approach to advertising
helped to boost Mary Wells' salary to
$80,000 a year by 1966. Her employers
asked her to sign a long-term contract,
but she elected to resign. Rich and Greene
also left, and the team renewed operations as Wells, Rich and Greene, Inc.
Braniff became the new firm's first client.
A number of other important accounts
were added and total billings were soon
in the $30 million range. By 1972 the
agency had $130 million in billings. She
was married to Braniff's president Harding
Lawrence in 1967, having been divorced

from Burt Wells in 1965. The Lawrences
have an apartment in New York, a house
in Dallas, Texas, a cattle ranch in Arizona,
and a villa at Cap Ferrat, Algeria.

Mary Wells always handles her firm's
presentations to clients, regarding this as
an especially critical part of client-agency
relationships. Her approach to management emphasizes what she found important during her rise: getting imaginative,
creative individuals who can be trusted
completely, then giving them considerable
independence. She gets to the office every
morning at 9, and works until 8 or 10 in
the evening. In 1972 she told an interviewer for *Vogue*, "For most of the past
23 years I have worked eight-day weeks."

She has been throughout her career
a popular subject of magazine articles—
many of them keyed to the question of
how it feels to be a woman in a man's
world. She turns the question away. "I've
got a successful track record so far," she
says, "and that's all that interests people."
One man who works with her has said,
"She's like steel, but not cold. Hot steel,
baby."

5. Purchase from a certain company may result in reciprocal purchases by that same company.
6. Products often need to be adapted or tailored to specific buyer
specifications.
7. The buyer must have a feeling that the product is the best overall
value for the money.

It is in the last factor that the possibilities for the marketing planner
are greatest. In selling to intermediate buyers, many transactions are
90 percent identical no matter who the vendor is. The remaining 10
percent of a transaction involves the buyer's "feeling" for the product.
It is in this area that he is open to the power of persuasion. The purchasing agent is a human being. It is the responsibility of the marketer
to invade that human being's psyche, determine the emotional needs
that may be satisfied in the process of the transaction, and claim the
10 percent of the purchase decision that lies outside the domain of the
purchasing system.

BUYER DEMAND

In addition to understanding the concerns that are likely to move the purchaser, the marketing planner needs to consider when, where, and how purchases are likely to be made. Decisions about advertising, location, promotion, packaging, and other elements in the marketing campaign depend upon these considerations. It obviously makes sense for an after-shave company to buy advertising time in connection with major sports events rather than during a daytime soap opera.

When People Buy

When people buy is of major importance in deciding about packaging methods, types of displays, kinds of outlets, and the time, placement, and emphasis of the advertising campaign. If purchases tend to be seasonal, the market planner may try to lengthen the season or multiply the number of seasons associated with the product. Retailers seem to begin their Christmas specials a little earlier each year, and greeting card companies regularly look for new days to commemorate. The outlets chosen will not be the same for a product that is generally needed on the spur of the moment throughout the 24 hours of the day as for one that tends to be chosen with care.

The "when" of purchasing is equally important in dealing with intermediate buyers. If items are used in daily operations or retailed to the public, the purchaser cannot afford delayed delivery. His entire business operation might be disrupted.

Where People Buy

It is equally important to know *where* the customers are most likely to buy. In this category the planner has to distinguish between the place of purchase and the place where the buying decision is made. If the buyer is likely to come into the store with his mind made up as to product brand, size, and price, then the seller will be wise to make his sales pitch earlier, ordinarily through advertising. On the other hand, if the buyer is likely to decide he needs the product at the point of purchase, the planner will emphasize displays or samples or other incentives inside the store. That is why candy, gum, and cigarettes are displayed at grocery check-out lanes, and not bleach or flour. Of course, both advertising and point-of-purchase promotion may be needed in a marketing campaign. Even spur-of-the-moment purchases will rely to some extent upon previous advertising and promotion.

How People Buy

The marketing planner must also give considerable attention to *how* his customers buy. For example, his choice of packaging will depend upon whether the customer buys on the run, under pressure, or purchases routinely from the same source every time. The "how" characteristics of one buyer will not be the same for every product. Is price likely to be the only determinant of a purchase? Is the package also influential, or should the development money go into some other aspect such as quality or quantity? Once the planner has formed a picture in his mind (and in the minds of his staff) of the buyer and the circumstances under which he is most likely to make his purchase, then he can take steps to make it easier for him. One helpful procedure is to dramatize the likely purchase situation: "Okay . . . here I come down to the corner store. . . . I am in a hurry. . . . My wife has sent me to the nearest store to shop. . . . I do not care about the brand. . . . I am concerned about price. . . . Still, I recognize that there are a lot of dollars wasted in trying to save pennies. . . . Now, let's name all the conditions which could possibly stand in my way or distract me from buying this particular product."

It is generally assumed that customers make choices between alternative products. Yet it is a rare housewife indeed who can stand to read all the labels on all the cans, juggle the information mentally, and make a calculated selection of the best value. More often she is going to rely on a brand she knows, on her own prior experience, or on someone's recommendation (even though it be from a movie star she has never met).

The planning of a marketing program will be a success or a failure according to the care with which the buyer's behavior is understood. The idea that a product can be rammed down the public throat by massive promotion is unfortunate because it is false. The art of inducing someone to buy was a certain resemblance to the art of enjoyable conversation: it is not the quantity of words that makes conversation pleasant, but rather a few words perfectly placed. For this reason, the most valuable time in the planning of a marketing approach is the time spent in analyzing the buyer and his likely behavior. Once the buyer is accurately pegged, the right approach will follow naturally.

PRODUCT LIFE CYCLE

The person who makes and markets a better mousetrap will be wise to set aside part of his income for the development of an even better mousetrap. Most products have life cycles: they are born, grow up, enjoy their peak years, and eventually wane. Not only is the average life of a product short, but it is getting shorter.

One research study found that the cycle for certain grocery products was declining from about 36 months for those starting in 1962 to 18 months for new items introduced in 1964. There is no longer any "lead time" for the company with an idea. The competition is so stiff, and the copiers so proficient, that any company that drags its feet over a new product may face its own product (with another name) as its major competition. A generation ago, Du Pont brought out nylon and had the new product to itself for 15 years. But recently, when it introduced Delrin—a product that it considered potentially as important as nylon—it took only two years for someone to bring out a closely competitive product. This shrinking of time advantages in the marketplace may soon make patent monopolies almost useless. What good is it to have a patent on some process if the life of the product is half the time required to get a patent violator into court?

Unless a company wants a rough ride on the waves of product life, it will take the wiser path of mixing its products and their life cycles. By staggering the new products, it is possible to avoid excessive start-ups and shut-downs and to produce a more or less continuous flow of products. The expense of seeing products through their introductory stages can be offset by the profits from products which have already weathered the introductory storms and have begun to supply a return on their investment.

Four periods in the life cycle of a product are generally recognized. These are depicted in Figure 10–2. *The introductory stage* invariably costs the company money. Not only are product development costs involved, but the company must go to considerable expense to convince the public to give the newcomer a try. The length of the introductory stage will vary, usually depending upon how easily the product can be tied to the success and reputation of its predecessors. As the introductory period comes to an end, the period of *market growth* begins. This period usually brings some profits. If the product is strong enough to make it beyond the introductory stage, it is likely to gather in a respectable portion of the market. Income from its sales continues to rise until the peak earning period begins, known as *market maturity.*

From the period of market maturity, the course is usually downhill. The period of *sales decline* will have been anticipated and even charted by the forward-looking organization. Provisions will have been made for the graceful demise of the product in skillful coordination with the

FIGURE 10–2

The Basic Life Cycle of a New Product

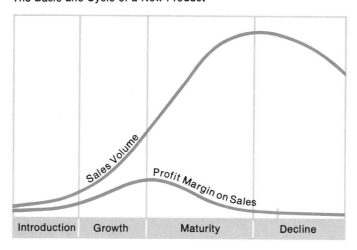

introduction of a "new, improved" product. At Procter & Gamble, Duz was the firm's leading detergent in the immediate postwar period. The public was humming, "Duz does everything." But the firm's shrewd management was quick to detect signs of declining public support, and after a time a new brand called Tide was introduced. The timing was so good that total company detergent sales showed no decrease.

The skill of a marketing effort can be measured by the smoothness of its product cycle charts. In the excitement of introducing a new product, it is easy to forget that mature products may produce ever larger profits because of lower advertising expenditures and the fact that development, tooling, and introduction costs have been paid off. If the company can move smoothly from one product's market maturity period to another product's market maturity period, then the marketing program is perfect. While a company's products may come and go, and its leading sellers vary from time to time, an efficient marketing approach can keep the organization on an even keel year after profitable year.

PRODUCT INNOVATION

"Because it is its purpose to create a customer," Peter Drucker has written, "any business enterprise has two—and only these two—basic functions: marketing and innovation."

Companies come into existence when somebody has a new idea or a

new twist on an old idea. If the idea isn't any good a company will fight an uphill battle even with the best marketing strategy. No company can remain in business with a product of questionable value. It was innovation that put the company into business, and it will be further innovation that enables it to succeed.

The innovative outlook can only be fostered by wise management. When Neil McElroy was chairman at Procter & Gamble, a customer wrote to him complaining that every box of Tide for over two years had claimed to be new or improved. She thought it dishonest and misleading to continue claiming credit for an old improvement. McElroy responded by saying he hoped that there would never be a box of Tide that was not new or improved. While the firm's legal department limited each specific improvement to six months' publicity, McElroy said, he and top management were committed to making at least two *major* improvements each year.

No company, of course, wants to go on record as opposing innovation. Everyone loves creativity—at least in theory. In actuality, innovation is difficult to handle. It never fits standard molds and methods. It calls for expensive and initially clumsy experimentation which often goes against the grain of production-oriented management. Only the wisest company executives will have the wisdom and patience to foster innovation.

The management consulting firm of Booz-Allen & Hamilton made a study of large companies and found that, even with careful planning, approximately 50 percent of their new-product introductions failed. The experience of 51 companies is summarized in Figure 10–3. The rate of failure is even higher for smaller companies.

Before a product even reaches the stage of development, many ideas must be investigated and discarded. The Pharmaceutical Manufacturers' Association reports that the odds are more than 6,000 to 1 that a newly discovered drug will never reach the market. In one year, 168,-000 substances were tested in pharmaceutical laboratories and only 28 became marketable drugs. J. H. Whitney and Co., a well-known investment firm, investigated 2,100 new-product propositions in several industries and found only 17 that were considered to have merit. Only two of these become conspicuously successful.

THE NEW-PRODUCT PLANNER

The first step in the development of new products is to *generate new-product ideas.* It is not difficult to generate ideas, for they are

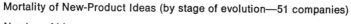

FIGURE 10-3

Mortality of New-Product Ideas (by stage of evolution—51 companies)

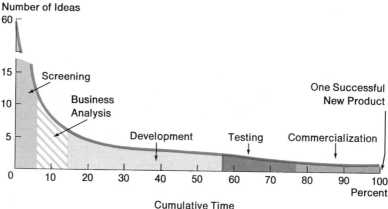

Source: Management Research Department, Booz-Allen & Hamilton, Inc.

already bubbling in the heads of innovative salesmen, consumers, and others associated with the product. The company's real job is to open the door to the idea people.

Screening

When the ideas flow in, they must be screened. In many ways, this is the most critical step of all. Initial investigation and discussion may be blocked by closed minds or traditional orientations. In screening an idea, management will decide whether or not the new idea "fits" the company. This is followed by a business analysis to see if the product would be profitable.

Next, technical research must be conducted to find out whether the product or process will work. This involves *development* of prototypes to see whether the idea can be produced, and *feasibility studies* to determine if it is economically feasible. When the pilot projects and technical refinements have been completed, it is time to test the product to see how well it performs in comparison with competitive products. Some technical adjustments will be made as a result of the product tests.

After planning the marketing and manufacturing programs, most firms take the product into a *test market*. Testing in limited geographical areas is wise because such tests are easier to control and monitor, and costs are lower.

The final stage is that of *full-scale production and marketing*. At the same time, development should be getting under way on this product's successor . . . even though it may be essentially the same product with just "a refreshing hint of menthol" added.

NEW-PRODUCT PLANNING

A few companies have organizational guidelines for developing new products. If, for instance, it is company policy that the firm will not in any way venture outside its specific field, there is no need to waste time investigating a new product in a related, but different, field. Many forward-looking marketing managers have found it useful to draw up specific policies for the development of new products. Robert Townsend suggests that by defining the business of Avis as "renting and leasing vehicles without drivers" he helped them stop considering the acquisition of related businesses such as motels, airlines, and travel agencies.

Product policies serve as guides for writing explicit policies about product development. Then the new-product manager does not have to spend time rethinking the grounds for accepting or rejecting every new suggestion that comes in. Many of them are bound to fall into the same categories and can be dealt with quickly if the new-product policies have been clearly stated.

When specific policy statements are made, it is possible to evaluate and even to quantify the company's potential interest in a new idea. Figure 10–4 illustrates how easily this can be done for a number of different factors at once. A company should also schedule a regular and thorough reevaluation of its existing line of products, and not assume that because a product was right for the company two years ago it is right for the company today. Some products simply become obsolete and need to be pruned away, lest they sap the energy that should go into developing new and more promising products.

It should be noted that "new product" can have a wide variety of meanings. It may be a product never before produced by the company, or it may simply be a slightly altered version of the old product. The Federal Trade Commission requires that for a product to be called "new" it must be either entirely new or changed in a "functionally significant or substantial respect." But the word "new" is so dear to American advertising that few companies are willing to do without it.

Product planning and product policy are important because they determine what the real direction of a company will be. Management should be willing to tell the truth at the policy-making stage. If profits are to be the prime objective of its products, management should say

FIGURE 10–4

Illustrative Screening Profile for a New Product

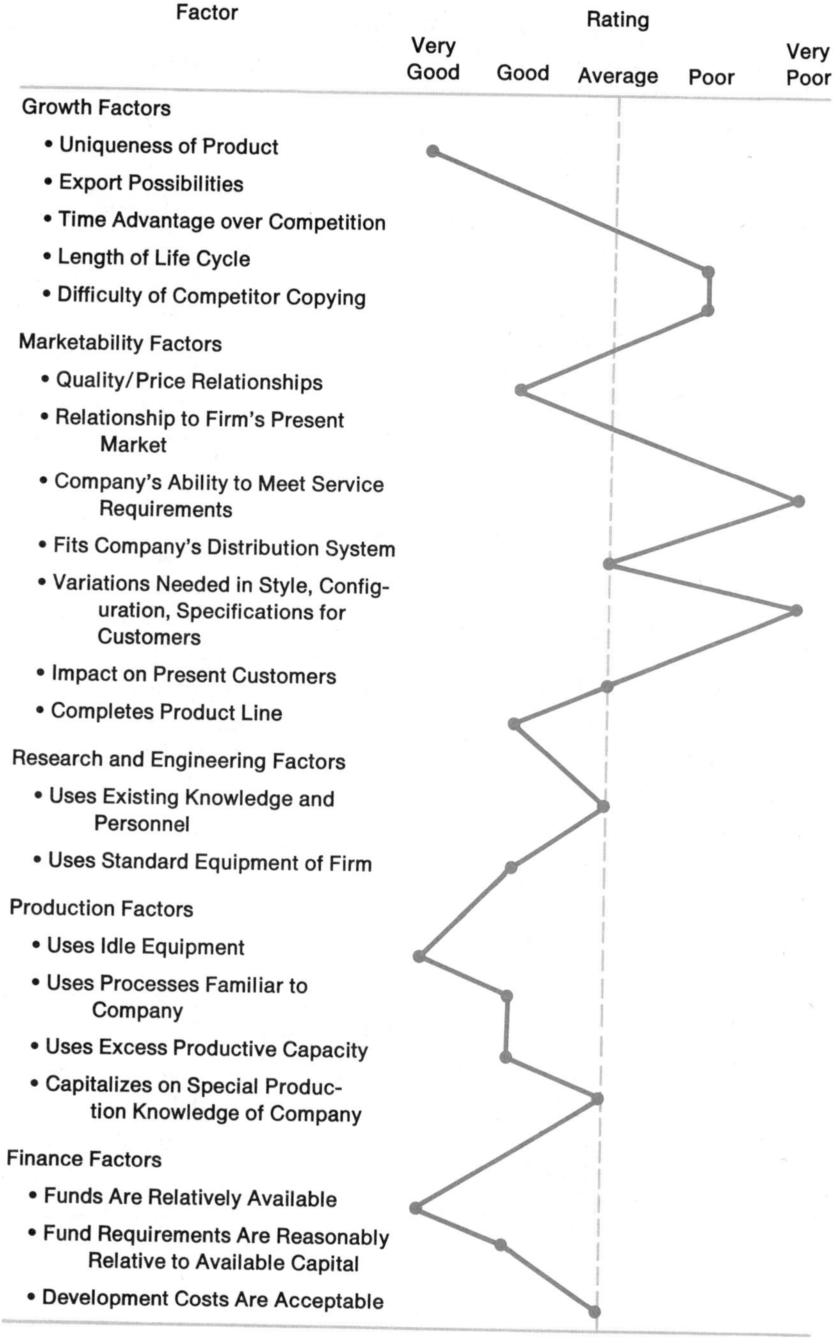

Source: G. A. Steiner, *Top Management Planning* (New York: The Macmillan Company, 1969), p. 584.

so . . . and not just talk about the nobility of the company's service to mankind. Expressions of concern about the responsiveness of product design to public need can become real influences only if they are hammered into policy. The great value of policy statements in any phase of business is the opportunity to make important decisions ahead of time so that cool reasoning can be done before the heat of a crisis.

NEW-PRODUCT DEVELOPMENT

Companies develop new products in many and varied ways. Some have departments charged with continuing research and refinement. Others utilize new-product executives or product managers to develop new ideas. Committees and departments assigned to product planning are often able to accomplish more because they work at the job full time. Many have specific directives to keep the company ahead of its competition. However, only the larger corporation can afford the luxury of setting up a whole new-product division, closely integrated with its research and development arm.

New-product planners have to do more than decide whether or not a product will be useful to consumers and can be sold at a profit. There are other considerations: the effect of the proposed product on current product lines, its effect on the company's product mix (or relative amounts of products of various kinds which will maximize profits), and the company's overall product strategy.

Few business leaders will admit that they deliberately design products to break down, wear out, or go out of vogue in a relatively short time. Ralph Nader and other consumerist leaders have pointed to the annual automobile model changes as proof of their charge that business tries to exploit the consumer through "planned obsolescence." Experience has shown, however, that customers usually demand the additional piece of chrome which makes last year's model obsolete. The practice of "planned obsolescence" has advantages for the producers and middlemen, since new models may help them out of the market maturity stage of the product life cycle and back into the more profitable market growth stage. But the recent success of Volkswagen, Pinto, and Gremlin with a minimum of year-to-year changes casts doubt on the necessity of planned obsolescence.

WHY PRODUCTS FAIL

Every year a multitude of new products come flowing into the public's consciousness on a great swell of jingles and fancy commercials.

With a few notable exceptions, there is little difference between the ad campaigns of those products that survive and those that fail. Investors might well wonder whether bringing out a new product is anything other than a gamble. Each year the marketing experts add to their knowledge of what it takes to make a product succeed. And each year the list of exceptions to their rules gets longer and longer.

Experienced product developers have learned that (1) you do everything you possibly can to make the new product fit the public need and market trend, (2) have it scrutinized by experienced marketers, and (3) hope that the public will buy it. Product developers can, in the final analysis, only do their best to remove all possible obstacles to success—the rest is in the great uncontrollable domain of public response.

It takes genuine creativity to recognize a new product. A new product is not just one that has never been available before. Many "new" products are merely updates of old ones, or modern applications of the same old basics. In a study conducted for the Conference Board, one of the authors was able to identify several types of innovations that are frequently considered new products.

1. *A new model.* This is a product which presents a technical improvement, packaging change, or other modification of an existing product. It is usually designed to be sold to the same customers for the same uses as the current product. Examples are a new model of automobile or cake mix.

2. *A new product in a familiar market.* In this instance, the product is new to the company but the market in which it is to be sold is one that the company is familiar with. For example, a company making and selling herbicides to control broad-leaf weeds may decide to sell one that controls narrow-leaf or grass-like weeds.

3. *A product not new to the market but new to the firm.* Transistor-grade silicon was a new product for Monsanto Chemical, but it had already been produced by competitors and sold in markets served by Monsanto.

4. *A totally new product introduced in a totally new market.* Du Pont's introduction of Corfam in an attempt to replace shoe leather is an example of this type of innovation.

Several trials must be endured before a new product is ready to make the big leap into the market. It is usually difficult for anyone to say a categorical "yes" or "no" to a new product. Checklists of winning characteristics will help the staff to edge up to the decision gradually. It is much easier to evaluate the contributing characteristics of a product than the product as a whole. One list of potential considerations was introduced in Figure 10–4. The following checklist may also help in the initial review of a product with promise. The more specific the characteristics, and the more definite the answers, the more accurate the prediction of success or failure.

1. Do the product and the product design have a comparatively long life?
2. Are the details of the product well designed?
3. Is the product useful and convenient?
4. Are the materials used practical for the product's end use?
5. Is the color right for use and environment?
6. Is the size right for best use?
7. Is the weight right for best use?
8. Does the product stand up well with its competition?
9. Are projected costs within limits?
10. Is the product easily understandable and usable?
11. Will maintenance pose special problems?
12. Is the product adaptable to all markets?
13. Are the product's raw materials readily available?
14. Will the product affect other products in the line?

PRODUCT DIFFERENTIATION

If a product is worthwhile, it will have competitors. The marketing plan should include provisions for meeting and mastering such competition. The two most common strategies for this are *product differentiation* and *market segmentation*. They are not mutually exclusive, and both can almost always be found in the history of a successful product.

Product differentiation is the headache of the advertising agency. It consists in finding (or creating) some quality in the company's product that sets it apart from the ranks of nearly identical competitors. Sometimes a product has no distinctive quality. Can you really feel which aspirin gets into your bloodstream first, or which deodorant keeps you drier, or which bathroom tissue is softer? Television watchers are familiar with the amazing ability of the ad men to wax eloquent about a millimeter's difference between one product and all the others. But even when there is no important difference, product differentiation succeeds in creating differences in the mind of the consumer. Tests show that the public believes that significant differences exist among products that are essentially alike.

MARKET SEGMENTATION

Market segmentation is **an attempt to escape from competition by** tailoring a company's product to a certain segment of the market. **Its ultimate degree would be represented by the custom tailor who fashions each suit for an individual buyer. A more common example of segmentation is the shoe company that specializes in cowboy boots. This approach to the market is quite common where a company sells to intermediate buyers, and there are many companies whose total product line is designed to meet the needs of a single intermediate buyer.**

While product differentiation endeavors to satisfy the majority of buyers fairly well, market segmentation is an attempt to render perfect satisfaction to a limited part of the market. **It is the difference between selling one-tenth of the buggies or ten-tenths of the buggy whips. Market segmentation has its dangers, however. When the aerospace industry began to decline, some of the suppliers were forced out of business because they had no other market.**

Even when a company designs its product for a limited part of the market, it must still differentiate its product from those of its competitors. And even the specialized cowboy boot company can hardly produce only one kind or style for everyone. It will have to expand its product line and differentiate each item to meet the demands of the market.

These changes occur at a rapid pace in the present-day business world. No company can afford to make leisurely marketing decisions. Nor can it feel its way by trial and error. The marketing planner must map out his product's life before it has even been born. He must think of ways to make it responsive to public need by changing it in the light of complaints or suggestions. He must also be prepared to change the public's need to fit his company's product. He must anticipate the anniversaries and milestones of his product's life . . . and its eventual demise and replacement.

SUMMARY

Marketing is more than selling. The field of marketing has expanded to include not only sales, promotion and advertising, but also all aspects of the business that affect the way the customer relates to the product. Companies are learning that to be profitable on a long-term basis their products must be designed, produced, distributed, and serviced with the consumer in the driver's seat.

The majority of customers are not final consumers but intermediate buyers, who intend to resell the item in one form or another. This industrial and commercial buying is usually handled by professional purchasing agents.

Market researchers try to find out who their buyers are and why they purchase a particular product. It is the task of the marketing executive to interpret these data so as to produce a mix of products that will meet customer needs and keep the company's product development moving smoothly. It is the job of marketing to get the right product into the right place at the right time at the right price.

Marketing planners must consider the normal life cycles of products. If the planning is done as well as possible, a company should maintain even financial progress because its various products will be spaced out so as to complement each other's ups and downs.

The capacity for innovation is one of the most important talents of an effective marketing executive. Having a feel for market trends and public needs involves much more than just reading the right statistics. The marketing planner must know his customers, his products, and the relationships which are likely to arise between the two.

KEY TERMS AND CONCEPTS FOR REVIEW

Total marketing concept
Ultimate buyer
Industrial buyer
Commercial buyer
Intermediate purchaser
Purchasing agent

Product life cycle
Market maturity
Test market
Product differentiation
Market segmentation

QUESTIONS FOR ANALYSIS AND DISCUSSION

1. What is marketing?
2. What are the major challenges of marketing?
3. How might a production-oriented firm move to the total marketing concept?
4. Why do many detergents still contain phosphates even after strong opposition by consumerist groups?
5. How might "writing paper" be purchased by ultimate, industrial or commercial customers?
6. How many of the major forms of customer motivation could be utilized in the sales effort for a new automobile? Explain.
7. Why do grocery stores not display dog food by their check-out lanes?
8. In what stage of the product life cycle are electric typewriters? Rotary automobile engines? Room air conditioners?

9. What pressures now exist in the marketplace to retard "planned obsolescence"?

10. If you could create a more efficient and economical energy source, would the world beat a path to your door? Explain.

11. Give an example of each of the major types of "new products."

SUGGESTED READINGS

Boone, Louis E., and David L. Kurtz *Contemporary Marketing.* Hinsdale, Ill.: The Dryden Press, 1974, chaps. 8–15.

Cundiff, E. W., et al. *Fundamentals of Marketing.* Englewood Cliffs, N.J.: Prentice-Hall, Inc., 1973, chaps. 10–19.

Gist, Ronald R.   *Marketing and Society.* New York: Holt, Rinehart, and Winston, Inc., 1971, chaps. 13–23.

Lipson, Harry A., and John R. Darling   *Marketing Fundamentals.* New York: John Wiley & Sons, 1974, chaps. 8–14.

McCarthy, Jerome   *Basic Marketing,* 5th ed. Homewood, Ill.: Richard D. Irwin, Inc., 1975), chaps. 15–28.

Schwartz, David J.   *Marketing Today.* New York: Harcourt Brace Jovanovich, Inc., 1973, chaps. 10–29.

UPI photo.

11

Marketing: Bringing Customers and Products Together

One of the freedoms available to each U.S. citizen is the opportunity to lose his shirt by going into business for himself. If he succeeds in business he will have to master some of the techniques of marketing. This is true even when his business grows out of a hobby. Emerging businesses often go through many of the phases of marketing development that American business as a whole has passed through.

A few years ago, Jim Gringleman made his first "cartop bedroom." It was his own design and a very clever little device. The "cartop bedroom" looked like an ordinary luggage rack until it was unfolded. When open, it provided camp-out sleeping space for two. It was Jim's own idea; he made it for his family. But one by one the orders began to come in from friends who also wanted cartop bedrooms. Jim soon found himself in business, flooded with work, and up to his ears in problems.

At first, his marketing had sort of taken care of itself. He was simply filling orders as they came. His situation had been much like that of the backwoods craftsmen of the nation's early years. In those days, production's job was to fill orders—not to beat the previous month's record output.

As Jim's business grew, its processes became so involved that he was no longer able to hold the marketing activity in his head. He knew that to prosper he had to make more, sell more, and induce folks to buy more. He began producing for anticipated orders, and at the same time pushing to find buyers. As had happened with many companies enjoying the success of a new product, Jim was letting the cart run ahead of the horse. His "make more, sell more" efforts eventually ran up against the terrifying possibility that the public might not want more! Sales dropped, and it began to appear that the public had absorbed all the cartoppers it could comfortably use.

At this point, he had a choice between two courses of action. On the one hand, he could stress advertising, hire aggressive salesmen, perhaps build a new kind of cartop to make the older one seem obsolete. Or he could try to find out what the public really wanted, and perhaps develop an entirely new camping product. The latter approach sounded more logical and certainly more high-minded. But pressured as he was by production quotas and sales goals, it was difficult to decide on a new course.

The oversimplified alternatives facing him were typical of the two most common approaches to marketing. For some companies, marketing entails only the operations necessary to "move the stuff we are making." Fortunately, Jim was wise enough to see that marketing should be a process through which communications flow in both directions—tying the producer, the consumer, and the product together. In modern marketing, production and engineering must become the servants of the customer, not his master or manipulator.

In our "affluent society," consumers may suffer from insufficient funds but seldom from insufficient choice. There are almost always more products than we can use or afford, and their distribution is expensive. Between 40 and 60 percent of the consumer dollar is taken up with moving a product from the factory to the purchaser. Intelligent corporation executives realize that such expenditures are self-defeating if they are used to promote products that serve no real need or that are identical to competing items. Company planning, policies, and operations must be brought into line with the needs of customers. Sound marketing is the best avenue to developing a healthy cycle of production and sales.

Jim Gringleman's investigations showed him that his simple cartopper was indeed approaching the limits of its market. Research also showed a tremendous need for a product of similar construction but with more expensive extras, such as electric lights, built-in transistor radios, and folding ladders. Jim's company sought to get a clear understanding of what the public would want in this new product. He also found that his customers wanted other camping equipment to go with the cartopper. Applying his design and production ability, Jim proceeded to enjoy financial success because he had been willing to find a need rather than force his product.

THE IMPORTANCE OF MARKETING

In many marketplaces of the world, the skills of marketing are relatively unnecessary. A rice salesman in underdeveloped portions of the Orient has no need of advertising, promotion, or warehousing. His customers stand in line waiting to purchase his product as soon as it is available. He can sell all he can get. He need not give away green stamps or offer chances on a late-model rickshaw. His marketing questions have automatic answers.

But a company that sells rice in the United States finds itself having to emphasize everything but the rice. The American rice buyer can choose many other foods that are equally nutritious, equally palatable, and equally available. Even if the consumer has a particular craving for rice, he will find an entire grocery shelf of choices. He must decide between enriched rice, instant rice, or rice with a recipe on the box. The cartons are all appealing, and there are even some variations in price. The decision is a difficult one.

Abundance Makes Marketing Critical

The difference between the two situations is one of *abundance*. Wherever there is abundance, marketing techniques are needed to keep the spiral of economic growth moving upward. Americans experienced a lack of abundance in recent times during a brief period after World War II. At that time many producers became obsessed with producing more and more, whether it was needed or not. Some of them overstuffed their warehouses and went quietly bankrupt.

During those postwar years a new marketing emphasis gradually developed. At first it centered on sales and merchandising. But as marketing managers gained experience, they gradually realized that it was far more sensible to make what people wanted to buy rather than to try to make them buy what they didn't ask for. Marketing began to enlarge its scope, taking over company activities such as market research and customer service—even down to the guarantees and repairs. Industries shifted from a production orientation to a marketing orientation. The domain of marketing grew until marketing could be defined in a leading textbook as "the performance of business activities which direct the flow of goods and services from producer to consumer or user in order to satisfy customers and accomplish the company's objectives."

Marketing today is no longer limited to the sales force. It is a total system of interacting business activities designed to plan, price, promote, and distribute want-satisfying products and services to present and potential customers. Between a fourth and a third of the work force is involved in such marketing-oriented activities as retailing, wholesaling, transportation, warehousing, and communications.

Marketing: The Tail That Wags the Company Dog

Virtually any company, and certainly any company with competitors, needs the ability to interest and reach willing buyers. It is no use coming out with a good product at an attractive price if the company cannot find buyers. Profits cannot be generated from the best-run factory unless its products are moved out to customers. While marketing is only a part of the operation of a business, it is the function upon which all the rest of a company depends. It is truly the tail that wags the company dog.

Business Functions Influenced by Marketing

The typical marketing department is likely to be responsible for those activities closely related to selling. These include not only the sales organization itself, whose job is to call on customers to induce them to buy, but also advertising and the formulation of sales promotion programs (such as special displays, contests, catalogs, free samples, "cents off" packages, and coupons giving customers a discount). In addition, the typical marketing department will have a group of market researchers whose job is to analyze the behavior of consumers, the market potential for a product, the products of competitors, and the many other things that tell the company why, when, where, and what people will buy.

Companies vary in the way their marketing departments operate. In some companies, everything is aimed at supporting the salesman who calls on customers. In a few, where advertising and sales promotion expenses can be high, as with Procter & Gamble, the customer is pre-sold the product and the salesman's job is primarily to make sure that

FIGURE 11-1

Different Market Mix for Different Market Segments

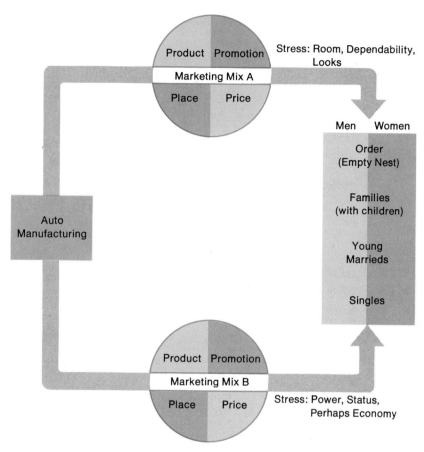

retailers place and keep the product on their shelves. Some companies have no field sales force at all, preferring to sell by mailing catalogs or other sales literature to potential customers, or placing advertisements asking a customer to mail in an order.

But for most businesses, personal selling is still the primary means of getting people to buy. More than 10 percent of all gainfully employed persons are engaged in selling, and sales people average among the highest paid of all occupational groups.

In addition to the activities that are ordinarily found in marketing departments, many other things done in a typical company are influenced by marketing considerations. These include deciding what new products to develop in engineering departments, controlling the quality and availability of products, determining where things are stored in warehouses, and deciding how goods are to be shipped and paid for.

MARKETING CHANNELS

The routes that goods follow as they journey from producer to user are referred to as channels of distribution, or marketing channels. Most people know that the corner drug store is a *retail* business, and that several "middle men" have to receive their commissions before the final consumer gets the product. And we all like to hear those golden words, "I can get it for you *wholesale.*"

This section will describe the varied channels through which companies market their products. In many cases, the categories overlap and a single business may be classified according to its products, its location, its sales practices, or even its customers.

If a company sells its products directly to the final users, it is said to be *retailing* its products. If, however, it sells to a purchaser who is buying for the purpose of resale, the company is marketing through *wholesale* channels. It is common for a product to go from its maker to a wholesaler, who resells it in bulk to a retailer, who resells it to the consumer. Among the groups that purchase for resale are industrial and commercial buyers. They may modify the product before passing it on to their own customers by repacking it. Strawberries don't grow in neat wooden boxes. At any rate, such purchases are almost always in large quantity—another characteristic of wholesale marketing channels.

Wholesalers

The men in the middle of the marketing process are usually known as *wholesalers.* In many instances, the wholesaler bridges the gap between the production-oriented manufacturer and the sales-oriented retailer. The wholesaler may help to bring the two together by performing services such as volume purchasing, transportation, storage, financing, and even delivery. "Full-function" wholesalers may perform all of these services. In other instances, either the manufacturer or the retailer may perform some or all of them. While it is possible to do without the wholesaler, his functions must be performed by someone. There are various special types of wholesalers:

1. *Wholesale merchants,* or *jobbers,* run a virtual "department store for retailers" by buying from many manufacturers and maintaining

stocks. An independent grocer may order a majority of his products from a jobber.

2. *Importers* and *exporters* buy from manufacturers in one country and sell in another country.

3. *Truck distributors* are much like small inventory jobbers on wheels. They buy goods that are in popular demand and take the goods directly to potential buyers. The man who used to push the fishcart in the early 1900s is a good example, buying from the fishermen and selling to the housewives, trying to make sure he had no leftover inventory at the end of the day. While once an important channel of distribution for many agricultural products, this form of wholesaler is relatively uncommon today.

4. *Rack merchants* have become quite common in the last few years and are likely to become even more so. These are salesmen who set up a display rack in a store, stock it regularly, and pay the store manager a commission on the amount sold. Magazine and candy racks are often maintained and serviced by representatives of these wholesale suppliers.

5. *Manufacturers' representatives* call on retailers to sell the products of certain manufacturers. A small company that does not wish to set up a sales force may choose such a representative to show its product (along with other noncompetitive products) as he makes the rounds of potential buyers.

6. *Brokers* are middlemen who negotiate sales without handling the actual commodity. A grain broker's tools may be order blanks, shipping schedules, and a special telephone or telegraph line. He is unlikely ever to touch any grain other than his breakfast cereal.

7. *Selling agents* are much like manufacturers' representatives in their relationship to the producer, and much like brokers in not carrying any inventory. Their principal function is to sell the products of a specified producer under definite contractual arrangements.

Retailers

The various kinds of retailers have in common that they bring the product to the ultimate user at an acceptable time, place, and price. Familiar forms of the retail outlet are: (1) department stores—Macy's, (2) single-line outlets—Midas Mufflers, (3) single-product shops—the Book Nook, (4) supermarkets—Safeway, and (5) discount stores—K-Mart. Other common approaches to the retail sales task are: (1) house-to-house selling—Fuller Brushes, (2) mail-order selling—Montgomery Ward, (3) selling of services at retail rates—H. & R. Block Tax Services, and (4) selling through vending machines—Vendo.

Another way of classifying retailers is by their ownership. There will always be major differences in product flow depending on whether a store is (1) independently owned and thus forced to buy through a jobber, (2) a member of a cooperative buying group receiving a certain cost advantage, or (3) part of a large chain of stores ordering through a bulk-buying home office.

Reformers who feel that markups are too high sometimes propose eliminating the wholesalers and other middlemen from the marketing channel. It only takes a little thought to see that these competitive middlemen perform vital services. The American pursuit of aggressive price-slashing would have pushed out the middlemen long ago if they had not been necessary. Some businesses are so large that they have been able to become their own wholesalers or jobbers. On occasion, chain stores and discount houses are able to undersell their smaller competitors by buying in large quantities directly from the manufacturer, and handling their own warehousing. But the middleman's job has to be done by someone. You can't cross a river without a bridge!

THE EQUILIBRIUM THEORY OF SUPPLY AND DEMAND

The gasoline and meat shortages of 1974 reminded everyone of a basic principle of marketing economics. Simply stated, this suggests that when the *supply* of a commodity is reduced and the *demand* for that item remains high, the price will almost certainly rise. In a competitive system, the relationship between supply and demand for goods or services tends to determine both the amount and the price at which goods will be sold.

Demand

Demand for a product is defined as the amount of the product that consumers will buy at a given price. Economists include in demand only what the customer is both willing and able to purchase. A 16-year-old boy may desire a Corvette Stingray, but his weekly allowance does not permit that desire to become genuine demand. Only when goods can actually be sold is there a demand for them. With most goods, when the price rises the demand for the product declines. As the price falls, more and more people are able and willing to purchase the product.

This relationship is illustrated in Figure 11–2A. The graph shows that, for the product in question, 200 units will be purchased when the selling price is $4.50. If, at a special clearance sale, the price is dropped to $1.50, approximately 1,075 items will be purchased. This line is called a *demand curve* or *schedule*. It shows the number of units that can be sold at each price level.

Supply

The quantity of goods or services offered on the market at a particular price is called the supply of that product. Like demand, supply depends primarily on the price of goods. When prices are high, more goods will be offered for sale. Fewer goods will be offered if the price

FIGURE 11–2

Typical Demand and Supply Curves

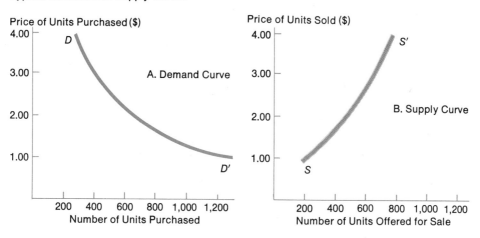

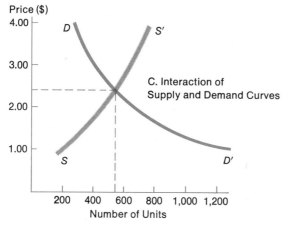

falls. When poultry is selling for $2.00 a pound, many people want to go into the chicken business. If the price drops to 10 cents per pound, no one wants to enter the business and many chicken farmers start looking for other sources of income.

Figure 11–2B illustrates the relationship between supply and price. The *supply curve* or *schedule* shows the number of units that will be made available at each possible price. As can be seen, the supply curve runs in the opposite direction from the demand curve. As prices increase, the quantity of goods supplied will rise while the demand for them will fall. This relationship can be shown by combining a supply curve and a demand curve on a single chart as in Figure 11–2C.

The graph in Figure 11–2C shows something that is basic in marketing economics. There is one price, and only one price, at which the quantity of goods brought to market will be equal to the quantity demanded. In other words, there is one specific price at which supply and demand are in balance. We see that suppliers are willing to sell 600 units at a price of $2.50 and buyers are willing to purchase 600 units at the same price. Under conditions of competition the market will tend to move to a point of equilibrium at which demand and supply are equal. This is known as the equilibrium theory of prices. Adam Smith thought it was sufficient to explain the working of the whole economy: market prices were the signals controlling all economic activity.

ASSUMPTIONS OF EQUILIBRIUM THEORY

The simple and appealing theory just described cannot be relied upon to explain the actual behavior of prices in every marketplace. In order for it to work, economists agree that certain conditions must exist.

1. The commodity produced by different producers must be identical. The concept of identical product is best illustrated in the agricultural field. Most consumers cannot distinguish between wheat grown on different farms.

2. Buyers must purchase on the basis of price alone, leaving aside impulse, whim, or other illogical factors. In reality, there are few products for which this assumption is wholly valid. Advertising, for example, attempts to get consumers to believe that two closely similar products are really quite different so that buying decisions will be made on the basis of brand name rather than according to which product is cheaper.

3. Buyers and sellers must have a complete knowledge of market conditions, including an understanding of the forces governing supply, demand, and price.

4. There must be so many different buyers and sellers that no one of them can affect the market by what he does.

When all of these conditions exist, we call it a state of *pure* or *perfect competition.* The theory of prices outlined above describes how prices behave under pure competition. The theory also helps to understand how prices behave when competition exists but isn't "perfect" since the basic tendencies existing under perfect competition are still likely to be fairly pronounced.

WHAT EQUILIBRIUM THEORY DOESN'T EXPLAIN

In many situations, the equilibrium theory does not explain how prices are actually arrived at. As mentioned before, if consumers believe there is a difference in quality between two products, they will not buy on the basis of price alone. Factors such as quality, service, prestige, and whim may have an impact on the buying decision and thus enable the manufacturer to influence the market price.

When the number of producers in a market is relatively few, there may be less competition among them and the sellers may be able to determine their own price to some extent. The extreme situation is when only one firm controls an entire market. This is called *monopoly.*

If a few large suppliers dominate the market, we say there is an *oligopoly.* In these conditions, if one seller lowers his price he will immediately draw customers away from other sellers. They in turn may be forced to lower their prices to get their customers back. It is often said that under these circumstances no seller will be willing to risk cutting his price for fear of setting off a price war. It is assumed also that one of the group, usually the largest seller, will be the leader in price changes and the others will follow. Some people claim that this means there is no real competition among them. But, as we saw in Chapter 1, fewness of firms does not necessarily mean lack of competition, especially since competitive rivalry may take other forms than price competition.

Sometimes, too, the loyalty that producers are able to develop through advertising will enable a particular brand of aspirin or toothpaste or other product to sell at a higher price than other products of comparable quality. The ability of a marketer to charge higher prices for his products is enhanced by the failure of consumers to read informative

Richard M. DeVos

Courtesy Amway Corp.

Richard M. DeVos is president of Amway Corporation, one of the largest personal selling companies in the world. "Amway" is an abbreviation for "American Way." The company manufactures and distributes a complete line of household cleaning and maintenance products, which are sold through a direct sales organization of more than 200,000 independent distributors. Amway's phenomenal growth rate is shown by its gross sales:

1966	$ 38 million
1967	50
1968	65
1969	85
1970	120
1971	165
1972	180

DeVos was born in 1926 in Grand Rapids, Michigan. After high school he served in the Air Force from 1944 to 1946, then returned to Grand Rapids where he attended Calvin College.

With Jay VanAndel, his close friend since high school days, DeVos started his first business venture—a flying school and air charter service called Wolverine Air

labeling, to be rational in their buying, or to inform themselves about prices of similar items in competing stores.

In addition to the forces of the marketplace and the other factors we have mentioned, the seller's price will obviously be influenced by the cost of producing the goods, the amount of profit he wants to make, and business conditions in general. Similarly, the price a buyer is willing to pay is determined by how much money he can spend, his desire for the product, the effect on him of advertising or sales effort, his knowledge of the market, and the general availability of the goods.

In these short paragraphs, we cannot adequately explain the complex problem of price determination. We have tried at least to introduce the reader to some of the more basic concepts that the marketing manager must consider.

PRICING POLICIES

Anyone who has ever gone through the ceremony of purchasing a used car knows that the process of putting a price on a product may

Service. In conjunction with it they built and operated a restaurant. In 1948 they sold out, bought a yacht, and set off on a year-long cruise of the Caribbean and South America. Their yacht sprang a leak and sank off the coast of Cuba, but they were rescued and spent the next six months traveling around South America.

Upon returning to Michigan the pair formed the Ja-Ri Corporation to import Latin American products. They soon switched to direct selling for Nutrilite Products, Inc., a food supplement business. During their 10 years with Nutrilite they built up an organization of 5,000 distributors. They also founded and operated a nationwide mail order distribution company, which they later sold.

In 1959, DeVos and VanAndel came into their own. They established the Amway Corporation, specializing in household cleaning products. The success subsequently achieved has been providing top-quality, easily-sold products that create and maintain a demand for repeat sales, and giving Amway's distributors the opportunity to build up their own businesses with a minimum investment. A typical Amway distributor is a man and wife working together to develop a source of extra income. Amway develops its own product lines through extensive research, standing behind every product with a 100 percent guarantee.

An Amway distributor is encouraged to enlarge his business by recruiting other distributors and becoming their wholesale supplier. There are no restrictions as to territories, franchise arrangements, or capital requirements. Each participant is free to develop his business at his own pace, depending on the time and effort he expends and on the effectiveness of his independent organization. Success depends upon selling to customers in their homes and developing a permanent clientele.

DeVos is deeply involved in church and community activities. He is also a popular speaker, having appeared before thousands of groups from coast to coast. His free enterprise address, "Selling America," has received the Alexander Hamilton Award for Economic Education from the Freedoms Foundation. The company's headquarters houses the Center of Free Enterprise, containing exhibits designed to interpret the American economic system to the public.

be very complicated indeed. From the very outset, the price of the car is puzzling—$1,995 instead of $2,000. Next, it appears that even that price can be adjusted downward: the salesman wants to "help" the buyer and will attempt to get his boss to approve a "special deal." This takes the form of a big trade-in allowance, a "free" tank of gasoline, and 5,000 trading stamps, which seem to whittle the cost down. But before it is all over, special equipment and time-payment charges have moved the price up again to a level that yields the dealer the profit he had hoped to make.

Price is one of those things that everyone assumes to be quite simple, and aren't. Doesn't the manufacturer just add up all his costs of producing and distributing the product, then tack on a profit margin? Hardly. The previous section introduced some of the basic complications in price determination. There are also many other factors influencing prices. Even after the product leaves the manufacturer, its price may undergo a number of changes before it reaches the final customer.

The price is not arrived at by simple addition. It does not arise automatically from the product's nature or characteristics. A price is simply the amount of money that needs to be exchanged for something. The price may include low profits or high profits. It may, in fact, be lower than the seller's costs.

The *list price* is the price printed on a package, or the "sticker" price on a new car, or the price carried in a catalog. It is usually only the point at which a transaction begins. It is the working price to which special charges must be added and from which special allowances may be deducted. Some sellers shrewdly set the list price at the highest level— including delivery costs, maintenance costs, and every possible additional cost. This allows the buyer to see the price go down with each thing he agrees to do for himself. Many products are never sold at their original list prices.

It is important that a company be absolutely clear about its *pricing objectives.* Considerable difference of approach can result if the company is aiming to "undersell all competitors" or if it is only trying to "maintain our current share of the market." Many larger corporations have realized that in pursuing increased sales as an unwritten policy, they have sacrificed necessary profits. Pricing policies should be specifically understood by producers lest they fall into the trap of self-deception.

Once the guidelines are clear, the game begins. The seller makes every concession and price adjustment that is necessary to help the buyer to an easy and comfortable transaction. The seller must not give more concessions than his costs will allow or he is out of business. (Perhaps the reader has heard of the man who was making gadgets at seven cents each and selling them at five cents each, in the hope of making up the difference through volume selling!) On the other hand, he must beware of making too great a profit lest he lose sales to a competitor or bring new competitors into the field who are ready to sell for less. He must also beware of incurring the attention of governmental regulatory authorities if his share of the market becomes too large. General Motors now has about half of the new car market, and could probably get even more by cutting prices. But if by doing so it drove American Motors out of business, the reaction of the federal government, and public opinion as well, would probably be immediate and strong.

For all these reasons, pricing is one of the most important factors in marketing. It is also one of the most difficult jobs of the businessman.

If his prices are too high he loses business. If his prices are too low, he loses his company.

Transportation costs are sometimes an important element in prices, especially of bulky goods. Most retail list prices include the cost of transportation, which is why some ads say "slightly higher west of the Mississippi." If the buyer is able to bear the transportation cost, the price may be reduced. Examples of this are the haul-your-own-and-save furniture discount house, or a supermarket chain that picks up its merchandise at the plants of suppliers. A commonly used term for this is F.O.B., meaning "free on board." A price that is stated "F.O.B. Detroit" means that the manufacturer in Detroit will see his products onto the truck or railroad car ready for shipment. After that, the risk and expense of transportation are the buyer's. It is easy to see that prices on the same object will differ considerably if quoted "F.O.B. manufacturer's loading dock" or "F.O.B. buyer's loading dock."

The *size of an order* often determines the discount allowable to the buyer. This is possible because the costs of delivery and of accounting are lower when large quantities go to the same destination. Rates and quantities are therefore scaled in such a way as to encourage customers to purchase in larger quantities. Whatever the commodity, bulk purchasing can almost always reduce its cost per unit through savings in handling charges.

Payment patterns are a very common cause of price differences on the same product. Every credit cardholder is familiar with the carrying charges on unpaid balances, which may add 18 percent, on an annual basis, to his costs. A homeowner who borrows $30,000 to buy his home may pay back in the course of 30 years as much as $80,000.

Business firms may, on the other hand, reduce their costs by paying bills within a specified period. Many sellers are willing to grant a 1 to 2 percent reduction in price if the bill is paid within 20 days. A familiar notation on many invoices is "2/10 net 30." It means that a 2 percent discount is available if the bill is paid within 10 days rather than 30 days. Two percent for 20 days may not seem like much, but on an annual basis it is equal to an interest saving of 36 percent a year. In other words, it would be worth borrowing money, even at an annual interest rate of 10 percent, in order to take advantage of this discount. (See Figure 11–3 for example.) A company that buys a million dollars worth of merchandise under such terms could save $20,000 by paying promptly.

The following terms are commonly used in invoicing:

FIGURE 11–3

Accept Discount or Pay Net?

The ABC Company purchases some items for inventory at a price of $1,000. The invoice states that the terms are 2/10 net 30. ABC does not have the cash on hand to pay the bill within the 10 day period, since it normally receives payment on its sales at the end of the month. Will it be profitable for ABC to borrow at 8 percent in order to pay the bill within 10 days?

Amount due in 30 days $1,000
Cash discount ($1,000 × .02) 20
Amount payable within 10 days .... $ 980

There is a saving of $20 by paying within 10 days.

Cost of borrowing $980 at 10 percent interest for 20 days: $980 × .10 × 20/365 = $5.36.

ABC will save $14.64 ($20.00 − $5.36) by borrowing and paying the invoice within the 10 day period.

---

1. *Net* means that payment for the face value of the invoice is due immediately.
2. *Net 30* means that payment is due within 30 days of the invoice date.
3. *1/10 net 30* means that one percent is deducted from the face value of the invoice if it is paid within 10 days.
4. *E.O.M.* (end of month) indicates free credit until the end of the month.
5. *R.O.G.* (receipt of goods) and *A.O.G.* (arrival of goods) usually mean that payment terms are in effect upon the receipt of the goods by the buyer.

A familiar type of reduction from the list price of retail goods is the trade-in on cars, tires, or typewriters. In some cases, the seller has no expectation of regaining anything on the item he takes as a trade-in. He has merely given a discount to the buyer as a way of promoting sales.

Sellers also commonly make price reductions for damaged goods and seconds. They also reduce prices for advertising purposes, and offer price reductions to sales personnel as incentive bonuses.

Trading stamps are a familiar retail device. They give the buyer the illusion that he is receiving something extra with his purchase, since the stamps can be redeemed for merchandise. Of course, the seller has to purchase the stamps from the company that issues them; he passes this additional cost on to his customers. Most observers feel that trading stamps are of advantage to the first concern to use them, but when everybody uses them the advantage lessens. The trading stamp ultimately adds to the list price of the retailer's goods. Many retailers spend from 2 to 3 percent of their total sales revenue for stamps. Customers ought not to think of the stamps as being something for nothing. They really represent a payment made on the merchandise for which they will eventually be redeemed, together with a large profit to the stamp company, especially if all the stamps issued are not redeemed.

The public tends to be rather cynical about the businessman's methods of pricing. People generally assume that any company tries to get all that the law allows. In some cases, this is true. But the seller is usually well aware of the danger of getting greedy, for if he isn't careful he is likely to encourage another company to "do it better . . . for less." And it is the chance of making a profit that is responsible for the product's being available in the first place.

Pricing is far more than just a matter of seeing how much can be squeezed out of the buyer. It is a component of the company's total marketing system. Even the man who builds a better mousetrap can't sell one for $10,000.

MARKETING STRATEGIES

If a company is to be successful it must supply its products at the time, place, and price they are needed. This is a difficult problem of organization.

A marketing executive must be quick to spot the appropriate markets and supply them with products. He will find specific needs all around him—some of them isolated, others overlapping. If the company is to do the marketing job properly, its executives must be concerned with understanding markets rather than pushing products.

One useful tool is the *market grid* shown in Figure 11–4. It is a charting method which can assist the planner in locating the market needs he may hope to meet. The grid is a checkerboard chart with various classes of customers listed along one side and the product characteristics they are interested in listed along another. The market grid for apartments shown in Figure 11–4 indicates that "sophisticated" customers tend to look for distinctive design, privacy, interior variety, and strong management. Job-centered apartment seekers want economy and a location close to where they work. A family looking for an apartment is likely to stress economy, facilities, and large rooms.

By using the market grid, the company may be able to focus on some particular market that it might otherwise overlook—the family market, the newly married market, the swinger market or some other specific

FIGURE 11–4

Market Grid for Apartments

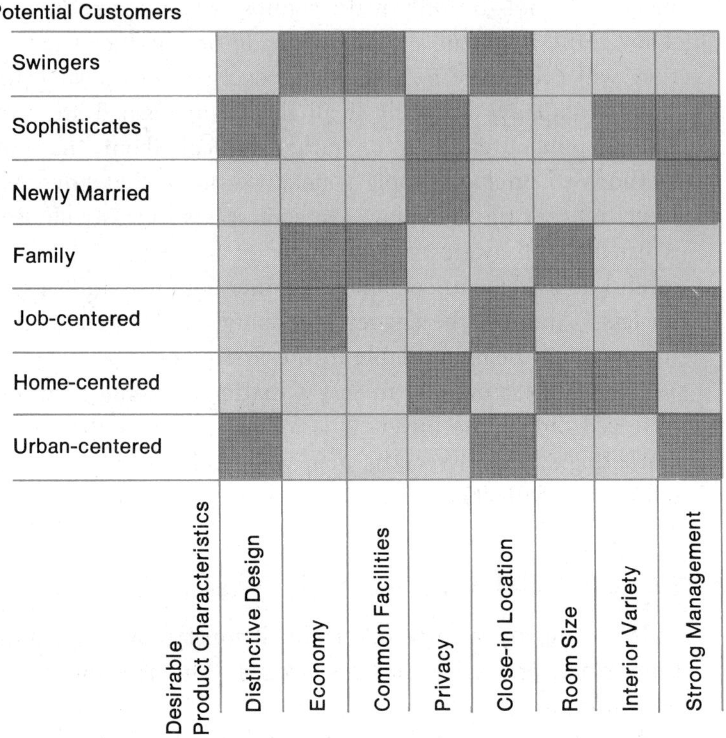

Potential Customers

group. Once the product characteristics of a market are pinpointed, it is easy to add other markets that have some of the same characteristics.

In laying out and discussing the market grid, planners can represent graphically the relative needs of different buyer groups. A second chart is often made that uses larger and smaller squares to show areas of differing need. The preparation and researching of such a grid enables the marketing executive to *know* products and probabilities and preferences. Otherwise his decision-making is only guesswork.

To get the right product, or product variation, into a specific market, the company may have to make changes in every phase of its operations. It can change such elements as the following:

1. The *product mix*—the arrangement of product lines.
2. The *distribution mix*—the assortment of methods for storing and transporting goods to the points of purchase.
3. The *communications mix*—the entire package of advertising, sales, promotional, and market research activities.

4. The *service mix*—the follow-up activities that assure customer satisfaction and product reliability.

By modifying and changing these packages of arrangements, the marketing executive attempts to control the life of his company's product.

He cannot control everything, of course. He cannot control (1) cultural and environmental changes and conditions, (2) political and legal occurrences, (3) the economic situation, (4) the prevailing business climate, or (5) the tide of public opinion. All the marketing executive can do with these factors is to appraise them and to allow for them in his marketing strategy. It is the ability to screen the situation and arrive at a successful marketing strategy that makes the marketing manager so essential to corporation management. He cannot be replaced by a computerized decision-maker.

PROMOTING SALES

The sales effort is only one part of marketing, but it is an important part. It has to be backed up by advertising and promotional efforts. Table 11–1 shows the sums spent on advertising in 1972 by the top 10 advertisers in the U.S. Procter & Gamble spent $275,000,000 (about 10 percent of total sales) for advertising alone, and its total marketing expenses usually ran to 20 percent of the sales dollar. Although Colgate-Palmolive spent about half as many dollars on marketing, its ad budget alone is over 20 percent of total sales revenue. Obviously, these firms believe in the value of aggressive advertising.

Table 11–2 shows how all companies spent their advertising dollars

TABLE 11–1

Top Ten in Ad Expenditures, 1972

1972 Rank	1962 Rank			
1	2	Procter & Gamble......................	$275,000,000	$139,150,000
2	12	Sears, Roebuck.......................	215,000,000	53,600,000
3	4	General Foods........................	170,000,000	101,000,000
4	1	General Motors.......................	146,000,000	160,000,000
5	14	Warner-Lambert......................	134,000,000	46,000,000
6	3	Ford Motor Co........................	132,500,000	106,000,000
7	8	American Home Products.............	116,000,000	65,500,000
8	9	Bristol-Myers.........................	115,000,000	65,000,000
9	6	Colgate-Palmolive....................	105,000,000	70,000,000
10	11	Chrysler Corp........................	95,415,400	54,062,000

Source: *Advertising Age*, November 21, 1973, p. 22.

TABLE 11–2

Advertising Expenditures in the United States in 1972

Medium	1972 Millions of Dollars	1972 Percent of Total	1975 Millions of Dollars Estimate*
Newspapers....................	$ 6,960	30.2	$8,742
National.....................	1,240	5.4	106
Local........................	5,720	24.8	735
Magazines....................	1,480	6.4	683
Weeklies.....................	600	2.6	531
Women's.....................	380	1.7	520
Monthlies....................	470	2.0	696
Farm National...............	30	0.1	33
Television....................	4,110	17.9	5,661
Network.....................	1,780	7.7	2,500
Spot.........................	1,375	6.0	1,786
Local........................	955	4.2	1,375
Radio.........................	1,530	6.6	1,943
Network.....................	75	0.3	106
Spot.........................	395	1.7	395
Local........................	1,060	4.6	1,442
Direct Mail...................	3,350	14.5	4,906
Business Papers...............	770	3.3	943
Outdoor......................	290	1.3	372
National.....................	190	0.9	239
Local........................	100	0.4	133
Miscellaneous.................	4,541	19.7	6,187
Total national..................	13,100	56.8	
Total local....................	9,960	43.2	
Grand Total..............	$23,060	100.0	$30,437

* Projections based on data provided by McCann-Erickson advertising agency.
Source: McCann & Erickson, Inc.

in 1972. Newspapers received 30.2 percent of the advertising dollar, television 17.9 percent, radio 6.6, and magazines 6.4. Direct mail advertising accounted for 14.5 percent. Local advertising absorbed 43.2 percent of the spending, and national advertising got 56.8 percent.

Critics of advertising say that it does not really sell things. Perhaps not. The sun does not put hay in the barn, but without it, little hay will find its way into storage. Advertising does not *make* sales, but it makes the public aware that a product or service is available. Trite as this may sound, the product must sell itself. Advertising can only make the introduction. It is the most dependable method of introducing a product so far discovered.

Just as a mix of elements may be used in the marketing, production, and distribution phases, so there will be a mix of techniques in the promotional phase. The person who plans the marketing effort must balance several factors in designing the promotional mix: (1) the amount of money available for promotion, (2) the nature of the market, (3) the nature of the product, and (4) the position of the product in its own life cycle.

The market being sought will strongly influence the approach to promotion. The approach will certainly differ for chewing gum and computers: chewing gum will employ the mass media and emphasize impulse buying; computers are more likely to be sold through personal calls by sales engineers. If the product is a grandson of a previously successful and well-known product, the promotional campaign will naturally seek to tie the newcomer to the old reliable.

The amount of money available for advertising or other sales promotion activities depends upon many factors.

1. Usually a small company will spend a greater percentage of its sales dollar on promotion than will a larger company.
2. But the larger company will probably spend more altogether, and reap better returns on what it spends.
3. New products require more promotion.
4. Some companies base their promotional allocation on a percentage of income from sales.
5. Some companies allocate a percentage of gross profits to promotion.
6. Some companies prefer to allocate a specific amount per unit produced.
7. Many companies follow the unimaginative course of copying their competitors' advertising methods.
8. The wisest, and rarest, approach to promotion is to determine first the exact goals sought. Then the company should "find" whatever promotion money is necessary to achieve those goals.

SALES MANAGEMENT AND SALESMANSHIP

Because salesmen are a special breed who live in a world of their own, it is especially important that a company's sales management be closely tied to the orientation and goals of the marketing plan. The 10 percent of our country's work force involved in personal selling march under a banner bearing the words, "Nothing happens until someone sells something." They cultivate a special brand of enthusiasm and personality.

While the oldtime traveling salesman with his sample case has nearly disappeared, the sales people of our day have many of the same characteristics. Hard work and enthusiasm are just as essential to the soft-sell methods of today as they were in the medicine show days. Today it is more important to have knowledge of one's product and industry, and to be able to discuss the customer's needs intelligently, but the gift of gab is still important. Product engineers make good salesmen only if they have sales aptitude to match their technical ability.

The man with the toughest job in selling is the sales manager. To begin with, he has probably come up through the ranks as a successful salesman, and may have little training or talent for management. Add to that the difficult task of keeping the salesmen enthusiastic about the product, and it is easy to see why good sales managers are so much in demand.

One of the primary tasks of the sales manager is often overlooked. The selection and orientation of new sales personnel provides the greatest opportunity for controlling the direction and momentum of a sales department, but it is often done carelessly. If a company keeps a close watch over the staffing process, it will help to eliminate future selling problems.

The sales manager should be more than a highly-paid cheerleader. He is the link for the transmission of the company's objectives, marketing orientation, and market research to the sales force. His people are in regular contact with the public. They can have an important influence on product changes and customer services by reporting back what they learn.

THE MARKETING MANAGER

In recent years, a number of new job titles have appeared in the marketing field. Company rosters list Marketing Managers, Directors of Marketing, and Vice Presidents for Marketing. The top marketing executive is often the highest paid executive of a company after the president.

The reason for this trend is easy to see. The experiments with the total marketing approach have proved so successful that many larger companies are adopting the idea.

The amount of authority and responsibility assigned to these positions is certain to increase as companies recognize the soundness of an integrated, systematic, customer-emphasis approach to their operations. Management will not abandon the quest for profits. But it is discovering that greater profits are possible for product lines that start from what customers want and follow this throughout the product's life cycle.

SUMMARY

Quality is not the only determinant of a product's success. No matter how good a product is, it won't make profits for a company unless it is delivered to the right person at the right time, and at the right price. The abundance of products in our industrial society results in strong competition among them. Businessmen have found it necessary, for the most part, to plan their marketing before the product has come off the drawing boards, in order to be certain that it will fit the needs of their customers.

The routes that goods follow from producer to user are called marketing channels. These may include various kinds of wholesalers, such as jobbers, importers, exporters, truck distributors, rack merchants, manufacturers' representatives, brokers, or selling agents.

Pricing is a more complex process than is generally realized. Prices are not determined entirely by the forces of supply and demand. In most situations, the marketer has some leeway in setting his list price. After he has decided on his list price, deductions may be made to arrive at the actual price to be paid in a given situation. Factors that may affect the final price paid by the consumer include: transportation costs, size of orders, payment patterns, trade-ins, trading stamps, damaged goods, cooperative advertising costs, incentive bonuses for salesmen, and profit guarantees.

A skillful marketing strategy will allow the marketing department to zero in on a specific market, as well as on the particular needs of customers. The marketing grid is a charting method which can assist in this task.

Sales are pushed by means of advertising, promotional programs, and personal selling. The greatest emphasis is still put upon personal selling, because the salesman is able to tailor his presentation to the customer. It is the job of the sales manager to communicate the corporate marketing approach to his sales force, as well as to make them a coordinated force of enthusiastic and aggressive salesmen.

316   *A Practical Introduction to Business*

KEY TERMS AND CONCEPTS FOR REVIEW

Marketing channel
Retailing
Wholesaling
Demand curve
Supply curve
Pure competition
F.O.B.

List price
Market grid
Promotional mix
Marketing manager
Equilibrium
Chain store

QUESTIONS FOR ANALYSIS AND DISCUSSION

1. Give examples of two marketing channels.
2. Identify two products that are frequently sold by rack jobbers.
3. Identify seven types of wholesalers.
4. Give an example (other than the one in the text) for each major form of retailing.
5. Why does a drought cause higher food prices?
6. Why does supply and demand not regulate the price for telephone service?
7. Why do different automobile dealers charge different prices for their cars?
8. If an $800 invoice for lumber reads "2/10 net 30," how much will a building contractor save by paying within 10 days?
9. Why are marketing managers paid better than some other corporate executives?
10. Why does Colgate-Palmolive spend a larger percentage of its sales on advertising than Allis Chalmers (farm equipment), or Procter & Gamble?

SUGGESTED READINGS

Boone, Louis E., and David L. Kurtz *Contemporary Marketing.* Hinsdale, Ill.: The Dryden Press, 1974, chaps. 1–7.

Cundiff, E. W. et al. *Fundamentals of Marketing.* Englewood Cliffs, N.J., Prentice-Hall, Inc., 1973, chaps. 1–9.

Gist, Ronald R. *Marketing and Society.* New York, Rinehart, and Winston, Inc., 1971, chaps. 1–5, 7–12.

Lipson, Harry A., and John R. Darling *Marketing Fundamentals.* New York: John Wiley & Sons, 1974, chaps. 1–12.

McCarthy, Jerome *Basic Marketing,* 5th ed. Homewood, Ill., Richard D. Irwin, Inc., 1975, chaps. 1–14.

Schwartz, David J. *Marketing Today.* New York: Harcourt Brace Jovanovich, Inc., 1973, chaps. 1–9.

12

Business in the Global Market

In our early school years some of us learned a very simple theory of international trade relationships: exports are the things a country sends out and *im*ports are the things a country brings in. If the country sends out (sells) more things than it brings in (buys), it accumulates the money of other nations. This oversimplified picture probably serves very well for comprehending the basic facts of international trade, although it doesn't consider the question of what a country is to do with the money it accumulates. Certain Arab countries found out in 1974 that they were receiving more foreign currency from sales of oil than they could easily make use of.

The theory also leaves out the normal complications of business, plus the additional question marks introduced by constantly changing technology, the problems of international finance, and world political upheavals.

Unfortunately, many people still assume that answers about foreign political and economic policy can be as clear-cut as the "ins and outs" of world trade theory may seem. Yet, there is a real danger in oversimplifying. This not only creates inaccurate expectations in the reader's mind, but we may be actually removing the natural objectivity and creativity by which we could have contended with the real situation.

Professor Marshall McLuhan has compared the world to a shrinking "global village." It is no longer possible for a nation or a tribe that doesn't like its neighbors to ignore them or to move somewhere else. A popular song of a few years back asked, "Where do you go when there's no place to go . . . and you don't want to be where you are?" The answer for us is that there is no place to go. We have to face our problems. Our shrinking world has left no more space for being alone, at least in business matters.

THE DEMISE OF COWBOY CAPITALISM

Economist Kenneth Boulding has used the phrase "cowboy capitalism" to describe the American economy of yesterday. He compares yesterday's capitalism to the early American West. The land was so rich, the resources so vast, that men were able to abuse their environment with impunity. They could cut down trees, kill the buffalo, plow the grassland . . . and if erosion began to take the land, or the animals got sparse, the answer was easy: move on to virgin territory and leave the wornout land behind. There was always plenty more just over the horizon!

Much as we might wish that our forefathers had been more thoughtful, there is nothing we can do to change the past. The cowboy is gone. Boulding is saying that the time of "cowboy capitalism" is also gone. The cowboy capitalist cannot operate successfully without a vast world of untapped markets. And it is easy enough to see that the untapped markets are getting fewer and fewer . . . faster and faster. No longer can the medicine show expect to dupe the folks in one town or county and move on to another. The time for quick and dirty profits has run out.

Another term to describe our world became popular in the 1960s. We are on "spaceship earth" according to some writers. All of mankind is part of one survival system, hurtling through space together. Each person's actions affect everyone else on the spaceship. We can no longer afford to use up resources; we must recycle them and use them over again.

Almost everything that is being said about natural resources in our crowding times is equally true of international business practice. The businessmen of the international global village must begin to recognize that the time of the cowboy capitalist is over. The abuse of any part of the world's environment must be increasingly seen as hazardous to the progress of all one's fellow travelers on spaceship earth.

A new awareness must accompany the teaching of world trade concepts. International marketing is no longer just a matter of language, distance, and politics. International trade and its meaning demand a place in the education of all businessmen who intend to survive in this global market.

THE INTERNATIONAL MARKET

Most Americans have little awareness of world trade. The United States throughout most of its history has been able to draw upon its own natural resources for most of what it needed. The unique land, climate and historical advantages of the United States have produced an unusual experience for Americans. Very few of the countries of the world could survive on their internal productivity. As Table 12–1 shows,

TABLE 12–1

Per Capita GNP (in 1970 dollars)

	1970	1980
USA	5,000	6,700
Communist Europe	2,000	3,800
Other developed nations	2,800	4,000
Less developed countries (non-Communist)	240	350
Communist Asia	120	200
Overall average	970	1,360

Source: The Hudson Institute Croton-on-Hudson, New York.

no section of the world enjoys the material standard of living which has become commonplace to Americans. And it would be very difficult to find a country on the globe which is not purchasing American goods or services. Americans assume that all trade revolves around us and will continue to do so. But it is now a questionable assumption with the rise of such trading countries as Japan.

The United States *is* the largest seller of merchandise on the world market. However, the *growth* of U.S. exports has not kept pace with the rises of the mushrooming economies of Japan, Italy, and Germany. The future holds several uncertainties, such as the day that the United States becomes number two—or three or four. There is also the uncertain future of trade with the Communist half of the world.

Currently, there are over four million workers in American industry and business whose jobs are *directly* dependent upon the health of U.S. world trade. In 1972, the United States exported 4.4 percent of its total production. Imports averaged about 5 percent of the goods we used. According to the simplistic grade school formula, the small difference between exports and imports would not appear to be great. Yet, the *trends* are disconcerting and the future of U.S. world trade is far from secure. British owners have taken over Gimbel Bros. department stores and Japanese interests are acquiring coal fields and real estate interests throughout the United States. Domination of the world market is less likely than ever. The political shifts and slips are sources of continuing danger. Devaluation of the dollar, foreign attitudes toward U.S. business and U.S. public opinion are likely to bring about some problems of our position in the world markets.

THE UGLY AMERICAN BUSINESSMAN?

World trade holds a moral responsibility for the American business-man. He must not only maintain and expand markets, but he must do it in the presence of general attitudes toward "the ugly American," the unwelcome "cowboy capitalist," and America as competitor rather than dominator. The future is not bleak for U.S. world trade—indeed, ex-panding world markets make it more *opportune* than ever before. De-spite problems, exports have grown and are expected to continue to grow (see Figure 12–1). The fact that the United States has owed more

FIGURE 12–1

United States: Exports and Imports of Goods and Services

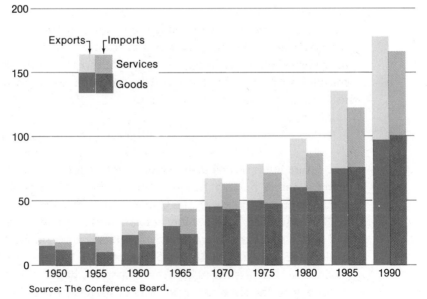

Billions of 1971 Dollars

Source: The Conference Board.

than $40 billion to other countries than it has exported to them has not been due to a lack of exports of goods and services in excess of imports, but rather to huge costs of military and foreign programs.

BALANCE OF TRADE

The phrase *balance of trade* refers to the difference between what a nation pays for imports and what it receives for its exports. This is a familiar term to Americans but not half so critical a term as it is in countries where an import license must be approved for every *personal* purchase from a foreign producer. An Egyptian may *like* a Chevrolet or American bourbon whiskey, but his government has not permitted their import. The citizens of some countries are forced to maintain portions *of their personal money* outside their home country in order to buy and sell freely. Businessmen throughout the world utilize Swiss bank accounts because of this flexibility and the secrecy they provide. Businessmen in some of the countries mentioned above must also keep banking accounts in countries where they transact a great deal of business. Only in recent years have Americans begun to feel the gradual weakening of the dollar as a global exchange. Can the day ever come when your purchase of a Japanese motorcycle will be dependent upon your ability to amass the sale price in some foreign (non-U.S.) currency? This is an everyday problem for the majority of world traders and U.S. traders must reckon with the possibility in their own futures.

The list of products which the United States *must* import is long. The materials are found in many of the "American" products we can think of: electronic components for telephones, transistors for computers, and sugar for Coca-Cola. Much of our oil, copper, chromium, and other materials must be imported.

The obvious conclusion is that new attitudes must be adopted which will soft pedal the nationalistic pride of world trade and emphasize the opening of doors and globalizing of the market. Though it will require a reversal of our traditional values, we must come to think less of the nation's competitive advantage and more of the world's competitive advantage. Why should the Swiss use expensive radios? Why should Germans not have access to the world's finest watches? By trading with their neighbors, they can produce what they do best and have a wider selection of goods to choose from. Of course, the intermediate steps are wobbly ones, but the time is gone forever when only a handful of nations could enjoy a top standard of living at the expense of all the other nations.

FIGURE 12–2

United States Trade with the World

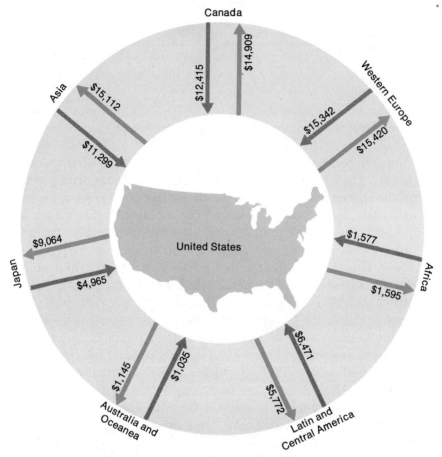

Source: *Statistical Abstract of the United States,* 1973, pp. 780–83.

COMPARATIVE ADVANTAGE

This is not to suggest that the workers must lose the reward of their labors. Instead, the principle of comparative advantage reminds us that the country that makes watches of equal quality at half the price should get the watch business of the other countries. If the United States makes watches for $100 and Japan makes watches of equal quality for $50, should the United States add a $50 import duty onto foreign watches to keep things equal? Or should the United States encourage its watchmakers to make computers or machines or some other product which Japan cannot make as well?

The answers are not simple. They always involve many variables.

Low cost of labor in some societies is often a major price factor. Other times, cheap labor is counteracted by increased efficiency or higher final quality. Some countries simply possess the right natural resources or the appropriate climate. How much sense would it make for Holland or Arabia to compete with the United States in the world grain market! Finally, the uncertainties of world politics can throw a monkey wrench into the best planned international transaction. But, perhaps, we have gotten the cart before the horse in the business-politics situation. Could it be that, instead of business and competition falling victim to changing political fortunes, they *could* be able to mold political progress? Could a common dedication to the raising of living standards through the world marketplace ever become the common denominator for world peace?

BASIC ECONOMICS OF INTERNATIONAL TRADE

As either an exporter or an importer, the United States is involved in almost 30 percent of all world trade. Therefore, for the time being we are very much a pivotal nation in the world's economy.

There are many nations in the world which allow higher percentages of their economy to be based on imports. While the United States imports 5 percent of the goods it requires, Japan imports about 10 percent, and Great Britain purchases 16 percent of its products from others. Even so, the mammoth trillion dollar American GNP (gross national product) places this country in a dominant role on the international monetary scene. If, for some reason, all international trade were stopped (1) many backward countries would hardly know the difference, (2) some countries like England would die out quickly, and (3) others like the United States, Canada, and Australia would survive on the merits of their great masses of land and natural resources (though the resulting standard of living would mean reverting to the "good old days" which would probably not seem too good any more).

While our total world trade in the United States is less than 10 percent of the national GNP (total value of all goods and services produced in a nation), the $56 billion of goods and services we imported in 1972 has a significant impact on the world economic situation. The causes of fluctuation in international trade advantage are many—and new causes arise each day. Different resources, technologies, production, population, and tastes can put different nations in advantageous positions or precarious economic imbalance.

No country has (or even expects) an exact and continuing *balance*

Akio Morita

Akio Morita, a slender, white-haired Japanese businessman who is president of Sony Crporation, was born in Nagoya, Japan, in 1921, the eldest of three sons. As the scion of a 300-year-old family of wealthy sake brewers, he had been expected to take over the management of the brewery for which his father had groomed him. But his interests lay in electronic physics, which he still pursues as his hobby. As a child he built his own record player. Ultimately he persuaded his father that the second son was more suited to the family's business, and went to study physics at Osaka University, graduating in 1944.

Morita served as Lieutenant Junior Grade in the Japanese Navy and worked as a technical engineer in the Naval Research Center. During this time he met Masaru Ibuka, another physicist and chief engineer at a precision instrument firm. In 1946, after a brief stint teaching at the Tokyo Institute of Technology, Morita and Ibuka founded the Tokyo Telecommunications Engineering Company with the equivalent of $500 in capital. Twelve years later the corporation's name was changed to Sony—one of the best-known trademarks in the world today.

Quartered in a bombed-out shell of a store, and later in a former army barracks, the company began by manufacturing voltmeters, amplifiers, and communications instruments. Its first consumer-oriented product was a bulky $500 tape recorder

of trade. It would be highly unlikely that the goods exported would ever equal exactly the goods imported during any given time. Further, there is no particular virtue in a perfect balance of trade. The real reason for all the attention to the balance of trade is its ability to index the economic health of a country. If the country regularly "spends" more than it "makes," it may be in serious trouble when time for payment arrives. On the other hand, a country that continually makes a large "profit" at the expense of its world neighbors may find it develops problems as to what to do with these "profits."

After World War II, the U.S. economic position went sky-high and the United States was building a considerable annual surplus from

that failed to sell except to schools. After the development of transistors by the Bell Telephone Laboratories in the U.S., the company acquired the first license to produce transistors in Japan. In 1955 it introduced the first transistorized radio. A string of firsts followed, including an all-transistor television set in 1959 and the first seven-inch color television set in 1968. In 1969 it brought out a home color video tape player, with an adapter for recording television programs.

Sony has invested heavily in research and development. In 1968, the company's special project team developed a new principle of color television and introduced it under the name of Trinitron. The Trinitron color television set was recognized for its excellence when Sony got an Emmy Award in 1973 from the National Academy of Television Arts and Sciences in the U.S.

Sony has been a pacesetter in improving the image of Japanese products and Japanese business in international markets since the close of World War II. Morita says that the company tests its products on the Japanese market first, "Then, with this experience, we can improve our product before we export it."

Morita has assumed responsibility for the company's international marketing. He lived in New York City for more than a year while setting up the American subsidiary's operations in the early 1960. He tells interviewers that he doesn't believe in doing market research on a product before it's developed. "We are the experts. We know what the technology will yield."

Sony now employs about 17,000 people. It was the first Japanese company to sell its stock in the United States, and in 1970 it became the first to be listed on the New York Stock Exchange. Presently over 40 percent of its stock is owned by Americans. Sony tends to depart to some extent from Japanese tradition in industry. A more relaxed atmosphere is maintained in its plants, where Morita and Ibuka are likely to be found wandering along the assembly line or discussing some problem with the company's technical people.

Morita himself published a critique of Japan's management practices which was a best seller in Japan in the late 1960s. He believes that the most serious mistakes made by management have to do with long-range decision making. The mistakes that show up right away are easy to correct, but in long-range planning a mistake may not become apparent for ten years or more. He has carried the theme to American business leaders in magazine articles and interviews and in numerous speeches and addresses.

Morita is now a board member of the IBM World Trade Corp., a member of the International Council of the Morgan Guaranty Trust Co. of New York, and a founding member of The Rockefeller University Council.

world trade. To keep from monopolizing the currency of the world, the United States began to aid countries left devastated by the war. This outflow of U.S. dollars equalized the balance of payments just long enough for the scales to tip to the other side. Even up to 1967, the United States was riding high with large trade surpluses and a strong, healthy dollar. Economic growth was rather slow, but steady, and largely free of the destructive influence of rampant inflation. Since that time, however, the United States has suffered significant trade deficits and seen the dollar devalued twice within a fourteen-month period. While inflation continues to erode the nation's productive capacity and makes its goods less competitive in the international market, there are hopeful signs.

The course of action taken in 1973 was to *devalue* U.S. currency, by lowering its value relative to all other currencies. Naturally, this made imports cost more in U.S. dollars and allowed foreign money to purchase more U.S. products. In April 1973, the United States had its first trade surplus in nineteen months with exports exceeding imports by nearly $200 million. However, the monopoly action of the world oil-producing nations, in quadrupling the price of oil, has again caused an unfavorable balance of trade.

RESTRAINTS ON INTERNATIONAL TRADE

International trade almost never is allowed to flow freely without government intervention. One reason for this generally is that goods or services crossing a border are so easy to tax. And, of course, what kind of a government wants to pass up a chance to levy a tax that will be popular with local merchants. Taxes fall naturally upon incoming goods for one of two major reasons: (1) to gain revenue for the government and (2) to protect the special interests within the importing country.

Of course, if a government slaps an import tax onto incoming goods, it will in reality collect the tax from its own citizens. The manufacturer or distributor is almost sure to raise his sale price enough to cover the extra tax. The final result is that the buyer pays his own government a tax for the privilege of buying goods from outside the country.

There is also some question about whether or not the protective tariff actually protects anyone. For as soon as Country A clamps an import duty on something from Country B, then Country B responds by raising tariffs on the imports from Country A. The round-and-round effects of protective tariffs make their final effect rather questionable. The only thing that is surely accomplished is that the domestic manufacturers *feel* protected—and consumer prices wind up being higher than they would be under freer trade.

TYPES OF TARIFFS

Tariffs are like many other things: Not necessarily good logic, but certain to exist nevertheless. Three methods of setting tariff amounts are common. An *ad valorem* duty is levied on a percentage of the value of the product (20 percent of the price). A *specific* duty is figured according to some measure of quantity ($2.25 per ton or 25 cents a pound). It is also common to find a *combination* of the value tax and the quantity tax. This combination approach may exact 10 percent of the sale price plus 10 cents for each unit sold. It is always interesting to remember that the man who foots the bill for all of this is seldom included in the trade discussions which establish the tariffs. Governments negotiate tariffs while the consumer pays the bill.

The markets of our world are so completely modified, controlled and counter-controlled that it is almost impossible to imagine a world in which trade were allowed to go on freely and without restrictions. There will always be tariffs as long as governments seek to: (1) gain revenue, (2) protect domestic industry, (3) increase the gains from trade, (4) guarantee that its own noncompetitive industries will stay in business to serve in case of war, and (5) punish other nations for some economic or political affront.

THE COMMON MARKET

One of the most interesting tariff developments of recent history has been the organization of the European Economic Community. This Common Market, or EEC, began with six nations (Belgium, France, Italy, Luxembourg, The Netherlands, and West Germany) in 1958. Commerce among these nations was agreed to be conducted upon equal tariff bases and each member agreed to charge the same tariffs to outside nations. In actuality, these countries produced a new, larger country for economic purposes. From 1963 to 1969, the EEC's gross national product grew by almost 50 percent. Although economic growth in member countries is not totally due to the EEC, the European economic market did sustain a higher growth rate during the past decade than the United States.

The entry of Great Britain, Denmark, and Ireland in 1973 has given the EEC additional impact and influence. The following GNP figures of EEC (in billions) suggest the impact of increased prosperity and increased size: 1963–$258, 1968–$384, and 1973–$695.

EEC has developed considerable negotiating power with other trading nations. Not only have economic conditions and standards of living been raised, but many observers see the EEC as the potential foundation of a united European nation in the near future. What great hurdles would prohibit the gradual addition of all nations of the world to this arrangement? Would it be desirable if we were to bring about a GEC–Global Economic Community? Are there some nationalistic barriers which can never be removed under any circumstances? What problems would arise if trade were conducted on equal bases among all nations of the world?

TAPPING INTERNATIONAL MARKETS

There are several routes by which domestic companies tend to enter the foreign markets. The first introduction comes about simply when the successful domestic company begins to have sizable foreign requests for its product. Or the planners of a company's marketing strategy may find some overseas market which is ripe for the harvest. Initially, the company becomes an *exporter*. It opens the minimal required offices to distribute, advertise, sell, and service its product. Many non-American companies are in this stage in U.S. markets, being represented by a single American distribution office but retailing the products via established American retailers.

A similar basic stage is when a company is an *importer* only. Such a company develops a flow of foreign products which it markets, or a flow of foreign raw materials which are incorporated into its own domestic products.

Licensing is the next most complicated approach. Frequently a domestic company sells a license or franchise to some foreign company. These license agreements depend greatly upon the careful wording of the contract. Many American firms have learned bitter lessons in the licensing arena. In some cases the franchise was granted without sufficient stipulations regarding quality control and actual control of the product. Some foreign holders of the franchise have merely learned the ropes through the license period, then introduced a similar—and often better adapted—product. Indeed, many licensing companies have found themselves to be training their own competitors.

The *joint venture* is similar to the licensing approach but stipulates the percentage ownership, and therefore the percentage control, of the participating companies. Some countries (such as Japan, England, and Mexico) will not allow an outside firm to own controlling interest in certain domestic joint ventures. The joint venture is, of course, more stable than the licensing situation, cheaper than holding the entire ownership, but is difficult to control because it involves cooperation across national boundaries.

A *wholly-owned* operation may be of two types. It may be a branch of the domestic corporation which simply does business in the foreign country. Or it may be a wholly-owned subsidiary which is frequently a company with its own management and objectives, but owned completely by a parent corporation outside the country.

Some American manufacturers have developed substantial overseas operations, either through joint ventures or wholly-owned operations. In companies such as Eastman Kodak, Warner-Lambert, Pfizer, Anaconda, Goodyear, Ford, IBM, IT&T, Corn Products, 3M, Exxon, Mobil Oil, Gulf Oil, National Cash Register, Singer, Colgate-Palmolive, H. J. Heinz, and Gillette, over 30 percent of their total sales are done abroad.

The day of the multinational company is no longer in the future. While corporations occasionally suffer abuse or even loss at the hands of political changes, as happened in recent years in Chile, it is becoming far more likely for the powerful foreign business interests to wield considerable power over the deliberations and decisions of the foreign government.

Students in the United States should remember that these multinational giants are not always American firms. In 1973, *Fortune* magazine reported that 105 industrial corporations outside the United States had sales of more than a billion dollars. Twenty-three of these firms reached the billion dollar level for the first time in 1972. Still, as shown in Figure 12–3, the United States is a powerful force in world trade. The top 25 firms, according to sales, are shown in Table 12–2.

THE MULTINATIONAL COMPANY—WHY?

The "multinational company" is an often used terminology even though very few folks can agree on exactly what a multinational company is. Some say that a company is multinational if it sells any of its products in another country—a loose enough definition to include almost any company which ever received a foreign order. On the other hand, a multi-national company is considered by most to require plant operations and managerial personnel and ownership from a mix of foreign countries.

One of the finest examples of true internationalism was recounted by Edward A. McCreary in his book, *The Americanization of Europe.* McCreary tells about the German victory parade up the Champs Elysees in Paris in 1940. The employees of the Paris office of the National Cash Register Company of Dayton, Ohio were watching the parade from inside their building. Suddenly, a tank left the parade and roared up the driveway and stopped in front of the Paris NCR building. A German major climbed out and introduced himself. Presenting his card, he made it known that he was the manager of the Berlin office of National Cash Register. He further requested that he be contacted

FIGURE 12–3

World's Largest Corporations, 1971

100 Largest, by Nationality

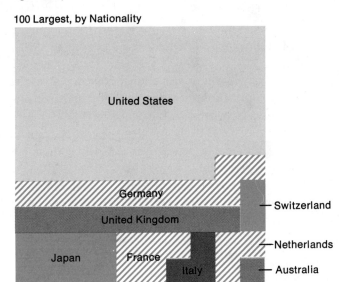

500 Largest, by Nationality

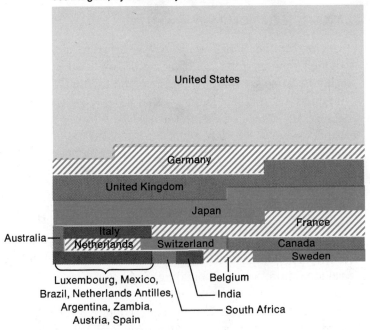

Source: U.S. Department of Commerce; The Conference Board, The World Economy in the 1970s: Trend and Issues, 1973, p. 39.

TABLE 12–2

The 25 Largest Multinational Corporations

Company	Total 1972 Sales (billions of dollars)	Foreign Sales as Percentage of Total	Foreign Earnings as Percentage of Total	Number of Countries Where Subsidiaries Are Located
General Motors (USA)	$30.4	19%	19%	21
Exxon (USA)	20.3	50	52	25
Ford (USA)	20.2	26	24	30
Royal Dutch Shell (Neth.-UK)	14.1	79	..	43
General Electric (USA)	10.2	16	20	32
IBM (USA)	9.5	39	50	80
Mobil Oil (USA)	9.2	45	51	62
Chrysler (USA)	9.8	24	..	26
Texaco (USA)	8.7	40	25	30
Unilever (Neth.-UK)	8.9	80	..	31
ITT (USA)	8.6	42	35	40
Gulf Oil (USA)	6.2	45	21	61
British Petroleum (UK)	5.7	88	..	52
Philips Gloeilampenfabrieken (Neth.)	6.2	..	..	29
Standard Oil of California (USA)	5.8	45	43	26
Volkswagenwerk (FRG)	5.0	69	..	12
U.S. Steel (USA)	5.4	54	62	..
Nippon Steel (Japan)	5.4	31	..	5
Standard Oil (Ind.) (USA)	4.5	..	..	24
du Pont (USA)	4.4	18	..	20
Siemens (FRG)	4.7	39	..	52
Imperial Chemical (UK)	4.2	35	..	46
Hitachi (Japan)	4.4	39	..	..
Goodyear Tire & Rubber (USA)	4.1	30	30	22
Nestle (Switz.)	4.1	98	..	15

Source: United Nations Department of Economic and Social Affairs, *Multinational Corporations in World Development,* 1973.

if he could be of any service to his Paris colleagues during the German occupation. After leaving his name and address in Paris, the German officer returned to his tank and rejoined the parade. Regardless of definition, no one could deny that such an incident proves NCR to be a multinational company!

It was not until the end of World War II that most companies began to pursue aggressively the fruits of multinational operation. In the late 1800s, there had been a few border crossings, with Du Pont purchasing a couple of Canadian powder mills and Edison starting the Canadian General Electric Company.

But it was not until the mid-1900s that the advantages of multinational status swung open the doors on an era of global cooperation which has not yet reached its zenith.

FIGURE 12–4

"Before we decide to lobby against foreign imports, may I remind you,
gentlemen, that 75% of <u>our</u> products are imports!"

Source: *Sales Management,* September 3, 1973, p. 27.

ADVANTAGES OF INTERNATIONAL OPERATION

There are three major reasons for the swing to international markets
and international production. The first and most commonly assumed
reason is *cheaper labor.* Once production processes have been streamlined as much as possible, the cost of labor is the remaining adjustable
variable. In many cases, the extra costs of transportation, construction
and tariffs can be regained many times over by reductions in labor costs.
Wages in other countries are generally much lower than in the United
States, but wages in certain countries like Germany and Japan have been
rising fast (see Figure 12–6). Of course, low wages must be accompanied
by reasonable productivity for this advantage to be significant.

A second reason for companies to establish foreign operations is the
location of *raw materials.* Why should a company buy its raw materials
in one country (which has cheaper labor or labor of equal cost) and
ship them to factories at home where labor is more expensive? If the
production facility can be set up where the resources are, there are sure
to be savings on transportation, tariffs, and talent.

FIGURE 12–5

Excerpts from *The Wall Street Journal*

'Multinational' Is And Isn't O.K. Now;

* * *

By a WALL STREET JOURNAL *Staff Reporter*

SPRINGFIELD, Mass.—It's official: It's all right to call a company a multinational company. But, the accompanying story notwithstanding, it isn't yet acceptable to call a multinational company just a "multinational."

That's the word from H. B. Woolf, editorial director for dictionaries at G. & C. Merriam Co. here, publishers of Webster's Collegiate and other dictionaries. In 1971, the adjective multinational was one of about 1,900 new words in an addendum to Webster's Third New International Dictionary, he says. And it is included in the Webster's Eighth New Collegiate Dictionary, which has just come out.

Among the meanings is "having divisions in more than two countries." Asked how an international company differs from a multinational one, Mr. Woolf confesses that "they sound synonymous to me." But business semanticists in New York claim that international is too broad and includes even small import-export firms while a multinational company is characterized by a global strategy of investment, production and distribution and, less specifically, by awesome size and power.

Mr. Woolf and his colleagues had sighted many, many citings of the adjective multinational by the time they decided to include it in the addendum. He says the first reference to the word that he is aware of occurred in the May 17, 1926, issue of Time, which referred to "a majority of the multinational citizens of what is now Hungary." The first known reference to a multinational company was in the June 3, 1927, issue of Science magazine, which wrote of "a well-known British author who on seeing a multinational publisher. . . ."

The current Webster's lists multinational as an adjective only, but Mr. Woolf says "I don't see why it shouldn't develop into a noun, the way national did." He says Merriam "might well list it as a noun in the next addenda," which will probably come out in 1976.

Source: *The Wall Street Journal*, April 18, 1973, p. 33.

Talk of the Globe

By CHARLES N. STABLER
Staff Reporter of THE WALL STREET JOURNAL

A random selection of facts about world trade:

—Of the 120 largest industrial corporations in Belgium, 48 are controlled partly or wholly from abroad. And it is forecast that in a few years one of every five Belgian manufacturing workers will work for a foreign—and probably American—company.

—German corporations now have more capital invested in South Carolina than anywhere else in the world except Germany. (The investment is in chemical and textile plants.)

—Some 90% of Europe's production of microcircuits is controlled by American companies.

—Switzerland's largest corporation, Nestle Alimentana S.A., does 98% of its business outside Switzerland.

—If a corporation's sales were to be equated with a nation's output of goods and services, then 51 of the world's 100 biggest money powers would be international corporations and only 49 would be countries.

—Large international companies currently do about $500 billion of annual business in each other's territories, or about one-sixth of the world's gross product. That's more than the entire gross national product of Japan.

A third type of expansion motivation is the availability of *new markets*. With competition getting stiffer at home, the corporation often realizes that there are untapped markets waiting across the border. Singer has "created" demand for sewing machines in places where no modern sewing equipment had ever been seen. In 1973 Pepsi-

FIGURE 12–6

Growth of Average Hourly Wage Around the World

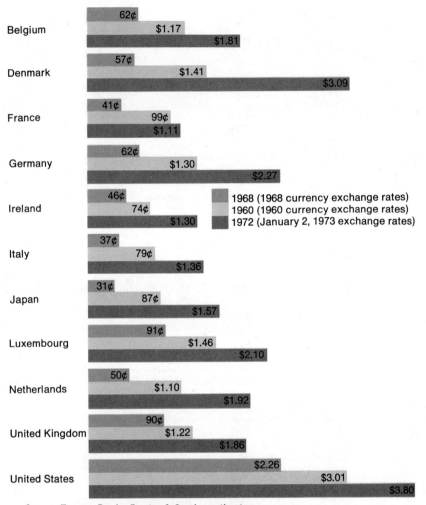

Source: Towers, Perrin, Forster & Crosby, estimates.

Cola was given permission to sell its products in Russia, a market where no American soft drink has ever been sold.

Besides these three positive motivators for making a company multinational, there have been some negative pressures which have pushed successful firms across borders whether they wanted to go or not. As certain companies grow larger and more powerful, they come under the scrutiny of governmental agencies with an eye out for monopolies.

Seeing impending difficulty connected with almost any domestic expansion, management moved its emphasis to the world markets. In many cases, this has proven a happy move though initially prompted by expansion limitations.

ORGANIZATION FOR MULTINATIONAL OPERATION

The international expansion of U.S. companies which began with exporting and importing, has moved through more sophisticated involvements to the point of true multinational status. These international operations must find their most appropriate organizational relationship in each company. This problem of organizational structure has usually been approached in one of four ways.

International Divisions

Some firms simply place all foreign concerns in one division which is separate and apart from the original corporation. The IBM World Trade Corporation, for instance, is a separate organizational entity from the rest of the IBM corporation.

Geographic Divisions

Another type of structure emphasizes a separate division of the company for each world market. Before becoming Exxon, the Standard Oil (New Jersey) conducted its world business via Esso Europe, Esso Eastern, Esso InterAmerica, and others.

Functional Divisions

A third organizational structure is based on function. Ford Motor Company is an example. The corporation is principally divided according to the jobs to be done. Thus, the marketing for the world-wide organization is planned by the Marketing Department. The Finance Department arranges international finance along with domestic plans.

Product Divisions

The fourth method of division is by products. A specific locale will handle the complete activity of producing and marketing its product. The Singer Company's operation in Chile is responsible for the manufacture and sale of sewing machines in that country while another Singer division will have a similar responsibility for Brazil. It will even market its product in the countries where its own sister companies are busily producing other products of the corporation.

The multinational company is a reality. The forms it may take in the future are still to be seen. It is already becoming obvious, however, that these organizations can become powerful agents in bridging the gaps which have divided nations for centuries.

PROBLEMS OF THE MULTINATIONAL COMPANY

It is very easy for domestic companies to make fatal assumptions as they rush into multinational expansion. Quite often, otherwise intelligent managers will make major decisions on the basis of a movie stereotype about a country or after making a single visit. The need for careful market planning is perhaps even greater in a foreign country since the manager has no experience to fill in the information gaps.

Problems have sneaked up on executives of multinational firms in the most unexpected ways, including the following:

Americans often take *reading skills* for granted, as they do a *common language*. But suppose you were given the task of planning the U.S. marketing approach for some product when only 15 percent of the American population could read and each state spoke a different dialect. Such is the plight of marketing managers who take a product into India or other similar countries. India has 500 million potential buyers—but only 15 percent are literate and 51 dialects are spoken. While Singer has been very successful in developing sales materials and instructions with pictures and drawings, picture language may be dangerous. One firm experienced a tremendous misunderstanding when a picture of a baby was placed on a baby food can. The illiterate buyers feared that the can contained ground-up baby!

Local attitudes about certain products may become very important. If a product is thought to be mainly for men, or mainly for children, or mainly for crooks, its sales could certainly be affected. International attitudes toward milk are a case in point, ranging from the Norwegians who drink 516 pounds per capita to the French and Italians who think milk is only for children.

Tastes vary from country to country. The sugar content of wine must be different for successful sales in France, in Belgium, and in Sweden. Same basic wine—different tastes across the borders.

Stereotypes about foreign countries are often incorrect and misleading. Would it make marketing different to discover that actually: the average Frenchman uses twice as many cosmetics as his wife; Italians eat only half as much spaghetti as the Germans; French and Italian housewives are not as interested in cooking as housewives in Luxembourg and Belgium?

Climatic differences and *currency problems* are two of the areas in which difficulty is anticipated but still encountered. Special scheduling and packaging is often required for protection from exceptional moisture, heat, or cold. Exchange of currencies can be more than irritating —it is sometimes prohibited by countries which must hold onto scarce American dollars for special needs.

Local laws, trade barriers, and *quotas* can make the free practice of business very difficult. Some countries will allow only limited numbers of certain commodities to be imported each year. Also special laws about taxation, shipping, and employment must be considered. Any U.S. businessman who assumes that all foreign ports will meet American standards in unloading ships or delivering goods deserves every delay he gets.

Business customs and *bargaining customs* are rarely part of written law. Nevertheless, they are sure to affect marketing strategy. Imagine trying to sell toothpaste in a marketplace where every sale must be bargained for—would the starting price have to be $5.00 per tube?

Anti-American feeling is a major point to be considered, even in pro-American countries. Many times, there is not outright hostility but a still harmful resentment of American domination of the market. Many countries have this problem, including our closest neighbors, Canada and Mexico.

The *number one* problem of the multinational corporation is not a function of the country at all. There is a critical shortage of qualified management personnel for the multinational operations. Schools are now training for international management. Some corporations are beginning to try to make overseas experience attractive and requisite for pyramid climbing within the corporation. And yet, the training of U.S. managers for foreign operations is only a half-step toward maturity for the multinational company. Full maturity cannot be realized until the managerial ranks of overseas subsidiaries include able personnel from the local scene and managerial ranks of American controlled multinationals include foreign nationals in headquarters offices.

Prejudice is common among Americans sent out to run local operations—not prejudice against a people necessarily, but the prejudicial assumption that "if it's not American, it's second class." Experience can usually solve this prejudicial attitude if the prejudice doesn't scuttle the experience first.

A final difficulty which often occurs at the upper echelons of the multinational company is the critical *interface of divisions.* These relationships between divisions can become strained when the typical competitiveness of division executives is increased by nationalistic pride. Great care for detail and fairness must be tied into the agreements and plans for marketing areas and responsibilities of each corporate arm. There is danger of "aggression" among national divisions of the multinational company. Boundaries and interrelationships must be specifically spelled out and carefully supervised lest they be allowed to be taken advantage of by the go-getter.

SUMMARY

Marshall McLuhan has suggested that our world has become "a global village" in which communication satellites have brought us together with people from other nations in the same way that citizens of a more primitive society might sit around the village campfire. Clearly, the "spaceship earth" has become the market place for many businesses. With world-wide business activity in economic growth, a new level of sophistication and statesmanship will be required of businessmen.

The concept of comparative advantage suggests that each nation would do well to emphasize the production of those things it does best. In other words, it might be more efficient for Switzerland to concentrate on the manufacture of watches even if it means that they must import computers from the United States and radios from Japan. To attempt the manufacture of all products which they might need would probably be inefficient and uneconomical. Of course, if they are to avoid a balance of trade problem, all nations must attempt to export approximately the same amount of goods and services as they import into the country.

Frequently, tariffs are used to keep foreign products from selling at a price below comparable goods which have been produced domestically. These tariffs provide revenue, protect domestic industry, preserve a nation's strength in "essential" industries, and may even be used to punish other nations. But they do end up in increasing consumer prices.

In order to eliminate some artificial tariff boundaries, the European Economic Community (frequently known as the Common Market or EEC) has agreed to allow commerce between member nations on an equal tariff basis and to charge equal tariffs to outside nations. Belgium, France, Italy, Luxembourg, The Netherlands, West Germany, Denmark, Ireland, and Great Britain have benefited greatly as a result of this international cooperation.

A firm may decide to become international or multinational in order to obtain cheaper labor, to secure cheaper raw materials, or to reach new markets. Although these motives are frequently logical and provide genuine benefits for the firm, the potential multinational businessman must consider the problems of language, local attitudes, and differences in tastes, culture, climate, laws, and other variables which exist between nations. Perhaps the greatest problem facing the multinational firm is the critical shortage of qualified management personnel.

In his book, The American Challenge, J. Servan-Schreiver predicts that the third ranking industrial power in the world (after the United States and Europe) may become U.S. industry in Europe. The rapid growth of Japan as a major economic force has cast some doubt on the validity of this prediction. With increased productivity in Japan and the rising impact of the European Economic Community, the potential scope of future prosperity or problems continues to grow dramatically. The danger of global trade wars, economic nationalism, and protectionism may lead to the regulation of multinational corporations. Jacques Maison Rouge, president of IBM World Trade Corporation, has suggested that it would be good for multinational corporations to have a counterpart which represents government. While the exact form of future regulation and controls is uncertain, the era of the multinational corporation is only dawning. Yet, it holds great promise for the future world peace and cooperation. Increased international trade has the potential of world harmony or increased dissension. The decision about which birthright will be claimed is in the hands of businessmen and politicians around the globe.

KEY TERMS AND CONCEPTS FOR REVIEW

Exports	Multinational corporation
Imports	Global village
Cowboy capitalism	Joint venture
Balance of trade	Comparative advantage
Tariffs	European Economic Community

QUESTIONS FOR ANALYSIS AND DISCUSSION

1. Was the "cowboy capitalist" a good guy or a bad guy?
2. Why is the world sometimes described as "spaceship earth"?

3. What would happen to Canada and England if international trade were stopped?
4. Identify the major types of tariffs.
5. What are the primary reasons for tariffs?
6. What are the most recent entries to the European Economic Market?
7. Why is the joint venture approach popular in Japan and Mexico?
8. Identify four major reasons firms wish to expand into foreign countries.
9. Why is India a very difficult market for American manufacturers?

SUGGESTED READINGS

Cateora, P. R., and J. M. Hess   *International Marketing* (2d ed.). Homewood, Ill.: Richard D. Irwin, Inc., 1971.

Haner, F. T.   *Multinational Management.* Columbus, Ohio: Charles E. Merrill Publishing Company, 1973.

Hays, R. D.   *International Business.* Englewood Cliffs, N.J.: Prentice-Hall, Inc., 1972.

Kolde, E. J.   *International Business Enterprise* (2d ed.). Englewood Cliffs, N.J.: Prentice-Hall, Inc., 1973.

Kriz, J. A., and C. J. Duggan   *Your Dynamic World of Business.* New York: McGraw-Hill Book Co., 1973.

Massie, Joseph L., and Jan Luytes   *Management In an International Context.* New York: Harper & Row, 1972.

Richman, B. M., and M. R. Copen   *International Management and Economic Development.* New York: McGraw-Hill Book Company, 1972.

Weston, J. F., and B. W. Sorge   *International Managerial Finance.* Homewood, Ill.: Richard D. Irwin, Inc., 1972.

13

Creating Goods and Services

If the American flag had been redesigned in the early 1900s, it might have had the words "A Better Way" stitched across it. The go-ahead spirit which had founded and settled this nation began, in the days of Henry Ford, to be obsessed with finding ways to do things better, faster, cheaper, or first. The U.S. had become a nation of strivers, experimenters, and efficiency experts.

Some men became famous because they did professionally what the culture glorified privately . . . the *improving* of something. Machines were not the exclusive invention of the United States. Other countries had equal access to the tools of mass production. But other countries had not been founded and nurtured so strongly on the doctrine of "A Better Way."

Suppose Henry Ford had proposed the mass production of automobiles in some other country or in another time. He might well have been run out of town by the centuries-old guild of buggy hand-crafters. He would certainly have been scorned as a money-mad monopolist. And his sanity might have been questioned as he proceeded to construct machines for which supplies, services, and roads were inadequate or nonexistent.

But in America in the early 20th century, there was excitement at the very news of mass production. Producing a horseless carriage that everyone could afford was enough to make a man President . . . or, perhaps even better, rich and famous! Do you remember who was President of the United States the year Henry Ford brought out his Model T?

Americans had the temperament for mass production, and the economy boomed. Mass production has now become an inescapable part of our life. Even the folks who demonstrate against the dehumanization of industrial life are sure to be found mass-producing their protest placards. It is interesting that those who want our society to return to the simple life almost always preach their doctrine via the mass media of newspapers or books or television. "And why not?" they would ask. "It's a more efficient way to tell lots of people."

Some of the most important characteristics of the American pursuit of a better way can be summarized in a few key words: competition, mechanization, automation, standardization, and specialization. They weren't invented in this country, but we have carried them farther than most other countries until recently.

Competition started it all and keeps it growing. One can take competition for granted, and even think it evil until one has the opportunity to live in a less competitive society. There people are often rewarded equally for working or for shirking. Premiums are not always paid for quality. In such countries one finds less efficiency and a lot more poverty. Competition is a hard taskmaster, but far better than the lack of it!

Mechanization means the use of a machine to do the work of a man or an animal. In 1850, the average American worker toiled 70 hours a week and produced approximately 27 cents worth of goods per hour. A hundred years later, the average worker was spending around 40 hours each week helping his machine turn out ten times as much per hour . . . and meeting with his union representative to demand better working conditions. Much of this progress can be attributed directly to the search for a better way, the effort to make things faster, easier, safer, and even better. The introduction of machines to do "human" work was greeted with some skepticism by those who predicted that machines would throw workers out of jobs. However, experience throughout the world has shown that machines tend to create rather than destroy jobs.

Automation goes one step farther than mechanization and makes the machines run themselves. Automated machines start and stop by themselves. They can be programmed by tapes to perform a series of different operations, and even to check themselves periodically. The advantage of automation, of course, is that it reduces labor costs, just as mechanization does. Consequently some people have predicted that automation would lead to unemployment. Rather than causing mass unemployment, however, automation has created many new jobs.

In the years 1965–1974, the only categories of jobs in which employment actually declined were laborers (by 2 percent) and people employed as farmers or farm workers (by 22 percent). The U.S. Bureau of Labor Statistics has estimated that technical and professional jobs increased by 45 percent during the same period. During the period 1975–1979, industry will need 350,000 new technicians, 138,000 new computer programmers and operators, and millions of new clerical employees. There have been short-term lay-offs, of course, but the long-term labor picture is far more favorable with continued automation than without it.

Standardization has long been one of the tools for finding a "better way." Eli Whitney, the inventor of the cotton gin, was also a successful manufacturer of rifles with interchangeable parts. He discovered that mass-produced rifles were not only cheaper to make, but also less likely to misfire and cost a marksman his eyesight. Today we take for granted that products will be standardized. We will pay a premium for a one-of-a-kind painting or other artwork, but if something has moving parts and we depend on it to perform some job, we want it standardized, synchronized, and guaranteed replaceable. Who would want to buy a handmade automobile for which each part had to be specially machined?

Another type of standardization that is less well known than product standardization is professional standardization. It has to do with systems, processes, and methods. For example, management consultants and certified public accountants may work with 50 different organizations in the same year. Without professional standardization, accountants could only work for a company after learning its unique record system. An understanding of basic business concepts, many of which have been introduced in this book, makes it possible for them to move quickly and efficiently from one assignment to another.

Specialization means dividing the work into its simplest components so that one worker can specialize in each. It is not a new idea. Adam Smith wrote a famous description of specialization and division of labor in an 18th-century British pin factory. But specialization has been carried much farther in the 20th century.

The manager of a factory and the engineers he employs are responsible for deciding how the work shall be carved up. They may divide it by processes, by workers, by chronological steps, by cost centers, or even geographically. Each specialty depends upon every other specialty.

Poor division of the component tasks, or poor performance of any task, places the entire operation in jeopardy. Because of this, wise management will anticipate the possibility of things going wrong and plan for corrective action.

The key words discussed above help to explain why the United States and certain other countries were able to get a head start on the rest of the world in modern industrial production.

MANUFACTURING PROCESSES

The methods by which production tasks are accomplished in the factory are called *manufacturing processes*. There are three ways of classifying them: according to the kind of activity involved, according to the time element utilized, or according to the product manufactured.

If we classify manufacturing processes according to the kind of activity involved, we may divide them into four categories. An *extractive* process involves primarily extracting some product from its natural place of occurrence. Mining gold and drilling for oil are extracting processes, as is wheat harvesting. *Analytic processes* remove one desired product from others with which it is first found. This happens in refining gold, oil, and wheat. *Fabricating processes* are sometimes called converting processes. These processes change the form of the material to make it more marketable. Fabricating processes applied to gold, oil, or wheat may produce a gold ring, motor oil, or flour. *Synthetic processes* bring together many diverse raw materials to form a single resultant product such as a gold-inlaid crown for a tooth, oil-base paint, or biscuits.

If we classify processes according to the time element utilized, we distinguish between continuous and intermittent processes. A *continuous* process goes on continually, perhaps 24 hours a day, 7 days a week. The shutting down of a continuous process, such as the huge furnaces used in steel production in Birmingham or the paper mills in Green Bay, may involve great losses. *Intermittent* processes are found wherever the nature of a product demands frequent changes, as with the work of a print shop.

When classified according to the product manufactured, processes may be either standard or custom. *Standard products* are made for a nameless buyer, each one exactly like the others. The customer must adapt to the standard products. But whenever the customer specifies the product characteristics he desires, a *custom process* must be created to meet his specifications. Each large tube of Crest toothpaste is essentially like other tubes. Yet the equipment used in producing the toothpaste is designed to fit Procter and Gamble's own specifications.

PRODUCTION MANAGEMENT

A production manager, of course, is someone who manages production. Each of us is a production manager, managing our own production. We may not be turning out a steady stream of identical objects, but each of us is involved in making expenditures of time and money, living within a budget, and continually reexamining our methods to see if there is a better way. It would be a narrow concept that saw production management only in factories and businesses producing tangible products. A doctor must manage the flow of his patients and supervise a staff that performs laboratory tests. An advertising agency has to bring together ideas, art, and media to produce its product: a change in buying behavior among the target audience.

When a student is assigned a class project, that student must become a project manager. Even though the steps toward a final, completed project may be accomplished at random, all must happen at sometime before completion. Have you ever seen a student sit down to type a paper only to realize that he needs paper or a new ribbon? The resulting trip to the store interrupts the flow of his production and wastes valuable time and effort. When a research paper is assigned, the efficient student goes through each of the same steps of production control used by production managers in large factories.

Planning is the first step. A production manager must take the customer's order and break it down into a complete list of necessary materials and processes. The student does the same. He listens to the professor's (customer's) description of the desired paper (job order) and makes mental notes of the materials needed (paper), locations to be visited (library), steps to be taken, and time to be used. The factory production manager compares his list of requirements with his machinery, his warehouse, and his manpower. The student does the same, though his estimates are usually made mentally rather than on paper. He may be able to afford the luxury of breaking his work flow to go and buy typing paper, but the production manager can't close up the factory while he sends off to have shipping boxes made for his product.

Routing is the step in planning that helps a manager avoid those last-minute hold-ups. With the aid of a charting system, he determines which things must happen before which other things, and what tasks can be done concurrently with other tasks. He is able to estimate the time required for the whole project. Occasionally, a student will attempt to cram five days of work into the final night before a product deadline. The deficiency is usually obvious, as obvious as it would be if Lockheed tried to produce a C5-A airplane in one week.

FIGURE 13–1

Activity Chart of a Team of Three Women Wrapping Eight Pints of Ice Cream in a Package

ACTIVITY CHART

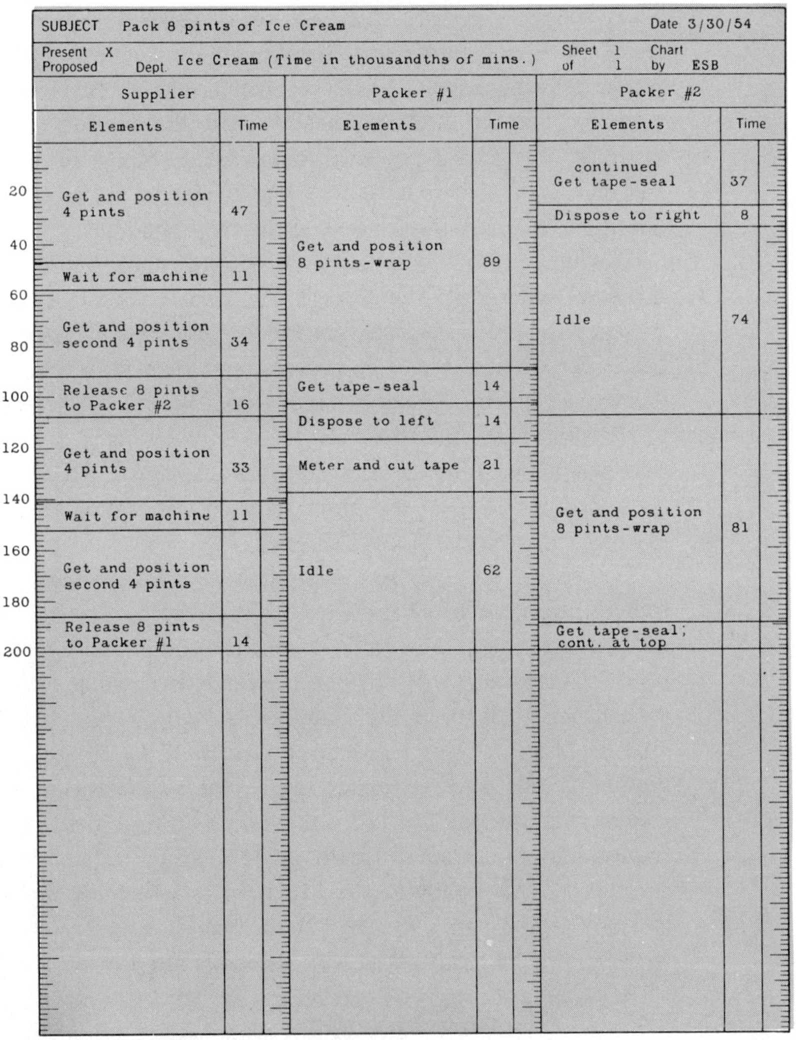

SUBJECT Pack 8 pints of Ice Cream				Date 3/30/54		
Present X Proposed Dept. Ice Cream (Time in thousandths of mins.)				Sheet 1 of 1	Chart by ESB	
Supplier		Packer #1		Packer #2		
Elements	Time	Elements	Time	Elements	Time	
				continued Get tape-seal	37	
20 Get and position 4 pints	47			Dispose to right	8	
40		Get and position 8 pints-wrap	89			
Wait for machine	11					
60						
Get and position 80 second 4 pints	34			Idle	74	
100 Release 8 pints to Packer #2	16	Get tape-seal	14			
		Dispose to left	14			
120 Get and position 4 pints	33	Meter and cut tape	21			
140						
Wait for machine	11			Get and position 8 pints-wrap	81	
160						
Get and position second 4 pints		Idle	62			
180						
Release 8 pints 200 to Packer #1	14			Get tape-seal; cont. at top		

Source: E. S. Buffa, *Modern Production Management*, 4th ed. (New York: John Wiley & Sons, Inc., 1973), p. 391.

Scheduling is where professional production managers show their mettle. When profit or loss depend upon well-timed production, the first-class production manager knows (and communicates to all involved workers) the intermediate deadlines along the way to the big final finishing date. In a major developmental project, the master schedule dictates departmental schedules, weekly schedules, and individual workloads. Everything must be ready at the right time. There is no allowance for cramming work in at the last minute.

In an assembly line operation, the various components of a job are physically dependent upon each other. In the following activity chart, the "supplier" can delay each of his coworkers by being slower than the schedule.

Would it be possible for a college term paper to be planned, routed, and scheduled according to a step-by-step production control system? If so, would that make writing it harder or easier? A sample approach to such an assignment is shown in Figures 13–2 and 13–3. A glance at Figure 13–2 will show how various things go on at approximately the same time and how, if certain activities are delayed (such as events 2, 3, 4, 8, 9), the completion of the paper will be delayed. How could such a system make a difference if the student happened to be working on several papers at the same time and needed to coordinate the input of other people? As we shall see later in Chapter 23, managers use the

FIGURE 13–2

Schedule for Producing a Research Paper

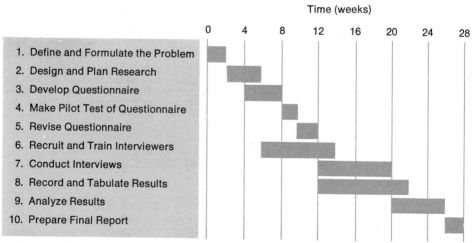

Source: Adapted from Robert G. Murdick, *Business Research: Concept and Practice* (Scranton, Pa.: International Textbook Company, 1969), p. 118.

Ray A. Kroc

Ray Kroc is living proof that success can come at almost any time in a person's life.

He was 52 and operating a small distributorship for milkshake mixers when the spark of his big idea was ignited—the idea that was to result in the creation of the McDonald's Corporation and, of course, the famous McDonald's hamburger. This idea revolutionized not only his life and the eating habits of millions of Americans, but also the fast food merchandising industry itself.

Kroc was born in Chicago in 1902. At 15 he dropped out of school to sign on with the Red Cross as an ambulance driver during World War I. After the war he worked for a time as a jazz pianist, then became music director of a radio station in Chicago. In this capacity he once hired a song-and-patter team who were later to become famous as Amos 'n' Andy. He left to sell Florida real estate until 1926, returning to Chicago stone broke. In 1937 he found out about a machine that could mix six milkshakes at one time, and began his own small company as exclusive distributor for the product. In 1954 he discovered that a small restaurant in San Bernardino, California, run by the McDonald brothers, was using eight of his mixers—more than any of his other customers. Kroc entered into an agreement to sell franchises for the McDonalds on a royalty basis. His principal objective at first was to increase the sale of his multimixers. But his partner, Harry Sonneborn, worked out a system that combined franchising and leasing. Often they would lease a site, develop it, and then release it to a franchisee.

The first of his new McDonald's units was opened in Des Plaines, Illinois, in April 1955. Two franchises were sold the same year. Kroc soon realized that his real profit potential was in hamburgers, so he sold his mixer company to raise capital for expansion. After a 1955 volume of $235,000, the

same basic techniques in planning and controlling their various operations.

Performance, follow-up, and control are an important part of the production manager's job, especially when the project is to continue. Wherever performance times or materials turn out to have been estimated unrealistically, savings can be made. If part of the operation needs strengthening, steps should then be taken to remedy that de-

company was able to report a $37 million sales total in 1960, from 228 outlets. In 1961 Kroc bought the McDonald brothers' interests for $2.7 million and by 1965 there were 738 units with sales of $170 million. In mid-1972 the 2,000th unit was opened, and 1972 sales exceeded $1 billion.

Although the fast food industry in general has experienced tremendous growth during the 1960s and 1970s, McDonald's has far outdistanced the other chains. This is attributable largely to the company's policies of reducing all elements of the business to a science, leaving little to chance. As 85 percent of the McDonald's outlets are franchise operations, some measure of centralized policy and control has been essential to maintain the firm's image, which is based on what Kroc calls QSC, the company motto: "Quality, Service, Cleanliness." The hamburger itself is rigidly controlled as to size, weight, and composition, and only certain cuts of beef may be used in its preparation.

Many people think that technology and efficiency are best applied to manufacturing operations. McDonald's has been a leader in applying production technology to the service industry. It has shown that a service company can enjoy unusual profits by combining technology, people, and a measure of good fortune.

Kroc moved up to chairman of the board in 1968, turning the presidency over to Fred L. Turner, who had not turned 40. Nevertheless, the corporation still adheres to many of the original policies established by its founder. It caters largely to a young family trade, making sure that its places don't become teenage hangouts. It looks for sites carefully before making a commitment, typically near shopping centers in residential neighborhoods of young families of above average income. Franchise owner-operators are sent to school at the company's "Hamburger University" in Elk Grove Village, Illinois. Regular inspections of all facilities bearing the McDonald's name are conducted by field consultants.

The average gross volume of a McDonald's restaurant in 1972 was in the $450,000 range. Some operators own franchises for several stores, and Kroc has estimated that at least 60 or 70 have become millionaires. Needless to say, there is a long waiting list for McDonald's franchises, which cost from $110,000 to $125,000, plus building costs.

Kroc reported in 1968 that he owned about two million shares of McDonald's stock, then worth about $50 a share. He is an important contributor to and supporter of various charities and institutions through his Kroc Foundation, and in 1972 was reported to have donated a total of $7,500,000 to them, in addition to his political contributions. In 1974 Kroc invested $12 million to buy the San Diego Padres baseball team.

A reporter who visited him at his winter home in Ft. Lauderdale said Kroc's place turned out to be just like any other 10,000 square foot home with a 72 foot yacht tied up in a canal out front. The doorbell, however, was somewhat unusual. When you push it, chimes play the opening of the McDonald's hamburger song: "You deserve a break today. . . ."

Kroc's personal credo has been widely published. "Press on," it begins. "Nothing in the world can take the place of persistence. Talent will not: nothing is more common than unsuccessful men with talent. Genius will not: unrewarded genius is almost a proverb. Education alone will not: the world is full of educated derelicts. Persistence and determination alone are omnipotent."

ficiency. The follow-up activity may also help a student to see which part of the job slowed him up the most.

As suggested earlier, every person is a manager of his own production. Some are very poor managers. Others have a natural desire to refine and perfect the methods by which they work or play. Thinking of oneself as a production manager enables one to do better the things he wants to do. Housewives, garbage men, artists, students, and fisher-

FIGURE 13–3

Charting a Production Program for a Research Paper

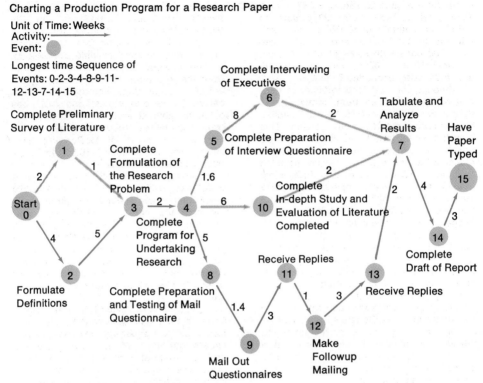

Source: Adapted from Robert G. Murdick, *Business Research: Concept and Practice* (Scranton, Pa.: International Textbook Company, 1969), p. 119.

men can always make life better for themselves by finding "a better way."

TECHNIQUES OF PRODUCTION MANAGEMENT

Several important techniques have been developed for the management of production. The most famous of them is time and motion study.

Anyone who has worked in a factory has noticed the occasional appearance of people with clipboards and stopwatches. These observers scrutinize the various movements required by workers to complete a job. They time the movements over and over, to see if any particular movement can be eliminated, combined with another movement, or made easier. The purpose, of course, is to arrive at a way of performing each operation without waste of time, motion, or effort. It may seem absurd to spend hours trying to save a few seconds, but a few seconds saved on a process that is repeated thousands of times can add up to a lot of time and money. An example of the way time and motion studies are used to direct workers' efforts is shown in Figures 13–4 and 13–5.

The *micromotion study* carries the process of analysis one step farther. It was developed from work originally done in 1911 by Frank Gilbreth, the efficiency expert whose family life became a popular movie of the 1950s—*Cheaper by the Dozen*. Micromotion study uses a motion picture camera to record the movements of a worker in conjunction with the face of a clock. The movements may be studied frame by frame to determine exactly where wasted motion occurs. This system has been used profitably by some Olympic track stars to analyze

FIGURE 13–4

A Capacitor, Showing Its Several Parts

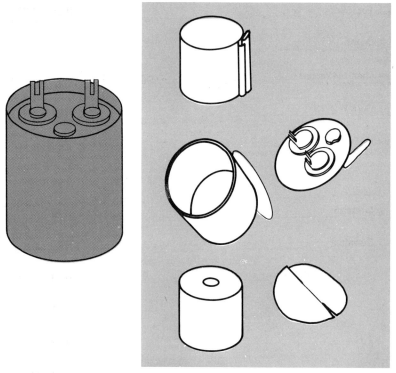

Source: E. S. Buffa, *Modern Production Management*, 4th ed. (New York: John Wiley & Sons, Inc., 1973), p. 245.

their running style. It is an expensive technique but valuable for rapid motions where timing is critical.

Other techniques of production management are discussed in Chapter 23. They are all designed to make graphic the kinds of things that tend to slip by the casual observer. The production manager cannot

FIGURE 13–5

Assembly Chart for Capacitor of Figure 13–4

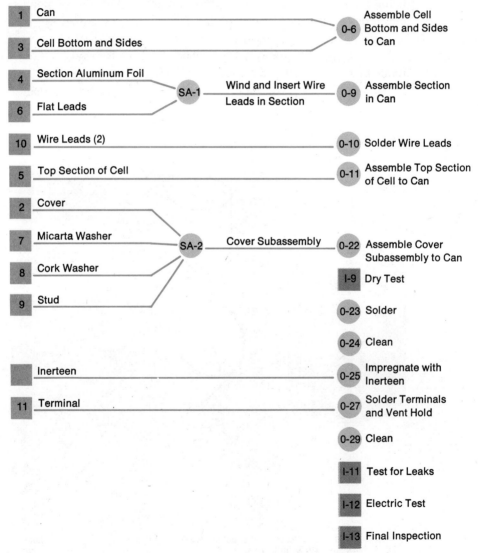

Source: E. S. Buffa, *Modern Production Management*, 4th ed. (New York: John Wiley & Sons, Inc., 1973), p. 253.

afford to be a casual observer. His job is to analyze, observe, and experiment . . . to find a better way.

QUALITY CONTROL

"Quality control" sounds like a phrase originated by some public relations firm to make its client look good. But it is really the name for a self-checking system used by manufacturers to make sure that their materials, processes, and craftsmanship are up to specifications. The more complex the operation, the more the need for regular and systematic inspection to guarantee that specifications are met.

Neither the practice of quality control nor any other kind of inspection of the production process should be regarded as a reflection on the workers. Products always vary, and management has to make sure that they do not vary more than by specified amounts. Even so, there is usually some resentment of quality control personnel on the part of other employees, who often regard them as snoopers or as nonproductive. It is best to have the inspectors report to the production manager or even to engineering, and not owe any allegiance, official or otherwise, to the line workers or their foremen.

Inspection can vary in thoroughness. The loosest approach is to inspect the raw materials as they arrive at the loading dock, and then inspect the final products as they are ready to be shipped. At the other end of the thoroughness scale, most materials for the space programs are required to receive 100 percent inspection—that is, to be inspected at every stage in their manufacture. Most products are inspected with some intermediate degree of thoroughness, depending on the nature and proposed use of the product itself. The kinds of tests made will obviously depend on the product; hardness, for example, is a more important test for the points of drills than for the tips of ballpoint pens.

Inspection may take place in a laboratory, in a special separate location, or right alongside the production line. In some cases the workers themselves act as intermediate inspectors, with final decisions made by someone else. Inspection tools may include gauges, scales, chemical processes, X-ray equipment, and electrical apparatus. A rejected piece may be reworked, thrown away, or sold at a reduced price as a "second." Of course, many firms, such as hardware manufacturers, cannot inspect every bolt or nail which they produce. Consequently, they inspect periodic samples of production runs.

One way that quality can be affected is through malfunction or breakdown of the machinery. The production manager must work out ways of maintaining the machinery and of handling breakdowns. He will have to be able to defend his approach to maintenance on a dollars and cents basis. He may find one of these four methods most appropriate:

1. *Preventive maintenance* seeks to prevent breakdowns before they happen by doing regular checking and correcting on a systematic basis. For example, bearings may be replaced in certain industrial machines after, 1,700 hours of use even though they often last for 2,000 hours.
2. *Routine maintenance* consists of upkeep, oiling, cleaning, and overhauling to help keep machinery going. It differs from preventive maintenance in that parts are not replaced until they wear out.
3. *Redundancy* is the use of double systems to assure that the entire operation will not break down if any single machine or source of supply fails. Many companies have emergency power supplies as well as multiple machines.
4. *Contract maintenance* by outside personnel may be feasible if the cost of keeping a full-time maintenance crew outweighs the losses from downtime (when a machine is out of commission).

RECENT DEVELOPMENTS IN TECHNOLOGY

In the last 30 years we have seen a stream of astonishing new products emerge from the world's factories and laboratories. The pace of innovation has been so fast that we fail to appreciate just how remarkable many of these developments are. The sight of men walking on the moon, broadcast by color television into millions of homes around the world, has made us yawn at things that are only slightly less spectacular.

Plastics used to be brittle, and only good for making a few shapeless toys. Today vinyl plastics are strong, lightweight, and can be used to make almost anything. *Fiberglass* is opening many new doors. Many *glues and adhesives* have been discovered that produce a joint stronger than the original material. New *alloys* have made it possible to produce steel that is lightweight and nonrusting. *Lighter, more useful metal products* are being made from titanium alloys, cermets (metal-filled ceramic materials), beryllium, chromium-based alloys, and aluminum.

New processes include fast-freezing with liquid nitrogen that freezes goods quickly to −320F. *The steel industry* has learned to refine low-grade ore previously thought to be unusable. Continuous casting, the oxygen furnace, and electrical discharge machinery are saving time and money in the production and finishing of steel.

Miniaturization has been one of the most remarkable developments. Only a few years ago a portable radio had to be the size of a small briefcase, but now better quality and performance can be found in an ear-plug unit. Astronauts carry with them a computer that only a few years ago would have had to be transported in a trailer truck. Parts for miniaturized equipment are assembled by workers peering through microscopes.

Sensing devices are now in use that can transfer three-dimensional photographs by telephone, or "feel" the shape of a mold to be duplicated in a metal die.

Perhaps the most amazing development of all has been *automation*. An automated machine runs itself. It starts, stops, and alters course according to its own monitory and sensing devices. These devices are called *servo-mechanisms*, and they are the brains and muscles of completely automatic machine tools. They are programmed to follow the instructions they are given. They are able to work in places not accessible to human beings: in blast furnace heat, at the bottom of the sea, and far inside the human body.

We are getting harder and harder to surprise, while our technology becomes more and more surprising.

THE EMERGING SERVICE INDUSTRY

Another phenomenon of the last two decades has been the growth of the service industries. Service industries have much in common with manufacturing industries, so far as the principles mentioned in this chapter about production management are concerned. *Planning* is as important in banking as in steel manufacture. *Routing* must be of major concern to a taxi driver. *Scheduling* should come at the top of the list for doctors and accountants.

Efficiency in the production of services is certainly worth the consideration of service industry managers. Too often they tend to set prices without any clear notion of their costs, because there is no visible, tangible product in hand. It is often difficult for workers in the service industries to justify increased prices or to evaluate their productive activities.

Several characteristics which apply to most service industries are:

1. *There is* no inventory of completed products in stock. A doctor is not expected to install an appendectomy, but to perform it. Similarly, an unsold airline seat cannot be stored for future sale.

2. *Small proprietorships* seem to be the dominant form of ownership, perhaps because of the small initial investment necessary. Even the burgeoning franchise industry consists mostly of small locally-owned operations.

3. *Limited areas* are generally served because the rendering of the service normally requires the personal presence of the worker.

4. *Skill* is more important than capital. Repeat business tends to be based on how well the service is rendered.

5. *Labor is the largest expense* in service industries because of the smaller inventories and the importance of skilled personnel.

6. *The* product of service industries is often intangible and often consists of maintenance. Haircuts, health care, and entertainment need to be replaced on a regular basis.

The service organizations and industries seem likely to dominate the business world of the future. Currently almost half our labor force is employed in service industries, and they account for approximately 40 percent of consumer expenditures. As automation frees labor for other pursuits, the service industries will certainly grow. This is good, since there are many services begging to be rendered.

FRANCHISING

The word "franchising" has come into everyday use in the last 20 years. It conjures up a picture of city streets crowded with fast-food business ranging from Burger King to Zuider Zee Seafood. Actually, these are only the most visible of the franchise operations. Automobile dealerships and soft-drink bottling operations were among the earliest franchise operations. Old-timers in Atlanta love to tell how Asa G. Candler bought the Coca-Cola formula for two thousand dollars and gave away the franchise for national bottling rights because he didn't want to be bothered with that detail. Franchising is now used for a wide variety of products and services, from paint sales to income tax services to automatic transmission repair.

By the end of 1973, franchises accounted for over $156 billion in annual sales, equal to nearly a third of total retail sales and 12 percent of the gross national product. There are some 500,000 franchised businesses in the United States today. New operations are being added at a rate of 21,000 annually, including overseas shops. When you are in Paris you can have wine with your burger at MacDonald's or if you go to Japan you can put up at a locally-owned Holiday Inn.

The principle of franchising is simple. Someone has an idea, perfects it, packages it, and makes money from it. Instead of owning all his own outlets, the franchisor simply sells the rights to use his idea and his name; frequently he also sells supplies or materials. The buyer or franchisee opens his own local shop, which must be identical to all the others. The public feels that it is dealing with local branches of a national chain. The advantage of franchising is that the extensive advertising, standardized procedures, and well-known merchandise of a national chain are added to local enthusiasm and aggressiveness. But if business is bad, the franchisee usually takes the loss—like any other small businessman. While a MacDonald's franchise in 1974 required $100,000 cash, a local franchise for *Sports Digest* magazine could be acquired for $15,000, and one might become an H. & R. Block tax consultant for less than $5,000.

SUMMARY

American methods of production have gained a head start on the rest of the world because of unique natural opportunities coupled with a passion for doing things better. Important elements in the pursuit of a better way are competition, mechanization, automation, standardization, and specialization. What America has done, other countries are now doing. In the early 70s U.S. productivity was increasing at an average rate of about 3 percent a year, while Japan's was increasing at almost 10 percent per year. Several other countries were also progressing at a more rapid rate than the U.S. Several other factors suggest that our leadership will continue to face real challenges. Almost 70 percent of Japan's machine tools were less than 10 years old in 1972, while almost 70 percent of ours were more than 10 years old. And Japan's rate of capital investment was double ours.

Manufacturing processes may be classified as extractive, analytic, fabricating, and synthetic operations. They may be either continuous or intermittent. When classified by product, they are standard or custom.

The principles of production management may be effectively applied to any task a human must do. Production managers are professional seekers for a better way. They do their work by planning, routing, scheduling, checking performance, and following up. Techniques used in production management include time and motion study, and micromotion study.

Methods of quality control assist in maintaining the consistent quality necessary for repeat business. The number and degree of inspections may vary from beginning-and-end inspections to a maximum of one inspection after every step in the process. Machine maintenance is important to quality control because of the impact of downtime and interruptions upon quality and cost. The manager must consider various alternatives in maintaining his equipment, and be able to defend his choice on a dollars-and-cents basis.

Recent developments in technology include plastics, fiberglass, glues and adhesives, new metals and alloys, new processes of fast freezing, miniaturization, sensing devices, and automation with its servomechanisms. These have allowed production to reach proficiency levels never before considered possible.

The mushrooming service industries already employ nearly half our work force, and continue to grow. Some of the characteristics of service businesses include: lack of product inventory, small proprietorship, limited market area, the use of specific skills, high labor costs, and an intangible product.

Franchising is now a major service industry in the U.S. It is based on the idea of selling the rights to an idea, a process, or an advertising system. Outlets are locally owned.

The principles of production management will become increasingly important as labor costs continue to soar. The important places where major savings are possible are in analytic, fabricating, and synthetic processes. The production manager is more than a pusher and prodder of reluctant workers. He can remove obstacles and make the operation more profitable for all concerned.

KEY TERMS AND CONCEPTS FOR REVIEW

Mechanization	Synthetic process
Automation	Standard product
Standardization	Custom product
Managerial standardization	Time and motion study
Specialization	Micromotion study
Extractive process	Quality control
Analytic process	Maintenance
Fabricating process	Franchising

QUESTIONS FOR ANALYSIS AND DISCUSSION

1. What is the chief advantage of automation?
2. In specialization, how may a task be divided?

3. How are manufacturing processes classified?
4. How do the authors classify manufacturing processes by activity?
5. How are manufacturing processes categorized by time element?
6. Describe the steps of production management.
7. What methods are available for handling defective pieces of production?
8. Identify the major approaches to maintenance.
9. In what ways are the service industries different from manufacturing?
10. Why does a McDonald's franchise cost so much more than a franchise for H & R Block?

SUGGESTED READINGS

Buffa, Elwood S. *Modern Production Management,* 4th ed. New York: John Wiley & Sons, 1973.

Chase, Richard B., and Nicholas J. Aquilano *Production and Operations Management.* Homewood, Ill., Richard D. Irwin, Inc., 1973.

Curry, J. A. H. et al. *Partners for Profits.* New York: American Management Association, 1966.

Garrett, Leonard J., and Milton Silver *Production Management,* 2d ed. New York: Harcourt Brace Jovanovich, Inc., 1973.

Niland, Powell *Production Planning, Scheduling, and Inventory Control.* New York: Macmillan, 1970.

Rosenberg, Robert *Profits From Franchising.* New York: McGraw-Hill, 1969.

Starr, M. K. *Production Management,* 2d ed. Englewood Cliffs, N.J., 1972.

14

Making Goods and Services Available

There is more than one way for a business to fail. Some fail because they make mistakes in handling money and men. Others fail because they can't find things —because they mismanage materials. Whether a company is an industrial giant or a small one-man operation, it must follow wise policies regarding the intake, storage, use, distribution, and transportation of material things. One reason for the high overhead costs in so many small businesses is their sloppy handling of these matters. A business may be built on a valid idea, but mismanage its *things* to the point of bankruptcy.

TYPES OF GOODS

The kinds of things handled by a business fall into five broad categories. One group of things is called *capital goods.* Capital goods are durable goods bought by a business to be used in carrying on the business. They range from blast furnaces or pneumatic drills to desks and ash trays. It is not uncommon for new businesses to overspend on capital goods and purchase the kinds of equipment that should only be available to well-grounded concerns. Good tools are essential in any business, but they should not be allowed to absorb too much cash and result in high operating costs.

Another group of materials common to all businesses are the *supplies* that are used up in running and maintaining the capital goods. Typewriters need paper, adding machines crave tape, furniture wants polish, machines need drills, soft drinks require packaging, and the sales department uses catalogs. The supplies used in operating a business should not be confused with raw materials. Supplies are necessary for the maintenance of the operation in which some product is produced and sold. Only by accident would supplies ever go into the actual product of the company.

Raw materials and parts form a third class of things. They include anything that will go into the manufacturing or processing of a company's final product, such as metal ores, chemicals, paper pulp, component parts, or electric motors.

Goods in process (also called semifinished goods) are raw materials or components that have been partially changed or processed but that need to be held in storage or on a production line until a later process converts them into the fifth category of things to be handled: finished goods.

Finished goods are the final outcome of the operation—the products a company sells. They often require warehousing and storage while awaiting shipment to customers.

Each of these categories of things to be handled overlaps with other categories. One company's raw materials or supplies are another company's finished goods. The largest category is often that of goods in process, since a factory will have many types of goods in process for each single type of finished product. In many factories, the partially completed component parts are stockpiled for future use. Sometimes a company buys components from outside suppliers instead of making them itself.

THE VITAL ROLE OF INVENTORY CONTROL

A stockpile of materials and components is good to have in case the source of supply should be cut off. But a stockpile can also be dangerous. What if there is a model change in the company's product? Or a particular component is found to be unsuitable? Also, the costs of storage may run high, or some materials may deteriorate over time. Most manufacturers try to steer between two disasters: that of being overstocked and that of running short. The right solution depends to some extent on experience and intuition. But in better-run companies it will be tied closely to known or forecasted needs.

"Inventory control" sounds like a job for an executive stock boy.

But, the importance of a skilled and creative controller of stock-flow cannot be overstated. Opportunities to save money in this area are numerous. The materials manager will be worth far more than his annual salary if he is able to eliminate waste in the quality of goods selected, in the quantities ordered and used, and in expenditures for transportation, storage, and distribution to markets.

When General George W. Goethals accepted the task of completing the Panama Canal, he looked with the greatest care for a supply officer. Finally he found an army engineer named Robert Wood. "I've made you quartermaster of the Canal," Goethals said to the 33-year-old lieutenant. "But the first day we run out of cement, you're fired." This was a big order considering that the rainy weather in Panama made stockpiling cement impossible. Wood was able through hard work and careful planning to keep the Canal in cement and all the other things that were needed. Fittingly enough, he later became president of Sears, Roebuck & Co.

ACQUIRING NEEDED GOODS AND SERVICES

Every large company employs people whose job is to buy things. In most industries they are called *purchasing agents*. In the retail field they are called *buyers*. The military likes to call the same job by a different name: *procurement*.

It may seem extravagant to employ people to do nothing but purchase, until we stop and try to picture what would happen if all the engineers or foremen of a large factory personally bought their own supplies. A good purchasing system always irritates people. When they are in a hurry it may seem slow and cumbersome. However, the impatience of an employee is a small price to pay for the major savings that can be achieved through careful purchasing.

What would you do if you suddenly found yourself responsible for the purchases of a company spending a million or more dollars per year for supplies? Suppose your first big request was for cellophane tape for each desk in the building. What would be your first move?

The simplest move would be to phone the local office supply store and order one reel of the most famous brand of cellophane tape for each worker. The store would certainly be pleased with the order, but your boss might like a special conference with you after the bill arrived. His first question might be, "Why do I need you, if you're only going to make a phone call?"

Your boss would be asking a good question. He hired you on the assumption that you were familiar with the meticulous system by which companies endeavor to get every penny's worth from the purchases they make. In the mid-1970s with shortages in many areas, the critical job of purchasing is becoming even more essential for business success.

The purchasing process usually begins when the person who will use the thing to be bought fills out a purchase requisition. His description and recommendation should be complete, accurate, and specific.

The Importance of Specifications

The purchasing agent needs to know precisely what is wanted. Then he can send out a simple letter containing the specifications and the quantities needed, the place and time requirements, and any special restrictions on bids.

Specifications make the purchasing job systematic. Otherwise the purchasing agent will be subject to an unending stream of salesmen with special prices on products that are "almost as good." But when the specifications are spelled out, he can look at the bids objectively and consider the more subtle distinctions between them. *Quantity* must be considered, for major savings can often be obtained on bulk amounts. It may be wise to purchase by the boxcar rather than by the half-truck. Before deciding on the size of the order, however, it will be necessary to consider a few other things.

Goods in storage must never be thought of as stored free of charge. The inventory manager must figure in rent on the storage space, record-keeping expense, handling charges, interest on the money tied up in stock, insurance, and the costs of obsolescence. Altogether, these carrying costs may total from 20 to 35 percent of the purchase cost of the inventory. To make a saving through bulk buying and then lose it in inventory is poor planning. The *rate of use* of the goods will be one factor to consider. Available *storage facilities* will be another. If inventory carrying charges are 25 percent a year, and if a company carries inventory equal to two months of sales, then the carrying cost is equal to more than 4 percent of each sales dollar.

Criteria for Purchasing Decisions

After thinking about quantity discounts and estimating storage costs, the purchasing agent should also consider the differences among major vendors with regard to delivery and service. Many companies make a policy of purchasing an item from more than one vendor. They will give half the order to each of the two lowest bidders so as to have alternative suppliers in case of delivery problems with either. This also helps to maintain competition among suppliers.

The industrial and military systems do their purchasing through bid or negotiation. The retailing field relies upon the skills of buyers. The retail buyers are like department heads who must "move" what they purchase because they are also usually in charge of sales of these items. Their tenure as buyers may depend upon their knowledge of what the public wants. Rather than dealing in specifications and carloads, they usually visit trade shows or wholesale showrooms where they pick and choose on the basis of their market research and of an intuitive feeling as to a product's value, cost, and customer appeal.

In all types of purchasing, small differences in specifications may mean large differences in costs. Most of us like the security of brand names and the margin of safety in top quality. Yet considerable savings can frequently be attained if the "good enoughs" are purchased consistently instead of the "sure things." Figure 14–1 shows some dramatic savings that were realized when each component of a purchase was subjected to "value analysis."

MOVING GOODS: TRANSPORTATION

In recent years a number of railroads and trucking lines have started advertising their services. The railroads use radio and television spots. Trucks carry slogans such as "Trucks pay their way," to remind us of the highway taxes they pay. These efforts are intended to prove to an ecology-minded public that trucks and railroads are well worth the noise and dirt they create. The transportation industries could make their point even more persuasively by simply going on strike for one day each month.

The Vital Role of Transportation

Freight transportation now accounts for about 9 percent of the gross national product. The ten largest transportation firms in 1973 had more than a billion dollars each in operating revenues (see Figure 14–2). Transportation has figured importantly in American economic history. The invention of the steamboat tied the great inland ports of the East together. The railroads opened the West. And the network of highways and trucking lines brought every small town within easy reach of the

FIGURE 14–1

How Value Analysis Slashes Costs

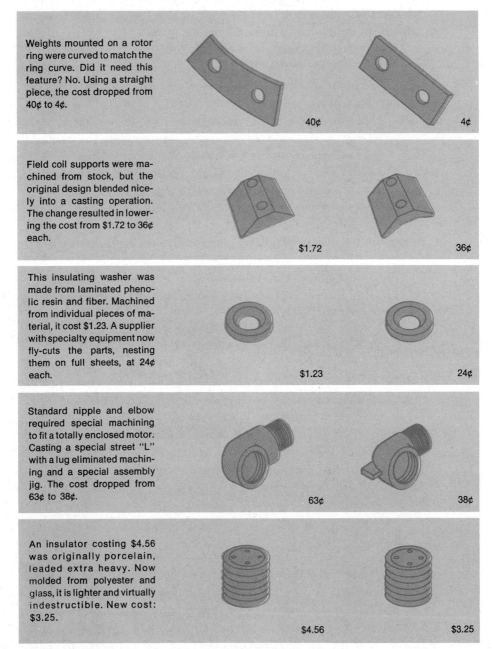

Weights mounted on a rotor ring were curved to match the ring curve. Did it need this feature? No. Using a straight piece, the cost dropped from 40¢ to 4¢.

40¢   4¢

Field coil supports were machined from stock, but the original design blended nicely into a casting operation. The change resulted in lowering the cost from $1.72 to 36¢ each.

$1.72   36¢

This insulating washer was made from laminated phenolic resin and fiber. Machined from individual pieces of material, it cost $1.23. A supplier with specialty equipment now fly-cuts the parts, nesting them on full sheets, at 24¢ each.

$1.23   24¢

Standard nipple and elbow required special machining to fit a totally enclosed motor. Casting a special street "L" with a lug eliminated machining and a special assembly jig. The cost dropped from 63¢ to 38¢.

63¢   38¢

An insulator costing $4.56 was originally porcelain, leaded extra heavy. Now molded from polyester and glass, it is lighter and virtually indestructible. New cost: $3.25.

$4.56 $3.25

Source: Reproduced with the permission of *Business Management* magazine, formerly *Management Methods* magazine.

FIGURE 14–2

The Ten Largest Transportation Firms

Rank	Company	1973 Operating Revenues ($000)
1	United Air Lines (Chicago)	2,060,268
2	Penn Central Transportation (Philadelphia)	1,963,673
3	Trans World Airlines (New York)	1,810,990
4	Southern Pacific (San Francisco)	1,551,265
5	American Airlines (New York)	1,481,927
6	Pan American World Airways (New York)	1,433,079
7	Burlington Northern (St. Paul)	1,331,524
8	Eastern Air Lines (New York)	1,259,808
9	Seaboard Coast Line Industries (Jacksonville)	1,230,055
10	Union Pacific (New York)	1,244,208

Source: *Fortune*, vol. 90, no. 1, p. 122 (July 1974).

factories. Air freight has become important in speeding deliveries and reducing inventories, carrying perishable items such as flowers, and handling delicate equipment with a minimum of packaging.

A company may find that its transportation costs are difficult to calculate, because the various routes and rate structures are highly complex. Some companies have been able to get rate reductions by convincing the railroads that this would enable them to ship more goods to more markets. Others have found that such arguments weren't necessary, because officials of the transportation companies often welcome the interest and support of their customers. They know that they grow by helping each other. The complicated rate system also leads to many honest errors. Companies should audit or at least spot check their transport bills before paying them.

Classification of Carriers

Railroads, trucking lines, and other forms of commercial transportation fall into two categories. The *common carriers,* holding themselves out to serve the public, are licensed and regulated by the government. They must maintain regularly scheduled shipping routes and accept goods they hold themselves out to carry from any customer. This serves to keep transportation predictable and within the domain of planning. Trains, planes, and buses are viewed as common carriers for passengers as well as for freight.

Contract carriers have fewer restrictions even though they are re-

Robert W. Prescott

Living by a motto he coined, "We'll fly any-thing, anywhere, anytime," Robert W. Pres-cott, founder and president of The Flying Tiger Line, has confidently stuck to his belief in the future of the commercial air cargo industry.

Born in Fort Worth, Texas, in 1913, Prescott was one of eight children of a truck driver, furniture salesman, and auc-tioneer. After high school he drove a truck and worked at other jobs until moving to California in 1934. There he attended Compton Junior College and studied law for a year and a half at Loyola University, still driving trucks or working in a tire fac-tory to finance his studies.

Joining the Navy in 1939, he completed flying school and became a flight instruc-tor. In 1941 he resigned his commission to volunteer for service with the Flying Tigers, which were being organized by Gen. Claire Chennault to fly for China against Japan. Later he flew for China National Aviation Corporation, carrying military supplies across the mountainous "hump" from India to China and completing more than 300 missions.

On his honeymoon in Acapulco in 1944, he met a group of Los Angeles business-men who were contemplating the establish-ment of an air freight line on the west coast. He convinced them that a transcon-tinental route would be better, and they agreed to match whatever capital he could raise.

Prescott recruited 11 other Flying Tiger veterans, who together were able to raise $89,000 for the venture. With that stake and the businessmens' matching sum, they bought 14 navy surplus craft and went into operation as the National Skyways Freight Corporation in 1945. Soon they changed the company's name to The Flying Tiger Line, Inc., which meant a lot more to the public.

Flying Tiger was one of 300 air cargo carriers established in the postwar years, mostly by former war pilots using surplus military aircraft. Few of these companies survived. Considerable determination and resourcefulness were needed in hustling whatever cash business was available. The Tigers hired out for charter flights and publicity stunts, and offered repair and maintenance services to foreign and do-mestic airlines.

quired to live within government regulations. They contract for spe-cific jobs. They usually do not maintain regular schedules. They may do odd jobs or work on a contract basis with a major shipper.

Many companies supplement the services of these carriers by owning their own railroad cars, trucks, barges, ships, and even aircraft. These private carriers constitute a third major category of transportation available to businessmen.

In 1946, the Air Transport Command opened bids on a contract to supply the occupation forces of General MacArthur in Japan. Prescott underbid his competitors by a tiny fraction and won the largest single airlift contract ever awarded a commercial carrier. For a year the Tigers flew 42 aircraft on a schedule of 8 flights daily carrying military passengers and cargo between the U.S. mainland, Hawaii, and Tokyo. Flown without a single accident, the performance drew strong praise from the military and established Prescott's company as a competitor to be reckoned with.

Plagued by lack of eastbound traffic for its transcontinental freight flights, the company got nonscheduled operators to lease its C-54 aircraft on turnarounds at Los Angeles, put in seats, and fly back east carrying passengers for $99. This was in 1947. Early in the 1950s, the Tigers started the first group tourist flights across the Atlantic, slashing passenger fares by more than half. But the company was eventually required by the Civil Aeronautics Board to confine its activities to carrying freight.

After a long legal battle, Flying Tiger was certificated by the CAB in 1949 to fly the nation's first scheduled cross-country cargo flights. This was a decisive competitive victory, and the airline earned a profit for the first time that year. During the subsequent Korean War, Flying Tigers carried supplies to the troops under one of the largest military freight contracts held by any company flying the Pacific. But commercial air freight business continued to range from spasmodic to unprofitable, and after several difficult years the company reported a net loss of nearly one million dollars for the 1959–60 fiscal year.

The problem of lack of business in the 1950s gave way to the problem of lack of funds for financing new jet aircraft in the 1960s. Competition with the large passenger carriers also became more intense, since they had been licensed for cargo operations as well. Prescott led the all-cargo carriers in their fight to convince the CAB that the all-cargo lines could handle freight more efficiently and economically than combination carriers. His campaign was partially successful. In 1966 the CAB gave the all-cargo lines the exclusive right to sell blocked space although the passenger lines continued to be the major factor in the general air freight business.

Profits grew during the Vietnam war, and in 1966 Prescott ordered 17 huge stretched-version jet freighters for a total cost of $206 million. These went into service in 1969 on transpacific flights. The 17,500-mile route from Boston to Bangkok meant the emergence of the Flying Tiger Line as a major carrier both domestically and internationally. Revenues skyrocketed from $76 million in 1968 to around $200 million in 1973.

In 1970 the company was reorganized into a holding company called Tiger International Corporation, of which Prescott is chairman. One of its two major holdings is the airline. The other is North American Car Corporation, the nation's fourth largest railroad car leasing organization, which with its subsidiaries is heavily engaged in many fields of equipment leasing.

From his offices in a new ten-story world headquarters at Los Angeles International Airport, Prescott has an unobstructed view of the Pacific where so much of the airline's history has been written. He admits that he never dreamt all this would grow out of the venture that began in a two-car garage at Long Beach, Calif., in 1945.

Carrier Rates

Common carrier rates are computed on three general bases. *Class rates* are used by the railroads to assign cost and value of service on more than 10,000 specific classes of goods. *Commodity rates* are usually set especially for bulky items like iron, coal, or lumber, which are shipped regularly and in volume. *Exception rates,* of course, are special rates for conditions not covered by the other rates. It is within this special rate area that concessions can often be bargained for by aggressive buyers of transport services. (This is not to imply that some transportation rates are vague, but rather that the rate setters are good businessmen who are willing to "give" a little to encourage growth which benefits them in the long run.) However, all rate setters must reckon with the regulations of state and federal agencies.

RAILROADS

Years ago, the railroads carried something like 80 percent of the nation's freight. At that time, rates were set for carrying bulky things such as coal at reduced rates, the idea being that large volume at small profits per shipment was best. Higher rates were charged on the more valuable but low-volume freight, such as finished merchandise. These arrangements worked against the railroads when trucks began carrying the lower-volume, lower-valued commodities at equal or lower rates than the railroads and with faster, more reliable service.

In recent years the railroads seem to have gone from one crisis to another. The stories in the newspapers, unfortunately, don't convey the strength and dependability of the country's rail services. Not only can railroads carry many goods cheaper than other carriers, but they are beginning to become more competitive in their services. They have developed new marketing approaches. For example, agreeing to ship by whole trainloads has made the railroads competitive with the barge lines in hauling commodities such as ore and coal. The tri-level car for new autos has enabled railroads to win back a major portion of the new-car shipping business from trucking firms.

Fast freight service has shown that not all trains are slow. For shippers with perishable or high-value goods, railroads have instituted 60 m.p.h. express services over long distances that compete well with trucks in speed and price.

Containerization has been taken up by both the railroads and the water carriers. Light-weight containers can be loaded at the factory and locked, delivered by truck to the railroad, easily shifted from rail to ocean to truck carrier, and finally opened at the destination.

Piggyback service takes the idea of containerization one step farther. In this case the container used is a truck trailer which is placed on railroad flatcars. It allows the shipper the economy of long-distance rail shipment and the convenience of local pickup and delivery.

In-transit privilege allows shippers to stop a shipment along the way, work on it, and then pick it up again for only a small charge. Telephone poles may be loaded in city A, dropped off in city B for a month or two to be creosoted, and sent on to city C. The shipper is not required to pay the local rates from A to B and from B' to C. Likewise, cattle may be stopped in transit for feeding and fattening.

Diversion in transit permits a shipper to alter the destination of his goods while they are in transit. A California shipper of lettuce, for example, may divert a shipment from New York to Baltimore if prices suddenly look better in Baltimore. If the new destination is in the same general direction as the original destination, and if the shipment is diverted at a junction point, there is only a slight additional charge.

Carload rates are given to shippers as often as possible. Because of the cost of loading, billing, and checking small shipments, railroads prefer not to carry them. The carload rate is normally below half the less-than-carload (LCL) rate per hundred pounds. Carload rates may be charged even if half the car is to be unloaded along the way, as long as the car meets minimum weight standards. Less-than-carload rail shipments have been declining. They dropped from $356 million in 1950 to only $34 million in 1971, while less-than-truckload shipments rose from $1,027 million in 1950 to $4,800 million in 1971. During the same time, air freight rose from $44 million to $896 million.

TRUCKS

Trucks, for many of us, are large vehicles that get ahead of us in traffic! But as freight carriers they are faster and more reliable than railroads, particularly for short distances.

Trucks are able to combine shipments by several different companies in one load. They can stop at any general store or crossroads along the way and drop off part of a load without the time-consuming reshuffling of cars that the railroads require.

For short distances and for higher valued goods, trucks must charge higher rates. They must make more of their profits here to be able to charge less on the long runs where the race with the railroads becomes more critical.

On the other hand, trucks have certain disadvantages. Bad weather usually slows down trucks more than railroads. Labor unrest seems to affect trucking more often than other forms of transportation. And, of course, trucks do not usually carry large loads as economically as the railroads.

We would not want to lose either the trucks or the railroads. A healthy transportation system needs their continuing competition.

WATERWAYS

The inland waterways of the United States were once the major mode of goods transportation. They are less used now that faster and more flexible means are available. But shippers with bulky, non-perishable products such as iron ore, grain, steel, petroleum products, cement, sand, gravel, chemicals, coal, and coke find that they can transport these things most cheaply by barge—providing, of course, that the customer is near a waterway. In 1972, more than 16 percent of all domestic freight between cities was carried by waterway.

The primary disadvantage of water transport is that it may be delayed by ice or fog. Many shippers attempt to plan around the seasons, even hauling the whole year's goods in the warmer months and warehousing for winter use. Movement of iron ore on the Great Lakes is concentrated in the months when freezing weather does not create unsurmountable problems.

The St. Lawrence Waterway System, completed in 1959, opened all the Great Lakes and the Midwest to Atlantic shipping. Eighty percent of ocean-going vessels can now sail right into the heartland of American commerce. These ocean-going ships may also carry containers of freight, and some even handle railroad cars. Thus it is possible for an ocean shipment to be carried first in the trailer of a truck, which is then loaded onto a piggyback rail car, which in turn will be loaded onto a railroad car-carrying ocean vessel. (But these railroad car-carrying boats usually ply between points within the U.S.)

PIPELINES

Pipelines, like other methods, are good for some purposes and poor for others. They serve quite effectively in transporting petroleum and natural gas along regular routes from source to refinery. Pipelines also carry gasoline, diesel fuel, and jet fuel from refineries to distribution points and even to airports. Almost every large city is laced with underground gasoline pipelines. But it would be inconvenient and costly to lay a pipe to every destination.

AIRLINES

Airplanes are the second most expensive cargo carrying system. (The most expensive is the rocket, but this will not be of interest to marketing planners until there is a colony on the moon.) The cost of shipping by air is, on the average, nearly three times the cost of truck shipment. The shipper must decide whether he wants to save time or money. Today, one can have flowers from Hawaii, strawberries from California, and French bread from Paris, regardless of the season. Highly perishable products often travel by air.

Some people look for the construction of supertransports that will put the airplane in competition for even more of the trucker's cargo. The cost of air freight will still remain higher, but the extra expense may be more than justified in time saved and storage eliminated. Even now, Sears often supplies its stores by air for certain items like clothing in order to speed customer service and to avoid carrying inventories near every market.

THE BEST METHOD

Trucking seems to have experienced the most rapid growth of any transportation medium in recent years, and truckers expect their share of the market to continue increasing (see Figure 14–3). The best method of transportation obviously depends upon the commodity being shipped, the market, and the ingenuity of the transportation officer of the company. Moreover, transportation is only one of the costs in moving materials and goods from producers to customers.

STORAGE

The problem of storage often occurs when the demand for a product is inconsistent with its supply. To avoid price fluctuations, companies may go to the extra expense of storing their products until demand increases. If your company produces Christmas toys, it can't make them only when they are selling, nor can it sell them all year long.

The manager must carefully compute the costs of alternative methods of getting his product to market. Storage costs money. On the other hand, if holding things off the market for a short while will increase their sale price, or if we must have them available in large amounts at peak periods, then storage pays. Also, storage at certain locations is often necessary in order to have a ready supply for local distribution and sale.

The warehouse has changed its image considerably in the last few years. The average warehouse used to be in the crowded center of a busy city, where parking was difficult and breathing impossible. It

FIGURE 14–3

Changing Shares of the Transportation Market

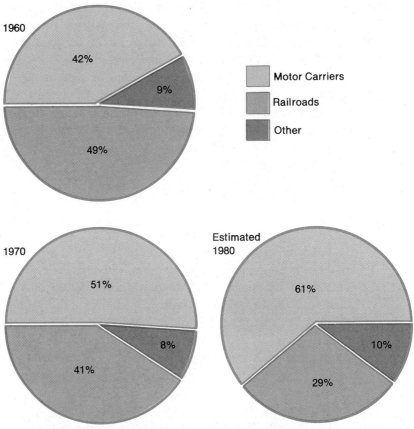

Source: American Trucking Association.

was an ancient building with several floors and a creaky freight elevator, ridden by reluctant workers. Today, many warehouses have moved to the suburbs; they are one-story, clean, light, and efficient. There is ample parking for employees and for trucks making pickups or deliveries. Inside, employees whiz around on silent forklift trucks, moving and stacking at the flick of a switch in minutes the amount of goods it used to take all day and a strong back to move. Even these methods are becoming obsolete in some cases, and it is possible that through the use of computers and automated handling many future warehousemen will never touch the goods they sort, stack, and store.

Storage places may be located almost anywhere along the way from the factory to the consumer. The greatest amounts of storage are

usually necessary at the production end, with needs gradually decreasing all the way to the retailer and to the final consumer, who
requires only minimum storage. One of the main decisions for the businessman is whether to own his storage facilities or to rent service in a
public warehouse. Unless the company's storage needs are very consistent and predictable, rental of warehousing service is likely to be
preferable.

DISTRIBUTION CENTERS

A relatively new development in goods movement is the distribution
center. Though it may look like a warehouse, it is really a place
where goods are reorganized for further shipment.

A distribution center is a sort of funnel. Trucks and trains unload
into it on one side, and trucks load out of it on the other side. Some
goods never stop moving, but go in one door and out the other.
Electronic data processing equipment has made possible the removal
of the "delivery lag" which used to be so common. Orders that come
in during the business day are telephoned or wired into a central
processing center, either at once or in the evening when communication expenses can be reduced by lower rates and group orders. The
requested items are picked from their warehouse slots, sometimes
mechanically, and sent on their way within 24 hours from the time
the order was placed.

Many companies have found that their warehousing and shipping
were based more on current output than on current orders. The
emphasis needed to be shifted to the other end of the line. The distribution center was the answer.

The Automated Warehouse

These distribution centers are of two kinds. Some have only "soft"
automation, in which the paperwork and goods selection system are
automated but employees must still collect, sort, and label the goods.
Others have "hard" automation: computers spin, motors whirr, and
machines gather various items from their slots and affix labels. The
goods are all but delivered to the customer (and someone may be
working on *that!*). IBM's warehouse in Endicott, N.Y., and A & P's
Canadian Division Distribution Center in Toronto process orders un-
touched by human hands.

THE PHYSICAL DISTRIBUTION MANAGER

"Move it—it costs money when it sits," is the watchword of a new kind of management. The physical distribution manager's job is to participate in the planning and locating of the entire operation. He does not, as did the old warehouse manager, simply keep goods on hand until somebody calls for them. His job is to see that materials and goods move in the fastest and most economical way from the supplier of raw materials and component parts to the factory, and from the factory to the warehouse and to the customer. His job would not be possible without the computer. Now it is not only possible, but imperative.

The physical distribution manager will have much to say about methods of packaging and handling the company's products. He will compare the costs of shipping goods by rail or truck and warehousing them against the cost of air freighting directly to the buyer without warehousing. He will be the person who knows what to do in case of an interruption anywhere in the transportation system.

Ultimately his job may involve much more. In a few companies the physical distribution manager is now responsible for the planning of raw material purchases and their transportation, the scheduling of production, the warehousing and shipping of finished goods, and the control of inventory levels.

More than anyone else in the company, the physical distribution manager will recognize the significance of where a company's plants and retail outlets are located. Figure 14–4 suggests the range of matters that fall within his scope.

LOCATION

Many factors must be considered in locating a manufacturing plant, a distribution center, a wholesale operation, or a retail store. The solution used to be simple—move to cities where services and skilled workers were available. Now the services can be moved to the site, or found where they are needed.

Manufacturing Plants

The following considerations must all be taken into account in seeking the best location for a manufacturing plant:

1. The *community* must be hospitable, convenient, and aware of both the advantages and disadvantages of gaining the new factory.

FIGURE 14–4

The Scope of the Physical Distribution Manager's Job

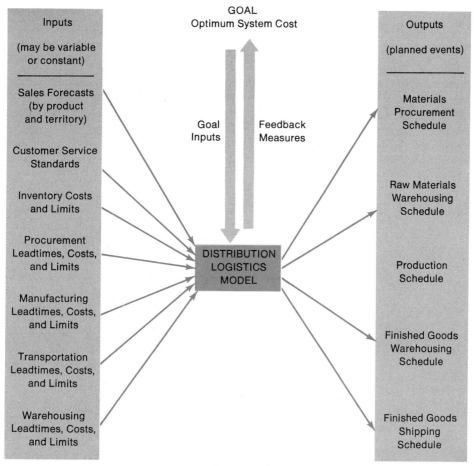

Source: Harold Koontz and Cyril O'Donnell, *Principles of Management*, 5th ed. (New York: McGraw-Hill Book Company, 1972), p. 621.

2. *Labor* must be of appropriate qualities, skills, and costs.
3. *Transportation* must be adequate to move raw materials, products, and personnel.
4. *Power* must be readily available.
5. *Ecological* considerations are becoming more and more important, particularly the question of waste disposal. Businessmen and the community in which they operate must have a clear understanding of what is involved in having a business in a certain location.
6. *Raw materials* must be nearby or economically transportable.
7. *Markets* must be accessible.

8. *Attitudes* of the company and the community must harmonize. There will be strains enough anyway, even if everything is made clear beforehand.
9. *Local and state taxes* may weigh considerably in a location decision.

Retail Stores

The choice of location for a retail store is equally complex. Though it does not always involve the long-range commitments of factory construction, a store must anticipate the movements of people and be willing . . . always . . . to pamper the customer.

The following considerations are necessary in picking a location for a retail outlet.

1. *Population* must be in the neighborhood, and likely to remain there for the projected life of the facility. People must not be expected to drive many miles unless the prices or products are unique. *Population trends* are as important as current population figures.
2. *Population categories* and *income levels* are extremely important.
3. The extent and methods of likely *competition* should be considered. Many businesses close after optimistically planning, but failing, to "out-hustle" the existing competition. Generally, people are slow to leave a store they know, even if a newer one has more to offer.
5. *Customer traffic* is very important. While nobody likes crowded intersections, a business must sell to people. Intersections are where the people meet.
6. The *future* of an area is of critical concern. While a planner cannot be a prophet, he should be wary of building a store in a place where conditions are changing.

SUMMARY

Even a well-made product, with strong customer loyalty, will not sell unless it is made available. Creating "place utility" is one of a businessman's most important challenges. Similarly, a well-designed factory with orders to fill may stand idle unless the necessary raw materials are available. The work of the skilled purchaser is important in all types of firms. He can make considerable savings in the acquisition of capital goods, supplies, and raw materials. Other savings can be made in the management, storage, and distribution of goods-in-process and finished goods.

Freight transportation now accounts for almost one tenth of the gross national product. Common carriers, contract carriers, and privately owned transportation facilities help move the nation's goods from point of production or storage to the place where the goods are needed. Although railroads no longer carry most of the nation's freight, they continue to be a major means of transporting bulky materials. Trucks, waterways, pipelines, and airlines are other commonly used means of transportation.

Warehouses, distribution centers, and automated warehouses handle products en route to their final destination. Efforts are constantly being made to reduce the amount of time that goods must be kept in storage, and to minimize human error in moving them from storage to their ultimate users.

The modern physical distribution manager must see that materials and goods move in the fastest and most economical way from the supplier of raw materials and component parts to the factory, warehouse, and customer. He must work diligently and carefully in choosing transportation and distribution locations, and should also have a voice in the location of manufacturing, wholesale, or retail operations.

KEY TERMS AND CONCEPTS FOR REVIEW

Inventory control	Warehouse
Value analysis	Distribution center
Common carriers	Automated warehouse
Contract carriers	Goods in process
Class rates	Commodity rates

QUESTIONS FOR ANALYSIS AND DISCUSSION

1. Identify the major categories of goods.
2. What two disasters must inventory control guard against?
3. What specifications must be considered by a purchasing agent in determining the needs of the company?
4. What is the most expensive practical means of transporting goods? When would this method be used?
5. What are the general bases on which common carrier rates are computed?
6. List the major transportation systems used in the United States.
7. Identify the new methods instituted to make railroads more competitive.
8. What factors should be considered in seeking a location for a manufacturing plant?
9. What factors must be considered in locating a retail outlet?

10. Identify the type of carrier you would recommend for each of the following products. Explain.
    a. Iron ore
    b. Orchids
    c. New automobiles
    d. Live cattle

SUGGESTED READINGS

Arbury, J. N. et al. *A New Approach to Physical Dstribution.* New York: American Management Association, 1967.

England, W. B. *The Purchasing System.* Homewood, Ill., Richard D. Irwin, 1967.

Heinritz, S. F. and P. V. Farrell *Purchasing,* 5th ed. Englewood Cliffs, N.J., Prentice-Hall, Inc., 1971, chaps. 8–13.

Heskett, J. L., N. A. Glaskowsky, Jr., and R. M. Ivie *Business Logistics,* 2d ed. New York: The Ronald Press Company, 1972.

Luna, Charles *The Handbook of Transportation in America.* New York: Popular Library, 1971.

15

Securing Human Resources

After plans are made and all the systems and safeguards have been designed, a business is only as strong as its human resources. Good people can make a poor plan succeed, but all the careful coaching in the world cannot produce success if the staff is unable or unwilling to carry the ball.

Finding people for a company is much more than merely filling positions and keeping them filled. In spite of its importance, however, the management of human resources is often one of the most neglected and poorly performed jobs in business. One of the reasons for this low batting average is that it is almost entirely "people work" and is, therefore, harder than paperwork. The functions of evaluating people and their potentials are very hard to reduce to a chart of simple steps. Staffing decisions involve subjective judgments and intuitive decisions. After all the tests have been scored and the interviews concluded, the businessman must decide between people—not percentile rankings. Organizations that have reduced the staffing procedure to computer decisions are certain to pass up people with great potential.

THE HUMAN BALANCE SHEET

Professor Rensis Likert of the University of Michigan argues that human assets are even more valuable than physical assets, and should be carried as assets on the organization's balance sheet. If you consider the time, effort, and money invested in recruiting and training each employee, and add what it would cost to find, hire, and train someone else to do the same job, you can begin to see the significance of "human resource accounting." Likert even argues that, during recessions, firms would be wiser to reduce inventories drastically and even sell machinery rather than dispose of their most important asset—people. Many businessmen would consider Likert's position extreme, but he does make a dramatic point about the importance of having a good staff.

It would be foolish for the president of a sizable company to try to handle all personnel activities himself. It would be equally foolish for him to relinquish control of them altogether. Nowhere is the clear statement of policy by management more imperative than in the screening and selection of people.

Promotion from within has been a popular term for the last 50 years. The idea is that "this company takes care of its own—stick with us and work hard and you can go all the way to the top." The fallacy lies in the fact that not all people have equal managerial talent. The same principle would require a professional football coach to choose his quarterbacks only from those who had played all other positions. What kind of proficiency would a team develop if all the players began on the line, worked their way up to ends, eventually became running backs, and finally played quarterback? When different skills are required, specialists must be brought in. A policy of *no* promotion from within could, of course, be equally shortsighted.

Many organizations that claim to have promotion-from-within policies manage to include an escape clause. The magic words are "whenever possible" or "unless we have no one who can possibly qualify." These loopholes allow management the advantage of promoting from within while retaining the right to hire from outside.

STEPS IN THE PERSONNEL PROCESS

Some of the steps to be taken in staffing an organization are fairly clear-cut, although the intangible human factor should never be disregarded. We shall discuss these steps briefly: (1) determination of needs, (2) selection and recruiting, (3) orientation and training, (4) performance appraisal, (5) compensation, (6) promotion, and (7) termination. These are not the "magic seven steps" of staff selection. They *are* seven areas which should receive careful attention from the manager who wants to assure business success. (The problems of choosing managers will be dealt with in Part Four of this book. Here we are concerned with nonmanagerial personnel.)

Determination of Needs

The logical first step of determining what the company needs is often overlooked by those embarking on the perilous business of managing people. We tend to shoot first and hang up the target later.

As we shall see in Chapter 21, many considerations enter into drawing up the organizational chart. Every position should be necessary to the achievement of a company's goals. In fact, once the organizational chart is drawn up, it may be a good idea to go over it and remove one position at a time to see whether any of them would be missed. Unless the organization would be harmed by its removal, a position should not exist.

Once the necessary positions have been established, the qualifications and expectations for each should be described. Descriptions should be in specific, down-to-earth terms, and the actual duties involved should be listed. Job specifications should include guidelines as to the education, ability, and minimum personal qualities required. Of course, such guidelines should never be allowed to become rigid, especially if they might cost the company an applicant who is qualified and capable.

Job descriptions should stress skills and performance rather than personality, experience, and education. These latter factors are useful only if they contribute to performance in a definite way. For example, possession of a college degree does not necessarily imply that the applicant can read and understand complex reports and plans. It is easier, however, to assume that college graduates possess such skills than it is to measure actual knowledge and ability.

When guidelines regarding qualifications, duties, and responsibilities have been spelled out, the whole staffing task becomes more precise. It may seem casual and sophisticated for an interviewer to say, "We want you on our team. There's no telling what we'll ask you to do but we've got a great bunch to work with. We want people who are ready for anything!" This kind of statement can be made only when people are being hired for their potential rather than their immediate ability to do anything specific. Large companies hiring potential managers may be able to do this, but smaller firms that need someone to make deliveries must make sure that an applicant has a driver's license —or can ride a bicycle.

In determining needs, it is also necessary to determine the *number* of new positions required and estimate the *dates* when they will be needed. By looking at those who are now employed, a manager can probably predict who will be there three or five years hence. If he compares the current picture with the ideal organizational chart, he may also see a need for reorganization or for creating new positions. When the present personnel have been promoted as far up the line as possible, it is time to go out and get new blood.

Selection and Recruiting

It may seem strange to mention selection before recruiting. Selection, however, involves more than picking names from a list of recruits. A great deal of advance work is required in the selection process, including the careful description of organizational needs and the delineation of job qualifications. Methods of selection must also be established in advance. If selection methods are not consciously present, it is likely that the manager will fall into one of three common traps.

First, businessmen sometimes make no provision at all for building a continuing strength into their labor force. They ignore the potential problems and then wake up one morning to realize that their entire work group is over 60 or that everyone is demanding simultaneous promotion. The top-notch manager carefully charts his people according to age, years of service, and "promotability." It is a foolish forester who does not realize that he must plant trees every year if he is to have a continuing harvest in the future, and winds up with a bumper crop one year and bare land the next.

A *second common pitfall of selection is to assume that "somebody will come along when we need him."* This is the kind of slipshod, catch-as-catch-can approach to staffing that puts untalented sons-in-law in positions of responsibility because they married the right girl. Similarly, the machinist who has been on the job for the longest period of time may be a poor prospect as supervisor of the machine shop. It is irresponsible to assume that the next person in line for promotion will be right for a highly specialized task. The businessman who picks his staff on a "who's available" basis probably has even more serious problems lurking around the corner. His planning may also be bad.

Third, many businessmen like to depend on their own personal judgment in recruiting. They are not swayed by work histories or by the results of psychological testing. They can tell "just by talking" with the candidate whether he is right for the job. Nonsense! While scientific indicators are not to be trusted blindly, neither are human impressions. A careful combination of the two techniques can balance the inadequacies in each and provide a more unbiased appraisal. The characteristic—and revealing—remark of the personal-impression selector is: "I knew that kid was right for the job the minute I laid eyes on him—reminds me of myself at that age!"

The approach to selection should be established at the outset. As time goes on and the manager gains experience in selection, recruiting, and training, he will probably be able to narrow the gap between the number of selectees and the number of possible openings. Larger, more experienced companies will recruit for the long-range future, regardless of economic or political fluctuations. They realize that sporadic hiring can eventually produce a poorly balanced age distribution on the staff, and that a regular recruiting program is a wise investment. It might even be said that when things are going badly, recruiting is more important than ever.

NONDISCRIMINATORY DISCRIMINATION

Screening is the first step in the recruiting process. This may take place when the firm's recruiting officer visits university campuses to interview potential candidates. Or, in a smaller company, one of the other corporate officers may have the task of selecting potential employees. The executive in charge of personnel may also be involved in selecting laborers, office workers, or other positions not involving management. Whatever his title and actual duties, the hiring officer should be far more than an errand boy. Being able to tell the company's story is important, but the recruiter's understanding of people is far more critical. A competent recruiter will develop personal relationships between his company and the placement counselors and business professors of colleges and universities nearby. He will always be acquainted with instructors at trade schools and technical high schools. Clear communication with those who know the applicant's daily performance is one of the most meaningful components of the selection process.

Each firm will establish its own minimum requirements. A good recruiter should be able quickly and accurately to eliminate candidates who do not meet those requirements. The sooner he spots an applicant's deficiencies, the better for all concerned. Most firms require applicants to file completed application forms or resumes so that they can make preliminary screening decisions. One type of resume outline and a sample resume are shown in Figures 15–1 and 15–2.

Companies must stay within the law when setting standards for

FIGURE 15–1

Possible Resume Outline

Name
Address, include zip code
Telephone, area code, home and office

Career objective:

Brief description of the type of position you wish to be considered for. If you are unwilling to relocate, your geographic preference should be indicated in this section.

Education:

Name of college/university, dates attended, degree received, and major field. List significant information about related courses, academic honors, field experiences, special skills—language proficiency, etc.

Experience:

List position, title, and description of duties, tasks performed, responsibilities, etc. This section may discuss your full and part-time work experience, summer jobs, volunteer experiences, extended research/study projects, and graduate assistantships.

Military experience:

If you have had military experience, list branch of service, dates, rank at time of discharge, and areas of responsibility.

Activities and interests:

In school and out of school.

Additional information:

If you have other assets, skills, or experiences significant to your career objective which are not easily organized or included under another heading, you may want to include them here.

References:

It is not necessary to list your references on your resume. You may simply state that they are available upon request. However, you should have several professors or former employers who can evaluate your ability to perform in a particular work situation ready to act as references. Be sure to request permission before you give the person's name as a reference. When an employer requests references, give their name, title or position, a complete and current address, and telephone numbers.

Source: Adapted from material submitted by Elizabeth M. Nuss and Kathleen Yorkis, Career Advisers, University of Maryland. *Placement Annual*, 1974, p. 26.

---

choosing employees. The Civil Rights Acts of 1964 and 1966 made it illegal to discriminate against any person on the basis of race, color, religion, sex, age, or national origin. When the law was first implemented, it applied only to employers of 100 or more persons. Currently, all employers with 25 or more workers are included. Job specifications must be limited to qualities, experience, skills, or other work-related information. An employer cannot legally refuse to hire a qualified managerial applicant just because she is black.

FIGURE 15–2

Sample Resume

Susan Sawdey
1234 College Drive
College Park, Maryland 20742   301-122-4000

Professional Objective: Retail Sales Management. Willing to relocate.

Education: University of Maryland, College Park, B.A. Marketing, 1974. Special emphasis on retail sales and merchandising; considerable work in consumer economics and accounting.

Experience:
Summer 1973—Sales Clerk, Housewares Dept. Duties included merchandise displays, assisting buyer, customer relations. Also assisted department manager in training new sales personnel, sold successfully on a commission basis. 1970–1973—Sales Clerk. Worked part-time in specialty clothing store. Assumed increased responsibility during time of employment. Duties included sales, window displays, assisting with inventory and ordering, and assisting with advertising and copy layout.

Summer 1969–1970—Lifeguard. Duties included general pool maintenance and swimming instructions for children and young adults.

Extracurricular Activities:
Program Chairman for American Marketing Association. Duties included planning programs, contacting speakers from area business community, and coordinating program.

Corresponding Secretary for national sorority. Responsible for all correspondence to national headquarters, alumnae, and others. Maintained files and records for group. Also responsible for ordering.

References: Will be furnished upon request.

Source: Adapted from material submitted by Elizabeth M. Nuss and Kathleen Yorkis, Career Advisers, University of Maryland. *Placement Annual,* 1974, p. 27.

Firms are allowed to set age limitations so long as these do not imply discrimination against older people. Most companies realize that it takes time to make a future manager, even from the most promising stock. If an applicant is 25 to 28 years old, this means that at age 45 or 48 he may be able to step into an upper-level executive position and render the firm approximately 20 years of service in that position before retiring at 65. Therefore, many enterprises set an upper age limit for management trainees of 25 to 30.

COURTSHIP AND MUTUAL APPRAISAL

In looking at applicants, the interviewer will try to "read between the lines" and can often discover a great deal about an applicant's attitude, drive, initiative, and common sense. If all systems are "go," the recruiter will encourage the applicant to become an active candi-

Arthur A. Fletcher

As the highest-ranking black official in the Nixon administration, Arthur A. Fletcher was largely responsible for implementing the President's program to improve employment conditions for minorities. He served as the Assistant Secretary for Wage and Labor Standards in the Department of Labor from 1969 to 1973.

A former football star and teacher, Fletcher came to the attention of Richard Nixon as a result of a successful community self-help program that he organized in East Pasco, Washington, in 1966. After taking office as Assistant Secretary of Labor, Fletcher concentrated on opening job opportunities, especially in the skilled construction trades, for blacks and other minorities. In his view, mandatory requirements were needed to overcome resistance by contractors and trade unions.

Arthur Allen Fletcher was born in a black ghetto in Phoenix, Arizona, on December 22, 1924. The family lived in a succession of ghettos, including the Watts district of Los Angeles, where Fletcher became a gang leader at 13. His mother, who had degrees in education and nursing but was unable to find professional employment, worked as a live-in maid. Fletcher was reared by various families, including Indians and Mexican-Americans.

In high school Fletcher distinguished himself in football; in 1942 he became the first Negro to be chosen for an all-state team in Kansas. He enrolled at Indiana University in 1946 on a football scholarship, but, unable to find suitable housing, decided to accept a scholarship offer from Washburn University in Topeka, Kansas. He got his B.A. in political science from Washburn in 1950. While there he earned Little All-American honors as the sixth leading rusher among small colleges.

date for the company's training program. He will discuss starting salaries, benefits, and opportunities for advancement, trying to "sell" the company but not to oversell it. An oversold employee may become dissatisfied once the honeymoon is over and his new job turns out to be duller than it was pictured.

Decisions to hire lower-level candidates may be made fairly quickly. In hiring managerial candidates, the normal procedure is to invite suc-

From 1950 to 1953, Fletcher played on several professional football teams. After trying unsuccessfully to find a job as a high school football coach, he took a factory job with Goodyear Tire and Rubber Company. In 1953–54 he did postgraduate work in economics and education at Kansas State University. He also taught in a rural school and, overwhelmed by the inadequacies of black education, helped raise funds for the historic *Brown* v. *Board of Education of Topeka, Kansas* case that was decided by the Supreme Court on May 17, 1954. In this decision the court declared that separate educational facilities are inherently unequal and therefore unconstitutional. As a result of his involvement with the Republican Party, Fletcher received a position in the administration of Governor Hall of Kansas.

After several political jobs, he was offered a position in the state of Washington in 1965 as director of a federally-funded manpower development project training hard-core unemployed in East Pasco, a small, isolated Negro community on the outskirts of the city of Pasco. Although Fletcher succeeded in training 380 men, differences with local welfare officials caused the program to founder. Meanwhile, on his own initiative, Fletcher organized the East Pasco Self-Help Cooperative Association to help the local residents cope with government plans for urban renewal. The association used local capital to buy land, build a service station, establish a credit union, and construct a $650,000 shopping center. All of the jobs and businesses were used to train people in skills that would enable them to work outside the ghetto. Fletcher served as a councilman in Pasco from 1968 to 1969.

Fletcher's work in East Pasco brought him to the attention of the national Republican Party organization in 1968. This won him an appointment as a special assistant to the newly elected Republican Governor of Washington, Daniel J. Evans.

On March 14, 1969, Fletcher was appointed Assistant Secretary for Wage and Labor Standards in the Department of Labor. He was responsible for the Office of Federal Contract Compliance, the Bureau of Labor Standards, the Women's Bureau, the Wage and Hour and Public Contract Divisions, the Bureau of Employees' Compensation, and the Office of Wage Determinations.

Emphasizing the need for economic security for blacks, Fletcher concentrated his efforts on using federal power to push for equal employment opportunities. His major vehicle was the power to cancel or suspend government contracts of firms that practice discrimination. He issued directives requiring that progress in equal employment be measured by actual numbers of minority group members on the job, not by project plans, and that firms receiving government contracts file monthly reports. The mandatory employment quotas for minorities are still subject to considerable controversy. There has not been enough time to judge the success or failure of his methods.

After leaving the government in 1973 he established his own firm, Arthur A. Fletcher & Associates, Inc., management consultants specializing in employment standards and personnel management. Mr. Fletcher served as Executive Director of the United Negro College Fund from December 1971 until April 1973. He was also an Alternate Delegate to the 26th Session of the United Nations General Assembly.

cessful applicants to one or more home office interviews. Although these interviews may be supervised by the officer in charge of the training program, other corporate executives are usually included. It is very important that the applicant's prospective boss and some of his staff interview the candidate. Interviews should definitely be more than small talk.

Final selection should be made in a discussion which includes all

FIGURE 15–3

Summary of a Selection Procedure

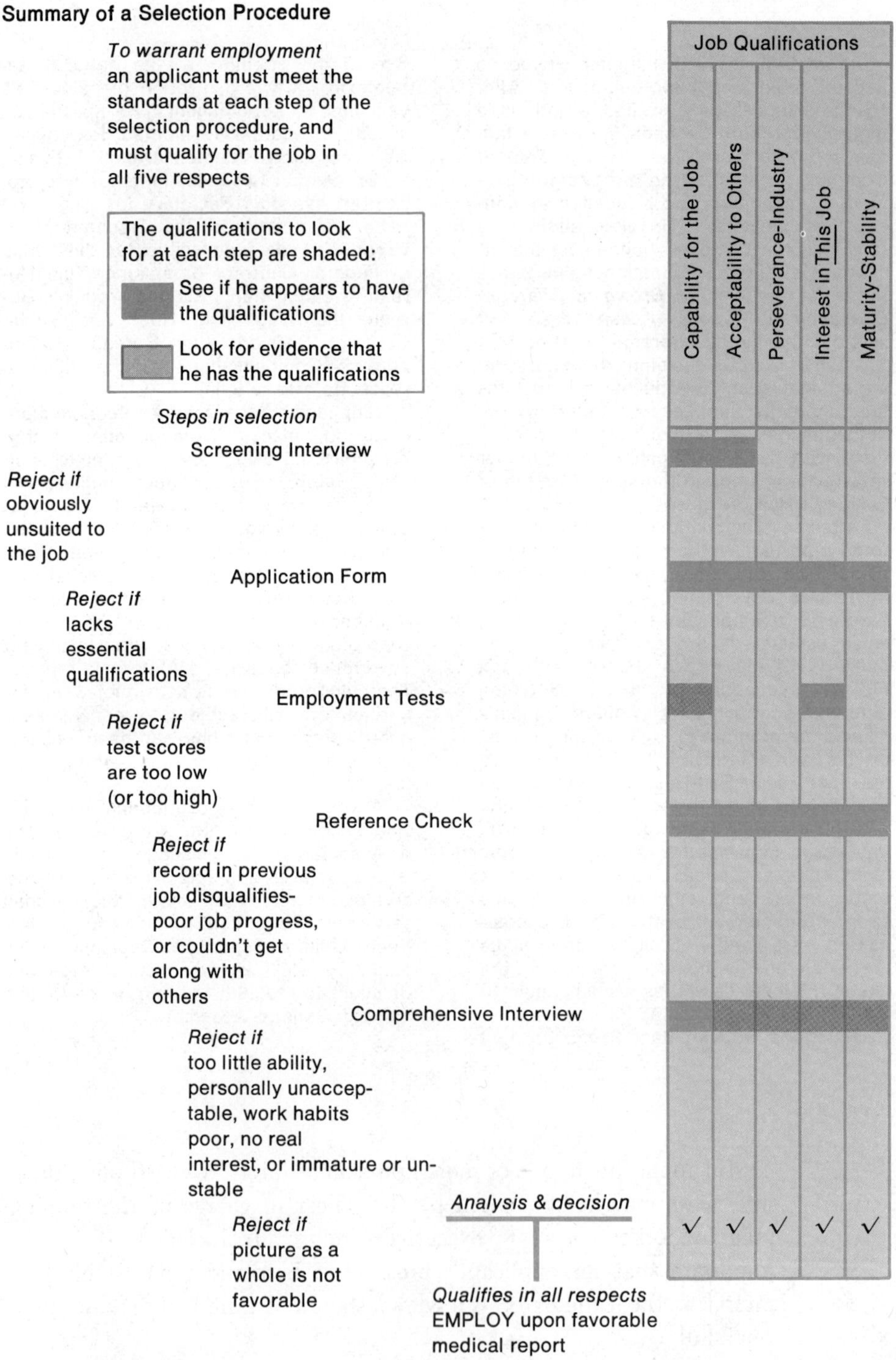

To warrant employment an applicant must meet the standards at each step of the selection procedure, and must qualify for the job in all five respects

The qualifications to look for at each step are shaded:

▓ See if he appears to have the qualifications

░ Look for evidence that he has the qualifications

Job Qualifications

- Capability for the Job
- Acceptability to Others
- Perseverance-Industry
- Interest in This Job
- Maturity-Stability

Steps in selection

Screening Interview

Reject if obviously unsuited to the job

Application Form

Reject if lacks essential qualifications

Employment Tests

Reject if test scores are too low (or too high)

Reference Check

Reject if record in previous job disqualifies— poor job progress, or couldn't get along with others

Comprehensive Interview

Reject if too little ability, personally unaccep- table, work habits poor, no real interest, or immature or un- stable

Analysis & decision

Reject if picture as a whole is not favorable

√ √ √ √ √

Qualifies in all respects EMPLOY upon favorable medical report

Source: Milton M. Mandel, *The Employment Interview*, Research Study No. 47 (New York: American Management Association, 1961).

who have interviewed the candidate. This final conference is not a time for "being nice" or overlooking concerns. A great deal of heartache, headache, and money can be saved if it can be determined that the applicant is not quite right for the position.

Such companies have developed selection formulas which include charts (like the one seen in Figure 15–3), psychological tests, and interviews and impressions. Companies should utilize whatever combination of methods works best for them—but almost any method is better than no method.

ORIENTATION AND TRAINING

The word "orientation" is commonly used today to describe a period of introduction. The original meaning was to show the newcomer which way was east—or toward the orient. During orientation we align the newcomer's compass with those of the old hands; we get our easts, wests, norths, and souths synchronized—or, in present-day language, we show him "which way is up."

A partial orientation may wisely be included in the interview and selection processes. Interviewers will want to observe closely the ease or difficulty with which the candidate grasps the company's main ideas. At this stage, orientation includes few things more confidential than general information about vacations and group insurance.

Most organizations also provide some sort of official orientation. It may be a classroom lecture, a movie, a group conference, or a personalized tour by a member of the personnel department. In many cases, unfortunately, the company puts its worst foot forward—like the television network that conducted its orientation entirely by the lecture method! An hourly employee may merely be shown where to work and "clock in."

The following types of subjects are usually covered in a thorough orientation program: (1) company history, products, and major operations; (2) general company policies and regulations; (3) relations between foremen and the personnel department; (4) rules and regulations regarding wages and payment, hours of work and overtime, safety and accidents, holidays and vacations, methods of reporting tardiness and absences, discipline and grievances, uniforms and clothing, and parking and badges; (5) economic and recreational services available, such as insurance plans, the credit union, pensions, and athletic and social activities; and (6) opportunities for promotion and transfer, job stabilization, and suggestion systems.

Of course, the new employee will remember very little of this information. The real purpose is overview and introduction. The actual orientation depends on the new employee's ambition—whether or not he makes friends at every level and asks questions of all. Probably more relevant orientation takes place during coffee breaks than in all the personnel presentations that will ever be produced. One company, realizing this, used a "roving conversation" orientation, providing the newcomer with a schedule of appointments for informal discussion with actual workers and managers in every phase of the operation.

PERFORMANCE APPRAISAL

In 1800, Robert Owen used what he called character books and character blocks to appraise the workers in his New Lanark cotton mills in Scotland. The character books recorded the workers' daily output. The character blocks, displayed at each worker's station, were of different colors according to a worker's performance—ranging from bad to good. We may not feel that character is best measured in terms of production, but Robert Owen was quite impressed by the way the workers' performance improved.

Whether it is colored blocks at the work station or a gold star on the chart, performance appraisal is here to stay. Nobody likes marks in school, and many people object to performance appraisal at work, but some method must be used to measure progress or the lack of progress. From management's viewpoint, appraisal is necessary in order to (1) allocate resources, (2) reward employees, (3) provide feedback for workers, and (4) maintain fair relationships and communication bonds.

The modern approach to appraisal includes: (1) performance orientation—to make the worker aware of the quality of his work; (2) a focus on goals—to make him aware of what the end results of his job should be; and (3) mutual goal setting—to give him an opportunity to understand his job and, above all, to allow him to contribute to its nature and content. Bosses are often surprised how much a subordinate knows about problems and how to solve them.

Mature managers think of the performance appraisal as a chance to discuss with the employee his progress and possibilities for improvement. Immature managers approach the appraisal session as a long-awaited chance to unload on the subordinate all the ill will and irritation they have stored up. Still other managers dislike to undertake appraisal at all because they feel it puts them in the position of "playing

God" with people. Many people seem to enjoy playing amateur psychiatrist. This can be tremendously dangerous in performance appraisal. Unless the manager always thinks first of the employee's progress, he can do irreparable damage.

Managing by Objectives

As we shall see in our discussion of planning in Chapter 20, one of the most significant recent concepts to arise in management is the idea of managing by objectives (MBO). It arose primarily out of dissatisfaction with performance appraisal. MBO has been welcomed by managers who were tired of traditional evaluation systems based on personal traits and work habits. (A portion of a traditional employee rating form is shown in Figure 15–4.)

Instead of grading the employee on the basis of whether or not he is dependable, shows good judgment, has initiative, and is cooperative, the manager may work with him to establish objectives. If an objective is accomplished, the employee has succeeded. It is a simple, direct approach to performance. Since managing by objectives and using results for appraisal are so much a part of the manager's task, managing by objectives will be further discussed in Chapter 20.

The problem with managing by objectives is that it often conflicts with our preconceptions about how an employee should use his time. If we see a worker busily slaving away with his sleeves rolled up, breathing heavily, we naturally assume that he is working well, while we frown upon an employee who appears to be relaxing with his feet up on his desk. Yet, if we really stop and think about it, why should we care how the worker *looks?* What we should be interested in is how he *works* . . . above all, in what kind of results he obtains. In short, the boss ought to adopt the motto, "Don't give me gold-plated reasons for your heroic failure—I'll be happy with clumsy, unheroic success."

By tying the performance appraisal to the concept of management by objectives, the emphasis is moved to the real goal. Managers will have to be clear, concise, and specific about what they want. Employees will know exactly what is expected of them. And the performance evaluation will be removed from the realm of office politics, favoritism, and subjectivity. It will be obvious to manager and employee alike whether the objective has been reached; there will be an exchange of intelligence instead of ignorance. Regular, on-going feedback is essential if performance appraisal is to be anything other than an annual ceremony. If objectives have been adequately identified, there will be few surprises

FIGURE 15–4

Appraisal and Progress Report

| | First | Initial | Last | | FOR PERSONNEL DEPARTMENT USE |

EMPLOYEE'S JOB TITLE

DEPARTMENT & LOCATION (City & Country)

BIRTH DATE   DATE LAST HIRED

(Form should be completed by Supervisor)

MONTHS IN
PRESENT POSITION   MONTHS SUPERVISED BY RATER

RATING
PREPARED BY   Name

EMPLOYEE'S NAME   Title

FACTOR TO BE RATED	FOR EACH FACTOR CHECK THE APPROPRIATE BOX WHICH MOST ACCURATELY DESCRIBES THE EMPLOYEE BEING RATED				
1. KNOWLEDGE OF WORK Knowledge and understanding of all phases of job.	Has an unsatisfactory knowledge of job.	Has fair job knowledge but needs more training.	Has a satisfactory working knowledge of job.	Well informed on most phases of job.	Has an extensive knowledge of job.
	Comments:				
2. QUALITY OF WORK Accuracy and thoroughness with which work meets recognized and accepted standards of performance.	Not acceptable. Needs continuous checking.	Sometimes acceptable but must be checked.	Satisfactorily meets accepted standards. Needs very little checking.	Consistently accurate and thorough and above standard.	Maintains exceptionally high standards.
	Comments:				
3. QUANTITY Volume of work based upon recognized standards of performance.	Always below minimum job requirements.	Barely meets minimum requirements.	Steady producer. Satisfactorily meets requirements.	Consistently turns out good volume ahead of deadlines.	Unusually high output.
	Comments:				
4. DEPENDABILITY Ability to do required jobs well and promptly with a minimum of supervision.	Is unreliable; requires close supervision.	Requires prompting and assistance.	Satisfactorily completes necessary tasks.	Consistently reliable; requires little supervision.	Optimim performer; requires minimum supervision.
	Comments:				
5. COOPERATIVENESS Cooperation with associates, supervisor, and others.	Uncooperative, careless and indifferent. Irritates others.	Indifferent to importance of cooperation.	Meets others half way.	Consistently helpful and cooperative.	Shows desired cooperativeness.
	Comments:				
6. ORGANIZING AND PLANNING Success in systematically devising, designing, or formulating a program of action.	Work poorly organized. Planning frequently ineffective or too late.	Planning and organizing sometimes incomplete, ineffective, or too late.	Required planning and organizing is thorough and prompt.	Planning and organizing is thorough, prompt, and effective over and above normal requirements.	Very successful planner and organizer even under adverse circumstances.
	Comments: (If organizing and planning is not applicable please indicate N/A.)				
7. INITIATIVE Ability to contribute, develop and/or carry out new ideas or methods.	Is not a self-starter, needs continuous prompting.	Shows reluctance to begin difficult tasks. Needs frequent prompting.	Generally initiates preliminary work on his own without prompting.	Consistently grasps situations and pursues in depth without prompting.	Extremely alert to what needs to be done. Initiates frequent innovations.
	Comments:				
8. JUDGMENT Decisions or actions based upon sound knowledge of values and logic.	Actions and decisions indicate lack of logic and practicability to unsatisfactory degree.	Does not carefully weigh alternatives. Needs common sense guidance in order to be effective.	Satisfactorily demonstrates objectivity and level-headedness and a careful weighing of alternatives.	Actions and decisions consistently based on sound reasoning.	Outstanding judgment.
	Comments:				

at the appraisal interview. By knowing in advance what is expected of them, people can hardly be surprised at appraisal time if they have missed their goals.

Performance appraisal can become a great asset, or it can be a meaningless routine. Performance will be appraised, in some way, whether formally or informally. It is the manager's job to make the experience meaningful and beneficial.

COMPENSATION

It is difficult for us to conceive of a society in which income would be the same for everyone. Our entire system of private enterprise is based on the premise that people should be paid or rewarded according to what they produce or how much risk they take. It doesn't always work out that way, but we are accustomed to making financial considerations major in our employment planning. Even those who recognize that many things are more important than money eventually discover that they're proud of how much money they make. Pay is a unique incentive—it can satisfy our lower-order need for security and our higher-order need for esteem and recognition.

Production Incentives

About 25 percent of manufacturing workers are under incentive plans such as "piece work" or productivity bonuses. *Piece work* means that a worker is paid for each item or piece he produces. More frequently, hourly workers are given a specific sum per hour but also have a chance to receive a *bonus* if they or their work group do more than the minimum required. In sales work, the same idea is followed with *commissions* or *salary plus commission* compensation plans. The main reason for the use of wage incentives is clear: they nearly always increase productivity while decreasing labor costs per manufactured unit. Workers under hourly wages usually have the capacity to increase their output. Wage incentives are one way to release that potential.

The amount of increased productivity that can be obtained with an incentive system is sometimes astonishing. Some industries have shown increases of over 100 percent. It should be admitted that such results may require considerable planning, but there is no way of arguing with the logic of that brilliant but unknown philosopher who said, "Money talks!" If compensation is a major motivator, it stands to reason that a worker's motivation can be increased if his compensation is increased.

There are countless cases where people have enjoyed a 50 percent increase in take-home pay, without working longer hours, because the reward made it worth while.

Managerial Compensation

Just as bonus plans cause production workers to produce more, the proper compensation can also have a powerful effect on the performance of managers. Obviously, the work of management differs from that of production. The assembly line worker is generally judged on whether he does his job. The manager's success, on the other hand, is measured more by how well he performs[1]—often in relation to some abstract standard. The principle of supply and demand is very much in operation in selecting and hiring a manager. His more subtle skills make him more costly. And, by the same token, the subtlety of his abilities makes him difficult to compensate and motivate with money alone.

Selecting forms of compensation for managers is a major decision, because both the employee and the employer must be satisfied. The employee needs cash income, protection of his earning power, a chance to accumulate an estate, and financial security after retirement. The company must do its best to meet these requirements and go beyond them if it wants to attract and retain good managers. Still, it cannot use up all its profits in building and maintaining its staff.

Some companies have developed complex forms of executive compensation. Before federal Internal Revenue Service regulations were tightened, many small companies paid owners or officers a very small salary plus an unlimited expense account that included use of a "company" house and "company" cars. Other companies have used various "fringe benefits" heavily, since executives often prefer increased tax-free services to increased taxable income. Group insurance, bonus plans, stock options, pension and retirement pay and other fringe benefits—all these must be added to cash income to determine the "pay" given a manager. It is not surprising to see companies picking up the tab for country club memberships, haircuts, and even clothing expenses, when this can be done without objection from the tax authorities. The owners of small companies are especially likely to be provided with such extras.

An executive of a large bank was once faced with a dilemma. Two of his best men were in line for promotion to one vacant position. Because of the difficulty of deciding between them, the manager called

---

[1] See Harold Koontz, *Appraising Managers as Managers* (New York: McGraw-Hill Book Company, 1972).

them in and laid the problem before them. One of the men had a simple solution. He suggested that the other man receive the promotion and that he be given instead the free parking space and other fringe benefits that went with the position. He calculated that this arrangement would net him more income than if he received the promotion without the fringe benefits, since extra expenses automatically accompanied the new title. The manager gave the astute young man the parking place . . . and the promotion too.

The relationship between incentive systems and human behavior in large organizations is both important and complex. Many questions must be considered. How much should people be paid, and in what form? What strings should be attached? What differences between people's pay are justified? Does seniority automatically deserve increased pay? What value should we place upon experience and training when setting salary scales?

Combinations of Incentives

Large corporations have complex combinations of compensation. Individual proprietorships and institutions are perhaps more limited in their methods. Every manager, however, must be aware of the variety of forms in use. In many cases, managers will need to create new and original ways of getting and keeping good people. The following list of types of compensation may be helpful when trying to achieve just the right combination for any particular job.

1. Wages—pay based on hours of work or specific units of work that have been completed.
2. Salary—pay based on time at work, in terms of weeks, months, or years, and paid on a weekly, semi-monthly, or monthly basis. Salaries are usually paid to managerial, professional, and technical personnel, but are increasingly being used for other employees.
3. Overtime pay—payment at 1½ times the regular hourly rate for hours worked in excess of the normal number. Managers, executives, professionals, and several other kinds of workers are exempt from the legal requirement of overtime pay.
4. Incentive pay—compensation aimed at increasing production or stimulating progress toward company goals. Types of incentive pay include piecework, commissions, and profit sharing.
5. Bonus—a cash award given for special performance, usually on the basis of a pool of money arising from profits.

6. Profit sharing—employee participation in the company's profits either in cash or in contributions to a pension plan.

7. Stock options—the opportunity for employees to purchase company stock for a period of five or ten years at prices existing at the time of award, with the hope that prices will go up before the option holder buys the stock so that he will reap profits.

8. Savings plans—company-sponsored employee savings or investment plans, often with company contributions of money based on the amount an individual saves.

9. Insurance—group life, health, and disability insurance paid in full or in part by the company.

10. Retirement or pension plans—provision for retirement income, often based on the employee's length of service and pay level, and often financed from a percentage of company profits. These are in addition to Social Security retirement benefits provided by law.

11. Paid vacations and holidays—time off with full pay.

12. Additional nonmoney benefits—discounts on company products, free use of company recreation facilities, special gifts such as Christmas turkeys, military leaves of absence, and many others.

Promotion

Advancement to a higher position is one of the most common forms of extra compensation. Usually promotion involves increased pay, but there are many appealing things about promotion that have nothing to do with money. The social, psychological, and personal gratifications inherent in promotion can often be more meaningful to a worker than a larger salary. A promotion is a direct form of praise—it says, "You have done such a fine job at your present position that we know you will meet this new challenge equally well."

Much controversy has raged over how to decide whether employees deserve wage increases and promotions. Under a merit rating system, an employee is periodically measured on his progress or lack of it, usually at six-month or one-year intervals. He is rated on such things as results, dependability, initiative, acceptance of responsibility, appearance, production, use of resources, amount of supervision needed, and judgment. A good merit rating entitles him to a raise. In practice, however, merit increases tend to be almost automatic.

A seniority system for promotions and salary increases is almost always preferred by union members. Under this system, promotions, layoffs, and recalls to work are determined according to employees' length of service. Naturally, this system does not always work to the company's or the employee's best advantage since the employee with the longest service record may not be the best qualified for promotion to the next higher position. But if employees perceive the company's merit system as unfair or prejudiced, they will almost certainly prefer some type of seniority system.

There are other problems in promoting people. It is easy to assume that because a worker does one thing well, he can automatically do the next thing just as well. The consequences of this have been dubbed "the Peter Principle."[2] The idea is that in any organization a person who is competent will be promoted as a reward for doing his job well. When he reaches a level at which he is no longer competent he will not be promoted again, and the organization will be stuck with an employee whose job exceeds his abilities. Everyone knows of instances of the Peter Principle. Often the demand for more money, prestige, or recognition drives workers into jobs they do not like or cannot do well. Other dangerous moves are those from labor to management, player to coach, teacher to administrator, or enlisted man to officer.

Almost everybody *wants* a promotion . . . but not everybody *needs* a promotion.

Termination

The ultimate "promotion" takes a worker right out of the firm. He retires, having earned the right not to work after a certain age. Theoretically, the pay he receives in retirement is money he earned during his productive years and set aside for deferred payment. Our current retirement rules leave much to be desired because they are applied more or less mechanically. Different people have different needs. Some would like to retire early, and others are never ready to retire. Perhaps companies will be able to find some more meaningful criterion than age by which to determine when an employee should be turned out to pasture. Some people remain good performers for a much longer time than others. At any rate, to retire a man on the basis of age alone is often shortsighted and in many cases heartless.

Employees often leave voluntarily to take jobs with other firms. Our society's mobility has made resignation a common occurrence; more and more workers are working for more and more companies. Psychologist Eugene Jennings has called the current generation of executives

----

[2] See Laurence J. Peter and Raymond Hull, *The Peter Principle* (New York: William Morrow, 1969).

the "mobile managers." Occasionally a letter of resignation serves as a lever to bring about some desired change or to focus attention on some wrong. More often, though, it is a recognition that greener pastures are to be found elsewhere.

A resignation should not be thought of as desertion or as a knife in management's back. If an employee leaves as an enemy of the company, then good riddance to him. If he leaves as a friend . . . what company doesn't need more friends among its competitors? For years, International Business Machines has smiled over its claim to have trained and launched many of the pioneers in the computer software field. Evidently, IBM has been able to keep on growing because of its ability to hire and retain enough good men to hold its position of leadership.

The unhappiest form of termination is dismissal, whether it comes through layoff (because the company is not doing well) or through firing (because the employee is not doing well). On the other hand, there are probably innumerable success stories that began when a dismissal shook loose a creative personality from a static position. Sometimes the best thing that can happen to a person is to be "fired with ambition."

SUMMARY

No businessman can ignore the importance of his human assets. Securing the right human resources is perhaps more difficult than securing raw material, or even customers. It involves determining needs, selecting people who will meet those needs, training them to perform their jobs effectively, reviewing their performance, paying them fairly, promoting them as they become ready for more responsibility, and deciding when and under what circumstances they should be terminated.

Accountants and engineers are seldom recruited in an unemployment office or union hall. Similarly, unskilled laborers or union craftsmen are not usually found in college recruiting programs. People must be found, hired, and supervised as individuals. Standardized procedures are useful, but they must be flexible enough to meet the needs of the nonstandard individuals to whom they are applied.

KEY TERMS AND CONCEPTS FOR REVIEW

Human resource accounting
Civil Rights Acts
Orientation
Promotion from within
Resume

Incentives
Peter Principle
Mobile managers
Piece rates
Layoffs

QUESTIONS FOR ANALYSIS AND DISCUSSION

1. What are the major steps in the personnel process?
2. What areas should be included in job descriptions?
3. What dangers exist if selection methods are not consciously preset?
4. What types of subjects are usually covered in an orientation program?
5. Why is performance appraisal necessary to management?
6. What are the main considerations of the modern approach to appraisal?
7. Under what conditions are wage incentives desirable?
8. What are the major types of compensation?
9. Contrast the merit rating system with the seniority system as a way of deciding who should be promoted.
10. What are the different types of termination? Describe them.
11. Do you think the human balance sheet will become popular during this decade? Explain.
12. Could Robert Owen's "character blocks" be used in a modern automobile assembly plant? Discuss.

SUGGESTED READINGS

Chruden, H. J., and A. W. Sherman, Jr. *Personnel Management,* 4th ed. Cincinnati, Ohio: South-Western Publishing Company, 1972.

French, Wendell *The Personnel Management Process* 3d ed. Boston: Houghton Mifflin Company, 1974.

Jucius, M. J. *Personnel Management,* 7th ed. Homewood, Ill., Richard D. Irwin, Inc., 1971.

Megginson, Leon C. *Personnel,* 2d ed. Homewood, Ill., Richard D. Irwin, Inc., 1972.

Miner, John B. *Personnel and Industrial Relations,* 2d ed. New York: Macmillan, 1973.

16

Reducing Risks through Insurance

As early as 3000 B.C., Chinese merchants recognized the advantage of spreading risks. They frequently had to ship their goods by boat downstream, and because of the treacherous rapids on the river some of the boats never arrived. To reduce the impact of losses to any one individual, the merchants decided to distribute their goods among each other's boats. When one of the boats was dashed to pieces on the rocks, the loss was shared by all rather than falling on one unfortunate individual.

This ancient bit of Oriental wisdom has become a universal practice in modern business. The risks that today's businessman must face are more numerous than those of his Oriental predecessor. Every subject discussed in this book deals with potential *risk*—the danger that something will happen to destroy the best-laid plans. The same ingenuity is required in dealing with the countless risks of modern business that the Chinese merchants displayed 5,000 years ago.

A business is subjected to a wide variety of risks of loss through some unexpected event. Of course, the greatest is the loss of profits through such things as changes in customer demand, competition, rises in costs, or poor management. But there are a number of other risks. Some, as we will see, may be covered by insurance, and others ordinarily cannot be insured against.

409

KINDS OF BUSINESS RISKS

Marketing Risks

In Chapter 10 we looked at some of the risks involved in marketing a new product. We saw that the probability of success for any new product idea is, at best, slim. Moreover, the loss associated with an unsuccessful introduction can be catastrophic. One of the means that companies sometimes use to help minimize the risks associated with their new product programs is test marketing.

Even after a product is successfully introduced to the market, risks continue to plague its existence. Every new marketing program is a potential disaster. A $10 million advertising campaign may conceivably alienate a sizable segment of the market. Product obsolescence and declining demand can also imperil a firm's financial position.

Equipment Risks

The purchase of special facilities and equipment can involve great risks. Utility companies with heavy investment in traditional generating plants have much to ponder in a time of fuel shortages and of possible solar-powered energy and nuclear generators. When new technology is emerging, any purchase of traditional equipment is subject to early obsolescence. At the same time, there is risk in being the first to make heavy commitments in new equipment or processes. The expensive equipment required to produce that new wonder drug may prove useless if the drug has dangerous side effects. Practically any major purchase decision—even the purchase of insurance—involves an element of risk.

Credit Risks

Each time a company extends credit to a customer, there is danger that the customer will not pay his bill. The credit manager must investigate the reliability of prospective customers in order to eliminate poor risks. But if he is too careful and screens out everybody who has ever been late with a payment, he runs the risk of restricting company sales.

Inventory Risks

Inventories also present the businessman with a dilemma. If he fails to buy adequate supplies, there is the danger of running out of stock. It is disheartening and often disastrous for a company to run out of its product in the middle of an aggressive sales campaign. Yet the maintenance of large inventories means heavy storage costs, plus potential dangers of theft, deterioration, obsolescence, or price declines.

Governmental Risks

Certain federal laws have added to the risks associated with being a businessman. "Product Liability" means that the manufacturer may be held liable if someone is injured because of a defective part in his product. While it may be expensive for General Motors to repair 200,000 steering columns on one model, this expense is considerably less than if a number of people were to be seriously hurt in automobile accidents and all were to file personal injury suits against the company.

Fire, Theft, and Casualty Risks

Every business, like every individual, is subject to possible losses due to fire, theft, and a variety of casualties. A factory or office building may be damaged by fire. A business may be robbed by burglars, or a dishonest employee may steal money or goods a business handles. Also, every business may suffer losses due to such casualties as windstorm or earthquake, employee accidents, mishaps caused by a company car or truck, suits against directors and officers by disgruntled stockholders, or failure of a product to perform in accordance with specifications.

After thinking of the risks a businessman must take, the student may decide that he would prefer a quieter career as a stunt pilot or a lion tamer. But fortunately, the businessman has ways of coping with his risks.

METHODS OF HANDLING RISKS

Avoiding Risks by Avoiding the Cause

The best way to reduce the chance of loss is through protective or preventive measures. Locking the barn door before the horse is stolen is less expensive than buying insurance. Armed guards, safety equipment, fireproof buildings, automatic sprinkler systems, and even adequate lighting are some of the means companies use to reduce their risks.

These measures can be most helpful, and may substantially reduce the chance of loss. They do not, however, eliminate it altogether. Guards may go to sleep, automatic sprinklers may fail to work, or an unforeseen danger may wipe out the entire operation. The astute executive is a professional pessimist. After eliminating the possibility that anything can go wrong, he will still ask, "What do I do when something does go wrong?"

Anticipating Risks

Many companies minimize risks by recognizing and anticipating potential risks. This usually means setting aside a financial reserve that can be drawn upon should the loss occur. This is called self-insurance, and is simple and easy to administer.

Self-insurance is more appropriate for large organizations than for the small business. A restaurant owner who has invested $100,000 in his business can hardly afford to set aside that much money to protect his restaurant. Even if he were to put aside $1,000 each year, he would not live long enough to accumulate enough to rebuild his property. If he owns a chain of 100 restaurants, however, the annual allocation of $1,000 for each unit would be enough to cover a disaster to any one of them.

As suggested in the preceding example, self-insurance should be used for protection only against certain risks. A group of doctors who joined together to operate a clinic, might practice self-insurance as it related to their own personal medical needs. They would probably not use that method to protect themselves against malpractice suits, since potential losses from that danger are much larger and more difficult to estimate. Even for large organizations, self-insurance is usually not a sufficient answer to all problems of risk.

Reducing Risks by Flexibility

Another method of dealing with risks seeks to reduce the potential impact of an undesirable event. Many firms carry a large number of items in their product line in order to minimize the danger of obsolescence. When product obsolescence hits a one-product firm, the results can be catastrophic. If Purex or Proctor and Gamble has to drop one of its products, the total corporate income statement may show no effect at all.

Some companies try to minimize the potential loss if a dynamic corporate president should die. They provide annual physical checkups, refuse to let him fly on the same plane with the chairman of the board, or take out a large life insurance policy on him. An even better way of dealing with the risk of his untimely death is to provide for flexibility by training subordinate managers who would be able to step into his position. Such flexibility is merely good management.

Transferring Risks through Insurance

The methods which have just been discussed help companies to protect themselves against the chance of loss or the impact of loss. The ultimate solution to the problem of risk is to *transfer* that risk to professional risk takers or insurance companies.

One of the simplest definitions of insurance calls it a process in which one party (the insurer) agrees, for a sum of money (a premium), which is paid by a second party (the insured), to pay the insured a specified sum if he should suffer a particular loss.

Going back to our illustration of the Chinese merchants, let us suppose that there were 10 merchants who owned junks valued at $1,000 which they used to transport goods downstream. If Lon Gung-Ho collected $105 (premium) from each of the merchants (the insured), he (the insurer) was able to reimburse an unfortunate merchant who later lost his junk, and also make $50 for his trouble. The insurance did not prevent *loss*, but it shifted the burden of the risk to someone who was a specialist in this type of problem.

Insurance should be considered a last resort in the management of risk. It always costs more than the statistically expected value of the loss covered. The insurance company estimates, on the basis of past experience, the amount it will have to pay in order to cover losses that will probably occur. In addition to covering the losses, it must also recover its own costs of operation. Although this may sound contradictory, the best buys in insurance involve those losses that are least likely to occur. The higher the probability of the loss, the less appropriate insurance is for dealing with the risk. A $100,000 life insurance policy on a man condemned to die in the electric chair would have to cost something more than $100,000. On the other hand, the average individual can buy $100,000 of flight insurance for less than $5.

The Law of Large Numbers

The obvious reason that an insurance company can afford to assume a $100,000 risk for such a small premium lies in the *law of large numbers* or the *law of averages*. The safety record of airlines is remarkably good. By insuring thousands of air travelers against a very unlikely occurrence, the company is able to charge a low premium against a high potential payout.

INSURABLE AND UNINSURABLE RISKS

Unfortunately, the most significant risk facing any business firm is uninsurable. That is the ever-present possibility that it will not make a profit. Although not to make a profit would be catastrophic from the standpoint of the owner, no insurer is willing to write this kind of coverage. Many of the risks identified in the opening section of this chapter are also uninsurable. No regular insurance company will insure the successful introduction of a new product, the adoption of new technology or the passage of favorable legislation.

Insurance is more than gambling. The insurance company is not betting $50,000 against your premium of $270 that your restaurant will not burn down. Gambling is the creation of a risk, while insurance provides for the transfer of an existing risk. One way to view insurance is to see it as a certain loss (*premium*) incurred to prevent a less certain but much larger loss.

Theoretically, it is possible to insure all possibilities of loss. Many contingencies are not, however, insurable at a reasonable price. An *insurable risk* will generally meet the following characteristics.

1. *The potential losses must be reasonably predictable.* Insurance is generally based upon the operation of the law of large numbers. Unless we are able to estimate the probability of loss, we cannot have a financially sound insurance program. Ideally, the risk should be spread over a wide geographic area. A company that writes flood protection coverage only for people who live near the banks of the Mississippi would be a poor insurance risk itself.

2. *The loss produced by the risk must be concrete and finite.* Insurance loss should be relatively difficult to counterfeit and should be subject to financial measurement. In other words, the insurance company needs to be able to tell when a loss has taken place or what the extent of loss actually is. Obviously, the terms of a life insurance policy are easier to establish than one for disability insurance. In every instance, the company must be able to make some measurement of the loss that a claimant has sustained.

3. *The loss must be accidental.* There is little reason to insure

FIGURE 16–1

COVERAGES APPLICABLE TO SMALL RETAIL STORES

Including:

Appliance Stores	*Glassware Stores*	*Music Dealers*
Booksellers	*Hardware*	*News Dealers*
Clothing	*Hosiery Shops*	*Notions*
Dept. Stores (small)	*Home Furnishings*	*Office Supplies*
Dry Goods	*Jewelers*	*Paint Dealers*
Florists	*Junk Dealers*	*Pawn Shops*
Furriers	*Leather Goods*	*Radio Stores*
Furniture Stores	*Lingerie Shops*	*Shoe Stores*
General Merchandise	*Luggage Dealers*	*Sporting Goods*
Gift Shops	*Milliners*	*Stationers*
		Variety Stores

Insurance for the smaller mercantile risks falls into three natural sub-divisions: Building, Contents and Business Operations. If the merchant is not the owner of the building he occupies, many of the coverages listed under Building can be eliminated. Contents, Furniture and Fixtures are his own property and require careful insuring accordingly. Particular attention should be given to the small merchant's need for Business Interruption insurance, complete Automobile coverage and adequate dishonesty protection, under "Business Operations."

BUILDING

Fire Insurance: Insures against direct loss or damage by fire or lightning, including destruction of building by civil authority to prevent further advance of fire from neighboring property. Standard policies are in force in the several states, with some variations. Watch carefully: Name of insured, additional interests, correct location of premises insured, accurate description of occupancy and mortgage, if any.
(Term credits: Usually 3 years, 2½ times annual rate; 5 years, 4 times annual rate.)

FIRE POLICY ENDORSEMENTS

Extended Coverage Endorsement
Windstorm, Hail, Explosion, Riot and Civil Commotion, Aircraft, Vehicle and Smoke Damage
Vandalism and Malicious Mischief
Contingent Liability from Operation of Building Laws Form
Rental Value Insurance Form
Leasehold Interest Form
Improvements and Betterments Form
Consequential Loss or Damage Form
Coinsurance Clause
Standard Mortgage Clause
Sprinkler Insurance
Earthquake Insurance
Glass Insurance
Electrical Signs

Boiler and Machinery Insurance: Insures loss as result of an accident to boilers or machinery from property damage (merchant's, as well as his liability for property of others) and may include liability because of bodily injuries to persons other than employees. The inspection service that is included is very valuable.

BOILER ENDORSEMENTS

Non-Ownership (Explosion)
Use and Occupancy

Source: Irving Williams and J. R. Gregory, *Coverages Applicable* 7th ed. Indiana: Rough Notes Company, Inc., 1971.

FIGURE 16–1—*Continued*

CONTENTS

Mercantile Stock and Fixtures: Insures merchandise, furniture, fixtures and other items in specified amounts. This form is used with Fire and Windstorm policies and Extended Coverage Endorsement. Merchandise covered should be accurately described on the form. Expense involved in removal from premises of property endangered by fire is covered.

(Term rate credit applies to furniture and fixtures only: 3 years, 2½ times annual rate; 5 years, 4 times annual rate.)

Extended Coverage Endorsement
Vandalism and Malicious Mischief
Inventory-Iron Safe Clause

Reporting Form: Insures stock, furniture, fixtures, improvements and betterments. If the merchant's annual Fire premium, exclusive of ECE, is more than $100 annually, and supplies of stock show marked seasonal variation, a Reporting Form may probably be used to his advantage. Attaches to standard Fire policy.

Mercantile Open Stock Burglary: Insures against burglary of and damage to merchandise, furniture and equipment on merchant's premises. Visible marks of forcible entry are required. Also insures payment of damage to property resulting from such burglary or attempt thereat.

(Term rate credit: 3 years, 2½ times annual rate if paid in advance, or 3 times annual rate if paid in equal annual payments.)

BUSINESS OPERATIONS

Business Interruption (Use and Occupancy): Reimburses merchant for profits he would have earned if fire or other hazard insured against had not occurred, including reimbursement for necessary continuing expenses such as taxes, payroll, etc. Written with or without Extended Coverage Endorsement.

(If building occupied by business is subject to term rates, Business Interruption may be written for the same proportionate rate credit.)

Accounts Receivable Forms
Transportation Floater
Deferred Payment Merchandise
Parcel Post Insurance (Coupon and Open Policy)
Tools and Equipment Floater
Installation Risks Form

Motor Vehicle Liability: Insures against loss or damage to merchant by reason of liability for bodily injury or property damage to members of the public from operation of his business autos, motorcycles, etc. Be sure to include Medical Payments.

Non-Ownership (Contingent) Liability
Hired Cars
Automobile Fire and Theft
Collision
Fleet Plan

Storekeepers' Liability: A package policy for stores classified as such in the O. L. & T. manual. Insures merchant's liability arising out of operation and his premises, including Product Liability, equipment rental to others and certain types of Contractual Liability.

FIGURE 16–1—*Continued*

Comprehensive General Liability

SPECIFIC HAZARD LIABILITY POLICIES

Owners', Landlords' and Tenants'
Elevator Liability
Contractual Liability
Owners Protective Liability
Products Liability

Storekeepers Burglary, Theft and Robbery: Insures against loss of money, securities and merchandise, not exceeding $250 per policy unit, in each of the following classifications: (1) robbery within premises, (2) robbery outside premises, (3) custodian forced to return to premises and open safe, (4) safe burglary, (5) loss of money and securities from night depository or custodian's home, (6) loss of merchandise by burglary and (7) property damage due to burglary or attempt. May be sold in a single policy or in multiples as may be required by smaller merchants.

Money and Securities (Broad Form): May be recommended where more than two units of Storekeepers Burglary would be required. Covers within or away from premises against loss of money or securities caused by destruction, disappearance or wrongful abstraction, except dishonesty of employees, war or forgery. Safe burglary, interior and messenger protection for the merchant's property other than money are provided.
(Term rate credit: 3 years, 2½ times annual rate if paid in advance, or 3 times annual rate if paid in equal annual payments.)

LIMITED COVERAGE BURGLARY POLICIES

Messenger and Interior Robbery
Mercantile Safe Burglary
Paymaster Robbery
Valuable Papers

Comprehensive Dishonesty, Destruction and Disappearance Policy: All risk protection for money and securities on and off the premises caused by dishonesty, mysterious disappearance or destruction. Provides insurance against loss due to dishonesty of employees, loss of money and securities within or without the premises, damage done to premises and equipment, loss of securities in safety deposit or forgery of outgoing instruments. OR:

Fidelity Bonds: For bonding store employees who handle money or merchandise. Indemnifies for loss due to embezzlement or wrongful abstraction of money, securities or other property. Four Fidelity bonds are available to merchants: individual, name-schedule, position-schedule and blanket.
(Rate credit: 3 years, 2½ times annual premium. If paid in installments of 50%, 30% and 20% at start of first, second and third years, add 5%.)

Depositors Forgery Bond
License Bonds

Workmen's Compensation: Insures loss due to statutory liability as result of personal injury or death suffered by employees of store in course of their employment, providing compensation in amounts prescribed by law. Workmen's Compensation is mandatory in most states for varying minimums of employees. Be familiar with your state's requirements.

Employers' Liability

LIFE INSURANCE: Sole Proprietorships: Provides cash to assist merchant's heirs in continuing or disposing of business without sacrifice, in event of death of owner. **Partnerships:** Provides cash to carry out a buy-or-sell agreement in case of the death of one of store owners. **Key Man Insurance:** Reimburses business for financial loss resulting from death of a key man in the business, and builds up a sinking fund to be available upon his retirement.

Group Life Insurance and Hospitalization Insurance
Accident and Health

against the inevitable. If the insurance company knows that an event is certain to take place, it also knows that it must collect a premium equal to the loss that it must pay plus its cost of operation. Most firms charge depreciation off as an expense rather than attempting to buy insurance against the depreciation of equipment.

4. *The loss should also be beyond the control of the insured.* A man who burns his factory down in order to collect the fire insurance will have two disappointments. In addition to being subject to arrest for arson, he will probably find that the insurance was invalidated by virtue of his action.

5. *The loss should not be catastrophic.* The insurance principle is based upon the idea of sharing losses. Inherent in this idea is the assumption that only a small percentage of the group will suffer loss at any one time. Damage which would result from a nuclear attack would be catastrophic in nature. Consequently, most property insurance carries the provision that the policy is invalid in the event of war or riot.

SOURCES OF INSURANCE

Insurance in the United States is a tremendous industry. There are almost 5,000 companies, employing over 1,600,000 people and with assets of more than $200 billion. In the 30 years 1945–1975, the number of people working in insurance rose from 600,000 to 1,638,000. Some of their characteristics and occupations are shown in Tables 16–1 and 16–2.

Government Insurance Programs

All states in the U.S. operate unemployment insurance programs which provide payment to certain unemployed workers whose employers have paid "premiums" during previous periods of employment. Almost half of the states have some form of workmen's compensation insurance. Five states have compulsory disability programs which provide income to workers who are disabled through nonoccupational causes, and four states have hail insurance coverage which protects against loss to crops from hail damage.

In addition to a wide variety of social insurance programs, federal and state governments have become increasingly active in the area of private insurance. In some cases they compete with private insurers and in other cases they operate monopolistic programs. In most in-

TABLE 16–1

Characteristics of Persons Employed in Insurance in the United States, 1975

Sex	
Male	862,000
Female	775,000
Total	1,537,000
Work related to:	
Life or life and nonlife Insurance	425,000
Nonlife Insurance only	713,000
Total	1,638,000
Type of work	
Sales: More than 50% of Income from life Insurance	275,000
Less than 50% of Income from life Insurance	287,000
Total Sales	562,000
Nonsales: In home office of Insurance company	550,000
In agency, field, brokerage, or other office	526,000
Total Nonsales	1,076,000
Total	1,638,000

Source: Institute of Life Insurance. Estimates based on projections.

TABLE 16–2

Occupations of Persons Employed in Insurance in the United States, 1975

Sales	562,000
Nonsales	
Managerial	207,000
Professional and Technical	69,000
Clerical and Other	800,000
Total Nonsales	1,076,000
Total Insurance Personnel	1,638,000

Source: Institute of Life Insurance. Estimates based on projections.

stances, the government has entered the insurance area when private insurers were unable or unwilling to provide the desired coverages.

As might be expected, the federal government is the largest insurer in the United States. Among the most important social and private insurance programs administered by the federal government are the following:

1. *The Social Security Program,* which provides life insurance, disability income insurance, retirement benefits, and health insurance to those covered. Over 90 percent of the workers in this country (and their dependents) are covered for at least some of the benefits of this program.

Arthur S. DeMoss

A pioneer in applying techniques of mass merchandising to the marketing of insurance, Arthur S. DeMoss is founder and president of National Liberty Corporation of Valley Forge, Pennsylvania. This 15-year-old insurance organization is today the fastest growing mass marketer of health and life insurance in the world. Since going public in 1968, the company has seen its new business grow by 60 percent a year, its premiums by 31 percent, and its earnings by 55 percent. The firm's assets now exceed $250 million.

Born in Albany, New York, in 1925, DeMoss began his insurance career at the age of 20. At 24 he owned four insurance offices, and during the 1950s he worked his way up to the ownership of a general agency covering nine states, with an annual premium volume of some $1 million.

It was at this time that several ideas began to jell for him. He had become keenly aware that millions of Americans who were not eligible for group health insurance coverage could not afford the expensive individual health policies offered by the insurance industry. The idea of applying a modern mass merchandising system to the marketing of insurance held a particular appeal for DeMoss. His new approach involved eliminating the agent and his renewal commissions by selling through advertisements and by direct mail. He began by developing a hospitalization policy that would pay supplementary benefits of $150 a week indefinitely and would

2. *The Federal Deposit Insurance Corporation* (FDIC) which provides a specialized form of insurance protection on bank deposits. Many financial institutions advertise that their deposits are insured up to $20,000 by an agency of the U.S. government. This means that if a bank were to fail, the federal government would prevent the small depositor from losing his money.

3. *The Federal Housing Authority* (FHA) which provides mortgage insurance to lenders to protect them against default by home purchasers.

4. *The Federal Crop Insurance Corporation* which sells crop insurance to farmers.

cost $20 a year. To this he added a special marketing strategy.

His conviction that a market existed resulted in his development of a custom-tailored program of supplementary income coverage during hospitalization which he called Special Protection for Special People. The "special people" to whom his initial marketing campaign was directed were the surprisingly large contingent of citizens who did not drink alcoholic beverages. He believed that such people would be receptive to a plan providing built-in rewards for total abstinence in the form of lower premiums. Unable to sell his idea to the larger insurers, DeMoss found backing through a small firm, and his Gold Star Plan went into effect in 1959. Response was so strong that an additional carrier was soon needed. DeMoss acquired the Imperial Life Insurance Company of Pennsylvania for a cost of $71,000 and changed its name to National Liberty Life Insurance Company. In its first full year of operation the company issued more than 15,000 new policies.

By 1967 his volume had grown to $22 million in premiums annually. He established National Liberty Corporation, a public stock company, as the parent firm holding the stock of five subsidiaries. These subsidiary organizations engage in insurance sales and underwriting, marketing, advertising, and computer processing. As the company has grown, the variety of policies offered has expanded. In 1969 the

door was opened to coverage for those not able to sign a nondrinking pledge—at a higher premium, of course. The company has committed itself to the attainment of a compound annual growth rate of 25 percent or more, and has instituted a comprehensive Management by Objectives system to implement and monitor its progress.

DeMoss attributes his success to a fervent belief in evangelical Christianity. "When We Have a Problem, We Pray" runs a message carved in letters of gold in the company's lobby. DeMoss was converted early in his business life, through a traveling evangelist. He and his closest associates believe that they are in partnership with God, and invoke His assistance whenever a major decision is to be made.

Another key ingredient in the company's success has been its practice of getting well-known persons to serve on its board, notably Art Linkletter and former Pennsylvania governor William Scranton. Linkletter's appeal to a broad segment of the potential market has been demonstrated in the company's advertising program.

In a recent listing of the largest 500 corporations by market value of capital stock published by *Forbes* magazine, National Liberty ranked 374th. In 1972 it was in the top 5 percent of *Best's Review's* listing of 1,800 American life insurance companies in terms of premium income.

5. *The Veterans Bureau* which sells National Service Life Insurance to veterans of previous wars.

Private Insurance Companies

In an earlier chapter, we briefly discussed the difference between capital stock companies and mutual companies. These are two major kinds of insurance companies. Stock companies are organized as profit-making ventures, with stockholders assuming the risk. A mutual insurance company is owned by the policyholders; instead of making a profit, the mutual company returns its surplus over costs to the policyholders in the form of a dividend, or else invests it in reserves.

Classification by Type of Policy

A more important distinction can be made among insurance companies on the basis of the coverage they provide. Until recently, companies tended to specialize in a limited area such as life insurance or automobile insurance. In recent years, most states have liberalized their laws to allow a single company to write many different kinds of coverage. The result has been that there are now two major types of insurance companies: (1) life insurance companies and (2) property and liability companies. While health insurance is written by both types of companies, in other respects they are usually quite distinct.

Persons who meet rigorous qualifying standards and then pass appropriate examinations are certified in each of these areas. The American College of Life Underwriters awards a designation, CLU (Chartered Life Underwriter), for specialists in this area. Similarly, the CPCU (Chartered Property and Casualty Underwriter) designation is awarded by the American Institute for Property and Liability Underwriters.

INSURANCE TO PROTECT AGAINST EMPLOYEE RISK

Insurance of various kinds can be a major fringe benefit for American employees. By helping all his employees achieve a certain degree of financial security, employers are able to provide a genuine service to their work force. Through collective buying, they can acquire insurance at lower cost than their employees could if they bought it themselves.

Life Insurance. As a fringe benefit, a hefty life insurance policy has been a real asset in the recruiting programs of many firms. Younger workers are attracted by the inexpensive but extensive coverage for those critical beginning years when their budgets are tightest and their security needs greatest. Employers can make group, term, or permanent life policies available both to hourly workers and to key executives at low cost. However, an employee should try to avoid having his total insurance holdings in the form of group plans, for this would make it difficult for him to leave the firm once he had aged into the upper premium brackets. If he left, he would be removed from the group and would have to pay much higher individual rates for his insurance. The primary value of group life plans is that they supply additional chunks of coverage at relatively low rates.

Disability Income Protection. One of the most needed and often neglected forms of coverage is the kind that reimburses the employee if he is unable to work because of sickness or accident. Most groups now have some sort of sick-leave plan which pays the worker's salary for a given amount of time regardless of his ability to continue work. However, if the disability proves to be of a permanent nature this coverage is not enough. After the short-term plan expires, the worker and his family face a lifelong problem.

Generally speaking, premiums are low on plans protecting income in case of total disability and the benefits are great, since there is a low probability that a claim will have to be made against the income protection plan. The usual procedure is to insure some percentage of the worker's salary, up to about 70 percent. Some of the more attractive policies also provide other payments for the insured.

Major Medical Insurance. Anyone who has just received a bill for a few days in the hospital will have no difficulty understanding what a lengthy stay in the hospital involving modern surgical and other treatment could mean. It does not take long nowadays to run up a hospital bill of $10,000 for a major sickness or injury. Major medical insurance is designed to cover this danger; it can mean the difference between financial difficulties and financial devastation. Most often, major medical is added on as a rider to a regular hospitalization plan. Major medical benefits vary, but usually pay 80 percent of all costs over a certain deductible amount, such as $100 or $500. Since 1951, over 40 million people have come under the protection of major medical plans.

Hospital Money Plans. Some plans offer a simple flat-rate payment for each day spent in the hospital. This type of plan is not suitable as total coverage, but as an add-on benefit it can be very attractive. There are almost always extra expenses resulting from hospitalization and sickness that are not usually covered by regular insurance.

Liability Plans. Members of some professions and industries have a particular need for protection against legal action. It may cost a great deal of money to defend oneself even when falsely accused. Because of the high cost of litigation, some groups have found it valuable to prepay their legal defense through insurance. If the group is especially open to legal attack—as are architects, corporation directors, and physicians—liability coverage is a necessity that can best be provided through special insurance.

Pensions and Retirement Plans. A majority of employees in the U.S. are covered by programs intended to supplement their anticipated retirement income from Social Security. Many employers have profit-sharing plans to fill this need. Others set up a group retirement insurance plan or maintain a separate operation to save and invest in behalf of their employees' retirement. Retirement plans can take the form of life insurance policies that develop cash value at a prescribed rate; or the employer may invest in variable annuities or mutual funds to build the principal.

Pension plans are either *vesting* or *nonvesting.* If his pension plan is vested, a worker can take the benefits with him when he leaves an employer before retirement. In nonvesting plans, the employee takes with him only his own contributions and none of the company's if he leaves before retirement.

INSURANCE FOR THE FIRM

There are approximately 3,000 insurance companies in the U.S. that sell policies related to the protection of property and other business liabilities. These companies have over $50 billion in assets.

Property insurance can protect against two types of losses. The first is *direct loss,* which involves the value of an asset. If a restaurant burns down, the direct loss is that of the property itself. A second loss relates to the *consequential* or indirect loss which results from the loss of use of that asset. If the restaurant was grossing $5,000 per week, and two months are required to rebuild it, the loss of operating income will be approximately $40,000. We shall see how a businessman can protect himself against both of these losses.

Since business firms are not as much alike as homeowners, they require many more forms of insurance to cover their particular needs. The following are some of the major features of business protection.

Building and Contents. Most fire insurance for businessmen is written to cover the building and its contents. Unless the policy specifies, there is no coverage for loss of improvements, rental value, or other expense associated with a fire. Often, the insurance is suspended if a building is vacant or unoccupied for more than 60 days.

Additional Perils. While the building and contents basic provision may cover only fire or other specified peril, coverage for the danger of vandalism or malicious mischief is generally added to the policy by paying an additional premium. Some properties are eligible for "all risk" coverage which will take care of damage or destruction regardless of the cause.

Coinsurance Clause. Under the provisions of the coinsurance clause, the businessman agrees to maintain insurance equal to some specified percentage of the value of his property (such as 80 percent) in return for a lower premium rate. This means that the coinsurance rate is a quantity discount.

To illustrate this concept, suppose that a businessman has purchased insurance on a $100,000 factory with an 80 percent coinsurance clause. This means he is required to maintain $80,000 in insurance coverage at all times. In the event of a $10,000 loss, he will receive full payment for the loss. In fact, as long as he maintains insurance amounting to 80 percent of the value of the property, any loss up to $80,000 will be covered completely. In the event of a total loss, the face value of his policy (in this case, $80,000) would be paid to him. The company would have to make up the additional $20,000 out of its own resources. When a businessman is insuring a piece of property that is not likely to be totally destroyed by fire, coinsurance may be a desirable alternative for him.

THE APPROACH TO SELECTING BUSINESS INSURANCE

The steps to be taken in setting up an insurance plan for a business are almost obvious. Logically, any firm should decide what it needs, check out available plans, and then contact the insurance company (or companies) which best meets its needs. Unfortunately, insurance selection is sometimes haphazard, and is often determined by the accident of having a brother-in-law who is in the insurance business, or being visited by an agent at a convenient time. Moreover, many companies (especially small companies) are not prepared to check out all the available plans or to identify the carrier that can best satisfy a particular need.

Rarely do insurance agents receive requests for simple bids on specified types and quantities of insurance. More often, the request is something like, "We are planning to make a few changes in our insurance program. Why don't you come by and tell us what we need and what you have to offer." This approach opens the door to confusion, since different companies quote rates on every imaginable combination of benefits.

Some smaller firms have found it desirable to purchase group insurance plans through their trade association. The Georgia Business and Industry Association provides a wide range of insurance programs for business firms in many industrial categories. Specialized trade associations such as the National Association of Wholesalers or the American Metal Stamping Association provide group insurance programs for corporate members.

Most large firms have an insurance department. In smaller companies, the controller or another key financial officer usually handles the insurance program. They will usually call in a broker who analyzes their

FIGURE 16–2

Types of Insurance Offered by One Insurance Agency

Oil—World Wide

Control Of Well
Land
Platform Rigs
Platforms
Underground Damage
Blowout and Cratering

Casualty

Automobile
  Mobile Home
    Comprehensive Physical Damage
  Motor Home and Camper
    Liability and Physical Damage
  Taxicab Liability and Physical Damage
  Truck
    Cargo
    Liability and Physical Damage
  Excess Auto Liability
Mexican
  Tourist Liability and Physical Damage
Surplus Lines
  Accountants Professional
  Adjusters Errors and Omissions
  Advertisers Libel and Slander
  Beauty Shop Malpractice
  Burglary, Robbery, Open Stock,
    Safe Burglary
  Community and Sports Events
  County Clerks Errors and Omissions
  Insurance Brokers and Agents Errors and Omissions
  Lawyers Professional Indemnity
  Lenders Single Interest
  Libel and Slander—Radio, TV
  Libel and Slander—Newspapers
  Livestock Mortality
  Malpractice
  Nursing Homes
  Personal Accident
  Pest Control—Exterminators
  School Board Errors and Omissions
  S.E.C. Liability
Liability
  Excess Maritime Employers
  Directors and Officers Financial Institutions
  Directors and Officers
  Primary and Excess General
  Primary and Excess General—Foreign
  Products
    Cosmetics, Pharmaceuticals, etc.
    Mechanical

Umbrella (wide-ranging casualty coverage)

Marine

Commercial Hull and Protection and Indemnity
Ship Repairers Legal Liability
Marine Builders Risk
Installation Floater
Warfingers Liability
Boat Dealers
Marina Operators
Cargo—Ocean, Barge, and Air
Yachts

Inland Marine

Jewelry
Furs
Personal Articles
Jewelers Block
Gun Floaters
Contractors Equipment
Bailees Liability
Radio Towers

Aviation

Hull and Liability Individual and Corporate
  Aircraft Including Excess Liability
Commercial Aircraft including
  FBOs
  Airlines
  Airport Liability Including Excess and Products, Hangerkeepers, Contractual
Workmens Compensation and Employers Liabilities (when written with commercial risks)
Personal Accident—Pilot and Crew

Property

Builders Risks (other than Marine)
Difference in Conditions and All Risks
Fire, Allied Lines, and Inland Marine
Surcharged Fire, Allied Lines
Installation Floater
Valued Use and Occupancy

Accident & Sickness

HiLimit Accident
Major Medical
Specific Disease
Weekly Income

Source: Cravens, Dargan & Company, Houston, Texas.

insurance needs and coverages, and together they work out the details. Other firms find it desirable to set up an insurance committee that includes employees representatives, to recommend insurance for employees.

Any insurance agent or broker is delighted to spend time with a potential prospect. Ideally, the initial round of discussion should include a number of consultants, brokers, or insurance company representatives. This will allow the company decision makers to become acquainted with recent developments in business insurance and help them refine their thinking. Deliberative action of this nature is far more promising than if an expensive plan is chosen because one salesman has a more elaborate sales presentation than the others.

Of course, insurance brokers receive commissions based on a percentage of premiums. Consequently their recommendations may be a bit biased although there are many brokerage firms that act as highly professional consultants.

As a beginning point, the executive purchasing insurance should make certain that his advisor is knowledgeable about the group and business insurance field, and that he receives exactly the same fee regardless of which company gets the business. An insurance broker is one who can write business for many different insurance companies. If he or his associates are CLUs or CPCUs, he should be qualified to design a program that will meet the specific needs of the firm. Figure 16–2 shows the variety of types of coverages offered by one insurance agency.

SUMMARY

This chapter has attempted to review the development of insurance as a means of meeting many forms of business risks. Obviously, good management on the part of the businessman is still his best insurance against the most serious risks he faces. Risks relating to marketing, purchasing equipment, extending credit, keeping too much or too little inventory, and meeting governmental regulation and supervision, can best be handled through good management. Frequently this means avoiding the risk by eliminating its cause, or, at least, by anticipating the risk. When anticipation or flexibility is not enough to avoid the risk, the businessman may wish to insure against it. In exchange for the payment of a regular premium, an insurance company will agree to pay the businessman a specified sum if he should suffer the loss he has insured against.

In order for a risk to be insurable, several characteristics should be present. First, the potential loss must be reasonably predictable. The loss should be concrete and measurable. The loss should also be accidental, beyond the control of the insured, and should not be catastrophic.

In recent years, insurance has become a major industry. Both private companies and government agencies provide insurance for businessmen and their employees. Competent professional help should be sought, however, so that the insurance decision will be as intelligent and well-informed as other important business decisions.

KEY TERMS AND CONCEPTS FOR REVIEW

Risks	Coinsurance
Law of large numbers	Premium
FDIC	Insurable risk
CLU	Life insurance
CPCU	Property insurance
Direct loss	Self-insurance
Consequential loss	

QUESTIONS FOR ANALYSIS AND DISCUSSION

1. What are the major types of risks faced by businessmen?
2. How can businessmen avoid or reduce their risks?
3. Why should the owner of two small retail stores not elect to handle his risks by self-insurance?
4. For a risk to be insurable, what factors should be present? Why would aging insurance for football players not qualify?
5. Is insurance against employee theft a better way of reducing risk than the careful screening of employees? Explain.
6. What type of underwriter would be most likely to write building and contents insurance?
7. What type of insurance is most helpful to an employee facing open-heart surgery?
8. Why is flight insurance less expensive than automobile insurance?
9. Identify the major forms of government insurance. Which of these directly involve you?

SUGGESTED READINGS

Best's Insurance Reports   New York: A. M. Best, annual.

Bickelhaupt, D. L.   *General Insurance,* 9th ed. Homewood, Ill.: Richard D. Irwin, 1974.

Greene, Mark R.   *Risk Aversion, Insurance and the Future.* © Bloomington: Graduate School of Business, Indiana University, 1971.

Heath, G. B. *Insurance Words and Their Meanings.* Indianapolis, Ind.: Rough Notes, 1972.

Mayerson, Allen *Introduction to Insurance.* New York: Macmillan, 1972.

Williams, C. A., and R. M. Heins *Risk Management and Insurance,* 2d ed. New York: McGraw Hill, 1971.

17

Managing Information

Everyone initiates and receives information in one form or another. It has been estimated that the average American adult is exposed to 560 advertising messages each day. In his home, at his place of work, and in transit between them, he is constantly receiving more information than he can possibly absorb. In one research-oriented organization, technical employees were found to spend 61 percent of their time dealing with information. (About 35 percent of their time was spent speaking and listening, 16 percent writing, and 10 percent reading.) Many business managers devote most of their time to handling information in one way or another.

Much of this information is perishable. It is constantly being replaced by new information, while the sum total of human knowledge grows ever faster. Stuart Flexner, senior editor of the *Random House Dictionary of the English Language*, points out that of the 450,000 "usable" words in the English language today, almost half are relatively new. In fact, only 250,000 of our words would have been comprehensible to William Shakespeare.

Dr. Robert Hillard, an educational specialist for the Federal Communications Commission, estimates that by the time today's children are 50 years old, 97 percent of everything known in the world will have been learned since they were born. What does this bit of information tell you about the difficulty of staying up-to-date in your chosen field?

MANAGEMENT IS INFORMATION

When he was chairman of the board of one of the nation's largest advertising agencies, Marion Harper coined a useful motto for business-men: "To manage a business well is to manage its future; and to manage the future is to manage information."

A progressive businessman is only moderately interested in the present and even less concerned about the past. His major concern must be for the future growth and success of his organization. He is constantly making decisions which will have an impact upon that future. One of the greatest difficulties he experiences is the inability to be certain his decision is the right one. An executive can never have all the facts to cover all the contingencies in a forecast. He makes his decisions partly on the basis of facts and partly by hunch.

But nobody wants to risk everything on a hunch. Decision makers throughout history, whether businessmen or kings, generals or popes, have felt the need to fortify themselves with as much information as they could get. They got their information in various ways, usually from wise men or men of experience or from scholars. It must be ad-mitted that the success of an advisor sometimes depended more on his ability to tell his master what he wanted to hear than on the accuracy of his information.

THE INFORMATION REVOLUTION

Today, we are well into an information revolution in which the supply of data is doubling every few years. For over a decade, we have had data processing machines that can absorb information or give it back at the rate of four full-length novels a second. The sheer mass of available data is increasing faster than we can build libraries to hold it. One critic has suggested that the storehouses where crop surpluses used to be kept might be converted to storehouses for surplus informa-tion.

DATA AND INFORMATION INDIGESTION

While there is something almost unpatriotic in criticizing the in-satiable American appetite for information, we must decide how much information is really necessary or even helpful. When confronted with too much detail, businessmen may react like the boy who was asked to summarize a book on peacocks. He simply wrote, "This book tells more about peacocks than I want to know."

The real question is how well can we use the mass of raw data currently available. Too many undigested facts can turn a man of action into a Hamlet, paralyzed by indecision. Just as the raw materials of industry must be converted into something, information must be processed, packaged, and marketed in a manner to make it useful.

We should not overlook the fact that nothing is information that does not inform. Data of all kinds may or may not be information. Look at a table of figures, a computer printout sheet, an accounting statement, or a statistical report. Does it inform you? If it does, it is information. If not, it is merely uninformative data.

MANAGEMENT INFORMATION SYSTEMS

Since data can be a source either of power or of paralysis to the manager, he must find a systematic way of dealing with it. Many firms have comprehensive *management information systems* for this purpose. A *system* is simply a collection of things that work together toward some common purpose. A pair of eyeglasses is a system composed of metal (frames and hinges) and glass. A more complex system will provide for change based on input received into the system. For example, a thermostat takes regular readings of the temperature in a room and decides whether the heat or air conditioning should be turned on. In a similar way, a management information system takes regular readings of various data and sends an appropriate message to the decision maker. The components of such a system are shown in Figure 17–1.

Systems for management information may be of several kinds. Three basic types of information systems are as follow:

1. *Environmental Information.*   This describes the economic, political, and social aspects of the environment in which a business is operating or is planning to operate in the future. It is perhaps the least formalized of the systems used. Most progressive firms attempt to generate and utilize information relating to population, price levels, transportation availability and cost, foreign trade potential, and labor trends. As we shall see in the chapter on planning, these facts often are the foundation upon which the plans for business activity are based.

2. *Competitive Information.*   This describes the past performance, activities, and plans of competing firms. An alert businessman always

FIGURE 17–1

Components of a Management Information System

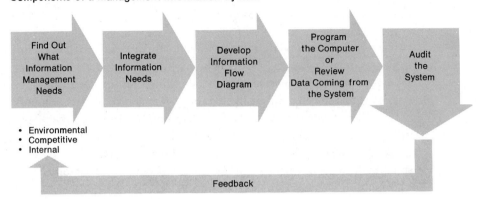

- Environmental
- Competitive
- Internal

wants to know how his competitors are doing. He seeks information on such matters as their profitability, their share of the market, and their return on investment, so that he can determine how his firm is getting along by comparison.

He will also be interested in his competitors' activities in such areas as product introduction, marketing changes, and price strategy, since such information can materially influence what his own firm does. One of the authors recalls that when he was employed at a large consumer goods company, it usually took four weeks for the company to decide on a price change. But on one occasion when a leading competitor had reduced its price in a major segment of the market, the decision to meet it was made in 48 hours.

The A. C. Nielsen Company and other market research organizations exist primarily to provide companies with information about how well their competitors are doing. Many retail organizations regularly use "comparison shoppers" who check on the price and quality of merchandise in competing stores.

Companies are also interested in their competitors' plans for the future. Such matters as contemplated acquisitions, plant expansion, or major research and development are all of vital interest. Some of the information is available through normal business channels. Plans that are within the jurisdiction of governing bodies such as zoning boards or the Securities and Exchange Commission become public knowledge. In some instances, companies may even engage in espionage. The major automotive manufacturers go to great lengths to disguise the features of their test models, even on their own "secret" test facilities. Some manufacturers have also observed reconnaissance planes flying over their proving grounds.

3. *Internal Information.* The third and most basic category of information necessary for business decisions consists of internal data aimed at identifying the major strengths and weaknesses of an organization. Quantitative data on the number of customer complaints, labor turnover, the company's share of the market, and its sales growth are of constant interest to management. Much of the internal information subject to regular scrutiny is financial: sales, cost of goods sold, expense figures, and almost every other component of the company's financial statements.

ACCOUNTING SYSTEMS ARE INFORMATION SYSTEMS

The most basic and fundamental information system within the organization is made up of the flow of accounting data. As suggested in Chapter 6, a very simple financial statement can provide a considerable amount of information about a firm. It can show, for example, what is happening to accounts receivable, to inventories, and to cash flow— matters of continuous concern to management. Financial statements are like windows through which we are able to look inside a business and see what is happening to it. Whereas an extensive market research study can be quite expensive, accounting data are generated in the daily activity of a company.

PRIMARY AND SECONDARY INFORMATION

It will be useful to list the main sources of information with which every businessman should be familiar. He should know which sources are likely to provide him with information about a particular problem. He should also be able to distinguish between reliable and unreliable information, and to tell whether or not it is pertinent to his needs.

Primary Information

Primary information is original data collected by an individual or firm for specific purposes. As suggested above, one of the finest sources of information is the company's own records. When properly sorted and analyzed, these sources will reveal much about the management, marketing, or financial problems of a business and their potential solutions. In addition to such basic documents as the balance sheet and the

H. Ross Perot

©Karsch, Ottawa.

The phenomenal growth of H. Ross Perot's Electronic Data Systems, Inc., during the late 1960s catapulted him into the public eye. Almost overnight he appeared on the scene as a leader in the information revolution and a shrewd financier. At the height of the 1969–70 bull market he was worth almost one and a half billion dollars, but after the ensuing shakeout on Wall Street he had the distinction of being perhaps the only man ever to lose one billion dollars.

Born in Texarkana, Texas, in 1930, son of a cotton broker, Henry Ross Perot lived, listened, and learned in an atmosphere created by his father's business interests. Discussions in the household routinely centered around trading, and young Perot learned by osmosis. His gift for selling became evident quite early. When he was 12 he persuaded the local newspaper to let him establish a paper route in the town's black slum area in return for 70 percent rather than the customary 30 percent in commissions on the subscriptions he collected. Setting out at 3:30 A.M. each day, he covered 20 miles on horseback before school began, and soon was making $40 a week. When the circulation department tried to back out of the commission arrangement, he carried his case all the way to the newspaper's owner.

Although a mediocre student in some respects, he showed his ability to rise to a challenge. In 1949 he secured an appointment to the U.S. Naval Academy, fulfilling a major ambition. Graduating 454th in a class of 925, Perot was elected life president of his class.

profit and loss statement, detailed records of sales transactions and various data on advertising, sales effort, inventory cost, equipment maintenance, wage rates, and productivity can be most useful.

Probably the most important single source of marketing information is the ultimate consumer. Surveys and interviews are widely used to find out what customers think about a particular product or marketing program. Telephone calls to institutional customers or reports from salesmen can frequently provide needed information.

Many companies employ outside research firms to collect primary information. The subjects they are asked to study may range from consumer reaction to a new cake mix to a detailed site analysis for a pro-

He served in the Navy until 1957 and then took his discharge as a lieutenant. He liked ships and the sea, but was disenchanted with the navy's promotion and seniority systems which he felt did not give enough recognition to a man's performance.

Perot went to work as a computer salesman for IBM in Dallas, where he made a phenomenal record. In his fifth year with IBM, he was able to meet his sales quota for the year by the end of the third week in January.

Sensing a need for a type of computer service that would design, install, and operate electronic data processing systems for clients on a contract basis, Perot left IBM and started his own company, Electronic Data Systems, in June 1962, on his 32d birthday, with $1,000 in savings. During the years that followed, the company doubled its business each year as branch offices were opened in major cities throughout the country and the work force grew to 3,500 employees. The company went public in 1968 with a stock issue of 11.5 million shares, of which only 650,000 were offered to the public—at a price of 118 times earnings. Perot himself sold 325,000 shares, for which he received $5 million in cash. Subsequently the market price of the company's stock rose from $16.50 a share to $160 a share in early 1970. Perot himself owned over 9 million shares—worth (on paper) almost $1.5 billion. Later it was to be worth less than $12 a share.

In 1971 Perot opened a new chapter in his career by entering the Wall Street brokerage business. He took over one of his data processing customers, duPont Glore Forgan, Inc., in order to save it from bankruptcy. In 1973 he assumed control of another brokerage firm, Walston and Co., and merged their retail business with duPont Glore Forgan. The new company, duPont Walston and Co., became the second largest brokerage house on Wall Street. Although he invested $100 million in the firm, it was unable to survive in the depressed state of the securities industry. After six months of red ink, Perot announced that duPont Walston was quitting the retail brokerage business and its many retail brokerage offices were sold to others or liquidated.

Personal wealth has not been a major target for Perot, who has steadfastly refused to lead the luxurious life that is within his grasp. He has stated that he doesn't want to deprive his children of the opportunities he had by bequeathing them large sums of money.

For a brief time Perot became famous for his attempts to free United States prisoners of war in North Vietnam, at an estimated cost to him of over $2 million. In the fall of 1969 he collected 26 tons of mail, food, clothes, and medicine, and set out for Hanoi in two chartered airplanes. Neither this nor later attempts succeeded in freeing the prisoners, although they helped to make their lives a little less onerous. His other philanthropic activities have included a wide range of educational and youth programs.

posed plant expansion. Wholesalers and retailers may also be useful sources of information for a manufacturer.

Secondary Information

Secondary information is data collected by government agencies, trade associations, and other agencies without an individual business' specific needs in mind.

The U.S. government publishes a vast quantity of business information. The Department of Commerce publishes regular statistics on population and business. The Department of Labor compiles statistics on wages and the cost of living. The Federal Reserve System publishes financial information. The variety of available data can be seen in the regular lists published by the Government Printing Office, which may be obtained by writing to the Superintendent of Documents, Government Printing Office, Washington, D.C. Of particular interest to the small businessman are the publications of the Small Business Administration.

The *Statistical Abstract of the United States,* published annually by the Department of Commerce, is an encyclopedic source of basic information for current and past years. Among the many topics included in this publication are statistics on population, employment, business expenditures, productivity, and the output of various industries.

Professional and Trade Organizations

There are several national research organizations that provide information to businessmen. The most prominent of them are the Conference Board, the American Management Association, the National Bureau of Economic Research, and the Research Institute of America. Each of these organizations conducts research and publishes reports on subjects of interest to its members.

Most of the business professions such as marketing, management, statistics, insurance, and economics have their own organizations that publish specialized journals. These journals often contain helpful information, although most of their articles are academic and reflect individual points of view.

There are hundreds of trade associations comprised of businesses in particular industries, ranging from air conditioning to window shades. One of their most important functions is to provide information to their member firms. This is especially important in associations that represent many small firms that cannot afford elaborate research programs of their own. They provide very helpful data concerning the industry, the economy, and the future of a specialized area. One of the authors has worked with several trade associations ranging from the National Management Association to the American Home Economics Association in helping these groups assess the future of an entire industrial or professional specialty.

Many trade associations also publish their own magazines containing extensive information about their industries. Persons in the drug field, for example, will be interested in reading *Drug Topics* or *The American Druggist.*

Anyone interested in business should read one or more of the general business publications such as *Fortune, Forbes, Business Week, Dun's Review,* and *Harvard Business Review.* Day-to-day information on business and economic conditions can be obtained from the business pages of the daily press or from business newspapers such as *The Wall Street Journal.*

FINDING SECONDARY INFORMATION

Many businessmen pay large sums of money to obtain information readily available in most libraries. This is because the average businessman doesn't have time to search through thousands of publications for specific information about wage rates in Arkansas or the details of a

FIGURE 17–2
Is This Student Seeking Primary or Secondary Data?

new financing method. He is better off paying someone to locate the information for him.

For those with more time, there are a number of ways to make research easier. Many libraries have trained personnel to help find the answers to specific questions. Everyone should be familiar with the most important periodical guides that catalog, by subject, articles in leading periodicals. The following are useful for business reference:

Reader's Guide to Periodical Literature. This index covers articles in general interest magazines, including most of the largest business magazines. It is a general reference, however, rather than a specialized business source.

The Public Affairs Information Service. Important articles and books relating to public affairs and economics are listed in this source. A distinguishing feature is that brief, one-sentence summaries of books are sometimes included.

Business Periodicals Index. Perhaps the most significant reference for individuals interested in business, this index lists articles from more than 170 business publications.

THE DANGER OF "FACTS"

Things aren't always what they appear to be. As every college student realizes, many of the statements one reads in leading publications are erroneous. In making decisions about acquisitions or purchases, businessmen know that enthusiastic salesmen sometimes are prone to exaggeration. Trade associations and government agencies may reflect a particular viewpoint in reporting their data. Likewise, even the most sophisticated of financial statements should be subjected to rigorous scrutiny. Every decision maker needs to be careful that his subordinates do not tell him what he wants to hear—or what they want him to believe.

Additionally, items which are as reliable and valid as any "fact" can be, may be totally inappropriate by the time a decision is implemented. The Edsel fiasco in the 1950s is reported to have cost the Ford Motor Company some $225 million. Extensive market research had been conducted to determine what the American public wanted in a new automobile. But the findings of early studies were not rechecked later on, before the Edsel went into production. During this lag time between research and final development, the fickle consumer began to shift his allegiance from the heavy, bulky, chrome-laden monsters of the early 1950s to the smaller, more economical cars of the late 1950s.

A fact is not always a fact. And even when a fact is correct, it may not remain so for long. Businessmen need to be constantly aware of changes in their information which may affect their decision-making.

NEED FOR EXPECTATIONS RATHER THAN FACTS

No one can do anything about the past. Facts are facts because they're over and done with. Today's decisions have to deal with the future. Therefore, the smart businessman will not ask for facts but for expectations—what knowledgeable people expect to happen in coming months or years. He will be interested in such things as forecasts of sales, or trends in prices, wages, and costs, or what new products are likely to appear on the market. He will also insist on knowing the assumptions behind the expectations.

This is why the practice of forecasting has become so important. While we can never be sure of the future, good forecasters are developing the ability to tell approximately what will happen to broad economic aggregates such as national income, capital spending, home building, or inventories. Any businessman would rather have knowledge of what is *expected* to happen, even with some degree of uncertainty or error, than accurate knowledge of what did happen last month or last year.

Even if the businessman can only get data on the past, he should use it with an eye to the future. After all, he must live in the future.

PRESENTATION OF DATA

Not only must data be comprehensive, accurate and timely, they must be presented in a form so that the appropriate decision maker can understand and act upon them. For the experienced executive, computer printouts may be adequate. He may merely want to look at a balance sheet or some other financial statement and draw his own conclusions. In other instances, considerable staff work will be done in order to summarize and evaluate tha data. While he was president of Procter & Gamble, Neil McElroy wanted the countless reports and tables which he reviewed to be summarized. You could submit several pages of tables, but the standing rule was that the summary could not be more than one page. "There is nothing that needs to be said about soap," he would tell subordinates, "that can't be said in one page." When he became Secretary of Defense, McElroy employed the same rule with his subordinates in the Pentagon. Other businessmen could profit from his emphasis on concise information.

Charts

Charts are a medium for explaining, interpreting, or displaying complicated collections of quantitative data in a simplified manner. They often employ lines, bars, circles, dots, or other symbols. A major criterion in the presentation of quantitative data is ease of comprehension, for they are meant to be understood by people who have had little to do with the collection of the data.

In developing charts, three basic questions should be answered: What? Where? When? The items being depicted should be clearly labeled, and only a limited amount of data should be shown on one chart.

The simplest chart to design is the *line graph,* showing relationships or patterns of movement. The simple line graph may be made a little more sophisticated by adding an additional line so that the reader may see the relationship between two variables. Thus figure 17–3 shows how

FIGURE 17–3

Simple Line Graph

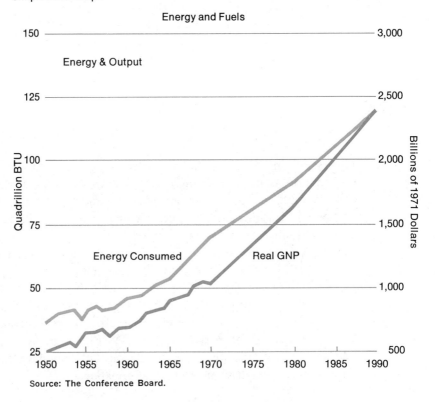

Source: The Conference Board.

FIGURE 17–4

Simple Bar Chart

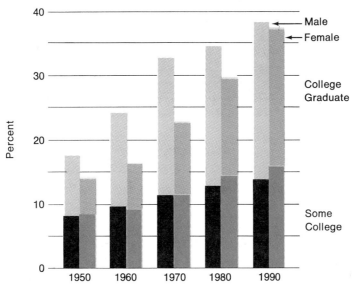

Education by Generation

Percent College Educated in Age Group 30-34

Source: The Conference Board.

the consumption of energy has grown over the years in comparison with the growth of national output. The trends are projected as far as 1990.

Another simple means of presenting data is a *bar chart*. This is especially appropriate when it is necessary to compare absolute changes over a period of time. Figure 17–4 shows how the percentages of men and women going to college or completing college have changed since 1950. It also shows the changes expected through 1990.

A very effective means of showing how something is divided up is the *pie chart*. This technique changes the data into percentages and presents them as segments of a pie. One example of the infinite number of uses for a pie diagram is shown in Figure 17–5.

SUMMARY AND CONCLUSION

In all likelihood, the management of information will continue to be among the unsolved problems of every business. The only way to keep it within manageable proportions is to hold each individual responsible for the information he demands and transmits. Hopefully, this require-

FIGURE 17–5
Pie Chart

Distribution of Land by Use, 1990

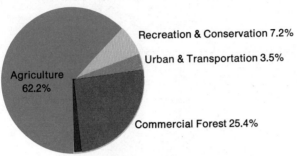

Recreation & Conservation 7.2%

Urban & Transportation 3.5%

Agriculture
62.2%

Commercial Forest 25.4%

Other & Unusable 1.7%

Sources: Bureau of Mines; Department of Commerce; Resources
for the Future; The Conference Board.

ment will cause him to think seriously about the problem of information, to give serious thought to proper definition of his information
needs, and to insist that the most efficient technique be used for sub-
mitting it.

The challenge of creating an information system to satisfy these
goals is not easy. Environmental, competitive, and internal information
will need to be thoroughly analyzed, presented in an understandable
form, and digested before it can be useful to the organization. Shopping
for the right kinds of information requires a knowledge of the product
you are seeking as well as the major primary and secondary sources of
supply.

While inflation will continue to affect both the quality and cost of
good information, no corporation can survive for long without a
steady diet of meaningful data.

KEY TERMS AND CONCEPTS FOR REVIEW

Information revolution
Information systems
Comparison shoppers
Primary information
Secondary information
Government as information source
When data are information

Periodical indexes
Facts
Line graph
Charts
Trade associations
Professional organizations

QUESTIONS FOR ANALYSIS AND DISCUSSION

1. How much time do technical employees spend in handling information?
2. Why is it so difficult for businessmen to stay up-to-date?
3. What is "information indigestion?"
4. Is this textbook a system? Explain.
5. How can firms collect competitive information?
6. Which of the following would be considered primary data for a business term paper?
    a) interviews with businessmen
    b) articles in *The Wall Street Journal*
    c) Government published statistics
    d) notes about your part-time job
7. Look at three business periodicals in the library. Which do you think would be most helpful to the owner of a small hardware store? Explain.
8. Why are "facts" sometimes dangerous?
9. Prepare a simple pie chart showing the approximate percentages of time you spend in study, classes, recreation, sleep, and all other activities. These five categories should cover 24 hours.

SUGGESTED READINGS

Weisman, H. M. *Information Systems, Services and Centers.* New York: Becker and Hayes, 1972.

Meltzer, M. F. *The Information Center, Management's Hidden Asset.* New York: American Management Association, 1967.

Kochen, Manfred   *The Growth of Knowledge.* New York: Wiley, 1967.

Meetham, Roger   *Information Retrieval.* Garden City, N.Y.: Doubleday, 1970.

Miller, Arthur R.   *The Assault on Privacy.* Ann Arbor: University of Michigan Press, 1971.

Stamper, Ronald   *Information in Business and Administrative Systems.* New York: Wiley, 1973.

Information Technology   New York: The Conference Board, 1972.

18

Information and the Computer

Most of us take the wonders of science and invention pretty much for granted. When the parents of today's students were young they were fascinated by the rapid pace of progress, and often tried to imagine what the distant future would be like. They followed the adventures of Buck Rogers and Flash Gordon in the Sunday papers as those men of the future went zooming through space in their rocket ships and talked to people on other planets by television. Everyone supposed such fantastic things were hundreds of years away. Nobody dreamed that in a few short years we would be able to watch astronauts driving an automobile on the moon, or that students would carry computers in their pockets enabling them to solve math problems almost instantly.

The electronic computer is a development of the last 20 or 30 years—almost within the lifetime of today's college freshmen. The first electronic computer was developed in the 1940s. It was very large compared to the present-day ones, and its hundreds of vacuum tubes gave off so much heat that an elaborate air-conditioning system was necessary. A new generation of computers was born about 1960. They used transistors, which are much smaller than vacuum tubes and do not give off heat. The new computers were many times faster than the old ones. But soon they too were outmoded and gave way to a third generation of computers, in which the transistors were replaced by units the size of a pinhead. Their tiny components had to be put together by workers looking through microscopes.

Computers are not only smaller now, but they remember more than they used to. One computer can hold enough information to fill 300,000 books. Its memory unit takes up about six cubic feet of space and costs far less than would a building large enough to hold that many books. And any bit of information in its whole memory can be retrieved in about 3/10 of a second!

The computer is having a revolutionary effect on modern business. Because of its speed in performing difficult calculations it can function as a kind of chief clerk. It can make up payrolls, check inventory, and bill customers. It can provide instant and up-to-date information on sales and shipments. It can even make certain kinds of executive decisions, such as choosing the best of several alternative solutions to a problem. For example, computers are used on toll highways to decide how many toll booths should be open at various times during the day.

Each day seems to bring some new use for the computer. You can reserve a place on an airplane, a bed in a motel, or a seat at a baseball game by dialing a telephone number, receiving a report of what is available, making a selection, and providing the operator with your credit card number.

HOW THE COMPUTER WORKS

Most of the computers used in American business are digital computers, that is, computers that use numbers in their operation. They reduce the numbers, however, to a simple code that resembles a set of yes-or-no answers. Every number or letter is described by the opening or closing of electrical circuits. By performing just this single kind of operation, these machines can add, subtract, multiply, divide, spell, and remember.

It may seem strange that vast amounts of information can be recorded by this yes-or-no system. It doesn't seem so strange if one thinks of that well-known guessing game in which the players find out some very complicated answers by asking questions that are answered yes or no. Computers use this yes-no system in the form of a *binary code*.

Basics of Binary

The binary code gets its name from the fact that it uses only two digits, 0 and 1. A "one" is indicated when an electrical circuit is on,

FIGURE 18–1

The Binary System

Decimal	0	1	2	3	4	5	6	7	8	9
Binary	0	1	10	11	100	101	110	111	1000	1001

and a zero is indicated when the circuit is off. It is possible to write any digit from one to nine by a combination of zeros and ones, as shown in Figure 18–1. Letters and symbols can also be written in this way (Figure 18–2). In fact, because of its multitude of tiny off-on switches, the computer can record any combination of numbers and letters and therefore any combination of words or other information. It puts together millions of these "bits" of information, but so rapidly that it seems to grasp them almost instantaneously.

Using its yes-no system, the computer performs five basic operations that underly even the most complicated task. These operations are (1) input, (2) memory, (3) arithmetic, (4) control, and (5) output. They are shown in schematic form in Figure 18–3.

Input is the activity of receiving information and instructions, in the form of a long series of yes's and no's. When punch cards are used, a hole in the card allows a tiny electrical impulse to go through, telling the computer that there is a "yes" in that position. If there were no hole, the lack of an electrical impulse would tell the computer to register a "no" in the position.

The yes's and no's can be fed into the computer by means of punch cards, lights, electric switches, magnetic tape, and other devices. When students are given a test that is to be graded by computer, they are

FIGURE 18–2

Developing a Binary Code

Decimal Number, *Letter, or Symbol*	*Binary Code*
1	000001
5	000101
9	001001
A	010001
B	010010
E	010101
I	011001
+	110000
$	111011
%	111100

FIGURE 18–3

The Essential Elements of a Computer

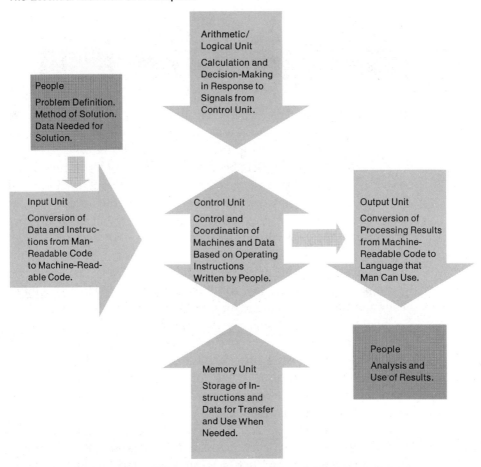

Source: International Business Machines Corporation, *More About Computers*, 1971, p. 8.

asked to use a special pencil for marking their answers. This is in order to make signals that can be read by the computer and matched with the information it has previously been given.

Memory is the distinguishing characteristic of the computer. Its memory consists of an intricate network of magnetic cores, which are tiny pinhead-sized pieces of magnetic material strung on vertical and horizontal wires (Figure 18–4). The cores accept and maintain an electrical charge in one direction or the other, depending on whether the message in the binary code is yes or no. Each core is always ready to tell its message instantly.

FIGURE 18–4

Magnetic Core Storage

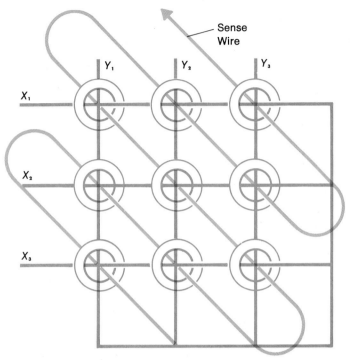

Source: International Business Machines Corporation, *More About Computers,* 1971, pp. 12–13.

Arithmetic for computers consists of adding, subtracting, multiplying, dividing, and comparing. These operations can be performed in combination or in sequence.

Control consists of instructions which are stored in the memory and can be brought forward when needed to tell the computer the next step to take. The instructions are in the same binary code as the rest of the information.

Output is the way in which the computer's storehouse of information becomes usable by men or by other machines. Sometimes the output is transmitted to an electric typewriter which "prints out" the information. Some high-speed computer printers can print 1,200 lines per minute. The printout may be in the form of accounts, financial statements, bills, invoices, checks, or even drawings and sketches.

Some computers write their messages on a small TV screen or cathode ray tube. You may have seen such screens in banks or airports, where the information doesn't have to be put on paper. Computer out-

Thomas J. Watson, Jr.

Courtesy Fabian Bachrach.

As chief executive of International Business Machines Corporation from 1956 until 1971, Thomas J. Watson, Jr. transformed the unwieldy monolith built by his father into perhaps the most efficient and responsive manufacturing and marketing operation in business history. Under his command, IBM became the world leader in the computer industry.

Thomas John Watson, Jr., was born in Dayton, Ohio, on January 8, 1914. His father, formerly vice president and sales manager of the National Cash Register Company, lost his job about the time young Thomas was born. He moved the family to New York to assume the presidency of the Computing-Tabulating-Recording Company. The company grew, and in 1924 its name was changed to International Business Machines Corporation.

Tom Watson, Jr. attended private schools in Short Hills, New Jersey and the Hun Preparatory School in Princeton. After being refused admittance to Princeton he entered Brown University, where he majored in geology and spent much of his time flying airplanes. Upon graduation in 1937 he went to work reluctantly for IBM as a salesman in New York's Wall Street area.

During World War II, Watson was a pilot, and logged 2,000 hours flying high-ranking officers around the Pacific. He was discharged as a lieutenant colonel and returned to IBM, where he was named assistant to the vice president in charge of sales. In June of 1946 he became a vice president, and in October a member

put need not be in readable form, however; the computer may be connected to switches that activate machines of various kinds. If the message of the computer is that the basement is filling with water, the output may take the form of throwing a switch to start the basement pumps.

While the total operation of a computer may make it seem a superhuman marvel, it is the product of a sequence of simple operations. Taken in its essentials, even the most complex activity is seen to be composed of a string of yes's and no's. (For some examples of computer arithmetic, see Figure 18–5.)

of the board of directors. Three years later, he was appointed executive vice president. In January 1952 he became IBM's president, his father moving to chairman of the board. In 1956 the younger Watson took over as chief executive officer. He became board chairman in 1961.

Watson took over a company that his father had built up from a tiny tabulating-equipment manufacturer to a corporation ranking eighth in sales in 1973 among U.S. manufacturers. But it was only at the beginning of a second great expansion, during which it was to be in the vanguard of the worldwide computer revolution. Watson began by reorganizing the company's management structure. He also launched a tremendous investment program in the field of electronics. IBM had been beaten to the draw by Remington Rand, which brought out the first commercially successful electronic computer—UNIVAC—in 1951. During the 1960s, IBM spent over 5 percent of its gross income on research and development, and this bore fruit in the mid-1960s with the introduction of the 360 computer, and again in 1970 with the 370 computer. These computers were a significant advance over existing computers, and gave IBM undisputed leadership in the industry.

Watson attributes IBM's success with computers to the large field force of salesmen and repairmen that it had developed in earlier years. They knew how to put the computers to work solving bookkeeping problems. IBM also had the financial resources to support a big research program.

The company's sales have expanded more than 20 times since Watson assumed the presidency in 1952. Revenues rose from $412 million in 1952 to nearly $11 billion in 1973. Since 1960, earnings per share have risen from $1.55 to $10.79 in 1973 (after a number of stock splits). IBM not only sells computers but has been very successful in electric typewriters and dictation machines, and has done well with photographic copiers.

Perhaps because of its remarkable expansion, IBM has become well known for its no-layoff policy. Watson has said that one of a manager's most difficult decisions is to fire people; this can be avoided, he holds, if the correct policies are followed in hiring, training, and promoting employees.

Watson retired as board chairman and chief executive officer in 1971, but remained as chairman of the executive committee. His retirement seemed to represent the end of an era for IBM. The company recently found itself involved in several large legal actions. Telex, one of IBM's competitors, was successful in obtaining a legal claim of over $350 million, although the case was appealed and the judgement decreased. A serious threat arose from a federal antitrust action that might possibly lead to a breakup of IBM into a number of smaller corporations. This seems rather unlikely, however, and most observers expected IBM to remain one of the giants of American industry.

COMPUTER HARDWARE AND SOFTWARE

When we hear the word "hardware" we usually think of electrical fixtures or garden tools. But during the early computer years, the term hardware came to be applied to the machinery of computers. By a simple extension, the term "software" was adopted for the ideas, systems, and methods required to run the hardware.

Types of Hardware

The hardware of any computer system can be divided into two categories. The first is the Central Processing Unit, or CPU. The second

FIGURE 18–5

Primer in Binary

The memory and arithmetic elements of an electronic digital computer are made so that they are either on or off, lit or unlit, closed or open, or magnetized clockwise or counter-clockwise. In a sense, these *bi-stable* elements have only two fingers on which to do their counting. The two-valued way of counting is called the *binary* or *base-of-two* system, in contrast to the *decimal* or *base-of-ten* system we usually use. The number base used in arithmetic is arbitrary and always has been chosen for convenience. The ancient Babylonians used a sexagesimal, or base-of-sixty scheme, that is carried over to our clocks and angle measurements. Some mathematicians advocate that we shift to the somewhat more convenient duodecimal (base-of-twelve) system.

A computer therefore counts in the following manner:

Binary Number	Computer Memory*	Decimal Number
0000	o o o o	0
0001	o o o x	1
0010	o o x o	2
0011	o o x x	3
0100	o x o o	4
0101	o x o x	5
0110	o x x o	6
0111	o x x x	7
1000	x o o o	8
1001	x o o x	9
1010	x o x o	10
1011	x o x x	11
1100	x x o o	12
1101	x x o x	13
1110	x x x o	14

* o = open relay; x = closed relay.

The binary system has blocks, or positions, arranged from right to left, worth 1, 2, and powers of 2 (such as 4, which is 2×2; 8, which is $2 \times 2 \times 2$; etc.). To build the number 3 from binary blocks requires one 1-block, and one 2-block, so it is written 11. To build binary 13 requires one 8 block, one 4 block, no 2-blocks, and one 1-block—written as 1101. The number 49 needs one 32, one 16, no 8, no 4, no 2, and one 1—written as 110001. In the yes-no language of electronic computers, when the binary system writes 100 as 1100100, it is really saying: "A block of 64, yes; a block of 32, yes; a block of 16, no; a block of 8, no; a block of 4, yes; a block of 2, no; a unit, no."

Addition in binary is simple. There are four basic rules:

$$0 + 0 = 0$$
$$0 + 1 = 1$$
$$1 + 0 = 1$$
$$1 + 1 = 0 \text{ plus a carry of 1.}$$

When we add columns that generate a carry, we consider the carry a 1, and add it to the next column to the left, as we do with carries in decimal addition. Carries are indicated by the letter "c." A long column may generate more than one carry, in which case all of them are added to the next column.

So,

```
cccc
 1101    or     13
+1011          +11
11000           24
```

or:

```
  c  c               1
ccccc
10111    or     23
+10011         +19
+11010         +26
1000100         68
```

Multiplication is hardly more difficult.

FIGURE 18–5 (Continued)

The whole binary multiplication table can be reduced to one rule: "One times one is one; any other product is zero." So,

$$\begin{array}{cc}
101 & \text{or} \\
\times\ 11 & \\
\hline
101 & \\
101 & \\
\hline
1111 &
\end{array}
\qquad
\begin{array}{c}
5 \\
\times\ 3 \\
\hline
15
\end{array}$$

Binary notation uses a "binary point" corresponding to the "decimal point" in decimal notation. Position values to the right of the binary point are successively halves, quarters, eighths, and so on. So the binary notation for the value "three and five-eighths" is 11.101.

The binary equivalent of any decimal number may be found by subtracting powers of 2 in the following fashion:

To find the binary equivalent of decimal 77, we say:

$77 - 2^6 = 77 - 64$ with a remainder of 13
$13 - 2^3 = 13 - 8$ with a remainder of 5

$5 - 2^2 = 5 - 4$ with a remainder of 1
$1 - 2^0 = 1 - 1$ with 0 remainder.

Thus, $77 = 1 \times 2^6 + 0 \times 2^5 + 0 \times 2^4 + 1 \times 2^3 + 1 \times 2^2 + 0 \times 2^1 + 1 \times 2^0 = 1001101$.

Problem 1

The binary number 101 actually is $1 \times 2^2 + 0 \times 2^1 + 1 \times 2^0 = 5$. What, then, is the decimal equivalent of 101.1?

Answer:
     5.5

Problem 2

How can the decimal number 6.375 be expressed in binary? Build the decimal up from *negative* powers of 2.

Answer:
     110.011;
     i.e., $6.375 = 1 \times 2^2 + 1 \times 2^1 + 0 \times 2^0 + 0 \times 2^{-1} + 1 \times 2^{-2} + 1 \times 2^{-3}$.

Source: William R. Corliss, *Computers*, Washington, D.C., U.S. Atomic Energy Commission, 1967, pp. 14–15, 53.

category contains all supporting devices of the Central Processing Unit.

The CPU controls the sequence and pacing of all operations. It receives information from its input units, shuttles that information into its memory unit, recalls and regroups the information in its arithmetic units, and sends appropriate signals to the output unit which translates the results for human comprehension. The Central Processing Unit is like a busy and efficient executive, giving orders, requesting services, and combining results. And, like that busy executive, the CPU must have its support services.

A basic installation will contain the following types of hardware: (1) the Central Processing Unit, (2) the Instruction Center, where the operator sits and gives instructions to the CPU, (3) the Card Reader, which scans and electronically "reads" the information on standard computer cards, (4) the Card Punch, which can punch and verify a hundred computer cards per minute, (5) the Storage Units,

FIGURE 18–6

Sample Computer Facility

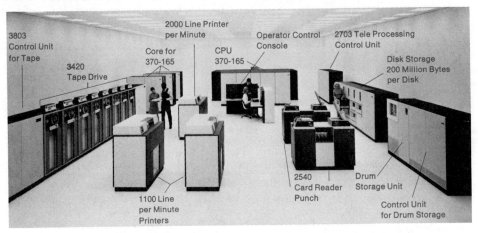

which may be magnetic tapes or disc units, and (6) a High Speed Printer, that prints up to 1,200 lines per minute. A typical computing system is shown in Figure 18–6.

New kinds of hardware are continually being developed which add to the jobs the computer can accomplish at the push of a button. Optical scanners can read printed matter and translate it for computer understanding. Data transmission equipment makes computer service available to anyone with a telephone. High-performance data storage and retrieval units are capable of automatic storage and recall of data. A sample of the computer hardware required by one firm is shown in Figure 18–6. The equipment in this illustration cost about $75,000–$125,000 a month to lease in 1974.

The cost of computers is high by any standard. Refinements are lowering the relative costs, but computer hardware for business purposes is still too expensive for many companies to buy or lease. However, as we will see below, companies can buy time on computers owned by others at a reasonable cost. The cost is high because manufacturing is intricate and highly specialized, requiring an environment free of dirt and moisture. Even after installation, most computer systems need pampering. Temperature, humidity, and power must be watched carefully to ensure efficient operation. Skilled people must be hired to program, operate, and repair the equipment.

Nevertheless, the cost and performance of computer hardware have improved at an accelerating rate. Figure 18–7 shows that in 20 years the speed of computers has increased between 10,000 and 100,000 times, while storage cost have fallen by a similar proportion.

FIGURE 18–7

Developments in Computer Technology

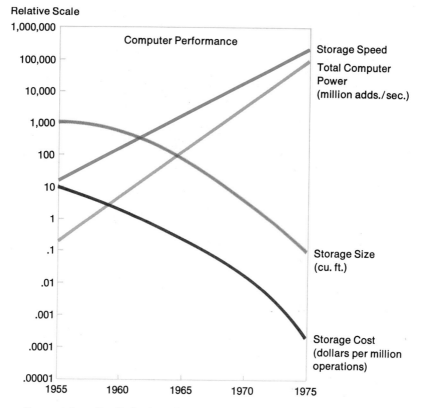

Relative Scale

Source: *Information Technology*, New York: The Conference Board 1972, p. 188.

Software

Hardware is costly, but software—data gathering and designing programs for proper computer inputs so that the computer will know what to do—is even more so. Whenever we want a computer to learn to do something new, we must first have it programmed by the software experts. Some computer hardware can be bought with ready-made answers built in, but not the big machines that are used for business purposes. It is comforting to realize that human imagination and direction are still needed. This is true in every field. Figure 18–8 diagrams the way hardware and software fit together. It shows how human language and logic must be translated into machine language and machine logic so that the computer will be able to process the data in the desired way.

FIGURE 18–8

Relationship of Hardware and Software

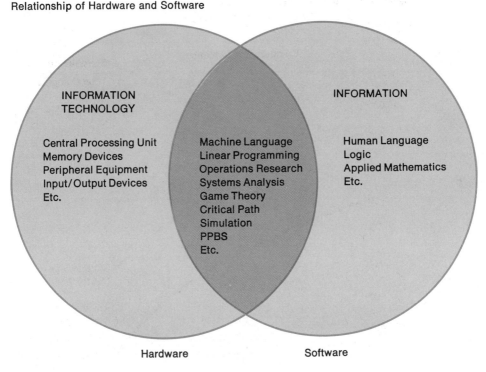

INFORMATION TECHNOLOGY		INFORMATION
Central Processing Unit	Machine Language	Human Language
Memory Devices	Linear Programming	Logic
Peripheral Equipment	Operations Research	Applied Mathematics
Input/Output Devices	Systems Analysis	Etc.
Etc.	Game Theory	
	Critical Path	
	Simulation	
	PPBS	
	Etc.	

Hardware   Software

COMMUNICATING WITH THE COMPUTER

One of the new jobs produced by the computer revolution is that of programmer. You may have seen advertisements for programmers in the help-wanted columns of your newspaper. A programmer is a person who is trained to tell the computer what to do. He or she (1) defines the problem that needs to be solved, (2) outlines each logical step required to reach a solution, and (3) writes down these steps in a language that the computer will be able to use. This is called the program.

Different computers speak different languages. A computer language is a collection of numbers (or computer words) that the computer is adjusted to understand. For instance, an IBM 1620 computer would know exactly what to do if given the following instruction: 21 02005 11509. It would know that 21 means "add." It would recognize that it was to take whatever amount was stored at memory location 02005 and add it to the number found at computer location 11509. The IBM 1620 would also know (because of the order of the words in the instruction) that the sum of the two numbers should be stored at memory location 02005.

If, however, the computer were set to communicate in COBOL (Common Business Oriented Language), the programmer would insert the word ADD instead of the computer word 21. If the language in use were FORTRAN (Formula Translation), a + would be understood as meaning add.

The multiplicity of languages is a result of the varying uses of the computer. IBM's PLI (Programming Language I) attempts to bridge the gap between scientific and business languages. More recently, APL (Applied Programming Language), a third-generation computer language, has begun to gain wide popularity; it is easier for the non-expert to learn and use because of its similarity to regular language. This simplicity, however, means that more of the computer's capacity is utilized for instructions that tell it what to do. A comparison of how the same operation is expressed in FORTRAN and in APL is shown in Figure 18–9.

Once we have found the proper language, there are several media through which we may talk to the computer.

Punched cards are the most familiar medium of communication with the computer. The card is called the Hollerith card after its inventor, Dr. Herman Hollerith, who developed it to tabulate census statistics in 1890. The card is 7⅜ inches by 3¼ inches and is made of moisture-resistant paper. Printed on it are 80 vertical columns and 12 horizontal rows. Holes are punched in the card here and there to represent numbers or letters. When the computer scans the card, the existence or absence of a hole at a certain place indicates a binary one or zero for that position.

Punched paper tape operates on the same principle as the punched card. Occasionally a loop tape is used if the same instruction is to be repeated continuously.

Magnetic tape is the most widely used medium for recording data. The tiny electronic charges deposited on magnetic tape can be read in significant combinations by a computer as fast as 300,000 characters per second. One reel contains as much information as 250,000 punched cards. Magnetic tape is economical, since old data can be erased and the tape used again.

Magnetic discs and *magnetic drums* use the same storage principle as magnetic tape, but permit somewhat faster retrieval of information.

An employee may carry on a conversation with a computer by typing in questions and reading out answers on a video screen. In some com-

FIGURE 18–9
Comparison of FORTRAN and APL

Computing the Average of a Set of Numbers

FORTRAN	APL

```
        FORTRAN                             APL
   DIMENSION X (100)                   (+/X) ÷ σX□
   READ (5,10) N, (X(I),I=1,N)
10 FORMAT (15/(F10.0))
   S=0.0
   DO 15 I=1,N
15 S=S+X(I)
   A=S/N
   WRITE (6,20)A
20 FORMAT (E15.2)
   END
```

Sorting a Set of Numbers

```
         FORTRAN                            APL
   DIMENSION X (100), Y(100)           X[ΔX□]
   READ (5,10) N, (X(I),I=1,N)
10 FORMAT (15/(F10.2))
   DO 20 I=1,N
   A=X(I)
   L=1
   DO 15 J=1,N
   IF (A-X(J)) 15,15,12
12 A=X(J)
   L=J
15 CONTINUE
   Y (I)=A
20 X (L)=100000.
   WRITE (6,30) (Y(I),I=1,N)
30 FORMAT (E15.2)
   END
```

puter applications, the computer will "interview" its user. The words on the screen say, "What is the name of the client?" The employee types in "John Doe Construction Co." The computer records this information in the right place and then responds, "Thank you. What is the client's address?" The "thank you's" and other responses sometimes make the computer seem more human than it is. In reality, computers are just robots that see, say, and do only what they are told.

APPLICATIONS OF COMPUTERS IN BUSINESS

The ways in which computers may be utilized are limited only by the imagination of their employers. They are like handymen who stand ready to carry out any task assigned to them.

Routine Procedures

Because of its speed in performing arithmetical calculations, we have suggested that the computer may be considered a kind of chief clerk. It can be put in charge of making out payrolls, keeping track of inventories, or billing customers. The computer has to be carefully supervised, however, because it will make the same mistake over and over unless it is given the correct instructions.

One of the first and most successful applications of the computer system has been in payroll accounting. Even companies with only a few employees find it quicker and more efficient to have a computerized payroll. It is economical because the payroll process involves so much more than just writing a check. Multiple deductions must be made for each employee, some of them in percentages and some of them in flat rates. Employees have come to expect that a statement of each deduction and the accumulated amounts of each type of deduction for the year will be provided on the vouchers of their paychecks. A computer can supply these easily, while a clerk would require many hours just to add up the various items. The computer can also store and update an employee's personnel file, catalog his promotions and job transfers, and even keep track of the times he has clocked in late.

Information Storage

Only a few years ago, sales data or shipment records in most firms took a long time to compile. Reports were usually made at the end of each month, and were about two weeks behind. Now, with the aid of computers, reports can be generated much faster than before, and can include the results of the previous workday.

Solutions to Problems

When there are several ways of solving a problem, the computer can render valuable aid by analyzing each approach and identifying the one that leads to the best results. The computer is much faster at this than humans are, and therefore it can get results that are beyond the scope of an individual working alone. For example, large contractors use the computer in preparing bids on major construction projects. The computers can weigh the relative costs of different types of building materials and different sources of supply, and estimate the cheapest way of building the project. All that's necessary is to provide the basic formula and the necessary data; the computer will then make the proper decision.

Sometimes management may ask the computer to help it decide a matter without rendering a final decision. From the infinite number of possible solutions to a problem, the computer may select three of the best approaches. At this point, management's judgment will be required. One solution may be less expensive than the others, but the businessman knows that it would not be as desirable from the standpoint of employee morale. He knows this because he is able to evaluate intangible or unquantifiable factors, and the computer cannot.

The importance of the human element can be seen in the forecasting of business conditions. Few companies will rely upon statistical forecasts alone, even when they are made with elaborate techniques employing a computer. For major decisions, the judgment of a wise, experienced executive is usually added to the recommendation derived from the computer.

Accounting and Billing

The computer can figure the most complicated bill with ease. It can also subtract payments and allowances, address the envelope, and send reminders when payments lag.

Besides sending the bill, the computer can also name the item sold and dispatch this information to the warehouse. In some retail stores, the cash register tape is the first step in a unified computer-controlled system. The cash register tape is fed into a memory input, which not only records the amount of the sale and the tax collected, but keeps track of inventory and sends orders for replacements. The information may also be broken down by type of product for the purpose of analyzing shopper trends or measuring the relative effectiveness of various forms of advertising.

Automation of Production

Computers have also been displacing skilled operators in production. They have learned to control complex industrial processes, and even to run machine tools. Figure 18–10 shows how a computer can be made to take directions from a blueprint and transform them into instructions that are then fed to machine tools by means of punched cards or magnetic tape.

FIGURE 18–10

Overall Programming System and Information Flow for a Numerical Control Program for Machine Tools

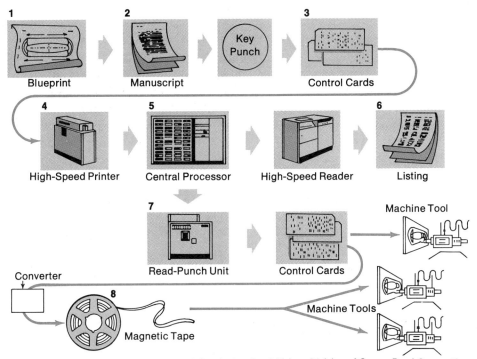

Courtesy Dr. Gastone Chingari, Remington Rand Univac Division of Sperry Rand Corporation.

Other Computer Applications

We mentioned at the start of this chapter how a person can reserve a seat on an airplane, a bed in a motel, or a seat at a baseball game by dialing a telephone number, receiving a report of what is available, making a selection, and providing the operator with your credit card number. This is only the forerunner of the worldwide information services that are sure to come.

Computers are already making it more and more difficult for anyone to drop from sight. They will sooner or later be able to provide a complete dossier on everybody, from his social security number to his past addresses, successes, and failures. Some people fear that the computer will lead to the extinction of our freedoms. Others reply that computers do nothing of themselves; they only make it easier for humans to do the good or evil that is in them.

KEEPING THE COMPUTER AT WORK

A company can make use of computers without actually purchasing one. Only a fairly large organization can afford to have its own data processing center.

Because of the need to get 24 hours of use out of every computer day, it has become the practice to sell computer services by the hour. Some data processing services do jobs for many different businesses on regular schedules, charging in proportion to the time consumed. Other companies that own their machines find they can handle their work during regular business hours, and lease out the machines in the remaining hours. These "timesharing" operations help to pay for the expensive equipment.

One way of economizing on computer time is to save up material until a sizable amount has accumulated and then process it in one batch. This is called "batch processing." A drawback of the batch method is that some of the material may be obsolete by the time it is processed.

The alternative to batch processing is "real-time" processing. With this method, data on things that happen are fed into the computer as they occur, and the results are instantly available for use. Real-time processing requires that the computer be set up in such a way that it can handle different kinds of inputs as they come.

THE LIMITATIONS OF COMPUTERS

Computers make excellent employees. They do not go out on strike, show up drunk, or ask for higher wages. Unfortunately, they also have their bad qualities. While a computer does not catch colds or suffer from Monday morning hangovers, it does break down occasionally. It also becomes obsolescent; there is always a newer, more efficient model coming out that just happens to be more expensive than the old even though it processes more data much faster. Then, too, the computer seldom lives up to all the expectations that the company had when it placed the order.

This is partly because many businessmen fail to define or even understand clearly what they want the computer to do. The computer is not a magic genie that makes all problems disappear. The glamour of computers adds to the problem—especially with businessmen who don't uninformed, there are many executives who simply refuse to acquaint themselves with the practical problems of using computers in their businesses.

Computer experts may contribute to the problem by overselling their wares. The systems engineer often knows very little about the problems faced by managers. Simplistic assumptions about these matters will only serve to reinforce the negative attitudes that some managers have about the new-fangled contraption.

Finally, every businessman should be clear about the difference between information problems and business problems. Hitching a computer to his inventories or his accounts receivable will not help move outdated products from his shelves or enable him to collect money from customers who can't pay.

SUMMARY

The rapid growth of the information-handling industries has had a revolutionary effect on modern business. Many operations that once required dozens of clerks are now performed in a few minutes by an electronic computer.

The computers used in business work with the binary code, a number system consisting of two digits, 0 and 1. One may think of the computer as a machine that operates by saying yes or no to everything. By means of its yes-or-no answers it can record any combination of numbers and letters. It can memorize information and instructions, make rapid calculations, and print out the answers faster than a person can read.

A computer programmer is a person who tells the computer what to do. The programmer studies the problem that needs to be solved, outlines it in a series of logical steps, and translates the outline into the computer's language.

The practical uses of computers in business are never-ending. They can calculate payrolls, keep track of inventories, or bill customers. They can store vast quantities of information and make it instantly available. They can help management make difficult decisions. Because of their high cost, computers must be kept busy. A small company may share part of a computer's time with other companies.

It is important to understand both the advantages and limitations of computers. They are useful machines that do a great deal of work, but they cannot solve all of a businessman's problems.

KEY TERMS AND CONCEPTS FOR REVIEW

Digital computers	Hardware
Binary code	Software
Input	CPU
Memory	Programmer
Arithmetic	Computer languages
Control	Timesharing
Output	Batch processing
Sequence of simple operations	Real-time processing

QUESTIONS FOR ANALYSIS AND DISCUSSION

1. What have computers contributed to the sophistication of business practices? Are the revolutionary changes attributable to computers actually necessary? Why? Why not?

2. How can a computer system based on a simple binary code solve complex problems? Can you explain how the code works? How is the number 9 written in binary code?

3. What are the five basic operations which enable a computer to process information? How are they interrelated?

4. How is the hardware of a system interrelated? What analogy can you draw to the hardware system (for example, the human body)? Why would you select such a representation?

5. How large must a corporation be before the use of a computer system can be justified? What can be done to make such systems available to more firms?

6. How is information "fed into" a computer? What are some of the factors which determine which device should be used?

7. What is the difference between "hardware" and "software"?

8. Why are the costs of computers so high? What do you project as the future costs of computer time?

9. Why have computers "grown hardier with each passing generation"? What effect does this have on maintenance and related costs?

10. What types of situations cannot be handled by a computer?

SUGGESTED READINGS

Arnold, Robert R. *Modern Data Processing.* New York: John Wiley & Sons, Inc., 1969.

Crowley, Thomas H. *Understanding Computers.* New York: McGraw-Hill Book Company, 1967.

Halacy, D. S. *Computers, The Machines We Think With* (2d ed.). New York: Harper & Row, 1969.

Kemeny, John C. *Man and the Computer.* New York: Charles Scribner & Sons, 1972.

Murphy, John S. *Basics of Digital Computers.* New York: Hayden Book Company, 1970.

Nikolaeff, George A. *Computers and Faculty.* New York: Wilson, 1970.

Woolridge, Susan, and Keith Louden *The Computer Survival Handbook.* Boston: Gambit, 1973.

Vazsonyi, Andrew *Introduction to Electronic Data Processing.* Homewood, Ill.: Richard D. Irwin, Inc., 1973.

part four

Managing a Business

Disney's Magic of Management

While almost all organizations have planning divisions or at least someone designated as planner, Walt Disney Productions has its own planning company. WED Enterprises, Inc. was started by Walt as a family-owned business which could experiment without having to explain every little thing to a bunch of skeptical stockholders.

During its history, WED has developed some important products. But its primary product is one that is intangible and often overlooked by management. This product is planning. In its atmosphere of creative freedom, the WED staff has brainstormed and picked clean the master plans for Walt Disney World and for other projects which may never occur. The idea of planning, to which so many companies have given lip service, has been made a reality by the management of Walt Disney Productions.

A major element in the planning machinery of Disney operations is control. Planning is as perfect as Cinderella's castle; nothing is left to chance. The company didn't just launch into the construction of Walt Disney World and hope for success. It negotiated a contract with the unions that made strikes unnecessary—an almost complete guarantee of continued work. Rather than take legal hurdles as they came, the obstacles were removed ahead of time through

© *Walt Disney Productions.*

meticulous planning. Even Florida state legislators fell into line with the orderly phasing of the master plan. At times it seemed that the weather had been planned so that rain fell only at prearranged times.

Disney World will always be a great place for the kids. Along with the opportunity for family togetherness, there is another appeal for the moms and dads: they have to marvel at a city that is so clean . . . so well-run . . . where everything *works.* The father coming fresh from morale troubles at the office cannot help but notice the attitudes of the hosts and hostesses in the magic kingdom. He will realize that such courtesy and helpfulness does not just happen—it is managed. It is carefully developed in the University of Walt Disney World, where there is a training course for every policeman, waitress, or Mickey Mouse to be employed. Skillful management is always obvious, especially in the hard-to-handle behavior of personnel.

Mothers will know that something must be happening in this magic place that keeps it so immaculately clean. Obviously, someone is moving mountains of trash, but the hidden operation is never seen by the visitors. Solid wastes are collected through an underground vacuum system designed into Disney World while it was on the drawing boards. It is out of sight, and very efficient.

Managerial support for planners is a tradition that Walt Disney built into the company from the first. Walt and his brother Roy made sure that whatever they did was planned, perfected, and absolutely controlled. They even went one step further and planned for the continuation of this attitude toward planning. When Walt died in 1966 the heirs to the throne had already been selected and groomed and indoctrinated with the Disney philosophy.

After Walt's death, the company was run by Roy Disney and the two crown princes: Donn Tatum and Card Walker. Roy Disney died in December 1971, and the management of Walt Disney Productions never missed a beat. Today the corporation is in the hands of Tatum, Walker, and two junior members of the executive committee. The control principle continues, and the two junior members—Ronald Miller (Walt's son-in-law) and Roy E. Disney (Roy's son)—are helping to run things the Disney way.

The overwhelming initial successes of Walt Disney World are certain to provide the corporation with many chances for diversification. Opportunities are great both at home and abroad. Many foreign countries are eager for a touch of the Disney wand upon their economies. But no glittering prospect or burst of entrepreneureal excitement is going to rush Walt Disney Productions into anything. The next big Disney coup, whether in real estate, urban services, or some totally unexpected field, will have been planned to the final detail by the people at WED Enterprises. The plan will be carefully executed and completely controlled, to the pleasure of the consumer and the financial reward of its authors.

19

Managers: Catalysts for Business Success

The quality and vigor of managers are the most important ingredients for the success of any enterprise. This is true not only in business but in government, charitable associations, churches, universities, or any other kind of organization. It is especially true for those at the top who lead an organization. But it is also true of managers at all levels, down to the first-line supervisor or foreman.

The business magazine *Forbes*, which has studied American companies for many years, has found that they succeed almost invariably to the extent that they are well managed. The Bank of America said in 1973 in its publication *Small Business Reporter*, "In the final analysis more than 90 percent of business failures are due to managerial incompetence and inexperience." Economists who have analyzed the billions of dollars of aid given to underdeveloped and developing countries after World War II have found that dollars were effective only in those nations where the programs were reasonably well managed.

Poor management is at the bottom of most business failures. The following newspaper account from the *Los Angeles Times* of July 5, 1973, is not unusual:

Royal Inns started out as a one-man hotel company under Earl Gagoisian in 1965, then put on a spectacular spurt of growth through 1971 when it earned $1.1

million on revenues of $30 million from 54 Royal Inn hotels, 46 restaurants, and 39 cocktail lounges.

The 1972 report shows a loss of $1.9 million. Losses have continued. For the latest quarter the company lost $1.2 million on revenues of $12.1 million.

What went wrong?

Basically, the company grew too fast and burst into a big league where it wasn't equipped to compete. It was a one-man operation. When it outgrew that, it could not make the transition to a larger administrative structure. As the hotels got bigger and their staffs got larger, they were in competition with other big chains. In that league the physical product was competitive but the organization was not.

Henke [the new president who succeeded the founder] blamed inadequate supervision in a business that requires "direct management supervision on a day-to-day basis" to control costs, service, and product quality.

MANAGERS EXIST IN ALL ORGANIZED GROUPS

Any organized group, even the smallest, must have a manager. Other than those small one-man businesses or partnerships where the owners do everything and have no employees, a business would be a group of people only accidentally working well together if there were no managers. We can hardly imagine a collection of salesmen, accountants, or factory workers making a successful business operation without someone in charge of departments and units. This is true whether a business is small or large. We can, therefore, define a manager as someone who is responsible for the performance of one or more persons reporting to him. As a business grows and has more people than the owner or chief executive can effectively manage, the problem will be solved by naming a second layer of managers. As the business continues to grow, a third layer of managers will be introduced who report to the second layer. In very large companies, there may be 10 or 12 levels of managers between the president and the workers on the factory floor.

Managers Are Found Everywhere

This, of course, does not only exist in business. Managers and levels of managers are found in large numbers in government agencies, hospitals, churches, and universities, and every other kind of human organization. As a matter of fact, we can hardly speak of any kind of operation being organized without the grouping of people under managers. Whether they are presidents, vice presidents, division general managers, department directors, superintendents, supervisors, or foremen, they are all managers. Likewise in universities and colleges we see presidents, chancellors, vice presidents, deans, and department chairmen. And in some church groups we see presiding bishops, bishops, district superintendents, pastors, and directors of music or religious education.

How Many Managers Are There?

We do not have an accurate count of all the managers in businesses and other organizations in the United States. The Census Bureau reports nearly 9 million "managers, officials, and proprietors," but this figure doesn't include foremen, of whom there are many, or military managers such as commissioned officers and noncommissioned sergeants. Nor does it include the multitude of unpaid volunteer managers in social organizations such as parent-teacher associations, scouting, political clubs, and similar groups. There are also many proprietors of one-man businesses (including farmers), and coequal partners who do not have employees and are, therefore, not counted by the Census. A reasonable estimate of the number of managers of all kinds, in all types of social organizations, would certainly exceed 12 million.

Approximately 71 million persons were employed in business in the U.S. in 1974, not counting the business operations of government. It is probable that about 8 million of those persons held managerial jobs.

WHAT IS A MANAGER'S JOB?

It is not enough to say that a manager's job is one where an individual is responsible for the work of a group of people or is one with people reporting to him. His job involves much more. He is responsible for designing and maintaining an environment in which individuals reporting to him can work together effectively in groups toward the accomplishment of desired goals. He must make things happen. This, of course, involves working with and for people and seeing that they have the resources and tools to accomplish their jobs.

Managers as Environment Creators

Too often managers are looked upon as individuals who sit in their offices and punch buttons, write letters, or boss people around. Or they are seen as amateur psychiatrists manipulating the lives, activities, and personalities of those reporting to them. A manager's primary job is to enable individuals and groups to accomplish the organization's goals with a minimum of wasted effort and with the personal satisfaction that comes from seeing tasks done well.

While some people have little or no interest in their jobs aside from their paychecks, most would like to accomplish something they regard as worthwhile. There is no greater source of pride for such people than a sense of accomplishment. It is up to managers to provide an environment that makes this possible.

Inherent in any managerial job is the existence of some degree of authority. While authority is literally the power to command or require people to act, the wisest manager regards it as the power to exercise discretion. In other words, he regards it as the right to use his judgment, within certain areas of an operation and subject to certain limitations, in a creative way to help those reporting to him do their jobs better and to gain satisfaction from them. This is not easy, but it is exactly why managing is so important and requires such exceptional talents.

No manager has unlimited power. Even the President of the United States is bound by the Constitution, the courts, Congress, voters, and the many social pressures existing in the country. No company president can issue orders that ignore the many restrictions imposed by the law, the wishes of stockholders and directors, various public pressures, and the feelings and attitudes of his employees. The first-line supervisor or foreman is limited by all of these and by many more—the company's policies, rules, procedures, and program requirements, as well as the extent of authority delegated to him by his superiors.

Elements in an Environment That Make for Performance

In designing an environment that will lead people to perform well, the effective manager must keep many things in mind. The following are of major importance:

1. The environment must provide *objectives or goals,* and plans that outline how they may be reached. The manager must see that these are clearly understood by the people involved. Everyone wants to work toward something, but no one can work toward a goal that isn't clear or follow a program of action that he doesn't understand. If we say, for example, that our goal is "fair profit" or "quality products" or "lowest costs," how much meaning will people attach to these words?

2. The environment should provide a *meaningful and understood structure of positions, or roles.* No one has a meaningful position or role unless it includes (a) a clear and verifiable goal or goals (that is, will he know, at some future date, whether he has accomplished it?); (b) an understanding of the end results areas for which he is responsible; (c) a definition of the discretion he can exercise; and (d) access to the information and tools he needs to do his job. It is obvious that a person's role or position involves far more than a box on an organization chart.

3. The environment should provide for the *removal of obstacles to performance,* to the extent that this is possible. A manager may be limited, of course, by obstacles such as rules or laws, or the lack of money, that are beyond his power to eliminate. Sometimes these problems may even be beyond the power of a manager's boss to whom he should appeal for help if he cannot eliminate them himself.

4. The environment should ideally *cause* people to do things in a desired way *because they want to do it that way;* sometimes it may lead them to do things in a certain way *because this is the way things get done;* and occasionally it directs them to do something *because they must.* It is surprising in how many well-managed companies people do things in certain ways because the situation encourages them to. Thus in the General Motors Corporation people are not told that they *must* seek the advice of certain staff specialists. They find out from experience that if they want their proposals approved by top management, they are more likely to succeed if they have the support of appropriate staff specialists. Also, sometimes things must be done because they must be. We may not want freedom, creativeness, or the right to "do our own thing" in every situation. "No Smoking" in a room with explosive gases may mean just that. A banker may not want a highly imaginative teller cashing checks. And and airline is not likely to want an innovative and experimental pilot at the controls.

5. The environment must recognize the importance of *human motivation*—the inner forces that make people "tick." This does not mean that the manager will try to be an amateur psychiatrist and manipulate people, but only that he will recognize that everyone has his own feelings, attitudes, and desires.

6. The environment should take into account the fact that *many people have considerable knowledge of problems and solutions in their areas of work,* as well as a desire to perform well. Experienced

managers are constantly amazed at how much people know, even at the bottom levels of a company. The environment should provide ways to tap these resources, not only to get needed answers to problems but also to take advantage of the satisfaction people get from being "in the act."

The Manager as a Catalyst

Most students are familiar with the process by which green plants turn water and carbon dioxide into food, known as photosynthesis. This chemical reaction takes place only in the presence of light. Without light, there is no reaction at all. The light acts as a catalyst—an agent that makes things happen. Up to a point, photosynthesis can be accelerated by adding more and more light. But if the catalyst becomes too strong, if there is too much light, the plant dies.

The analogy is obvious. A good manager is a catalyst. He is an agent that makes a business operate effectively. The results of a catalytic manager can be easily measured by the successful performance of his group. Poor management, on the other hand, is an anti-catalyst. In chemical language an anti-catalyst is an agent that paralyzes activity or slows it down. A manager with poor judgment, who doesn't know his job, or who is clumsy at human relations, can hinder the smooth operation of his department.

A manager often does not do many of the things for which he is responsible. His main objective is accomplishment through others. The head of Firestone may know how to make tires, but he can't do so and at the same time manage the company. A visitor to a large plant may receive the impression that the people in the front office are not really involved in the making and selling of products. Walking among the noise and excitement of assembly lines and conveyor belts, it would be easy for him to decide that the *real* work is happening on the factory floor. But on a closer look he will recognize the importance of the quiet, catalytic activities of the front office. The coordination of intricate programs and operations is a job that is fully appreciated only when something goes wrong. The catalytic manager moves calmly and methodically about the business of making the business itself move calmly and methodically.

THE GOAL OF ALL MANAGERS

The reader will recall that when we discussed profit in the first chapter we referred to it as "surplus." Profits are, of course, only the amount by which sales dollars exceed expense dollars. They arise only because a group of people, working together in business and following programs developed and fostered by managers, have turned out products or services that people want at a cost low enough to yield a surplus of dollars when they are sold.

As we saw in the first chapter, a surplus is logically and practically the goal of every manager, regardless of his position in a company and irrespective of whether he is in business or some other type of organization. But if he is to strive for a surplus, he must know as specifically and concretely as possible what his goals are and what it will cost to accomplish them. A manager must also do everything possible to assure that an environment will exist where people will be able to contribute, as effectively as they can, to the accomplishment of desired objectives.

There is really no other workable measure of how good a manager is or how good the group of people reporting to him is.

MANAGING: SCIENCE OR ART?

It is often asked whether managing can be made a science, in which everybody who follows the same rules can get precisely the same results, or whether it will always be an art. This is putting the question the wrong way. Of course managing is an art. But so are medicine, architecture, music composition, engineering, and baseball. All require practical skill. But a moment's thought will show that the practitioners of these arts will tend to do their jobs better, and be more successful, if they possess the basic knowledge underlying their art and know how to apply it to real life problems.

Thus science and art go hand in hand. Science is organized knowledge. Art is the application of knowledge to achieve a desired result in practice. The best engineering designers—those who can devise workable new products—are individuals who are well grounded in such underlying sciences as physics, electronics, or chemistry. The best businessman and manager is also likely to be one who knows the sciences pertaining to his job. When we are being operated on we want a surgeon with great knowledge as well as great skill. But few people think of their bosses in this way, even though an ignorant manager may create great havoc.

Knowledge alone does not assure that an individual will be a good practitioner. A person may know everything there is to know about music composition but be unable to compose a good piece of music. A genius in physics may not be able to design a piece of equipment. In the same way, a manager may know all there is to know about manage-

Harold S. Geneen

Harold S. Geneen has been called "the world's best manager." He had already made a name for himself as Raytheon's executive vice president when he took over as president of International Telephone and Telegraph Corporation in 1959.

Since that time, he has completely transformed ITT from a holding company operation involving mostly foreign business to a major conglomerate deriving more than half its business from within the North American continent. In effecting this change in the company's direction, and in achieving a succession of new records in sales and earnings, Geneen has been widely acclaimed for his dramatic and unique approach to the process of management.

He was born in Bournemouth, England, in 1910 and moved to New York when only a few months old. His father was a manager of concert performers. When he was 16, Geneen became a page on Wall Street while studying accounting at night. After receiving his degree he went to work for Lybrand Ross Brothers and Montgomery, where he was an accountant for eight years.

He left the accounting firm to work in a series of corporate finance positions at American Can Company, Bell and Howell, and Jones and McLaughlin Steel, moving steadily higher in responsibility.

The opportunity arose to join Raytheon Company as executive vice president in 1956, with a mandate from the company's president to develop some profit potential. He set out to tighten up the firm's finances, collect its old bills, arrange new bank credit sources, and spread profit con-

ment, yet be unable to manage effectively. The good practitioner needs not only to have knowledge, but also must know how to apply it.

THE IMPORTANCE OF KNOWLEDGE FOR EFFECTIVE MANAGING

Though knowledge is not enough in itself, any manager who thinks he can "fly by the seat of his pants" is courting failure. Probably in no area of human practice are the requirements of knowledge greater. At the same time, there are many fields of management in which the

sciousness within the company. Raytheon's earnings increased four-fold during his three years there.

In 1959 an executive recruiting service sought Geneen's services for the top job at ITT, and he resigned at Raytheon. ITT was already a giant, but was highly vulnerable to the uncertainties of international politics and economics. Geneen centralized its worldwide operations and also set up a corporate headquarters in Brussels for the company's European manufacturing activities, its major profitmaker at that time.

Building up a management system centered around communications and control, he laid down a tight reporting system covering both financial and operational aspects of all members of the ITT family. A network of management meetings was established as the nerve center for this reporting system. The byword at ITT is that Geneen wants "no surprises." The system was designed to ensure that problem situations would be reported and tracked from their inception onward to their solution.

Geneen's method of "management by review" or "management by meetings" is a way of achieving the total kind of in-depth communication and trust that control of his far-flung organization requires. A former employee estimates that travel and salary expenses for these "analysis and review sessions" run about $4 million per year. Although it seems cumbersome in operation, and makes heavy demands on every top executive's time, everyone agrees that this method is effective.

Geneen's other goal was to develop a management system in which all levels of management would participate in running the company, each individual making his maximum contribution to the company's success. While the organization has a clear and complex structure, Geneen tries to deemphasize structure and levels and to open up the communication channels.

His system is obviously quite demanding, and often irritating. Geneen has not been without his critics, including some former team members who dropped out along the way. But despite the 60-hour weeks expected of ITT managers, the constant availability demanded of them, the profusion of meetings and reporting requirements, and the strong personality of the executive himself, there is universal admiration and affection for him in the ranks. A favorite ITT joke runs: "Is the G in Geneen pronounced as in God or as in Jesus?"

ITT absorbed more than 70 companies in Geneen's first 10 years. Its activities include telecommunications, industrial and consumer products, services, natural resources, and space and defense. A settlement with the Department of Justice in an antitrust case in 1971 requires that ITT not take over any more U.S. companies with sales of $100 million or more.

In 1973, the firm set a new record of 528 million in earnings, before extraordinary items. That year Geneen was the nation's sixth highest paid executive, with salary and bonuses of $814,299. His goal of doubling profits every five years had been met and exceeded.

present state of knowledge is crude and inexact. In part this is because managing is an exceptionally complex task. When we consider that human beings all have different attitudes and desires, and come from varying backgrounds, we can see that managing them is not easy. When we consider that each manager of a department must gear his activities to those of other managers in the same company, and when we realize that every business must be responsive to a broad and complex external environment, the intricate nature of management is easy to see.

Our knowledge of management is crude and inexact for another reason: we have not done much research and development in the field. Even today, not much effort is going into management research. We do not have many inventions—such as budgeting or cost accounting— to help the manager do his job. It is estimated that perhaps 2½ percent of all expenditures in the United States go for all kinds of research, and that only 1½ percent of what is spent on research goes into research in the social sciences. Of the very small amount devoted to the social sciences, probably less than one twentieth is useful for management. Thus, not more than 2/1000 of one percent of all our expenditures for everything is at all useful for management.

But, as little as we do know, we are too seldom using, as well as we might, what we do know. Perhaps most managers are like the farmer who was criticized for not taking courses in agriculture to learn more about farming. He replied that he did not need to know more because he was not even using what he already knew.

THE KNOWLEDGE A MANAGER NEEDS

We can get a better idea of what a manager needs to know by pointing out what he must be. In his varied fields of everyday activity he must apply the insights of the historian, the psychologist, the sociologist, the logician, the futurologist, and the management scientist.

Learning from the Past

One of the ways a manager can increase his skill is by studying the experiences of successful managers as well as the reasons why some managers have failed. The effective manager will not merely study successes and failures on the basis of exactly what happened but rather by looking at the basic causes of what worked or did not work. Unfortunately, this idea that history repeats itself is a little too simple for complicated reality. What exactly worked or did not work in the past may not work or may not fail to work in the future.

Experience can be an expensive teacher in the field of management, and a foolish one as well. This is why we hear it said so often in business that "we want someone who doesn't know this can't be done." There is even danger in experience. One of the authors of this book once heard a vice president of a company urge an organizational change as a means of solving a problem the company faced. He used as his main argument that the company for which he formerly worked (which had been one of the largest and best managed companies in the industry) had once had the problem and solved it in the way he recommended. By chance, the author knew that the vice president's former company was then having the same problem again. But now, in the face of different circumstances, it was solving the problem in an entirely different way. The famous industrialist Alfred P. Sloan's best-selling book *My Years with General Motors* proved a disappointment to many small businessmen who had expected to get ideas from it on how to organize their much smaller operations. They failed to realize that what had worked for General Motors would probably not work for them.

The effective manager does not attempt to copy the experience of others but to distill useful conclusions from it. He does this so he won't have to rediscover the wheel or reinvent the typewriter. He learns from experience, but he applies his knowledge to the real situations he faces today and expects tomorrow.

Studying People

The effective manager also pays attention to the characteristics of people he deals with. He knows that people are people, and he also has an understanding of basic psychology—the science of relationships among people. He should not try to be an amateur psychiatrist, however. His job is to understand what motivates people, what they like and dislike, and how and why they respond to things he does as a manager.

He must try to combine what he knows about psychology with a commonsense understanding of human behavior. Managers who get the greatest benefit from psychology are those who listen carefully, sift realistically, and utilize their knowledge wisely. A manager must ever recognize that his job is to help people work together.

Understanding Group Behavior

The manager must also remember that people are members of groups. He must know that people who work or live together develop certain ways of feeling and behaving. Many of these ways of feeling and behaving are passed down from parents to children. Others are acquired from friends. For example, consider how you feel about going to school, or making money, or attending church, or getting married. Ask yourself why you feel as you do. The chances are that you got some of these feelings from your family or your friends, or from people with whom you have worked.

Many of the contributions of sociologists, social psychologists, and cultural anthropologists have been useful for the effective manager. The manager deals constantly with groups—the group of people who report to him, other groups within his company, groups of customers, groups of sellers, groups of government officials, and so on. And of course every person he meets is a member of many other groups, such as the Parent Teachers Association or the Friday Night Bowling Club, a family, a church, a neighborhood, a country. That is why the manager needs to know something about groups and how groups influence the behavior of people he works with.

Thinking Rationally

One of the major tasks of any manager is to make decisions—what to buy, what to sell, how much to charge, whom to hire, how much to pay people, what machine to use, how much to produce, how to raise money, what product to make, and a host of other things. Every manager is, therefore, a professional rationalist, not just an ordinary one. He gets much of his pay for making correct decisions.

To be rational or logical a manager must have a *clear goal* in mind. Unless he has a goal to achieve, how can there be a problem? Problems are sometimes looked upon as states of confusion, chaos, or uncertainty. However, if one's goal is confusion, chaos, and uncertainty (as it sometimes seems to be for some managers), how can we have a problem? Demands for rational thinking only arise when we want to achieve something we do not have—such as more profits, greater production, higher sales, or better product quality.

Given a goal, the professional rationalist looks at the different ways of accomplishing it—the *alternatives* in the situation. He weighs them in terms of the goal he is trying to reach, and selects the alternative that offers the most promise.

This is relatively easy to do when we have definite quantities to work with. For example, if we must choose among several different ways of making soup, and if each way costs a specific amount for each case of soup, then a choice may be easy. But in marketing the soup it may be much more difficult to decide which kind of TV program or "commercial" to use, since the results are not so easy to measure.

Putting things into mathematical form often helps us to clarify our thinking and to discover elements we had overlooked. With the aid of the computer we can even routinely solve many problems that we could have hardly tackled a few years ago. But the effective manager will never forget that mathematics, as well as the computer, is a tool and not a substitute for managing.

Thinking of the Future

A manager must always look ahead, and sometimes far ahead. Decisions made today may not produce their full effects until some years from now, when it will be too late to change them. Since business success depends on developing, producing, and selling products or services, and this can only be done over time, every manager must think of what the situation will be at some future date when the decision he makes today will bear fruit.

It is often said that the major task of a manager is to manage change. Certainly he must be able to meet change. But because it takes time to get ready to meet change, the most successful manager is one who can forecast changes. If a maker of women's clothing waits until he sees that styles have changed, he will be hard pressed to catch up with competitors who have anticipated the change and are ready with the new-style clothing for sale. This is even more important if he makes products that take longer to design and produce, such as television sets, automobiles, or airplanes. For example, the Magnavox company, long the most profitable of the television manufacturers (in terms of profits as a percentage of sales), lost markets and profits in the early 1970s when it delayed going completely into solid-state circuitry, which had greater reliability and customer appeal.

This means that the manager must rely heavily on forecasts of economic trends, technological advances, and coming changes in political and social patterns. In other words he must be a "futurologist." He must be concerned with the future and even live in it, since that is where his business will succeed or fail.

Working Scientifically

We might sum up our discussion of what the manager needs to know by saying that he has to use knowledge much as a scientist does. He is not a scientist in the sense of manipulating mathematical formulas and symbols or doing laboratory experiments. But he works in a scientific way to the extent that he collects knowledge and uses it to solve problems. Knowing is not enough. His most demanding and challenging task is to apply his knowledge to problems in a way that will achieve success.

THE DEMANDING NATURE OF THE MANAGERIAL JOB

It is easy to see that the job of the business manager, whether he is president of the company or only a first-line supervisor, is a highly demanding one. He must constantly be concerned with achieving the goals of his department and his company. He must think of those who buy the company's output, and of those from whom he purchases his supplies. He must be keenly aware of the governmental regulations and laws under which he operates. And while keeping an eye on what goes on inside the company, he must also peer constantly around him and into the future.

This isn't all. His most important single concern must be people—those who report to him and for whom he is responsible, those he must work with in other departments, and those to whom he reports. They are all individuals with their own personal goals that are not usually the same as those of the company or department. Joe Doakes does not usually live and die for old Paragon Steel, but for himself and his family.

Moreover, people need tools, machines, and materials to do their work. According to estimates made in 1973, the capital invested per employee in the United States ranged from about $8,000 in furniture manufacturing to more than $160,000 in oil refining—an average of about $35,000 for all manufacturing. Capital, of course, includes buildings as well as tools, machines, and materials. It is part of the manager's job to provide these things, in the right kinds and amounts.

People also need to know the goals they are trying to achieve, what their specific tasks are, how much discretion (or authority) they have, how their jobs relate to those of others, for what and to whom they are responsible, when and where they are to work, how much and how they get paid, what policy and procedure guidelines they must follow, how well they are performing, how to get obstacles to performance removed, and a multitude of other things if they are to work together effectively and efficiently.

It is no wonder that managers are among the highest-paid occupational groups in our society, second only to doctors and lawyers.

HOW DOES AN EXECUTIVE REALLY SPEND HIS TIME?

While it is clear what a manager must and should do to be effective, very little is really known about how a manager really spends his time and what he really does. Because of the importance of planning, one would think that an effective manager would carefully plan his time since time is the most universal of all limitations on human activities.

An interesting study was made of a sample of 52 executives some years ago.[1] While this study was of upper- and top-level executives who should have had considerable freedom to organize their activities, surprisingly enough they often failed to do so in the way they had intended. For example, a head of a company department could plan his day within the organization, but often had to meet a variety of demands on his time imposed without notice from his superiors. Also, many unexpected crises occurred which could not be foreseen and had to be dealt with, taking away time from other activities. Table 19–1 shows

TABLE 19–1

How an Executive Spends the Day

	Minutes per Day	Percent of Day
Handling mail—reading and dictating................	45	7.0
Telephone...	32	5.0
Reports—reading, writing, dictating...................	50	7.8
Making decisions.....................................	38	5.9
Conferences—committees............................	7	1.1
Conferences—staff and subordinates................	252	39.1
Conferences—customers and visitors................	48	7.4
Lunches—mostly with customers or staff............	69	10.7
Travel...	96	14.9
Public relations.......................................	3	.5
Miscellaneous..	4	.6
Total..	644	100.0

how the sample of executives used a typical day of 10 hours and 44 minutes.

These executives evidently used a large portion of their time meeting and talking with people, and a small portion of their time thinking and studying. However, one should bear in mind that: (1) the sample did not include evening hours when many executives do much of their planning and thinking; (2) much planning and other managerial work goes on during meetings and conferences; and (3) the typical executive does some of his thinking during the time he spends in travel.

The higher a person is in the ranks of management, the more time he is likely to spend in meetings. As a matter of fact, when John De

---

[1] Fred E. Case, "An Executive Day," *California Management Review*, vol. 5, no. 1 (Fall 1962), pp. 67–70.

Lorean, the six-feet-four General Motors superstar, surprisingly quit an executive vice-presidency paying him $550,000 in salary and bonuses at age 48 and took a Cadillac agency in Florida, one of the reasons he gave was that he had to spend too much of his time in meetings. The fact that his job paid so much in salary and bonuses did not compensate him for having too little time left over to be an automotive engineer or to enjoy sports and music.

COORDINATION: THE ESSENCE OF MANAGING

We have already seen that a manager has to coordinate the work of those for whom he is responsible. One might suppose that this is only one of the things a manager does. On closer examination, however, the coordination of people and what they do appears to be the essence of management. It is perhaps the closest thing to a synonym we can find for management.

What makes coordination so important is that individuals often perceive the goals of their group differently, and also tend to seek different ways of reaching these goals. A coordinator keeps everyone together, while at the same time drawing out individual strengths and ambitions. The combined result of a group's work should be a composite of the strengths and contributions of each member. It is the central task of the manager to reconcile differences in approach, timing, effort, or interest, and to harmonize company and individual goals.

The larger a business gets, the more important coordination becomes. And as a business grows and the efforts of dozens, or hundreds, or thousands of people must be made to fit together, coordination becomes crucial. The successful manager is truly the catalyst through which this coordination is made possible.

UNDERSTANDING THE MANAGER'S TASK

If the success of a business depends on the quality and skill of those who manage it, and if knowledge is important in becoming an effective manager, how can we best get an overview of this knowledge? We have seen that managing involves setting an environment that will encourage performance. This is an interesting concept but not too useful as a specific guide. How can we tie down more specifically what a manager does?

One way is to analyze the major functions of managers, the things managers typically do, and see what the major kinds of problems are and how they handle them. We shall do this in the chapters that follow, on planning, organizing, leading, and controlling. As we shall see, the task of *planning* is to design the foundation of management. The job of *organizing* is to establish a structure of roles for performance. The purpose of *leading* is to energize the organization in the same way that a battery energizes an automobile starter. The need for *controlling* is to enable the manager to make as sure as possible that his plans are succeeding.

In addition, managers must be keenly aware of labor unions and of their impact on the running of a business. Labor-management relations are sometimes a vital element in business management.

SUMMARY

Evidence over the years has shown that the quality and vigor of managers are the most important ingredients for the success of a business. This is also true for such nonbusiness organizations as government agencies, charitable associations, churches, and universities— indeed, for any kind of operation where people work together in groups to accomplish given objectives. Managers, therefore, can be found in all organized groups and at all levels in them.

We can define a manager as someone who is responsible for the performance of one or more persons reporting to him. But to understand what a manager is, we really must say more. He is responsible for designing and maintaining an environment in which individuals can work together effectively. His task is to act as a catalyst for the group and its operations. His primary job is to make it possible for individuals and groups to accomplish desired organization goals with a minimum of wasted effort and with the highest possible degree of personal satisfaction. It is to accomplish these things that a manager is given authority —the right and power to use his discretion in a creative way to help people do their jobs better.

Among the most important elements in an effective environment are the following:

1. *The provision of clearly understood objectives or goals, and of plans to meet them.*

2. *The provision of a meaningful and understood structure of roles so that people know the position they play in an operation and how what they do relates to what others do.*
3. *An environment in which, to the maximum extent possible, obstructions to the performance of people are removed.*
4. *An environment that will lead people to do the right things, preferably because they want to, often because they find that a given way is the way things get done, and sometimes because they must.*
5. *An environment that recognizes the importance of human motivation.*
6. *An environment that takes into account the fact that many people have knowledge of problems and the solutions to them.*

In carrying out his duties, every manager has both a logical and moral obligation to strive for a "surplus." He must aim to reach his organization's objectives with the minimum use of materials and money, as well as the minimum of effort and dissatisfaction on the part of his people. Or else to accomplish as much as he can of the organization's objective with the material and human resources made available to him.

To do their jobs most effectively, managers need to be acquainted with the science of management and the techniques and approaches underlying it. This is not to say that managing in itself is a science. It is rather an art, like medicine, engineering, accountancy, or baseball. But like all other arts, it is one in which the practitioner succeeds best by applying organized knowledge to real problems.

The knowledge a manager needs is extensive. He should understand the lessons of past experience. Because his task involves dealing with people, he must understand the elementary aspects of psychology. Since he deals with groups of people he must understand something of why groups of people behave the way they do. He is also a professional rationalist in that one of his major tasks is to make decisions. Moreover, because decisions operate in the future, he must also keep an eye on what is likely to come. All these things mean that the successful manager must indeed be a scientist as well as a practitioner at the same time.

The chapters that follow take a closer look at the major functions of managers. They examine the areas of planning, organizing, leading, and controlling. Furthermore, since the manager must often deal with organizations of his employees, a chapter is devoted to management and labor unions.

KEY TERMS AND CONCEPTS FOR REVIEW

What a manager is
The manager's job
Managerial authority
Major elements in an environment for
  performance
The manager as a catalyst
The goal of managers
Management as a science

Management as an art
Why management knowledge is crude
Experience as the manager's teacher
Psychology and the manager
Group behavior and the manager
The manager as a rationalist
Meeting change by managers

QUESTIONS FOR ANALYSIS AND DISCUSSION

1. Businesses are not the only organizations needing managers. Explain.
2. Companies sometimes appoint their best salesman as the sales manager. Would you believe this is a good practice?
3. When we speak of a manager as being responsible for the design and maintenance of an environment for performance, what do we mean? What are the major elements necessary in this environment? How can we undertake such a design?
4. People working for a manager usually refer to him as "the boss." This implies that he has great power over them. Yet in this chapter his job of environment design is emphasized. Are these two positions consistent?
5. It is often debated whether management is a science or an art. Which is it?
6. Some people say that managing can only be learned on the job by doing, and that colleges and books cannot make a person a good manager. What do you believe?
7. Why is experience often a dangerous teacher for managers?
8. Why is so much stress placed in this chapter on the importance of managers in making a business succeed?

SUGGESTED READING

Bower, M. *The Will to Manage.* New York: McGraw-Hill Book Company, 1966, chap. 1.

Drucker, P. F. *Managing for Results.* New York: Harper & Row, 1964, chap. 1.

Drucker, P. F. *Management: Tasks, Responsibilities and Practices.* New York: Harper & Row, 1974.

Fulmer, R. M. *The New Management.* New York. Macmillan Publishing Company, Inc., 1974, chaps. 1–4.

Koontz, H., and C. O'Donnell *Principles of Management* (5th ed.). New York: McGraw-Hill Book Company, 1972, chaps. 1–5.

Koontz, H., and C. O'Donnell *Essentials of Management.* New York: McGraw-Hill Book Company, 1974, chaps. 1–4.

Sloan, A. P. Jr. *My Years with General Motors.* New York: Doubleday and Company, 1964.

20

Planning: The Foundation of Management

One of the major causes of business failure is lack of planning. No one would think of taking an automobile trip without deciding where he wanted to go and laying out a route to get there. But people often decide to start a business or produce a new product without knowing exactly what they wish to accomplish and how. As Bernard Baruch, successful businessman and adviser to U.S. presidents, once observed: "Whatever failures I have known, whatever errors I have committed, whatever follies I have witnessed in public and private life, have been because of action without thought." Any student who has rambled in an examination or in a term paper without thinking through what he was going to write can understand what Baruch had in mind.

Failing to plan means, in the final analysis, planning to fail. Whatever the activity, whatever the business, a person who refuses to plan is likely to go off in all directions; he is trusting to chance. If you do not know where you are going or are on the wrong road, it does not matter how fast you travel.

Planning is, therefore, the primary task of management. Without it, the other functions of management cannot be exercised. There is no sense in setting up an organization and hiring people to fill positions in it if nobody knows what is to be accomplished. If there is to be leadership, the leader must have a goal. Obviously, taking steps to assure that plans are being accomplished—the task of control—is useless if we do not have any plans.

WHAT PLANNING IS

Planning involves the selection of goals and the means of reaching them. Planning is essentially choosing among alternative courses of action. Planning is deciding in advance what to do, how to do it, when to do it, and who is to do it. Planning bridges the gap from where we are to where we want to go.

Planning is looking to future action. The job of planning is to make something happen that would probably not otherwise occur. Planning is not avoiding risks; the future is always subject to uncertainties. Planning requires that we see the future as best we can, recognize areas of uncertainty and risk, and assess the size of the risks we are taking. Any intelligent businessman would like to have an idea of the size and nature of the risks he is taking before he invests heavily in a new product, a new process, a piece of machinery, or an advertising program. He can achieve this only by trying to foresee the future as best he can. Only by then can he make provision as to how he will cope with possible risks when they confront him.

Planning is the most intellectually demanding portion of a manager's job. It is a mental tendency to do things in an orderly way, to substitute clear thinking for guesses and hunch. Because it is such intellectually hard work, this may be the reason that planning is perhaps the thing managers do least well. For most of us it is easier and more exciting to meet crises, fight fires, or kill snakes—to make many decisions without much thought. And certainly it is more fun!

WHAT ARE PLANS?

As the great French industrialist, Henri Fayol, said over six decades ago, planning involves assessing the future and making provision for it. But businessmen sometimes forget that there are many types of plans. We can identify seven types: objectives, policies, strategies, procedures, rules, programs, and budgets.

Objectives or Goals

Objectives, or goals, are the end points toward which we aim. If we plan a trip from New York to Los Angeles, the latter city is our objective. If a businessman aims to go into the business of producing and marketing filing cases at a profit, that is his objective. Or if he sets out to purchase three lathes or hire a new plant superintendent, these are his objectives.

As has been noted, objectives can be fairly general and fuzzy or they can be clear and verifiable. Our objective of travelling to Los Angeles is fairly clear, but we may set a much more definite goal of travelling to the home of our Aunt Susie on Maple Avenue in Los Angeles. We would be even more clear and precise if we were to say that our goal is to arrive before six o'clock in the afternoon on January 16.

An objective is meaningful if its achievement is verifiable—that is, if a person can tell at some specified time in the future whether he has accomplished it. Thus our objective of buying three lathes would be far more meaningful if we said three lathes of certain specified characteristics, to be delivered by a certain time, and not to exceed a certain cost. Then we would know when we had truly accomplished it.

Objectives, or goals, are types of plans because in achieving them we have to think out specifically what we want to accomplish and have some idea how to go about it. It hardly makes sense to say that we have an objective if we have no idea whether it can be achieved.

Policies

Policies are also plans in that they are statements or understandings which guide thinking in decision-making. Those who make decisions must have discretion, and policy exists to guide and limit their discretion. The purpose of policy is to assure that those who make decisions within a company will do so consistently and in the best interest of the firm.

The discretion allowed is often quite broad, as with the requirement that a customer must always be satisfied (which of course has its obvious limits—we can't give him the company). But the discretion may also be quite narrow. A company may, for example, have the policy of buying from the lowest of three qualified bidders. This policy leaves to the purchasing agent's discretion only the determination of who are "qualified bidders."

The area of discretion in most policies is quite general. For example, a typical company policy on employee acceptance of gifts from suppliers (see Figure 20–1) states that "except for token gifts of purely nominal or advertising value, no employee shall accept any gift or gratuity from any supplier at any time." On the other hand, a policy

FIGURE 20–1

Example of a Company Policy

	Policy No.: MANAGEMENT-2
Gifts, Gratuities, and Entertainment	Issued: _____ Effective: _____ Supercedes: _____

Good management of our relation with vendors, many of whom compete with each other because of our policy of having two or more suppliers of the same material, transportation or service, requires complete impartiality on our part.

     1.   ACCEPTANCE OF GIFTS AND GRATUITIES

Gifts from suppliers   1.1   Except for token gifts of purely nominal or advertising value, no employee shall accept any gift or gratuity from any supplier at any time.

Return of gifts   1.2   Should a supplier send a prohibited gift or gratuity to an employee, it shall be returned immediately with a letter of regret explaining Company policy.

     2.   ENTERTAINMENT

Lunches, dinners, free tickets   2.1   Suppliers' representatives may at times substitute lavish or repeated entertainment (lunches, dinners, trips, hotel bills, free tickets for various events, etc.) in place of other gifts or gratuities. Employees are required to exercise their good judgment in accepting such entertainment and avoid subjecting themselves or the Company to any possible claim of partiality or favoritism.

may spell out fairly specific requirements for the area of discretion, as in a policy allowing sales managers to change prices. Such a policy might stipulate that the sales manager can set prices differing from list prices if (1) such a price meets the legal requirements of the fair trade laws; (2) the price is not more than 10 percent below the list price; and (3) a competitor's price requires such a reduction to get the business.

Policy should be regarded as a means of encouraging discretion and initiative, but within limits. It is a way of delegating authority to people without losing control of the company. Policies must be planned and regularly revised. No company's employees should ever be able to say, "We don't know why we do it; it's just our policy." Nor should a company look upon its policies as unchangeable as the Ten Commandments. After all, a company's policies are designed to guide actions for the future.

Strategies

The word "strategy" is of military origin, and it means large-scale planning drawn up in the light of what an enemy may do. Business managers, like generals, have to consider what actions their opponents or competitors may take. Some years ago Volkswagen decided to put its "beetle" on the U.S. market when it detected a demand for a small, maneuverable, and economical car that American manufacturers were not prepared to supply. This was a strategy designed to take advantage of market opportunities provided by Volkswagen's competitors.

In business usage, strategy has a broader meaning than its military connotation. It denotes a general program of action with an implied deployment of money and manpower to attain overall company objectives. A strategy usually includes within it several major policies, for example, the marketing policy of Avon Products: Avon markets through a network of housewives who sell cosmetics to their neighbors and friends. This marketing policy is also a cornerstone of Avon's entire company strategy. Avon's strategy is to design products for this market, to package them attractively, and not to sell through regular drug and cosmetic stores.

A strategy serves to determine and communicate, through a system of major objectives and policies, a picture of the kind of company envisioned by management. A strategy does not attempt to outline exactly how a company is to accomplish its objectives, since this is the task of countless major and minor plans. But it provides the framework for planning and for deploying resources. A company with a clear strategy can avoid much aimless groping on the part of those who make and carry out decisions.

Procedures

Although procedures are not often thought of as plans, they really belong to planning since they control and specify future action. Procedures are definite ways of doing things. Their essence is chronological sequence: first do this, then do that, and afterward do that; send the

FIGURE 20-2

Typical Company Procedure for Personnel Status Changes

All personnel status changes are initiated by the supervisor with the proper approvals and forwarded to Corporate Employee Relations Office for review and processing.

A.   New Hires
     A Personnel Change Form (PX4412–4) must be completed on each new employee, indicating employee's department, position description, code number, position title, starting salary, and effective date of hire.

B.   Promotions and Demotions
     All changes of this type must be initiated on Personnel Change Form (PX4412–4). The personnel change form shows the employee's former position classification and salary, and the new position classification and salary.

C.   Transfers
     All transfers must be initiated on Personnel Change Form (PX4412–4), indicating the employee change in status. Transfers involve a change from one position to another with the same salary range, or change from a position in one department or division to a position of equal value in another department or division.

D.   Merit Increases
     As in the above status changes, all merit increases must be initiated on Personnel Change Form (PX4412–4). In addition, a Performance and Progress Review Form (PX4421–1) must be completed and attached to the merit increase request.
     Upon receipt and review for proper approvals and conformance to Company policy, the Performance and Progress Review form will be returned to the designated supervisor. This action signifies to the supervisor that the merit increase has been approved and can be discussed with the employee. After discussion, the Performance and Progress Review form will be sent to the appropriate and designated office for filing in the employee's personnel jacket.

green copy to shipping, the yellow copy to production, and the white copy to accounting. Procedures are truly guides to action. A pure procedure permits no discretion.

The reasons for having procedures—the "red tape" of business—are two. One is to point out the best way of doing things; if we have found that the most efficient way to make out expense reports is to follow a certain form, why let everyone experiment? A second reason for having procedures is for purposes of control, to assure that a thing will be done in a certain way and not in any other way. In the filing of expense reports, it is more convenient if travel, hotel, food, entertainment, tips, and other items are reported by everyone in the company in the same way.

While procedures are necessary in every kind of organization, they often tend to develop with a momentum of their own, without regard to their original purpose, causing unnecessary paperwork and effort.

It has been estimated that at least 20 percent of all expenses in American industry and government arise from procedural paperwork, and some estimates go much higher. One cannot help but wonder whether, if better planning of procedures were done, much of this cost could not be avoided. This is a problem not only for large companies but for small businesses as well. Think how much procedural paperwork you do in your own daily life, and ask yourself how much of it is really necessary.

Rules

Rules are required actions or nonactions. Since they control future action they are a form of planning, just as in the case of procedures, which might be called sequences of rules. They may vary all the way from the "no smoking" rule in a fire hazard area to the rule adopted by the president of Xerox that no person who has been with the company for eight or more years can be laid off or discharged without the president's personal approval.

Rules are, of course, often necessary and wise. But too often they are established simply to assure that no one will make a mistake, and in such instances they may unnecessarily limit the use of discretion and imagination. Before making a rule a manager should always ask himself whether a policy guideline, allowing some individual discretion, would serve just as well.

Programs

A program is a complex of goals, policies, procedures, rules, job assignments, steps to be taken, manpower or money to be used, and other things necessary to carry out a desired course of action. It is usually supported by its own budget, covering operating expenses and capital expenditures.

Programs may be major or minor. They may be as major as the program of Continental Air Lines to acquire and install a fleet of DC-10 airplanes. Or they may be as minor as a program of the same company's engine maintenance foreman to train five mechanics to disassemble and assemble an engine accessory.

Programs are usually interconnected. One seldom finds a program standing by itself. Thus, a program to acquire a DC-10 fleet would need many other programs: to provide spare parts, to set up maintenance facilities and procedures, to schedule aircraft over the route structure, to train pilots and stewardesses, to advertise flights, to provide food services, and so on. Each of these would be a program in and of itself. But each would have to be coordinated with the others. The development, coordination, and implementation of all the programs necessary to make most businesses operate profitably is an extraordinarily difficult and complex task.

Budgets

Although budgets are usually thought of as means of controlling a company, and will be discussed later in the chapter on control, it should not be forgotten that a budget *should be* a numberized plan. As a matter of fact, the operating revenue and expense budget is often called a "profit plan."

A budget then, as a plan, is simply a statement of expected results expressed in numerical terms. It may be couched in dollars, in man-hours, in units of product, in machine hours, in number of sales made, or in some other measure. Since budgets translate programs into sets of numbers, they allow a precise measurement of the performance expected, and give managers concrete standards to use for control.

But unless budgets truly represent plans, they can become forked sticks to prod people with instead of yardsticks for guiding and measuring. When they become devices for oppressing people, they are resisted. Most subordinates have ways of beating their bosses at the "numbers game." One of the most common ways is to pad the budget with unnecessary expenses to allow some leeway. One of the authors, when he was a business manager, had a boss who customarily sliced off 10 percent of every budget submitted to him. The result was that budgets were submitted with 10 percent more expenses than necessary, so that the boss could cut off his usual 10 percent without reducing the total below what was needed to do the job.

HOW TO PLAN

Planning proceeds by simple steps that we can outline. Any planning process, whether in business, in school, or in one's private activities, follows a certain sequence based on common sense. In practice, of course, these steps may often be taken almost simultaneously. Experienced managers, in approaching the solution of a business problem, often go through them almost intuitively. If any step is left out, however, they will feel that something is wrong.

FIGURE 20-3
The Planning Process

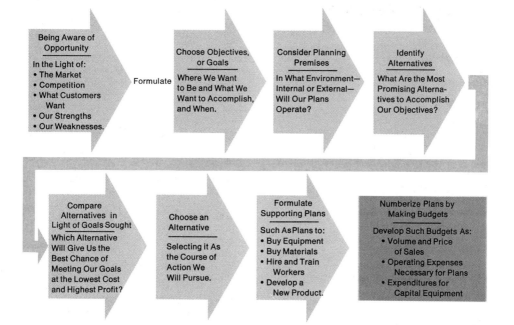

The student will be wise to apply these steps of the planning process to his own life situations. Memorizing the list will be meaningless in itself, but if he uses it to plan some personal activity he will see how practical it is and how easily the steps can be applied to a business problem (see Figure 20-3).

1. *Be Aware of Opportunity.* The first step in planning comes before the actual planning and is therefore not strictly a part of the planning process. The awareness of an opportunity (or a "problem" since problems are merely opportunities waiting for a solution) is the real starting place for planning. This awareness also involves an analysis of the opportunity or problem.

The analysis will probe in various directions. One thing it will consider is the market for the products and services we wish to offer. What do customers want, what can be sold, how much can be sold, and for what price? In this connection, too, we will want to look at our competitors. What are they doing in the field? What are they likely to do in the future?

Another subject for analysis is ourselves. What kind of company are we? What business are we in? What can we make and sell? Do we have, or can we get, the necessary money and skilled people to do

David Packard

In 1938, two young Stanford University graduate engineers—David Packard and William R. Hewlett—formed a part-time partnership to design and manufacture electronic instruments for testing and measurement. While still taking university work and acting as research assistants, they started making things and a professor helped them find odd jobs. They made a diathermy device for the Palo Alto Clinic, a motor control for a large telescope, and a foul signalling device for a bowling alley. But their first important product was a new-type circuit for an audio oscillator, built in a garage behind the Packard home in Palo Alto, California.

The organization that grew out of the partnership is known today as the Hewlett-Packard Company. It now has 22 plants worldwide, with sales of more than $660 million a year.

David Packard, born in Pueblo, Colorado, developed an interest in electronics at an early age. He read every book on electricity and science that he could find, and built his first radio when he was still in grade school. This interest continued during his high school days, but he also found time for athletics—particularly track and basketball. At Stanford his six-foot-five frame soon attracted the attention of the football coach, and he was persuaded to join the team. He limited himself to this one sport to allow sufficient time for his studies.

Through his participation in the athletic program and his interest in electrical engineering, he came under the influence of Professor Frederick Terman, a highly respected authority in the emerging field of radio engineering. It was also during this period that he met a fellow student, and team-mate, Bill Hewlett.

After graduating from Stanford in 1934, Packard accepted a job with General Electric in Schenectady, New York, but kept in touch with Hewlett and Prof. Terman. In 1938 he took a leave of absence from GE to return to Stanford on a research fellowship arranged by Professor Terman to complete work on his master's degree. By that time Hewlett had received his master's from M.I.T., and had also returned to Palo Alto.

Terman played an important role in the development of the Hewlett-Packard Company. As a professor, he stimulated the two students' interest in electronic engineering. He worked out a fellowship for Packard to return to Stanford. He encour-

what we may wish to do? Do we know how to make and sell the new product or service? Can we produce it at a profit? How soon can we get our product on the market? Can we get the raw materials we need to do it? Will we have to expand our plant or buy new machinery?

We must ask these and other questions before we can set objectives. There is no sense, after all, in setting objectives that we cannot reach. A small company cannot usefully go into automobile manufacturing,

aged Hewlett and Packard to go into business for themselves. He got them some initial part-time jobs. He has been an important adviser over the years. He served on the company's first board of directors and still serves as an honorary director.

Hewlett had developed a promising design for an audio oscillator, and the two young men decided to go into business for themselves. Although their starting capital was only $500, they did not feel undercapitalized because they produced the instruments themselves. Their first big order was from Walt Disney Studios for eight audio oscillators. Sales for the first year totalled about $5,000.

One of the partners' early management decisions was to build test and measurement instruments of a general-purpose nature, available to a broad range of customers. They made several policy decisions of long-range importance. They avoided taking on specialized contract work that would require a "hire and fire" operation, preferring instead to build a strong, loyal, stable work force. They also planned that their growth would be limited only by their ability to develop and produce technical products satisfying customer needs, and that their growth would be financed by internally generated earnings so that they would not have to be unduly controlled by money lenders. Another early management policy was to hire young people right out of school and train them on the job so that the company could expand from within.

One of the key ingredients in their ultimate success has been the loyalty and dedication of their employees. Most of the 28,000 HP people are non-union—the only exceptions being in countries where union membership is mandatory. According to Packard, employees have faith in the company and the company demonstrates that it has faith in them. A paragraph in the HP Corporate Objectives reads, "We want people to enjoy their work at HP, and to be proud of their accomplishments. This means we must make sure that each person receives the recognition he needs and deserves. In the final analysis, our human resources are our most valuable asset."

Packard has often emphasized the importance of good working conditions. "We recognize that our employees spend about half of their waking hours in our plants and offices. It is very important to make that an attractive part of their lives." When sales fell off in 1970–71, the company reduced wages and work weeks by 10 percent instead of laying workers off. Most of the employees took their pay cuts without protesting.

In 1969 Packard was appointed Deputy Secretary of Defense, a post he held for three years. He had to give up nearly $1 million a year in income—$125,000 in salary, $135,000 in profit-sharing, and $700,000 in dividends from his stock. He put his stock in trust for a variety of educational and charitable institutions with the understanding that all the dividends plus any increase in the value of the stock should go to them. As a result, these institutions received about $22 million in dividends and stock value increases over the three-year period of Packard's government service.

Packard and Hewlett have always worked closely together, Hewlett specializing in the technical side of the company and Packard doing the managing. During Packard's stint in Washington, Hewlett took over as chief executive officer as well as president. Packard currently serves as chairman of the board.

except perhaps to produce one or two hand-made racers for the Indianapolis 500. A company without a special marketing organization cannot go into the hospital supply or toothpaste business. In assessing his opportunities, a businessman must also realistically take stock of his financial and human resources and his strengths and weaknesses.

Even the largest company has its limits. Some years ago the Hughes Aircraft Company had a group of scientists and engineers who had developed an advanced data processing system with a view to competing with the International Business Machines Corporation. The system was good and very advanced, but the question arose as to whether the company had the people and facilities to market and service it. After the lead of IBM in these areas had been considered, and a consultant had estimated that it would cost at least $60 million to develop the necessary service and marketing capabilities, the company decided that the program was too risky and abandoned it.

2. *Choose Objectives.* As pointed out earlier, every plan must have an objective or goal. To be meaningful, an objective must be clear, verifiable, and reasonably attainable. Choosing the objective is certainly the first step to take after we have studied the opportunity.

It is usually assumed that profit is the main objective of a business. In a sense it is. But as pointed out in the first chapter of this book, profit is merely a measure of the surplus of sales dollars over expense dollars. A business must make a profit if it is to survive. However, in speaking of planning objectives, it is more realistic to think of a business objective as producing and selling a certain kind of product or service (computers, watches, washing machines, hair dressing, or what not) for a certain market (business or government, homeowners, or women).

These objectives may give rise to other supporting goals, such as raising a certain amount of money by sales of stock or bank loans, building a new factory of a certain kind and size, constructing and operating a new supermarket, acquiring certain machinery by a certain date, hiring and training a given number and kind of factory workers or salesmen, or installing and developing suitable programs for a new computer.

As can be seen, company objectives guide us toward major plans; these, in turn, give rise to departmental objectives; then to section objectives; and so on down the line. Clearly, the objectives of lesser departments and subordinate managers will be better chosen, if everyone down the line understands the company objectives.

3. *Identify and Communicate Planning Premises.* Since plans always operate in the future, it is necessary for planners to make assumptions as to what the future will be like. These assumptions, or premises, may be forecasts of economic conditions, population growth, price levels, company policies that are expected to prevail, the fact that we have plants in Chicago and Dallas, that a certain amount of cash will be available, and so on. Planning premises are a picture of the environment in which a plan is expected to operate.

Forecasting is obviously important in setting planning premises.

What kind of markets will exist? What will our sales be? What prices can we expect to get? What will our costs be? What technical developments may be expected? What will happen to wage rates? To tax rates? What new plants will the company build? What new products will be offered by our competitors?

Actions we have already taken may become premises for plans. We may have decided that we will not engage in long-term borrowing. Or we may have decided that we will only market our products in the western part of the United States. Or that we will only sell through our own salesmen. Or that we will not spend more than 4 percent of our sales income on advertising.

As planning moves down the line in a company, the major plans already made at higher levels become premises for supporting plans at lower levels. If, for example, we have decided to build a plant in New Jersey, this becomes a premise for our plans for hiring labor or shipping our product. When Westinghouse and General Electric decided to go into the production of nuclear electric generating plants, this decision became an important premise for the planning of their engineering, manufacturing, and marketing departments.

A company's planning premises must be consistent. Since decisions are made at various levels and by various people in the company, it is important that decision makers utilize consistent planning premises if plans arc to "fit." The use of different sets of planning premises can be extremely costly. Imagine the lack of consistency in plans if the sales manager of a company based his sales and advertising programs on a forecast of high sales and prosperity while the manufacturing head based his on a forecast of low sales and a business recession!

The problem of premising may be illustrated by what actually happened to one airline. The struggling company had no money to waste. It ordered ten airplanes from a manufacturer who gave a series of dates on which each plane would be delivered. The sales head of the airline assumed that they would be delivered when promised; he developed his advertising programs, his hiring and training of reservations agents, and his other activities on this premise. The chief pilot believed that the airplanes would be delivered six months later than promised, and based his hiring and training of pilots on that premise. The airplanes were actually delivered three months late. The result was that half of the company—the sales group—had been spending money for three months with no airplanes to fly; and after the new airplanes were delivered, it was another three months before there were trained pilots to fly them.

A major responsibility of managers, starting at the top, is to make sure that subordinate managers understand the premises on which they are to plan. If people do not know they will, consciously or unconsciously, make their own assumptions, and it would be an accident if the many different planning programs were to fit together. No top manager can afford to be careless in formulating, communicating, and coordinating all of the planning premises throughout his company. There is probably no other area of planning that can be more troublesome and costly if it is not handled properly.

4. *Identify Alternatives.* As Billy Goetz, one of the early writers on planning, has said, "a planning problem arises only when an alternative course of action is discovered." As a matter of fact, experienced managers have learned that the process of looking carefully at the most promising alternatives can cause the decision to "make itself." Too often, however, the destiny of an individual or an organization is sealed without recognition of all the options that were open.

In his famous poem, "The Road Not Taken," Robert Frost suggests the importance of remembered alternatives:

> Somewhere ages and ages hence
> I will be telling this with a sigh.
> Two roads diverged in a wood, and I,
> I took the one less traveled by—
> And that has made all the difference.

Although there may be regrets about roads not taken, the regrets are not likely to be as severe if all roads are given some consideration. Obviously, every alternative cannot be considered in detail. Managers learn to identify quickly those alternatives which are unrealistic because of the resources they require or because of policy limitations. It is better to consider too many alternatives than to fail to recognize an important option.

At the same time, a manager usually cannot afford to look at too many alternatives. In almost any problem there are so many different solutions that we could not look at them all even with the aid of a computer. Sometimes people spend so much time in looking at alternatives that they never get around to making a decision. This has aptly been called "paralysis by analysis."

Sometimes it helps to look for the limiting or critical factor. In every problem situation, there is always one factor or a few factors that make the most difference to the desired solution. If we can identify them, and if we can pick the alternative that makes the *most* difference, we will save a great deal of time.

The principle may be put this way. Suppose something goes wrong with your automobile. You *could* tear it down piece by piece, put each part of a canvas and inspect it, repair or replace any doubtful part, re-assemble it in accordance with manufacturers' specifications and blue-prints, put gasoline and oil in it, and it would run. But you are more likely to study the car and its motor, find out that a faulty ignition wire is keeping it from running, and replace the wire. Some people are by nature automobile disassemblers—they want to look at everything. But the successful business manager doesn't have the time to do this. He must look for critical, or limiting, factors. Indeed, we can all apply this principle in making our personal decisions. Try it.

5. *Compare Alternatives in the Light of Goals Sought.* After identifying the most likely alternatives, the next step in planning is to compare them as ways of reaching the goals we have chosen. Which path is best? Which alternative promises to yield the results we want at the least cost? This is truly the stage of analysis. It is in this stage that the techniques of operations research—using mathematics and the computer—can be of great help. But perhaps of greatest help to the business manager is the computer of the human brain, and that un-common quality called "common sense."

In analyzing alternatives, again, the principle of the limiting, or critical, factor can be used effectively. What makes the most difference in the situation? Is the critical factor our inability to buy the most efficient tools and machinery? Is it the cost of advertising? What is it?

6. *Choose a Course of Action.* If our goals are clear, if we have had a look at the most promising alternatives, if we have been able to compare alternatives in light of the goal sought, then the final decision should be rather easy. The trouble with real-life situations is that our alternatives may not be as clear as we would like, our analysis not as certain, and that our decisions must operate in an uncertain future. As a consequence, we can seldom make a clear, easy, and riskless decision. Imagine the study and worry that RCA went through a few years ago when it decided to dispose of its computer business at a $450 million loss. Or the risk and high stakes involved in Walt Disney's original venture into Disneyland.

Sometimes the best thing for a manager to do is to decide not to decide, to postpone a decision. But this is usually a costly and danger-ous course. If it results in a drifting organization, in which people work aimlessly, the costs can be considerable. Good people will leave for better jobs under more courageous leadership. Competitors will gob-ble up opportunities that the company missed. A manager must not be like the proverbial donkey that starved to death between two bales of hay because it couldn't make up its mind.

7. *Formulate Supporting Plans.* At the point where a decision is made, planning is seldom complete. Other steps must be taken. A major plan almost invariably requires supporting, or derivative, plans. The airline that decided to acquire a fleet of new airplanes triggered a host of derivative plans dealing with the acquisition and positioning of spare parts, the development of maintenance facilities, scheduling, advertising, financing, and hiring and training people.

8. *Numberize Plans with Budgets.* To wrap up a plan and make it meaningful to people in an organization, a budget has to be established for it. The budget expresses the plan in terms that people can understand, such as costs, work loads, or output. Budgets set up standards against which to measure performance. Budgeting also gives a kind of definiteness to planning, since it is difficult to translate programs into numbers without defining them.

PLANNING: AN EXERCISE IN RATIONALITY

As can be seen from the planning steps outlined above, planning is simply a rational, or logical, approach to the future. Business, or any other kind of organized effort, would be accidental or random without planning.

The forces at work in planning can be illustrated by the diagram in Figure 20–4. In the diagram, progress toward any goal (more sales, lower costs, the completion of a training program) is measured along the vertical axis, and time is measured along the horizontal axis. X indicates where we are now (at time t_o) and Y indicates where we want to be at some time in the future (t_n). The line XY indicates the path of a plan which will take us from X to Y.

If the future were completely certain and we could anticipate all the forces that might affect the operation of a plan, the line XY would be fairly easy to draw. But this is never the case, and therefore we have to identify the most critical planning premises which will affect our program and make provision for them. For example, an electric utility company must premise population shifts and changes in the demand for energy that will influence the size of generating plants and the location of transmission lines. And in recent years, it would have had to make assumptions as to how environmental protection laws would affect the location of generating plants and transmission lines.

The essential logic of planning applies regardless of the time interval

FIGURE 20–4

Rationality of Planning

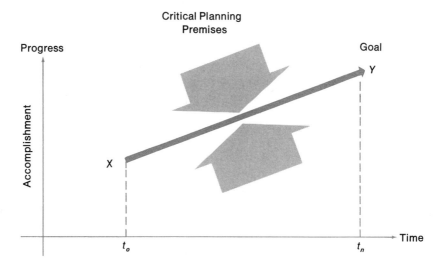

between t_o and t_n, whether ten minutes or ten years. However, the extent to which we carry through all of the planning steps will naturally depend on the time available and the importance of the planning program in terms of dollars, reputation, or other factors.

HOW FAR AHEAD SHOULD WE PLAN?

Most businesses try to plan for five years. A few companies, like Weyerhouser Lumber Company, plan for as long as 50 years, and some companies probably do not look farther ahead than 5 minutes.

Decision Commitment: The Guide

The length of time for which a company plans depends on the commitments it makes. A plan is only an idea or a study until a decision is made to do something. A decision implies a commitment of money, man-hours, direction, raw materials, sales effort, or reputation, among other things. If a company buys a computer and figures on writing off the cost (including interest on the money invested) over ten years, we can say that commitment has been made for ten years. If it orders steel to be used in manufacturing a machine, and it will take only four months before the raw steel has been converted into a finished machine and sold, the commitment is for four months. The reason Weyerhouser

Lumber Company plans for 50 years is that this is the time it takes for the company's trees to grow to a size suitable for cutting.

A manager should attempt to assure, as best he can, the fulfillment of decisions he makes today. So-called long-range planning is not planning for future decisions, but planning to fulfill commitments involved in decisions taken today. It is only common sense to try to look as far ahead as necessary to support the kinds of decisions we are making.

Since the future is filled with uncertainties, it may not be possible to assure the fulfillment of the commitments we make today. This is one of the major sources of business risk. When a company buys a computer, for example, how can it be sure the computer will be useful for long enough to pay back the investment? When Colgate invests $5 million in an advertising campaign for its toothpaste, how can it be certain that it will get this money back in increased sales?

Building Flexibility into Programs

One way to insure against losses from long-time commitments is to build flexibility into a program—that is, the ability to make a change without undue cost or embarrassment. An office building, for example, represents a flexible investment because it can be used by all kinds of businesses needing office space. The same can be said for a warehouse, or a general-purpose lathe. But what of an oil well, a pipeline to an oilfield, or a refinery? These represent large investments that can hardly be turned to other uses. Perhaps that is the reason why our large oil companies have long been known for their thoroughness as long-range planners.

Sometimes a businessman can build flexibility into his plans as he makes them. A builder of a three-story office building may, for example, put strong enough construction into it so that he can later make it a six-story building. A businessman may put extra money into a factory he is building so that it can be used for other purposes than its original one. For example, when Lever Brothers built a soap and detergent factory on the west coast some years ago, it added $5 million to the $30 million construction cost so that the factory could be converted into a chemical plant later on if the company wanted to do so. Likewise, a storeowner may take a short-term lease of 5 years rather than a 20-year lease at a lower annual rate, so that it will be easier for him to move to different quarters later on.

There are many ways to provide for flexibility in our planning decisions. But flexibility almost invariably costs money. While the intelligent businessman will always try to be flexible in his planning decisions, he must also weigh the costs involved.

ASSURING SUCCESS THROUGH MANAGING BY OBJECTIVES

One of the newer approaches to making planning more effective, an approach which has swept American industry in the last few years, is called managing by objectives. This recognizes that a company exists to accomplish objectives. It also recognizes that groups of people in a company, as well as individuals within these groups, also work to accomplish objectives. It is an awareness that people have to work toward something. But they can only do this if they know what their objectives are in specific and verifiable terms.

Managing by objectives is, therefore, simply common sense. Like so many simple things, it is not easy to accomplish in practice. But if a company makes it possible for every employee, from president to hourly worker, to know what he is expected to accomplish in as clear terms as possible, if it gives him the tools and assistance he needs to accomplish these things, if it removes obstacles to his performance, and rewards him for achieving his goals, the company will certainly be more productive and will have more satisfied employees.

These are some of the things a company must do to make managing by objectives work:

See That Goals or Objectives Are Verifiable

As pointed out earlier, if goals or objectives are to be meaningful, they must be verifiable—that is, a person must be able to tell whether or not he has reached them. The easiest way of making goals verifiable is to state them in numerical terms: dollars of sales, dollars of costs, units of output, hours of work, pieces of paper handled, and so on.

There are, however, many things in business that cannot be put into numerical terms. In such cases we can make objectives verifiable by spelling out their characteristics and setting a time for each objective to be accomplished. Thus we might set as a goal the development and installation of an advertising program by June 30, the program having such features as (1) appealing to housewives, (2) emphasizing the high quality of a product, (3) utilizing only daytime television, and (4) giving the housewife the feeling that she will be showing her husband how intelligent she is by using the product.

Coordinate Goals So They Represent an Interlocking Network

Care must be taken that the goals of one department or individual do not work at cross purposes with those of another. It would be disastrous for a production manager to have a goal of minimizing costs if that meant he only produced one item when the sales department needed a full line of products to sell their customers. If the goal of the credit manager was to minimize credit losses, and he did so at the price of turning down many desirable customers, the results could be very serious.

No manager can overlook the fact that his operation is only part of the total operation of his company. Goals must support and be consistent with each other.

Make Goals Realistic and Reasonably Attainable

If goals are set so high that people cannot reach them, they become meaningless. They also lose their meaning if they are set so low that everyone can reach them without any special effort. The problem and the challenge is to set goals at a level where they are reasonably attainable with a certain amount of "stretch" or "pull." People like to reach for the difficult, but they are discouraged by the impossible.

Give People Adequate Tools and Help

If people are to accomplish objectives, their bosses must do their best to see that they have all the assistance possible. This means not only adequate tools, machinery, or workspace. It also implies an understanding of the company's objectives and strategies, a knowledge of planning premises and policies, and a clear understanding of the amount of authority a person has in his job.

Let People Have a Voice in Setting Their Own Objectives

People will always feel more desire to accomplish an objective that they have a part in setting. They will also have a better understanding of what is expected of them. And people on the job, whether managers or workers, usually know better than anyone else what the problems in their area are and how best to solve them. By letting them participate in setting goals, the boss not only opens lines of communication but is likely to learn from them. In one detergent plant, for example, the foreman in charge of the packaging line pointed out to his superiors some small changes that would increase output by 25 percent. Had it not been for joint goal setting, this opportunity to reduce costs might have been buried indefinitely in the foreman's mind.

Giving people a voice in setting their own objectives does not mean that the boss lets them do anything they want. He must have the final say on what is a reasonable goal. In practice, we often find that people tend to set their goals too high and that the boss must lower them to an attainable level. In some ways, we are all alike. Anything is possible a year from now, two months from now it is a little more difficult, but it becomes impossible next week.

Be Willing to Appraise People in Terms of What They Accomplish

Managing by objectives makes it possible for us to appraise people according to what they accomplish, rather than what kind of a person they are or how they spend their time. What is the use of rating people's "loyalty," "friendliness," or "intelligence" if they do not accomplish results? Who cares how hard and long a person works if he does not achieve anything? The standard on which people should be judged, and on which most people like to be judged, is the results they accomplish.

ESTABLISHING AN ENVIRONMENT FOR EFFECTIVE PLANNING

If effective planning is so important to business success, and if the manager's primary task is to establish an environment in which people can perform, what, in summary, are some of the most important things a manager can do? Several suggestions can be made, most of which arise from the previous discussion.

1. *Clarify and Communicate Business Objectives and Strategies.* People at all levels and in all jobs can gain if they understand the company's objectives and strategies. These are difficult to communicate, especially in large companies. But they cannot be communicated at all if they are general, fuzzy, or nonexistent. One difficulty some businessmen have in communicating is that they have nothing to communicate.

Employees are interested in what the company is, what business it regards itself as being in, and what it is trying to do. They can often make worthwhile contributions if they know these things. A group of research scientists in a large company once expressed the opinion that they could do their work better if they knew more about what the company was trying to accomplish. Rather than just working on the development of a certain electronic instrument, they believed they might come up with entirely new approaches to solving the company's problems. One of the authors of this book found that in a certain company a group of 450 foremen were intensely interested in the company's financial planning and problems. He was surprised. But on second thought he realized that, after their families, the company was probably the most important thing in their lives, and company financial matters were therefore important to them.

2. *Make Goals Verifiable and Interlocking.* The importance of doing this has been emphasized above. Otherwise planning tends to be meaningless.

3. *Clarify and Disseminate Important Planning Premises.* As pointed out earlier in this chapter, those who take part in the planning process must base their decisions and actions on certain assumptions about the future. Obviously, they should use the same premises if their plans are to be coordinated.

4. *Clarify Job Responsibilities.* Making and implementing plans are the responsibilities of everyone in a company. Unless an individual knows what his job is and what his duties are, he can hardly contribute much to making or carrying out plans. A structure of verifiable goals helps. A knowledge of the amount of discretion (authority) a person has is essential. It also helps him to know what the company's policies are so that he can use his authority in a consistent way. One element of job responsibility that is often disregarded is the need for information. It takes information of all kinds to make and achieve plans. The business executive who keeps information from those people in his company who need it will find he has a group of ignorant, lackadaisical, and inefficient employees.

5. *Never Overlook the Importance of Regular Review of Plans and Progress.* Sometimes plans get out of date. A new law, an unexpected new product from a competitor, a sudden increase in the price of an important raw material, the failure of a machine, or a number of other unforeseen things may upset a well-thought-out plan. Think what happened to importer of foreign made toys when the dollar sank to unexpected lows in 1973. Or to many other companies when oil products became unexpectedly scarce and more expensive. Obviously one cannot make plans and then forget about them.

Furthermore, no responsible business manager can take for granted that people in his company or department are actually accomplishing plans as expected. He cannot wait to take action until after the company has suffered a large loss or gone bankrupt. The old adage about locking the barn door after the horse is stolen applies especially in business.

Planning progress must be monitored. This is a major part of a manager's job. He is responsible for doing what he reasonably can to assure that plans are being achieved. How he should go about it is the subject of a later chapter on managerial control.

SUMMARY

One of the major causes of business failures is the lack of effective planning—that is, the selection of goals and the means of reaching them. Planning is the foundation of managing a business because everything else a manager does depends on it.

To realize what planning involves, it is necessary to understand the various types of plans. All of them shape and control the future actions of people in a company, and they may be summarized as follows:

1. *Objectives, or goals—the endpoints toward which business activities are aimed.*
2. *Policies—guides for people in using discretion in their decision making.*
3. *Strategies—general programs of action, including major objectives and policies, with an implied deployment of resources, to attain overall company objectives.*
4. *Procedures—chronological sequences of specified actions.*
5. *Rules—required actions or nonactions in a specific area.*
6. *Programs—complexes of goals, policies, procedures, rules, job assignments, steps to be taken, manpower or money to be used, and other things necessary to carry out a desired course of action.*
7. *Budgets—statements of plans and expected results expressed in numerical terms.*

The logical and rational approach to planning may be outlined as follows:

1. *Being aware of opportunities through diagnosis of business markets and the strengths and weaknesses of the company.*
2. *Choosing clear, verifiable, and attainable objectives.*
3. *Identifying and communicating planning premises—the expected future in which plans will operate.*
4. *Identifying alternatives by which goals may be reached.*

5. *Comparing and analyzing alternative courses of action in the light of goals sought.*
6. *Choosing from among alternatives—that is, making a decision as to which course of action to follow.*
7. *Formulating necessary supporting plans.*
8. *Numberizing plans through budgets to give them meaning and definiteness.*

In determining what period of time to plan for, it is best to try to assure that commitments made in the planning decisions taken today can be fulfilled in the future. But for many important long-term commitments, we may not know enough of the future to assure their fulfillment. In this event, a manager can try to build a degree of flexibility into his plans that will allow him to change his plans, if necessary, without undue cost or embarrassment.

One of the most promising approaches to planning in recent years is that of managing by objectives. This commonsense approach to managing requires a number of things to make it work. Goals must be verifiable, must interlock with other company goals, and must be reasonably attainable. People must be given adequate assistance, should have a voice in setting their own objectives, and should be appraised on the basis of what they accomplish.

The discussions in this chapter suggest a number of ways in which a manager can establish an environment for effective planning. In general, they consist of doing things that help people to plan, and of making sure that they do plan.

KEY TERMS AND CONCEPTS FOR REVIEW

What planning is	Steps in planning
Types of plans	Planning premises
Objectives or goals	Selecting an alternative
Making objectives verifiable	Principle of the critical, or limiting, factor
Policies	
Strategies	Rationality in planning
Procedures	Decision commitment
Rules	Flexibility in planning
Programs	Managing by objectives
Budgets	Goals as an interlocking network
	Regular review of plans and programs

QUESTIONS FOR ANALYSIS AND DISCUSSION

1. Why is planning referred to as the primary task, or foundation, of management?

2.   A company president once remarked that he could not understand all the fuss about objectives and managing by objectives since he and everyone in his company knew that the objective of the business was profit. What do you feel about his statement, and what would you say to him?

3.   Since policies guide people in their planning, some believe that they can hardly be called plans. Do you agree? Why? Why not?

4.   Because paper work is such a large expense in businesses and other organizations, and since it arises mostly from procedures, it might be argued that a company should do away with procedures. Do you agree that this might be a good thing?

5.   All kinds of plans must be interrelated. Why?

6.   Why are planning premises important to correlated company planning?

7.   Take a problem you have in which you are not clear what you should do. Identify the critical or limiting factor(s) and solve for it(them). Did doing so help you resolve your problem?

8.   Why may planning be looked upon as an exercise in rationality? Why does following certain steps help in coming to a rational decision?

9.   "Long-range planning is not planning for future decisions but planning the future impact of today's decisions." Explain.

10.   "The best plan is not always the most flexible plan." Explain.

11.   A large number of American businesses are operating under programs of managing by objectives. Yet not many are satisfied that their programs are working well. Have you any idea why this is probably so?

12.   If the task of the manager is to design and maintain an environment for the performance of people, how can a manager develop an environment to assure him that planning is done well?

SUGGESTED READINGS

Cannon, J. T. *Business Strategy and Policy.* New York: Harcourt, Brace & World, Inc., 1968.

Fulmer, R. M. *The New Management.* New York: Macmillan Publishing Company, Inc., 1974, chapters 8–9.

Kepner, C. H., and B. B. Tregoe   *The Rational Manager.* New York: McGraw-Hill Book Company, 1965.

Koontz, H., and C. O'Donnell   *Principles of Management* (5th ed.). New York: McGraw-Hill Book Company, 1972, chapters 6–11.

Koontz, H., and C. O'Donnell   *Essentials of Management.* New York: McGraw-Hill Book Company, 1974, chapters 5–9.

Paine, F. T., and W. Nauman   *Strategy and Policy Formulation.* Philadelphia: W. B. Saunders Company, 1974.

Raia, A. P. *Managing by Objectives.* Glenview, Ill. Scott, Foresman & Company, 1974.

Steiner, G. A. *Top Management Planning.* New York: Macmillan, 1969.

21

Organizing: Making Teamwork Possible

One of the difficult problems every businessman faces as soon as his business requires more people than he can personally supervise is how to organize his operations. It will be recalled that in Chapter 19 we stated that a successful manager must design an environment for performance. One of the major elements of such an environment is a structure of roles. Not just any structure of roles, but an intentional one that has been designed for the purpose and in which it is possible for people to perform.

REQUIREMENTS FOR STRUCTURED ORGANIZATIONAL ROLES

It will be remembered that individuals in an organization must have roles to play just as football players must have specified positions on the team. A person's role should include: (1) verifiable goals; (2) end-result areas for which he is responsible; (3) a specified area of discretion (or authority); and (4) the needed information and tools to perform tasks.

Furthermore, if individuals are to make a meaningful contribution to business success, what they do—their roles—must be coordinated. Imagine a football player who knew that his position was to be left tackle, but did not know what he was to do or how he fitted in with the other players!

This is what organizing is all about. It

involves establishing a network of roles for people to fill. **A good organization makes it possible for people to feel responsible for tasks because they actually are responsible.** It gives each person a clear idea of how his role relates to others. It furnishes an environment in which people can and will perform. And, hopefully, it makes it possible for people to be employed to their fullest capacities.

Sociologists call this sort of organization a *formal* organization as distinguished from *informal* organizations. The latter kind of organization is without design; it springs up of itself, like the office grapevine or the group around the water cooler.

CRITICISMS OF FORMAL ORGANIZATIONS

Many writers who have studied business enterprises, especially large ones, have been critical of their formal organization structures. Some years ago William Whyte wrote a popular book on *The Organization Man,* picturing him as forced to be a conformist with little or no opportunity to remain an individual and to exercise his imagination. A few years later, Professor Chris Argyris of Harvard made the point that a business structure based on formal organization principles (as he then interpreted them) led to individual frustration, personality conflicts, loss of perspective, and even mediocrity.

Other critics have contended that a manager should operate his company as a team. They seem to forget that members of athletic teams play given positions for which they are specially trained, follow play patterns that have been worked out in advance, and obey signals that someone calls from the field or the bench. Still other critics have said that the manager should simply be a leader, like a symphony orchestra conductor. They overlook the fact that the fine cooperation of a symphony orchestra is that of accomplished musicians playing specific instruments, following scores written for those instruments, and responding to the exact interpretation of the orchestra conductor. A symphony orchestra conductor would not let his clarinetist do any kind of "tootling" he wished.

It is true that many businesses, government, and other organizations do unnecessarily stifle people, and that people sometimes feel like cogs in a machine. It is also true that some jobs require little imagination and give little opportunity for creativity.

Some of the inadequacies of organizations arise from poor practice rather than from the fact that they are organizations. There is no reason from the standpoint of organization *principles* why a role cannot give a person opportunities for discretion, utilization of his creative talents, and recognition of his individual likes and capacities. There are many such roles in business.

Nevertheless, we must recognize several facts of life. In the first place, all human cooperation—indeed, just living together—implies some degree of conformity; we must obey traffic lights, we must work or play at certain times, and we must respect other people's rights. In the second place, the need to reduce costs requires having many routine jobs with very little discretion in them. Much as we may be dismayed by the automobile assembly line, cars would be impossibly expensive if we put them together one by one. In the third place, it is a fact that some people are satisfied with, and even challenged by, tasks that look deadly dull to some of us. One of the authors recalls meeting a man who had spent 30 years keeping account of the fuel consumption of loco-motives on a railroad, and was convinced that he had the most im-portant job in the company!

ORGANIZATION CHARTS

One way of depicting an organization is to use an organization chart. It may resemble that of the small electronics factory shown in Fig-ure 21–1, or that of the department store shown in Figure 21–2, or that of the huge General Motors Corporation shown in Figure 21–3.

These charts show something of the way in which companies are organized, and some of the things they do. The charts even give a clue to the roles of the various managers. But they provide only a skimpy guide to the structure of roles in these companies. In the first place, they do not show the title and position of everyone who works in them. In the second place, there is no information on the exact goals of each manager, and only a general idea of the end-results for which he is responsible. Third, there is no information on how much authority each manager has. Can the various managers in the department store

FIGURE 21–1

Organization of a Small Electronics Company

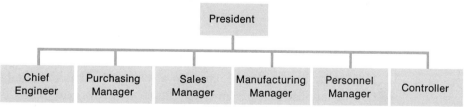

FIGURE 21–2

Organization of a Department Store

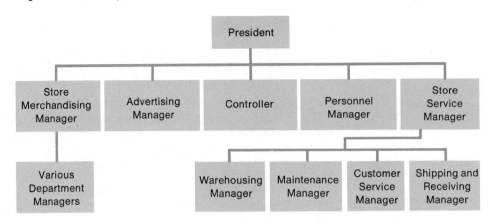

buy all they want of anything? Can the chief engineer design any electronic product that suits his fancy? Can the general manager of Chevrolet develop and market any size or kind of car he likes, and sell it for any price he wishes?

This is the trouble with organization charts. They give an outline of how a company is organized, and show the principal authority relationships for decision-making. As such they are a handy tool, but the businessman who thinks he is organizing his company when he draws boxes on an organization chart is like a person who thinks he knows a country by looking at a roadmap. In particular, there are a number of difficult problem areas managers must recognize if they are to be successful organizers.

THE PROBLEM AREAS IN ORGANIZING

As simple as organizing seems to be in outline, the best-designed organization structure may unintentionally lead to friction and waste. Every businessman should look at this part of his job with great care. The following discussion deals with some of the problem areas and some of the fundamental principles that are important to effective business organization.

We can bring these problem areas into focus by addressing ourselves to a few simple questions:

1. How many people should report to a manager? (It is this limitation of number that accounts for the fact that we have levels of organization).

2. What are the major organization structures (or patterns of grouping activities), and why are different structures used?
3. What kinds of authority relationships exist in an organization structure? (This is the problem of line and staff.)
4. How is authority delegated within an organization?
5. To what extent should authority be dispersed in an organization? (This is the problem of centralization and decentralization.)
6. Why should organization structures be planned?

HOW MANY PEOPLE SHOULD REPORT TO A MANAGER?

No manager can supervise an unlimited number of people. Some are able to supervise a few more than others, but effective supervision and control require that the number of immediate subordinates be relatively few. This is known as the "span of management" or "span of control" problem. Can you imagine the confusion if the hundreds of thousands of people in the General Electric Company reported directly to the chairman and chief executive officer? At the other extreme, think of how many managers GE would need if each boss had only two people reporting to him—and the multitudinous levels of managers that would result.

The Bible tells us that even Moses, when he was leading the Israelites out of Egypt 3,000 years ago, had a span of control problem. In Exodus 18:17–26, we find Moses' father-in-law telling him how to solve it.

> The thing thou doest is not good. Thou wilt certainly wear away, both thou and this people that is with thee; for this thing is too heavy for thee; thou art not able to perform it thyself alone. Hearken now unto my voice, I will give thee counsel. . . . Thou shalt provide out of the people able men . . . and place such over them, to be rulers of thousands, and rulers of hundreds, rulers of fifties, and rulers of tens. And let them judge the people at all seasons; and it shall be, that every great matter they shall bring unto thee, but every small matter they shall judge; so shall it be easier for thyself, and they shall bear the burden with thee. If thou shalt do this thing, and God command thee so, then thou shall be able to endure, and all this people shall also go to their place in peace.

Moses followed this advice and built an organization that aided him considerably in leading his people to the Promised Land.

Levels Are Expensive

We have already seen that the fewer persons reporting to each manager, the more levels of organization there will be. As levels in-

FIGURE 21–3
Organization of General Motors Corporation (July 1973)

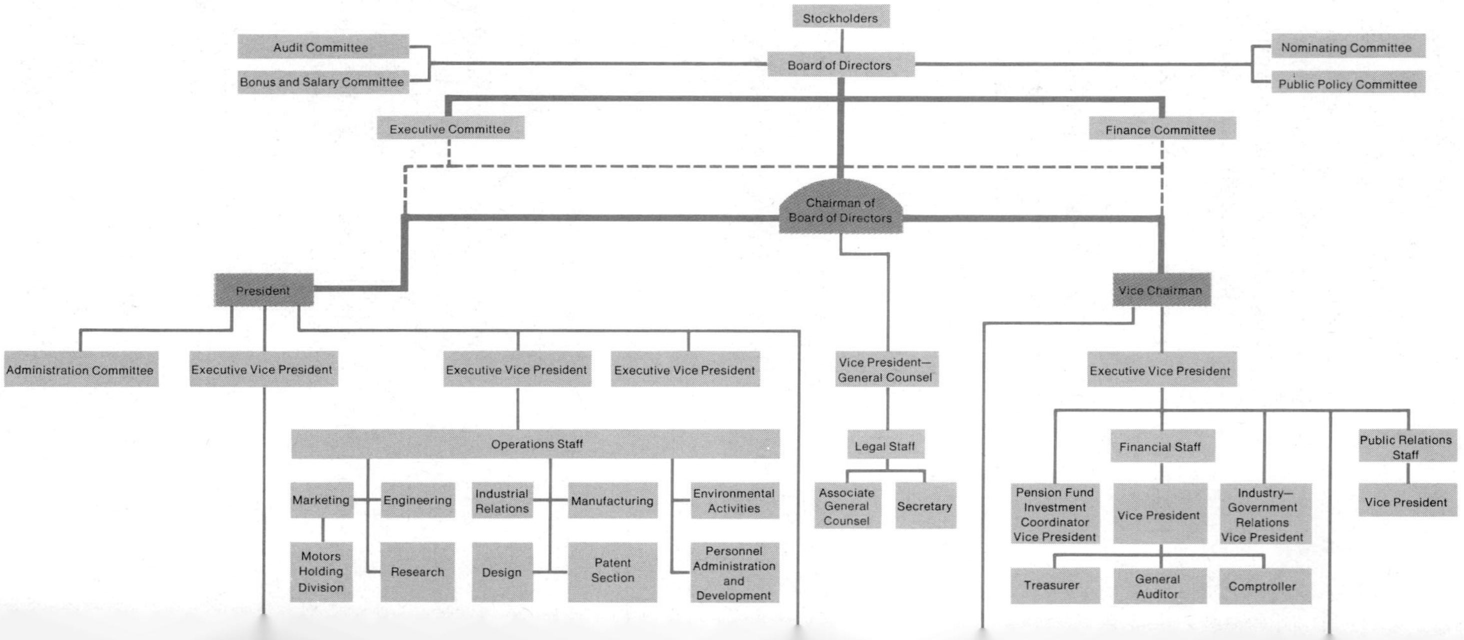

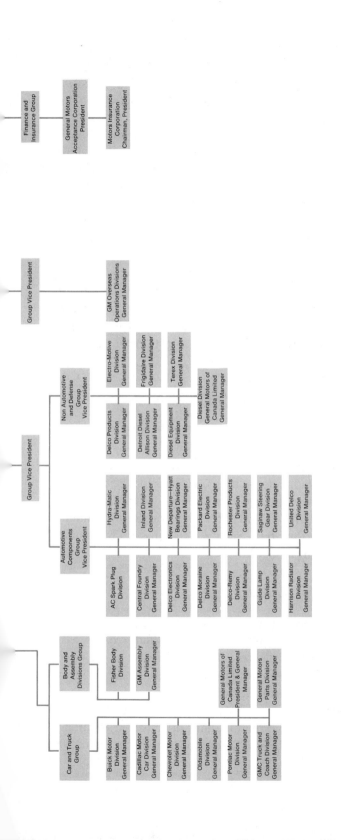

crease, more and more effort and money must be devoted to managing, not only because of additional managers required, but also due to the costs of staffs to assist them, the costs of coordinating more depart- ments, and the costs of office space and other facilities. Accountants refer to such costs as "overhead" or "burden" in contrast to the "direct" costs—the costs for factory, sales, and engineering labor who directly produce the goods or services that make business profits. Levels above the "firing line" are predominantly staffed with managers and their as- sistants who are not directly productive and whose cost it would be desirable to eliminate *if that were possible*.

Also, the more levels a company has the more complex its communi- cations become. A company with many levels has greater difficulty in communicating objectives, policies, and plans to the operating level than does one in which the president can speak directly with operating employees. Communication back from the "firing line" to the top also becomes more difficult. Each level filters out some of the information passing through it; researchers have estimated that as much as 75 per- cent of a communication may be lost in passing through only four levels.

Too Many Subordinates May also Be Expensive

While additional levels of management cost money and create difficulties in communication, too few levels may also be expensive. The manager who has a large number of people reporting to him may not have the time to make the decisions people need for their work, to help and counsel them, and to give them policy guidance. This can result in a group of frustrated subordinates who twiddle their thumbs waiting to get in and see their boss. Such a manager is really a bottle- neck and costs the company money.

How Many People Should Report to a Manager?

This question, as we have seen, is as old as Moses, but we still do not know much more about the answer than Moses did. Experts seem to feel that around 4 to 8 subordinates is the right number at the upper levels of management and 8 to 15 at the lowest levels. Studies made of management show that, as broad averages, these figures correspond to what happens in practice.

At the same time, one finds wide variations in actual organizations. The Pope, as head of the Catholic Church, apparently has some 1,900 people reporting directly to him. The President of General Motors had only three executive vice presidents and one group vice president reporting to him in 1973. One of these executive vice presidents had 9 executives reporting to him, and the vice president in charge of the automotive components group had 14 subordinates reporting to him. The president of a railroad that is generally regarded as well managed had 10 top executives reporting to him in 1973, and one of these had 11 subordinates. Yet the head of another carrier, not regarded as so well managed, had only seven major subordinates.

Examples could be given of successful business managers with as few as 1 subordinate or as many as 30. But when the number gets above ten, we suspect that too many people are reporting directly to a single superior. When the span is as large as that of the Pope or the President of the United States, we find that a crew of staff assistants actually make many of their boss's decisions. This was illustrated by the Watergate scandal which caused President Nixon so much trouble in the mid-1970s.

The important thing for a businessman to realize is that the span problem cannot be solved by a rule. There is no set number that can be applied in all situations. But certain general considerations do apply. The businessman who wants to avoid too large a span on the one hand or too many levels on the other would do well to give his attention to these.

Factors Underlying the Number of People

Various factors bear upon the number of people a manager can effectively supervise. The major ones are the following:

1. The clearer plans are, and the better a subordinate understands them, the less time the boss will have to spend explaining what should be done and how to do it.

2. The clearer a person's job, and the more definite his authority, the less time his boss will have to waste in making decisions his subordinate should have made, in correcting decisions his subordinate should not have made, and in explaining his subordinate's job and how it relates to other people's jobs.

3. The more training a person has for his job, the less time his superior will have to spend showing him how to do it and correcting his mistakes.

4. The more stable a company is, and the slower the pace of change, the easier it will be for its employees to understand plans, job defini-

tions, and the delegation of authority. Of course, many businesses are in fast-moving fields where new products and stiff competition require rapid change; in such cases the load on managers may be so great as to require narrow spans.

5. Since most managing requires communication—of goals, policies, plans, authority delegations, and information—the better a manager is as a communicator, the more people he can effectively manage.

6. Since a manager who delegates tasks to his subordinates never loses his responsibility for what they do, he must have ways of assuring himself that they are doing what was intended. The more efficient a manager is in setting up standards of performance that are easy to monitor, the more people he can effectively manage.

7. Since many managerial relationships require face-to-face contacts with subordinates, and since personal contacts tend to be time consuming, the more contacts that are necessary, the fewer persons a manager can supervise.

8. Because time is the major limitation in all of the things we do, the amount of time a manager can devote to supervision will affect his span of control. Managers usually have other managers over them and must spend time meeting with them and with other people in the company. In addition, no manager manages all the time since he spends some of his time doing the activities he supervises, such as selling, engineering, or accounting.

WHY DIFFERENT ORGANIZATION PATTERNS ARE USED

The purpose of an organization structure, it will be recalled, is to provide an environment in which people can perform. The internal environment is, of course, influenced by the external environment—markets, competition, geographic location, government actions, and other factors. Organization is also affected by the technology of a business. Out of experience and logic, a number of patterns have developed. The wise businessman will select a pattern of organization that will fit his needs, and not just copy that of another firm, no matter how successful it may be.

Functional Organization Structures

One of the patterns most commonly used organizes a company according to functions—the major things the company does. In a manufacturing company, these are likely to be production, marketing, finance, and engineering. In an insurance company, they are likely to be selling, investments, controllership, and actuarial (mathematical calculations about what types of policies can be offered, and their cost). In an oil company, the major functions will probably be exploration, production, refining, marketing, and finance.

A typical functional organization pattern is shown in Figure 21–4. The major advantages and disadvantages of this pattern are summarized underneath the diagram.

Territorial Organization Structures

Territorial, or geographic, structures organize a company or a part of it around the places where operations are located. The Prudential Life Insurance Company, for example, has a west coast office in Los Angeles that almost duplicates the headquarters in New York. Sears Roebuck groups its stores in regions across the United States. Most companies organize their sales departments by geographic districts and regions. Production plants may be in various locations, sometimes near raw materials and sometimes near markets. Naturally, the plant managers on the spot are in charge.

While sales or manufacturing operations are frequently organized on a territorial basis, this is seldom the basis for organizing major segments of a company or its top management. Territorial organization is found in large insurance companies, such as Prudential, in large management consulting firms with offices over the country, in large supermarket chains, and in the overseas operations of most companies.

A typical territorial organization structure is shown in Figure 21–5, together with a summary of the major advantages and disadvantages of this form of organization.

Product Organization Structures

As companies have grown larger and have sought to involve more of their managers in the responsibility for profit-making, it has become common to organize them according to product lines. The Buick, Cadillac, Chevrolet, and other divisions of General Motors are well-known examples of this. Each of them is much like a separate company, with its own engineering, manufacturing, and marketing departments. Product organization is found in most large U.S. firms, at least wherever a closely related grouping of major functions related to a product line can be made. The product organization structure is also applied to

Robert C. Townsend

Robert C. Townsend is known for his best-selling book, *Up the Organization* (1970). He is also a management consultant whose career has included a three-year stint as president and chairman of Avis, Inc., the auto rental firm.

Townsend was born in Washington, D.C., in 1920, of a well-to-do family. He attended elite schools, graduating from Princeton in 1942 with a degree in English. He was a Navy gunnery officer in the Pacific during World War II. Afterward he returned to graduate school at Columbia, taking business administration courses, and then worked for a Wall Street brokerage house.

From 1948 to 1962 Townsend worked for the American Express Company, where he became director of Hertz American Express International, Ltd. (owned jointly by American Express and Hertz Rent A Car). He advanced to senior vice president in charge of the company's investment and international banking activities. During his time at American Express, he found himself in what he later described as a "near-perfect learning environment" for the study of how not to handle organizational problems.

In 1962 Townsend was hired by the international banking firm of Lazard Fieres & Company to head up Avis, Inc., which had just come under the banking company's control. He was offered $50,000 a year, but insisted on taking only $36,000 since the company was chronically in the red. But when Avis moved into the black, he still refused an increase, believing that the company should emphasize profit sharing, rather than high salaries, for its key employees.

divisions within a company: the marketing division, for example, may have people in charge of various product lines, and so may the engineering division.

Sometimes the technology of an industry makes product organization impractical. An oil company, for example, could not have separate gasoline, jet fuel, motor oil, heating oil, or asphalt divisions for the simple reason that all these products come from the same wells and refineries. But it might have separate product marketing groups. For the same reason a passenger airline would not have separate divisions handling

His policy at Avis was based on promotion from within, the promotion itself providing the motivation for people to grow into their jobs. His method of problem-solving was what he termed the "Man from Mars" approach: The manager pretends he is a man from Mars who knows everything about earth people and their society except what has been done in the past by his firm or by other companies to solve similar problems. This ran counter to what he called the "policy manual" approach, based largely on "the way we've always done it."

Townsend's originality led to a whole new way of doing business at Avis, resulting in a 28 percent increase in the company's share of the car rental market. One change he made was to get rid of the company's advertising department and give the account to Doyle Dane Bernbach, the leader in Madison Avenue's trend toward low-key but imaginative, often humorous, advertising. They came up with the slogan "When you're only number two, you try harder," and made it into a household phrase. Within three years the company's internal sales growth rate increased from 10 percent to 35 percent, and operations started to show a profit—$2.8 million in 1965.

On the day in 1965 when Avis was acquired by International Telephone & Telegraph Company, Townsend resigned. Since then he has been a free-lance management consultant and publisher of the *Congressional Monitor,* a Washington newsletter for which subscribers pay a $285-a-year subscription fee.

During a consulting job with the C.R.M. Company, publisher of *Psychology Today,*

Townsend developed what he called "The A.B.C. Survival Manual," copies of which were mimeographed and distributed to all of the company's employees. At the suggestion of an executive of the company, he revised the manual and published it as *Up the Organization: How to Stop the Corporation from Stifling People and Strangling Profits.* Designed to communicate his own brand of managerial wisdom in a folksy way, the book is arranged in 97 short chapters. He concerns himself with people in the organization, their ego and development needs, and the sort of climate that will motivate people to achieve common objectives. *Up the Organization* has been translated into 12 languages and has sold over 2 million copies.

One of Townsend's maxims is: "Try to create an organization around your people, not jam your people into those organization-chart rectangles. The only excuse for organization is to maximize the chance that each one, working with others, will get for growth in his job."

Townsend's critical approach to organization made many businessmen rethink their organization practices. But many of the more talented company organizers have come to the conclusion that: (1) Townsend was right in certain of his criticisms and ideas; (2) in certain areas of management and organization he did not know what he was talking about; and (3) his phenomenal success at Avis was due to imaginative advertising, marketing, and leadership, and not to effective organizing. As author of *Up the Organization,* Townsend did, however, carve a popular and lasting niche in management.

passengers, mail, and freight, since these usually go together in the same plane.

A typical product organization structure is shown in Figure 21–6, along with a summary of its principal advantages and disadvantages.

Customer Organization Structures

Some companies focus their organization structure on the customer, particularly in sales operations. Book publishing companies are likely

FIGURE 21–4

Typical Functional Organization Structure for a Manufacturing Company

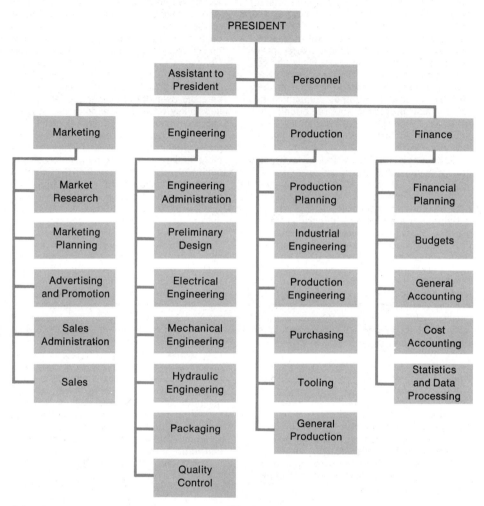

Advantages
—Logical reflection of functions
—Follows principle of occupational
  specialization
—Maintains power and prestige of
  major functions
—Simplifies training
—Means of tight control at top

Disadvantages
—Responsibility for profits at the
  top only
—Overspecializes and narrows view-
  points of key personnel
—Limits development of general
  managers
—Reduces coordination between
  functions

FIGURE 21–5

Typical Territorial Organization Structure for a Manufacturing Company

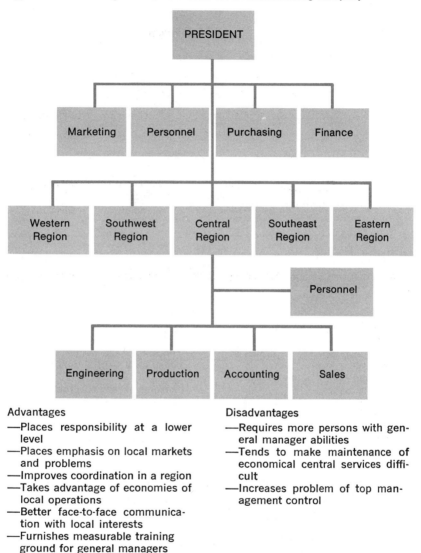

Advantages
—Places responsibility at a lower level
—Places emphasis on local markets and problems
—Improves coordination in a region
—Takes advantage of economies of local operations
—Better face-to-face communication with local interests
—Furnishes measurable training ground for general managers

Disadvantages
—Requires more persons with general manager abilities
—Tends to make maintenance of economical central services difficult
—Increases problem of top management control

to have departments for the different kinds of readers they sell to: elementary school, secondary school, college and university, professional, reference, and trade (that is, customers who buy novels, biographies, and other books sold through general bookstores). Each of these departments in a book publishing company may be a fairly separate operation with its own editing, production, and sales groups. In other

FIGURE 21–6

Typical Product Organization Structure for a Manufacturing Company

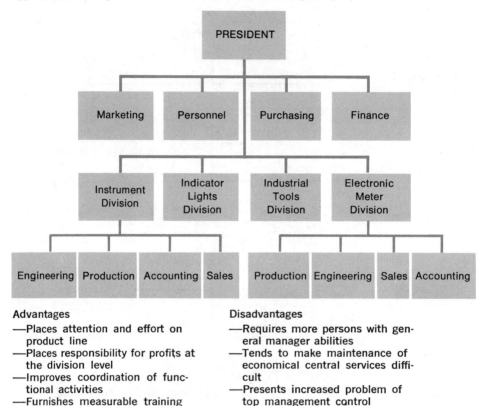

Advantages
—Places attention and effort on product line
—Places responsibility for profits at the division level
—Improves coordination of functional activities
—Furnishes measurable training ground for general managers
—Permits growth and diversity of products and services

Disadvantages
—Requires more persons with general manager abilities
—Tends to make maintenance of economical central services difficult
—Presents increased problem of top management control

companies a sales department may be divided into separate groups selling to industrial customers, homeowners, office building managers, and others.

This kind of organization, particularly in sales, has the advantage of keeping people close to customers and their needs. But there can be drawbacks. Each customer manager may want special attention for his own customers, and coordination among them may be difficult. Also, employees who are oriented toward customers sometimes lose sight of the fact that their product may be useful in other markets. For example, in one company making synthetic materials, so much attention was given to selling the product to automobile and furniture upholsterers that its use for women's handbags and apparel was for a time overlooked.

Process, or Equipment, Organization Structures

Some companies organize their activities around processes or equipment. A manufacturer, for example, may have heat-treating, paint, punch press, and electronic data processing departments.

This kind of departmental organization obtains economic advantages by concentrating on a process or a group of machines. Sometimes the nature of the machines demands it, as in the case of large computer installations that require heavy capital investment, have tremendous capacity for handling data, and cannot be economically divided into departments.

Service Department Organizations

Plant maintenance, the stenographic pool, accounting, personnel recruiting, and electronic data processing are examples of the service departments commonly found in companies. Although often confused with staff functions, to be discussed below, they are actually grouping of activities as in any other kind of department.

The reasons for service departments are two. One is that lower costs can be obtained by combining activities. Another is that they enable centralized control. By having everyone's typing work to go to a central group of stenographers, we utilize the typists' time more efficiently. By putting accounting work into a single department, we not only save money by having specially trained people do it but we assure that accounting records will be kept accurately and consistently.

There are dangers in overdoing service departments. A stenographic pool may save money in getting letters typed, but lose much more money if important letters written by key executives and engineers are delayed. An accounting department may concentrate accounting activities to a point where the plant manager or sales manager who needs information may not get it soon enough or in a form he can understand. The problem is often this: we can easily see that we can save the cost of a clerk or technician by concentrating activities in a central department; but we cannot as easily see how much this will cost in terms of frustration and delay to the people the department is designed to serve.

Matrix Organization Structures

A form of organization coming into increased use is variously referred to as "matrix," "grid," or sometimes "project" or "product management" structure. The essence of a matrix organization, as we normally find it, is the combining of functional and product patterns in a single structure. Figure 21–7, depicting matrix organization in an engineering department, shows functional managers in charge of engineering functions and an overlay of project managers responsible for specific projects.

Matrix organization is common in engineering and research and development operations. It is found also in marketing, when a company wishes to give a manager overall responsibility for a product, such as "Ivory" soap or "Cascade" dishwashing detergent, but not put directly under him the people engaged in sales, advertising, or production.

Matrix management represents a kind of compromise between functional and product organizational arrangements. As companies have become increasingly interested in end results—that is, in the final product or project—they have wanted to hold someone responsible for assuring such end results. This could, of course, be accomplished with product organization alone. But technology may not permit it, as in the oil business. Or it may be wasteful; a test laboratory and a skilled mathematician may be more economically used if they are not restricted to a single project. Moreover, professionally trained people like scien-

FIGURE 21–7

Matrix Organization in an Engineering Department

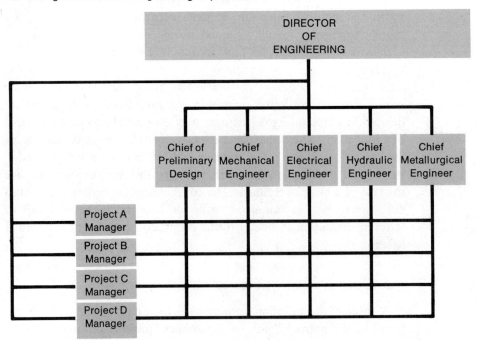

tists, engineers, lawyers, and college professors often prefer to be identified with their technical specialties, and to report to a boss of their own kind.

Matrix organization results in people having more than one boss. This often spells confusion and conflict. Also, it is hard for people to feel loyalty to two bosses.

But such problems can be avoided to some extent by carefully defining the separate roles of the functional managers and the project managers. In engineering, for example, we can give the project manager authority over the project budget, relationships with customers, and the integrity of the total project design. We can make it clear that the functional managers are responsible for their people, for getting work done that they have promised a project manager in return for his budget money, and for the quality of the design work they turn out.

MIXING ORGANIZATION STRUCTURES IN PRACTICE

In practice, businesses mix the forms of organization structure. This is because no single organization pattern may fit a particular business. The form of organization structure chosen depends, in the final analysis, upon practical needs. The question is: Does it work? Does it help to assure business success?

At the top of a typical large company we may find functional heads of manufacturing, engineering, marketing, personnel, and finance. But we may find product divisions at the next level. Within the Chevrolet Division of General Motors, for example, we find functional departments. Within the sales department of Chevrolet, we find territorial managers in charge of districts and zones, and special departments devoted to retail dealers and fleet customers.

THE PROBLEM OF LINE AND STAFF

An important distinction in every area of organization is that between line and staff. Probably no organizing leads to more misunderstanding, more friction, jealousy, and even open warfare than do those that arise from differences between line and staff. A business does not have to be very large before it encounters this problem.

The Importance of Understanding Line and Staff

An example from real life will illustrate the importance of knowing the difference between line and staff. The president of a company hired an exceptionally brilliant young man to be his staff assistant. This young man had a master's degree from a major university, was a certified public accountant, and had some good industrial experience. The president charged his young assistant with finding means and places to reduce costs. The assistant gathered around him statisticians, economists, production-efficiency experts, planners, and other specialists. With their help, he readily discovered many places where costs could be reduced and management improved.

But he was doomed to fail. He thought all he needed to do was to tell his findings to the key line operating executives, and they would be required to follow them. But the line operating executives resented the intrusion of the president's young staff assistant; they didn't want to take orders from him, and insisted that the young man be replaced. Faced with a choice between supporting his chief line lieutenants or supporting his assistant, the president had to replace the assistant with someone who knew how to sell his ideas to the line executives.

This kind of problem is repeated over and over in the business world. People, and often very intelligent people, get into trouble because they fail to understand the difference between line and staff roles.

The Meaning of Line and Staff

Some experts look upon the line employees as those who have the responsibility for accomplishing the major objectives of a business, and the staff as "other people." Those who hold to this view usually classify production and sales (and sometimes finance) as line functions and all other functions, whether purchasing, accounting, personnel, or plant maintenance, as staff functions. This widely-held idea identifies line and staff with types of activities. But is not a person who supervises buyers or maintenance workers just as much a line manager as one who supervises salesmen?

While this concept is not completely wrong, it implies that we have two kinds of people in a company: those who work toward the attainment of objectives, and other people. But surely, if we are going to operate a business efficiently we should not have anyone on the payroll who is not working to help the company achieve its objectives! Except, possibly the president's brother-in-law!

A more precise and logically valid concept of line and staff is that they are simply relationships. A person in a line position—that is, having line authority—is in a supervisory relationship; he has the power to

FIGURE 21–8

Line and Staff Relationships

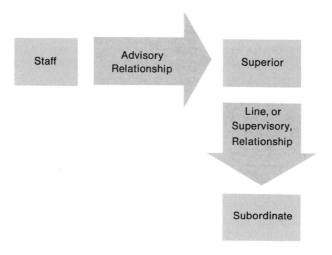

direct, to make decisions, to command. A person in a staff role is in an advisory relationship; he has the power to advise, recommend, or counsel, but not to give orders. These two relationships are shown in Figure 21–8.

Line relationships are supervisory and staff relationships are advisory. In practice, we usually find both relationships in the same position. Thus a company chief engineer will operate in a line capacity when he supervises his engineering group. He will also be called upon for advice by the president and others in the company; when he gives advice he will be operating in a staff capacity. There are certain departments which are primarily service departments but, because they are made up of specialists are likely to be relied on for advice and tend to be called staff departments. These include the legal, public relations, and personnel departments.

What the Concepts Mean in Practice

An understanding of line and staff is very important, and especially for the younger person in business. He must always ask himself what elements in his job are line and what are staff. When he is responsible for people and their actions, he is working in a line capacity. When his responsibility is to give advice, to sell ideas and recommendations but not to tell anyone what to do, he is functioning in a staff capacity.

This does not mean that a person with only the power to advise is powerless or useless. Most businessmen require and appreciate the advice of specialists and others who have something to contribute to the solution of problems. It is a rare businessman who does not have more problems than answers. But the intelligent boss wants sound advice, well thought out, based on analysis and study, and taking into account both the dangers and the advantages in a course of action.

Functional Authority

Departments that are primarily staff in nature are often given limited authority over people who do not report to them. This is also true of many service departments. For example, a company controller is almost invariably given the authority to prescribe the kind of accounting records and reports all managers must make. A personnel manager is usually given authority to prescribe how employee grievances and union relations are to be handled. A public relations officer may be given the power to approve all statements to the press or to television. A chart of these relationships is shown in Figure 21–9.

The functional authority of the personnel director or public relations director is really a slice of the president's authority which he has

FIGURE 21–9

Line and Functional Authority Relationships

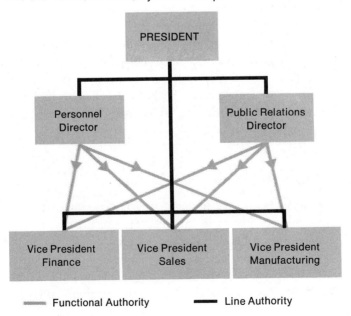

PRESIDENT

Personnel Director

Public Relations Director

Vice President Finance

Vice President Sales

Vice President Manufacturing

▬▬▬ Functional Authority   ▬▬▬ Line Authority

given them to use on his behalf. **Functional authority is generally un-avoidable.** An organization needs the decisions of many specialists, and the only other way to get them would be to have these specialists pass their advice on to the chief, who would automatically approve it and pass it on down. But functional authority has its negative aspect, since it means that people can receive instructions from a number of bosses. It is not unusual for people, especially far down in an organization, to have to take instructions from many persons who are not their direct superiors.

Moreover, specialists often have a way of seeing the whole business through their own eyes. A controller, for example, told one of the authors that he realized his authority was limited to accounting matters only, and therefore he insisted on approving only proposals with a dollar sign attached. If his colleagues were allowing him to have the deciding voice on all expenditures, he was actually running the company.

The danger that specialists may exercise too much power is a serious one. The least a top manager should do is to make sure that the specialist and the people he gives orders to understand exactly what his functional authority is. Few businesses seem to do this. The result too often is confusion and resentment on the part of those to whom such orders come.

DELEGATION OF AUTHORITY

The main cause of business failures is poor management. The main cause of managerial failures, in turn, have been shown to be poor or inept delegation of authority.

What Delegation of Authority Is

Authority is delegated when a superior gives a subordinate the power to make certain decisions. The process of delegation involves: (1) determining the results expected of a subordinate; (2) clarifying the tasks he is expected to undertake; (3) giving him the authority necessary to accomplish these tasks; and (4) holding him responsible for using his delegated authority properly.

Underlying Principles of Delegation

Although delegation is often done badly, the principles underlying it are simple. They may be summarized as follows:

1. *Delegate by results expected.* A superior should not simply parcel out his authority to a subordinate; he should decide what results he expects, and make sure his subordinate has the authority to accomplish them. If bosses follow this principle, they will sometimes find that a subordinate simply does not have the power to accomplish what is expected of him.

2. *Maintain unity of command.* As far as possible, subordinates should have only one boss. While this is not always possible, as we noted in the cases of matrix organization and functional authority, it decreases the chance that there will be conflicts in instructions and increases the sense of loyalty and responsibility a person will feel toward his boss.

3. *Responsibility is absolute and cannot be delegated.* A superior can delegate authority but he cannot delegate responsibility for the acts of his subordinates. If your boss called you in and asked about a mistake made by a person reporting to you, would you tell him that you had delegated the authority and so he had better talk to your subordinate?

4. *Authority and responsibility should be equal.* No subordinate should be held responsible for more than he has been given power to do, nor should he be held responsible for less.

5. *Decisions should be made at the point where necessary delegated authority exists.* Each manager should make whatever decisions he can in the light of the amount of power he has had delegated to him, and only those decisions beyond his power should be referred upward. To do otherwise is to make delegation meaningless and to shift decision-making back to a boss who already has provided for his subordinate to do it.

Delegation Is Also an Art

The principles of delegation are widely understood, and when managers fail to apply them it is usually because they are unable or unwilling to do so. Delegation is necessary if a company is to grow. Men who are building their own businesses often find it difficult to delegate. This is natural. A man starts his business in a garage, and does much or all of the engineering, selling, manufacturing, and even the accounting. As the business grows he finds it difficult to delegate decisions he has long been in the habit of making.

Since delegation as an art is so much a matter of personal attitudes, perhaps we can point out some of the requisites for becoming a good delegator. One of these is a willingness to give other people's ideas a chance and to let them make decisions in their own way. Another is a willingness to "let go," to realize that even if we can make all the decisions better and more easily than a subordinate can, we should save our time and effort for the more important decisions.

Another personal quality the good delegator must have is a willingness to see subordinates make mistakes. People learn that way. However, not all mistakes are alike. No manager would sit idly by and let his subordinate destroy the company, any more than a flight instructor sitting in an airplane with his student would let his student make a mistake that would crash the airplane.

A major reason why many managers are reluctant to delegate is that they fear losing control of their company or their department. They are afraid of what their subordinates will do. As we shall see in the chapter· on Management Control, the answer to this fear is to find a way of making sure that our subordinates are using their delegated authority to accomplish the desired goals and programs.

CENTRALIZATION AND DECENTRALIZATION

Centralization and decentralization are really aspects of the delegation of authority. A company is said to be centralized when there is little delegation and decisions are mostly made at the top. The ultimate of this is a company in which only one man, usually the owner, makes all the decisions. But such a company can hardly be said to have an organization structure at all. Decentralization, on the other hand, is the tendency to disperse authority widely throughout a company. The ultimate of decentralization would be to push all decision-making power down into the bottom of the organization. But this again would result in no organization structure because there would be nothing to tie together all the dispersed decision makers.

Consequently centralization and decentralization are not absolutes but matters of degree, like "hot" and "cold." They reflect styles of managing. Decentralization requires careful selection of what decisions to push down into the organization structure and what to hold near the top. Properly applied, it is a system of managing that relies on verifiable objectives, clear policies, and adequate controls.

A manager cannot be either for complete centralization or for complete decentralization. Even the most determined despot will find it impossible to make all the decisions in his company, for lack of time.

Factors Determining the Degree

Perhaps the most important factor determining the degree of decentralization is cost. Decisions involving large amounts of money are likely to be held close to the top. An airline's decision to buy a fleet of new airplanes will certainly be made at the very top of the organization, while the decision to hire maintenance mechanics will be made down below.

Another factor influencing the degree of decentralization is the importance attached to having uniform policies. One can be sure that in an automobile company any major decision concerning dealers will be made at the very top, both because of the strength of the dealer organizations and because of the importance of the dealers to the companies.

The degree of decentralization is also influenced by the size of a company. An owner of a small plumbing supply shop with a half-dozen employees can probably make all the decisions himself. But in larger companies, top managers have no choice but to decentralize to some extent. One cannot imagine the top management of the Bank of America trying to approve all of the thousands of loans made each day.

Still another important factor is the history of the business. If it has developed from a very small company to a large one, there will be a tendency for the founders to try to hold decision-making power at the top. If it has grown by the acquisition of dozens of once independent companies, as Litton Industries did, decentralization will be considerable because the former owners will want to hold on to as much authority as possible.

Furthermore, some top managers are by their very nature autocrats who grasp and hold onto power. Others are believers in democracy. Their attitudes are bound to have some influence on the degree of decentralization, although necessity may often overrule them.

An executive may be forced to centralize certain kinds of authority, whether he wants to or not. Government tax policies and regulations have a centralizing effect, since companies want to assure themselves of being within the requirements of the law and therefore, in order to have adequate control, must centralize decisions concerning them. Many companies would like to give their foremen more authority over subordinates, but the risks of getting into trouble with a union prevent them from doing so.

The Importance of Balance in Decentralization

One of the most difficult things for a businessman to do as his company grows is to strike the right balance between centralization and decentralization. In a company's early years, authority tends to be too centralized at the top. Then, when the company sees the need to disperse authority in order to remove managerial bottlenecks and permit efficient growth, it may decentralize too far. The result will sometimes be to give a subordinate manager power to make decisions that can prove very costly. This happened with the General Dynamics Corporation a few years ago; its Convair Division acquired so much power that it was able to lose $480 million on an ill-timed and poorly controlled jet airplane program. This huge loss almost bankrupted the very large parent.

Many companies seem to go through a cycle of decentralization and recentralization. For example, General Electric, which had been highly centralized until 1954, decentralized too much. Pushing almost complete authority onto some 130 operating departments, each of them fairly independent of the others, the top management lost too much control. When this became apparent, as costs rose and profits fell, action was taken to retrieve some of the delegated authority.

Proper balance requires that top management decide which decisions should be made at the top and which can be safely delegated. In a well balanced company, the top group retains authority on matters necessary to safeguard the company's future. These are likely to include such matters as acquisitions and mergers, raising of money, major capital expenditures, summary operating budgets and profit plans, new product programs, personnel policy, executive compensation, and the basic nature of the organization structure.

If proper balance is to be achieved, indeed if delegation is to be effective, it is necessary that the degree of delegation be made clear. Every manager should know the extent of his power to commit the company. And steps should be taken to make sure that people use their power exactly as prescribed.

ORGANIZATION STRUCTURE SHOULD BE PLANNED

Many businessmen overlook the importance of planning their future organization structure, especially as their companies grow. Organization structures change as businesses change, as they enter new markets, build new plants, or acquire other companies. The company that finds a simple functional organization suitable today may need a divisional-ized product organization some years hence.

Position requirements also change over time. It is a rare growing company that has not appointed someone to a position at one time that the person later was unable to fill. A typical case is an industrial and medical instruments company that grew because of the founder-president's genius for inventing new products. In its early days, when the company had only a few employees, the president was fearful of losing a key engineer and gave him the title of vice president for en-gineering. But the man had no talent for engineering management, and when the company grew he could not handle his managerial responsi-bilities. This had sad consequences, because it is virtually unworkable for any person to be demoted, when this problem occurs, a company usually has no choice but to seek a replacement. It lost a poor ex-ecutive and a fine engineer.

Proper organization planning helps a company anticipate the kind of people it will need for positions tomorrow. This is also the only way a company can develop enough people for future key positions. It is common for management to think that it has an adequate number of young "comers" for future executive positions. But it is often mistaken. In one company, for example, an organization plan disclosed the need for 45 key people in five years. This came as a shock to top manage-ment, who had felt that the 15 "comers" it had identified would be sufficient.

However, an organization structure cannot be planned if a company has no other plans for its future. The purpose of organization structure, as we have emphasized repeatedly, is to provide an environment for performance, a structure of roles to help people do their jobs. But if we have no idea what kind of company we will have in 5, 10, or 15 years, we can hardly plan an organization structure for it. Nor can we plan for the number and kind of people we will need, or for recruiting and training programs for them.

This is another indication that managing is an indispensable element in business success. It also illustrates how planning is the foundation of management.

SUMMARY

One of the difficult problems a businessman faces is how to organize his company so that people can work together effectively. Individuals must have roles to play in business just as football players must know their positions on a team. In business, if a person is to have a meaning-ful position he must (1) know what his goals are, (2) be clear as to the end results he is responsible for, (3) understand the degree of discretion or authority he has, and (4) have available to him the information and tools necessary to perform his job. Organization charts cannot show all these things. They can, at best, only be a simple kind of road map showing the arrangement of organizational positions.

One of the problems in developing an effective organization structure is to decide how many subordinates a manager should have. There is no precise number that can be applied to every situation. A manager's span of management depends on various factors: (1) the clearness of company plans, (2) the clearness of job specifications and authority, (3) the amount of training required and possessed by subordinates, (4) the pace of change in a company, (5) a manager's ability to com-municate, (6) a manager's effectiveness in monitoring his subordinates, (7) the extent to which face-to-face contacts are required, and (8) the time a manager has to devote to supervision.

Another problem is to select the pattern of organization that will best fit a company's needs. The organization can be structured around (1) the functions to be performed, (2) geographic territories, (3) prod-ucts or projects, (4) customers, (5) special processes or equipment, (6) service departments, or (7) a matrix combining functional or-ganization with product or project organization. The typical business organization structure is a mixture of several patterns.

A third major problem area in organizing involves the distinction between line and staff. These concepts are often misunderstood, re-sulting in needless inefficiencies and frictions. If we remember that line and staff are relationships between positions of an organization, and that most positions involve both line and staff relationships, many of these difficulties will disappear. It should be noted that a line relation-ship is a supervisory one and a staff relationship is advisory. It is not unusual to give staff specialists a limited type of authority—called func-tional authority—to decide on certain matters affecting people who do not report to them. Confusion can be avoided by making clear to all concerned exactly what the authority of the staff specialist is.

A fourth major problem area in organizing has to do with delegation of authority. The principles of delegation are clear enough, but man-agers are not always able to practice them. In a company as a whole, the problem becomes one of how much decision-making power to de-centralize and how much to retain at the top. Many companies have difficulties in this area. It is apparently hard to strike a proper balance in dispersing authority. The key to balance is to decide what decisions must be made at the top in order to safeguard the company's future, and what can be safely delegated downward.

Since organization structure changes as a company changes, it is desirable to plan an organization structure well ahead of time. By doing so, we can have a better idea of the number and kind of people we will need in the future, and can avoid putting a person in a job today that he cannot perform tomorrow.

KEY TERMS AND CONCEPTS FOR REVIEW

What an organization role should include

Organization as an intentional structure of roles

Span of management

Organization levels

Functional organization

Territorial organization

Product organization

Customer organization

Process, or equipment, organization

Service departments

Matrix organization

Line

Staff

Functional authority

Delegation of authority

Principles of delegation

Delegation as an art

Centralization of authority

Decentralization of authority

Factors determining the degree of centralization and decentralization

QUESTIONS FOR ANALYSIS AND DISCUSSION

1. Why should a structure of roles be intentional?
2. To what extent do organization charts show an organization as an intentional structure of roles?
3. If organization structures are intended to create a structure of roles in which people can perform effectively, why do company organizations often cause confusion and friction between people?
4. Why are levels of organization regarded as expensive, but often necessary? Why may too few levels also be costly?
5. How many people should report to a single manager? Why? How would you determine the proper number in a given situation?
6. What are the major advantages and disadvantages of using a functional organization structure? A territorial organization structure? A product organization structure?
7. It is often said that the technology of a business can influence an organization structure. How?
8. What are service departments and why should we use them?
9. Why are matrix organization structures common in engineering, research and development, and marketing?
10. Why is it important for people in a company to understand the difference between line and staff?

11. Why is functional authority in organization regarded as both unavoidable and dangerous?

12. It is said that the principles underlying delegation of authority are simple. Yet, studies have found that inept delegation leads the list of causes of managerial failure. How can you explain this?

13. Why may it be difficult for a businessman to obtain the right balance between centralization and decentralization of authority as his company grows?

14. Why is it important for a businessman to plan a company's future organization structure?

SUGGESTED READINGS

Bower, M. *The Will to Manage.* New York: McGraw-Hill Book Company, 1966, chapter 5.

Dale, E. *The Great Organizers.* New York: McGraw-Hill Book Company, 1960.

Fulmer, R. M. *The New Management.* New York: Macmillan Publishing Company, Inc., 1974, chapters 7 and 12.

Glueck, W. F. *Organization Planning and Development.* New York: American Management Association, Inc., 1971.

Hutchinson, J. G. *Organizations: Theory and Classical Concepts.* New York: Holt, Rinehart and Winston, 1967.

Koontz, H., and C. O'Donnell *Principles of Management* (5th ed.). New York: McGraw-Hill Book Company, 1972, Chapters 12–20.

Koontz, H., and C. O'Donnell *Essentials of Management.* New York: McGraw-Hill Book Company, 1974, chapters 10–15.

Lawrence, P. R., and J. W. Lorsch *Organization and Environment.* Boston: Harvard Graduate School of Business Administration, 1967.

McFeely, W. M. *Staff Services in Smaller Companies.* New York: The Conference Board, 1973.

22

Energizing the Business through Leadership

We have seen the importance of planning for growth, and the importance of having a sound organizational structure, but more than these are needed if a company is to succeed. It must be energized through effective leadership.

Leadership is the ability to influence people to strive willingly toward accomplishing group objectives. It is hard to think of any group of people accomplishing all they can without capable leaders. In a company, of course, the various departments and sections also have their group objectives and therefore must also have leaders. People will always fill in their time somehow, but the question is whether they will do the right things and do them willingly and enthusiastically.

GROUP PRODUCTIVITY ARISES FROM SYNERGY

"Synergy" has become a widely used word. It means that when two or more elements are mixed together they sometimes add up to more than the sum of the parts. Instead of $2 + 2 = 4$, we get $2 + 2 = 5$.

In 1885; the World Series of the Mule Team Competition was held in Chicago. The winning team of mules was able to pull 9,000 pounds. The second-place team pulled slightly less. Someone came up with the idea of hitching the first and second teams to a single load. Together, the teams pulled 30,000 pounds. This example of synergy was duplicated in Death Valley when a young foreman named Stiles noticed that a team of 12 mules was hauling loads twice the size that 8 mules could handle. This set him to thinking and experimenting. In the end, a 20-mule team wound up pulling 10 tons—about half the capacity of a modern railroad freight car. This was synergism in action. It is interesting to note that the team had a leader in the form of the driver who handled the reins and also a lead mule to help the other mules coordinate their efforts. It was also the origin of "Twenty Mule Team Borax," which became a household phrase and an international trademark.

A leader's goal is to draw synergy from a group of people. He needs help in the form of workable goals and plans, a clear and logical organization structure, the proper selection and training of people, and so on, but his distinctive task is to spark the group so that synergy results.

LEADERSHIP AND MANAGEMENT

The title of manager does not make its holder a leader, although, as we shall see, good managers tend to be good leaders. And not all leaders are managers. The leader of a mob can hardly be called a manager. Often a research scientist without managerial responsibility becomes the leader in a research group because of his superior knowledge. In one fairly large company, the secretary to the president became the real leader; this happened because the president was not doing his job, and the secretary obtained the confidence of his subordinates.

Leadership is an important part of managing, but not all of it. If an individual is a strong leader and a weak manager, he may lead people to the wrong destination. Conversely, a manager who is no leader, may do everything right but not be able to get people to work together enthusiastically and effectively. It does not matter how much a manager knows if he cannot get people to contribute to the success of his operation.

MISCONCEPTIONS OF LEADERSHIP

There are many misconceptions of leadership. One is that leadership is the same as popularity. Many times leaders are chosen for their popularity regardless of their ability to set goals and to guide groups toward them. This is as shortsighted as to assume that the best machinist will automatically be the best supervisor of machinists. It is also quite common for people in leadership positions to make wrong decisions out of a desire to be popular. On the other hand, some managers cultivate unpopularity because they confuse unpleasantness with efficiency and leadership. Neither popularity nor unpopularity is a sign of leadership.

Leadership is often thought to require aggressiveness and enthusiasm. These may be part of good leadership, or they may not. Sometimes a leader does best to stay in the background, keeping pressure off the group, allowing other people's ideas to emerge, and calming the group in time of panic. It has been said that a good leader leads from three positions: at the front of his group, pointing the way; in the middle, encouraging the majority; and at the rear, picking up stragglers.

THE PRACTICAL MEANING OF LEADERSHIP

In practical terms, leadership is followership. A leader is someone people follow. Why do people follow one individual and not another? The simplest answer seems to be that they follow individuals in whom they see promise of fulfilling their own personal goals and wishes.

If we look at great political leaders, we see this is true. The Germans flocked to Hitler because they thought he would lead them out of confusion, despair, unemployment, and humiliation following World War I. The Chinese followed Mao Tse-tung because they saw in him the hope of solving their problems of food, shelter, and self-respect. One of the reasons Americans elected Richard Nixon was that they saw in him a means of getting out of the Vietnam conflict with honor. A moment's reflection will bring the reader to similar conclusions about people he regards as leaders and would be willing to follow.

This means that if we are to be leaders we must pay attention to what our followers want. In a company, it will probably be the paycheck and what it will buy, the satisfaction of working with others, the feeling of accomplishing something worthwhile, or the pride of having status in the company. In a bowling club, the follower may want fun and recreation at modest cost, the pleasure of associating with congenial people, and the stimulation of friendly competition and a good score.

Many scholars of leadership say that the leadership process is a function of the leader, the follower, and the situation. Therefore, if a businessman is to understand leadership and practice it successfully, he needs to know his followers and what motivates them in the situation of a plant, sales office, or engineering department.

WHAT MOTIVATES PEOPLE?

There have been many studies of what motivates people—what makes them strive to accomplish things. In general, these studies come to similar conclusions.

Maslow's Hierarchy of Needs

One of the commonly quoted summaries of human motivations is that developed by the psychologist Abraham Maslow. Maslow held that human needs fall into an ascending order, starting with basic, or lower-level, needs and going on to higher-level needs (see Figure 22–1). He thought that when one level of needs was satisfied (for example, food, clothing, and shelter), they ceased to motivate a person and higher-level needs took command. Maslow listed needs in the following order:

FIGURE 22–1

Maslow's Hierarchy of Human Needs

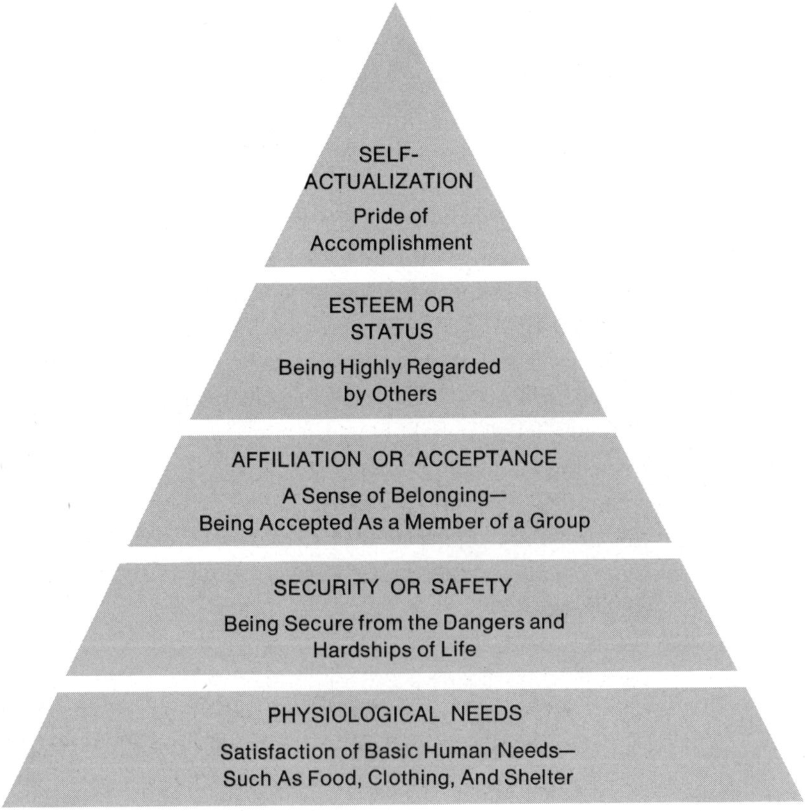

SELF-
ACTUALIZATION
Pride of
Accomplishment

ESTEEM OR
STATUS
Being Highly Regarded
by Others

AFFILIATION OR ACCEPTANCE
A Sense of Belonging—
Being Accepted As a Member of a Group

SECURITY OR SAFETY
Being Secure from the Dangers and
Hardships of Life

PHYSIOLOGICAL NEEDS
Satisfaction of Basic Human Needs—
Such As Food, Clothing, And Shelter

1. *Physiological needs.* These are the basic needs of human life—food, clothing, and shelter. Maslow held that until these needs were satisfied to the degree necessary to maintain life, no other needs would motivate people.
2. *Security (or safety) needs.* These are the needs to be free from physical danger and from the fear of loss—of a job, property, food, clothing, or shelter.
3. *Affiliation (or acceptance) needs.* Since people are social beings, they have needs to belong to a group and to be accepted by others.
4. *Esteem needs.* Once people begin to satisfy their needs to belong, they tend to want to be held in esteem both by themselves and by others. This need, according to Maslow, produces such satisfactions as power, status, prestige, and self-confidence.
5. *Self-actualization.* This was regarded by Maslow as the highest in his hierarchy of needs. It is the desire to become what one is capable of becoming, a desire to maximize a personal potential, to accomplish something.

Maslow's classification of human needs has of course been challenged by some scholars. His belief in an order of needs is open to question. When, for example, are physiological needs satisfied? One of the authors knew a movie actor who considered himself practically at the "starvation" level unless he had three new Cadillacs in his garage. (Of course, this may have represented the status level in his hierarchy of needs.) Most Americans seem to be partially satisfied on all levels at once, and partially unsatisfied, enjoying relatively more satisfaction at the physiological and security need levels and less at the higher levels.

Arch Patton's Managerial Motivators

Arch Patton, a management consultant and expert on executive compensation, has identified things that he sees as motivating managers in business. His list is similar to Maslow's except that it does not include physiological and security needs, which he assumes are fairly well satisfied for people in managerial positions. Unlike Maslow, he does not try to rank them in order of importance. His motivators are as follows:

1. *The challenge we find in work.* If this is to be maximized, a man must know the purpose and scope of his job responsibilities, what his authority is, and what is expected of him; he must also have a belief in the value of what he is doing.
2. *The desire for status.* Although the importance of status has been

recognized for centuries in the church, in the military, and in government, industry has come to recognize it only in recent years. The attributes of status include titles, promotions, an impressive office, "executive" secretary, a company car, and memberships in clubs.

3. *The urge to achieve leadership.* While difficult at times to distinguish from a desire for power, this is a desire to be a leader among one's fellow men.

4. *The lash of competition.* This important motivating factor is present in many aspects of life.

5. *Fear.* This takes many forms, including fear of errors, fear of losing one's job, and fear of getting a smaller bonus.

6. *Money.* Its position at the bottom of the list does not mean that it is the least effective motivator; on the contrary, it is most often more than mere money, being generally a reflection of other motivation.

Motivators and Business Success

These two lists of motivating factors, one made by a psychologist and the other by a management consultant, are different in approach but have a strong similarity. They are useful to the businessman in showing how he may expect people to behave. A major task of the leader is to design an environment that fits human motivations and connects them with the work to be done.

As one might expect, people's motivations vary. Some are mainly interested in their paychecks. Most people, however, want other things: to do a job, to feel a sense of accomplishment, to belong, to be appreciated. Most like to know when they are doing well and to be given a pat on the back. Even small status symbols, such as having one's name on his desk or at his workplace, can be powerful satisfiers.

These considerations are important in the manager's job. He must create and maintain an environment for *individual* performance that will make use of them all.

APPROACHES TO UNDERSTANDING LEADERSHIP

For almost as long as there have been leaders, there have been people who wondered about them and studied what makes leadership. Some have concentrated on the traits of individuals who were leaders; some have emphasized the behavior of leaders; and, most recently, some have studied leader behavior in relation to specific kinds of situations.

THE TRAIT APPROACHES

It is natural to look for something a leader has that distinguishes him from other people. *Physical traits* probably received the earliest attention as determinants of leadership. The authority of many ancient leaders doubtless rested on the fact that they were the strongest. Anyone who challenged a leader would have to be prepared to defeat him in physical combat. But physical strength alone is not sufficient to explain leadership. Even the strongest person needs followers. Even "the fastest gun in the West" cannot lead people where they don't want to go.

Through much of history, even into modern times, political leadership has gone to a chief who owned a great deal of land and had retainers who would fight for him. Since land was inherited, leadership would often be inherited along with it. The concept of aristocracy and of the divine right of kings to rule over their people was a way of maintaining a feudal society and of preventing continual warfare among aspiring leaders. Eventually, as cities grew and the factory system developed, the old aristocratic system decayed. People today do not believe in the inheritance of leadership. We like to believe that "all men are created equal," and nobody will follow a leader simply because he or she is taller, faster, stronger, blonder, or "the seventh son of a seventh son."

Mental traits play a greater part in successful leadership today than do physical powers. We like to hear that our leaders not only read 2,000 words per minute but also surround themselves with a "brain trust." Politicians can gain votes by affiliating with the leaders of the educational community, so long as they are careful not to sound like "ivory tower intellectuals."

Leaders tend to have somewhat higher intelligence scores than the average person, although the difference is not enough to explain why they are leaders. It is true that a leader requires analytical ability to see into the broad problems and complicated relationships with which he deals. His communication skills must be good enough to convey ideas, motivate others, and enable him to understand what others are saying to him. Most of us would agree that a leader must be smart, but common sense tells us that the smart ones are not always leaders. In fact, if a person seems too smart he may not be acceptable as a leader.

Those who maintain that leaders are distinguished by certain *personality traits* probably come closer than any of the other trait theorists to a satisfactory explanation of leadership. This is because most interrelationships of physical, mental, and social factors tend to fall under

W. Clement Stone

W. Clement Stone, insurance company executive, publisher, philanthropist, and civic leader, was born in Chicago in 1902. He began the accumulation of a personal fortune of $400 million by selling newspapers in downtown Chicago at the age of 6, his father having died three years earlier. At 13 he was managing his own newsstand.

His first contacts with the fundamentals of insurance came during the summers of his early teens, when he helped his step-father in the operation of a small agency. His mother moved to Detroit when he was 16 to open another insurance office, and he joined her that summer to begin his career as an insurance salesman. Although he suffered at first from shyness, he rapidly overcame it and developed the sales approach and optimistic attitude on which he has built financial and business success.

Stone dropped out of high school but he later completed school at night, and also took some law school and college courses. At 20 he invested his savings of $100 in his own insurance agency in Chicago. By 1930, at the young age of 28, he had about 1,000 agents throughout the country selling insurance for him. He says that he met the challenge of the depression of the 1930s through more effective management. In 1939 he became president of the American Casualty Com-

the broad classification of personality. One can hardly go wrong in saying that a leader's personality is the key to his success. The problem comes when we try to group the types of personality according to whether they are likely to be successful or not. Two leaders with completely opposite personality types may succeed because each has the right personality for the group he is leading—but this suggests that they might not succeed if they were in other groups.

Leaders tend to have broad interests and activities. They are emotionally mature so that they are neither crushed by defeat nor smitten by victory. They can stand a lot of frustration. Their antisocial attitudes, such as hostility to others, are minimal. They are self-assured and have reasonable self-respect.

Leaders have strong personal motivation to keep accomplishing things. They continually strive toward fulfilling their ultimate needs—

pany of Dallas and organized the Combined Mutual Casualty Company of Chicago. In 1946, he purchased the Pennsylvania Casualty Company of Philadelphia, a stock company licensed to sell accident and health insurance in states throughout the country. Although Pennsylvania Casualty had $1.6 million in liquid assets, Stone was able to make the purchase with only $25,000 of his own money by borrowing from the Commercial Credit Company of Baltimore, which owned the insurance firm. In 1947 he changed the firm's name to the Combined Insurance Company of America and merged it with his Chicago operation. A number of subsidiaries have since been acquired.

Stone's early inspiration came largely from his reading of Horatio Alger's stories of poor young men who rose through their strength of character and dedicated efforts to become wealthy businessmen. He regards his life and career as exemplifying the results to be gained from what he calls PMA—Positive Mental Attitude. With evangelical fervor he has indoctrinated his own salesmen and employees in this outlook, and written books and articles focusing on success through self-help, inspiration, and PMA. He also is editor and publisher of a monthly magazine, *Success Unlimited,* founded in 1954. Self-motivation, enthusiasm, and energy are the ingredients of the faith by which he lives.

Stone has been an ardent political activist. He contributed more than $7 million to about 50 candidates for state and national office between 1968 and 1972. He has given time as well as money, serving on many committees and in various offices in civic, government, and political groups. These include membership in the National Advisory Committee to the President, the executive vice chairmanship of the Republican National Finance Committee, and the vice chairmanship of the National Center for Voluntary Action.

Along with his politically-oriented activities, Stone has involved himself with charitable organizations in the areas of mental health, youth welfare, religion, and education. These include, to name only a few, the John Howard Association, an agency active in prison reform; the National Council on Crime and Delinquency; the Boys Clubs of America; the Black P. Stone Nation, an organization of young blacks on Chicago's south side; the National Music Camp at Interlochen, Michigan; the Chicago Chamber Orchestra; and the Lyric Opera of Chicago. Since 1958, his family's foundation has contributed $73 million to these causes. He often requires recipients of his grants to raise specified sums of self-help money through their own efforts. His basic goal is simply "to help make the world a better place for this and future generations to live in."

those at the upper levels of Maslow's hierarchy. They are more concerned with satisfying their inner drives than with external rewards. They tend to accept responsibility eagerly.

Successful leaders realize that they get their jobs done through other people. Therefore they develop an understanding of how people interact, and acquire the skills for dealing with them. They have a healthy respect for people, if for no other reason than that their success as leaders depends on the cooperation of others. They approach problems more in terms of personalities than of the technical elements involved.

The trait approach to leadership has many things to recommend it. The traits do exist, and often they seem to provide the identifying marks of leaders. Yet it is difficult to be certain whether the trait makes the leader a success or the leader's success makes the trait noticeable. Eugene E. Jennings, practical researcher and consultant on leadership, has said, "Fifty years of study have failed to produce one personality trait or set of qualities that can be used to discriminate leaders and nonleaders."

LEADER BEHAVIOR

Some writers on the subject of leadership have sought in the leader's "way of doing things" the unique quality that distinguishes him. They feel that traits are rather evenly distributed throughout the population, but that patterns of behavior among leaders tell us more about leadership in action.

In general, these behavior patterns may be divided into three kinds. One is that of the leader who is highly autocratic, who tells people what to do. Another is that of the leader who is very democratic or participative, who consults his followers and works with them and usually gets their agreement on courses of action undertaken by the group. A third pattern is that of the "free-rein" or "laissez-faire" leader who gives people a minimum of guidance and direction, letting them "do their own thing."

In practice, of course, leaders are likely to follow all three patterns, depending on the situation and the people involved. A leader can hardly use the participative approach when he is the only one who has information. Can you imagine a person asking his boss when a new machine will be ready so that he can use it, and his boss saying to him, "What do you think?" Also, it would be difficult for a boss to be highly participative in deciding how to set up an assembly line.

If his subordinates are research scientists or college professors, the superior is likely to give them a good deal of free rein. But he may become autocratic if they start missing work or are found smoking in a dangerous "No Smoking" area.

McGregor's Theory X and Theory Y

In his classic book on the *Human Side of Enterprise* some years ago, psychologist Douglas McGregor classified managers according to two behavior patterns that he called "Theory X" and "Theory Y." He defined Theory X managers as those who are highly autocratic and handle their employees on the basis of the following assumptions:

1. The average human being has an inherent dislike of work and will avoid it if he can.

2. Because they dislike work, most people must be coerced, controlled, directed, and threatened with punishment to make them put forth adequate effort toward the achievement of organization objectives.
3. The average human being prefers to be directed, wishes to avoid responsibility, has relatively little ambition, and wants security above all.

At the opposite extreme McGregor found what he called the Theory Y manager, whom he obviously felt was a better and more productive leader. He handled his employees according to these assumptions:

1. The expenditure of physical and mental effort in work is as natural as play or rest.
2. External control and the threat of punishment are not the only means for getting people to work toward organization objectives; they will exercise self-direction and self-control in the service of objectives to which they feel committed.
3. Commitment to objectives is a function of the rewards associated with their achievement.
4. The average human being learns, under proper conditions, not only to accept but to seek responsibility.
5. The capacity to exercise a relatively high degree of imagination and creativity in the solution of organization problems is widely, not narrowly, distributed in the population.
6. Under the conditions of modern industrial life, the intellectual potentialities of the average human being are only partially utilized.

As a general rule, the modern manager lies in the direction of Theory Y. Very few managers in the last several decades are Theory X managers. If the reader will refer back to Chapter 19, where the nature of the manager's task was analyzed and the elements of the environment he should design outlined, he will see that we are really talking in this book about a manager who is fairly much a Theory Y type of leader. But believing in the Theory Y approach does not imply that a manager must be a weak, indecisive, or permissive leader who allows his subordinates to make all the decisions and do anything they wish to do.

McMurry's Benevolent Autocrat

Psychologist Robert McMurry believes that the manager, or leader, must be a person who makes decisions and is a kind of autocrat. But he should also listen considerately to his follower's opinions before he makes his decision. McMurry, along with many other writers, believes that the American emphasis on democratic processes—"the will of the people"—should not be applied in an organized group situation where it is necessary to get things done by coordinating individual efforts. We may use democratic processes in voting for a mayor or governor, or even in deciding whether we want a new park or sewer system, but we can't vote on every decision made by an administrator attempting to run a city, a state, or a business.

Robert McMurry believes that systems of democratic leadership are unworkable in business. He would probably agree that too many participants spoil a decision. Anyone who has ever tried to accomplish something with a committee must have sighed for a benevolent autocrat who would take the committee in hand and guide it decisively toward its goal.

The benevolent autocrat in McMurry's conception is a powerful and prestigious manager who can be communicated with and who is personally interested in his subordinates' problems. When difficulties arise within his jurisdiction he is able to take prompt remedial action.

In support of his benevolent autocrat theory, McMurry offers the following reasons for the failure of democratic leadership, especially in business:

1. The climate within businesses is unfavorable to democracy. The "captains of industry" have worked hard to attain their positions in the managerial hierarchy. They are hard drivers who want to control the destiny of their firms, and are not likely to delegate major decision-making power.

2. Since most companies must make rapid and difficult decisions, it is in their best interest to maintain the control of operations in a centralized group of managers. Freedom of action is constrained by the need to make rapid decisions, and democratic leadership is not feasible because it encourages freedom of action.

3. Democratic leadership concepts are relatively new and unproven. Successful firms have historically followed bureaucratic principles, which are generally compatible with autocratic, but not with democratic, leadership. Once a firm has begun to follow bureaucratic guidelines and to develop autocratic leaders, these leaders tend to perpetuate themselves.

McMurry argues that a benevolent dictatorship is not only faster moving, but is a more effective system for managing a business. Of course, many leaders who have never heard of Robert McMurry have adopted the benevolent autocrat approach because it suited their personalities. This type of leader functions on the assumption that he understands and his subordinates do not. He is willing (and in some cases eager) to hear and consider the ideas and concerns of his underlings. But when the chips are down he is likely to be more autocratic than benevolent.

Neither benevolent autocracy nor democratic leadership can be declared categorically superior, since each appears to work for some leaders. The leader and the *situation* tend to determine the behavioral pattern which can best succeed. Possibly the benevolence of a leader depends on one's point of view. Is a leader benevolent as long as his decisions agree with yours? And does he become pure autocrat when he listens to your advice but makes the opposite decision?

WORK-ORIENTED VERSUS PEOPLE-ORIENTED LEADERSHIP

Behavior patterns vary depending on the personality of the leader and the situation he finds himself in. Some people by their very nature tend to be the Theory X type. Some situations call for strong leaders to make quick decisions: when a fire department is fighting a fire, there is no time to hold a meeting to decide how to put it out; when a plant's machinery breaks down, or when a company must respond quickly to a competitor's price-cut, immediate and decisive action may be called for.

On the other hand, when we must decide on long-range goals, or what new products to develop, or how to reduce costs, or how to formulate a new advertising program, we usually want as many people as possible to contribute something. But discussion can't go on indefinitely. As the great industrialist, Clarence Randall, said: "The counsel of war is held the night before in an army; but when the dawn comes, the general does not hold a town meeting. He gives the command to fire."

Leadership as a Continuum

Robert Tannenbaum and Warren Schmidt have depicted the range of leadership styles on a continuum. As indicated in Figure 22–2, they see leadership varying from a task-oriented style, which tends to be highly autocratic, to a people-oriented style which tends to be democratic. At the autocratic extreme the manager makes a decision and then tells his subordinates about it; at the democratic extreme he lets

FIGURE 22–2

Continuum of Leadership Behavior

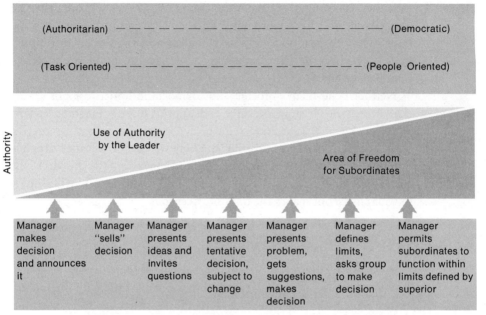

Source: R. Tannenbaum, et al, Leadership and Organization: A Behavioral Approach (New York: McGraw-Hill Book Company, 1961), p. 69.

his subordinates make the decision. Tannenbaum and Schmidt find that leadership styles change from time to time, depending on the personality of the leader and the situation in which he finds himself.

Leadership and the Managerial Grid

Managers need to think of the work to be done as well as of people. This is illustrated in the popular managerial grid developed by Robert Blake and Jane Mouton. The adaptation of their grid, shown in Figure 22–3, assigns places to managers in accordance with the degree of their concern for both people and production.

Although many different combinations can be shown, Blake and Mouton selected five for illustrative purposes. These types of management may be characterized as follows:

1,1 *Impoverished.* "Don't make waves; do as little as possible to keep the boss off our backs."

9,1 *Task.* "The objective's the thing. We'll take that hill even if all the troops are lost in the battle."

FIGURE 22–3

The Managerial Grid

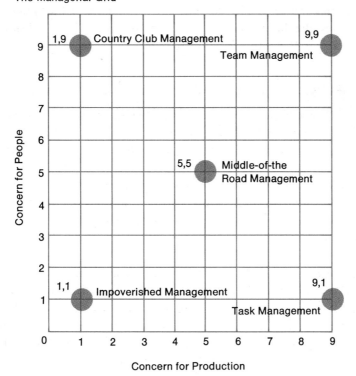

Concern for Production

1,9 *Country Club.* "Why should I worry about progress? My boys like each other and have a good time."

5,5 *Middle-of-the-road.* "People and production . . . they are both important."

9,9 *Team.* "Yes sir! This is the finest staff that anyone could want to work with. They really work as a team to accomplish team goals!"

Source: Adapted from Robert M. Fulmer, *The New Management* (New York: Macmillan, 1974), p. 329, based on Blake and Mouton, *The Managerial Grid* (Houston: The Gulf Publishing Company, 1964).

The grid suggests that the ideal leader or manager is the person who does his utmost to be concerned with people as well as production. While the grid is only a simple illustration of the two areas that every manager should be concerned with, it has proved to be a powerful teaching device for analyzing leadership styles. How would you rate yourself and the people you have worked with?

The leader most concerned with goal achievement initiates action, keeps members' attention on the goal, clarifies the issues, and develops plans. On the other hand, the group-centered leader keeps interpersonal relations pleasant, arbitrates disputes, provides encouragement, gives the minority a chance to be heard, stimulates self-direction, and increases the interdependence among members. The best leaders, according to Blake and Mouton, do both.

OUTSIDE INFLUENCES AFFECTING LEADERSHIP

We would not be able to see the whole picture of leadership if we focused only on the leader and his characteristics. Other factors enter into the picture, which may help or hinder a leader in his performance.

The size of the organization within which the leader must function plays a definite part in the extent to which he will succeed. There is an almost unvarying correlation between organizational bigness and organizational slowness. An elephant carries more weight than a monkey, but an elephant can hardly leap from one tree to another.

The degree to which people interact in a company also influences the extent to which leadership talents may flourish. Some operations have a greater need for interaction than others. In many cases, modern technology demands contributions from many experts throughout the company. As the need for interaction, cross-checking, and collective thinking increases, the organizational structure and the leader's style must be adapted to permit the free flow of information and ideas.

Leadership is easier when there is *compatibility of goals*—when everybody in the company is heading the same way. When the goals of a company and those of its members are harmonious, participative processes and a less formal leadership can work well. Unfortunately, this is not always the case. When organizational goals and member goals are divergent, greater reliance must be placed upon authoritative processes and formal direction so that adequate control is assured.

The *level of decision-making* can have important consequences on the quality of leadership. Decision-making (and therefore leadership) tends to be most effective if it is practiced at the level where it will be put to use. That is, if the boys in the shipping room have a part in making decisions and determining the course of their operations, then chances are that the shipping room will reflect effective leadership.

The *health of the organization* can have a lot to do with the amount and variety of leadership. Some companies cannot afford the luxury of democratic leadership. When an organization is in relatively poor health, more authoritative processes of motivation and structure may be required.

MANAGERIAL LEADERSHIP ENHANCED THROUGH CAREFUL SELECTION AND TRAINING

The job of the manager in energizing his organization is made vastly easier if the people in his company have been carefully selected and trained. People who fit their jobs, who feel comfortable because they know what they are doing, are always easiest to lead and manage—whether they are factory workers or vice presidents.

As pointed out in Chapter 21, a major task of organizing is to make sure that jobs and groupings of jobs are designed so that people can know what their roles are and how their work relates to that of others. Moreover, a good manager will try to design positions so that they can be filled by the kind of people he can obtain, and will build into them characteristics which motivate people.

The Need for Careful Selection

But all the efforts put into planning, organizing, and leading will come to nothing if people are not carefully selected for the positions they are to fill. This is fairly easy to do when we are hiring machinists or typists. We can give people skill tests and tell very quickly whether they can do the job. But as we move up the ladder, and especially into managerial positions, the selection process becomes very difficult. It may take several months or a year to tell whether an engineer or manager is right for his job. If we make a mistake, we not only lose money but something more important than money—time.

Perhaps the best gauge of ability for a person who cannot be evaluated on the basis of simple skill tests is his performance in another job. This is not always easy to know, especially if he is new to a company or has had little or no work experience. Letters of recommendation are not always reliable because previous employers and friends will seldom say anything negative about a person.

This problem has led to the use of many psychological tests. Most experts would agree that intelligence tests and perhaps aptitude tests are fairly reliable. But there is a wide difference of opinion on the reliability of most other tests.

Most companies interview candidates for positions. However, unless the interviewer knows what he is looking for and is highly skilled at finding out these things, interviewing may be superficial. The typical interview by an executive, quickly done and usually interrupted by telephone calls, leaves much to be desired. Superficial impressions may have some value but their reliability is open to question.

Selection for all except the simpler jobs is still pretty largely an art, and a risky art at that. The record of a person is probably the best indicator, whether this is a work record, college record, or report of outside activities. But most companies simply do not spend enough time and effort on the selection process. This may be costly to a company, but it is also costly, both to the company, and to the candidate who suffers real harm by being selected for a job he cannot fill.

The Need for Adequate Training

The successful business will also do what it can to train and develop its employees. Most companies engage in this. Indeed, there is probably as much educational work being done in industry, government, and other organizations as in our universities and colleges.

Training is more than taking courses and seminars or attending conferences. Perhaps the best training comes from working on the job, particularly if a person's boss will coach and teach him. Unfortunately, such bosses are all too rare. Most are not good teachers, and are so preoccupied with getting a job done that they understandably feel they cannot take the time to teach. A young person going into business is fortunate indeed if he has a boss who is interested in helping him develop and knows how to do it.

MANAGERIAL LEADERSHIP STRENGTHENED THROUGH ACCURATE APPRAISAL OF INDIVIDUAL PERFORMANCE

Most people want to know how well they are doing. They do not want to know how well someone *thinks* they are doing, but how well they are actually accomplishing their job. They naturally are highly motivated when their boss can find reason to praise their efforts, and any intelligent manager will go out of his way to find something in a person's work to praise. Having done this, he will find that his criticisms of shortcomings become far more palatable.

Deficiencies of Appraisal Systems

For too many years it has been common to appraise people on the basis of their personal abilities and work traits. The usual appraisal system provides for rating people on such qualities as intelligence, ability to get along with others, industriousness, job knowledge, adaptability, judgment, and the quality and quantity of their work. Each of these may be rated on a scale ranging from "unsatisfactory" to "average," "good," "superior," and "outstanding."

It is obvious that such standards emphasize what a boss *thinks* of a person rather than what he *does*. There is simply no way that an appraiser can be sure of grading accurately on these qualities. Most superiors tend to rate people on the high side of their performance simply because they may not be able to defend a lower grade or do not want to harm a subordinate's career. It is hardly surprising that a study made of the United States Navy's appraisal of officers found a statistical paradox: 98.5 percent of all Navy officers were rated as "excellent" or "outstanding," and only 1 percent were "average"!

Appraisal Against Objectives

The greatest single improvement in appraisal systems has occurred in recent years. When a company is able to set up a program of having everyone establish verifiable objectives (as described in Chapter 20), it is fairly easy to rate people on their ability to establish and achieve objectives for themselves. What a superior thinks of a person's manners or intelligence or other traits really does not matter, since the important thing is how he performs.

This kind of appraisal has so far been applied mostly to managers. It could also be applied to nonmanagerial personnel, since their jobs certainly call for accomplishing goals or objectives. It must be admitted, however, that many programs of managing by objectives in American business are not working very well, and some are little more than paperwork exercises. But to the extent that it is done well, this is a far better approach to appraisal than the traditional trait and work habit systems.

Appraising Managers as Managers

In addition to appraising managers on their ability to set and achieve objectives, it makes sense to appraise them on their ability to manage. We would hardly want a manager who knew everything about managing but could not perform. By the same token, since performers sometimes look good or bad through luck or other factors beyond their control, it would seem logical to appraise managers also on their ability to manage. For standards in this area we can look to the fundamentals of managing found in any good basic management textbook. We can then use the principles of good management as standards against which to measure an individual's quality of managing. When combined with his ability to perform by achieving objectives, we now have a double-barreled and highly effective approach to appraisal.

EFFECTIVE MANAGERSHIP MAKES FOR EFFECTIVE LEADERSHIP

The discussion of leadership in this chapter should bring into focus the fact that an effective manager is also likely to be an effective leader. This is not surprising. When we consider what motivates people and why people follow, we see that there is a very close relationship between good managing and leading. The proof may be found in the following summary considerations:

1. Clear goals and plans to meet them give people a sense of knowing what is expected of them, where they are going, and how they are best likely to get there. We can hardly have a sense of accomplishment and with it a degree of security, good pay, or status without these. This is, of course, the purpose of managerial planning.

2. A clear understanding of organizational positions and how they relate to each other enables people to see how they fit into the company and what part of a task is theirs.

3. Understanding the extent of one's authority, and being able to get prompt and clear decisions from a superior, opens the door to accomplishment.

4. If a manager links people's desires and motivations to every aspect of his operation, he will naturally cause people to want to follow him.

5. Carefully selecting individuals for jobs, giving them every opportunity for improving themselves through training, and accurately appraising their performance will encourage them to do well and help to give them a feeling of accomplishment.

6. Checking up to see how well people are progressing toward the accomplishment of goals, and when they are missing goals, and why, will also help to motivate them and make them happy to follow a boss who shows that much concern. Good people want to know how well they are doing. This is the purpose of control, to be discussed in the next chapter.

If a manager does all these things, he is almost certain to be a strong and effective leader.

SUMMARY

To be successful, a business must be energized through effective leadership on the part of those in charge of a company and every department in it. Leadership is the ability to influence people to strive willingly toward accomplishing group objectives. A leader's goal is to assure synergy in an organization, that is, to draw from the joint efforts of people working together a result that is more than the sum of their individual efforts. While not all leaders are managers and, unfortunately, not all managers are leaders, the best managers are good leaders.

Perhaps the most practical way to understand leadership is to understand followership. People tend to follow individuals in whom they see promise of fulfilling their own personal goals and wishes. This implies that the effective manager must understand what motivates people.

There have been many studies of what motivates people. Perhaps the most widely quoted are the needs identified by the psychologist Abraham Maslow. He found that people respond to the following needs: (1) physiological, (2) security or safety, (3) affiliation or acceptance, (4) esteem, and (5) self-actualization. These needs are similar to those found for managers by an emiment management consultant, Arch Patton.

What makes for leadership? One can try to identify certain physical, mental, and personality traits of leaders, but this approach has not proved to be useful. Another approach is to study leader behavior. The best known study of leader behavior among managers is that of Douglas McGregor, who classified them as "Theory X" or "Theory Y" managers, the former being highly autocratic and the latter highly democratic in their dealings with people. Another popular and persuasive approach to leadership is that of Robert McMurray who believes that the most effective managerial leader is the benevolent autocrat. He believes that such a manager must be concerned with people and their welfare, but also be willing to make unpopular decisions.

Recent students of leadership in an organizational setting have tended to emphasize both concern for production and concern for people. Tannenbaum and Schmidt have seen leadership as ranging from autocratic to democratic, depending on the situation. Blake and Mouton have popularized this basic notion and the idea of concern both for production and for people with their useful managerial grid.

It is not enough to study leadership from the standpoint of the leader's behavior. There are many other influences which may help or hinder his performance: (1) the size of the organization; (2) the degree to which people interact in a company; (3) the compatibility of company goals; (4) the level at which decisions are made; and (5) the health of the organization.

To supplement a manager's leadership, it is important that the people in a company or department be carefully selected and trained for their jobs. It is also important that they be appraised as accurately as possible. This requires gauging their ability to set and accomplish goals and, if they are managers, their ability to manage.

An individual who knows how to manage well is almost certain to be an effective leader. By making it possible for people to accomplish their goals, and showing them how well they are doing, the manager is not only taking advantage of one of the strongest human motivations but also serving the needs of his company.

KEY TERMS AND CONCEPTS FOR REVIEW

Leadership	Free rein leadership
Synergy	McGregor's Theory X and Theory Y
Motivation	McMurry's benevolent autocrat
Maslow's hierarchy of needs	Leadership as a continuum
Trait approaches to leadership	The managerial grid
Leader behavior approach to leadership	Outside influences affecting leadership
Autocratic leadership	Managerial appraisal
Participative leadership	

QUESTIONS FOR ANALYSIS AND DISCUSSION

1. "Good managers tend to be good leaders, but leaders are not always managers." Comment and explain.
2. If you wanted to become a leader of a group, whether in a company or elsewhere, what are the things you would try to do?
3. Analyze your own motivations—your own needs. To what extent do they fit Maslow's list of needs? Do you feel that your own needs can be identified as a "hierarchy"?
4. How does Patton's statement of managerial motivators fit into, or agree with, Maslow's? Which statement do you see as the most accurate for yourself, and for other people you know?
5. As you think of various leaders (in school, sports, or elsewhere) you have known, to what extent do you see that their physical, mental, or personality traits helped make them leaders?
6. Which kind of leader would you most likely follow—one who is autocratic, one who is participative, or one who gives you a "free rein"? Why? Would the conditions at a certain time make a difference?
7. Considering the various leaders you have known, do they come closer to McGregor's Theory X or Theory Y? In working in a company, which kind of boss would you rather have? Why?

8. Would you prefer a boss who fits McMurry's "benevolent autocrat" to either a Theory X or a Theory Y boss?
9. Which approach to managerial leadership—Tannenbaum and Schmidt's continuum, or Blake and Mouton's grid—seems to you to best explain the kind of leader-manager you should be if you were in business as (1) a factory manager, (2) an office manager, (3) a chief engineer, (4) a sales manager, or (5) a factory assembly line foreman?
10. Why does the selection of managers become more important and more difficult as we move up the ladder in a company's organization?
11. If you were being appraised as a supervisor, what kind of appraisal approach would you prefer? Why?

SUGGESTED READINGS

Blake, R. R., and J. S. Mouton *The Managerial Grid.* Houston: Gulf Publishing Company, 1964.

Cribbin, J. J. *Effective Managerial Leadership.* New York: American Management Association, Inc., 1972.

Fulmer, R. M. *The New Management.* New York: Macmillan Publishing Company, Inc., 1974, chapters 14–16.

Hersey, P., and K. H. Blanchard *Management of Organizational Behavior.* Englewood Cliffs, N.J.: Prentice-Hall, Inc., 1969.

Koontz, H., and C. O'Donnell *Principles of Management* (5th ed.). New York: McGraw-Hill Book Company, 1972, chapters 21–28.

Koontz, H., and C. O'Donnell *Essentials of Management.* New York: McGraw-Hill Book Company, 1974, chapters 16–23.

McGregor, D. *The Human Side of Enterprise.* New York: McGraw-Hill Book Company, 1960.

Patton, A. *Men, Money and Motivation.* New York: McGraw-Hill Book Company, 1961.

Tannenbaum, R., I. R. Weschler, and F. Massarik *Leadership and Organization: A Behavioral Approach.* New York: McGraw-Hill Book Company, 1961.

23

Controlling: Assuring that Plans Succeed

Every businessman hopes and plans for success. If goals in every part of a business were automatically achieved, if people were able to carry out plans as intended and if the plans were always right, and if every one knew what he was supposed to do, business success would be virtually assured.

Real life is not that certain. One can plan for rising sales, adequate profits, products that will sell, low costs of production, salesmen who will sell, and managers who will assure that all these things happen. But people make mistakes and fail to do what was expected of them. Competitors, labor unions, new products, government regulations, changing business conditions, and a host of other things can interfere with the best-made plans. The purpose of managerial control then, is to assure that plans succeed by watching what is happening, detecting errors and misses, and taking action to get back on the intended course.

This is the task of every manager, whatever his position in a business. Just as he is responsible for making plans and supervising people, he also has the task of making sure that things go as intended.

THE PROCESS OF CONTROL

Control processes are found everywhere in our lives, but they are so automatic that we are generally unaware of them. Our bodies have a number of automatic controls built into them. For example, we have a thermostat that regulates temperature. In cold conditions our pores close and the blood vessels in our skin contract, reducing heat loss. In hot weather, the body perspires and utilizes a simple evaporation process to get rid of heat. The average person rarely even thinks of these processes except when he is suffering from fever or chills.

Perhaps the best example of the process of control is the familiar room thermostat. We may set it at 72 degrees. If the temperature falls below this setting, an electrical impulse starts the furnace. When the temperature comes up to the desired setting, another electrical impulse turns off the furnace. As most of us have found out, the thermostat does not keep the temperature at exactly 72 degrees but probably between 70 or 71 and 74 or 75. This is because of time delays in the system. It takes a while for the radiators to heat up, and heat may continue to come from them after the thermostat has shut the furnace down.

Managerial control in business works very much like a thermostat. Instead of controlling body room temperature, it acts on cash flow, costs, office procedures, product quality, morale, or anything else that is important to the company's operations.

The Basic Control Process

Wherever it is found, the basic control process can be boiled down to three steps:

(1) establishing standards;
(2) measuring performance against standards;
(3) taking action to correct deviations from standards.

As a backwoods grocer explained to his son, control is (1) "sayin' how things ought to be"; (2) "seein' how things is"; and (3) "straightenin' out what's crooked."

Standards

The dictionary defines standards as "criteria of performance." In business, goals and plans are the standards against which we measure performance. If we have clear and verifiable goals, they become important standards. But since we do not usually want to wait until a job is completed to measure how well it is being performed, and since a manager cannot watch every detail of his subordinates' operation, the effective manager will pick out a few key items to watch in order to be certain that things are going well. For example, an airline vice president in charge of operations may watch the daily on-time performance of his airline on the assumption that if the plans are operating on time, many other activities and programs under his control such as maintenance, pilot training and availability, and spare parts purchasing, are probably working as intended.

In practice, standards are usually expressed in terms of money, time, quotas, speed, volume of output, or other terms. The manager must ask himself: What will best show me how things are going in my department? What will show me most quickly? On what can I get adequate information?

Measuring Performance

In some areas of a company's operations, it is fairly easy to find specific standards for measuring performance. For example, if our standard on a packaging line is 300 cases of soap per hour, we can quickly tell whether we are meeting it. If our standard for a salesman is 12 customer calls per day, we can easily determine whether he is meeting it.

In many kinds of business operations, however, standards and measurement are not easy. For example, definite standards are difficult to develop for the work of the finance vice president or the director of industrial relations. It may be necessary to rely on such vague standards as the financial health of the business, the accuracy of cash plans, the absence of strikes, the kind of settlements made with labor unions, the enthusiasm and loyalty of employees, or the apparent success of training programs. As we move away from the assembly line, from accounting machines, and from the local sales office, standards and measurement become more difficult, even though no less important.

Perhaps the best standards for measuring the performance of middle- and upper-level departments or managers are the verifiable goals they set. We can tell whether they have met or missed them. It is difficult, however, to tell whether the goals were set right and whether or not the reasons for missing them are excusable. If the marketing manager has a goal of selling a million dollars of a product in a year, and sells less, he may offer as reasons the business climate, the fact that a competitor has a better product, or that the manufacturing department was slow in making and delivering the item. The problem his boss faces is whether these are the real reasons, or whether they are excuses for failures in the sales or advertising effort.

The smart manager would like to measure not last month's or even yesterday's performance, but next month's or tomorrow's probable performance, simply because past mistakes can never be corrected. It is not often practicable to do so, but there are some management techniques for predicting what will happen. For example, companies do not usually wait to find out in May that they did not have enough cash in the bank to cover their checks in April. Instead, they forecast their cash resources and their cash needs to make sure their checks will not bounce.

Correcting Deviations

Measuring and evaluating are not control. No production manager would feel that he had a satisfactory quality control system if the inspectors merely filled barrels full of unsalable rejects. Real control implies that something will be done to correct deviations from plans.

Correcting deviations from plans may take many forms. The business manager may decide that he needs to revise his plans. A marketing manager who missed his sales goal may decide that he needs a new advertising program, or that an instrument the company produces needs redesigning to be more attractive to customers. Or he may decide that the sales department needs reorganizing so as to give individual salesmen responsibility for types of customers rather than territories. Or he may conclude that his sales force needs more training and perhaps that some poor performers should be replaced. He may also decide that the kind of inducements the company gives its salesmen—commissions, company cars, or expense accounts—need overhauling.

THE MANAGEMENT CONTROL SYSTEM

The whole system of management control is diagrammed in Figure 23–1. The steps correspond to those of the thermostat system described above. Actual performance is measured against the desired standard, deviations are identified, and corrective action is taken. In a business situation, however, the process is likely to require a much longer time. In the case of the marketing manager, for example, it may be a month or two before he is sure his sales program is failing to meet its goals. Then it may take him days or weeks to find out where and why the program is missing its goals, still more time to figure out what to do,

FIGURE 23–1

Management Control Loop

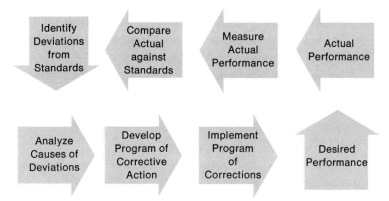

and weeks or months to implement the changes he finds desirable. This is why some managers develop ulcers.

A look at the control loop will show why computers won't solve the problem of management control, as so many computer enthusiasts seem to believe. The computer with its fast information processing may make it possible for a manager to know more about his operation and to know it faster, but it will not solve his problems for him. Much of the information the computer gives him is about the past. Even where a computer system can give us information on what is happening as it happens—right now—the time required for analysis and correction is such that even this information is too late. A manager needs instead better methods of forecasting the future. When he looks at statistics on his operation, he must examine them for what they can tell him about what is likely to happen tomorrow.

INFORMATION NEEDS FOR MANAGERS

When we walk into the office of a businessman and see stacks of computer printout sheets or volumes of statistical reports, we may wonder what he does with all the data. Too often, not much. The trouble today, with the thousands of computers grinding out miles of printout sheets of data, is whether the business manager is really getting information. Data are not information, since nothing can be called information unless it informs.

If we want to know whether the data we are receiving are really information, it is helpful to ask the following questions.

1. *Is the Information Timely?* It does little good for the owner of a business to find out in June that he went broke in April for something he did in February. He should try to find out before February what is likely to happen in April if he does not do something.

2. *Are Appropriate Units of Measure Used?* Statistics can be slippery communicators. We have all heard the saying that "figures don't lie, but liars figure." It is important that gains, losses, and mistakes be explained in terms that are clear, accurate, consistent, and relevant to the real things the numbers represent. Statements of quantity should not be permitted to conceal differences in quality. Producing 3,000 units in a given month may be a questionable accomplishment if they are so bad that 2,500 dissatisfied customers turn up the following month.

3. *Is the Information Reliable?* With the aid of the computer, information can be transferred more rapidly and accurately than before. When information is not reliable, the reason will usually be found at the source. Employees often become bored with filling out reports, and tend to do them hastily and carelessly. What good are data on labor costs if workmen and foremen do not fill out time cards accurately? It is worth taking trouble to assure that such information is correct.

4. *Is the Information Valid?* Information may be correct but not valid—that is, it may not enable us to draw the right conclusions about the matter to which it relates. An example of misleading information occurred a few years ago during an international road trial between the U.S. and the U.S.S.R. Only two cars were entered, and the American car won. The Russian press reported that while the Russian car finished second, the American car came in next to last. The reporting was accurate, but the conclusion was wrong.

5. *Is the Information Being Channeled to the Proper Person?* A good information system channels the right information at the right time to the right person. Control information needs to go to the person who is designated as being responsible for the operation and who has the authority to change its direction.

WHAT MAKES A CONTROL TECHNIQUE GOOD?

Business managers employ various techniques to control their operations. One of the most universally used is a budget. Other techniques include statistical reports and charts, special studies of problem areas, personal observation, and the many so-called "systems" techniques that have developed in recent years.

A company's control techniques should be specially tailored to its requirements. These will vary, with a company's plans, its organization structure, and the personalities of the people concerned. Some techniques, to be sure, are pretty well standardized. But it should always be borne in mind that their purpose is to help a particular person control *his* operations.

Controls Must Be Tailored to Plans

A control system should reflect the job it is intended to serve. A system useful to the vice president in charge of manufacturing will almost certainly be different in coverage and nature from one employed by the shop foreman. Controls in the purchasing department will differ from those in the sales department. A large business will need controls somewhat different from those required in a small business. And many of the controls used by an aerospace company will not be the same as those used by an insurance company.

Controls Must Reflect Organization Structure

Control information is not very helpful if it says, "Something is wrong somewhere in our operation" but does not tell where. If a report tells the head of manufacturing that production costs are too high, this is just an interesting piece of information; it should tell him that the costs are out of line in the machine shop, or the parts production department, or the shipping room.

To be effective, control information must pinpoint the spot in the company where variations from standards are taking place. This means, of course, that controls must be designed to reflect the organization structure.

Controls Must Be Tailored to People's Personalities

People differ in their ability to understand information. Statisticians and accountants may like to read statistical reports and tables. Most managers want their information in chart form so that they can see the trends and not get bogged down in a mass of figures. The authors have known certain scientists who preferred to receive their information in mathematical symbols and formulas.

However a person wants his control information, this is the way he should get it. The importance of having control information is to inform people who can and will take action. It does not matter whether a person cannot understand, or will not understand, what he does not understand he will not use. As a matter of fact it is not too ridiculous to say that if an individual will only understand information in comic book form, this is the way he should get it.

Controls Should Be Objective

If controls are to be efficient and effective, the information they are based on should be objective. This means if at all possible that controls should be cast in verifiable or numerical terms so that there can be no doubt whether an individual is achieving his target. Thus if a person has a budgeted cost of $8,500 for his operation, and costs exceed $10,000, there can be no doubt that he has missed. On the other hand, if an individual is charged with developing a workable and promising advertising program, or a plan to improve the quality of customer service, it becomes a matter of judgment whether his performance is good enough. We may be able to tell after the program is operating whether it was good. But often we simply cannot develop objective standards of control.

Unless a standard and its measurement are objective, a boss often has a difficult time proving to his subordinate that he has not done the job well enough. The subordinate may think he has done an adequate job and his boss may think not. Even though the boss's evaluation will probably prevail, the corrected or criticized subordinate may think he is being unfairly treated.

Controls Should Point Up Exceptions at Critical Points

One of the major requirements for an efficient control system is to have controls that disclose exceptions to standards at critical points. Managers cannot possibly monitor everything. As a general rule the efficient manager should pay real attention only to exceptions—that is, to those activities which are not meeting desirable standards.

But that time-honored principle is not enough. There are exceptions and exceptions. A manager should be concerned only with the important, or critical, exceptions that make a difference. If the cost of postage stamps exceeds the budgeted amount by 20 percent, the manager might not be overly concerned; but if labor costs are 5 percent over the mark, that is a different matter.

Controls Should Be Economical

As a famous manager said years ago, it is not just a question of finding costs but of knowing how much it costs to find costs. How much should a company pay for its control system and its information? There is no simple answer. It is easy to say we should not pay more than the controls are worth, but trying to assess the value of controls is like trying to determine whether seat belts in a car are worth what we pay for them. One may use a seat belt for many years and never need it. But if the belt saves your life just once, you will probably feel that your investment was worthwhile.

There are times when controls clearly cost too much. One of the authors once found a loophole in the controls of a bank that would have enabled two cooperating employees to embezzle money. He called this to the attention of the bank's chief operating officer, who pointed out that the chances of theft were really very small and that it would cost the bank more to close the loophole than it would lose if the employees stole. If a mistake cannot cost more than five dollars, we are not justified in spending a hundred dollars to put in a control system.

Controls Should Lead to Action

A control system should do more than flash a red light or ring a bell. It should disclose where failures are occurring, who is responsible for them, and exactly what responses ought to be forthcoming. And above all, it requires people to see the red lights, hear the bells, and take action.

The need for people to respond with action may seem too obvious to mention. But some people tend to ignore developing problems in the hope that they will go away. This is apparently what happened to the manager of a major project in a defense contract. His project was millions of dollars over its budget and had fallen months behind schedule. Yet he took little action; he did not even tell the company president of his difficulties until a three-star general from Washington walked into the president's office to cancel the contract. Bosses are basically the same. They do not like to be surprised. This chief executive replaced his project manager that day.

Some people overlook warning signals. The operations head of a chemicals company had a foreman in whose area a serious explosion

Henry Crown

Henry Crown, the power behind the scenes at General Dynamics Corporation, was born in Chicago in 1896, one of five sons of a Lithuanian immigrant who worked most of his life as a suspender maker. Henry quit school at 14 to go to work, but studied commercial subjects in night school. In 1916 his older brother, Sol, set up business as a steel broker, and Henry joined him as a partner.

In 1919 Henry, with his brothers Sol and Irving, organized Material Service Corporation with a capitalization of $10,000. It was eventually to become the largest construction supply firm in the midwest. After Sol died of influenza in 1921, Henry became president and general manager of the company. Material Service relied heavily on bank financing in its expansion. Crown undertook a strategy of bidding low to obtain a steadily increasing volume of contracts. By building up his own fleet of trucks, shipping via canal whenever feasible, and keeping profits low, he was successful in competing against larger, more firmly entrenched suppliers.

Crown was named chairman in 1941, after accumulating a considerable fortune. He volunteered for wartime service and became a Colonel in the Army, serving as Chief of Procurement in the Corps of Engineers.

After the war Crown enlarged his activities, investing in real estate, coal mines, railroads, and sugar plantations. In 1946 he put up $4 million for the defaulted bonds of the Chicago, Rock Island and Pacific railroad, which had been in receivership for a number of years. When the legal battles over the railroad were resolved, Crown had tripled his investment.

Crown met Conrad Hilton in 1944, and played a prominent role in acquiring the Stevens Hotel in Chicago for him, later named the Conrad Hilton. Crown and Hilton, together with other associates of Hilton, bought Chicago's Palmer House and then organized the Hilton Hotels Corporation. Growth was rapid in the following ten years with the acquisition of the Statler chain, the Waldorf-Astoria in New York, and many other hotels throughout the world.

In 1951 Crown led a group that pur-

occurred. It was an area where at times the gas in the air reached dangerous proportions. The company had installed gas detectors and warning lights and bells at great cost to give notice when the air was becoming dangerously contaminated. When the foreman was asked why he did not take the men out of the area before the explosion, he replied that the bells were ringing so loudly he could not hear the plant superintendent yelling at him.

chased the Empire State Building in New York. Over the next few years Crown and his family bought out the other investors for approximately $150 million. His innovating and modernizing efforts restored the Empire State Building's former prestige and filled it with major tenants. He sold the building in 1961 for $65 million.

Over the years Material Service Corporation continued its steady growth until it became the world's largest cement distributor. Its gross sales, increased from $45 million in 1951 to $115 million in 1958, when Crown negotiated a merger with General Dynamics Corporation. It continued to operate autonomously, however, as a division of General Dynamics. Crown became chairman of the executive committee of General Dynamics.

When its commercial jet program failed in 1960, General Dynamics had the dubious honor of losing more money on a single program than any other U.S. company. Business publications ran stories titled "How a Great Corporation Got Out of Control." But the company was only at the beginning of a decade of misfortune.

In merging Material Service into General Dynamics, Crown accepted a convertible preferred stock which paid an annual dividend of 5 percent and could be redeemed by the company at a 10 percent premium over the market price. In 1966 interest rates were low, and some of the directors decided to call the preferred stock and replace it with borrowed funds. Crown expressed doubt as to the wisdom of exchanging $100 million of equity for that much debt. The temptation to substitute tax deductible interest for dividend payments was extremely attractive, however, and the preferred stock was called at the 10 percent premium. Crown resigned, saying that he had no interest in serving on the board of a company in which he had no financial stake.

With the $100 million he got from his interest in General Dynamics he set up his own investment firm to manage his family's interests, sticking to more conservative policies. He was soon offered blocks of General Dynamics stock at prices substantially lower than the redemption figure of $65. He started buying in the high $30s and down into the $20s. When his acquisitions reached 10 percent he was invited to return to the board of directors, with the understanding that he would again be named chairman of the executive committee.

Crown was instrumental in bringing in a new management group early in 1971 that embarked on a long-range program to turn General Dynamics around. The company had a host of problems, some of them stemming from losses on defense contracts and others from poor management. One insider described General Dynamics as "a bunch of divisions looking for a corporation. They had no pride, no cohesiveness, and in some cases little incentive." The new management set out to trim the losses in defense operations and to build up its commercial business in such fields as sand and gravel and electromechanical telephone equipment. It was also on the lookout for new acquisitions to give it profitable growth.

One of Henry Crown's most cherished projects is setting up funds at many colleges to give students of business administration an opportunity to practice making investments and to learn about finance by actual participation. Although he never finished school, he has been active in the affairs of half a dozen universities, including Chicago, Syracuse, Loyola, and Brandeis.

TRADITIONAL TYPES OF CONTROL DEVICES

Most control devices are used for both planning *and* control. This is because planning and control are the Siamese twins of management: plans set the standards of control, and control has as its purpose to see that plans succeed. There is no way of knowing whether you are going where you want to go unless you first know where you want to go.

Many kinds of control devices have long been used in business, including budgets, the Gantt Chart, statistical data, special reports and analyses, and personal observation.

Budgets

Already referred to as a type of plan in Chapter 20, budgeting, or "profit planning" as it is often called, is the most commonly used device of control. It simply means putting plans into numerical terms. As such, a budget represents anticipated results expressed in numbers. A budget may be expressed in financial terms, as with sales and expense or capital expenditure budgets. It may, however, be in nonfinancial terms, such as direct labor hours in a factory, units of output from an assembly line, or physical units of sales.

A simplified sales and expense budget for a company as a whole might look as follows:

Sales

Product A.....................................	$180,000
Product B.....................................	375,000
Product C.....................................	236,000
Product D.....................................	87,000
Total Sales.............................	$878,000

Expenses

Direct factory labor..........................	120,000
Direct materials..............................	260,000
Factory overhead.............................	240,000
Engineering Expenses........................	60,000
Sales & advertising..........................	85,000
General administrative.......................	42,000
Total Expenses	807,000

Budgeted profits before taxes................	$ 71,000

The engineering department budget for the same period might be as follows:

Direct engineering personnel......................	$25,000
Technicians...	15,000
Engineering supplies..............................	6,000
Engineering overhead.............................	14,000
Total Budgeted Expenses...................	$60,000

Budgets force definiteness in planning. They also show where in the organization structure certain activities and expenditures are expected and authorized. If properly done, they also become a useful and objective standard of control. As a matter of fact no company is too small not to operate with budgets, since the only way to be reasonably sure of making profits is to plan for them.

At the same time, there are many dangers in budgeting. If budgets are done in too much detail or become inflexible guides, they can put a straitjacket around managers. In one company with such a budget, the sales head found that he could not buy paper for sales promotion letters to potential customers because he had expended his office supplies budget, even though his department as a whole was well within its total budget.

Another danger is that the budgets of various departments may not dovetail with each other. In one case an engineering department would not furnish the sales department with information it needed to sell the company's technical products on the grounds that there was no provision in the engineering budget for doing this.

Budgets sometimes have a way of continuing from year to year on precedent. The engineering group that had a $60,000 budget last year and asks for a $70,000 budget next year may only be required to defend the extra $10,000. This assumes that last year's budget was right, instead of more logically looking at the entire $70,000 to see how much of it is actually needed for the work to be done next year. Unless a budget is thoroughly examined each year, looking at every item of expense to see if it is necessary for the next year, the budget can become an umbrella under which many inefficiencies may hide.

Budgets are inherently inflexible. It is not unusual for conditions to change during a budget year, with sales exceeding or falling short of the plan, or for other unforeseen changes to occur that may modify needs for expense money. If a manager is forced to live within an obsolete budget, this will of course defeat the whole purpose of budgeting as a planning and control instrument. In good managerial practice, provisions are made for adapting budgets to important unforeseen developments.

The Gantt Chart

Early in the twentieth century, management pioneer Henry L. Gantt devised a bar chart that he used in scheduling work. This simple invention has been called the most important social invention of the first half of the twentieth century.

An example of a simplified Gantt Chart for the construction of an

FIGURE 23–2

Simplified Gantt Chart for Construction of an Office Building

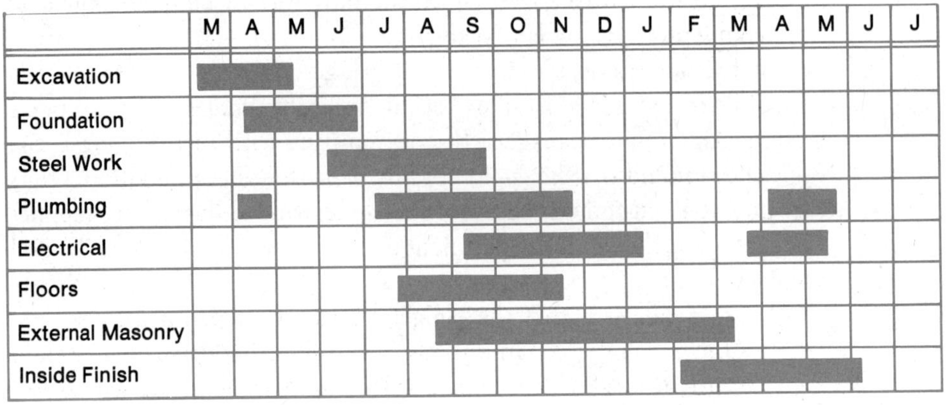

	M	A	M	J	J	A	S	O	N	D	J	F	M	A	M	J	J
Excavation	███																
Foundation		████															
Steel Work				████													
Plumbing		█			████									███			
Electrical						████							███				
Floors					████												
External Masonry						██████											
Inside Finish											██████						

office building is shown in Figure 23–2. Displayed on it are the various major tasks, when they will start, and when they are scheduled to be completed. Some tasks overlap. The installation of plumbing starts before the foundation is poured, since some of the plumbing must be laid under the foundation. The plumbers then take a break and return to the project after the steel framework has begun to rise, following the steelworkers upward. After the plumbers come the workers who install electrical conduits. Later, after another break, the plumbers return again, along with the electricians, to complete their work.

The advantage of using the Gantt Chart is that it forces people to plan in specific time frames. It takes into account when different jobs must be done, makes visual the passage of time, and is fairly easy to construct and read. It provides a definite means of control. It has deficiencies, however, unless it is refined by identifying each piece of a job and how it relates to others. For example, in Figure 23–2 some of the steelwork—that of putting the girder footings into the foundation— is started before the foundation is completed. But the chart does not show clearly just when and what part.

Presentation of Statistical Data

Some managers have no difficulty in interpreting statistical data from a mass of tables or computer printouts. But most people, as indicated above, like it best in chart form because they can more easily see trends and relationships.

If data are to be meaningful, whether in tables or on charts, they should be presented so that comparisons with some standard can be made. If a manager looks at a chart and sees that sales have risen ten percent, he will want to know how this compares with his goal for the year. If costs have risen, he will want to know how much his expense budget allows him. The chart should also show which department is responsible for whatever has happened. There is a great deal of art involved in designing a chart. It should be a tool to enable the user to see trends so that he can make his own judgment as to what may happen in the future. Good charts are powerful sources of information for control.

Special Reports and Analyses

Sometimes a problem requires special study in depth to discover where corrections are needed. Occasionally a company will hire an intelligent young analyst and ask him to dig into some problem area. Such an analyst may be able to smell out a difficulty or suggest an improvement that is worth many times his salary.

One airline had a young college graduate, not too experienced in the airline business, who wondered why the company kept six aircraft tied up in the overhaul base at the same time. His curiosity led to a study, and he was able to offer a plan that enabled overhauls to be done with one less airplane in the base. The result was the same as if he had saved the company the purchase of one plane costing more than $5 million.

Such results do not indicate that operating personnel are stupid, but only that it pays to take a fresh look once in a while. An individual or a small team with time to research problems can often come up with answers that busy operating managers and their staff easily overlook.

Personal Observation

Finally, despite all the sophisticated control techniques available, managers should not forget to use their own eyes. A stroll through the plant or the office, or a visit to the field, can often give a manager impressions and information that no reports will convey. Experienced managers can detect, almost by intuition, how things are going in a shop or office. They don't have to be told; they can "feel" problems and inefficiencies. They can also learn a good deal about their business operation by merely listening to others.

NEWER TECHNIQUES OF CONTROL: PERT

Planning and control in business have become increasingly sophisticated much more so than we can even begin to show in this textbook. However, we may mention one of the newer techniques known as PERT, which stands for Program Evaluation and Review Techniques. PERT and its companion CPM (Critical Path Method), which is different in some respects but follows the same basic principles. Both can be regarded as an outgrowth of the Gantt Chart.

These two planning tools were invented almost simultaneously in 1958. PERT was used by the Navy to coordinate the development and production of the Polaris Missile. DuPont originated CPM about the same time as a means for reducing the downtime required in equipment maintenance. PERT is credited with saving two years on the missile project, and CPM is said to have cut downtime in duPont's maintenance by 22 percent.

PERT represents a considerable refinement of the Gantt Chart. It really adds two features: (1) it breaks down planned programs into identifiable parts, or "milestones" and (2) recognizes that the various parts of a project have network relationships. From these innovations, some interesting opportunities for improving planning and control have resulted.

Milestones

To understand milestones, let us take the example of the office building in Figure 23–2. Excavation is a major part of the job. But it can be broken down into such identifiable tasks as (1) laying out the area to be excavated; (2) bringing in the excavation machinery; (3) providing trucks for carrying away the dirt; (4) providing a place for disposal of the dirt; (5) relocating pipe and sewer lines that may be in the way of the excavation; and (6) obtaining permission from the city to block a lane of street in front of the building so that the trucks may operate. These are specific tasks that must be done in a certain order and at certain times. Similar milestones might be laid out for the other major programs in constructing the building.

The advantage in identifying these milestones is that they give the manager an opportunity to lay out his plan in some detail, to see more specifically what must be done and when, and to establish checkpoints for control.

There are few planning programs that cannot benefit by being broken down into parts, or milestones. Imagine the number of separate things that have to be planned in setting up an automobile assembly line. The Apollo moon shot program could not have been done without this kind of planning, when we consider that more than 60,000 suppliers contributed some product or service to it.

Many projects are more complex than they appear. One plant manager found that 34 separate steps had to be taken in a certain way in installing a new automatic machine. The preparation of the monthly accounting reports in a company also requires a large number of steps, such as getting reports from operating departments, checking these reports for completeness, allocating sales and expenses to proper accounts, putting information into the computer, running the computer program, and putting the report in a form demanded by management.

Setting Milestones into Networks

The Gantt Chart does not show all the milestones in each program, nor does it recognize clearly how milestones in different programs fit together in a network. In other words, the various parts, tasks, or milestones of a planning program are interconnected. A network will show this and how the start or completion of one depends on another. In the office building example, some plumbing work had to be done before the foundation was poured, much of both the plumbing and electrical work could only be done after the steelwork was up, and some (such as putting fixtures in place) could not be done until the inside finish work was well under way.

This is the way most plans are. We can see it easily in an automobile assembly line. The engine has to be completely assembled before it goes to the main assembly line, bodies have to be painted before they are put in place, and the various accessories must be ready to be installed as the car moves down the line. The same kind of network planning goes into almost everything in life. Would the intelligent student wait to get groceries for his breakfast until he was ready to sit down and eat, or wait to buy pencils and paper until it was time to write a term paper?

Figure 23–3 shows how the PERT planning and control technique can be regarded as a refinement of the Gantt Chart. This is a simple schedule for a manufacturing operation involving purchasing (Task A); parts manufacture (Task B); product assembly (Task C); advertising (Task D); and the sales program for the product (Task E). In an actual situation, of course, there are many more program tasks. Each

FIGURE 23–3

Transition from a Gantt Chart to PERT

I.   **Gantt Chart**

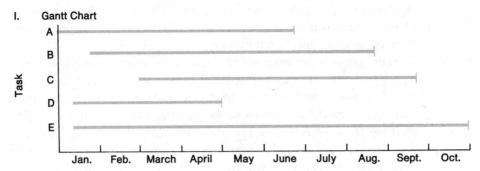

II.   **Gantt with Milestones**

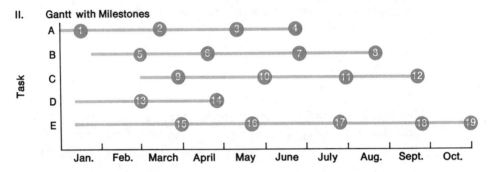

III. **Gantt with Milestones and Network of Milestones**

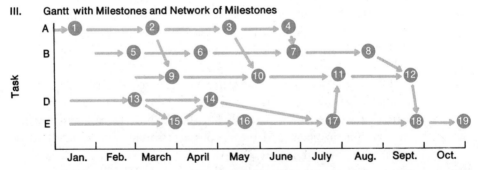

task is broken down into milestones. In purchasing, for example, there are milestones such as preparing specifications for materials needed, selecting suppliers who will be asked to bid on items to be purchased, asking for bids, evaluating bids, selecting successful bidders, and issuing purchase orders.

Each milestone within each major task is then related to all the others in a network fashion. For example, until it has been determined which parts are to be purchased and which are to be manufactured in the plant, parts production cannot go ahead. Until the overall sales program has developed to a certain point, the advertising program cannot be decided on. And until the product becomes available, the sales force cannot go to work.

The Critical Path

After we have developed the network and estimated the time each milestone event will take, we will know which series of events takes longest and therefore has the least amount of slack time. If, for example, we are planning to have the product ready for sale (milepost 18 in Figure 23–3, Part III) in 36 weeks, and if customers are relying on delivery at that time, and if it is discovered that the time required to do mileposts 1–2–3–10–11–12 will be 35 weeks, and no other series of events will take longer, then we call this the critical path. A delay in any of the events 1–2–3–10–11–12 of more than a week will certainly result in a delay in the delivery of the product.

If, however, the series of events 13–15–14–17–11–12 is scheduled to take 32 weeks and a delay of more than three weeks occurs in event 14, then this will become the critical path. Delays at various points and times can change the critical path.

Adding Costs

The original PERT system was applied to engineering projects such as the Polaris missile, and it was concerned with time rather than with costs. This is probably sufficient for such projects, since engineering costs tend to vary with time; if a project takes six months to do it is likely to cost half as much as if it took 12 months. But it is possible to refine the PERT system to take account of the specific costs for each milestone. Introducing the cost element makes PERT programming much more complex, although it need not be so complex as to be unintelligible to people who must see it.

Advantages of PERT and Network Planning

There are many advantages in network planning. Perhaps the most important is that it forces people to think through what a project involves before they start on it. Another is that it gives managers more accurate control over the progress of a plan. It helps them pinpoint critical deviations from plans and shows them where corrective efforts will do the most good.

One of the most exciting features of network planning and control is that it is a means of seeing problems in advance. For example, in the network shown in Figure 23–3, Part III, if event 10 is on the critical path and there is only one week of slack time, and if event 10 gets delayed for two weeks, a manager knows that he will have to do something if he wishes to meet the scheduled delivery date. He may, for example, reduce the time planned for event 11 or 12 by putting his work crew on overtime. This gives managers what they really want: a chance to correct things before real trouble develops.

OVERALL CONTROL

Sometimes a company wants to apply controls to the overall operation of a division or department—such as an integrated product division that has its own engineering, manufacturing, and marketing activities. This type of control is designed to measure a key manager's total operation.

The two principal overall controls are financial: (1) the measurement of profit and loss; and (2) the measurement of return on investment. This is what might be expected, since money is the best measure of total performance—the best way to add up the various parts of an operation.

Profit and Loss Control

Under this system, each major department or division makes up a profit and loss statement much as if it were a separate company. The department or division details its sales revenues and expenses—normally with a prorated share of the headquarters overhead—and calculates a monthly, quarterly, or annual statement of profit or loss.

The idea back of this kind of control is that, if it is the purpose of the company to make a profit, then it should be the purpose of each of its parts to make a profit or avoid a loss. Parts of a company are thus measured by the same standard used to measure the success of the whole company.

Simple and sensible as the idea is, it is often difficult to apply. The Ford Motor Company, for example, has marketing divisions such as Ford, Lincoln-Mercury, and Customer Service. There are other divisions that manufacture parts, produce engines, make transmissions, and assemble automobiles. The expenses of each division are fairly easy to know, but at what "price" should the engine division sell to the assembly division, or the assembly division to the Ford division? Neither the engine division nor the assembly division sells to outsiders, so there is no market price for their output. Consequently the establishment of mutually agreed-upon formulas for determining these "prices" can be very difficult.

Another problem is how to allocate headquarters expense among the divisions. It is fairly easy to allocate expenses such as those of personnel department training operations or of the central computer. We can allocate them according to the extent each division or department uses such services. But some costs cannot be traced to divisions or departments, such as the expenses of the president, the controller, or the treasurer. There is no completely accurate way. In practice, companies allocate such headquarters expenses by levying on their departments and divisions a "service charge" equal to, say, two or three percent of their sales.

Control through Return on Investment

By far the most generally used form of overall control is to measure a division's or department's return on investment. This carries profit and loss control a step farther, since it expresses a division's profit as a percentage return on the assets it uses in its operations. In this way, the company is looked upon as a kind of banker furnishing funds to division and department managers. They are then evaluated on the basis of how well they use these funds.

This technique of measuring performance was invented by Donaldson Brown of the duPont Company in 1914, and has been used by that company ever since. Many large companies, like General Motors, adopted it in the 1920s. Since World War II, and especially in the last 20 years, it has been used almost universally by companies large enough to be able to identify separate departments or divisions that can be seen as truly responsible for profits.

Using percentage return on investment as a standard puts smaller divisions on the same footing as larger ones. A division with $10 million in sales and profits of $2 million on an investment of $12 million has a rate of return of 16.67 percent. A division with $100 million in sales and profits of $10 million on $125 million of assets, will have a return of only 8 percent on its investment. Dollar for dollar, it follows that the much smaller division is doing a better job with the funds the company has invested in it.

Of course, this measure of performance also has problems. In the first place, it is subject to the same problems of allocating costs and determining profits as the other system is. In addition the calculations are complicated by the need to know exactly what the investment in the division is. And since both systems focus on financial factors, they will not give information on things that may not yet have affected profits, such as employee satisfaction or business reputation.

A third problem may arise if either of the two systems is used on a short-term basis. In any given year, a manager can show high profits by such manipulations as not maintaining his plant, cutting engineering expenses and not developing new products, or cutting back advertising expenses.

There are obviously limitations in any control technique. A manager cannot rely on any single method for all of his control requirements. Techniques help him, but they should not replace his judgment.

DIRECT CONTROL THROUGH CONTROLLING THE QUALITY OF MANAGEMENT

Perhaps the most direct form of control is to control the quality of those in charge of managing a business at all levels. Most control tools and techniques are based on correcting the mistakes of managers or detecting them before they occur. To be sure, many errors and deviations in plans are beyond even the best manager's control. An unexpected new product put on the market by a competitor, a sudden strike, a change of government policy on taxes, unexpected tightening of money supply by the banks, or new government regulations, are a few of the things that make trouble for even the best manager.

But to the extent that variations from plans are caused by managerial mistakes, it is obvious that the most able and best trained managers are likely to make fewer of these. Moreover, if we can effectively appraise these managers against their ability to set and achieve verifiable objectives and against standards of what good management is, we can take steps to assure the quality of our company managers.

In addition, it would be good to have some way of appraising the quality of the *total management* of a company. After all, we make financial audits of a company to assure stockholders, bankers, and the tax authorities that the books of account are properly operated and that the profits are as reported. But would it not be even more important to investors, bankers, employees, those who sell to companies, and even its customers, to know how well it is managed? Would not such an audit be important to students who plan to go with a company?

An accounting audit only tells us what has happened in the past.

The company's future is in the hands of those who run it, from the board of directors on down. An audit of management would give us a look ahead—not a prophecy, but at least an assurance of what to expect. Perhaps some day we shall have this kind of audit.

SUMMARY

The purpose of managerial control is to assure that plans succeed. We do this by watching what is happening, detecting errors and misses, and taking action to get operations back on a planned course. Control is a task for all managers not only in business but also in other kinds of organizations.

The managerial control process involves the same steps as any other control process—for example, that of a simple room thermostat. It requires: (1) establishing standards, (2) measuring performance against standards, and (3) taking action to correct deviations. Standards are simply criteria of performance. A manager could use an entire program as the standard but, since he usually cannot watch everything, he picks out critical points that can show him easily and quickly how things are going in his area of operation.

Management control can be looked upon as a system. Seeing control as a system makes clear the delays that will occur in obtaining corrections. It emphasizes the need for techniques and information that will allow a manager to see his problems early enough so that he can take corrective action as soon as possible. Even the computer, with its ability to process information quickly, is not good enough for the most effective control.

Control information should be timely, appropriate, reliable, valid, and channeled to the person who can and should take action. A manager's control techniques must be tailored to his plans, to the organization structure, to individual personalities, to requirements for objectivity, to the need to point up exceptions at critical points, and to economic managing. Moreover, controls must lead to action.

Typical control devices can be divided into two groups: those that have been used for a number of years and can be regarded as traditional, and the newer control devices. Among the traditional devices of control are budgets, the Gantt Chart, meaningful statistical data, special reports and analyses, and personal observation of performance. An example of the newer techniques of control is network planning and control, or PERT. This approach recognizes that planning programs can be better understood if broken down into a network of events, or milestones.

This enables us to see better how the pieces of a plan fit together and how one event depends on another. We are then in a better position to follow events and to correct deviations in time.

Many large companies apply controls to the overall operation of a division or department. These are usually financial in nature. One technique is to measure the performance of a division by calculating its independent profit or loss. Another is to measure its profit as a percentage of the assets a company has put at its disposal. This rate-of-return-on-investment system makes it possible to compare more accurately the effectiveness of smaller divisions with that of larger divisions of a company.

Perhaps the most direct form of control is to control the quality of managers in a business. Better managers, after all, make fewer mistakes, and, therefore, require fewer special controls to assure that they are carrying on their jobs effectively. Perhaps in the future we will develop ways of auditing the quality of the total management of a company. If we could be more certain than we are now that a business is well managed, we could have more confidence in its success. Certainly such information would be useful to investors, creditors, employees, students who plan to cast their lot with a company, and to the company managers themselves.

KEY TERMS AND CONCEPTS FOR REVIEW

Management control	PERT and CPM
The process of control	Milestones
Standards	Networks of planning and control
Management control loop	Critical path
Data versus information	Overall control
Tailored controls	Profit and loss control
Budgets	Control through return on investment
Gantt chart	Direct control

QUESTIONS FOR ANALYSIS AND DISCUSSION

1. Why is management control necessary for a successful business manager?
2. Why are merely measuring and evaluating activities not enough for effective control?
3. With all its fast data processing, why cannot the computer solve the problem of management control?
4. "Data are not information." Why is this true? Explain how a businessman can make sure he has the information he needs for control.
5. It has been emphasized that control techniques and approaches, to be effective, must be tailored. How can a business manager do this? Suppose that you were asked by your boss to tailor your own controls for your job, how would you go about it?

6. Management control techniques are planning *and* control techniques. Why is this so? Referring to three control techniques or approaches described in this chapter, show how they are both planning and control techniques.

7. Budgets are the most commonly used type of management control. Yet there are many dangers and difficulties in budgeting. How would you set up a budget to avoid them?

8. It is sometimes said that the modern control technique known as PERT is an outgrowth and an improvement of the Gantt Chart. Explain how this is so.

9. Take any project you wish (a term paper, preparation for an examination, a school dance, a vacation trip, a search for a job, or any other project) and set up a PERT network for it. Has doing so helped you with your planning and control?

10. "Profit and loss control is simple and sensible, yet difficult." Explain.

11. Why do so many businesses use rate of return on investment as their most important simple control technique? What care should be taken in using it?

12. Why is controlling the quality of management regarded as the most direct type of control? If you were to undertake an audit of a company's management, how would you go about it?

SUGGESTED READINGS

Anthony, R. N. *Planning and Control Systems: A Framework for Analysis.* Boston: Graduate School of Business Administration, Harvard University, 1965.

Bower, M. *The Will to Manage.* New York: McGraw-Hill Book Company, 1966, chapter 7.

Koontz, H., and C. O'Donnell *Principles of Management* (5th ed.). New York: McGraw-Hill Book Company, 1972, chapters 29–32.

Koontz, H., and C. O'Donnell *Essentials of Management,* New York: McGraw-Hill Book Company, 1974, chapters 24–27.

Levin, R. I., and C. A. Kirkpatrick *Planning and Control with PERT/CPM.* New York: McGraw-Hill Book Company, 1966.

Mockler, R. J. *The Management Control Process.* New York: Appleton-Century-Crofts, 1972.

Welsch, G. A., and B. H. Sord *Management Planning and Control.* New York: Financial Executives Research Foundation, 1968.

UPI photo.

24

Management
and Labor
Unions

In many companies, and in almost all of the larger ones, managers have to deal with strong labor unions. These organizations, representing as they do a large portion of the employees, have goals of their own. Their goals are essentially to protect and promote what they regard as the interests of their members.

Often the interests of unions have placed them in conflict with the managers of business, sometimes, as in the case of the railroad and construction industries, to the detriment of business efficiency. At other times, as with the coal miners' union, they encourage business efficiency but see that the benefits of lower costs are translated into higher wages. In some instances, union pressures have forced autocratic and incompetent managers to change their ways for the better and to see what their real tasks as managers are. It is probably no accident that the rise of modern management occurred just before World War II at the same time as the rise of strong, militant national unions.

Rights and Responsibilities

No field of business or industry is immune to the problem of employer-employee relations, and in recent years it seems that no field is immune to the special problems associated with organized labor. Certainly, there are two sides to the apparent conflict between labor and management. Management has certain rights, but along with these rights go obligations to the employees. Labor also has rights which must be respected, but in return labor should offer the employer loyalty and productivity.

Full production and higher standards of living require that management and employees jointly increase their productivity and lower their costs. Thus the goals of both management and labor can be reached along the same road. To stay on that road, however, every tool in human relations, not merely labor relations, must be used to good advantage.

UNIONS

The activities of labor unions are well known to most of us from reading our newspapers. We are familiar with terms such as "union leader" and "strike." The following terms are also in common use in management-labor relations, and a brief review of their meanings will help to introduce the concepts to be discussed in the rest of this chapter.

- LABOR AGREEMENT—a contract between management and a union specifying the terms and conditions of employment.
- COLLECTIVE BARGAINING—the process of negotiating a labor agreement between management and labor representatives.
- COOLING-OFF PERIOD—a period during which there can be no strike. The President of the United States can call for an 80-day suspension of any strike that would threaten the public interest. Hopefully, during this time the parties will reach an agreement.
- MEDIATION—the procedure in which a neutral third party tries to persuade both parties in a dispute to reach a compromise. The mediator has no authority over either party.
- ARBITRATION—the procedure for resolving a dispute under the terms of a labor contract. An objective third party hears both sides of the case and makes a decision, often representing a compromise of the opposing positions. Ordinarily, the arbitrator's decision is binding upon both parties.
- GRIEVANCE—an employee's demand that his employer honor a particular aspect of the labor agreement or of law. A labor contract will usually include a step-by-step procedure for settling grievances, ending with arbitration as a last resort.

Organized Labor: Image and Reality

The man in the street has fairly definite opinions about labor unions. Usually his opinion depends upon whether he has most recently crossed the path of union corruption or benevolence. The concept of the labor union is certainly not a wishy-washy topic with most folks—they either love the idea or they loathe it.

Most people have a picture of the labor-management relationship that is rather different from the actual one. One popular picture is of a bad businessman giving his good workers a hard time, and of the workers joining together to bargain for what they want. Actually, the bargaining is not between labor and management. It is really between the business *managers* and the labor union *managers*. In the effort to achieve certain goals, labor has thus taken on a second set of managers. As shown in Table 24–1, managers for labor are generally paid well.

With two sets of managers, the worker has twice as many chances at everything. He has two chances to receive fair treatment and two chances to be abused. But there is an even higher probability that the ultimate agreement will be fair to the worker.

It is worth considering the possibility that two of the students reading this book may someday find themselves on opposite sides of a negotiating table. The principles of effective management are equally important to the manager of a cheese factory and to the one who represents the cheesemaker's employees in negotiations with the "big cheese" himself.

The historic role of unions has been to provide a counterbalance to

TABLE 24–1
How Much the Top Labor Leaders Earned in 1972

		Salary	Allowance	Expenses	Total Compen- sation
1.	Frank E. Fitzsimmons, pres., Teamsters.........	$125,000	$ 2,745	$ 3,736	$131,481
2.	Murray W. Miller, sec.-treas., Teamsters.........	100,973	4,295	8,960	114,228
3.	Hunter P. Wharton, pres., Operating Engineers...	80,833	22,200	—	103,033
4.	Joseph Curran, pres., National Maritime Union...	85,257	5,200	1,636	92,093
5.	C. L. Dennis, pres., Railway Clerks..............	70,000	—	21,069	91,069
6.	John H. Lyons, pres., Iron Workers..............	48,000	15,120	18,071	81,191
7.	James T. Housewright, pres., Retail Clerks......	60,000	13,000	8,082	81,082
8.	Peter Fosco, pres., Laborers.....................	75,000	—	5,599	80,599
9.	Edward J. Carlough, pres., Sheet Metal Workers..	50,000	19,490	8,166	77,656
10.	George Meany, pres., AFL-CIO...................	72,960	—	1,816	74,776
11.	Terence O'Sullivan, sec.-treas., Laborers........	70,000	—	3,410	73,410
12.	Ed S. Miller, pres., Hotel & Restaurant Employees.	49,999	12,810	8,841	71,650
13.	David S. Turner, sec.-treas., Sheet Metal Workers.	45,000	19,490	6,345	70,835
14.	Jos. D. Keenan, sec., Electrical Workers (IBEW)...	55,000	—	15,640	70,640
15.	I. W. Abel, pres., Steelworkers..................	60,000	—	9,937	69,937

Source: *Business Week,* August 13, 1973, p. 63, based on union reports to the U.S. Department of Labor.

the employer's economic power. The employees, through elected representatives, negotiate the terms of employment with company officials. The agreement thus reached by "equals" provides a set of rules for the parties as long as the contract lasts.

The union is much more than an economic institution. It may seek to use political power and public opinion to accomplish its goals. Even "collective bargaining" is a more complicated process than it appears to be. A broad definition of collective bargaining would be that it is a process by which employers and the representatives of employees attempt to arrive at agreements governing the conditions under which employees will contribute their services and be compensated therefor.

HISTORY OF ORGANIZED LABOR

Labor unions have existed in the United States since the Revolutionary War, but only within the last 80 or 90 years has the union movement been able to flex any muscle. The American Federation of Labor (AFL) was formed in 1886, and by the 1930s nearly all of the country's unions were affiliated with it. In 1935, some of the industrial unions—those representing workers in factories or mines as distinguished from skilled craftsmen like carpenters and bricklayers—dropped out of the AFL to form their own group, called the Congress of Industrial Organizations (CIO). The CIO proceeded to organize workers in manufacturing industries such as the automobile and steel industries. In 1955 the two organizations reunited and took the name American Federation of Labor-Congress of Industrial Organizations. The name was a little clumsy, and it was shortened in use to AFL-CIO.

Law and Labor

The reason for union growth in the 1930s lay largely in changes in the laws. Until the 1930s, labor unions could not gain much momentum because of legal bulwarks created against them. Businessmen could often ignore the unions so long as the law did not require employers to recognize them and bargain with them. The courts were prepared to issue injunctions prohibiting unions from engaging in strikes, boycotts, picketing, and efforts to increase their membership. Finally, a company could require its employees, as a condition of employment, not to join unions; this kind of stipulation came to be known as the "yellow dog contract."

The Roosevelt administration in the 1930s passed new legislation favorable to union organizing. The first important change came in 1932 with the Norris-LaGuardia Act. This placed severe restrictions upon the use of court injunctions intended to curb or limit union activities, and outlawed yellow-dog contracts. In 1933, the National Industrial Recovery Act gave employees the right to organize and bargain collectively. Union growth accelerated as a consequence.

When the NIRA was declared unconstitutional on May 27, 1935, Congress immediately passed the National Labor Relations Act (known as the Wagner Act). This gave employees the right to organize and made it mandatory for employers to bargain collectively with representatives of the employees. It outlawed certain "unfair" labor practices of employers. Subsequent federal legislation has added measures designed to protect the employers against unfair labor practices of unions. Specifically, the Labor Management Relations (Taft-Hartley) Act was passed in 1947, over President Truman's veto. This amended the National Labor Relations Act, which many people felt had gone too far in giving advantages to labor organizations. The new act contained a list of unfair labor practices in which unions were not allowed to engage.

In 1959, the Landrum-Griffin Act was passed to control racketeering and financial irresponsibility in certain unions. Now every union must file a detailed financial report with the Secretary of Labor and make the information in this report available to its members.

Labor Legislation in States

A number of states in the U.S. have legislation supplementing the federal laws. Some states ban strikes by public employees, forbid the closed shop (in which no one can be hired unless he is already a union member), or prohibit compulsory joining of unions. The federal Taft-Hartley Act permits state legislatures to pass such laws, and this has led to the enactment in many states, especially in the south and southwest, of so-called right-to-work laws which stipulate that no worker can be required to join a union in order to obtain or keep his job (Table 24–2).

TABLE 24–2

States with Right-to-Work Laws in 1973

Texas	Arkansas	Florida
Nevada	Mississippi	Utah
Georgia	Iowa	Nebraska
North Carolina	Arizona	Virginia
South Carolina	North Dakota	Kansas
Tennessee	South Dakota	Indiana
Alabama		

FIGURE 24–1

Structure of the AFL-CIO
Organization

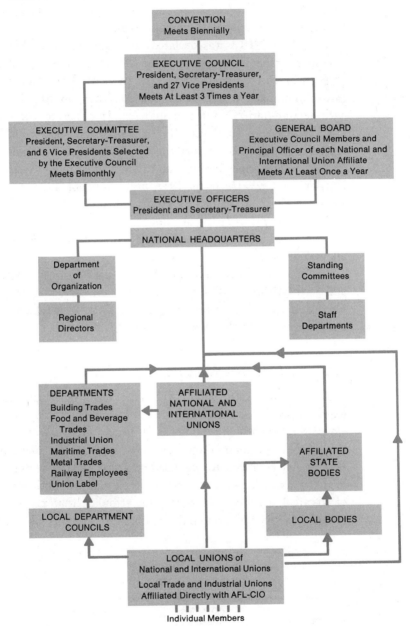

UNION ORGANIZATION

Local Union Organizations

In the United States, the basic unit of organized labor is the local union comprised—if it is an industrial union—of workers in a particular industry or group of related industries within a local area, or—if it is a craft union—of workers in a particular craft in the local geographic area. For example, the carpenters in a local construction labor market are likely to be members of the local carpenters union. Similarly, workers in an automotive assembly plant will probably be members of a United Automobile Workers local, regardless of their particular job function.

Present union membership in the U.S. is estimated at almost 20 million workers out of a total civilian work force of over 89 million. About half of the workers in manufacturing belong to unions. In construction the proportion is around 75 percent, but in the distribution and service industries only about 10 percent. Ironically, while workers have joined unions to combat the impersonalization of large corporate employers, they frequently find themselves far removed from the center of power in their union organization. Figure 24–1 shows the elaborate organization structure of the AFL-CIO.

National Union Organizations

There are about 190 national or international unions in the United States. The largest are the International Brotherhood of Teamsters, Chauffeurs, Warehousemen and Helpers of America (usually called Teamsters), the United Automobile Workers, and the United Steel

TABLE 24–3

Largest Unions and Their Membership in 1972

1.	Teamsters	1,855,000
2.	Auto Workers	1,400,000
3.	Steelworkers	1,400,000
4.	Electrical Workers	957,000
5.	Machinists	865,000
6.	Carpenters	820,000
7.	Retail Clerks	633,000
8.	Laborers	600,000
9.	Meatcutters	529,000
10.	State, County, Municipal Employees	529,000
11.	Hotel Workers	458,000

Workers of America, with memberships of more than a million. At the other extreme, the Journeyman Stonecutters Association of North America has a membership of 1,900 and the International Association of Siderographers (engravers on steel) has a total membership of 29.

Most local unions are affiliated with national or international unions, the latter having members outside the United States (usually in Canada).

Federations of Unions

The next level in the union structure is the federation of national unions or their locals. Federations may exist on the city, state, or national level. Every large city has a labor federation composed of local unions that come together because of their common interest in municipal problems, or for political reasons.

The AFL-CIO is a federation on the national level. Not every national union belongs to it, however, and some former members have withdrawn from it. The United Mine Workers left the CIO in 1942 and never returned, the United Auto Workers withdrew in 1967; and the International Brotherhood of Teamsters was expelled in 1956.

The primary functions of the federation are political and mediatory. A federation will represent the labor movement in dealing with public officials and helping to settle disputes between various affiliated unions. Federations are sometimes the conscience of the labor movement, and may take broader positions on public issues than do national or local unions which exist primarily for economic collective bargaining.

Craft and Industrial Unions

Craft unions draw their membership from a skilled trade, such as electricians, plumbers, and carpenters. Their members often have a very short attachment to particular employers. For example, in the building trades, the craftsmen change employers each time a project is finished. They tend to rely on their unions to find them jobs. Thus the union's hiring hall may become the primary placement agency for skilled jobs in a local labor market, so long as the employers are not able to hire nonunion workers. The unions also have considerable control over the supply of new workers because of their apprenticeship system, which often requires members to go through a long period of training as apprentices before they become qualified members or "journeymen."

Industrial unions, on the other hand, have very limited control over hiring. Most of their power comes from controlling the internal labor market in a particular firm. For example, an industrial union may have considerable impact in determining promotion priorities within a firm, or the classifications of jobs. It will attempt to establish seniority as the main factor in determining promotion; it will want to have a say in grievance procedures; and it will exert some influence on wage rates. Nevertheless, industrial unions typically have much less control of the labor market than do the craft organizations.

UNION CONTRACTS

While unions differ widely in the power they possess, the range of subjects covered in most union contracts is about the same. They usually include a management rights clause, recognition of the union as bargaining agent, hours of work, wages, vacations and holidays, seniority, working conditions, layoffs and rehirings, grievance procedure, arbitration and mediation, and clauses governing renewal of the contract. The details and treatment of these subjects differ so much that it is impractical to cite examples here. To some extent, the union contract deals with many of the subjects that should be included in good personnel practice. But it often covers much more, such as promotion by seniority or the restriction of work assignments.

Today, unions and management each argue that the other has too much power. Both agree that the government is becoming too large and too powerful. And each feels that it is at a disadvantage relative to the other two.

Actually, all three sectors—labor, management, and government—have become increasingly powerful. It is of utmost concern that some balance be maintained between them, for only in this way can the public's interest be protected. Figure 24–2 shows how unions, manage-

FIGURE 24–2

The Business Balance

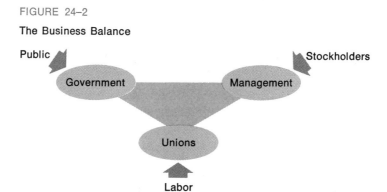

Marvin Miller

United Press
International photo.

Although Marvin Julian Miller has been said to epitomize the "new breed" in union leadership, his early childhood is traditional Americana. He was born in New York City in 1917 to children of European immigrants. His childhood heroes were athletes such as Babe Ruth, Dazzy Vance, and Tarzan. True to the Horatio Alger tradition, he secured his first job at the age of ten, as a paperboy. Soon he moved up from the *Brooklyn Eagle* to the *New York Times.* Later, he worked as a soda clerk and as a Wall Street runner.

He attributes his interest in unionism to the influence of his father who was one of the early organizers for the Retail Wholesale and Department Store Employees Union. His father, a salesman in a woman's clothing store, typically worked 10 to 12 hours a day including Saturdays and Sundays.

Miller graduated from public schools in Brooklyn, received a B.S. from New York University where he majored in economics, and did graduate work at the New School for Social Research.

During World War II, he was an economist with the Wage Stabilization Division of the War Labor Board and subsequently a hearing officer in the Disputes Division. Later, he helped modernize the United States Conciliation Service. His first full-

ment, and government ought to relate to each other. We may point out that they have one thing in common: all three represent people, in their capacities as union members, stockholders, and voters. Many businessmen today feel that the balance of power is weighted on the side of the unions. They point out that striking workers can collect government unemployment benefits. This, to a businessman, means that the government and businesses on which unemployment taxes are levied are helping the unions and making management's job more difficult.

THE PROCESS OF NEGOTIATION

Negotiating with a union is one of the businessman's greatest responsibilities because so many parties will be affected by what he does. His employees and stockholders are most immediately concerned with the outcome, but his customers, creditors, and suppliers will also feel the impact of the negotiations.

time union job began in 1947 when he became affiliated with the International Association of Machinists. Three years later, he moved to Pittsburgh to work with the United Steel Workers of America where he became known as an intelligent, articulate, and imaginative labor leader. He was instrumental in resolving the record breaking 1959 steel strike of 116 days. Among his ideas was a committee of representatives from management, union, and neutral outsiders to resolve major problems. Miller was appointed to the National Labor-Management Panel by President Kennedy in 1963 and was reappointed to that position under President Johnson.

In 1966, Miller was nominated for the position of executive director of the 700-member Major League Baseball Players Association. He campaigned aggressively for the post, touring the major league training camps that spring to speak with the players. He overwhelmingly defeated the owner-backed candidate and took office on July 1, 1966.

Although he at first was received coldly by the owners, he soon was able to establish a solid basis for collective bargaining. One of his first major victories was to gain the right for an impartial arbitrator to resolve grievances between players and team management. Miller argued that it was unfair for the baseball commissioner, who was chosen by management, to handle player grievances.

In 1972, major league baseball players staged a historic 13-day general strike. The strike caused the cancellation of 86 games. One critic accused Miller of hypnotizing the players. *The Sporting News,* however, suggested, "If the active players did the voting, the guy they would immortalize and put in the Hall of Fame is Marvin Miller."

Through Miller's negotiations, players obtained a minimum salary guarantee of $15,000, improved living expenses and conditions, an increased share in World Series receipts (minimum of $20,000), and vastly improved pension plans. During Miller's first seven years on the job, players won over $20 million in increased salary and pension benefits.

Marvin Miller is 5'9" tall and weighs 160 pounds. His wife says, "He can eat all he wants without putting on weight—it's disgusting." He dresses conservatively and plays aggressive tennis. His wife is a clinical psychologist at Kingsborough Community College in Brooklyn. She and her husband recently won the college's faculty mixed doubles tennis tournament. They have two grown children. The Players' Association pays Miller $80,000 per year.

A businessman dealing with a union should first acquire some knowledge of industrial relations, as well as a sense of what he wants to achieve. Union negotiators are prepared. They bring facts and figures with them, and they also have a feeling of moral rightness. They see the employer as a foe of the worker, and they believe that their mission is to protect the worker from exploitation. In actuality, of course, neither side is right or wrong; each side is working in behalf of its own interests. A labor union leader is really a businessman—in the business of satisfying the union members who support him through their dues. Management, for its part, is in the business of satisfying its stockholders. But it needs to have a positive approach to industrial relations that stresses healthy employer-employee relationships as well as material compensation and benefits. Otherwise it cannot sit down at the bargaining table and hold its own.

Management's viewpoint must be backed up with some notion of how it wants to proceed in the give-and-take of the bargaining sessions.

One of the chief employer pitfalls in union negotiations is the lack of a "battle plan," or failure to carry such a plan through. Having a plan on paper is important, but management must be willing to use the plan to best advantage if it hopes to gain points in collective bargaining. The employer's plan should be positive and aggressive, and he should be able to make demands upon the union.

To deal effectively, the negotiator must also have information on wages and benefits, company labor costs, additional costs that would be imposed by a new labor contract, plans for any changes that might affect labor costs, and possible "booby traps" that can occur in union proposals.

As a rule, the negotiating process passes through several distinct stages. The following is a general guide as to what to expect of collective bargaining.

Probing. As a management and union prepare for bargaining negotiations, they begin very early to probe and feel out each other's positions. The union signals its demands, and management responds by keeping policy-making officials uncommunicative and by debating the validity of the union's demands.

A most serious consideration at this stage is not to push the opposition, especially the union leader, so far that he cannot later recede from his early position. Both sides must be able to leave the bargaining table with a claim of victory.

Dressing. Each party builds up a much-publicized justification for its proposals or counterproposals. The purpose of this "dressing" is to weaken the position of the other party by softening and undermining the foundation upon which its major proposals and counterproposals are based, and to lead it to question the logic behind its position.

Simulated Real Position. Management and union generally sit down at the bargaining table with major proposals backed by bargaining cushions that can be depressed from a maximum to a minimum as the need develops during the negotiation process. For example, the union may demand an increase of 95 cents per hour, but has secretly decided it can settle for 45 cents. Management states it can give no raise, but privately decides it can agree to a 35-cent increase. The area between the company maximum and the union minimum may be termed the true area of bargaining expectancy.

Since both parties want to emerge from the negotiations with some portions of their cushions intact, they sometimes advance the impression that they are at breaking-off points where further negotiation is fruitless. These stratagems are called false breaking-off points and may involve one party's stalking from the meeting room while the other remains impassive and unmoved. They may be accompanied by well-publicized strike preparations, or by pessimistic announcements that the business may be forced to close its doors.

Real Position. As the parties respectively move toward the limits in their ranges of concessions, they compress their bargaining cushions. When they find simulated positions of no avail, they reach their real positions on given proposals. At this point, strike threats by the union take on real significance, and management obstinancy probably means that the company is willing to sustain a strike rather than make any further concession.

Trading Positions. In a previous stage, the union may have made concession to the extent of reducing its demands to 75 cents, and the company may have moved to the point of conceding 25 cents. In this situation the parties may compromise on a figure below 75 cents and above 25 cents. Or one party may concede on this matter, and use the concession to gain something elsewhere. Often a loss in one area is set off with a gain in another.

Take Position. Having made their trades, the parties have now reached what may be called their "take positions," each taking what the other is finally offering. They are more or less content, knowing that every proposal has been squeezed dry. A strong "wrap-up" psychology pervades all corners of the bargaining room, and the final contract becomes the handiwork of both parties.

If a Strike Occurs. In concluding, it may be observed that collective bargaining continues even during a strike. For a limited time the parties may draw apart and widen the area of disagreement, even going back to their original demands. But as the strike continues, pressure toward settlement accelerates the tempo with which the parties move from simulated to real to take positions and to final settlement.

With this general pattern in mind, the negotiator should be able to put each stage of the bargaining process in proper perspective. Knowing the direction the negotiations will probably take, he will be able to make demands at strategic times.

Signed Contracts. Once contracts are signed, everyone on both sides must be thoroughly oriented to the new limitations and opportunities. Management, supervisors, and line production staff all need to be familiar with the new contract requirements which will influence every decision they make . . . until the contract expires.

CRITICISMS OF LABOR UNIONS BY BUSINESS

Businessmen have naturally been critical of labor unions. Most of their criticisms have to do with programs and actions of unions that seem to interfere with the efficient operation of business. Although not all of the criticisms can be listed here, the following appear to be the most significant ones.

Monopoly Power

Perhaps the strongest criticism of unions is that many of them are able to control the labor supply. The Pilot's Union can shut down an airline. So can unions of mechanics, air traffic controllers, cargo handlers, and even meteorologists. The United Automobile Workers can shut down any plant of Ford, General Motors, Chrysler, or American Motors. A single one of the numerous railroad unions can shut down the entire railroad industry. The few thousand dockworkers on the west coast were able to shut down the entire west coast water shipping industry for many months in 1971, and could do it again at any time. In 1972 there were 5,010 work stoppages in the U.S., involving 1,714,000 workers. This meant that 27,066,000 man-days of work were lost in labor disputes that year.

Thus unions are monopolies in that they are able to take their members off the job while keeping businessmen from hiring replacements. It is argued that if monopolies in business are to be outlawed (except for public utilities), it is inconsistent to have laws that protect labor monopolists.

In reply, unions make the point that if they did not have monopoly power their strikes might not be effective and they would have no way to enforce their collective bargaining demands. They also point out that companies in the same industry are permitted by law to join together to meet a strike threat against an individual company. Most railroads, for example, have an agreement that a strike against one is a strike against all. Also, most airlines have an agreement that if a union strikes one of them so that it loses business to its competitors, it is entitled to receive some of their windfall profits.

But neither of these arguments protects the general public when a company or an industry is shut down. To be sure, there are laws that permit the government to delay a strike for a period of time, such as the Taft-Hartley Act mentioned above. And in the case of such essential industries as the railroads, Congress has occasionally passed special legislation forcing the end of a serious strike.

Make-Work Rules

Certain unions have been criticized for requiring employers to hire workers they do not want. For many years, the railroads were required to keep firemen on diesel locomotives, although there were no longer any steam boilers to fire. They are still required on passenger trains despite the fact that the head brakeman riding in the cab with the engineer can give him any help he needs. On many lines the modern locomotives are almost as automatic as a building elevator.

Railroads have also been required to carry minimum crews of from five to seven on freight trains, whether they were needed or not. At one time certain unions threatened to strike unless engine and caboose crews were given extra pay as radio operators after radio telephones had been installed.

But the railroads have not been the only industry where such practices are found. Airlines are required to include a "flight engineer" on the crew of every medium to large passenger plane, even though there may be little for an engineer to do. Movie studios are forced to use larger crews than they want: electricians whose only duty is to plug in a light once a day, carpenters to drive a few nails, or stagehands to move a single piece of furniture. Painters' unions were able for years to limit the width of the paint brush a union painter could use. Movie theatres sometimes must hire stage hands. Oceangoing ships may be required to use two operators on a loading winch, each to operate one control, when one person could handle both more easily.

Make-work has been carried farthest in the transportation industries, where most unions are organized around crafts such as engineers, signalmen, mechanics, dispatchers, pilots, and dockworkers. The practice is less common among industrial unions. The mine workers and auto workers have generally not attempted to force business to hire unnecessary labor, preferring the higher wages to be gained from greater efficiency.

The student may wonder why craft unions enforce rules that require unneeded labor. The union argument is that, if employers were not required to respect craft lines, they would destroy the crafts' integrity. The craft unions also argue that clear distinctions between crafts have to be maintained so that workers will not be overloaded with work, and that technological improvements do not justify laying off workers. When shipping lines on the West Coast wanted to adopt the container system, requiring less manpower to load and unload, they paid the longshoremen's union a substantial fee for permission to do so. The union argued that these payments were necessary to compensate the dockworkers for loss of jobs. The money was used to provide for early retirement, a move to another area, or retraining.

Interfering with the Prerogatives of Management

Unions have also been accused of interfering with the essential rights of managers. Most unions require that hirings, layoffs, and promotions be based on seniority. Sometimes a manager can hire only union members. In many contracts, once a person has been on the job for a trial period, usually three months, he cannot be fired without a clear cause acceptable to the union. In other instances, unions may insist upon a flat rate of pay and forbid piecework or incentive pay based on the amount a worker produces. Restrictions may also be placed on moving workers from one job to another, or requiring them to work overtime.

These and other provisions of course limit the rights of a manager to manage. If they limit his right to hire or fire, they take away much of his authority over his subordinates. But unions maintain that if they are to protect workers against capricious management practices they must have such rules. They favor seniority because, since it is based on concrete facts, it eliminates prejudice and favoritism in promoting people or laying them off.

Assuming All Productivity Increases Are Due to Labor

One union attitude that especially concerns businessmen is the tendency to assume that all increases of productivity are due to labor. It is true that we usually calculate productivity in terms of output per labor hour. To do this, we take total company output and divide it by the number of labor hours spent in its production. Unions then use this as an argument for increased wages.

As can be readily seen, the output of a company is influenced by expenditures for tools, machines, new ways of doing things, and other factors not directly related to how hard or efficiently any individual worker works. Clearly, if *all* increases in total output per labor hour were passed on to workers in increased wages, there would be nothing left to pay for the costs of machines and other efficiency-improving items. The same would be true if all increases in productivity were passed on to consumers through price reductions.

There is no way of settling the dispute to everyone's satisfaction. When a new machine is installed, who ought to benefit most from the increased productivity? The employees of the plant? The company's stockholders? The customers who buy the product? Or should they all benefit equally?

The logic of the case probably does not matter much anyway. On the premise that the union is really a business concerned with getting the best possible deal for its members, union negotiators can be expected to use any reasonable argument that comes to hand.

CRITICISMS OF MANAGEMENT BY LABOR

Unions for their part are quick to say that management has been less than perfect in its dealings with workers. Even the most rabid adversary of management would agree that its attitude toward workers has substantially improved during this century, but many workers still resent certain things that management does.

Perhaps the most frequently mentioned is a tendency for management to be impersonal and arbitrary. When companies transfer people from one job or one city to another without consulting the employee, or when they discharge employees if business takes a downturn, workers are likely to feel that management has little consideration for their problems. Better human relations have reduced the impact of this concern, but for many, it still exists.

As suggested earlier in this book, management's essential job is to secure adequate profits for the owners of a company. Many workers do not understand the vital function of profits. Moreover, they frequently assume that profits are much higher than they actually are. It is only natural for many workers to feel that the primary purpose of business ought to be to provide jobs rather than to make profits. Many union members feel that management is too preoccupied with the profit objective.

The development of modern cost accounting has led workers to feel that their position in the company is similar to that of machinery or raw materials. Although it may look that way on the income statement, management certainly should be well aware that labor is more than a cost of production. Workers are human beings and will insist upon a recognition of this fact. Any company that wants to introduce technological improvements will find that it has to reckon with deepseated feelings in this area.

Achievements of Unions

Unions can point to many specific accomplishments in their long history. Union efforts have played a major role in the achievement of higher wages for workers, a shorter workday and workweek, the abolition of child labor, better working conditions, greater job security, extensive fringe benefits, workmen's compensation, old age insurance, medical care, greater equality of opportunity, and, in some instances, profit sharing or a guaranteed annual wage.

While some people feel that unions may have outlived their usefulness, few union leaders are likely to agree to this. They consider their future to lie in organizing those who are still unorganized—the younger, better-educated workers as well as white-collar workers and government employees. The success of unions in these areas will determine whether they grow or decline. Beyond this, the challenge for union leaders, as well as for businessmen, is to recognize the social responsibility that goes with power.

THE FUTURE OF COLLECTIVE BARGAINING

At the 1972 White House Conference on the Industrial World Ahead, Secretary of Labor J. D. Hodgson made some interesting comments about the future of collective bargaining. He stated that the conditions which once made collective bargaining one of the real forces in the world of industrial relations do not now exist. He predicted that the future may see a sharp decline in the incidence and efficacy of collective bargaining.

He saw two developments threatening collective bargaining. One is the big, crippling strike which affects the public much more than the strikers. In the early days of union formation, strikes hurt employers and workers much more than the general public. Now, however, markets are so closely tied together and workers are concentrated so heavily that a major strike can cripple the entire country. Consider, for instance, the panic that occurs when the dockworkers or teamsters go on strike!

Another factor is the part strikes play in pushing up prices. If wage settlements are higher than labor productivity, business has no choice but to raise prices. We call this "cost-push" inflation. Price increases tend to reduce the buying power of the higher wages gained from striking. This leads to further demands for wage increases and creates a continuing upward spiral. Efforts by government to control wages can be of only temporary usefulness. Neither labor nor management completely trusts the government's ability to make wise, fair decisions on wages or prices.

Secretary of Labor Hodgson predicted that public opinion will determine whether or not we will continue to have collective bargaining. The wishes of labor or of management will not prevail—only the will of the people who are ultimately affected by crippling strikes and inflationary wage settlements. As shown in Figure 24-3, public support for labor is not especially high.

FIGURE 24-3

What the Public Thinks of Labor

71% oppose the continued growth of unions.

55% believe unions have too much power and this power should be curbed. (Among union members, 41% agree.)

68% think strikes hurt everybody too much. (Among union members, 61% agree.)

59% blame costly union settlements for causing the U.S. to price itself out of world markets. (Among union members, 68% agree.)

68% blame higher prices and living costs on unions (57% of the unionists agree.)

62% believe unions should be subject to tighter government regulation.

65% say the government shoud intervene in strikes that hurt the public.

63% would bar strikes by firemen, 62% by policemen, 65% by teachers, and 54% by sanitation workers—but the percentage of those against public employee unionism is down since the late 1960s.

46% would bar food stamps and other forms of public assistance to those on strike.

65% rate the job that union leaders are doing as "fair to poor." (Among union members polled, 8% said "excellent" and 26% "good," but 59% rated leaders as "fair to poor.")

Source: Opinion Research Corp., 1972.

THE FUTURE OF THE WORLD OF WORK

The 1972 White House Conference also addressed itself to several key questions bearing on the character of tomorrow's working world. The way in which these questions are answered will ultimately decide who works at what and for how much.

Does Every American Have the Right to a Job? The right to work is nowhere guaranteed in the U.S. Constitution, but has come to be accepted in many circles as the self-evident right of every citizen. It is held that everyone who wishes to work should be able to find a job. No one questions the desirability of increased employment opportunity, but to *guarantee* everyone a job poses problems of incentives and costs that will not be easy to resolve.

Should Every Citizen Who Is Able to Work Have an Obligation to Do So? This is the issue of whether everyone should be guaranteed some minimum level of income whether he works or not. The problems of "work relief," guaranteed income, and the burgeoning welfare rolls will be subjects of major controversy in the next decade. Regardless of how they are answered, the practical problems will be staggering.

What Do We Mean By Equal Opportunity to Work? Doesn't this imply that access to jobs should be based on ability without regard to race, creed, color, sex, or age? Minority groups are disproportionately represented in the ranks of the unemployed and in low-status jobs; women have very little access to higher-paying and higher-status occupations. The fuller implementation of this principle (already adopted in law) will be a necessary feature of tomorrow's world of work.

What Should Be Done about Education and Training for Work? There are fewer and fewer jobs that can be done without specialized training of some sort. Even so, education at most high schools, universities, and colleges focuses on a general curriculum that does not prepare the student for any particular line of work. The shockingly high unemployment rate among young people testifies to the need for suitable training. Another related problem is that of changing occupations—a worker's skills become obsolete much more rapidly now. A person training for a particular occupation today may have to retrain later on when his type of work is taken over by a machine or when new procedures cause his job to be downgraded. People will have to have more than one career. Even when they don't, the rapid developments in technology will require them to undergo further training to keep up-to-date in their jobs.

What Role Should Work Play in Personal Fulfillment? Social scientists have learned that good mental health and interesting work go hand in hand. More and more people are seeking ways to make their jobs more varied and fulfilling. It is increasingly believed that one's work should be interesting as well as useful, and that the worker should know how his particular job contributes to the general welfare of society.

The main thrust of all these questions can perhaps be summed up in this way: work and the way work is organized are going to be increasingly influenced by social and human needs, and private interest will have less to say in these matters.

Private enterprise has always added much to the quality of American life, even as it created some of the problems concerning us today. It is highly likely that the solutions to these problems—and the people who will provide the solutions—are to be found in the private sector of our economy. Business leaders will be expected to assume more responsibility for meeting social goals in the future, and there is no reason to doubt that they will do so.

SUMMARY

In many companies, particularly the larger ones, managers have to deal with strong labor unions. They do not have total control over the selection, the compensation, the promotion, or even the termination of employees.

Although many businessmen resent the fact that their power to make decisions is limited by unions, they have no choice but to accept the situation. Organized labor has a strong position in the historical, legal and contemporary scene. Business managers and union managers have to understand each other's needs and ways of thinking. Enlightened understanding can enable both labor and management to achieve their mutual goals of greater productivity, financial rewards, and meaningful work.

The growth and strength of the union movement will certainly have a bearing upon the businessman's situation sooner or later. The negotiator has the opportunity to emerge as a hero or a heel from the collective bargaining room. He can serve both mankind and company; he can serve one and alienate the other; or he can serve neither and look for a job somewhere else . . . in which case, he becomes someone else's labor problem!

The future of work and the implications for workers are topics which must be explored thoroughly and dealt with positively. Some of the more pressing questions are (1) the right to work, (2) the obligation to work, (3) equal opportunity to work, (4) education and training for work, and (5) the role of work in human fulfillment. Sensitive and creative handling of these major problems is essential if the world of work in the near future is going to be pleasant and meaningful.

KEY TERMS AND CONCEPTS FOR REVIEW

Labor agreement	National Labor Relations Act
Collective bargaining	Labor-Management Relations Act
Cooling-off period	Landrum-Griffin Act
Arbitration	Closed shop
Mediation	Union shop
Grievance	Craft union
AFL-CIO	Industrial union
Yellow dog contract	Cost-push inflation
Norris-LaGuardia Act	

QUESTIONS FOR ANALYSIS AND DISCUSSION

1. What is the most basic labor unit?
2. List the three largest unions in the United States.
3. Diagram the union structure.
4. What are the primary functions of the federation?
5. Contrast the craft union with the industrial union, emphasizing the primary tasks of each.
6. What subjects are usually covered in the union contract?
7. List and describe the basic elements in the negotiation process.
8. What are the major criticisms of labor unions by business?
9. What answers do unions give to these criticisms?
10. What developments threaten collective bargaining?
11. What factors will determine the character of tomorrow's working world?

SUGGESTED READINGS

Bakke, E. W., et al. *Unions, Management and the Public* (3d ed.). New York: Harcourt, Brace & World, 1967.

Beirne, J. A. *Challenge to Labor.* Englewood Cliffs, N.J.: Prentice-Hall, 1969.

Bok, D. C. *Labor and the American Community.* New York: Simon and Schuster, 1970.

Harrington, Michael, and Paul Jacobs (eds.) *Labor in a Free Society.* Berkeley: University of California Press, 1959.

Marceue, Leroy (ed.) *Dealing with a Union.* New York: American Management Association, 1969.

part five

Why Go into Business?

Disney: Can It Ever Happen Again?

The Disney story gets more amazing the more we learn about it . . . from Donald Duck of Disneyland to the diversified developments planned for Walt Disney World. The wide-eyed amazement of a child at his first Mickey Mouse movie can hardly compare with the expression on the face of the business student studying the management methods of the Magic Kingdom. Walt Disney Productions has a unity of purpose, method, and result that is perhaps greater than most of any other business group or conglomerate today.

The calculated and complete control exercised by the firm is all the more fascinating because it goes on behind a facade of cartoons. Who would suspect that the bungling, slapstick characters of the Disney films conceal so much incisive managerial acumen? Disney planners not only know *what* they are working toward, but *why*. They illustrate the difference between businessmen who "make plans" and those who "plan the future."

Of course the Disney brothers did not sit in their little garage office and plan the sequence of events that would lead to Walt Disney World and beyond. But Walt and Roy showed their managerial magic in producing their first cartoon . . . and the second. As one successful project followed another, their accumu-

Copyright, 1966, Walt Disney Productions.

lating wealth became the foundation for the success of bigger endeavors.

As one part of the master plan for Disney World, WDP plans to build an Experimental Prototype Community of Tomorrow (EPCOT) where, as Walt Disney said, "people actually live a life they can't find anywhere else in the world today."

EPCOT will be a "living blueprint of the future" where a projected 20,000 citizens will live and work in a fully operating community. Here American free enterprise will constantly introduce, test, and demonstrate new concepts and technologies—years ahead of their introduction to the general public.

The enormous complexities of building an entire city—especially one conceived as a "blueprint of the future" and a showcase for private enterprise—will require the cooperation of other major business firms plus considerable research and development before it becomes part of the second phase of Walt Disney World.

Many of America's major corporations have already expressed interest in the concept. U.S. Steel, Monsanto, RCA, and Aerojet-General are among those now working with WED Enterprises to develop systems and materials to be applied in EPCOT.

The Disney story confirms every platitude in the cockeyed optimist's book of favorite ideas: dedication to quality, hard work, value for payment, and benevolent autocracy. The Disney empire today comes closest of all corporations to being a perpetual success machine. Only a siege of unprecedented bad luck could slow this machine down.

The Mickey Mouse empire has all the things that every business giant seeks. It has a protected product, a solid-gold financial status, a balanced management team, and a promising future. On top of that, its public acceptance is close to 100 percent. While the ecology and anti-establishment forces are picketing everybody else, nobody thinks of bothering the company that gave us Cinderella and Disney World. The Disney corporation really has everything going for it.

The normal American businessman's reaction to such a success story is, "Why didn't that happen to *me?*" We have the rags-to-riches concept ingrained in us from birth; we believe that the right mixtures of ideas, opportunities, and hard work can still do the trick for us, even in our crowded and competitive society.

Can this great success story repeat itself in the future, or did the days of real opportunity disappear twenty years ago? Is there another young company beginning today in a garage or a back room that will grow into a financial empire and influence millions of lives just a few years from now? And, if it is still possible to become big and rich in a short time, can a company go on beyond these first plateaus and become stable and secure? The answer is that our system still allows dreams to come true. New success stories are being written every year.

Several bits of advice for would-be entrepreneurial giants can be gleaned from the Disney experience. First, do your own thing— the thing that will bring you satisfaction. Second, do it well, and demand absolute quality from beginning to end. Third, make sure that your own thing happens to be in an area of life important to the public, and that is certain to become more important as current trends continue. Fourth, maintain important control of your operation—its finance, creativity, and direction. Finally, if the Disney story is any guide, the road to success is best travelled by those who enjoy the trip too much to worry about reaching the destination!

25

The Business of Tomorrow

Nobody can predict exactly what business will be like in tomorrow's world. But one thing is certain—tomorrow's business will not be a repeat of things we have seen before. Though the foundation principles of business enterprise—buying and selling to make a profit or provide a service—will no doubt persist, it is becoming more and more obvious that changes in our society will make the activities of businessmen different in scope, intent, and procedure.

Sometimes the future can be read in the past. The student is probably aware of the sweeping changes that have taken place in American agriculture in the past two or three generations. Agri-business approaches to growing crops have opened the doors to production rates that seem fantastic to most of the world's farmers. Because of this we do not need to keep most of our population in the countryside to provide us with food, as we did when the U.S. was an agricultural society.

Agriculture is still a vital force in the United States today, supplying most of our food and fibers and accounting for nearly a quarter of our exports. Even so, no one would describe this country as an agricultural society. Agriculture employs less than four percent of our work force. It is not the source of major innovations in our society. And, perhaps most significantly, it no longer determines our values and way of life.

Something similar seems to be happening in industry. When agriculture was ousted from the throne, industry took its place. America's strength and position in the world today are the result of the great advances in production and technology that occurred when the farmers began to leave the fields and go to the factories. The blue collar worker became the backbone of our economy all through the earlier part of this century.

THE POSTINDUSTRIAL SOCIETY

Today, manufacturing is faced with agriculture's problem of success. The secondary industries (those that process primary products) are beginning to lose their predominance much as primary activities (farming, forestry, fishing, mining) did after 1870. Just as fewer farmers now raise more food than in the days when we were an agricultural society, fewer factory workers now turn out more industrial goods than ever before. Some observers believe that this decline in the role of manufacturing signals a postindustrial society with primary emphasis on the service businesses.

The share of the secondary industries in employment and gross national output is a steadily declining one. They are being overtaken by the *tertiary* industries (which supply services to primary and secondary occupations) and the *quaternary* sector (which supplies services to tertiary activities and to society as a whole). The quaternary sector is primarily concentrated in education, the professions, and government and nonprofit institutions. More and more of our economic exchange is taking place in this quaternary sector, outside the traditional market economy. This means that the sector of profit-making activity is decreasing as a proportion of total economic activity.

Figure 25–1 shows the extent to which different sectors of the U.S. economy have been growing at different rates. It also includes estimates of the rates at which they will grow in coming years. The fastest growing industries are utilities and communication. Among the slowest growing are mining and agriculture. In comparing growth rates by type of product, the chart suggests that in the years from 1970 to 1990 the output of services and of durable goods will increase at a faster pace than the output of nondurable goods (food, clothing, and other products that we use up soon after purchasing).

People who study human society are cautious about making predictions. But it is possible, nevertheless, to perceive certain trends. Futurists—those who make a profession of studying such trends—use the term "postindustrial society" to mean the kind of society we are

FIGURE 25–1

Past and Predicted Rates of Growth in U.S. Output

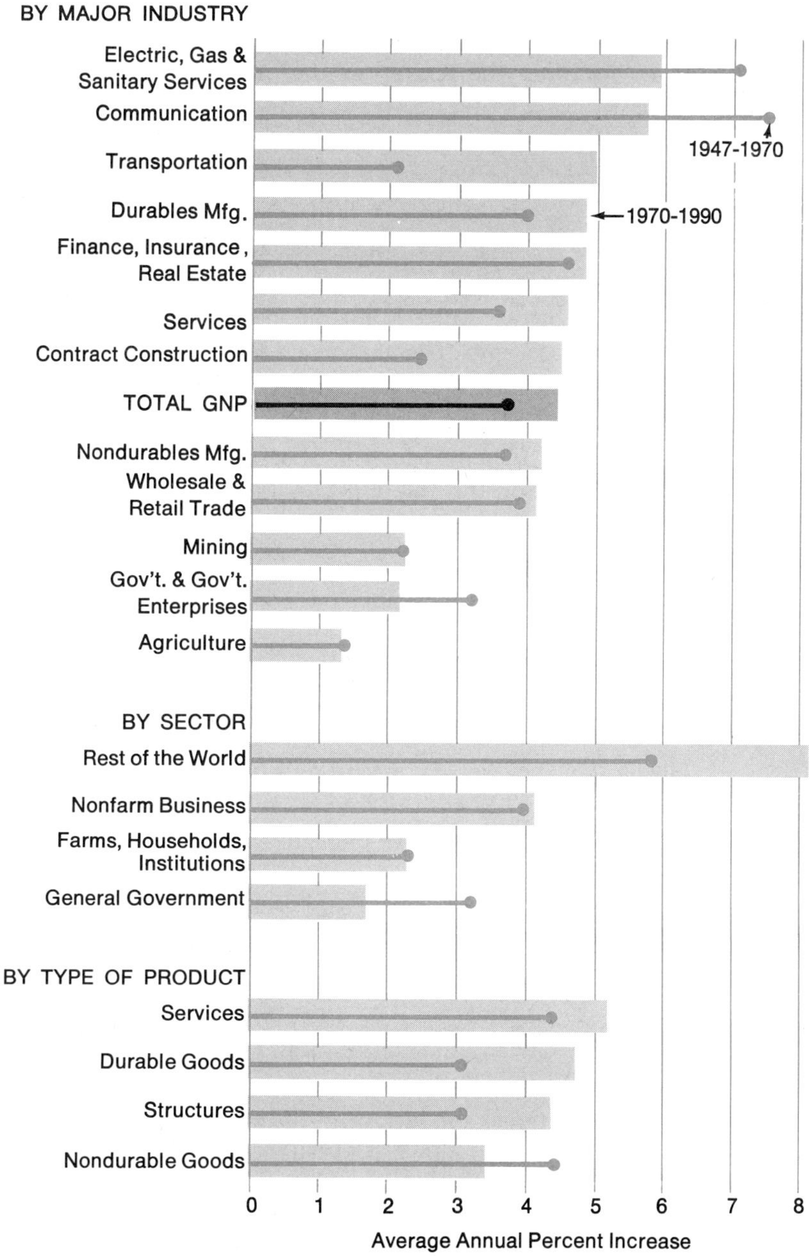

Horizontal lines show average annual percentage rates of growth in the period 1947–70. Bars show predicted rates of growth for 1970–90.

Source: U.S. Department of Commerce, The Conference Board.

heading toward in the United States and other developed countries. Every age has its dominant institutions. As we have already seen, agriculture and industry have taken turns on the throne of our economy. But now, in an era of chemistry and automation, the scepter is likely to go to either the tertiary or the quaternary sector. Which will receive it?

The quaternary sector (education, government, and public services) seems likely to become the new dominant sector. It includes some of the most rapidly expanding fields. Now that we have the ability to supply our material needs, it is natural that we should devote more of our resources to satisfying our inner needs and our social needs.

The quaternary sector is, for the most part, characterized by smaller, less-centralized units. Among these a leading role is likely to be played by academic institutions, particularly the strong universities. The academic community has the potential to surpass even government in its dominance of the next age. This is because, in the next age, importance will be placed on the ability to innovate and on theoretical knowledge and skills, rather than on routine administration or production.

THE NEW EDUCATIONAL STATE

The university has the chance to lead us into the new age, but there is no certainty that it will actually do so. Like other potential leaders, it may fail to seize its opportunities. Educational institutions have a tendency to look inward and become too concerned with their own problems. The costs of leadership are high. Educators will lead the next age only if they move outward toward society instead of looking inward.

The charts in Figures 25–2 and 25–3 show how two key activities of the quaternary age, education and medical care, are expected to increase in importance. The resources devoted to health are rising rapidly (Figure 25–2) and by 1980 there will be 150 physicians for every 100,000 people in the United States. Expenditures on health (also shown in Figure 25–2) are expected to consume over 10 percent of the gross national product in 1980, as compared to about 8 percent of a much smaller GNP in 1950. An increasing percentage of students will complete high school and go on to college. Of persons 30 to 34 years old in the year 1990, about 38 percent will have been to college and 25 percent will have completed college. In 1950 only about 15 percent of the persons in this age group had some college (Figure 25–3).

FIGURE 25-2

Resources Devoted to Health

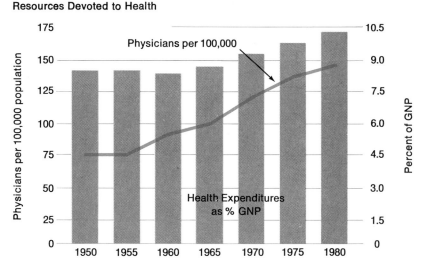

The solid line shows the number of physicians per 100,000 people, measured on the left-hand scale. The vertical bars show expenditures on health services as percentages of the gross national product, measured on the right-hand scale.

Sources: Department of Commerce; Department of Health, Education, and Welfare; The Conference Board.

EDUCATION FOR MEANING AS WELL AS FOR JOBS

There will be a continuing growth of junior colleges, together with higher expenditures for private, in-the-home, and adult education. Computer-assisted instruction will make programmed learning available to all. Within the next 10 years, the average student will probably have available to him 14 years of free schooling, plus greatly expanded scholarship and loan funds to carry him through college. Even after this lengthy period of formal education, he will continue the process of learning and retraining throughout his career. In-service training and continuing education programs will increase as schools and universities establish new ties with business, government, and non-profit organizations. More and more, people will try to relate to each other and find personal fulfillment through education.

As recently as 1959, this nation was spending as little as three percent of its gross national product on education. Today, that percentage has more than doubled, and it is anticipated that the doubling will continue. More money, more facilities, more courses, new methods—these physical manifestations are merely reflections of a new public attitude

FIGURE 25–3

Educational Attainment

Years of School Completed, Persons 25 Years and Over

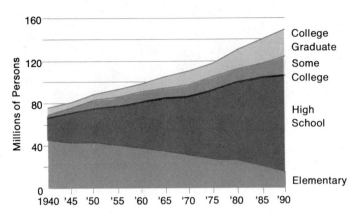

Percent College Educated in Age Group 30-34

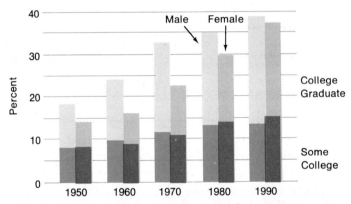

The top chart shows how many people 25 years and older have completed only elementary school, only high school, some college, or are college graduates. The data are projected to 1990. The lower chart shows what percentages of people in the age group 30–34 have had some college or are college graduates, in various years projected to 1990.

Sources: Department of Commerce; Department of Health, Education, and Welfare; The Conference Board.

toward education and learning. Americans have always placed value on education for economic reasons. The coming age will value education more for the ways it can help solve problems and make people happier.

Times of rapid change demand versatility and flexibility; these require education and a continuing flow of new knowledge.

For centuries, education and knowledge have been important factors in society. In the postindustrial society, both the degree and the character of their importance will be quite different. In the past, education has been largely concerned with the transmission of accumulated knowledge and the perpetuation of a way of life. From now on, the university's task will be to teach people to prepare for change. Knowledge formerly consisted mainly of practical information about observable and tangible phenomena. In the postindustrial era, the value of theoretical knowledge will become more widely recognized. This may mean that funds for new buildings will be hard to find while proposals for improved programs will be viewed with greater favor.

This increased valuation of education also results, in part, from a new way of looking at the school years. Workers' education is now looked upon by economists as a form of capital investment that will increase tomorrow's output. The years in training are therefore regarded as an *investment* period rather than a consumption period. School years have come to be seen as a way of capitalizing time. Education used to be considered the secret passageway to wealth. Now it is a force for meaningful change in the nation's future.

Education and the Individual

Today we want to learn to make a living but we are equally concerned with education's other values. The well-educated person has more self-respect; is more concerned with being treated as an individual; is far less tolerant of authoritarianism and organizational restraints; and has higher expectations of what he wants to put into a job and what he wants to get out of it. These attitudes will be reflected in the personalities of those working in managerial, professional, and technical jobs tomorrow. Similar attitude changes will be found among graduates who become production or service workers.

Writing job descriptions will become more difficult because jobs will have to be redesigned to fit the new type of worker. Not all jobs will require this; there will still be some unskilled and transient workers. But job enlargement is sure to become essential for holding the interest and motivating the performance of tomorrow's better educated work force.

Federal agencies are pouring dollars into inner-city educational facilities. This money, along with increasing revenue from private sources, should help to eliminate some of the inequalities in our public education. Because of society's increased emphasis on education, students from poor families will tend to stay in school longer. Non-

Herman Kahn

Herman Kahn is founder and director of the Hudson Institute, the prestigious New York think tank, and perhaps the world's best-known living futurist. He has been described as a 300-pound intellectual sponge, as the most important prophet since Isaiah, and as one of the world's greatest talking machines.

Before he left to start the Hudson Institute in 1961, Mr. Kahn was associated with the RAND Corporation for approximately 12 years. At RAND, a Pentagon-supported research organization in southern California, he worked on problems in applied physics and mathematics, operations research and systems analysis, weapon design, particle and radiation diffusion, civil defense, and strategic warfare. He became an overnight celebrity in 1961 with his book *On Thermonuclear War,* in which he coolly explored the threat of the hydrogen bomb, discussing the various ways in which it might be used and the probable amounts of devastation that would ensue. The book horrified many reviewers because of the detached way in which Kahn talked about "megadeaths"— millions of deaths—and a "doomsday machine" that would destroy the whole world. Less excitable critics realized that Kahn was really engaged in exploring the strategies by which civilization might be preserved in an age of galloping technology.

During the past decade, he has at-

academic training programs, sponsored by both government and industry, have already been started in an attempt to prepare the unemployed for the thousands of positions requiring space-age skills.

PERSISTENT SOCIAL PROBLEMS

Some problems in our society have been with us a long time. One of these social problems is the urban crisis. It is predicted that, by the year 2000, nearly 74 percent of the U.S. population will be living in 300 major metropolitan areas. Unless action on these problems is taken, the air will be dirtier; the slums more unlivable; the traffic more immovable; and the psychological tolls of overcrowding even greater.

Conditions must improve. Nobody denies that we have the ability

tempted to analyze the politics, economics, and technology of the future on a global scale. According to Kahn, the "conceptual, doctrinal, and linguistic framework" of the world is changing so fast that it is impossible to make firm forecasts that are meaningful. Consequently, he often presents his predictions in the form of triple "scenarios"—hypothetical sketches of the outcome based on various assumptions, including one that is moderately optimistic, one that is moderately pessimistic, and one that seems "most probable."

Kahn has written several other books, including *The Year 2000: A Framework for Speculation on the Next 33 Years* (with Anthony J. Wiener), *The Emerging Japanese Superstate,* and *Things to Come.* A group of leading futurists has called *The Year 2000* the most significant book ever written about the long-term future.

Kahn enjoyed a very productive career at RAND, but found its security-conscious atmosphere somewhat of a burden. Also, as one of his friends has said, "He was becoming more important than RAND." With some friends he put together $10,000 and took over a former estate at Croton-on-Hudson, N.Y., where he has built up a staff of several dozen researchers. During the past decade, he has raised several hundred thousands of dollars to support futuristic research relating to the corporate environment of the 1980s.

Kahn's life has been devoted to doing what he likes—reading, thinking, and talking. He was born in 1922. His mother was divorced when he was quite young, and the family was often on welfare. He got a B.A. in physics from U.C.L.A. in 1945, and did graduate work in applied mathematics and physics at the California Institute of Technology, where he got his M.S. In 1948 he joined RAND, with no clear idea of what he wanted to do. For a time he considered going into business, and even acquired a California real-estate license. Over the years at RAND he moved from projects in mathematical theory and physics to research in military and political strategy.

Kahn is a family man. But at the Hudson Institute he puts in 18-hour days bossing his research staff, reading, writing books, and lecturing. The institute does research on a contract basis for various public and private institutions, and also for foreign governments. As a lecturer, Kahn has been known to speak continuously from morning to night, drawing on his prodigious memory. He is not easily overawed. Once he told a group of senior military officers in Vietnam: "There are six or seven acceptable ways to win this war, two or three unacceptable ones, and only one way to lose it—and you've found it."

His institute is continuing its research in alternative world futures and long-run (10 to 15 years) political, economic, technological, and cultural change.

to solve our problems whenever we are ready to make the necessary effort. It is to be hoped that improvement in the quality of city life can come about from the practical application of present technological knowledge. Research efforts are now underway to discover methods for combating such chronic problems as air pollution, inadequate transportation, water shortage and overcrowding. It is reasonable to expect that the urban environment of the 21st century will be more pleasant, at least physically, than the one in which we are now living. The optimistic editors of *Newsfront* magazine believe that the "massive challenges of city planning are not too great to be overcome by a combination of imagination, technical know-how and hard cash." In a paper on how cities should be, N. A. Owings of the famous architectural firm of Skidmore, Owings & Merrill, gives us some interesting, but probably impractical, ideas, as the following excerpt indicates:

Cities as They Should Be[1]

The cities of this country are already there. Their locations are fixed points at the crossing of desire lines of people and goods. Those who talk of new cities in unspoiled open space are simply walking away from a problem they have failed to solve. What right have they to start a new one when they cannot solve the old one? I firmly believe that the solution is before us, and possible within the next 20 years.

Our central cities should be low rise, high-density habitat, where the central city is taken over and treated as one great unit. Every city has at least a third to a half of it in streets. At the lowest levels of this habitat structure, I propose the heaviest things would be done: heavy transportation, heavy traffic, heavy industry. Then, rising through successive layers of wholesale, retail, light industry, cottage industry, would be open parks, terraces, green space, on which rest apartments and housing for the city dwellers—and there must be city dwellers. They could rest up on top where the sun is.

The Secretary of the Interior recently suggested that the land-use policy of the United States is one of the prime objectives and necessities to be established before any working order could be arranged. This land-use policy should require housing within the city, walk-to-work operations, the elimination of the automobile within those cities and the cleaning up of the open space around. All of this involves long-term commitments, heavy machinery, heavy industry, all forms of manufacture.

I see the end of the single-purpose skyscraper, and of the senseless burgeoning of the little cubicles in which human beings sit at sterile, faceless desks punching little buttons, never seeing the beginning of the process or the end. It seems intolerable that we should ask young people, or anybody, to do this. Why shouldn't that be relegated to the computer? Why not use half or more of each of these great structures that we at Skidmore, Owings & Merrill are designing and building for housing of the people who work in them —or at least work in the city? Why not raise the high art of topiary, or horticulture, or service trades, to the point where the 85 or 90 percent of those who live in town can find employment? We must find ways and means of raising the dignity of human labor to the point where it will be acceptable again, or I really see no answer to the future. We must develop service industries to help fulfill the void between the rat race of manufacturing expendable products and getting back to the slower, lower key kind of living involved in the full recognition of the development of habitat.

---

[1] From *A Look at Business in 1990* (Washington, D.C., Government Printing Office, 1972), p. 162.

A Nation of Crises

The crises in the city are complicated by threatening shortages in the nation's supply of power and raw materials. For years, isolated voices have warned that we are using up our natural resources at too fast a rate. But nobody paid much attention until we began having to wait in long lines to buy gasoline at much higher prices. The high cost of gasoline and other fuels will probably slow down the rate of economic growth, for it means that many other things will also become more expensive. Suddenly the prospects for roadside food operations, international travel, and even suburban real estate development seem dimmer, to mention only three examples. What kinds of business operations can you think of that will benefit from an energy crisis?

The public seems to spend much of its time trying to figure out whom to believe: the ecological alarmists or the ecological pacifists. On the one hand, experts are declaring that air and water are irrevocably contaminated and that the earth is a dying planet. Other experts insist that technology can and will meet these problems and even create better ways because of the necessity. The charts in Figure 25–4, compiled by The Conference Board, illustrate the trends in use of national basic commodities.

There is growing public pressure for solutions. The public is turning to governments, universities, businesses, and to foundations and other nonprofit institutions. In each case, it demands fast action with a minimum of red tape. If acceptable solutions are not forthcoming, more drastic action will eventually be taken. The failure to produce results will be punished—in political circles, by failure to get reelected; in business circles, by the incursion of governmental control into such areas of management as hiring, testing, and plant location.

DOING THE JOB IN LESS TIME

There is a popular misconception that the people of the future will not work much. While automation and increased efficiency may reduce the workweek somewhat, projections of current labor force trends indicate that the workweek will not shrink spectacularly in the next 20 years. And it is highly unlikely that the following 15 years will bring the kind of economic paradise that some have foreseen, in which the average breadwinner works only one day out of seven.

On the contrary, the more productive we become the more things we are likely to want. Consumer and industrial demand will keep pace

FIGURE 25–4

Trends In Use of U.S. National Basic Commodities

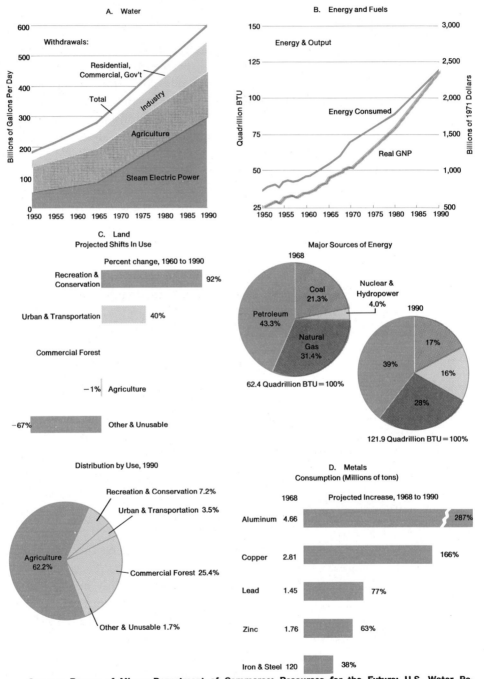

Sources: Bureau of Mines; Department of Commerce; Resources for the Future; U.S. Water Resources Council; The Conference Board.

FIGURE 25-5

Average Hours Worked Per Week—Private Sector

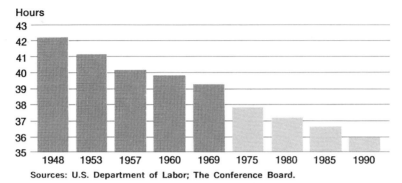

Sources: U.S. Department of Labor; The Conference Board.

with rising productivity, The booming service industries will create new jobs to offset those lost as we become more productive.

It has been estimated that in 1900, leisure absorbed 26 percent of the average person's day. In 1950, the average American was at leisure 34 percent of the time. If this trend were to continue, leisure could absorb 44 percent of our time by the year 2000, and 57 percent by 2050. The downward trend in the number of hours the average person spends working is shown in Figure 25–5, which projects it to 1990. An average workweek of 36 hours in 1990 would still keep most people moderately busy.

It may be anticipated that vacations will grow longer and holidays more frequent. Retirement will come earlier, and, as the lifespan stretches, men and women will look forward to decades instead of years when they leave their jobs. It may very well become possible for almost anyone who wants more leisure to have it, thanks to rising wage scales and increasing opportunities for part-time work. The real problem lies in the fact that the average American already has more leisure than he seems to know how to handle effectively.

THE CHANGING WORK FORCE

While people are going to work somewhat fewer hours, the total number working will increase. More and more women are entering the labor force and this trend is expected to continue. The total labor force of the United States is expected to grow at an average rate of 1.2 percent a year between now and 1990, when it will include 117 million persons. Figure 25–6 shows the trends in two major aspects of the labor force: employment by sex and by age group.

FIGURE 25–6

Developments in the Labor Force

A. Growth by Sex

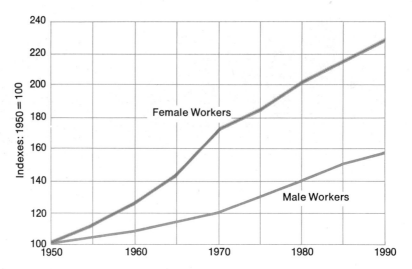

B. Composition by Age

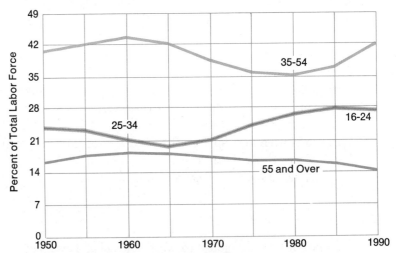

Chart A suggests that the number of women workers in 1990 will be more than double the number in 1950, whereas male workers will have increased by around 50 percent. Chart B shows expected trends in employment by age group. In coming years, workers in the 16–24 age bracket will increase as a proportion of the total labor force. What will happen to other age groups?

Sources: U.S. Department of Labor; The Conference Board.

There is certain to be a large increase in women working. In 1975, there were approximately 33 million women in the U.S. work force, increased by 27 percent, or three times the increase for males in the increase has come from women aged 45 and over, whose numbers increased by 27 percent, or three times the increase for males in the same age bracket. But the numbers of younger workers will increase much more, until by 1990 they amount to nearly two-sevenths of the total labor force.

NEW KINDS OF WORK

Some fields will acquire more workers while others lose them. New jobs will be created and old jobs will become obsolete. The Council on Trends and Perspective of the Chamber of Commerce of the U.S. predicts that the growth of service-producing activities will continue. Already the United States is the only country in the world that employs more than half of its labor force in the production of services rather than goods. The fastest growing segment of the service-producing industry is that of government employment, particularly state and local government.

By 1980, it is predicted, nearly 17 percent of U.S. workers will be engaged in government service. Another 20 percent will earn their livings by buying and selling. Only 3 percent of the labor force will be needed in the agricultural sector of the economy. Less than 25 percent will be employed in manufacturing. In other words, the service category will account for more than two-thirds of civilian employment by 1980 (see Table 25–1).

The changing profile of the business community will have consequences in the political and cultural spheres. There will probably be a relative decline of basic industry as a prime force in our society. This will result from its diminishing percentage of employment, income and wealth.

Increasingly, businessmen will have to develop an instinct for survival in a political world. Managers will need to become more involved in governmental and community affairs, particularly in the problem-solving sphere. The public will expect business to place greater emphasis on "the quality of life." This means that companies will be expected to take interest in the continuing education and personal development of their employees, to improve the quality of their products, and to do what they can to reduce their contribution to urban problems, such as pollution and noise.

TABLE 25–1

Projected Civilian Employment in Various Industries, 1980 (percent distribution)

Goods Producing Sector....................................	31.7%
Agriculture, forestry and fisheries.......................	3.2
Mining..	0.6
Construction..	5.5
Manufacturing..	22.4
Durable...	13.3
Nondurable...	9.1
Service Producing Sector.................................	68.4
Transportation, communication and public utilities.......	5.0
Trade...	20.6
Finance, Insurance and Real Estate.....................	4.7
Services, including households..........................	21.2
Government...	16.9
Federal...	3.0
State and Local	13.9

Source: *The U.S. Economy In 1980: A Summary of BLS Projections*, Bulletin 1673 (U.S. Department of Labor, Washington, D.C.: U.S. Government Printing Office), p. 49.

There will be more government regulation and more government pressure on business to meet higher public service standards. The activities of consumer groups and the increasing public concern with environmental hazards will bring about more legislative restrictions on business. Business leaders surveyed in a nationwide poll said that governmental regulations and restrictions would be their biggest problem in the next decade.

NEW ATTITUDES TOWARD WORK

Workers are going to expect more from their jobs in the future. This is happening for several reasons: a rising standard of living, more education, continuing automation at the workplace, and vast changes in the environment. Our traditional respect for hard work has already been called into question by the younger generation. As the 65-year-old worker with an eighth or ninth grade education is replaced by a youth with a high school diploma and perhaps some college study, the work expectations of the labor force will reflect this change.

To the problem of rising expectations will be added another problem: that of finding jobs for the hard-core unemployed. We have learned how to avoid mass unemployment of the kind the U.S. experienced in the 1930s. But while the right fiscal and monetary policies can keep the economy expanding, and provide jobs for perhaps 96.5

percent of the labor force, this still leaves several million workers who are unable to find employment. Many of them lack the necessary education or training; many have little motivation to work; and some happen to live in areas where few jobs are available. The problem of the hardcore unemployed will yield only to a cooperative effort on the part of business, government, and educational institutions. We may get some help in this effort from our experience in training workers during World War II, when the labor force had to be greatly expanded, as well as from experience in employing the blind and handicapped.

A REASON TO WORK

The changing value systems of workers and the changing demands of production are going to create some unprecedented motivation problems. For companies interested in getting and keeping capable employees, paychecks and fringe benefits will probably come to mean less than job satisfaction. The help wanted ads of the future may include, along with the salary being offered, a description of the opportunities for education, self-development, and self-fulfillment. In fact, many ads already do this.

Another expected trend is the gradual disappearance of the wage-salary difference among workers. The growth of benefit programs (especially income security programs and short workweek provisions) over the past 20 years has laid some groundwork for a shift to salaries for workers who are now paid by the hour. And regular workers in some industries may gradually get guarantees of annual earnings. Labor market conditions may make such guarantees of salaried status necessary in order to attract and hold skilled workers. Actually, the cost of substituting salaries for hourly wages in an economy with high employment and few layoffs may be negligible.

Income maintenance is another trend. There will be programs to raise and maintain the income level of employed workers who are not earning enough to keep their families above the poverty level. These will probably be extended to unemployed workers as well. Income maintenance will be financed through some sort of "negative income tax"—that is, people below a certain level of income will receive payments from the government according to their income, instead of making payments. As they rise out of the poverty level the benefits they receive will taper off. It is generally expected that some form of income maintenance program will be enacted during the 1970s.

One problem with income maintenance is the need to reassure the public that those receiving government assistance will not lose their incentive to work. That is the reason for using a sliding scale that reduces allowances as earned income rises, instead of the current public welfare practice of deducting from cash payments 100 percent of any income earned. If all of a person's earnings are deducted from his benefits, he may feel that it doesn't pay to work.

People are not going to be retiring much earlier. Truck drivers, airline pilots, and policemen may be exceptions to this, since their job requirements may dictate retirement before the age of 60. Pensions are likely to rise to a point at which, together with social security benefits, they may total 80 or 90 percent of pre-retirement earnings. Workers who change jobs will be able to take their pension rights with them to a greater degree than they can now.

THE PROMISE OF THE AMERICAN ECONOMY

Most long-range studies foresee continued economic growth for the United States. A series of projections made by the U.S. Chamber of Commerce includes the estimate that by the year 2000 the gross national product will reach $2.4 trillion (in 1967 prices). This is especially impressive when we realize that the GNP reached $1 trillion only in 1971. It means that in the last 30 years of the century our economy will more than double its output of goods and services according to these projections and family purchasing power will be about 70 percent above the present level. Prices in the year 2000 will be considerably higher, but wages tend to increase about twice as fast as prices, so buying power will rise. In 1972, median family income increased to $10,000, and per capita disposable income to $3,800. In the 1980s, almost half of U.S. families will be earning more than $15,000 annually. By 2000, hourly wages will average $7.50, and family consumption will average almost $20,000. Our output of goods and services will have risen almost four times as fast as our population. As average family income rises, more and more families will reach what is now the top income bracket of $25,000 and over. One prediction, shown in Figure 25–7, is that by 1990 some 27 percent of U.S. families will have reached the $25,000-and-over bracket (in terms of 1971 dollars).

Continued economic expansion will mean increasing affluence for U.S. consumers, who are already pretty high up on the income ladder by world standards. We will see great changes in the way they spend their money. As incomes rise, consumers do not simply buy more goods or better quality goods: they begin buying different kinds of goods and

FIGURE 25–7

Rising Income Levels

(Total families each year = 100%; based on 1971 dollars)

Income Class

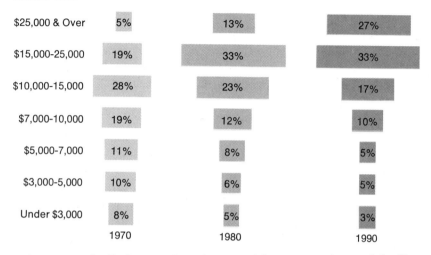

Income Class	1970	1980	1990
$25,000 & Over	5%	13%	27%
$15,000-25,000	19%	33%	33%
$10,000-15,000	28%	23%	17%
$7,000-10,000	19%	12%	10%
$5,000-7,000	11%	8%	5%
$3,000-5,000	10%	6%	5%
Under $3,000	8%	5%	3%

As average family income rises, larger and larger percentages of families will move into what are now the upper income brackets, and smaller percentages will remain in each of the lower brackets.

Sources: Department of Commerce; The Conference Board.

services because their preferences change. They begin to eat more meat and to take more expensive vacations. They hire others to cut their grass and mind their children. They add to their bank accounts, buy more insurance, and become interested in the stock market. In short, nondurable goods such as food, beverages, clothing, and household supplies come to represent a smaller proportion of their total spending, while services grow in importance. More money is spent on education and other self-improvement activities; on recreation and other leisure-time activities; on travel; and on personal and family activities.

The U.S. market has developed historically from one of subsistence wants to one of luxury wants. It is now becoming a market of "human fulfillment" wants. The new American consumer will place less emphasis on subsistence needs and more on psychological and social needs. He will want to develop his talents, improve himself as a person, create an attractive environment, eliminate suffering and poverty, and in general achieve a new quality of life. This represents a new market— estimated by one top business research executive at $100 billion a year over the rest of this century.

POLITICS AND BUSINESS

Business does not take place in a vacuum. When we set out to forecast business trends we must also take into account ideas. Political forecasting is even more hazardous than economic forecasting, but if we are careful we can make certain generalizations that will probably hold true for the next 10 or 20 years.

We will probably see less actual operation of domestic economic programs by the federal government, which will tend to confine itself more to the establishment of policy while leaving the implementation of programs to state and local governments. Federal power and influence will remain strong. But there will be some decentralization of power from the national to state and local levels of government. The federal government will play a major policy and funding role, with state and local governments making the main operating decisions in fields such as transportation, education, and pollution. Business will become involved in managing government-sponsored projects, leading to a deeper and more effective partnership between government and business in many "public need" areas.

This shift in the functions of the federal government from the operation and management of programs to a role of goal-setting, funding, catalyzing, and measuring will be slow but steady. There will not be, even by 1985, a complete shift away from the "do it" role, but the changed direction will be unmistakable. The space program has successfully demonstrated that even federally managed programs do not have to be federally operated. Beyond this, there is a growing concern that the nation, like an overcentralized company, may otherwise get neither well-run programs nor a well-designed set of national goals and priorities.

Goal-setting is becoming more important, as well as more difficult, and it is fitting that this should be recognized as a function of the federal government. But how are national goals to be established? How will they be formulated, discussed, and decided upon? This is a political question of the first magnitude, and we may be moving toward a new way of answering it.

Is the Party (System) Over?

The changing role of government may be accompanied by changes in the way Americans line up at the polls. Since the New Deal days of the 1930s, liberals have believed in a strong federal government that would be involved in the economic and social life of the country. Conservatives opposed this tendency. But there are indications that this will no longer be the main axis of American politics. Liberals are starting to call for a strengthening of government below the federal level (for example, stronger local governments). Conservatives for their part have begun to accept some of the principles of economic management (such as the use of fiscal and monetary policies to stabilize the economy). At the state and local levels, conservatives and liberals will probably continue to differ over issues such as urban renewal in its broadest sense; urban-suburban relationships; and, of course, taxation and the financing of government.

Political issues today are more complex and shifting than in the past. The composition of parties and political groups changes from time to time. More and more voters are likely to register and vote as "independents" rather than as members of parties. The area of critical concern to businessmen in American politics is likely to be the nature, and order, of national goals and priorities. The need for business skills, especially those related to planning, will grow in importance.

While many voters will be independent of parties, the polarization of political opinion will probably intensify. That is, there will be an enlargement of political effort at the conservative and liberal extremes. The voters will thus tend to fall into three groups, with splinter parties on the right and left, and a reduced but still dominant middle ground over which the Republicans and Democrats will contend. Interestingly, a similar pattern appears to be developing in the labor force. At one extreme are the 15 percent of affluent, mobile, highly educated and motivated professionals and managers. At the other extreme are the 15 percent of poor, poorly educated, and poorly motivated ghetto dwellers. Both in politics and in the labor force it may be that the divergent needs of the extremes will determine policies and directions, rather than the wishes of the center.

THE PROBLEMS AND THE PROMISE

A great many developments and transitions obviously lie ahead of us. Whether the outcome is blessing or not, the problems and promises of the future are worth thinking about.

Among the answers we must find are: (1) an alternative to industrial strikes that will allow management and labor to achieve solutions that are just to both parties, (2) a sane way of dealing with our environment, (3) new ties between our society and its estranged youth, (4) a realistic public attitude toward the ability of technology to solve problems, (5) fair and just profit structures that will allow business to "live and let live," and (6) systems of honest, direct communication between governments and people.

To state the problems is not to say that answers will be found. But if we manage to organize our society so that it better serves our purposes, we will open the way to a future full of astounding and delightful things. Some of the new inventions which are already off the drawing board and undergoing tests include the following, as compiled by the editors of *Newsfront* magazine:

1. *Boron fibers:* Hailed as the greatest single advance in materials in 3,000 years, this new material possesses more strength and stiffness per unit of weight than any other material.
2. *Super-hard glass:* New, chemically-cured glass may become the material for constructing cars, tanks, or anything requiring super-strength.
3. *Light-sensitive glass:* Already in use in newer buildings, this photo-sensitive glass announces the coming of many new uses of glass products.
4. *Synthetic rubber:* "Nordel" is made from petroleum raw materials and already possesses demonstrable resistance to temperature change, abrasion, chemical attack and the effects of ozone which cracks conventional rubber.
5. *Rat poison:* New materials have almost unbelievable specifications, like the new rat poison which kills only rats, leaving humans and pets unharmed.
6. *Stretch fabrics:* Advances in fabric and textile industries may soon follow the space-age one-suit-for-all-occasions. Materials will be tougher than steel and stretchy enough for one size to fit everyone.
7. *Newspapers by wire:* Already in experimental use in Japan, daily newspapers will soon flash electronically to homes instead of following the cumbersome hand delivery methods.
8. *Electronic data transmission:* Microwave radio networks are today matter-of-factly flashing 40,000 words per minute from one place to another.
9. *Pushbutton libraries:* Computerized storage, research, and screening systems will make the students' job a snap.
10. *Message transmission:* New methods will enhance everyday miracles like the telephone. One cable will now carry one million telephone calls or 1,000 television broadcasts. Messages will also travel by laser beam faster and farther.

11. *High powered microscope:* The combination of television with the electron microscope has enabled magnification up to 2 million times normal size.
12. *Air floors:* "One-man-power" can move three tons of load across a level warehouse floor with the assist of new air floors.
13. *Photography:* A new duPont process makes immediate positive photos, bypassing the time-honored negative-first process.
14. *Sleep machines:* A slumber more refreshing than natural sleep has been produced by a new electronic device.
15. *Self-propelled bullets:* Jet-propelled bullets will be faster and quieter with no fumes and no recoil.
16. *Gasoline from coal:* Relief for critical petroleum supplies could be produced by 100 octane gasoline from the nation's plentiful reserves of coal.
17. *Atomic mining:* Canals and coal mines may soon be dug in a flash by means of strategic atomic explosions.
18. *Fertile deserts:* Silicone coating can make the desert retain its rainfall instead of washing away immediately.
19. *Controlling plants:* Many accomplishments with chemical hybridization, synthetic diets, fish farming and computerized high-rise greenhouses promise to end the food crisis in the years to come.
20. *New life for wood:* Advances by the lumber industry will enable accelerated growth of trees, superstrength lamination, and chemical treatments making wood tougher than steel.

SUMMARY

The Postindustrial Society will be characterized by an increase in importance of the service (tertiary and quaternary) sectors of society and a relative decrease in the numbers of people working in the industrial sector. Because of growing emphasis on innovation and problem-solving skills, a new educational state will emerge, with the universities enjoying a leading role. Education will be more available to a higher percentage of workers, both as young people and as adults.

The rising cost of fuels and raw materials, and the crisis of the cities, will require the cooperative efforts of business and government to overcome them. In the future people will enjoy more leisure, but not to the degree imagined by science fiction writers of the past. The U.S. civilian labor force will grow to 135 million by the year 2000.

Businessmen will have to develop an instinct for survival in a political world. The nature of work will alter, with people becoming as concerned with what they do as with how much they get paid. There will be higher percentages of women, non-whites, and college graduates in the work force.

Businessmen will have to move faster, know more, and accept some of their pay in forms other than money. Vacations will be longer, retirement earlier. Prices will rise but workers will earn more, and their buying power will be greater.

Voting patterns and political groupings will probably change, and so will the role of the federal government.

KEY ITEMS AND CONCEPTS FOR REVIEW

Tertiary industries

Quaternary sector

Education as investment

Full employment

Guaranteed annual wage

Human fulfillment wants

Political polarization

Future role of leisure

Changing labor market

Social costs

Postindustrial society

QUESTIONS FOR ANALYSIS AND DISCUSSION

1. Give one example of a business in each of the following categories:
   a) primary
   b) secondary
   c) tertiary
   d) quaternary
2. Why should educational institutions become more important during the next few years?
3. Identify three persistent social problems which confront the United States.
4. For a private business, what should be the average workweek in 1980? 1990?
5. What major changes will take place in the work force between 1960 and 1980?
6. What major changes will take place in the work or employment patterns of workers between 1960 and 1980?
7. How does advanced education affect a person's attitude toward work? Why is this true?
8. Do you favor the "guaranteed annual income" idea? Why?
9. What major political changes do you anticipate by 1990?
10. Of the business ideas discussed in the text, which do you believe has the greatest potential? Explain.

SUGGESTED READINGS

Kahn, Herman, and A. J. Wiener *The Year 2000.* New York: Macmillan, 1967.

Kahn, Herman, and B. Bruce Briggs *Things to Come.* New York: Macmillan, 1972.

Dunstan, Mary J., and Patricia W. Garland (eds.) *Worlds in the Making.* Englewood Cliffs, N.J.: Prentice-Hall, 1970.

Toffler, Alvin (ed.) *The Futurists.* New York: Random House, 1970.

Meadows, D. H., et al. *The Limits to Growth.* New York: Universe Books, 1972.

Toffler, Alvin *Future Shock.* New York: Random House, 1970.

The Wall Street Journal "Here Comes Tomorrow." Princeton, N.J.: Dow Jones and Company, 1967.

Clarke, Arthur C. *Profiles of the Future* (rev. ed.) New York: Harper & Row, 1973.

A Look at Business in the 1990's Washington, D.C.: U.S. Government Printing Office, 1972.

NOTES CONCERNING OCCUPATIONAL ASSESSMENT TESTS

Although very sophisticated tests are available to determine occupational preference and job aptitudes, you may enjoy taking this rather simple quiz, which will give some general insight into the types of jobs which you might find most interesting. Because of the brevity of this test, we make no claim that it is a valid indicator of your real potential. It should, however, provide some general insight into your own personality and the types of jobs which you are most likely to enjoy. After completing this simple exercise, you may want to check with the Counselling or Testing Center at your own college or university. Experts on testing and evaluation should be able to provide much more detailed assistance to you in evaluating your interests and abilities.

What Kind of a Job Is Best for You?

"Doctor, lawyer, merchant, chief?" Fortunately we are not all suited to do the same thing. It would be a sorry world if everyone wanted to be a farmer or a truck driver or a dentist. This quiz will give you some hints about yourself and the kinds of jobs for which you have the greatest aptitudes.

Yes or No

—————   1. When you read a murder mystery, do you often know who the criminal is before the author tells you?

—————   2. Would you rather attend a concert than a rock 'n roll session?

—————   3. Has it always been easy for you to spell correctly?

—————   4. Are you bothered if a picture on the wall is crooked?

—————   5. Would you rather read nonfiction than a novel?

—————   6. Do you usually remember facts you have read or heard?

—————   7. Would you say you tend to do one thing very well rather than a number of things fairly well?

—————   8. Do you enjoy checkers or bridge?

—————   9. Do you conscientiously keep some sort of budget book?

—————   10. Do you enjoy learning what makes things, such as clocks, switches, or motors, work?

—————   11. Do you enjoy changes in your daily routines and feel that you are flexible?

—————   12. In your leisure time would you prefer to participate in some sport rather than read a book?

—————   13. Are arithmetic and mathematics difficult for you?

—————   14. Do you enjoy being with people who are younger than you are?

Yes or No

_____   15. Can you list five people whom you think of as friends?

_____   16. Do you enjoy parties?

_____   17. Do you dislike small detail work?

_____   18. Do you read rapidly?

_____   19. Do you think the old adage "Don't put all your eggs in one basket" is good advice?

_____   20. Do you enjoy new people, places, and things?

Scoring:
There are no right or wrong answers to this quiz! Your answers merely show how you tick.

1. Circle all your yes answers.
2. Count the number of Yes answers for the first ten questions.
3. Count the number of Yes answers for the last ten questions.
4. Compare the two numbers.

A. If you have a great many more Yes answers in the first ten questions than for the second ten, you are an intensive person who will do well with meticulous jobs requiring patience, care, and research—for example, doctor, lawyer, scientist, research & development, materials manager, accountant, financial manager, production manager, quality control, market research analyst, repairman, technician, editor, engineer, skilled worker.

B. If you have a great many more Yes answers for the last ten questions than for the first ten, you are an "extensive" person whose greatest strength will be in jobs dealing with people. You will have the ideas but prefer to have someone carry them out for you. Such jobs include personnel director, consultant, receptionist, sports director, labor negotiator, actor, salesman, advertising manager, marketing manager, insurance agent.

C. If your Yes answers are fairly evenly divided, you will do well with jobs that require detail work coupled with good human relationships. Even in this case, however, you can see where the weight of your aptitude lies and select your job accordingly. You might be best as a teacher, secretary, business executive, entrepreneur, lecturer, politician.

Source: Adapted from J. S. Singer, *What You Should Know About Yourself* (New York: Meredith Press, 1969)

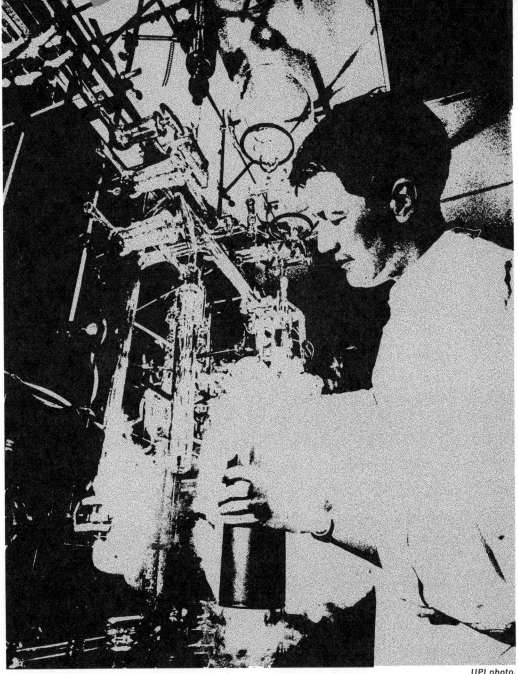

26

Challenging Opportunities in Business

In the previous chapters we have seen some of the realities and some of the challenges involved in business. It may seem strange that many college students apparently feel that "business is for the birds." This was especially noticeable a few years ago when we used to see headlines in newspapers and magazines saying: "Top Students Sell Business Short," "Are American Students Flunking Capitalism?", "Is Business for the Birds?", or "Can Business Attract the Young?" Various polls showed that business did not enjoy a high place in the opinion of many college students. One poll, taken in 1966, reported that only 12 percent of 800 college students would choose business as "the career they would like best."

The attitude of some students seemed to be that business did not have any intellectual challenge and that it was something people went into if they didn't have enough intelligence to do anything else. Many students see in business little that is stimulating, challenging, creative, or oriented toward helping others. Most agree that a person can make a good living in business, but some question whether this would give them a sense of accomplishment. As one student put it, "Could I feel that I had done something worthwhile if, on my retirement forty years from now, I could only look back and say that I was in a company that produced three billion tires?" Again and

657

again, one hears students say such things as "I want a job where I can do something useful," or "I want something where I can be involved."

Often, too, students have the idea that there is something wrong in making profits, that businessmen are dirty money chasers, and that business tries to enslave its workers and take advantage of its customers. Some college students have the idea that businesses want their employees and managers stamped out with the same degree of conformity and impersonality as electrical appliances and automobile parts. And possessing as little excitement and challenge.

IS BUSINESS REALLY FOR THE BIRDS?

To be sure, the "business is for the birds" attitude is not as widespread today as it was a few years ago. As the pressures of the unpopular Vietnamese War and the compulsory military draft passed into history, and as jobs became less plentiful with business slowdown after 1972, many students changed their minds. College placement officers—both for the community colleges and the four-year colleges—report that their offices have been crowded with students asking for appointments with business job recruiters.

Even when the "birds" attitude was said to be so prevalent, campus placement officers reported that it was really held by only a small group of campus militants and had been greatly exaggerated by the news media. At the very height of this reported attitude, the Princeton University career-services director declared, "If business is for the birds, then this campus is something of an aviary."

The fact is that most college students eventually make business their careers. Others, to be sure, go into government, but many of these end up in the business side of government or in a government-owned business. Some take up the professions of law, medicine, dentistry, or architecture, or follow their idealistic desires by going into teaching, social work, the ministry, or the Peace Corps.

Although college students do not show by their actions that "business is for the birds," it is undeniable that most of them want a career that is meaningful, in which they can accomplish something or contribute to the solution of pressing social problems, and still earn enough to enjoy the "good life." These desires are real. They are understandable. They are a part of the usual idealism of youth. While they may have been more vocally expressed in recent years, and have taken on a greater sense of urgency in a time when so many major social problems have been occupying our attention, they are really not very new.

Are there no challenging opportunities in business? The authors of this book, both of whom have been in business and continue to be active as business consultants, believe there are many such opportunities. The older of your authors got a Ph.D. many years ago because, as a college student, he thought business would be an unrewarding career. Unable to afford law school, and turning down opportunities to be a bond salesman, go into a chemical company, or join a soap company, he took scholarships and went on to graduate school. Later he found that exciting and challenging opportunities existed in railroads, airlines, aviation manufacturing, the chemical business, and even in soap!

How does modern business stack up in terms of challenging opportunities?

BUSINESS FILLS AN ESSENTIAL SOCIAL NEED

The young person who wants to work in something that contributes to the welfare of society should not forget that it is business that produces the goods and services upon which the life of society depends. We sometimes overlook how much we rely upon the humble activities of those who provide us with our food, clothing, housing, transportation, medical supplies, soap, or dry cleaning. We are reminded of this when the filling station runs out of gasoline, or when we must cut back on our electricity use, or when we can't find porterhouse at the meat counter. After all, what is more "relevant" than the ready availability of those material goods and services upon which we base our lives?

Those who say "business is for the birds" usually don't appreciate how much skill and creativity it takes to provide us with our standard of living. We could still be living like cavemen or Robinson Crusoes if we didn't have business firms competing with each other for the consumer's dollar, and, in the effort to do so, coming up with new products, devising ways of producing what we want most cheaply, and investing huge amounts of capital to do so? Where would we be if our labor produced barely enough to eat or to wear, instead of making it possible for us to enjoy the higher standard of living Americans have? It is business that has marshalled the talent and ingenuity that make the "good life" possible for so many of us.

EVERY FIELD HAS ITS SOCIAL MISSION AND OPPORTUNITIES

The social mission of business is to produce goods and services of an economic nature. Its mission is to satisfy customers, it must do so, at least in the United States, in a predominantly competitive climate. To achieve better products, more efficient production and distribution, lower prices, and higher profits presents difficult and challenging opportunities to everyone involved.

Every other field has its mission and its opportunities. People in government service have as their mission the supply of top-quality police service, fire protection, military defense, and human health and welfare programs. In medicine and dentistry, doctors have the important mission of administering to the health needs of their patients. Lawyers have the mission of assuring that people receive their legal rights. In music, the mission of the composer or musician is to create pleasure for listeners. Teachers have the mission of training people for more useful and satisfying lives and imparting the accumulated knowledge of our society.

Every mission has its challenges. We want to do it as well as we can, and so efficiently that as many people as possible can benefit from our efforts.

Challenges are really opportunities, because they involve the solution of problems. Problems exist only when we encounter something that stands in the way of successfully accomplishing a mission. Losers tend to give up when they encounter problems, while winners get interested in the problems and try to solve them. It is thus well said that problems are opportunities—opportunities for someone to come up with an answer.

EVERY FIELD HAS ITS DISSATISFACTIONS AND FRUSTRATIONS

Some students are turned off because they feel that business is full of dull tasks and boredom. It is true that there is much dull work in any business. Doing paperwork, calculating tables of statistics, making entries in accounting books, performing repetitive operations on an assembly line, counting inventories, loading baggage on an airplane—these and many other things are certainly not the stuff of romance and excitement.

But we have some dullness in every field. Dentists have been known to find filling teeth day after day boring, physicians often find treating people day after day for imaginary or minor aches and pains a chore, and musicians find hours of practice tedious. As for lawyers—one only needs to spend a few days in court watching a libel action or damage suit, or a case dealing with the value of real estate, to come away with a sense of wonder that a group of educated men can spend weeks or months on such details. It is well, before glamorizing any occupation, to recognize that there must be ever so many elements of dullness in it. Even college professors find grading papers and attending long committee and faculty meetings somewhat less than exciting.

Then too, the constant obstacles everyone faces in his work and the inability to solve problems readily cannot help but be frustrating at times. The frustration increases with the difficulty of the job and the level of its responsibility. It has been said that the higher a person goes in management, the higher must be his "frustration tolerance." This is particularly true if he has to deal with many people, since people can create the most frustrating problems of all.

So we face dullness and we face frustration in every walk of life. Some jobs may be just plain dull without much challenge to them. Others may be frustrating because the problems they involve are so difficult. That is one part of the picture. But a frustrating situation may also be interesting and challenging because of the demands it makes upon our abilities. Moreover, a job that seems dull to one person may be full of challenge to another. One person may find all the challenge he wants in keeping an accurate record of the fuel burned by an airline. Another may find enough demand upon his talents in making sure the pistons fit properly in automobile engines on an assembly line. But to another person, life may seem worthwhile only when he is closing a big sale or designing a new computer.

In short, we must not think we can escape dullness or frustration by choosing one career over another. If the grass looks greener in another field, let us make sure that we are looking at all the grass.

EVERY FIELD HAS ITS UNETHICAL OPERATORS

Some people believe that business practices are often unethical or dishonest, that businessmen will do anything for a dollar. Of course, there are instances where business behavior has been dishonest, fraudulent, or unethical. The Equity Funding Company scandal of 1972, in which a small group of executives were found do have written phony life insurance policies and sold them to other insurance companies, is only one example of dishonesty in business. Sometimes customers are taken in by misleading or dishonest advertising. Sometimes borrowers have been deceived by moneylenders who buried their hidden charges in the fine print of a loan contract. We all know of many other cases.

But the degree of unethical or dishonest behavior is not large when one considers the millions of businesses, the billions of transactions carried on each year, and the number of people of varying character who work in business. In fact, it is a rare business executive who does not place honesty and integrity very high on his scale of values.

At the risk of laboring the obvious, we must remember that dishonesty and unethical behavior can be found in all walks of life. There are surgeons who do unnecessary operations, professors who fail to live up to their obligations to their universities and students, lawyers who gouge people, social workers who connive with their clients to help them collect welfare checks they don't deserve, politicians who accept bribes, policemen who look the other way for a price, judges who have been bought, and students who cheat on examinations. We do not think of damning the medical profession for a few charlatans, or social workers for the few who are dishonest, or our legal system for its shysters.

Moreover, business is heavily controlled and policed. The controls are not limited to the thousands of laws designed to keep business honest, ethical, and regulated. They also include the millions of buyers who cannot be fooled for long, the force and threat of competition, and above all the fact that most transactions within a company, between companies, and between companies and their customers are carried on by word and honor and not by detailed written contracts.

WHAT DO STUDENTS WANT IN LIFE?

Students are human beings after all, and it is reasonable to suppose that they want in life what people generally want. In Chapter 22, we saw that Maslow's identification of human needs has been widely accepted as a summary statement of what people want. Maslow felt that human needs could be classified as follows:

1. Physiological needs—for food, clothing, and shelter.
2. Security needs—for freedom from physical and other dangers.
3. Affiliation needs—for belongingness and acceptance.
4. Esteem needs—for status, prestige, and power.
5. Self-actualization needs—for accomplishment, for becoming what one is capable of becoming.

What Do College Students Want?

What we know about college students fits the Maslow pattern exceedingly well. Various studies have been made of what college students look for in a career. At the top of most lists is work that is intellectually stimulating and challenging. They apparently neither want nor expect a series of routine and unexciting jobs, in which they will not have a chance to apply what they have learned and where the work will be too easy.

Another desire of college students is for careers that give them a chance to do something creative and worthwhile. This motive ties in closely with the desire for stimulating and challenging work. The feeling is expressed by today's "in" word, "involvement."

Still another major desire of the modern college student has been to be of service. With today's student it is tied in with the increased concern for major social problems—war, pollution, poverty, sickness, crime, discrimination, and the problems of the large and congested cities. Today's generation sees the seriousness of these problems and wants to be able to play some part in solving them.

Interestingly enough, the surveys of college students have shown little concern with what Maslow called "security" needs, and none at all for physiological needs. The students expressed surprisingly little interest in making money. Today's student probably takes these things for granted. Almost any job will pay him enough so that material concerns are not a major factor in his choice of career. Since 1972, however, when jobs have been harder to find and when many trained and experienced workers have found themselves unemployed, students have begun to show more concern with money and security.

What has been shocking to those in business is that so many students do not see a business career as satisfying their higher needs—as offering them stimulating and challenging work and a chance to be at service to society. When asked about this, some students find basic business values "sadly wanting." Others feel that business is a rewarding career only for a person "willing to endure an extended apprenticeship involving conformity, boredom, and spiritual starvation."

The reader of this book will surely realize by now that students who feel that way about a business career can hardly know what business is all about.

Can College Students Find What They Want in Business?

When we look at the various kinds of work available to the trained, educated, highly motivated person, we cannot help but see that challenging opportunities do exist in business. We find them in the various functional operating areas—in marketing, engineering, production, finance and accounting, and transportation. We find them also, and these are opportunities of especially high order, in the demanding task of being an effective manager.

To be sure, there are still managers in companies (as there are in government, universities, churches, and hospitals) who either cannot or will not develop an environment that turns people on. Managers like these do not encourage innovative goal setting, organize work to make it interesting, allow participation, or delegate decision making. But even this is changing. New tendencies are emerging in management that are of great importance to those considering business careers.

DEVELOPMENTS IMPORTANT TO A SATISFYING CAREER

In the past few years there have been a number of developments in modern business that increase its attractiveness to a person seeking a business career. Those have arisen from markedly improved management, greater understanding of human needs, and a number of positive social pressures. Let us consider a few of them.

Business Cannot Be Conservative or Reactionary

Some people think that business is normally conservative or reactionary—that it resists change, doesn't accept new ideas, is concerned with holding onto its present position. But for companies that want to stay in business nothing could be further from the truth. To resist change, to be reactionary, is to invite disaster. Competitors will take advantage of new product ideas, develop ways of reducing costs, or find new ways of appealing to the buying public.

In a very real sense businessmen must be ranked among the revolutionaries in our society. In political matters they may be conservative, since they understandably fear the inroads of government and the penchant of political leaders for heaping regulations on them that interfere with their ability to do business. They may also resist the efforts of some labor unions to introduce and maintain work rules that make it difficult to operate efficiently. But they are anything but conservative in other respects.

Many radical changes in the quality and character of American life have been brought on by businessmen in recent times. Mass production, mass distribution of goods and services, automation, modern food growing and processing, electronic data processing, television, our whole transportation system—these are only some of the consequences of businessmen's drive to produce and sell. These business-led revolutions have surely altered our daily lives more deeply and broadly than have all the innovations in the highly respected professions of law, medicine, or the arts.

Nor do we see any letup in this revolutionary zeal. It brings oil and gas from the wastes of the Arctic, the depths of the oceans, and the backcountry of Siberia. It explores the ocean floor for minerals and other resources, develops new ways of transportation, and uses space satellites to carry messages. To think of doing these things is one matter; to organize them and make them practical realities is quite another. If we go behind the scenes we find enormous energies deployed—we find businessmen planning, thinking, persuading, inspiring, organizing, arranging, investing, and spending. They will go on doing these things as long as our society lets them and encourages them.

Business Is Increasingly Relying on Individual Initiative

Business firms, particularly larger ones, are often pictured as places of conformity where everyone marches in lock step. A fair degree of conformity does exist in every business organization. People are expected to work certain hours, operate within existing policies, make decisions only within the authority delegated to them, file expense reports in a certain way, work on assignments that are considered a part of their jobs, and conform to various rules. By the same token, a football player assigned to the position of offensive guard is not expected to call signals or run with the ball. Even a college professor is expected to meet classes, give examinations, and see students.

The highly competitive nature of business, particularly in a private enterprise system, puts a premium on creativity and innovation. It constantly calls for new products, new ways of controlling costs, new ways of selling, and new ways of solving the countless problems that always seem to crop up—from laying out a new advertising program or a new production line to selecting and promoting people, or deciding where best to put the limited financial and human resources of a company or department. As businessman-inventor Edwin H. Land, founder of the Polaroid Corporation, once emphasized, the process of marketing a product calls for exactly the same creativity and invention as does the most advanced field of science.

It is no wonder that business leaders increasingly say that they want more people "who do not know that a thing cannot be done." They realize that differences of opinion and ideas go farther in making progress than do conformity and ready agreement. They know that dif-

Charles H. Percy

One of the handicaps of Charles Percy when he ran for the U.S. Senate in 1966 was that he seemed too good to be true. He was handsome. He was young, only 47. He was a self-made man who had risen out of poverty to become president of Bell & Howell at the age of 29. Despite all this he was able to defeat incumbent Senator Paul H. Douglas, one of the top vote-getters in Illinois political history, by more than 420,000 votes. In 1972 he was reelected by a 1,146,000 vote margin, the largest plurality ever received by an Illinois senatorial candidate. He carried all of the state's 102 counties, the only time a state-wide candidate has ever accomplished this in Illinois.

Percy was born in 1919. His father was the cashier of a bank that failed in 1931, and for several years the family lived in deep poverty. Young Percy's business abilities were evident at an early age. In high school, he held four jobs at the same time. He worked his way through the University of Chicago, beginning with waiting on tables and finally starting his own business as a central purchasing agent for all the fraternities. He got volume discounts for food, coal, laundry services, and the like, and was said to be grossing $150,000 a year at the time of his graduation. He was also president of his fraternity, captain of the water polo team, and university marshal, the highest honor accorded a senior student.

Working during his summer vacations at Bell & Howell, he attracted the attention of the firm's president with a cost-saving scheme for answering customers' complaints. After graduation he went to work there full time in 1941. He convinced Bell & Howell's president that participation in defense work was necessary to the firm's future success. When the U.S. entered

ferences in thinking can do much to develop ideas, help to keep troublesome but useful questions alive, and goad people to make second efforts. Some individualists like General David Sarnoff, who built and led RCA for many years, put such a premium on differences that he even felt indebted to his competitors and enemies. He said that he was grateful for his enemies because "in the long-range movement to progress, a kick in the pants sends you farther along than a friendly hand does."

World War II six months later, Percy, who had been put in charge of Bell and Howell's defense efforts, was able to capitalize on his foresight by building the war contracts division into a prosperous operation. In 1942, at the age of 23, he was made a director of the company. A year later he enlisted in the Navy, but kept in touch with Bell & Howell through a monthly report he sent to the president.

He returned to the company in 1945 and was promoted to corporate secretary, with responsibility for industrial relations and manufacturing programs. On the president's death in 1949, Percy became president at the age of 29. That year he was named one of the "ten outstanding young men in the country" by the U.S. Junior Chamber of Commerce.

During his tenure at Bell & Howell, the firm's sales grew from $13 million to $160 million annually, and the number of employees increased from 1,600 to more than 10,000. The company pioneered in profit-sharing for employees, favored reductions in import duties even though Japanese cameras threatened its sales, and gained public attention by sponsoring controversial television documentaries in prime time.

Percy attributes his remarkable success in business—his ability to discover opportunities and capitalize on them—to having good men on his staff, to his strategy of delegating a major share of decision-making authority to his key people, and to his willingness to take risks. "In business," he has said, "you have got to take risks. The more risks you are willing to take, backed up by solid reasoning, judgment, and research, the more a business can afford to pay you. One of the qualities that brings success is, I think, the ability to take risks, to not make too many mistakes, but to make enough."

Percy became chairman of Bell & Howell in 1961. Simultaneously with his business career he had been involved in politics. Starting in 1946 as a Republican precinct worker, he went on to become president of the United Republican Fund of Illinois, raising more than $4 million for the party in four years during the 1950s. He was vice chairman of the Republican National Finance Committee from 1955 to 1959, and served as chairman of the Republican Platform Committee in 1960. In 1956 President Eisenhower sent him to the presidential inaugurations in Bolivia and Peru as his personal representative with the title of Ambassador. In the late 1950s he rejected offers for high appointive offices, saying that if he entered public life he wanted to run for elective office so he could learn the business of government and politics as he had learned the business of business at Bell & Howell.

In 1964 Percy ran for governor of Illinois and was defeated. In 1966 he committed himself to a political career, resigning from Bell & Howell to wage a full-time campaign for the U.S. Senate. His experience in 25 years at Bell & Howell formed a solid foundation for public service. The principles upon which his earlier success was based have found new application in government, both in his activities as Senator and in his approach to government. He has employed management consultants to aid him in the operation of his office. He keeps up regular communications with his constituents, even devoting his personal resources—he is a multimillionaire—to defraying the costs. And he has applied the principles of good organization and delegation of authority to the management of his political activities.

It would be incorrect to imply that all business managers encourage innovativeness. Most top business leaders do. But unfortunately there are many lower level managers, in business as elsewhere, who do not share this attitude. These are the unimaginative, usually insecure, bosses who do not wish to "rock the boat," who resist change, and who thrive on rules and procedures. But these people seldom move up the ladder. And they may even feel indebted to subordinates who diplomatically offer them new ideas that they can present to their own bosses in turn —and look good as a result.

Increasing Complexity, Problems, and Opportunities in Modern Business

Business is becoming more complex. New products and services, new production methods, new approaches in transportation, new ways of selling and marketing, new accounting and financial techniques, the ever widening use of electronic data processing—all these make for increased complexity, even in small firms. Also, the job of the manager, at all levels and in all companies, is becoming more complex and difficult as we come to understand more about people and about methods of managing.

Complexity means greater costs and greater risks. Problems must be recognized in time to do something about them, and this requires analysis and intelligence. It also requires that people be aware of how their decisions affect the work of people in other parts of their company. For example, those in sales are preoccupied with what customers want and with how to beat competitors; those in engineering are concerned with problems of design; those in manufacturing are interested in production costs; and those in the financial department think mainly of accounting questions and of how to obtain funds. Obviously, they will sometimes have conflicting interests, and the job of reconciling them may be very complex.

But this is not all. The complexity of modern business is made greater by the necessity of responding to a social and political environment that is continually throwing up new challenges. Business has always been subject to forces of the market and to changes in technology. And these spell complexity. But the demanding nature of new social and political forces makes for even more complex problems.

As pointed out above, problems spell opportunities. Complex problems mean even greater opportunities. The rewards to those who can help in solving these problems are certain to become ever greater, and those who can contribute in any way will be appreciated accordingly.

The New Day of Equal Opportunity

Pushed on by a series of laws and administrative orders, and culminating with the Civil Rights Act of 1964, the federal government has placed itself solidly behind the effort to do away with discrimination in hiring and promoting people. It is illegal to discriminate on the basis of race, age, or sex in employment practices, and tremendous strides have been made toward translating this from words into reality.

To be sure, human nature hasn't been transformed. There are people in companies and unions who are still prejudiced and who even secretly practice discrimination. But when a company states in its advertisements that it is an "Equal Opportunity Employer," this means that it is committed to certain nondiscriminatory procedures in its hiring practices. Today the jobseeker can expect an even break, especially from larger companies. In fact, many companies aggressively seek out minority people, and even offer well qualified persons high financial and other inducements. There can be no question that this is a new day.

Serious Recognition of Human Needs in Modern Business

In better managed businesses there is an increasing awareness that human beings have individual attitudes, needs, and desires. Part of this greater recognition of human needs arises from the work of behavioral scientists in this area. Part is due to the fact that businessmen themselves are becoming better educated in the subjects of motivation and leadership. And part of it is due to greater awareness by business leaders of human motivations and to an appreciation that a well motivated employee will be more efficient and productive.

There are many evidences of the recognition of human needs in practice. The rapidly growing practice of managing by objectives, discussed in Chapter 20, is one important development. The effort being made to enrich jobs is another. An increasing number of companies are accepting the idea that the college graduate wants work that is meaningful and challenging. They have tried to cut down on long training and orientation assignments, and on making graduates do trivial jobs so that they can learn from the ground up. Every new employee needs some orientation, of course, but many companies now throw the college graduate early into the water of company problems to see if he can swim. At the same time, there is no job that does not involve some dull and routine work. Even company presidents do much routine work; they cannot spend all their time on exciting new challenges.

The Modern Manager

Another factor causing businesses to recognize human needs more than they ever have before is the development of more intelligent and better trained managers. Such managers realize that their task is not to give orders or to push buttons but to design and maintain an environment in which *individuals* can perform (see Chapter 19). They are not interested in coddling people; they simply recognize the human factor as important to business success, and that they must show concern for human needs.

As an environment creator, the modern manager has many things to think of. His job is to establish an environment in which people can work toward meaningful objectives. He has the responsibility of making sure that his part of the company is well organized so that people can know the significance of what they do and how their roles relate to those of others. He must also see that people are well selected, appraised, trained, and compensated. He must make sure that his subordinates have adequate guidance, and that they are informed as to the progress they are making.

ENVIRONMENT AND OPPORTUNITY VARY IN DIFFERENT BUSINESSES

Businesses are not all alike. One cannot expect the same problems and opportunities in the railroad business as in the oil or chemical business. They will not be the same in a department store and a tire company. A slow-growing or declining industry will have fewer opportunities than a fast-growing one: obviously, the faster growing a business is, the more challenges and opportunities it will offer, and the greater the chances for an able person to go quickly up the ladder of promotion.

Perhaps it will be easiest to summarize these differences by comparing the environment and opportunities a person who starts his own business with those of a person who goes into a small business or into a large business. Let us take a brief look at the three alternatives.

Going Into Your Own Business

Some people find the greatest satisfaction in having their own business, whether it is a store or an electronics factory. A person may have his own business by taking over a family business, by buying control of an existing business, or by starting a new one. We do have in the United States exceptional freedom for a person to have his own business, whether he acquires it or starts it. Of course, depending on the kind and size of business, money is required as well as a willingness to work hard and assume the risks of possible failure. Despite the number of people with limited financial resources and the fact that a large number of businesses fail, it is remarkable how many businesses succeed and how many of their founders accumulate sizable fortunes.

There are many advantages in going into your own business. One of the greatest is the opportunity to be your own boss. A person can do pretty much what he pleases, he does not have to please a boss with whom he may disagree. He need answer only to himself. However, having your own business is not quite that independent. A person must cater to customers and win over competitors. He must meet the requirements of bankers and suppliers. He must consider the attitudes of his employees. And there are always government regulations and licenses to deal with, not the least being the exacting demands of the tax authorities.

Another major advantage of being in business for yourself is that it is possible to make far more money than you can expect as an employee. If the business succeeds and grows, not only does the owner draw a high salary but the value of his investment may grow very fast. One small business owner was surprised to discover that the combination of these two factors made his after-tax personal wealth increase annually by an amount higher than the after-tax salary and bonus of the chairman of General Motors. But growth takes money and hard work. It may require years of putting all except the small amount needed for personal living expenses back into the business. It may require heavy borrowing from banks, suppliers, and others. It usually demands long hours; a 75-hour week is not unusual for the small business owner. And then everything may disappear if the business fails. Failure may come about because of the incompetence of the owner, a shift in the market for his products, a loss on a large contract, a sudden shutting down of bank credit, or a business recession. The freedom to succeed is also the freedom to fail.

Still another reward for having your own business is the satisfaction gained from building something, from accomplishing something and seeing and feeling it. If the business succeeds, also, the owner is likely to enjoy a high reputation in his community as a success.

Joining a Small Company

When most college students think of entering business, they think of a career in a large company. But there are also rewards and opportunities in a small company. The Small Business Administration defines a small business as a manufacturing company with 250 or fewer employees, or a retailing or service company with $1 million or less of annual sales. To many people, of course, "small" is much smaller than this.

One can usually get as much salary, insurance, pension, and other compensation with a smaller company as with a large one, at least in starting or middle-level positions. Admittedly, unless one is the owner, the pay scales will not go as high at the top in a smaller company as in a larger one.

One of the important advantages of a career with a smaller company is that a person gets a feeling of being nearer the top. As a matter of fact he is nearer the top, since there are not as many levels of management in the smaller company. He is more likely to have a stronger sense of identity with the company, and a feeling of being in the middle of the action, of knowing what is going on.

Being close to the action may also give a person a feeling of accomplishment. Smaller companies have much the same problems, and almost as many of them, as larger companies. Therefore, those in a smaller company tend to have more direct exposure to those problems. In a large company a person may find himself immersed in accounting, engineering, or sales, without any chance to gain knowledge of other departments.

In the small company a person may gain a broad experience in a variety of fields. He will almost surely have a better opportunity to interact with specialists in different fields, and to learn from them.

In small companies, also, there may not be as many rules and restrictions, as many forms to fill out, or as many reports to be made. Nevertheless, one should not assume that small companies are free of these things. As soon as a company becomes larger than one man can manage—say, more than 20 or 30 employees—it has to rely on accounting, personnel, purchasing, and other procedures.

Some college graduates see an advantage in the smaller company because competition for positions may not be as strong. The smaller company cannot hire as many college men and women as the larger company, or build up a backlog of highly qualified people for future promotions. This will mean less competition among college-educated career people in the company, to be sure, but the number of openings for promotion will also be fewer.

Joining the Large Company

There are many reasons why a person may prefer to join a large company. Salary and other financial benefits may not be greater in the beginning, but they will almost certainly be greater as one moves up the ladder. Pension benefits are likely to be larger, and some of the other benefits may be attractive. For example, some employees of Ford or General Motors can buy cars at reduced prices; and employees of General Electric can buy appliances at factory cost. Small companies cannot offer such benefits.

Perhaps one of the major advantages of being associated with a large and well known company is the element of prestige. Friends and neighbors are often impressed when an individual is a part of a large company and may not even have heard of the small company he might be employed by.

A person may also feel more secure with a large firm than with a smaller company. For one thing, it is unlikely to fail. If he is a manager or a specialist in one of the operating areas of the company, he may not be subject to layoff in case of a business downturn. But as many aerospace managers and engineers, some with long service records who were laid off, have found, this security is not at all absolute. A person may feel a greater sense of security with a larger company in that the decisions he makes are likely to be so small or so thoroughly doublechecked by others that a mistake will not cause him great embarrassment or cost him his job.

Another advantage the large company may offer is a chance to move around into various divisions and operations. In companies that have a policy of rotating people among various jobs, a person may get meaningful experience in sales, marketing research, advertising, engineering, production, finance, or even overseas operations. He thus has many new challenges and greater opportunities to grow.

Larger companies also are likely to have many types of training and development programs that give a person a chance to continue his learning. They are also likely to have other personnel practices, such as appraisal and selection programs, which can be of great assistance to employees, particularly to those in specialist or managerial positions.

But working for the large company has its disadvantages, too. It is easy to get lost or forgotten among those thousands of employees and hundreds of departments and managers. People also understandably see that it is a long way from their starting position to the top with a slim chance of going far up the ladder.

A large company must necessarily have many policies to guide decision making and assure its consistency and many procedures to make sure that certain things are done and done in a given way. These are often frustrating to individuals who see their freedom curtailed. However, where a company is well managed, policies can become charters for making clear the extent of freedom in decision making and procedures need not be unduly burdensome. Even most large companies can put the more burdensome procedures, like those in personnel, purchasing, or work scheduling, on a computer so that people hardly need to be bothered with them at all.

Perhaps one of the greater disadvantages to an aspiring young person in a large corporation is a sense of insignificance. As a very small wheel, he can't feel that the few decisions he makes are of great importance to the company. If he decides to buy motor parts from one supplier rather than another, he may not be able to see how this makes a difference to a General Electric or a Westinghouse.

A career with a large corporation may also require moving around from Phoenix to Detroit, or from Los Angeles to New York, and then to Pittsburgh, and a few years later to Atlanta. Moving may be a good path to promotion, but it can be rough on a person's family and one's own desire to put down roots. Some people, on the other hand, are good at making these adjustments; they find moving on to new environments and friends a broadening and wholesome experience, even for their children.

CHALLENGING OPPORTUNITIES IN OPERATIONS

We often make the assumption that everyone wishes to become a manager, largely because this position is seen as one of power, prestige, and high financial reward. But many people would rather be salesmen, engineers, financial analysts, chemists, physicists, or personnel specialists.

Opportunities for the college educated lie in both directions, or in a combination of both. One may become a specialist in some operating area such as marketing, sales, engineering, production, purchasing, personnel, accounting, or finance. Or one may become a manager in one of these areas with a view to rising possibly to the position of a division general manager or even chief executive. In the normal course of events, career opportunities lie in both directions. An individual may start out in sales, or production, or accounting as a specialist in these fields and then start the climb up the managerial ladder.

Some larger companies, especially those in high-technology industries, recognize this and provide ladders of promotion for specialists that can yield rewards equivalent to those of managers for individuals who prefer not to take the managerial route. For example, the duPont Company makes it possible for a research chemist to go to a position of very high pay and prestige without being a manager. Some of our oil companies do the same for their geologists. And it is not unusual for a highly successful salesman to earn more in salary and commissions than the company's sales manager. Some life insurance salesmen make more than the president of the company. Let us look at some of the challenges and opportunities in business operations.

Marketing and Sales

As business has become more and more competitive, career opportunities have multiplied in the field of marketing and sales. In order to sell, a company may need more than salesmen. It is likely to require people who can study and analyze customer behavior, markets, competitors, and prices. A company that relies heavily on advertising to get the customer's attention, and often to presell him, will need creative people —if not on its own staff, then on the staff of its advertising agency. It takes a certain genius, as well as much hard thinking and work, to come up with such slogans as Avis's "We Try Harder" (because "We are Only No. 2"), or Crest toothpaste's "Look Mom! No Cavities!" But it is not so much a matter of finding a catchy message as of understanding how a message in an advertisement influences potential buyers. This means understanding the buyers as well as the product.

Virtually every position in the sales and marketing area requires imagination, as well as hard work and intelligence. In selling a technical product, a company naturally looks for people with appropriate technical expertise. But for most products a broad education in many areas of business is the best preparation, since, after all, sales and marketing people are usually the major link between a company and the outside world.

Engineering and Research

There are as many fields of engineering and scientific research as there are fields of scientific specialty. These range from the mathematician in the actuarial department of an insurance company who figures the risks underlying the premiums, to the research chemist in a drug manufacturing company. Engineering and research opportunities exist in almost every kind of business. They have increased in recent years as products and services have become more complex and based on advanced sciences.

The opportunities may be as simple as designing a new screwdriver, or as complex as building a space satellite. Companies now look for people with a bachelor's degree, and even with master's and doctor's degrees. It is true that the great inventor Thomas Edison did not even graduate from grade school, but—as one business executive put it—"We do not have time to look for an Edison."

Production

Many opportunities exist for specialists in the production field, whether the products involved are automobiles or typewriters, department store services, or cattle. The work may include laying out an efficient production line, planning the flow of materials and production, doing statistical analyses of costs and quality, developing new ways of producing something, attempting to design enriched production jobs, setting up incentive pay programs, or even overseeing actual production operations.

Even in the service industries there are great opportunities for inventiveness and imagination, as well as for careful analytical work. Insurance companies, banks, and brokerage houses have been inundated with paperwork. As a matter of fact, failures of many brokerage houses in recent years have been due to inefficiency in handling masses of stocks, bonds, and the paperwork involved in security transactions. The opportunities for people who can simplify, control, and automate through computerizing the flow of paperwork are exceptionally great.

Information Processing

A business lives on information. It has even been said that to manage a business is to manage information. The advent of the computer has created a need for a new kind of specialist—and not just someone who can program the computer but someone who knows how to relate a computer program to the specific needs of a business. High salaries and opportunities for accomplishment in this area exist in almost every business.

Purchasing

One of the more important and rapidly developing areas of business is buying the wide range of materials, supplies, parts, and components businesses need. In a large company, more than half of every sales dollar may be accounted for by purchases. Even in smaller companies it is not unusual for purchases to amount to 30 percent or more of sales.

Purchasing is a demanding occupation. To do it well, the purchaser must know his suppliers thoroughly, and their record for costs and performance. He must understand the needs of his company, and when he can substitute parts or materials for those ordered. Purchasing also requires a knowledge of prices, quantity discounts, and methods of delivery. Those in purchasing, because of their close relationship to suppliers are also an important pipeline of information on new products and developments being undertaken by suppliers and which might be beneficial to their company.

For many items purchased, buyers must also be able to exercise the fine art of negotiation in order to make the best possible deal. This does not mean automatically taking the lowest price offered. Judgment and diplomacy are often required. If a supplier of some part has been developing new products of great use to the buying company, it is usually poor practice to give a follow-on order to another supplier who merely copies the new development and underbids by a few pennies. The wise buyer maintains a reliable and helpful supplier.

Accounting and Finance

One of the most interesting and promising careers in business is that offered by accounting and finance. Strictly speaking, accounting involves the recording and interpretation of whatever data are needed to tell the story of what is happening in a company. Most accounting deals with the financial data necessary for the construction of income statements and balance sheets. The field of finance is closely related to accounting, but its emphasis is on assessing needs for money, analyzing the returns earned on investments, working out arrangements to obtain needed capital, and forecasting and analyzing cash flow.

The accounting and finance area affords a person a chance to look at the company's operations as a whole and to see how they fit together. This is because accounting and finance reduce all the operations to a common measure—money. Because accounting and finance are essential tools for all managers, top managers in particular, people working in this part of a company are likely to have a close association with managers and managerial problems.

As business has become more complex and competitive, and as information requirements have become more exacting, there has been a growing demand for specialists in accounting and finance. Even during the business recession of the early 1970s, the demand for specialists in accounting and finance outran the supply. Nor is there any reason for the demand to be less in future years. But the need is not just for people who know accounting, but for people who also have analytical abilities and imagination as well.

CHALLENGING OPPORTUNITIES IN MANAGEMENT

Since the quality and vigor of management are the most important factors in business success, it is not hard to understand why those who can manage reap the greatest challenges and rewards. The science of management is fairly crude, but it is developing rapidly. Management, after all, is the most complex of all jobs. This is evident when we consider the variables that managers must deal with—variables in people and their personalities, in associates and superiors, in problems of making every part of a business operate, in the demands of customers and suppliers, and in the multitude of forces pressed on a business by government and society.

The challenges are numerous. Managers need to prepare for and meet change. They have the continuing problem of balancing the needs for conformity in an organization, with giving people the opportunity for being creative or innovative. Managers must try their best to create an environment in which there is an incentive to perform, and where people will find it in their own interest to help the company accomplish its goals. Managers must ever realize that it is a part of their job to help their subordinates: through accurate appraisals of their work; by giving them chances for training and development; by removing obstacles to their performance; and by giving them guidance, information, and tools —including clear goals and accurate control information.

Managing is also challenging in that it requires the effective manager to keep abreast of the new knowledge in his field, and have the imagination and creativeness to apply it to his job. This includes important knowledge developing in the behavioral and physical sciences. He should also be challenged by the expanding use of advanced computers and by having an appreciation of their information processing potentials as they relate to his job.

The demand for effective managers is likely to continue high. Researchers such as John B. Miner (see the *Harvard Business Review,* November–December, 1973) predict that by the mid-1980s the major limitation on company growth will not be money or materials but a shortage of managerial resources. Some even believe that this shortage will restrict profitable business growth. It is hardly surprising that managers get increasingly higher pay and higher status in the community.

Yet, while the opportunities for reward, for contributing to the welfare of society, and for experiencing a sense of accomplishment are clearly available in a managerial career, a genuine desire to manage is essential. People who go into management because of the rewards it promises are not likely to succeed unless they also have a desire to manage and are willing to put into the job the intelligence, hard work, and imagination it requires.

CHOOSING A CAREER[1]

Some young people know what they want to be from the time they are in grade school, and never waver from this choice. All of us have heard of people who wanted to be a doctor, a lawyer, or an engineer all their lives. But most of us are never sure so early. Many of us are not even sure by the time we enter college. One thing is certain. Unless we are going to be dropouts we must select and follow some kind of career, even though we may change our career plans a number of times. One hears of the young man who became a minister, then went into banking and became a young vice president, and finally settled down as the owner of a boys' camp in the Appalachian Mountains. Or of the promising young man who started out in the newspaper business, switched to a career in law, then joined the Air Force, and ended up in business.

What Is Important in Choosing a Career?

Most writers of books like the one you are reading have their own ideas as to what is important in selecting a career. And the authors of this book are no exceptions. It seems to them, rightly or wrongly, that the following are the most important things to consider:

1. Above all, do what you want to do, what gives you pleasure, what interests you. Be sure, however, that you match your aptitude— what you are able to do—with what interests you. This is normally not much of a problem, since we seldom enjoy doing something we cannot do well.

2. Pick a career and a company and position in which you can learn and continue to learn. People who do this not only get more satisfaction from their work but also are ready for higher job opportunities when they come. The years before 38–40 should be regarded as years of training for the big opportunities that lie ahead. Remem-

---

[1] Many books and monographs have been written to help people choose a career. A selected list will be found in Appendix B.

ber that we may learn from even the dullest task—it will give us an appreciation of many details that are important in business, and also give us in later life, after we have moved up the ladder, a feeling of sympathy with the workers who must do these dull jobs. On the other hand, experience is not the same as learning. Twenty years of experience may really be just one year of meaningful experience done 20 times over.

3. Try to get a job with a good boss. This means a boss who is a good manager and can show you by his own actions what good managing is or what good selling or accounting practice is. This means a boss willing to coach and who takes pride in seeing his subordinates develop and get ahead. One of the best reasons for quitting a job is having a boss who is incompetent, selfish, and uninterested in his subordinates.

4. Pick a career and a job in which you can have a feeling of being useful, of accomplishing something, of doing something worthwhile. Nothing is more frustrating and even embittering to a person than to spend years doing something that does not give him a feeling of personal reward beyond his paycheck.

Planning a Career

Most vocational guidance specialists emphasize the importance of planning one's career. Know as early as possible what career you are going to follow, they say, and plan your high school and college courses to prepare for it. Choose summer and part-time work that will help in your career. Become familiar with the field you want to work in, and even study the industry or company in which you expect to be.

This is all very well. Certainly there are advantages in doing these things. But the experience of many successful men and women has shown that it is not always possible. In fact, many young people "paint themselves into a corner" by overpreparing for a career that they later find they do not enjoy or cannot do well in. A very large number of young people simply do not know where they want to go and what they want to do. Many do not find their proper career niche until years after college.

The best advice we can give the student who is not completely sure what career he wants to follow—and this, we suspect, is most students— is not to worry about it. Take college courses that seem interesting and challenging. Include some courses that are basic—such as writing, speaking, science, engineering, or accounting—because these will help you in almost any field. Then look for a job that seems interesting in a company or other organization that seems interesting. After all, life is too short and precious to make it orderly at the cost of making it dull.

And finally, if you find you have chosen the wrong position in the wrong organization, and if you have given the job a fair trial, then have enough guts to quit and try something else.

OPPORTUNITIES AND CHALLENGES DO NOT COME TO THE OBSOLETE

If anyone is to enjoy and take advantage of the opportunities and challenges of business, or for that matter any other field of work, it is important for him or her to be constantly aware that these only come to people who do not allow themselves to grow obsolete. The knowledge required in almost any career keeps expanding. We speak of scientists being obsolete ten years after they have finished their graduate studies because they have not kept up with new developments in their field. This is true in every area of modern business and it is especially true in management.

This means that the person who enters on a career must continue to keep up and expand his knowledge. Some of this he will get from his job and from his boss or his associates. Some he will get from reading books and magazines in his field. Some he will get from training courses provided by his company, which naturally has an interest in keeping its people from becoming obsolete. He can also profit from part-time courses at a nearby university; most universities have extension programs for precisely this purpose of "life-long learning."

Opportunities and challenges exist in business. But the most satisfying and important of these are mainly open to those who are prepared to take advantage of them. We should never forget that, as Alfred North Whitehead, Harvard philosopher, once said, "Knowledge keeps no better than fish."

appendixes

appendix A

The Financial Flow of the U.S. Economy

We have used the words National Income and Gross National Product in this book. An understanding of these terms and what they describe is important for anyone who wants to be able to follow discussions of economic policy. Figure A–1 summarizes the flow of funds in our economy, and the various tributaries and rivulets that form the stream called Gross National Income (which is the same as Gross National Product). The following discussion attempts to show:

- How business production of goods and services creates the gross national income, and what national income is.
- How this national income is comprised of personal income, government income, and savings.
- How personal income, government income, and savings return to the productive system in the form of personal consumption expenditures, government purchases, and gross private investment.
- And, in sum, the cyclical nature of expenditures and investment within our system, coming back to form tomorrow's national income and then to be respent and reinvested.

Let us see how the system works step by step, referring to the numbered items in Figure A–1:

1. Probably consumer spending is as good a place to break into the cycle as any, since consumer needs and wants are the moving force of every economic system.

2. and 3. Starting with needs and wants—and a system of private ownership of property operating on the profit motive—private business goes into action, investing in capital goods and basic resources and hiring labor to produce, distribute, and exchange the goods and services which private enterprise believes will satisfy those needs and wants. The

685

FIGURE A–1

The Financial Flow of the U.S. Economy

Key

Personal Consumption Expenditures
Government Purchases—Expenditures
Gross Private Investment—Savings

total value of all goods and services produced within a period of time is labeled Gross National Product or GNP. Because what is produced soon becomes income, the total value of GNP is equivalent to Gross National Income (GNI) within a given period. In other words, production costs and expenditures plus profits become income for the nation. This is a self-feeding system.

4. But Gross National Income does not go directly into the pockets of individuals. First we must deduct business savings for the replacement of capital goods. These enable businesses to maintain their productive processes by having buildings, machinery, and other capital continuously in operating condition.

5. Next we must deduct the many indirect business taxes which are included in the selling price of a product. These include sales taxes, taxes on imported goods, and excise taxes on such items as alcoholic beverages and cigarettes. They get siphoned into Government Income (B) before ever reaching the National Income level.

6. What remains is called National Income, which is generally broken down into the following elements: business profits; salaries and wages; income from property rentals; and interest paid on such things as savings accounts and bonds.

7. Our income flow is further diminished by the income taxes that corporations pay to the government.

8. Also siphoned off are the savings of corporations, which represent profits retained by the firm and not paid out either in taxes or as dividends. These corporate savings will find their way back into the system through investment. (This simplified scheme does not take into account the international transfer of funds.) The remaining income stream is called Personal Income (A) because it flows through the pockets of individuals.

9. Ah, but alas, Personal Income isn't completely at the disposal of the recipient—as you may have expected—since the individual income tax goes to swell the stream of Government Income (B); in fact, it forms the largest single source of government funds. What remains is called Disposable Personal Income.

10. Disposable Personal Income is the amount individuals can spend as they choose. Some of it is channelled off into Savings (C) by various routes, including bank accounts, insurance policies, and the purchase of securities.

11. The remainder is spent to meet consumers' needs and wants, and is labeled Personal Consumption Expenditures. This is the largest

portion of the GNI, and it now returns into the production cycle through the creation of business income as the basis for further production.

12. Meanwhile, part of the income stream marked Savings (C) has gone into the purchase of government bonds. It merges with the rest of Government Income (B).

13. All of the government income—including that portion borrowed through government bonds—is poured back into the private economy by means of government purchases, thus becoming part of the production cycle.

14. The rest of the income stream marked Savings (C) becomes gross private investment and forms the basis for further expansion of the productive forces. Naturally, the savings must be drawn into the business investment stream by expectations of interest payments or profits.

We have traced the flow of the U.S. economy, showing how the GNP becomes Personal Income (A), Government Income (B), and Savings (C)—which are recycled into a new GNP through Personal Consumption Expenditures, Government Purchases, and Gross Private Investment.

Admittedly this is a very simplified picture of our total economy since it makes no allowance for the important sector of international trade and capital movements. Nor does it take into account the transfer of income from taxpayers to particular groups in the form of social security pensions, unemployment compensation, and welfare assistance; these are called "transfer payments." However, it is meant to provide the business student with a basic insight into the dynamics of our economy.

appendix B

Selected Sources of Information
on Careers in Business

General Sources of Career Information

Angel, J. L., *Modern Vocational Trends Reference Handbook*, World Trade
Academy Press, Inc., 50 East 42nd St., New York, N.Y. 10017. 1970.
815 pp. $17.50.*

This handbook presents analyses of the professions most in need of
personnel. Included are job descriptions, training requirements, opportunities, remuneration, typical program of studies to prepare for
particular professions, scholarships available, leading schools offering
training, and sources of additional information. The handbook also lists
selected positions for men and women according to occupational aptitudes and attitudes. Four supplements containing current bibliographies
in the fields covered in the handbook are issued each year.

Arco Career Guidance Series, Arco Publishing Company, Inc., 219 Park
Ave. South, New York, N.Y. 10003. $1.95 each.

A series of 40 books containing information about specific careers.
Among the fields covered are accounting, banking, computer programming, hospital work, insurance, law enforcement, and real estate.

Career Briefs and Summaries, Careers, Inc., P.O. Box 135, Largo, Fla.
33540. $21.60 per year. Individual titles available at 20¢ each for sum-
maries and 35¢ each for briefs.

A set of 110 career items, all current, released on a monthly basis
through the normal school year. Titles range from nonskilled through
semiskilled, semiprofessional and professional occupations.

Career Information Monographs, World Trade Academy Press, 50 East
42nd St., New York, N.Y. 10017. Each about 24 pp. $1.25 per booklet.

This is a series of 76 separate monographs containing information about
each of several specialties within the fields represented by the titles.
Typically they include a description of the work, training, opportunities,

---

* All prices subject to change.

remuneration, and typical places of employment, lists of educational institutions and private organizations offering scholarships and fellowships in the various fields, and a bibliography with approximately 20 references in the specific field of interest.

Careers for Tomorrow (a series of books on careers), Henry Z. Walck, Inc., 19 Union Square West, New York, N.Y. 10003. Each book has about 100 pp. $4.50.

Gives current information on job opportunities in each field, description of qualifications required, a comprehensive overview of the field itself—how it functions, subdivisions in the field, opportunities for advancement, and a comparison of activities and status in the present day. Twelve careers are covered: School Teaching; Protective Services; Foreign Languages; Modern Nursing; Natural Resource Conservation; Department Store Merchandising; Building Trades; Writing; Library Careers; Airlines Operations; Engineering; and Music.

Careers in Depth, Richards Rosen Press, Inc., 29 East 21st St., New York, N.Y. 10010, 1969–1973. Approximately $3.99 each.

A series of 98 small hardcover books, written by prominent men and women, covering most of the major careers and written in practical terms for the young man or woman who is interested in more than "just a job."

Careers Research Monographs, The Institute of Research, 610 South Federal St., Chicago, Ill. 60605. Each about 24 pp. $2.00 per booklet.

This is a series of 292 separate vocational monographs presenting detailed information about each career. They include the nature of the work, description of job, personal qualifications, training, educational requirements, opportunities, earnings, attractive and unattractive features of the work. Each also lists schools offering appropriate specialized training and professional associations in the field, and includes a reading list.

Concise Handbook of Occupations, J. G. Ferguson Publishing Co., 6 North Michigan Ave., Chicago, Ill. 60602. 1971. $11.95.

Detailed, up-to-date information on 305 of today's most popular jobs ranging in educational requirements from an eighth grade certificate to a Ph.D. Each job description is complete on one page and includes information on type of work done, necessary personal qualities, educational requirements, average earnings, working conditions, advancement possibilities, and long-range employment outlook.

Dutton Career Books Series, E. P. Dutton & Co., Inc., 201 Park Ave. South, New York, N.Y. 10003. Approximately 200 pp. each. Prices range from $4.95 to $6.95.

Books on contemporary fields of employment which give an account of the work, qualifications needed, educational requirements, salaries, and diverse opportunities. Fields covered include: astronautics; chemistry; commercial art; computer science; electronics; engineering; fashion; journalism; music; physics; science; sports; retailing; and medical sciences.

Encyclopedia of Careers and Vocational Guidance, J. G. Ferguson Publishing Co., 6 North Michigan Ave., Chicago, Ill. 60602. 1972. 2 volume set $39.50.

Volume I contains 71 general articles describing every major career field. Each article describes the nature and basic functions of that field, gives a brief history, discusses present developments, trends, and future outlook, and defines the areas of opportunity and general prospects for employment and advancement. Volume II gives specific facts about over 650 occupations. All occupational categories follow the latest *Dictionary of Occupational Titles* Occupational Group Arrangement. Each occupational field is introduced with an overview and then each occupation is described in detail: entry requirements, necessary training and/or education, working conditions, employment outlook, beginning and future earnings, and sources of additional information. Each occupation is cross-referenced to the career fields in Volume I.

Goldenthal, Allan B., ed., *Your Career Selection Guide*, Simon & Schuster, Inc., Regents Publishing Company Division, 200 Park Ave. South, New York, N.Y. 10003, 1968. 128 pp. $1.95 (paperbound); $3.95 (clothbound).

A detailed guide to aptitudes and scholastic prerequisites for 100 occupations now in high demand.

Handbook of Job Facts, Science Research Associates, Inc., 259 East Erie St., Chicago, Ill. 60611. 1972. 134 pp. $5.75.

Contains concise summaries of basic data on 300 major occupations— brief description of the typical duties and functions; the main industries and areas of the U.S. in which the occupation is found; educational and training requirements; and data on earnings.

Job Fact Sheets, Alumnae Advisory Center, Inc., 541 Madison Ave., New York, N.Y. 10022. 50¢ each.

A series of 75 titles on jobs from accounting to X-ray technology. Each job fact sheet contains information for job hunters, career counselors, and students on *what* and *where* the jobs are, the education needed, kinds of employers, and sources of further information.

The Job Family Series, Science Research Associates, Inc., 259 East Erie St., Chicago, Ill. 60611. 44 pp. each. $1.50 each, $24.25 per set.

A series of 20 booklets. Jobs are described in occupational categories, such as Jobs in Technical Work, Jobs in Selling, Jobs in the Performing Arts, Jobs in Clerical Work, etc.

Norton, Joseph L., ed., *On the Job*, J. G. Ferguson Publishing Co., 6 North Michigan Ave., Chicago, Ill. 60602. 1970. $7.95.

A collection of 65 actual work diaries compiled over a ten year period, giving the feel, the pace, the flavor of a job. Each shows the many facets of a job that a worker experiences day-to-day, but which are rarely told to young people during the time when they are making career decisions.

Occupational Briefs, Chronicle Guidance Publications, Inc., Moravia, N.Y. 13118. 4 pp. 35¢, 8 pp. 50¢.

Over 470 occupational briefs describing jobs ranging from accountant to zoologist. History of the occupation, work performed, working conditions, qualifications required, training requirements, and hours and earnings are covered in each brief. (This is revised every four years.)

Occupational Briefs, Science Research Associates, Inc., 259 East Erie St., Chicago, Ill. 60611. 49¢ per booklet.

These illustrated occupational briefs contain information on the major job areas. Each brief includes a description of the occupational field, qualifications, training required, earnings, opportunities, future outlook, advantages and disadvantages of the particular field, and selected references for further reading.

Occupational Outlook Handbook, 1972–73 Edition (Bulletin 1700), United States Department of Labor, Bureau of Labor Statistics. For sale by the Superintendent of Documents, United States Government Printing Office, Washington, D.C. 20402, or by the regional offices of the Bureau in Boston, New York, Philadelphia, Atlanta, Chicago, Kansas City, Dallas, and San Francisco. 879 pp. $6.25.

An "encyclopedia of careers" covering 800 occupations and 30 major industries. Information is included for each job on what the work is like, job prospects to 1980, training and educational requirements, working conditions, earnings, and chances for advancement.

VGM *Opportunities In:* Vocational Guidance Manuals, 235 East 45th St., New York, N.Y. 10017. Clothbound $3.75; paperbound $1.95.

A series of books dealing with 62 different occupations, including accounting; acting; foreign service; market research; sales; public relations; law enforcement; opticianry; environmental careers. Each book presents a comprehensive insight into all facets of the subject, the educational background required, and the opportunities for employment. A list of schools, job sources, and information sources is included in each book.

Zimmerman, O. T., and M. K. Zimmerman, *College Placement Directory*, Industrial Research Service, Inc., Masonic Building, Dover, N.H. 03820. $17.00 each issue.

This volume contains a list of more than 1,500 companies, giving the types of jobs each offers, as well as a listing of job classifications with names of companies offering jobs in each field. Companies are listed by state and city.

Careers in Accounting and Finance

Accounting for Your Future, United Business Schools Association, 1101 Seventeenth St., N.W., Washington, D.C. 20006.

Accounting Is Business Leadership, American Accounting Association, 1507 Chicago Avenue, Evanston, Ill. 60201.

Ankers, R. G., *Opportunities in An Accounting Career,* Vocational Guidance Manuals, Inc., 235 East 45th St., New York, N.Y. 10017.

Careers in Accounting, Accounting Careers Council, American Institute of CPA's, 666 Fifth Ave., New York, N.Y. 10019.

Careers in Financial Management and Controllership, Financial Executives Institute, 50 West 44th St., New York, N.Y. 10036.

Locklear, Edmond, Jr., *Your Career in Accounting,* Richards Rosen Press, Inc., 49 East 33rd St., New York, N.Y. 10016.

Management Accounting Opportunities Unlimited, National Association of Accountants, 505 Park Ave., New York, N.Y. 10022.

The Professional Practicing Accountant: Who Is He? What Does He Do? Public Accounting As A Career For You, National Society of Public Accountants, 1717 Pennsylvania Ave., N.W., Washington, D.C. 20006.

Wanted: Financial Executives, Financial Executive's Institute, 50 West 44th St., New York, N.Y. 10036.

Why Not Choose Accounting? American Women's Society of CPA's, 327 South La Salle St., Chicago, Ill. 60604.

Careers in Banking

A Career for Women in Banking, National Association of Bank Women, Inc., 111 East Wacker Dr., Chicago, Ill. 60601.

Banking: An Opportunity for You, American Bankers Association, 1120 Connecticut Ave., N.W., Washington, D.C. 20036.

Banking Opportunities and the College Graduate, American Bankers Association, 1120 Connecticut Ave., N.W., Washington, D.C. 20036.

Careers in the Trust Departments of Banks and Trust Companies, Institute of Research, 610 South Federal St., Chicago, Ill. 60605.

Career Opportunities in Consumer Finance, National Consumer Finance Association, 1000 Sixteenth St., N.W., Washington, D.C. 20036.

Occupation Briefs in Banking, American Bankers Association, 90 Park Ave., New York, N.Y. 10016.

Savings and Loan Occupational Guides, American Savings and Loan Institute, 111 East Wacker Dr., Chicago, Ill. 60601.

Careers in Computers and Data Processing

Bibby, D. L., *Your Future in the Electronics Computer Field*, Richards Rosen Press, Inc., 29 East 21st St., New York, N.Y. 10010.

Carroll, J. M., *Careers and Opportunities in Computer Science*, E. P. Dutton & Co., 201 Park Ave. South, New York, N.Y. 10003.

Computer Careers, American Federation of Information Processing Societies, 210 Summit Ave., Montvale, N.J. 07645.

IBM Engineer: A Lifetime of Opportunities, International Business Machines Corp., Old Orchard Rd., Armonk, N.Y. 10504.

IBM: The Problem Solvers, International Business Machines Corp., Old Orchard Rd., Armonk, N.Y. 10504.

Programmers, Science Research Associates, Inc., 259 East Erie St., Chicago, Ill. 60611.

Careers in Insurance

Anderson, K. L., *Invitation to A Career*, Research and Review Service of America, Inc., 3500 De Pauw Blvd., Indianapolis, Ind. 46206.

Careers in Insurance, American Mutual Insurance Alliance, 20 North Wacker Dr., Chicago, Ill. 60606.

Careers in Life Insurance, Institute of Life Insurance, 277 Park Ave., New York, N.Y. 10017.

Careers in Property and Liability, Institute of Life Insurance, 277 Park Ave., New York, N.Y. 10017.

Life Insurance Career Facts, Occidental Life Insurance Company of California, P.O. Box 54905, Terminal Annex, Los Angeles, Calif. 90054.

Sommer, A., and D. P. Kedzie, *Your Future in Insurance*, ARCO Publishing Co., Inc., 219 Park Ave. South, New York, N.Y. 10003.

Careers in International Business

Angel, J. L., *Looking for Employment in Foreign Countries Reference Handbook*, World Trade Academy Press, Inc., 50 East 42nd St., New York, N.Y. 10017.

Calvert, Robert Jr., *Your Future in International Service*, Richards Rosen Press, 29 East 21st St., New York, N.Y. 10017.

Casewit, C. W., *How To Get A Job Overseas*, Arco Publishing Co., Inc., 219 Park Ave. South, New York, N.Y. 10003.

Employment Abroad: Facts and Fallacies, International Group, Chamber of Commerce of the U.S., 1615 H St., N.W., Washington, D.C. 20006.

Liebers, Arthur, *How To Get The Job You Want Overseas*, Pilot Books, 347 Fifth Ave., New York, N.Y. 10017.

Careers in Management

Marting, Elizabeth, *Invitation to Achievement: Your Career in Management*, American Management Association, Inc., 135 West 50th St., New York, N.Y. 10020.

Careers in Marketing, Retailing, and Advertising

Advertising: Career of Action and Variety for Exceptional Men and Women, American Association of Advertising Agencies, 200 Park Ave., New York, N.Y. 10017.

Career As a Retail Merchandise Buyer, Institute of Research, 610 South Federal St., Chicago, Ill. 60605.

Careers in Industrial Advertising, Association of Industrial Advertisers, 271 Madison Ave., New York, N.Y. 10016.

Careers in National General Merchandise Chains, Institute of Research, 610 South Federal St., Chicago, Ill. 60605.

Jobs in Advertising, American Advertising Federation, 1225 Connecticut Ave., Washington, D.C. 20036.

Manufacturer's Representative, Careers, Inc., P.O. Box 135, Largo, Fla. 33540.

Marketing Research Workers, Science Research Associates, Inc., 259 East Erie St., Chicago, Ill. 60611.

Opportunities in Market Research, Vocational Guidance Manuals, 800 Second Ave., New York, N.Y. 10021.

Opportunity In Retailing, National Retail Merchants Association, 100 West 31st St., New York, N.Y. 10001.

Orent, Norman B., *Your Future in Marketing*, Richards Rosen Press, 29 East 21st St., New York, N.Y. 10017.

Scott, George A., *Your Future in Retailing*, Richards Rosen Press, 29 East 21st St., New York, N.Y. 10017.

Singer, Jules B., *Your Future in Advertising*, Richards Rosen Press, 29 East 21st St., New York, N.Y. 10010.

Supermarket Manager, Careers, Inc., P.O. Box 135, Largo, Fla. 33540.

Willinsky, Harriet, *Careers and Opportunities in Retailing*, National Retail Merchants Association, 100 West 31st St., New York, N.Y. 10001.

Your Career in Direct Mail Advertising, Direct Mail Advertising Association, Inc., 230 Park Ave., New York, N.Y. 10017.

Your Opportunities in Sales and Marketing, Marketing Executives-International, 630 Third Ave., New York, N.Y. 10017.

Careers in Personnel

Employment Interviewer, Careers, Inc., P.O. Box 135, Largo Florida 33540.

Employment Service Interviewers, Science Research Associates, Inc., 259 East Erie St., Chicago, Ill. 60611.

Employment Supervisor, Chronicle Guidance Publications, Inc., Moravia, N.Y. 13118.

Job Analyst, Chronicle Guidance Publications, Inc., Moravia, N.Y. 13118.

Mack, David, *Opportunities in Personnel Management,* Vocational Guidance Manuals, 235 East 45th St., New York, N.Y. 10017.

Personnel: A Challenging Career in Management, International Association of Personnel Women, 358 Fifth Ave., New York, N.Y. 10017.

Personnel Administration Occupations, Careers, Inc., P.O. Box 135, Largo, Fla. 33540.

Personnel Supervisor, Chronicle Guidance Publications, Inc., Moravia, N.Y. 13118.

Pond, John H., *Your Future in Personnel Work,* Richards Rosen Press, Inc., 29 East 21st St., New York, N.Y. 10010.

Careers in Production

Career as a Production Manager in Manufacturing, Institute of Research, 610 South Federal St., Chicago, Ill. 60605.

Industrial Designer, Chronicle Guidance Publications, Inc., Moravia, N.Y. 13118.

Careers in Public Relations

An Occupational Guide to Public Relations, Public Relations Society of America, 845 Third Ave., New York, N.Y. 10022.

Careers in Purchasing

Purchasing Agent, Chronicle Guidance Publications, Inc., Moravia, N.Y. 13118.

Your Career in Purchasing Management, National Association of Purchasing Management, Inc., 11 Park Place, New York, New York 10007.

Careers in Owning Your Own Business

Allen, L. L., *Starting and Succeeding in Your Own Small Business*, Grosset & Dunlap, 51 Madison Ave., New York, N.Y. 10010.

Baumbach, C., P. Kelley, and K. Lawyer, *How To Organize and Operate A Small Business*, Prentice-Hall, Inc., Englewood Cliffs, N.J. 07632.

Dibble, Donald M., *Up Your Own Organization*, Entrepreneur Press, Mission Station, Drawer 2759, Santa Clara, Calif. 95051.

Metz, Robert, *Franchising: How To Select A Business of Your Own*, Hawthorne Books, Inc., 260 Madison Ave., New York, N.Y. 10010.

Ota, L., and N. M. Rodgers, *How To Establish and Operate Your Own Small Business: Thirty-Nine Varieties*, The Business Library, 34 Commerce St., Newark, N.J. 07102.

Shreier, J. W., and J. L. Komives, *The Entrepreneur and New Enterprise Formation: A Resource Guide*, Center for Venture Management, 811 East Wisconsin Ave., Milwaukee, Wis. 53202.

Small Business Administration. This federal government agency with offices in all major cities publishes a wide array of booklets on how to found and organize a business in various fields. These booklets can be obtained at any Small Business Administration office or by writing to the Small Business Administration, Washington, D.C. 20416.

Winter, Elmer L., *Your Future in Your Own Business*, Richards Rosen Press, 29 East 21st St., New York, N.Y. 10017.

Methods of Seeking a Job

Angel, J. L., *Employment Opportunities for the Handicapped*, World Trade Academy Press, 50 East 42nd St., New York, N.Y. 10017. 1969. 411 pp. $12.50.

Angel, J. L., *Why and How to Prepare an Effective Job Resume*, World Trade Academy Press, 50 East 42nd St., New York, N.Y. 10017. 506 pp. 1973. $12.50.

Blackledge, Walter L., et al., *You and Your Job*, South-Western Publishing Co., 501 Madison Ave., Cincinnati, Ohio 45227. 1967. 103 pp. $1.96.

Calvert, Robert, Jr., and John E. Steele, *Planning Your Career*, McGraw-Hill Book Co., Inc., 330 West 42nd St., New York, N.Y. 10036. 1963. $3.75 (hard cover), $1.95 (paperback).

Do You Want a Job? U.S. Department of Labor, Manpower Administration, Washington, D.C. 1971. 8 pp. 10¢ Available from the Superintendent of Documents, U.S. Government Printing Office, Washington, D.C. 20402.

Dreese, Mitchell, *How to Get THE Job*, Science Research Associates, Inc., 259 East Erie St., Chicago, Ill. 60611. 1971. 52 pp. $1.02.

A Guide for Job Seekers, American Management Associations, 135 West 50th St., New York, N.Y. 10020. Reprint. $1.00.

Merchandising Your Job Talents, U.S. Department of Labor, Manpower Administration, Washington, D.C., 1971. 26 pp. 25¢. For sale by the Superintendent of Documents, U.S. Government Printing Office, Washington, D.C. 20402.

Miller, Theron F., *How to Write a Job-Getting Resume*, Vantage Press, 516 West 34th St., New York, N.Y. 10001. 1967. 122 pp. $3.75.

Resumes That Get Jobs, Arco Publishing Co., Inc., 219 Park Ave. South, New York, N.Y. 10003. 160 pp. 1967. $2.00 (paper); $5.00 (cloth).

Worthy, James C., *What Employers Want*, Science Research Associates, Inc., 259 East Erie St., Chicago, Ill. 60611. 1971. 46 pp. $1.02.

glossary of key terms and concepts

acceptances, trade or bank (See trade, or bank, acceptances.)

account payable The amount a company owes to a supplier for goods or services received but not yet paid for.

account receivable The amount a buyer owes a business for goods or services delivered to him but not yet paid for.

accrued taxes Taxed owed but not yet paid.

acid test, or quick assets, ratio The ratio of cash plus accounts receivable to current liabilities. It measures the ratio of assets that can be turned into cash quickly to current liabilities—liabilities that are normally expected to require cash in a short time.

advances, Federal Reserve Bank Lending funds by a District Federal Reserve Bank to a member commercial bank on the security of notes, securities, or other valuable business paper.

AFL/CIO The American Federation of Labor/Congress of Industrial Organization which is the largest federation of labor organizations in the United States.

agricultural support programs Programs provided by the federal government to aid agriculture through subsidizing crops and crop prices to assure farmers a fair and adequate income for their produce.

alternative, selecting an In selecting an alternative from among others, the decision maker will compare and an-alyze the various alternatives to select the one which shows the most promise of achieving the goal desired.

analytic process The removal of one desired element from others with which it is found.

antitrust laws A series of laws, starting with the Sherman Act of 1890, passed by the federal government to forbid attempts by business firms to develop monopolies or to restrain trade (that is, to eliminate competition through mergers and other kinds of combinations). Essentially these laws were designed to enforce competition in business (except public utilities).

appraisal of managers (See managerial appraisal.)

arbitration The procedure for resolving a dispute under the terms of a labor contract in which an objective third party hears both sides of the case and makes a decision, often representing a compromise of the opposing positions.

arithmetic/logic The mechanical operations including adding, subtracting, multiplying, dividing, and comparing.

authority, centralization and decentralization, balancing of Balancing requires a definite determination of what decision-making authority must be kept at the top of the company and what can be safely decentralized. In a well-balanced company, the top group retains authority over those matters necessary to assure or safeguard the company's future.

authority, centralization of The tendency to hold decision-making authority at the top of an organization or company.

authority, decentralization of The tendency to disperse decision-making authority widely throughout an organization or company.

authority, delegation of (See delegation of authority.)

authority, factors determining the degree of centralization or decentralization Centralization or decentralization of authority in any organization or company will be dependent on (1) costliness of certain decisions; (2) the need for uniform policies; (3) the size of a company; (4) the history of a business; (5) the attitudes and beliefs of top managers; (6) external forces such as government regulations and labor union rules.

autocratic leadership (See leadership, autocratic.)

automated warehouse A distribution center in which the paper work and goods selection system are automated.

automation The process of using machines which run themselves.

balance of trade The difference between what a nation pays for its exports and what it receives from its imports.

balance sheet The accounting statement that summarizes the relationship of assets (the left side of the balance sheet), on the one hand, and the claims against these assets by creditors or owners (the right side of the balance sheet), on the other.

batch processing Computer operators "save up" the work and run all of one kind of work at the same time.

"bear" market A market for securities where prices are falling and buyers are not interested in buying securities.

binary code A process using the unlimited yes-no system which uses only two digits: zero and one.

"blue sky" laws State laws aimed at regulating the issuance of new securities to assure that when a stock or bond is issued, the issuing company sells something of reasonable value and gets something of reasonable value in return for the sale.

board of directors A group of individuals given the power by law and by vote of stockholders to manage a corporation. Usually only common stockholders are given the right to vote for directors, although preferred stockholders may sometimes be given this right.

board of governors The governing body of the Federal Reserve System with seven members all appointed by the president of the United States to serve single, 14-year terms.

bond discount Although bonds carry a promise to pay the holder a specified interest rate and the face amount of the bond at some time in the future, a bond may sell at any time for less than this amount, generally because the interest rate the bond pays is below the interest investors are willing to accept. The amount by which the market price of a bond is below its face value is referred to as bond discount.

bondholder trustee (See bonds.)

bond premium Although bonds carry a promise to pay the holder a specified interest rate and the face amount of the bond at some time in the future, a bond may sell at any time for more than this amount, generally because the interest rate the bond pays is above the interest rate investors are willing to accept. The amount by which the market price of a bond is above its face value is referred to as bond premium.

bonds Bonds are debts of a corporation evidenced by the existence of a special contract between the corporation and a trustee for the bondholders (who have loaned money to the corporation). This contract specifies, among other things, the specific credit position of bondholders and what the corporation may or may not do in its operations. These provisions are designed to assure protection of the bondholders' credit position. (See also mortgage bond, collateral trust bond, debenture bond, sinking fund bond, and convertible bond.)

bond yield "Current yield" is the amount of interest, in dollars, a bond pays divided by the price at which it can be bought on the market. "Yield to maturity" is the interest an investor will receive taking into account the interest in dollars paid, the amount of money the bond will repay when it is due, the years the investor will have to wait for repayment, and the present market price of the bond.

brokerage houses Firms whose business is to buy and sell issued corporation and other securities on behalf of investors who wish to buy or sell them.

budgeting capital expenditures A plan for a business showing how much, for what purposes, and when expenditures will be made for such capital items as buildings, machinery, office equipment, and computers.

budgeting sales, expenses, and profits A plan for a business showing how much it will receive from sales in a given period of time (usually a month, three months, or a year), what its expenses will be, and what its profits should be. (See also budgets.)

budgets Statements of plans and expected results expressed in numerical terms.

"bull" market A market for securities where prices are rising and buyers are interested in purchasing securities.

business environment (See environment of business.)

business, the business of business Economic enterprises, whether large or small and whether privately or publicly owned, have as their purpose (or "business") the production or sale of products or services to people who want and can buy them.

business responsiveness The need for any business to respond to the total environment in which it operates, whether the environmental elements be economic or market, technological developments, social and cultural forces, the political setting, or legal pressures and requirements.

business trust A form of business ownership where individuals (trustees) hold actual ownership of the business but hold it for the benefit of investors to whom the trustees issue certificates of beneficial interest (trust shares). Since the trustees actually own the business, the individual investors have limited liability and can usually freely transfer their shares.

business, what a business is Any person, group, company, or government department or agency whose purpose is to produce or sell products or services.

capital Sometimes used to imply the buildings, machinery, tools, equipment, materials, and money a business must have to operate; sometimes used to describe the amount of ownership in a business.

capital expenditures Expenditures for investing in such long-term company assets as new buildings, machinery, and equipment.

capital invested in a business This usually refers to such things as buildings, tools, machines, and materials which people need in order to produce a product or service.

capitalism Ordinarily used to apply to an economic system which relies predominantly on individual initiation of business enterprise and private ownership of business. It is thus used to imply private capitalism, although, strictly speaking, government-owned businesses could be called capitalistic in the sense that they use capital in their business operations.

cash dividends Payments made in cash to common or preferred stockholders as compensation for their investment in the company.

cashier's check A check written by a bank and signed by one of its officers, the cashier, payable to a designated party.

centralization of authority (See authority, centralization of.)

certificates of deposit Deposits which are made by business firms or individuals for a certain period of time, bear interest, and usually cannot be withdrawn during the certain period of time without the depositor suffering a penalty.

certified check A business or personal check which a bank stamps "certified" and immediately deducts the amount of the check from the issuer's account to assure the person receiving the check that funds are available to cover it.

chain store One of a group of stores which operate under one name and order merchandise through a bulk-buying home office.

changing labor markets Changes are taking place in the composition of the population which are sure to have definite impact on the traditional ideas about age, education, sex, and work patterns.

charts A medium for explaining, interpreting, or presenting complicated collections of quantitative data in a simplified manner by the use of lines, bars, or other graphic devices.

civil rights acts Legislation which made it illegal to discriminate against any person on the basis of race, color, religion, sex, age, or national origin.

class rates Rates used by the railroads to assign cost and value of service on more than 10,000 classes of goods.

clearinghouse A central agency to which checks drawn on one bank in favor of another bank may be sent. Since banks have checks drawn on and in favor of each other, the clearinghouse is a means by which checks can be collected and charged without a significant amount of money changing hands between banks. In other words, many checks cancel each other out.

closed shop A business where a person is not hired unless he is a union member.

CLU A Chartered Life Underwriter which is a certification awarded by the American College of Life Underwriters for individuals in the field who pass a series of qualifying examinations.

coinsurance Insurance in which the businessman agrees to maintain insurance equal to some specified percentage of the value of his property in return for lower premium rates.

collateral Any kind of valuable property pledged as security for a loan. (See secured loans.)

collateral trust bond A bond issue in which the principal security for bondholders is the pledging of certain stocks and bonds of other companies held by the borrowing corporation.

collective bargaining The process of negotiating a labor agreement between management and labor representatives.

commercial banks Banks that specialize in (1) accepting deposits of money and making funds readily available to depositors on demand and (2) lending money, usually for short terms, to businessmen and individuals. They also normally offer many other banking services.

commercial buyer Those organizations which do not generally alter their purchases before resale. Many of the materials purchased are intended to be used up in the production of a service or resold in a retail store without significant change.

commercial finance companies Companies that help businesses of all kinds and sizes to finance their accounts receivable, sometimes purchasing the receivables at a discount and other times lending money to businesses on the security of their accounts receivable; these companies also make loans to businesses on the security of their inventories, machinery, or equipment.

commission brokers Brokers who buy and sell securities for individuals or other brokers and receive their compensation by charging a commission.

commitment, decision (See decision commitment.)

commodity rates Transportation rates set especially for certain items like iron, coal, or lumber which are shipped regularly and in volume.

common carriers Businesses selling transportation services. They hold themselves out to serve the public and are licensed and regulated by the government.

common stock A share of ownership in a corporation, evidenced by a certificate, which carries no preference and ordinarily carries with it rights to (1) vote for corporation directors; (2) share in earnings of the corporation, subject to priorities of creditors and preferred stockholders, when these earnings are declared as dividends; and (3) share in the assets of the corporation if it is liquidated, subject to prior claims of creditors and preferred shareholders.

communism In its original meaning, a political system of government, or public, ownership where people contribute to production of goods and services in accordance with their abilities and receive such goods and services in accordance with their needs. In

practice, communist societies tend to represent not only government ownership of business and other wealth but also enforce many restrictions on the freedom of individuals.

company "insiders" Company officers, directors, and anyone else owning more than 10 percent of its stock.

comparative advantage The concept that each country should produce that which it can produce most economically and thereby get the most from its material and human resources, even if it imports items which it could produce at a lower cost.

comparison shoppers Shoppers who check on the price and quality of merchandise in competing stores.

compensating balances The practice of banks to require that a borrower maintain in his deposit account a minimum balance equal to a percentage of the loan. This, of course, means that borrowers are actually borrowing less than the full amount of the loan while paying interest on the full amount of the loan. It is actually a means of increasing the rate of interest.

competition The situation in which persons strive among each other to sell the most at the best price and profit. (See pure competition.)

competition, effective Competition is said to be effective when suppliers of goods and services are in open and free rivalry with each other for customers, and where customers are in open and free rivalry for the products and services of suppliers.

competition, responsible Competition is said to be responsible when it is fair, does not ruthlessly destroy or unfairly discriminate against competitors, and is socially acceptable and ethical.

competition, role of Competition, or rivalry, in business is designed to assure that both producers and consumers will be protected against unreasonable prices, poor quality, or inadequate service and that consumers will obtain the products and services they want at the lowest possible prices.

computer control The instructions which are stored in the memory and brought forward when needed to tell the computer the steps to take.

computer hardware The machinery of computers.

computer input The activity by which the computer receives the information and instructions it needs to do any required job.

computer languages Collections of numbers (or computer words) which the machine is set to understand.

computer output The function by which the computer's storehouse of memory becomes usable to men or to other machines. Sometimes called "printout."

computer software Ideas, systems, programs, and methods required to run the computer machinery or the hardware.

consequential loss An indirect loss which results from the loss of the use of an asset—such as the loss of income while fire damage is being repaired.

consumer finance companies Companies that specialize in making personal loans to individuals for any purpose.

contract carriers Transportation businesses that contract for specific jobs rather than just carrying whatever is offered it.

control, computer (See computer control.)

controlling or management control Assuring that plans succeed by watching what is happening, detecting errors and misses, and taking action to get back on the intended course; making sure that things go as intended.

control loop (See management control loop.)

control process The basic control process involves (1) establishing standards, (2) measuring performance against standards, and (3) taking action to correct deviations from standards.

controls, tailored (See tailored controls.)

control through return on investment An overall type of control that measures a company division or department on its ability to earn a profit on the investment placed in it. This is done by showing profit as a percentage of the assets the division or department uses in its operations.

convertible bond Bonds issued with the provision that the holders may trade (convert) them for the corporation's stock at an agreed upon price or at an agreed upon number of shares per $1,000 bond.

cooling-off period An 80-day suspension of any strike that would threaten the public interest. Under the Taft-Hartley Act, the president has the authority to call for such a period in "national emergencies."

cooperative associations or cooperatives A form of business ownership where members share in profits—after payment of interest on their investment—in accordance with the amount of business each member does with the cooperative association.

copyright monopolies By giving authors or publishers the exclusive right to own, sell, or otherwise use a written work, the government gives the copyright holder a monopoly position.

corporation An artificial being, or "person," endowed by law with most of the rights, powers, and obligations of natural persons—among these, the rights to own property, incur debts, and be sued for damages. Because of the legal "fiction of the corporation as a person," a corporation is the proprietor, or owner, of an incorporated business.

corporation charter The contract between a state and the individual persons setting up a corporation authorizing the creation of a corporation.

cost of goods sold or **cost of production** The record of what goods cost to produce. This includes (1) the cost of materials used; (2) the cost of labor directly utilized in the production of a good or service (direct labor); and (3) overhead or "burden" costs involved in production, such as supervision, electricity, production machine maintenance, and labor "fringes."

cost-push inflation A situation in which wage settlements are higher than labor productivity, causing businesses to raise prices—which, in turn, reduces the buying power of higher wages, again causing a demand for higher wages and creating an upward spiral.

cowboy capitalism The term describing methods used in achieving quick and easy profits.

CPCU A Chartered Property and Casualty Underwriter which is a designation awarded by the American Institute for Property and Liability Underwriters for individuals in the field who pass a series of qualifying examinations.

CPM Critical Path Method is a planning and control technique similar in its essentials to PERT. (See PERT.)

CPU The Central Processing Unit which controls the sequence and pacing of all operations.

craft union Unions made up of individuals with special skills which may have taken them some time to acquire (for example, electricians, plumbers, and carpenters).

credit An accounting term indicating a transaction that reduces assets, reduces expenses, increases sales, increases liabilities, or increases net worth—in other words, a transaction that reduces the left-hand side of a balance sheet or increases the right-hand side of a balance sheet.

credit rating The credit standing of an individual or a business. There are some credit agencies, like Dun & Bradstreet, that regularly rate the credit standing of a business.

credit unions Cooperative savings associations of people who have a common tie, such as a company for which they work or a union to which they belong. Depositors, or members, own the cooperative, and loans are normally made only to members.

critical, or **limiting, factor** This is the factor, or factors, in a problem that makes the most difference in the solution of the problem.

critical path In a PERT or CPM network, this is the path of tasks (or milestones or events) that take the longest time and are therefore the most important in terms of accomplishing a program or project on time.

crudeness of management knowledge Management knowledge is crude and inexact due to (1) the exceptional complexities of the manager's job and the many variables he must deal with; and (2) the small amount of research and development that has been done in the field.

cumulative or **noncumulative preferred stock** A preferred stock is cumulative if any amount of preferred dividends not paid in a given year accumulates and must be paid at some time in the future before common stockholders can be paid. A preferred stock is noncumulative when any preferred dividends not paid in a given year are *not* allowed to accumulate from year to year.

cumulative voting A system of stockholder voting in a corporation where stockholders are given the right to have as many votes for directors as the number of shares each holds multiplied by the number of directors to be elected. In this way a stockholder can accumulate his votes for one or more directors, and minority stockholders may be able to elect one or more directors.

current assets An asset is classified as "current" if it is expected that it will be turned into cash within a year.

current liabilities A liability is classified as "current" if it is expected that it must be paid within a year.

current ratio The ratio of current assets to current liabilities.

customer organization Grouping activities in a department in accordance with the type of customer being served, as in the case of an industrial sales department or a homeowners store.

custom product A product specially produced to meet the exact specifications of a specific customer.

data versus information Data—in the form of figures and computer printout sheets—are not necessarily information, since nothing can be called information unless it informs someone.

debenture bond A bond issue in which no specific property is pledged as security—the security being the earning power of the borrowing corporation plus the security of the corporation's assets not otherwise pledged against loans.

debit An accounting term indicating a transaction that increases assets, increases expenses, reduces sales, reduces liabilities, or reduces net worth—in other words, a transaction that increases the left-hand side of a balance sheet or reduces the right-hand side of a balance sheet.

debt to net worth ratio The ratio of the total debt of a company to stockholders' equity, or proprietorship, of the company.

decentralization of authority (See authority, decentralization of.)

decision commitment Since every decision involves, among other things, a commitment of money, man-hours, direction, raw materials, or reputation, the decision maker should attempt to assure, as best he can, the fulfillment of decisions made *today*.

deficit A state in a business when the net worth of a company (assets less liabilities) is less than zero.

delegation as an art As an art, delegation depends heavily on personal attitudes: (1) a willingness to give others a chance to make decisions; (2) a willingness to let go of decision-making authority; (3) a willingness to see subordinates make mistakes; and (4) the ability to overcome a fear of loss of control by exercising managerial control effectively.

delegation of authority The granting of authority by a superior to a subordinate to make decisions within the power of the superior.

delegation principles Those principles underlying delegation of authority are: (1) delegate by results expected; (2) maintain unity of command (each person should have one boss); (3) responsibility is absolute and cannot be delegated; (4) authority and responsibility should be equal; (5) decisions should be made at a point where necessary delegated authority exists and not above.

demand curve A graph of the demand schedule. The line shows the number of units which will be demanded (that is, purchased) at each price level.

demand deposits Deposits made by individuals or companies that can be withdrawn on demand. Interest is normally not paid on these deposits.

demand, or sight, drafts A draft payable whenever a payee presents it to the drawee. (See drafts.)

depletion The cost of reduction of assets of a business due to bringing up certain natural resources (for example, oil or minerals) in the ground owned by the business.

deposit insurance   (See FDIC.)

depreciation   The cost of reduction of assets of a business due to wear or obsolescence.

digital computers   Computers which deal solely with simple digits, in the same way a simple adding machine does but with much greater capacity and speed.

direct control   This is control aimed at measuring and assuring the quality of those in charge of managing a company. It is referred to as "direct" since most other controls are based on correcting the mistakes of managers, and the best qualified managers make fewest of these mistakes.

direct loss   The damage or destruction of property which involves the loss of the value of an asset.

discount   A method of charging interest where the lender subtracts the interest due on a loan and submits to the borrower the loan amount less discount.

distribution center   A center for the reorganization of goods. Large quantities of goods are usually delivered to it, processed, then sent on to various customers.

dividends   Payments to stockholders of money or other things of value from the earnings of a corporation, if and when they are declared by the corporation board of directors.

dividends   (See cash dividends and stock dividends.)

double-entry bookkeeping   The essence of accounting and the balance sheet is the fact that every item of property has a claim, or right, against it; thus, every business transaction that increases or reduces property must have a corresponding effect on some property right. Double-entry bookkeeping recognizes these two kinds of events.

double taxation   In the case of a business corporation, the corporation pays income taxes on its profits; then, when profits are distributed as dividends to stockholders, they pay income tax on the dividends (beyond a small amount that is exempt from taxes), thus resulting in double taxes on the same profits.

Dow-Jones Bond Averages   An index of bond prices comprised of an average of 40 selected bonds equally divided between high-quality railroad bonds, second-quality railroad bonds, public utility bonds, and industrial bonds.

Dow-Jones Stock Averages   An index of stock prices, published since 1884 and comprised of an average of 65 leading stocks, of which 30 are industrial stocks, 20 are transportation company stocks, and 15 are public utility company stocks.

drafts   An order made in writing by one party (the "drawer") addressed to a second party (the "drawee") ordering the drawee to pay to a third party (the "payee") a certain sum of money. As can be seen, an ordinary bank check is a draft.

economic environment   The economic or market factors that influence business operations, such as customer desires and ability to pay for goods and services, the demand by customers for lowest possible prices, the availability and cost of capital, the level of productivity in a society, the quality of entrepreneurship, the availability of intelligent and able managers, and the size of markets.

economic system   The system of organizations utilizing land, labor, and capital to produce, distribute, and exchange goods and services to meet the needs and wants of consumers in any kind of a society. This description of an economic system clearly implies its task—to use the resources of society to meet the needs of society.

education as investment   Due to the

increased value of education, many firms and individuals have found that money spent on education will bring about increased productivity, efficiency, and income.

effective competition (See competition, effective.)

entrepreneurship The ability of a person to see a business opportunity, to get together the capital he needs to take advantage of the opportunity, and to start a business, taking the risks of failure with the hope to reap the gains of success.

entry into, and abandonment of, service Government regulation of many businesses, particularly public utilities and transportation companies, requires permission to enter into, expand, or abandon facilities of these businesses. This regulation is designed to assure that customers get adequate and responsible service.

environmental control laws Laws passed by the federal government, as well as by many state and local agencies, to protect people against such environmental nuisances or dangers as pollution of air and water, noise pollution, chemical or health hazards.

environment of business The conditions external to a business which affect its operations. These include market and economic factors, as well as those technological, social, political, and ethical factors that influence a business.

environment, social and cultural Those factors influencing a person or a business operation which arise from people's attitudes, desires, degrees of intelligence and education, beliefs, and customs.

equity (in property) (See ownership.)

European economic community The organization comprised of Belgium, France, Italy, Luxembourg, the Netherlands, West Germany, Great Britain, Denmark, and Ireland which agreed to conduct commerce upon equal tariff bases and to charge the same traiffs to outside nations.

experience as a manager's teacher Experience may be both expensive and dangerous as a teacher because what happened in the past will almost certainly not happen in the future. If a person distills experience to learn what *fundamentally* happened in the past and applies these conclusions to future problems, he may learn something valuable from experience.

exports The products or services sold from one country to other countries.

extractive process A process which is involved primarily in extracting some resource from its natural place—for example, mining gold or coal.

fabricating process The changing of the form of the material to make it more marketable.

factoring companies Companies that help finance businesses by purchasing their accounts receivable at a discount and handling the collection of these accounts from a firm's customers.

facts Accurate representations of historical occurrences.

FDIC The Federal Deposit Insurance Corporation which provides a specialized form of insurance protection on possible losses by bank depositors in case a bank should fail.

Federal Open Market Committee A committee, composed of the Board of Governors of the Federal Reserve System plus five representatives of the twelve District Federal Reserve Banks, with the power to require district banks to buy or sell government bonds and thereby decrease or increase the supply of money and credit in the nation.

Federal Reserve System Legislation passed in 1913 established a system of 12 District Federal Reserve Banks, privately owned, whose operations are under the control of the Federal Reserve Board. The principal function of the District Federal Reserve Banks is to make loans to commercial banks that are members of the system. District banks also influence money supply by the purchase and sale of government bonds.

Federal Trade Commission Act A national law, passed in 1914 and amended many times since, to enforce a degree of fair and responsible competition between businesses.

financial forecasts These are of two principal kinds: (1) a forecast of sales and other income items, less expenses, to anticipate business profits; and (2) a forecast of the cash that a business will receive (from investments, loans, from its operations, etc.) and the cash it will require (to meet such things as capital expenditures or dividend payments).

flexibility in planning Building into planning decisions an ability to change the direction of the decision without undue cost or embarrassment.

f.o.b. Stands for "free on board" meaning that transportation costs are paid by the producer to the point mentioned after the f.o.b. designation—for example, "f.o.b. manufacturer's loading dock" means that the buyer pays the freight from this point; or "f.o.b. buyer's loading dock" means the seller pays the freight to the buyer's loading dock.

franchising The business situation in which one person, the franchisor, develops an idea but, instead of operating the business himself, sells the rights to the idea, the methods, and frequently some supplies or materials to another person, the franchise, who opens his own local shop which must be almost identical to others in the franchised business.

free-rein leadership (See leadership, free-rein.)

full employment A situation in which, for all practical purposes, the entire labor force is employed.

future role of leisure The potential for increased leisure time due to increased automation, efficiency, and shorter working hours.

functional authority This exists where individuals in a staff, operating, or service department are given limited authority to prescribe some action for people who do not otherwise report to them.

functional organization Grouping activities in departments according to the things a company does. In manufacturing, for example, the first-level functional groupings in departments are likely to be production, marketing, finance, and engineering.

Gantt chart A bar chart developed by the management pioneer, Henry L. Gantt, that is used in scheduling work by showing major tasks to be done in accomplishing a program as a line (bar) set against the time required to do the task.

general partner (See partner, general.)

global village A term used to describe a shrinking world in which all citizens must learn to live together in cooperation.

goals as an interlocking network Since goals of departments and individuals must fit together if company goals are to be achieved, and since the accomplishment of one goal normally goes on while others are being achieved, the structure of goals represent not only a network but must also be interlocking.

goal of managers To manage in such a way that their groups achieve a "surplus" either in the sense of accomplishing an objective with the least input of human and material resources or accomplishing as much of an objective as possible with the human and material resources they have.

goals (See objectives.)

goods in process Raw materials or components which have been partially changed or processed but which need to be held in storage or on a production line until a later process converts them into finished goods.

government as information source The largest source of business information in the entire world, it provides extensive information which can help the businessman.

government fiscal policy Those actions of government that influence the availability of money and credit and the price level.

government tax policy The practice of government in levying taxes—both the amount of taxes collected and the way a government levies them—on business profits, on people's income, sales, or real estate values. The ways taxes are levied can have varying effects on business.

grid organization (See matrix organization.)

grievance An employee's demand that his employer honor a particular aspect of the labor agreement or of the law.

gross profit Net sales minus cost of goods sold.

group behavior and the manager Since groups of people develop certain attitudes and patterns of behavior and since all individuals have been members of many different groups, a manager will do well to understand the basic elements of the sciences of group behavior—sociology, social psychology, and anthropology.

guaranteed annual wage A program to maintain the income level of employed workers who are guaranteed a certain level of income over a year.

hardware, computer (See computer hardware.)

health and sanitation laws Government action to require certain standards of cleanliness in the manufacturing, packing, and handling of foods, drugs, and other items intended for human consumption.

human fulfillment wants The emerging American consumer placing emphasis not as much on subsistence needs as on psychological and social needs.

human resource accounting Rensis Likert's concept that human assets should be considered even more valuable than physical assets and should be accounted for in the same manner.

import quotas Government specification of the amount of a product that can be imported into a country, often with the purpose of protecting a nation's businesses from foreign competition.

imports The products or services bought by one country from other countries.

import tariffs Taxes levied on goods coming into a country, often with the purpose of protecting a nation's businesses from lower-cost foreign competition.

incentives Methods used by an employer to increase employee productivity while decreasing labor costs per produced unit—generally based on the idea that superior performance should receive superior compensation.

income before income taxes Income from operations less deductions or plus additions of various miscellaneous expenses and income.

income from operations Gross profit less operating expenses.

income statement A financial statement summarizing sales for a period of time and subtracting expenses incurred in the same period to arrive at a profit or loss for the period; often called a profit and loss statement or a statement of income.

incorporation laws Laws set up by the various states which provide for the establishing of a corporation and detail how persons may create a corporation.

industrial buyer The purchaser of goods for resale as is, or for resale in altered form, or for use in the production of another product.

industrial union   A union made up of individuals of a particular industry, such as automobile workers, retail clerks, and beverage workers.

information revolution   The current situation in which the supply of data is regularly increasing in geometric terms.

information   (See data versus information.)

information systems   A group of information sources which together provide a regular reporting of various data. On the basis of the report and analysis received, the system sends an appropriate message to the decision maker.

input, computer   (See computer input.)

insolvent   A state of a business when the value of creditor claims exceeds the value of property—where liabilities exceed assets.

insurable risk   A contingency which can be insured against at a reasonable price.

interest   Payments to creditors for the use of their money.

intermediate purchaser   One who purchases products to remake or resell them.

Interstate Commerce Act   The first such act was passed in 1887 with the purpose of regulating the country's railroads to avoid their use of monopoly power in charging shippers for transportation. Later amendments have extended this power to many other kinds of carriers and to almost every aspect of their businesses.

inventory   The raw materials, purchased parts, partly manufactured goods, finished goods, and other materials a company accumulates in order to produce or sell goods to customers.

inventory control   The elimination of waste in the quality of goods selected, the quantities ordered and used, and the expenditures for transportation, storage, and distribution to markets.

The attempt to maintain efficient levels of inventory to minimize the cost of storage and the danger of running out of stock.

inventory turnover   The ratio of sales to inventory. It measures the number of times a company inventory turns over in a year, or how fast the company is using and selling its inventory.

investment banking   (See investment banks.)

investment banks   Firms that specialize in handling the sale of stocks and bonds of other companies to public investors.

investment trust   A type of business trust where trustees invest funds, contributed by trust shareholders, in securities of various kinds, real estate mortgages, or other means of investment.

joint venture   A form of partnership—usually set up for special purposes and normally of short duration, ending when the purpose is accomplished—providing for one or a few general partners to manage the venture and including provisions that death or withdrawal of a partner does not affect the life of the partnership. Also called a syndicate. Also, a method by which two or more companies join together to form a company jointly owned by them in accordance with some agreed upon percentage of ownership; in foreign operations, the two or more companies are often from different countries.

labor agreement   A contract between management and union specifying terms and conditions of employment.

Labor Management Relations Act   An act containing a list of unfair labor practices in which unions are not allowed to engage.

laissez-faire leadership   (See leadership, free-rein.)

Landrum-Griffin Act   The act which requires every union to file a detailed financial report with the secretary of labor and make the information in this report available to members.

law of large numbers The situation in which the probability of something happening or not happening is high. Also known as the law of averages.

layoffs A situation in which a company is in a slump and does not require the services of all its employees. Workers are then terminated or "laid off."

leader behavior approach to leadership Analyzing leadership by identifying and studying various leader behavior patterns ("ways of doing things").

leadership The ability to influence people to strive willingly toward accomplishing group objectives.

leadership as a continuum The idea advanced by Tannenbaum and Schmidt that there is a range of effective leadership styles varying from a task-oriented and autocratic style to a highly people-oriented and democratic style; that the most effective leadership style varies from time to time and depends on the personality of the leader and the situation at a given time.

leadership, autocratic A behavior pattern of a leader where he tells people what to do and does not consult with them.

leadership, free-rein A behavior pattern of a leader where he gives his subordinates a minimum of guidance and direction, letting them "do their own thing." Often called "laissez-faire" leadership.

leadership, outside influences affecting Among the more important outside influences that may affect leader behavior are (1) the size of the organization; (2) the degree to which people interact in their work; (3) the compatibility of goals; (4) the level at which decision making is done; and (5) the health of the organization.

leadership, participative A behavior pattern of a leader where he consults with his subordinates and usually gets

their agreement on courses of action undertaken by the group.

leasing companies Companies that make a business of purchasing and leasing to others, primarily business firms, all kinds of assets, including buildings, equipment, machinery, automobiles, and computers. By renting such assets, a business need not spend its funds to have and use such assets.

legal environment The various laws and court-decision regulations imposed by government that influence our lives and business operations.

level of public utility and transportation rates The average of prices charged. By regulation, this level must be limited to an amount which will cover reasonable operating expenses of these businesses plus a fair return on the capital invested in the business.

liabilities In accounting terms, the claims of all kinds of creditors against property.

life insurance Coverage which promises to pay a specified benefit in the event of the death of the insured.

limited liability The case where an individual owner of a business is not liable for the debts of a company beyond the amount he has invested in it.

"limited" order An order to a broker to buy a security not higher than a specified price, or sell a security not lower than a specified price.

limited, or special, partner (See partner, limited or special.)

line of credit An arrangement made by a company or an individual with a bank, giving the company (individual) the right to borrow funds as needed up to a certain amount.

line graph A chart showing, by lines, the relationships, or patterns, of data.

line, in organizing Refers to an authority relationship where someone (a manager) is responsible for people by having the power to direct, make decisions for, and command these people. It is also called a supervisory relationship.

listed and unlisted stocks A stock is "listed" if it is listed on an organized exchange and may be traded through its facilities. Otherwise, the stock is referred to as "unlisted."

list price The price printed on the package or in a price list, the basic price from which discounts or allowances may be given.

long-term liabilities Liabilities are classified as "long term" if it is expected that they need not be paid for at least a year in the future.

McGregor's theory X A pattern of leadership which psychologist Douglas McGregor saw as being highly autocratic, based on the assumptions that (1) the average human being has an inherent dislike for work and will avoid it if he can; (2) most people must be coerced, controlled, and threatened with punishment to make them put forth adequate effort; (3) the average human being prefers to be directed, wishes to avoid responsibility, has relatively little ambition, and wants security above all.

McGregor's theory Y A pattern of leadership which psychologist Douglas McGregor saw as being highly permissive, based on the following assumptions: (1) The expenditure of physical and mental effort in work is as natural as play or rest; (2) people will exercise self-direction and self-control in the service of objectives to which they feel committed; (3) commitment to objectives is a function of the rewards associated with their achievement; (4) the average human being learns, under proper conditions, not only to accept but to seek responsibility; (5) the capacity to exercise a relatively high degree of imagination and creativity is widely, not narrowly, distributed in the population; (6) in modern industrial life, the intellectual potentialities of the average

human being are only partially utilized.

McMurray's benevolent autocrat A belief by psychologist Robert McMurry that an effective leader must be a person who makes decisions—one who is a kind of autocrat, but who also listens to his followers' opinions before he makes a decision.

maintenance All the activities which are required to keep equipment or other capital goods at a desired level of performance.

major elements in an environment for performance (1) Provision of objectives or goals and plans to reach them; (2) provision of a meaningful and understood structure of positions or roles; (3) provision for removal of obstructions to performance of people; (4) where people do things because they want to, find it worth their while to, or must; (5) where the importance of human motivations are recognized; (6) where it is recognized that many people have considerable knowledge of problems and solutions in their areas of work.

major traditional American beliefs Belief in private property, competition in business, and faith in better ways of doing things.

making a market in a security A broker making a market is one standing ready to purchase or sell a given security—usually, therefore, purchasing an inventory of it to have it available.

management control (See controlling.)

management as an art As all arts are the application of knowledge to achieve a desired result in practice, so management, or the act of managing, is an art—that is, practice.

management as a science Organized knowledge underlying and contributing to effective managing.

management control loop Seeing the process of management control as a closed loop involving (1) actual performance; (2) measuring actual performance; (3) comparing actual performance against standards; (4) identifying deviations from standards; (5) analyzing causes of deviations; (6) developing a program of corrective action to correct deviations; (7) implementing the program of correction; (8) and thereby attempting to obtain the desired performance.

manager A person responsible for the work of a group; an individual who has other persons reporting to him.

manager as a catalyst A manager gives an organization the extra element that makes a business (or other kind of enterprise) operate effectively.

manager's job Designing and maintaining an environment in which individuals reporting to him can work together effectively in groups toward the accomplishment of desired goals.

managerial appraisal The task of appraising the quality of a manager's work. In general, it is believed that managers can be appraised best by using two approaches: (1) appraising managers on their ability to set and to achieve verifiable objectives, or goals; and (2) appraising managers on their ability to manage.

managerial authority The power to exercise discretion, to use judgment in certain areas of an operation.

managerial grid An approach to identifying and studying effective leadership by developing a two-dimensional grid and rating managers, or leaders, on the basis of their concerns in two areas: concern for people and concern for production. From this comes the idea that the ideal manager, or leader, is highly concerned with both people and production.

managerial standardization The interchangeability of systems, processes, and methods.

managing by objectives A system of managing by which verifiable objec-tives are set for groups and individuals within a company so that people will know clearly what goals they are working toward and when they have accomplished them.

margin trading When a person purchases a stock or bond and borrows a portion of the purchase price from his broker, using the security purchased as collateral for the loan.

market grid A charting method which can assist the planner in locating the appropriate market needs which he may hope to meet.

marketing channel The sales and distribution route that goods follow as they move from producer to user.

marketing manager The person assigned the authority and responsibility of a company's total marketing approach.

market maturity The peak sales period of a product.

"market" order An order to a broker to buy or sell a security at the best prevailing market price.

market segmentation An attempt to identify and meet the specialized requirements of a given market segment.

Maslow's hierarchy of needs Psychologist Abraham Maslow found that human needs fall into an ascending order, starting with basic physiological needs (such as food, clothing, and shelter), then going to security or safety needs, then to affiliation or acceptance needs, then to esteem or status needs, and finally to the highest need, the need for self-actualization or pride of accomplishment.

matrix organization Sometimes called a grid organization, this is structuring activities in both functional and product (or project) organizational arrangements. It becomes a matrix when we consider that there are both functional and product managers, with various degrees of authority over activities performed by the same people.

mechanization To use a machine to do the work of a man or an animal.

mediation A neutral third party tries to persuade both parties in a dispute to reach a compromise. The mediator has no authority over either party.

meeting change by managers In order to meet change most effectively, a manager should forecast the future situation in which his decisions will operate so that he will have the time to prepare for change.

memory The part of the computer which stores and retains the information given it.

micromotion study A study using a motion picture camera which records the movements of a worker along with the face of a clock. The movements may be studied frame by frame to determine the exact amount of time and motion required for each activity.

milestones The specific tasks, or parts, of virtually all planning programs, or projects, that must be done in a certain order and at certain times.

mining partnerships A special type of partnership, usually with one general partner and a number of limited partners who own shares and can dispose of them to anyone without affecting the life of the business.

mobile managers The characteristic of many young managers to put individual advancement by frequent job changes ahead of loyalty to, and continuing with, a single firm.

monopolistic combinations The combination, by merger or otherwise, of two or more companies that may tend toward the development of a monopoly or severely limit competition.

monopolistic competition The case where otherwise competitive companies build in an element of monopoly in their businesses by making buyers believe that their individual products are different, whether they are or not.

This practice, often called product differentiation, is made possible by brand name, packaging, slight appearance changes, and advertising.

monopoly The case where there is a single supplier of a good or service.

monopsony The case where there is a single buyer for a good or service.

mortgage bond A bond issue in which the principal security for bondholders is the pledging of certain specified property, usually real estate.

motivation That which makes people strive to accomplish something.

multinational corporation A company which has plant operations, managerial personnel, and ownership in a variety of foreign countries.

mutual banks Banks where depositors are the owners. These are usually savings banks, although all federally chartered savings and loan associations and some state chartered associations are also mutually owned.

mutual companies A form of business ownership, similar to cooperatives, where the customers (policy owners in life insurance companies, depositors in savings and loan companies) own the business.

national banks Commercial banks chartered by the federal government.

National Labor Relations Act The act which gave employees the right to organize and made it mandatory for employers to bargain collectively in good faith with the representatives of the workers.

negotiable notes Promissory notes that a lender, or "payee," may sell to someone else who will have the same claim against a borrower that the original lender had. If the purchaser of a negotiable note may return it to the original lender for his money in case the original borrower does not pay, this is referred to as purchasing the note "with recourse."

net income or **profit** Income before income taxes less the taxes owed to various government agencies on this income. This is the true profit of a company after all expenses and taxes.

net sales Actual sales during a period less any returned merchandise, any discounts allowed for prompt payment, or any other allowance (such as a reduction in price for any defective goods) to arrive at the net amount a company receives from a sale.

networks for planning and control The interconnection of the various tasks, parts, or milestones of a planning program showing how each relates to another and how the start or completion of one depends on another.

net worth Claims of owners against property after claims of all kinds of creditors have been deducted. Also called capital or proprietorship.

New York Stock Exchange Index An average of all stocks traded on the New York Stock Exchange, using the number 50 as the index base representing average stock prices on December 31, 1965 and moving the index up or down since that time as the average of stock prices move up or down.

nonprofit corporation A corporation set up, usually to own and operate charitable, religious, educational, or social organizations, and not to make a profit.

no par value A share of stock with no stated value, indicating only that the share is what it really is, a pro rata portion of the ownership of a corporation.

Norris–La Guardia Act The act which placed severe restrictions upon the use of court injunctions intended to curb, or limit, union activities and outlawed yellow-dog contracts.

note receivable An amount owed to a company or individual and evidenced by a note promising to pay.

objectives (or goals) The end points toward which plans are aimed; the results expected from plans.

objectives, verifiable An objective or goal is verifiable when a person can tell at some specified time in the future whether he has accomplished it.

odd-lot dealers Brokers who buy or sell stocks in "round lots" (usually 100 shares) and buy from, or sell to, other brokers such stocks in smaller lots, or "odd lots." For this service, odd-lot dealers receive a special commission.

oligopoly The case where there are so few sellers in a market that what any one of them does to influence buyers will be immediately and definitely felt by others.

operating expenses In an accounting statement, these include various expenses not directly related to the cost of actually producing a good or service —expenses such as rent, most utilities, engineering, sales expenses, insurance, depreciation of buildings, accounting expenses, and the expenses of the general managers and officers of a company.

orientation A period of introduction in which a new employee is informed as to company policy and practices.

organizational role A person's organizational role should include (1) verifiable goals; (2) end-result areas for which he is responsible; (3) a specified area of discretion (authority) he can exercise; and (4) the needed information and tools to perform tasks.

organization as an intentional structure of roles An effective organization structure must be intentionally, rather than accidentally, structured so that roles people fill will fit together and contribute effectively to achieving a company's objectives.

organization levels As managers have more people reporting to them than they can effectively manage, subordinate managers must be appointed.

Each level of managers is referred to as an organization level.

output, computer (See computer output.)

overall control A technique of control that measures the overall operation of a division or department of a company, such as an integrated product division that has its own engineering, manufacturing, and marketing activities.

over-the-counter markets A system by which brokers buy and sell securities for investors without the use of a security exchange, but rather through an electronic information system whereby brokers can find who has certain stocks and bonds for sale, who wishes to buy, and at what price.

ownership What a person owns are rights to something valuable—cash, buildings, machinery and equipment, materials, or other items of marketable value—*less* the claims of others, usually lenders, against these rights. Ownership may also be referred to as equity.

participating preferred stock A preferred stock which participates with common stocks in the earnings of a company, when these are declared as dividends. It usually participates only after common stockholders have received dividends equal to the amount preferred stockholders first receive.

participative leadership (See leadership, participative.)

partner, general A partner who, regardless of the percentage of ownership in a partnership, has authority to act as an agent for the partnership, normally participates in its management, and is liable as an individual for all of the debts of the partnership (in other words, his personal liability for partnership debts is unlimited).

partner, limited or special A partner in a partnership who, in accordance with a specific agreement, usually contributes capital and shares in profits

in accordance with some agreed upon ratio, but whose liability for loss is limited to his capital contribution. His limited status must be known to creditors to be effective.

partner, silent or dormant A partner who is not active in the partnership and may or may not have limited liability. Usually a "silent" partner is known to the public, while a "dormant" partner may not be.

partnership A form of business ownership in which two or more persons own the business.

partnership agreement An agreement between persons creating a partnership, usually specifying such things as the amount of money to be invested by each partner, the division of partnership profits and losses, the position responsibilities of each partner, and the amounts of money each partner may withdraw. Whether the agreement is oral, implied by actions of the partners, or in written form, it has the force and effect of a legal contract.

par value A stated value of a share of stock indicating the amount which has been contributed in money or property by the original stockholders when they received the stock. After a corporation is operating, par value has no necessary bearing on the actual market value of a share of stock.

patent monopolies By giving inventors the exclusive ownership and use of a novel idea—whether a product, a physical or chemical composition, a process, or a design—the government confers on the patent holder a monopoly position.

perfect competition (See pure competition.)

periodical indexes Reference sources which catalog, by subject, articles in the leading periodicals.

PERT Program Evaluation and Review Technique is a planning and control tool that shows for a program the identifiable parts or tasks ("milestones") which must be accomplished, assigns a time or cost for accomplishing each, and shows how the tasks relate to each other—that is, how the start or completion of one task depends on another.

Peter principle This principle, developed by Professor J. L. Peter, suggests that a person who is competent is promoted, as a reward for doing his job well, until he reaches his "level of incompetence" where he will remain in a job that exceeds his abilities.

piece rates A pay scale based upon the number of pieces or items of work which are completed. Frequently, workers are paid on the basis of how many units of production they are able to complete in a single shift.

planning Planning is the selection of goals and the means of reaching them; the choosing among alternative courses of action; the deciding in advance what to do, how to do it, when to do it, and who is to do it.

planning premises The future environment in which plans are expected to operate; forecasts of future conditions which a company will face plus actions and policies already taken that will control plans.

planning steps The logical steps in planning are (1) being aware of opportunities through diagnosis of opportunities that exist for a business and its limitations; (2) choosing clear, verifiable, and attainable objectives; (3) identifying and communicating planning premises; (4) identifying alternatives; (5) comparing and analyzing alternative courses of action in light of goals sought; (6) choosing a course of action from among alternatives; (7) formulating necessary supporting plans; and (8) numberizing plans through budgets.

plans, types of The various types of plans are (1) objectives or goals; (2) policies; (3) strategies; (4) procedures; (5) rules; (6) programs; and (7) budgets. All are plans because they shape and control future actions of people in a company.

policies Guides for people in using discretion in their decision making. Policies may allow much or little discretion.

political environment The factors in our environment that are due to actions of legislators and other government or political figures.

political polarization An enlargement of political effort at the extremes.

postindustrial society The commonly accepted term among futurists used to identify the characteristics of the next dominant age of society in which it is expected that a wide variety of service industries will predominate.

preferred stock A share of ownership in a corporation, evidenced by a certificate, which ordinarily carries with it preference over common stock in matters of payment of dividends and liquidation of the assets of the corporation. Preferred stock may or may not be given the right to vote for corporation directors.

premium A sum of money paid by the insured to the insurer who, in turn, promises to pay the insured a specified sum if he should suffer a particular loss.

prepaid expenses Expenses like rent and insurance premiums, paid in advance, and office supplies which have been paid for but will be used over a period in the future.

price/earnings (P/E) ratio The ratio of the present price of a share of stock to the current earnings per share of the stock.

price equilibrium The one specific price at which the quantity supplied and the quantity demanded are equal.

price levels and inflation Price levels refer to the general average of prices for the things we buy. When price levels rise, particularly if they rise rapidly (at, say, 8 to 10 percent or more in one year), this is referred to as inflation. With inflation, dollars buy less, and consequently inflation is often referred to as a drop in the value of dollars (or any other national money).

primary information Original information collected by an individual or firm for specific purposes of its own.

prime rate The interest rate commercial banks charge to their best customers with unquestioned credit rating; usually the lowest rate charged by such banks for short-term business loans.

principles of delegation (See delegation principles.)

Private capitalism (See capitalism.)

procedures Chronological sequences of specified actions; definite ways of doing things in a certain order.

process of control (See control process.)

process, or equipment, organization Grouping of activities around processes or equipment used, as in the case of a heat-treating, punch press, or electronic data processing department.

product differentiation Finding or creating some quality or appearance about the company's product which sets it apart from nearly identical competitors. (See also monopolistic competition.)

productivity The ability of labor and capital to produce; the amount of output of goods and services compared to the input of labor and capital. The difficulty in measuring productivity of either labor or capital is knowing how much increase in output is caused by either factor.

product life cycle The stages through which a product moves from its introduction, through its market growth, market maturity, to its period of sales decline.

product organization Grouping activities together that are related to prod-

uct or product line, such as the Chevrolet or Buick divisions of the General Motors Corporation.

product packaging and labeling laws Government action requiring businesses to package and label goods so that the buyer can see what he is getting.

professional organization Individual membership organizations which often provide information to professional people or businessmen in special areas of interest. The Society of Personnel Administrators and the American Medical Association are professional organizations.

profit and loss control An overall type of control that measures a company division or department on its ability to show a profit or a loss.

profits The measure of surplus of business income from sales over expenses incurred in producing the products and services sold. (See also surplus.)

programmer The person who is the software expert, who speaks the computer's language, and who is able to reduce a problem to a series of computer actions.

programs, planning Complexes of goals, policies, procedures, rules, job assignments, steps to be taken, manpower or money to be used, and other things necessary to carry out a desired course of action.

promissory notes A written promise by a borrower (the "maker") to pay a lender (the "payee") a certain amount of money plus a specified amount of interest after a certain period of time or on a specified date.

promotional mix The balance of several factors including the amount of money available for promotion, the nature of the market, the nature of the product, and the position of the product in its own life cycle.

promotion from within The promotion policy in which current employees are promoted into higher positions instead of going outside the firm to fill vacancies.

property Items that may be owned, such as buildings, machinery, office equipment, raw materials, purchased parts, merchandise, supplies, and cash; the assets of a business.

property insurance Insurance coverage which insures against the damage or destruction of the insured property.

property rights Since all property is subject to some right or claim against it, whether by owners or creditors, these rights are called property rights.

proprietorship A business owned and controlled by one person. Claims of owners against property after claims of all kinds of creditors. Also called capital or net worth.

prospectus A fairly detailed summary of certain information filed with the United States Securities and Exchange Commission when a company registers a new stock or bond issue. The prospectus must be printed and made available to prospective investors. (See registering a security.)

proxy A device by which corporation shareholders grant rights to vote their stock to an individual or a committee.

psychology and the manager Since psychology is the science of understanding relationships among individuals and why individuals behave the way they do, knowing the basic elements of psychology can be helpful to a manager in his job.

public market In speaking of the public market, we are referring to the system and facilities by which thousands of individual and other investors buy and sell business corporation stocks and bonds and government bonds.

public ownership of business The case where businesses are owned and controlled by government agencies.

public utility and transportation rate discrimination The practice of charg-

ing different prices to different customers to take into account differences in quantities purchased, in costs of serving various customers, and in variations in customers' ability or willingness to pay. Regulation requires that the degree of discrimination be reasonable and fair.

purchasing agent The person who handles the buying for a purchaser.

pure competition The market in which there is a completely similar product, free entry and exit from the market, no artificial restraints, and numerous buyers and sellers such that no one of them has a significant impact on the market. Complete knowledge by buyers and sellers makes the model that of perfect competition.

pure food and drug laws Government action to regulate the quality of food and drug products produced by businesses and sold to the public.

quality control The regular and systematic inspection of production to guarantee that specifications are met.

quality of public utility and transportation service Government regulation of these businesses provide, for control of the quality of service offered —such things as adequacy and safety.

quaternary sector The sector which supplies services to tertiary activities and to society as a whole. Car washes or barber shops would fall into this category.

rationality and the manager Since managers make decisions and good decision making requires thinking rationally, a manager should realize that rationality requires (1) a clear goal, (2) the looking at alternative ways of accomplishing a goal, and (3) weighing alternatives in the light of a goal to determine which alternative offers the most promise of reaching a goal.

rationality in planning The steps in planning are simply an exercise in rationality. In other words, rationality implies a clear goal, an analysis of alternatives to reach the goal, and the selection of the alternative that appears most likely to be the one which is most promising in reaching the goal. (See also rationality and the manager and planning steps.)

real-time processing Data are processed into, and available from, the computer as the events they reflect occur.

rediscounting The Federal Reserve Bank practice of purchasing business and other commercial loans from commercial banks which had originally made such loans.

registered traders Brokers who are registered by the exchange under government regulation and who buy or sell securities on an exchange for their own investment and profit.

registering a security Registering a new security—stocks or bonds—with the United States Securities and Exchange Commission involves considerable information concerning the company, its operations, its financial statements, its products and competition, its management, and other things thought to be useful to a potential investor in deciding whether to purchase a company's security. The registration is accomplished by filing this vast amount of detailed information in what is called a registration statement which is open to public inspection.

responsible competition (See competition, responsible.)

responsiveness of business (See business responsiveness.)

resume A summary of personal, experience, and educational data frequently used by job applicants to summarize their qualifications for a specific position.

retailing The process by which a business sells its products or services to the ultimate consumer. Retailing includes all the businesses from which individuals typically make their purchases.

return on investment (See control through return on investment.)

review of plans and programs One of the most effective ways of assuring planning is regular and formal review of every individual's plans and programs. This not only sets an environment where people are required to plan but can go far in assuring that plans do not become out-of-date and that people are actually accomplishing plans.

revolving credit An arrangement with a bank for a certain level of credit over a period of time under which the borrower may borrow or repay loans within this limit; essentially, a line of credit.

risk The possibility that a venture will fail or incur loss versus the possibility that the venture will succeed. In areas of insurance, this usually means the degree of probability that a loss will occur; thus not every homeowner or automobile driver will suffer a loss in any year, but all have a risk of having a loss. In insurance, the risks of loss are pooled, and each homeowner or car driver pays a proportionate share.

Robinson-Patman Act Federal government legislation passed in 1936 to eliminate unreasonable price discrimination whereby sellers give certain buyers favorable prices which tend to reduce the effectiveness of competition.

role of competition (See competition, role of.)

role in organization (See organizational role.)

rules Required actions or nonactions in a specific area.

sales finance companies Companies that specialize in financing installment purchases of individuals and businesses.

savings and loan associations Associations of depositors who place funds in them on the basis of savings accounts. These associations have as their purpose the investment of savings in mortgages on homes and other real estate.

savings banks Banks designed to serve smaller savers as a means whereby their savings can be pooled, investments made by the bank, and interest arising from these investment earnings are paid to depositors.

savings deposits Deposits placed in a bank as a means of accumulating savings and, like time deposits, not ordinarily drawn on demand. Interest is normally paid on these deposits.

secondary information Published information, generally available, which can be used by other individuals or firms.

secured loans Loans secured by some property, such as stocks, bonds, life insurance policies, accounts receivable, equipment, or inventories.

Securities Act of 1933 The first entry of the federal government in the field of regulation of the issuance of stocks and bonds, this law places its main reliance for protection of investors on requiring businesses to provide investors complete and accurate information on stocks and bonds issued.

Securities and Exchange Act of 1934 Federal government regulation of trading in stocks and bonds to protect investors against unscrupulous, unfair, or misleading practices of those handling securities purchases or sales in the public markets.

security exchanges Associations of brokerage firms which furnish places and facilities where brokers may buy or sell securities.

security speculation The practice of buying securities with a view to making money by the rise in price of a security, or selling securities with a view to making money on the fall in price of a security. These purchases or sales are normally made with the objective of making money on short-term up-and-down price movements.

selecting an alternative (See alternative, selecting an.)

self-insurance The setting aside of a financial reserve by a business or an individual that can be drawn upon when a loss occurs.

sequence of simple operations The activities through which a computer proceeds from the input to the output.

service departments Grouping of activities in a department for the primary purposes of efficiency or control, or both, as in the case of plant maintenance, stenographic pool, accounting, or personnel recruiting.

short selling When a person sells a stock or bond which he does not own, but his broker borrows the security for delivery. Of course, at some time in the future, the person selling must buy the security to "cover" his short sale.

short-term liabilities Generally the same as current liabilities.

silent, or dormant, partner (See partner, silent or dormant.)

sinking fund bond Bonds issued with the provision that a company will provide for their repayment, either by accumulating a special fund for this purpose or by promising to reduce the bonds outstanding by repurchasing them on a schedule over the years.

social action Demands and pressures of people in a society for certain things, such as removing pollutants from air and water, providing health insurance, improving automobile safety, and stopping racial or other minority discrimination. Social pressures usually lead to legislation by national, state, or local governments.

social and cultural environment (See environment, social and cultural.)

social attitudes and beliefs Those attitudes and beliefs that any group develops, such as beliefs in the importance of private property, competition in business, faith in better ways of doing things, and the right of all people to a better life without discrimination because of sex, race, religion, or age.

social costs The costs of production which must be borne by society as a whole (for example, water pollution). Although caused in part by production, the cost of cleaning up streams may be generally borne by all of society.

socialism An economic system in which businesses are predominantly owned and controlled by governments —that is, by public ownership.

social responsibility of business A concept, commonly used very unclearly, to indicate that business has responsibility for social problems. In its more exact sense, since the purpose of business is the production and sale of economic goods and services, it is more appropriate to see the social responsibility of business as acting in a way of being responsive to the entire social environment in which it operates. (See also social responsiveness and business responsiveness.)

social responsiveness The necessity for any business to be aware of, and respond to (in the sense of living within and being affected by) the elements in its social environment— elements such as people's attitudes, desires, degrees of intelligence and education, beliefs, problems, and customs.

social security The program of the federal government, administered either by its agencies or by state agencies, to provide benefits for workers in the event of involuntary unemployment,

retirement, disability, death, or health problems.

software, computer (See computer software.)

span of control (See span of management.)

span of management The fact that there is a limit to the number of persons an individual manager can effectively supervise; but this limit cannot be expressed for all managers in exact numbers. The number will differ depending on certain underlying factors: (1) how clear plans are; (2) how clear a person's job is; (3) how well trained people are for a job; (4) how fast the pace of change in a company is; (5) how adequate communication is; (6) how effective a manager is in assuring himself how well his subordinates are performing; (7) the time required for necessary face-to-face contacts; and (8) the time a manager has to devote to supervision.

special insurance Insurance which insures against a specific risk.

specialists Brokers on the floor of a security exchange who are assigned to special locations on the floor and who specialize in certain securities, buying and selling for their own account and executing orders in these stocks for other brokers.

specialization Dividing the work into similar components.

staff Refers to an organizational relationship where an individual or a department has only the power and duty to advise, recommend, or counsel, but not to give orders. It is also called an advisory relationship.

Standard & Poors Averages An index based on the performance of 500 stocks. The index is not an average of stock prices but is based on the percentage change of prices using prices for the period 1941–43 as the base number of ten.

standardization   The process in which machinery parts are interchangeable.

standard product   A product made exactly like the one before it and the one after it.

standards   Criteria of performance; criteria against which performance is measured.

start-up costs   The unusual expenses incurred in starting a new business, embarking on a new product development program, or going into a new plant. These include many unforeseen costs: the low productivity and high cost of labor until workers learn how to produce a product or service efficiently, the cash needed for inventory and accounts receivable until sales are made and accounts collected, and other needs for cash at the beginning of a business or new program.

state banks   Commercial banks chartered by one of the 50 states.

steps in planning   (See planning steps.)

stock dividends   Payments made on shares of stock to common or preferred stockholders, but usually only to common stockholders, as a kind of compensation for their investment in the company. It should be noted that stock dividends do not increase a stockholder's total ownership interest in a company but only give him more shares of stock.

stock exchange "post"   Since various securities traded on an organized security exchange are assigned to special locations on the floor, these locations are referred to as "posts."

stock exchange "seat"   A membership in an organized security exchange which a member purchases and can sell.

stockholders' equity   In a corporation, the net worth of stockholders; the claims these owners have against a corporation's assets after claims of all kinds of creditors have been deducted.

stock splits   The practice of giving stockholders more shares of stock, such as giving a stockholder an additional share for each share he holds or one share for each two shares held. It should be noted that like stock dividends stock splits do not increase a stockholder's total ownership interest in a company but only give him more shares of stock.

"stop" order   An order to a broker to buy or sell a security only when it reaches a certain specified price. When the price of the security reaches the "stop" price, the order then becomes a "market" order.

strategies   A general program of action (including major objectives and policies) with an implied deployment of resources, to attain certain company objectives.

supply curve   A graph of the supply schedule. The line represents the number of units that will be offered for sale at different price levels.

surplus   (See goal of managers.)

syndicates   (See joint venture.)

synergy   Instances when two or more elements are mixed together and add up to more than the sum of the parts; where the joint efforts of people working together bring a result which is greater than the sum of their individual efforts.

synthetic process   The bringing together of diverse raw materials to form a single resultant product which is significantly different from its components.

tailored controls   Control techniques or information that are especially tailored to plans, that reflect organization structure, that suit people's personalities and their ability to understand, that are as objective as possible, and that are economical.

taking a position in a security   A broker purchasing a stock or bond for his own account in order to have an inventory for resale.

tariffs Taxes placed upon goods or services crossing a country's borders.

task of economic systems (See economic system.)

technological environment The state of technology that influences our life. In business, it is the state of technology that affects how a business develops new products, how it produces and sells products and services, and how well it understands individual and group behavior.

technology The sum total of knowledge of ways of doing things.

territorial organization Grouping activities in departments according to geography, places where operations are located.

tertiary industries Industries which supply services to primary and secondary occupations. Common carriers fall into this category.

test market The introduction of a new product in a limited geographical area to test its market appeal.

time and motion study A study timing the motions required to do each part of a job in order to arrive eventually at the best way to do it with no wasted motion, time, or effort.

time deposits Deposits which are made in a bank by individuals or companies for a period of time (often a specified period) and which are not ordinarily drawn on demand. Interest is normally paid on these deposits.

time drafts A draft payable to a payee at a specified time in the future. (See drafts.)

time-sharing The concept in which several businesses share in the use and the expense of computer time.

total marketing concept The practice of looking at marketing as involving more than selling and advertising; of seeing marketing also as being involved in helping a company discover what things customers want, of making sure the company produces them,

and of assuring that customers get good delivery service and any needed help after a product is delivered to avoid any dissatisfaction.

trade journals Published magazines which contain extensive information about a particular industry.

trademark monopolies By giving businesses the exclusive right to register certain product or process names, or "marks," the government introduces a monopoly element in business.

trade, or bank, acceptances A time draft which is drawn by one person, sent to the drawee, and which is, upon the drawee's acceptance of it by affixing his signature, binding on him. It usually becomes a negotiable piece of paper in that it can be bought and sold. If accepted by a business firm, it is a *trade* acceptance; if accepted by a bank, it is a *bank* acceptance.

trait approaches to leadership Approaching the analysis of leadership by studying physical, mental, and personality traits of leaders.

transferability of ownership The ability of a business owner to transfer his ownership to other persons.

Truth-in-Lending Act A federal law passed in 1971 that requires lenders to spell out clearly for the borrower what interest he is paying for on loans and for goods bought on time payments.

ultimate buyer The final purchaser of all products; the consumer.

underwriting Investment banks "underwrite" new security issues when they agree to buy these securities and resell them to the public. In other words, they guarantee the sale of such securities by an issuing company.

unfair competition Practices by competing businesses which are regarded as unfair or deceptive, such as false and misleading advertising, misbranding of commodities, copying another business firm's trade name or coming close to doing so, procuring business by spying or bribery, or making false or disparaging statements concerning a competitor's products.

union shop A business where an employee must join the union within a 30-day period after hiring to maintain his employment.

unlimited liability The liability of a proprietor or a partner for claims against a business that is not limited to his ownership in a business, but extends to any other items of value the person has.

unsecured loans Loans not specifically secured by any property, but having as their security only the borrowers' credit ratings and ability to repay.

usury laws Laws limiting the amount of interest a lender may charge a borrower for money.

value analysis The examination of product design, components, and proposed purchases to determine if they are really essential or worth what they cost.

verifiable objectives (See objectives, verifiable.)

warehouse A facility used for the storage of products at some point between the factory and the consumer.

when a business "monopolizes" Unlawful business combinations tending toward a monopoly are still not clearly defined, but some guidelines are: (1)

combinations of two or more businesses must be "reasonable"; (2) combinations must not use their power in a monopolistic way; (3) joint price fixing between businesses cannot be engaged in; (4) combinations must not be designed to squeeze out competitors; and (5) combinations must not lead to unusual power in a single company that might substantially lessen competition.

wholesaling The process in which the purchaser buys goods for the purpose of resale, usually to retailers.

with recourse (See negotiable notes.)

working capital In accounting terms, the amount by which the current assets of a business exceed the current liabilities. Since this excess almost always exists in a business, and indeed should exist if a business is to have a good credit standing, working capital represents an amount that must be available on a long-term basis.

yellow-dog contract A contract in which the business insists upon making employees agree, as a condition of employment, not to join unions. This is now illegal.

zoning laws Laws, usually passed by local governments, providing limits on the use of land, generally classifying permitted land uses as residential, commercial, light industrial, or heavy industrial.

index

Index

*This book has been set in 10 point and 9 point
Electra, leaded 3 points. Part numbers are 30
point Helvetica Medium. Chapter numbers are
72 point Caslon Old Style No. 540 and chapter titles are 24 point Helvetica. The size of
the type page is 26 by 46 picas.*

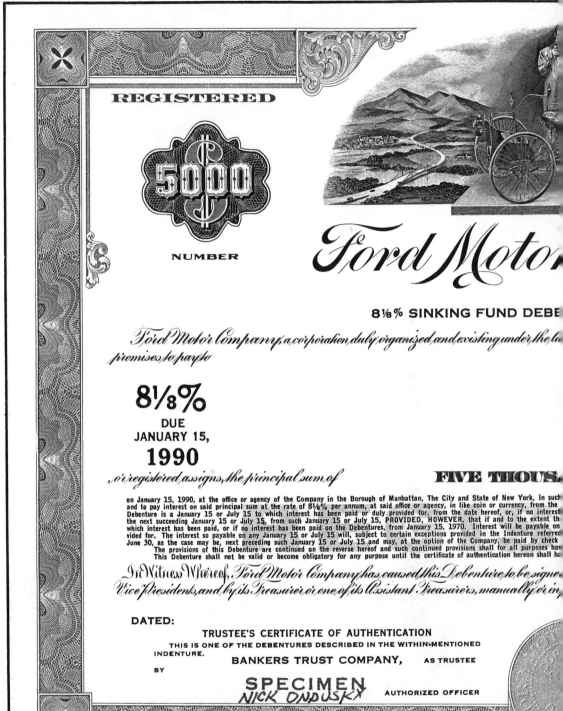

REGISTERED

$5000

NUMBER

Ford Motor

8⅛% SINKING FUND DEBE

Ford Motor Company, a corporation, duly organized and existing under the la promises to pay to

8⅛%
DUE
JANUARY 15,
1990

, or registered assigns, the principal sum of

FIVE THOUS

on January 15, 1990, at the office or agency of the Company in the Borough of Manhattan, The City and State of New York, in such and to pay interest on said principal sum at the rate of 8⅛% per annum, at said office or agency, in like coin or currency, from the Debenture is a January 15 or July 15 to which interest has been paid or duly provided for, from the date hereof, or, if no interest the next succeeding January 15 or July 15, from such January 15 or July 15, PROVIDED, HOWEVER, that if and to the extent th which interest has been paid, or if no interest has been paid on the Debentures, from January 15, 1970. Interest will be payable on vided for. The interest so payable on any January 15 or July 15 will, subject to certain exceptions provided in the Indenture referred June 30, as the case may be, next preceding such January 15 or July 15 and may, at the option of the Company, be paid by check

The provisions of this Debenture are continued on the reverse hereof and such continued provisions shall for all purposes ha This Debenture shall not be valid or become obligatory for any purpose until the certificate of authentication hereon shall ha

In Witness Whereof, Ford Motor Company has caused this Debenture to be signe Vice Presidents, and by its Treasurer or one of its Assistant Treasurers, manually or in

DATED:

TRUSTEE'S CERTIFICATE OF AUTHENTICATION

THIS IS ONE OF THE DEBENTURES DESCRIBED IN THE WITHIN-MENTIONED INDENTURE.

BANKERS TRUST COMPANY, AS TRUSTEE

BY

SPECIMEN
NICK ONDUSKY

AUTHORIZED OFFICER

© SECURITY-COLUM